Moroccan

THE AUSTRALIAN
Women's Weekly

Moroccan

acp
books

Contents

Morocco, in the vibrant north-western corner of Africa, is home to one of the world's most diversified cuisines. Its culinary traditions are a reflection of the indigenous Berber culture and strong Arab, Middle-Eastern, Persian and Andalusian influences that have reigned at various stages of Morocco's history. This combination of cultural influences has created a magical and exciting fusion of flavours.

The main meal of the day is usually served at midday, and begins with a series of hot and cold salads, followed by a tagine, or a succession of tagines, and an enormous platter of couscous. Bread is very important and is eaten with every meal. Moroccan bread is round, heavy-textured and spicy. It is highly absorbent and ideal for soaking up the sauces of tagines, and also acts as a kind of utensil to scoop up the food. Meals are traditionally finished with fruits and nuts, and a glass of simple, soothing, sweet mint tea.

Food in Morocco also has significant religious importance, and certain dishes are eaten in relation to the religious calendar. Being a predominantly Islamic country, pork and alcohol are not consumed. Couscous is traditionally served for lunch on Friday, the Islamic holy day, although it is also eaten at numerous other occasions, especially feasts. During Ramadan, the holy month of fasting, not a bite of food or drop of water is consumed between sunrise and sunset. The fast is traditionally broken at sundown with a thick, hearty bowl of harira soup followed by dates, honey cake and milk or coffee.

Couscous is often thought of as the crowning achievement of Moroccan cuisine. Simple but brilliant, these hand-rolled grains of golden semolina are steamed above a simmering tagine until they swell and become soft and fluffy, flavoured by the tagine.

Tagine refers to the name of the unique cooking pot as well as the wonderful rich stews that are cooked within it. The traditional tagine pot is made of clay and consists of a flat round base with low sides (which doubles as a serving dish), and the tall cone-shaped lid which acts like a closed chimney trapping the moisture and circulating the steam and flavours during cooking. Tagines were traditionally cooked over coals or an open flame, but you can use them in your kitchen over a gas flame, on an electric stove or in the oven. When using a tagine at home, follow the manufacturer's instructions.

Moroccan essentials

Saffron Available in strands or ground form; expensive because it consists of the hand-gathered stigmas from a crocus flower. Buy it only from a reputable source. It colours food golden and has a bittersweet almondy taste.

Chickpeas Also called garbanzos, channa or hummus, this legume is prized for its full, nutty flavour and crisp texture. It's the essential ingredient in hummus – the dip made with blended chickpeas, tahini, olive oil and garlic.

Split peas These are available in both green and yellow varieties; they have a sweet, strong pea flavour. Best known for pea and ham soup, split peas can also be found in Middle Eastern soups and stews.

Za'atar This blend of roasted dried thyme, oregano, marjoram, sesame seeds and sumac is found in many Middle Eastern kitchens. Za'atar is traditionally sprinkled on toast spread with ricotta, or try it tossed with roasted potato wedges.

Sumac A purple-red spice ground from the berries of a small Mediterranean shrub. Adds a tart, lemony flavour to dips and dressings and goes well with meat, chicken and fish, tomato and avocado.

Burghul Best-known in the refreshing Middle Eastern salad, tabbouleh, burghul is cracked wheat that is hulled, dried and then ground to various degrees of fineness. Before use, it is soaked briefly in water to soften and swell the grains, then squeezed dry.

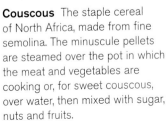

Couscous The staple cereal of North Africa, made from fine semolina. The minuscule pellets are steamed over the pot in which the meat and vegetables are cooking or, for sweet couscous, over water, then mixed with sugar, nuts and fruits.

Baharat A spice blend used throughout the Middle East, baharat typically includes ground coriander, paprika, black pepper, cumin, cassia, cloves, cardamom and nutmeg. Rub it over fish, beef or lamb before cooking.

Preserved lemons

10 medium lemons (1.4kg)
¾ cup (165g) coarse cooking salt (kosher salt)
8 whole cloves
4 cardamom pods, bruised
½ teaspoon coriander seeds
4 bay leaves
2 cups (500ml) lemon juice, approximately

1 Wash and dry lemons; cut into quarters lengthways. Place lemons in large bowl; sprinkle evenly with salt.
2 Pack lemons into sterilised jars (see tips) with spices and bay leaves.
3 Pour in enough juice to cover lemons completely; secure lids. Stand in a cool, dry place for at least three weeks before using.

prep + cook time 10 minutes (+ 3 weeks standing)
makes 1.5 litres (6 cups)
nutritional count per tablespoon 0.1g total fat (0g saturated fat); 17kJ (4 cal); 0.5g carbohydrate; 0.2g protein; 0.5g fibre
tips To sterilise jars, wash jars and lids in warm soapy water; rinse well. Place jars in large saucepan and cover with water. Bring to the boil; boil 10 minutes. Carefully drain water from jars; transfer jars and lids to a baking tray lined with a clean tea towel. Cover with a sheet of foil and place in a slow oven until dry. Use straight from the oven.
To use lemons, remove and discard the flesh from the lemons. Chop or slice the rind and use in tagines or dips, with lamb dishes or sprinkled over fish. This recipe is best made a month ahead. Refrigerate the preserved lemons after opening.

Harissa

45g (1½ ounces) dried long red chillies
2 teaspoons each cumin seeds and coriander seeds
100g (3½ ounces) roasted red capsicum (bell pepper), chopped coarsely
3 cloves garlic, crushed
2 teaspoons sea salt
¼ cup (60ml) extra virgin olive oil
¼ cup (60ml) water
extra virgin olive oil, extra

1 Trim and discard chilli stems; place chillies in small heatproof bowl.
Cover with boiling water; stand 1 hour. Drain.
2 Meanwhile, dry-fry cumin and coriander seeds in small frying pan
until fragrant. Cool. Use mortar and pestle to coarsely crush seeds.
3 Process chillies until chopped finely. Add crushed seeds, capsicum,
garlic, salt, oil and the water; process until mixture forms a thick paste.
4 Spoon harissa into small sterilised jars (see tips); drizzle extra oil over
surface and secure lids. Refrigerate.

prep + cook time 25 minutes (+ standing) **makes** 2½ cups
nutritional count per tablespoon 1.8g total fat (0.3g saturated fat);
75kJ (18 cal); 0.2g carbohydrate; 0.1g protein; 0.1g fibre
tips To sterilise jars, wash jars and lids in warm soapy water; rinse well.
Place jars in large saucepan and cover with water. Bring to the boil;
boil 10 minutes. Carefully drain water from jars; transfer jars and lids
to a baking tray lined with a clean tea towel. Cover with a sheet of foil
and place in a slow oven until dry. Use straight from the oven.
Large, dried chillies are available from Asian food stores.
Harissa is extremely hot. Serve in small amounts with meat, poultry and
couscous. Harissa will keep in the fridge for up to 10 days.

Chermoulla

½ cup (125ml) olive oil
⅓ cup (80ml) lemon juice
6 shallots (150g), sliced thinly
4 cloves garlic, crushed
1 teaspoon ground cumin
1 fresh long red chilli, sliced thinly
¼ cup each finely chopped fresh coriander (cilantro),
    mint and flat-leaf parsley

1 Combine ingredients in small bowl; season to taste.

prep + cook time 15 minutes **makes** 1 cup
nutritional count per tablespoon 9.6g total fat (1.3g saturated fat);
376kJ (90 cal); 0.7g carbohydrate; 0.3g protein; 0.4g fibre
tip This Moroccan blend of herbs and spices is traditionally used for
preserving or seasoning fish or meat. It may also be used as a quick
sauce for fish or seafood or as a baste or marinade.

Ras el hanout

2 teaspoons cumin seeds
1 teaspoon each caraway seeds, coriander seeds and fennel seeds
¼ teaspoon saffron threads
1 teaspoon each ground allspice, ginger, cinnamon and smoked paprika
½ teaspoon each ground turmeric, nutmeg and cardamom
¼ teaspoon each ground clove and cayenne pepper

1 Dry-fry seeds in small frying pan until fragrant; cool.
2 Crush seeds and saffron in mortar and pestle until fine.
Stir in remaining spices.

prep + cook time 15 minutes **makes** ¼ cup
nutritional count per teaspoon 0g total fat (0g saturated fat);
0kJ (0 cal); 0g carbohydrate; 0g protein; 0g fibre
tips With a name that loosely translates as "top of the shelf", ras el
hanout is a Moroccan blend of the best a spice merchant has to offer;
allspice, cumin, paprika, fennel, caraway and saffron are all generally part
of the mix. Although traditionally the spice blend may contain more than
30 spices, including several exotic and unusual spices not commonly
found, our version is a delicious and simple interpretation. Store in an
airtight container.
Stir a little ras el hanout into steamed couscous to add colour and aroma.
Ready-made ras el hanout is available from Middle Eastern and specialty
spice stores if you don't have the time to make it yourself.

Drinks & Snacks

Mint tea

1.25 litres (5 cups) boiling water
1 cup firmly packed fresh mint leaves
¼ cup (55g) raw sugar
15g (½ ounce) green tea leaves

1 Combine 1 cup of the water and ⅔ cup of the mint in medium heatproof jug; drain, reserve mint.
2 Stir drained mint, the remaining water, sugar and tea in medium saucepan over heat until sugar dissolves. Bring to the boil.
3 Strain tea into large heatproof jug.
4 Serve cups of tea topped with remaining mint.

prep + cook time 15 minutes **makes** 1.25 litres (5 cups)
nutritional count per 1 cup (250ml) 0.1g total fat (0g saturated fat); 247kJ (59 cal); 14.3g carbohydrate; 0.4g protein; 0.9g fibre

Almond milk

2 cups (320g) blanched almonds
2 cups (500ml) buttermilk
2 cups (500ml) milk
⅓ cup (75g) caster (superfine) sugar
½ teaspoon orange blossom water
pinch ground nutmeg

1 Blend nuts, buttermilk and half the milk until smooth.
2 Stir remaining milk and sugar in small saucepan over heat until sugar dissolves. Cool.
3 Combine almond mixture and milk mixture in large jug; stir in orange blossom water. Refrigerate 3 hours or until required.
4 Serve almond milk over ice; sprinkle with nutmeg.

prep + cook time 20 minutes (+ refrigeration) **makes** 1.5 litres (6 cups)
nutritional count per 1 cup (250ml) 34.6g total fat (5g saturated fat); 1994kJ (477 cal); 23.3g carbohydrate; 17.4g protein; 4.7g fibre

Green apple and rosewater milk

4 medium green-skinned apples (600g),
    peeled, cored, chopped coarsely
½ teaspoon rosewater
2 cups (500ml) milk
2 tablespoons caster (superfine) sugar

1 Process ingredients until smooth.
2 Strain mixture into large jug; serve over ice.

prep time 15 minutes **makes** 1 litre (4 cups)
nutritional count per 1 cup (250ml) 5g total fat (3.2g saturated fat);
727kJ (174 cal); 27.6g carbohydrate; 4.6g protein; 2.3g fibre

Spiced coffee with rosewater cream

8 cardamom pods
3 cinnamon sticks
4 cloves
¾ cup (30g) instant coffee granules
1 litre (4 cups) water
¼ cup (55g) light brown sugar
⅓ cup (80ml) pouring cream
1 teaspoon rosewater

1 Dry-fry spices in small frying pan until fragrant.
2 Combine spices, coffee, the water and sugar in medium saucepan;
stir over heat until sugar dissolves. Bring to the boil. Reduce heat;
simmer, stirring occasionally, 10 minutes.
3 Meanwhile, beat cream and rosewater in small bowl with electric mixer
until soft peaks form.
4 Strain hot coffee into serving cups; serve topped with rosewater cream.

prep + cook time 15 minutes **makes** 1 litre (4 cups)
nutritional count per 1 cup (250ml) 8.7g total fat (5.7g saturated fat);
589kJ (141 cal); 14.6g carbohydrate; 1.4g protein; 1.2g fibre

Citrus sparkler

⅔ cup (160ml) each strained lemon, orange and ruby red grapefruit juice
½ cup (110g) caster (superfine) sugar
½ teaspoon orange blossom water
1 small ruby red grapefruit (350g), quartered, sliced thinly
½ cup loosely packed fresh mint leaves
1.25 litres (5 cups) chilled sparkling mineral water

1 Stir juices and sugar in large jug until sugar dissolves.
2 Stir in remaining ingredients. Serve over ice.

prep time 20 minutes **makes** 1.5 litres (6 cups)
nutritional count per 1 cup (250ml) 0.2g total fat (0g saturated fat);
451kJ (108 cal); 25g carbohydrate; 0.9g protein; 0.6g fibre

Capsicum dip

4 large red capsicums (bell peppers) (1.4kg)
3 cloves garlic, unpeeled
2 tablespoons olive oil
1 tablespoon red wine vinegar
1 tablespoon lemon juice
1 tablespoon finely chopped preserved lemon rind
½ teaspoon hot paprika
2 tablespoons finely chopped fresh coriander (cilantro)

1 Preheat oven to 220°C/425°F. Oil oven trays.
2 Quarter capsicums; discard seeds and membranes. Roast, skin-side up, with garlic about 30 minutes or until skin blisters and blackens. Cover capsicum and garlic with plastic or paper for 5 minutes, then peel away skins.
3 Blend or process capsicum, garlic, oil, vinegar, juice, preserved lemon and paprika until smooth. Stir in coriander; season to taste.
4 Serve dip with toasted pitta bread or crusty bread.

prep + cook time 45 minutes **makes** 1½ cups
nutritional count per tablespoon 2.2g total fat (0.3g saturated fat); 155kJ (37 cal); 2.7g carbohydrate; 1.1g protein; 0.9g fibre

Eggplant dip

2 large eggplants (1kg)
½ cup (125ml) olive oil
6 medium tomatoes (900g)
3 cloves garlic, crushed
⅓ cup each coarsely chopped fresh flat-leaf parsley and coriander (cilantro)
1 teaspoon ground cumin

1 Preheat oven to 200°C/400°F.
2 Pierce eggplants all over with fork or skewer. Place eggplants on oiled oven tray; drizzle with 2 tablespoons of the oil. Roast eggplants, uncovered, about 50 minutes or until softened.
3 Meanwhile, place tomatoes on another oiled oven tray; drizzle with 2 tablespoons of the oil. Roast tomatoes for last 15 minutes of eggplant cooking time. Cool 20 minutes.
4 When cool enough to handle, peel eggplants and tomatoes; discard skin. Seed tomatoes; chop tomato and eggplant flesh coarsely.
5 Heat remaining oil in large frying pan; cook garlic, eggplant and tomato, stirring occasionally, about 20 minutes or until thick. Add herbs; cook, stirring, 5 minutes. Transfer mixture to medium bowl, stir in cumin; cool 20 minutes. Season to taste. Serve with crusty bread.

prep + cook time 1 hour 20 minutes (+ cooling) **makes** 3 cups
nutritional count per tablespoon 3.3g total fat (0.5g saturated fat); 150kJ (36 cal); 0.9g carbohydrate; 0.4g protein; 0.8g fibre

Hummus

800g (1½ pounds) canned chickpeas (garbanzo beans),
    rinsed, drained
¼ cup (90g) honey
¼ cup (60ml) lemon juice
¼ cup (60ml) olive oil
4cm (1½-inch) piece fresh turmeric (20g), grated
2 cloves garlic, crushed
1 teaspoon ground cumin
¼ teaspoon cayenne pepper
1 tablespoon finely chopped fresh coriander (cilantro)

1 Blend or process chickpeas, honey, juice, half the oil, turmeric, garlic, cumin and half the cayenne pepper until smooth. Transfer mixture to medium bowl; stir in coriander, season to taste.
2 Serve hummus sprinkled with remaining cayenne pepper and drizzled with remaining oil. Serve with toasted pitta bread or crusty bread.

prep time 10 minutes **makes** 2 cups
nutritional count per tablespoon 2.7g total fat (0.4g saturated fat); 234kJ (56 cal); 6.2g carbohydrate; 1.4g protein; 1.1g fibre

Goat's cheese with chickpeas and capsicum

2 large green capsicums (bell peppers) (700g)
2 large red capsicums (bell peppers) (700g)
2 tablespoons olive oil
1 medium red onion (170g), sliced thinly
2 cloves garlic, crushed
1 teaspoon ground cumin
½ teaspoon hot paprika
400g (13 ounces) canned chickpeas (garbanzo beans),
    rinsed, drained
2 teaspoons finely grated lemon rind
1 tablespoon lemon juice
⅓ cup coarsely chopped fresh flat-leaf parsley
60g (2 ounces) soft goat's cheese

1 Preheat oven to 200°C/400°F. Oil oven trays.
2 Quarter capsicums; discard seeds and membranes. Roast, skin-side up, until skin blisters and blackens. Cover capsicum with plastic or paper for 5 minutes; peel away skin, then slice capsicum thinly.
3 Heat oil in large frying pan; stir onion and garlic, until onion softens. Add spices and half the chickpeas; cook, stirring, about 2 minutes or until fragrant. Add capsicum; cook, stirring, until heated through. Remove from heat; stir in rind, juice and parsley. Cool.
4 Meanwhile, coarsely mash remaining chickpeas with cheese in medium bowl.
5 Stir capsicum mixture into cheese mixture; season to taste. Serve dip with soft bread rolls or toasted pitta bread.

prep + cook time 50 minutes **makes** 3 cups
nutritional count per tablespoon 1.5g total fat (0.3g saturated fat); 121kJ (29 cal); 2.3g carbohydrate; 1.3g protein; 0.8g fibre

White bean dip with pitta crisps

1 clove garlic, crushed
¼ cup lightly packed fresh flat-leaf parsley leaves
400g (13 ounces) canned white beans, rinsed, drained
1 teaspoon ground cumin
⅓ cup (80ml) olive oil
6 pitta bread (480g), cut into sixths

1 Preheat the oven to 200°C/400°F.
2 Blend or process garlic, parsley, beans and cumin until combined.
With the motor operating, add oil in a thin, steady stream until mixture
is smooth.
3 Place pitta on oiled oven trays; bake 8 minutes or until browned lightly.
4 Serve dip with pitta crisps and chilli marinated green olives.

prep + cook time 20 minutes **serves** 8
nutritional count per serving 10.6g total fat (1.5g saturated fat);
1062kJ (254 cal); 31.9g carbohydrate; 6.4g protein; 2.5g fibre
tips We used butter beans but you can use any canned white beans
you like.
This recipe can be made a day ahead. Store pitta crisps in an airtight
container.

Carrot dip

4 medium carrots (480g), chopped coarsely
2 cloves garlic, peeled
1 teaspoon ground cumin
1 tablespoon honey
2 tablespoons lemon juice
¼ cup (70g) greek-style yogurt
1 tablespoon coarsely chopped fresh coriander (cilantro)

1 Cover carrots and garlic with water in small saucepan; bring to the boil. Reduce heat; simmer, covered, about 20 minutes or until carrots are soft. Drain.
2 Blend or process carrot mixture with cumin, honey and juice until smooth. Add yogurt; blend until smooth.
3 Sprinkle dip with coriander; serve with toasted turkish bread.

prep + cook time 30 minutes **makes** 2 cups
nutritional count per tablespoon 0.2g total fat (0.1g saturated fat); 46kJ (11 cal); 1.9g carbohydrate; 0.3g protein; 0.5g fibre

Broad bean dip

500g (1 pound) frozen broad beans (fava beans)
1 clove garlic, crushed
1 teaspoon ground cumin
½ teaspoon smoked paprika
2 tablespoons olive oil
1 tablespoon lemon juice
1 tablespoon finely chopped fresh mint
1 tablespoon olive oil, extra
¼ teaspoon smoked paprika, extra

1 Cook beans in medium saucepan of boiling water until tender; drain, reserving some of the cooking liquid. When cool enough to handle, peel away grey-coloured outer shells from beans.
2 Blend or process beans with garlic, spices, oil, juice, mint and enough of the reserved cooking liquid until mixture is smooth.
3 Serve dip drizzled with extra oil and sprinkled with extra paprika.

prep + cook time 20 minutes **makes** 1¾ cups
nutritional count per tablespoon 2.7g total fat (0.4g saturated fat); 150kJ (36 cal); 0.5g carbohydrate; 1.7g protein; 1.5g fibre
tip Dip can be made a day ahead; store, covered, in the refrigerator.

43

Vegetarian fillo cigars with harissa yogurt

1 medium red capsicum (bell pepper) (200g)
1 tablespoon olive oil
1 clove garlic, crushed
1 small eggplant (230g), chopped finely
1 large zucchini (150g), chopped finely
1 large tomato (220g), seeded, chopped finely
1 teaspoon each ground cumin and sweet paprika
1 tablespoon finely chopped fresh mint
6 sheets fillo pastry
75g (2½ ounces) butter, melted
harissa yogurt
½ cup (140g) yogurt
1 teaspoon harissa
1 teaspoon finely grated lemon rind

1 Preheat oven to 200°C/400°F. Oil oven trays.
2 Quarter capsicum; discard seeds and membranes. Roast, skin-side up, until skin blisters and blackens. Cover capsicum with plastic or paper for 5 minutes; peel away skin, then chop capsicum finely.
3 Meanwhile, heat oil in large frying pan; stir garlic, eggplant, zucchini and tomato about 5 minutes or until vegetables soften. Add spices; cook, stirring, about 5 minutes or until fragrant. Stir in capsicum and mint; cool. Season to taste.
4 Brush 1 sheet of pastry with butter; top with a second pastry sheet. Cut layered sheets lengthways into 3 rectangles. Halve pastry rectangles crossways. Press 1 tablespoon of vegetable mixture into a log shape along one short end of each rectangle. Roll pastry over filling; fold in sides then roll up to form a cigar shape. Repeat to make a total of 18 cigars.
5 Place cigars, seam-side down, on oven trays; brush with remaining butter. Bake about 20 minutes or until browned lightly.
6 Meanwhile, make harissa yogurt; serve with cigars.
harissa yogurt Combine ingredients in small bowl.

prep + cook time 55 minutes **makes** 18
nutritional count per cigar 4.8g total fat (2.5g saturated fat); 276kJ (66 cal); 4g carbohydrate; 1.3g protein; 0.8g fibre

Lamb fillo cigars

1 tablespoon olive oil
1 medium brown onion (150g), chopped finely
2 cloves garlic, crushed
500g (1 pound) minced (ground) lamb
1 teaspoon each ground coriander, cumin, cinnamon and ginger
2 tablespoons roasted slivered almonds
1 teaspoon finely grated lemon rind
1 tablespoon lemon juice
⅓ cup finely chopped fresh coriander (cilantro)
18 sheets fillo pastry
155g (5 ounces) butter, melted
½ cup (140g) yogurt

1 Heat oil in large frying pan; stir onion and garlic, until onion softens. Add lamb and spices; cook, stirring, until lamb is browned. Stir in nuts, rind, juice and half the coriander; cool. Season to taste.
2 Preheat oven to 200°C/400°F. Oil oven trays; line with baking paper.
3 Brush 1 sheet of pastry with butter; top with 2 more sheets, brushing each with butter. Cut layered sheets lengthways into 3 rectangles. Press a rounded tablespoon of lamb mixture into a log shape along one short end of each rectangle. Roll pastry over filling; fold in sides then roll up to make a cigar shape. Repeat to make a total of 18 cigars.
4 Place cigars, seam-side down, on oven trays; brush with remaining butter. Bake about 15 minutes or until browned lightly.
5 Meanwhile, combine yogurt and remaining coriander in small bowl; serve cigars with yogurt and lemon wedges.

prep + cook time 1 hour **makes** 18
nutritional count per cigar 11.6g total fat (6.3g saturated fat); 715kJ (171 cal); 8.7g carbohydrate; 7.8g protein; 0.6g fibre

Minted tuna triangles

1 tablespoon olive oil
1 medium brown onion (150g), chopped finely
4 drained anchovy fillets, chopped finely
2 teaspoons ground cumin
425g (13½ ounces) canned tuna in brine, drained, flaked
1 egg, beaten lightly
⅓ cup finely chopped fresh flat-leaf parsley
¼ cup finely chopped fresh mint
12 sheets fillo pastry
90g (3 ounces) butter, melted
2 teaspoons poppy seeds

1 Heat oil in large frying pan; cook onion and anchovy, stirring, about 5 minutes or until soft. Add cumin, tuna, egg, parsley and mint; cook, stirring, about 30 seconds or until egg starts to set. Remove from heat, season to taste; cool.
2 Preheat oven to 200°C/400°F. Oil oven trays; line with baking paper.
3 Brush 1 sheet of pastry with butter; top with 2 more sheets, brushing each with butter. Cut layered sheets crossways into 5 strips. Place 1 rounded tablespoon of tuna mixture at one short end of each pastry strip. Fold one corner of pastry diagonally over filling to form a triangle. Continue folding to end of strip, retaining triangle shape. Repeat to make a total of 20 triangles.
4 Place triangles on trays; brush with remaining butter, sprinkle with poppy seeds. Bake triangles about 20 minutes or until browned lightly. Serve with yogurt and lemon wedges, if you like.

prep + cook time 55 minutes **makes** 20
nutritional count per triangle 5.7g total fat (2.9g saturated fat); 393kJ (94 cal); 5.1g carbohydrate; 5.4g protein; 0.4g fibre

Sweet anise rolls

1½ tablespoons dried yeast
¼ cup (60ml) warm water
½ cup (110g) caster (superfine) sugar
2 cups (300g) plain (all-purpose) flour
2 tablespoons sesame seeds
3 teaspoons anise seeds
¼ cup (60ml) milk
60g (2 ounces) butter, melted
1 egg
1 tablespoon orange blossom water
1 egg yolk
2 teaspoons sesame seeds, extra

1 Combine yeast, the water and 2 teaspoons of the sugar in small heatproof bowl, cover; stand in warm place about 10 minutes or until mixture is frothy.
2 Combine sifted flour, remaining sugar and seeds in large bowl. Stir in yeast mixture, milk, butter, egg and orange blossom water. Knead dough on floured surface about 10 minutes or until smooth and elastic. Place dough in oiled medium bowl, cover; stand in warm place about 1 hour or until doubled in size.
3 Preheat oven to 180°C/350°F. Oil oven trays.
4 Divide dough into 12 pieces; roll each piece into a ball. Place balls, about 5cm (2 inches) apart, on oven trays; cover loosely with oiled plastic wrap. Stand in warm place 20 minutes.
5 Discard plastic wrap. Brush balls with egg yolk, sprinkle with extra sesame seeds. Bake about 20 minutes.

prep + cook time 50 minutes (+ standing) **makes** 12
nutritional count per roll 6.8g total fat (3.3g saturated fat); 798kJ (191 cal); 27.5g carbohydrate; 4.6g protein; 1.2g fibre
tip These rolls (also called krachel) are sweet, fragrant rolls flavoured with anise seeds, sesame seeds and orange blossom water. They are perfect served warm, with butter, for morning or afternoon tea.

Chilli, cumin and garlic prawns

1kg (2 pounds) uncooked medium king prawns (shrimp)
¼ cup (60ml) olive oil
3 cloves garlic, sliced thinly
1 fresh long red chilli, sliced thinly
3cm (1¼-inch) piece fresh ginger (15g), cut into matchsticks
1 teaspoon each cumin seeds and sweet paprika
¼ cup each loosely packed fresh flat-leaf parsley and
    coriander (cilantro) leaves

1 Shell and devein prawns, leaving tails intact.
2 Heat oil in large frying pan; stir garlic, chilli, ginger and spices
about 2 minutes or until fragrant. Add prawns; cook, stirring, about
5 minutes or until prawns are changed in colour. Season to taste.
3 Serve prawns sprinkled with herbs; accompany with lemon wedges.

prep + cook time 40 minutes **serves** 6 as a starter or snack
nutritional count per serving 9.7g total fat (1.4g saturated fat);
660kJ (158 cal); 0.3g carbohydrate; 17.3g protein; 0.5g fibre

Moroccan-style lamb cutlets

24 french-trimmed lamb cutlets (1.2kg)
1/4 cup (40g) moroccan seasoning
2 teaspoons cumin seeds
250g (8 ounces) prepared baba ghanoush
3 green onions (scallions), sliced thinly

1 Sprinkle lamb with the seasoning. Cook lamb on heated oiled grill plate (or grill or barbecue) until browned and cooked as desired.
2 Meanwhile, dry-fry cumin seeds in small frying pan until fragrant; cool.
3 Top each lamb cutlet with a teaspoon of baba ganoush, cumin seeds and onion. Serve immediately.

prep + cook time 10 minutes **makes** 24
nutritional count per cutlet 6.4g total fat (2.4g saturated fat); 355kJ (85 cal); 0.6g carbohydrate; 6g protein; 1g fibre
tips Moroccan seasoning is a dry spice seasoning mixture available from most supermarkets.
Baba ghanoush is a Middle Eastern-style eggplant dip, also available from most supermarkets or delicatessens.

Salads

Chickpea and silver beet salad

8 spring onions (200g)
600g (1¼ pounds) canned chickpeas (garbanzo beans),
    rinsed, drained
1kg (2 pounds) silver beet (swiss chard), trimmed, shredded finely
1 large red capsicum (bell pepper) (350g), sliced thinly
paprika dressing
⅓ cup (80ml) mustard seed oil
2 teaspoons sweet paprika
1 tablespoon lemon juice
1 tablespoon light brown sugar

1 Make paprika dressing.
2 Trim green tops from spring onion bulbs. Cut bulbs into wedges;
thinly slice three of the green tops, discard remaining tops.
3 Combine onions with remaining ingredients and three-quarters of
the dressing in large bowl; season to taste.
4 Serve salad drizzled with remaining dressing.
paprika dressing Place ingredients in screw-top jar; shake well.

prep time 20 minutes **serves** 6
nutritional count per serving 13.9g total fat (1.7g saturated fat);
882kJ (211 cal); 14.2g carbohydrate; 5.8g protein; 4.7g fibre
tips Mustard seed oil can be found in most large supermarkets or
health-food stores.
A 1kg (2-pound) bunch of silver beet should give you about 250g
(8 ounces) of leaves after trimming.

Cucumber and fetta salad with za'atar

2 lebanese cucumbers (260g), peeled, sliced thinly
90g (3 ounces) goat's milk fetta cheese
2 tablespoons finely chopped fresh mint
1 tablespoon lemon juice
1 tablespoon olive oil
2 teaspoons za'atar

1 Arrange cucumber on large serving platter.
2 Combine cheese and mint in small bowl; sprinkle cheese mixture over cucumber. Drizzle with juice and oil, then sprinkle with za'atar.

prep time 10 minutes **serves** 4
nutritional count per serving 9.9g total fat (4.1g saturated fat); 468kJ (112 cal); 1.2g carbohydrate; 4.3g protein; 0.7g fibre
tip Za'atar is available from some large supermarkets, delicatessens and Middle Eastern food stores. Replace it with dried oregano if unavailable.

Roasted capsicum and beetroot salad

500g (1 pound) baby beetroot (beets)
1 small red capsicum (bell pepper) (150g)
1 small orange capsicum (bell pepper) (150g)
1 small yellow capsicum (bell pepper) (150g)
cooking-oil spray
½ small red onion (50g), chopped finely
1 tablespoon finely chopped fresh flat-leaf parsley
1 tablespoon thinly sliced preserved lemon rind
1 tablespoon lemon juice

1 Preheat oven to 220°C/425°F.
2 Trim leaves from beetroot; wrap each beetroot in foil, place on oven tray. Place capsicums on baking-paper-lined oven tray; spray with oil. Roast beetroot and capsicums about 30 minutes or until beetroot are tender and capsicums have blistered and blackened.
3 Cool beetroot 10 minutes then peel and quarter. Cover capsicums with plastic or paper for 5 minutes. Quarter capsicums; discard seeds and membranes. Peel away skin, then halve each quarter lengthways.
4 Arrange beetroot and capsicum on large serving platter. Sprinkle with onion, parsley and preserved lemon; drizzle with juice.

prep + cook time 50 minutes **serves** 4
nutritional count per serving 1.6g total fat (0.2g saturated fat); 397kJ (95 cal); 13.9g carbohydrate; 3.9g protein; 4.8g fibre

Salad of herbs

60g (2 ounces) baby rocket (arugula)
½ cup each loosely packed fresh flat-leaf parsley and
    coriander (cilantro) leaves
2 cups (230g) firmly packed trimmed watercress
½ small red onion (50g), sliced thinly
⅓ cup (55g) seeded mixed olives, chopped coarsely
preserved lemon dressing
1 clove garlic, crushed
1 tablespoon olive oil
¼ teaspoon sweet paprika
2 tablespoons lemon juice
1 tablespoon finely chopped preserved lemon rind

1 Make preserved lemon dressing.
2 Combine ingredients and dressing in large bowl; season to taste.
preserved lemon dressing Place ingredients in screw-top jar;
shake well.

prep time 15 minutes **serves** 4
nutritional count per serving 5.3g total fat (0.7g saturated fat);
339kJ (81 cal); 3.9g carbohydrate; 2.6g protein; 3.5g fibre

Tomato and preserved lemon salad

750g (1½ pounds) baby egg (plum) truss tomatoes, halved
1 small red onion (100g), sliced thinly
½ cup firmly packed fresh coriander (cilantro) leaves
preserved lemon dressing
⅓ cup (80ml) lemon juice
2 tablespoons olive oil
1 tablespoon finely chopped preserved lemon rind
1 tablespoon finely chopped fresh flat-leaf parsley
1 clove garlic, crushed
½ teaspoon white sugar
¼ teaspoon ground cumin
pinch sweet paprika

1 Make preserved lemon dressing.
2 Combine tomato, onion, coriander and dressing in large bowl; season to taste.
preserved lemon dressing Place ingredients in screw-top jar; shake well.

prep time 10 minutes **serves** 6
nutritional count per serving 6.3g total fat (0.9g saturated fat); 355kJ (85 cal); 4.5g carbohydrate; 1g protein; 2.4g fibre

Sweet cucumber and orange salad

2 large oranges (600g)
1 telegraph (hothouse) cucumber (400g)
2 cups loosely packed fresh mint leaves
honey lemon dressing
¼ cup (60ml) avocado oil
1 tablespoon finely grated lemon rind
1 tablespoon lemon juice
2 teaspoons honey

1 Make honey lemon dressing.
2 Segment oranges over small bowl; reserve juice.
3 Use vegetable peeler to cut cucumber into thin ribbons. Place cucumber in medium bowl with mint, orange segments, reserved juice and dressing; toss gently to combine. Season to taste.
honey lemon dressing Place ingredients in screw-top jar; shake well.

prep time 20 minutes **serves** 4
nutritional count per serving 14.3g total fat (1.7g saturated fat); 840kJ (201 cal); 13.5g carbohydrate; 2.6g protein; 4.6g fibre
tip Traditionally served as an accompaniment to spicy dishes, this recipe would also make a great light vegetarian starter.

Spicy lentil and rice salad

1 cup (200g) basmati rice
¼ cup (60ml) olive oil
30g (1 ounce) butter
4 medium red onions (680g), sliced thinly
4 cloves garlic, crushed
2 teaspoons each ground coriander, cinnamon, cumin and sweet paprika
4 green onions (scallions), sliced thinly
400g (13 ounces) canned brown lentils, rinsed, drained

1 Cook rice in medium saucepan of boiling water until tender; drain. Rinse under cold water; drain.
2 Meanwhile, heat oil and butter in large frying pan; cook red onion and garlic, stirring occasionally, about 20 minutes or until onion is lightly caramelised.
3 Add spices; cook, stirring, about 1 minute or until fragrant.
4 Remove from heat; stir in green onion, lentils and rice. Season to taste. Serve warm.

prep + cook time 35 minutes **serves** 6
nutritional count per serving 13.7g total fat (4g saturated fat); 1258kJ (301 cal); 37.3g carbohydrate; 5.9g protein; 3.5g fibre

Orange and radish salad

4 medium oranges (960g)
500g (1 pound) red radishes, trimmed
1 tablespoon olive oil
2 teaspoons white wine vinegar
¼ cup finely chopped fresh mint

1 Finely grate 2 teaspoons rind from half an orange. Segment oranges over small bowl; reserve 1 tablespoon juice.
2 Using mandolin or V-slicer, slice radishes as thinly as possible.
3 Whisk reserved juice, oil and vinegar in medium bowl. Add rind, orange segments, radish and mint; toss gently to combine. Serve immediately.

prep time 25 minutes **serves** 4
nutritional count per serving 5g total fat (0.6g saturated fat);
535kJ (128 cal); 15.6g carbohydrate; 2.7g protein; 4.8g fibre
tips You need a bunch of red radishes for this recipe.
This recipe is best made just before serving; it will become soggy
if left standing.

Carrot, raisin and herb salad

1.2kg (2½ pounds) baby carrots, trimmed
1 teaspoon each ground cumin and sweet paprika
½ teaspoon ground cinnamon
¼ cup (60ml) olive oil
¼ cup (60ml) orange juice
2 tablespoons lemon juice
⅓ cup (50g) raisins
⅔ cup coarsely chopped fresh flat-leaf parsley
¼ cup firmly packed fresh mint leaves

1 Preheat oven to 200°C/400°F.
2 Combine carrots, spices and half the oil in large shallow baking dish; roast, uncovered, about 15 minutes or until carrots are tender. Cool 20 minutes.
3 Meanwhile, make dressing by combining juices, raisins, remaining oil and half the parsley in large jug; season to taste.
4 Serve carrots drizzled with dressing; sprinkle with mint leaves and remaining parsley.

prep + cook time 30 minutes (+ cooling) **serves** 6
nutritional count per serving 9.4g total fat (1.3g saturated fat); 698kJ (167 cal); 16.2g carbohydrate; 1.9g protein; 5.9g fibre
tip You need 3 bunches of baby carrots, also known as dutch carrots; they're available from supermarkets and greengrocers.

Eggplant and tomato salad

6 baby eggplants (360g)
¼ cup (60ml) olive oil
½ teaspoon each ground coriander, cumin and smoked paprika
1 medium tomato (150g), seeded, chopped finely
1 small red onion (100g), chopped finely
2 tablespoons (20g) seeded black olives, chopped finely
1 tablespoon finely chopped fresh flat-leaf parsley
2 teaspoons finely chopped fresh mint
1 teaspoon finely grated lemon rind
2 teaspoons lemon juice

1 Carefully cut eggplants lengthways into four slices, leaving tops intact.
Combine eggplant and half the oil in medium bowl; season to taste.
2 Cook eggplants on heated oiled grill plate (or grill or barbecue),
flattening and fanning with the back of a spatula, until eggplants
are tender.
3 Meanwhile, dry-fry spices in small frying pan until fragrant; cool.
Combine spices, remaining oil and remaining ingredients in small bowl;
season to taste.
4 Serve eggplant; drizzled with tomato mixture.

prep + cook time 35 minutes **serves** 6
nutritional count per serving 9.3g total fat (1.3g saturated fat);
435kJ (104 cal); 3.3g carbohydrate; 1.1g protein; 1.8g fibre

Spicy tuna salad

2 teaspoons caraway seeds
½ teaspoon ground cinnamon
425g (13¾ ounces) canned tuna in oil
300g (10 ounces) canned chickpeas (garbanzo beans),
   rinsed, drained
1 small green capsicum (bell pepper) (150g),
   cut into 1cm (½-inch) pieces
⅓ cup (40g) seeded black olives, chopped coarsely
200g (6½ ounces) red grape tomatoes, quartered
2 green onions (scallions), sliced thinly
2 teaspoons finely grated orange rind
2 tablespoons orange juice
1 tablespoon harissa

1 Dry-fry spices in small frying pan until fragrant; cool.
2 Drain tuna; reserve 2 tablespoons of the oil. Flake tuna coarsely.
3 Combine tuna, reserved oil, spices and remaining ingredients in
large bowl; season to taste. Serve with toasted turkish bread.

prep + cook time 25 minutes **serves** 8
nutritional count per serving 12g total fat (1.8g saturated fat);
782kJ (187 cal); 6.2g carbohydrate; 12.7g protein; 2.1g fibre

Tomato, olive and radish salad

1½ cups (200g) seeded black olives
200g (6½ ounces) red grape tomatoes, halved
14 trimmed red radishes (210g), sliced thinly
200g (6½ ounces) button mushrooms, halved
½ cup loosely packed fresh flat-leaf parsley leaves
moroccan dressing
2 teaspoons moroccan seasoning
½ teaspoon each ground coriander and sweet paprika
2 tablespoons red wine vinegar
⅓ cup (80ml) extra virgin olive oil

1 Make moroccan dressing.
2 Combine salad ingredients and dressing in large bowl. Cover;
refrigerate 3 hours before serving.
moroccan dressing Place ingredients in screw-top jar; shake well.

prep time 15 minutes (+ refrigeration) **serves** 8
nutritional count per serving 9.5g total fat (1.3g saturated fat);
506kJ (121 cal); 6.7g carbohydrate; 1.5g protein; 1.8g fibre
tip Salad can be prepared a day ahead; add the dressing up to 3 hours
before serving.

Radish and cucumber chopped salad

4 trimmed red radishes (60g), sliced thinly
2 lebanese cucumbers (260g), peeled, chopped finely
1 small red onion (100g), sliced thinly
½ teaspoon sea salt
1 clove garlic, crushed
2 tablespoons lemon juice
¼ cup (60ml) extra-virgin olive oil
½ cup coarsely chopped fresh mint
60g (2 ounces) baby rocket (arugula) leaves
2 medium vine-ripened tomatoes (300g), chopped finely
¼ cup (30g) seeded small black olives

1 Place radish, cucumber and onion in salad bowl, sprinkle with salt; leave to stand for 5 minutes.
2 Pour combined garlic, juice and oil over vegetables in bowl; toss gently to combine. Cover; refrigerate 2 hours.
3 Just before serving, stir in mint, rocket and tomatoes. Serve salad topped with olives.

prep time 15 minutes (+ refrigeration) **serves** 6
nutritional count per serving 9.4g total fat (1.3g saturated fat); 468kJ (112 cal); 4.5g carbohydrate; 1.5g protein; 2g fibre

Tomato and herb salad

5 medium tomatoes (750g), chopped coarsely
¼ cup coarsely chopped fresh flat-leaf parsley
2 tablespoons each coarsely chopped fresh mint and dill
dressing
2 cloves garlic, crushed
2 tablespoons lemon juice
1 tablespoon olive oil
2 teaspoons white wine vinegar

1 Make dressing.
2 Combine tomatoes, herbs and dressing in medium bowl.
dressing Place ingredients in screw-top jar, season to taste; shake well.

prep time 15 minutes **serves** 4
nutritional count per serving 4.8g total fat (0.7g saturated fat); 309kJ (74 cal); 4.1g carbohydrate; 2.2g protein; 2.8g fibre

Watermelon, mint and fetta salad

2 teaspoons white sugar
¼ cup (60ml) lime juice
100g (3 ounces) fetta cheese, crumbled
½ small red onion (50g), sliced thinly
½ cup coarsely chopped fresh mint
850g (1¾ pounds) seedless watermelon, cut into wedges

1 Dissolve sugar in small jug with juice.
2 Place juice mixture in medium bowl with cheese, onion and mint, season to taste; toss gently to combine.
3 Spoon cheese mixture over watermelon.

prep time 10 minutes **serves** 4
nutritional count per serving 6.2g total fat (3.8g saturated fat); 506kJ (121cal); 10.1g carbohydrate; 5.4g protein; 1.5g fibre
tips Don't chop the mint until just before making this salad – it tends to blacken and go limp after it's been cut.
We used a fairly bland fetta here so that its flavour didn't overpower the melon.

Radish and herb salad

2 large pitta breads (160g), cut into wedges
1 medium green capsicum (bell pepper) (200g), chopped finely
1 lebanese cucumber (130g), seeded, chopped finely
1 medium tomato (150g), chopped finely
4 red radishes (140g), grated coarsely
½ cup finely chopped fresh flat-leaf parsley
⅓ cup finely chopped fresh mint
¼ cup coarsely chopped fresh coriander (cilantro)
2 tablespoons olive oil
2 tablespoons lemon juice
2 cloves garlic, crushed

1 Preheat grill (broiler).
2 Place bread on oven trays; toast under grill about 5 minutes or until browned both sides and crisp.
3 Combine remaining ingredients in medium bowl; season to taste.
4 Serve salad with pitta crisps.

prep + cook time 25 minutes **serves** 8
nutritional count per serving 5.2g total fat (0.7g saturated fat); 468kJ (112 cal); 12.6g carbohydrate; 2.8g protein; 1.9g fibre

Baby carrot and beetroot salad

800g (1 ½ pounds) baby carrots, trimmed
2 large beetroot (beets) (400g), grated coarsely
¼ cup (70g) yogurt
1 teaspoon ground cumin
1 tablespoon finely chopped fresh mint
2 tablespoons orange juice
1 tablespoon olive oil

1 Boil, steam or microwave carrots until tender; drain. Rinse under cold water, drain.
2 Squeeze excess moisture from beetroot.
3 Combine yogurt, cumin, mint, juice and oil in small bowl; season to taste.
4 Serve vegetables drizzled with yogurt mixture.

prep + cook time 25 minutes **serves** 8
nutritional count per serving 2.6g total fat (0.4g saturated fat);
318kJ (76 cal); 9.2g carbohydrate; 2g protein; 3.9g fibre
tips Beetroot will discolour your skin, so always use disposable gloves when handling them.
Baby carrots are also called dutch carrots; you rarely need to peel them.
Beetroot, carrots and the yogurt mixture can be prepared a day ahead. Assemble salad at serving time.

Sumac, onion and mint salad

4 small red onions (400g), sliced thinly
2 tablespoons olive oil
2 tablespoons finely chopped fresh mint
1 tablespoon lemon juice
1 tablespoon sumac

1 Combine ingredients in medium bowl; season to taste.

prep time 10 minutes **serves** 8
nutritional count per serving 4.6g total fat (0.6g saturated fat);
238kJ (57 cal); 2.8g carbohydrate; 0.7g protein; 0.7g fibre
tip Any small mint leaves can be left whole, rather than chopped.

Spiced cabbage, orange and radish salad

1 medium orange (240g)
2 cups (160g) finely shredded green cabbage
2 red radishes (70g), trimmed, sliced thinly
½ cup loosely packed fresh mint leaves
cumin and orange dressing
1 teaspoon cumin seeds
¼ teaspoon hot paprika
2 tablespoons olive oil
1 tablespoon white balsamic vinegar

1 Segment orange over small bowl; reserve 1 tablespoon juice
for dressing.
2 Make cumin and orange dressing.
3 Combine orange segments, remaining ingredients and dressing
in large bowl.
cumin and orange dressing Dry-fry spices in small frying pan
until fragrant; cool. Place spices in screw-top jar with oil, vinegar and
reserved juice, season to taste; shake well.

prep + cook time 25 minutes **serves** 4
nutritional count per serving 9.3g total fat (1.3g saturated fat);
472kJ (113 cal); 5g carbohydrate; 1.3g protein; 2.9g fibre

Tomato and pomegranate salad

1 teaspoon cumin seeds
2 medium tomatoes (300g), chopped finely
1 medium red capsicum (bell pepper) (200g), chopped finely
1 small red onion (100g), chopped finely
1 fresh long red chilli, chopped finely
¼ cup finely chopped fresh flat-leaf parsley
1 tablespoon pomegranate molasses
2 tablespoons olive oil

1 Dry-fry seeds in small frying pan until fragrant; cool.
2 Place seeds in medium bowl with remaining ingredients, season to taste; toss gently to combine. Serve with toasted turkish bread.

prep + cook time 20 minutes **serves** 8
nutritional count per serving 4.6g total fat (0.6g saturated fat);
234kJ (56 cal); 2.3g carbohydrate; 0.9g protein; 1g fibre

Couscous

Roasted vegetable couscous

1 medium red onion (170g), cut into wedges
4 small zucchini (360g), halved lengthways
10 baby carrots (175g), halved lengthways
2 tablespoons olive oil
1 cup (200g) couscous
1 cup (250ml) boiling water
450g (14½ ounces) bottled roasted red capsicum (bell pepper),
   drained, sliced thinly
2 tablespoons finely chopped fresh thyme

1 Preheat oven to 220°C/425°F.
2 Combine onion, zucchini, carrot and oil in large shallow baking dish;
season to taste. Roast, uncovered, about 20 minutes or until vegetables
are tender.
3 Combine couscous with the water in large heatproof bowl, cover; stand
about 5 minutes or until liquid is absorbed, fluffing with fork occasionally.
4 Stir vegetables and remaining ingredients into couscous; season to taste.

prep + cook time 35 minutes **serves** 6
nutritional count per serving 8.3g total fat (1.3g saturated fat);
995kJ (238 cal); 32.1g carbohydrate; 6.7g protein; 3.3g fibre
tip You can use any leftover or store-bought roasted vegetables
in this recipe.

Spiced cauliflower couscous

1 tablespoon olive oil
1 small brown onion (80g), sliced thinly
1 teaspoon ground coriander
½ small cauliflower (500g), cut into small florets
2 tablespoons water
⅓ cup coarsely chopped fresh coriander (cilantro)
1¼ cups (250g) couscous
1¼ cups (310ml) boiling water

1 Heat oil in large saucepan; cook onion, stirring, until soft. Add ground coriander and cauliflower; cook, stirring, until fragrant. Add the water; cook, covered, about 10 minutes or until cauliflower is tender and water is absorbed. Stir in half the fresh coriander.
2 Meanwhile, combine couscous with the boiling water in large heatproof bowl, cover; stand about 5 minutes or until liquid is absorbed, fluffing with fork occasionally.
3 Stir cauliflower mixture into couscous; season to taste. Serve sprinkled with remaining fresh coriander.

prep + cook time 25 minutes **serves** 6
nutritional count per serving 3.4g total fat (0.5g saturated fat); 844kJ (202 cal); 34.2g carbohydrate; 7.1g protein; 1.9g fibre

Pumpkin, apricot and cheese couscous

750g (1½ pounds) pumpkin, unpeeled, cut into wedges
2 tablespoons olive oil
1 cup (200g) couscous
2 tablespoons finely grated lemon rind
1 cup (250ml) boiling water
1 cup (150g) dried apricots, halved
½ cup (80g) pepitas
2 tablespoons lemon juice
2 tablespoons finely chopped fresh flat-leaf parsley
125g (4 ounces) soft goat's cheese, crumbled

1 Preheat oven to 200°C/400°F.
2 Combine pumpkin and oil in medium shallow baking dish. Roast, uncovered, about 20 minutes or until pumpkin is tender.
3 Meanwhile, combine couscous, rind and the water in large heatproof bowl, cover; stand about 5 minutes or until liquid is absorbed, fluffing with fork occasionally.
4 Stir apricots, pepitas, juice and parsley into couscous; season to taste.
5 Top couscous with pumpkin; sprinkle with cheese.

prep + cook time 30 minutes **serves** 6
nutritional count per serving 16.1g total fat (4.3g saturated fat); 1643kJ (393 cal); 45.5g carbohydrate; 13.6g protein; 5.4g fibre

Spicy red couscous

1 tablespoon olive oil
1 tablespoon harissa
2 teaspoons sweet paprika
4 green onions (scallions), sliced thinly
1 cup (250ml) chicken stock
½ cup (125ml) water
1½ cups (300g) couscous
1 tablespoon lemon juice

1 Heat oil in medium saucepan; cook harissa, paprika and half the onion, stirring, about 2 minutes or until fragrant.
2 Add stock and the water to onion mixture; bring to the boil. Remove from heat, add couscous; cover, stand about 5 minutes or until liquid is absorbed, fluffing with fork occasionally.
3 Stir juice into couscous; season to taste. Serve sprinkled with remaining onion.

prep + cook time 15 minutes **serves** 6
nutritional count per serving 3.6g total fat (0.6g saturated fat); 928kJ (222 cal); 39.4g carbohydrate; 7g protein; 0.7g fibre

Preserved lemon couscous

1 ¼ cups (250g) couscous
1 ¼ cups (310ml) boiling water
15g (½ ounce) butter
400g (13 ounces) canned chickpeas (garbanzo beans), rinsed, drained
½ cup (60g) seeded green olives, chopped coarsely
2 tablespoons lemon juice
3 green onions (scallions), sliced thinly
2 tablespoons finely chopped fresh flat-leaf parsley
1 tablespoon thinly sliced preserved lemon rind

1 Combine couscous with the water and butter in large heatproof bowl, cover; stand about 5 minutes or until water is absorbed, fluffing with fork occasionally.
2 Stir remaining ingredients into couscous; season to taste.

prep time 15 minutes **serves** 6
nutritional count per serving 5.3g total fat (1.8g saturated fat); 1020kJ (244 cal); 38.5g carbohydrate; 8.5g protein; 3g fibre

Baked tomato couscous

1 cup (250ml) chicken stock
1 cup (200g) couscous
15g (½ ounce) butter
2 trimmed medium silver beet (swiss chard) leaves (160g),
   shredded finely
410g (13 ounces) canned tomato puree
½ cup (60g) coarsely grated gruyère cheese

1 Preheat oven to 200°C/400°F. Oil shallow 1-litre (4-cup) ovenproof dish.
2 Bring stock to the boil in medium saucepan; remove from heat, add couscous and butter. Cover; stand about 5 minutes or until liquid is absorbed, fluffing with fork occasionally. Stir silver beet into couscous; season to taste.
3 Spoon couscous into dish; press down gently. Pour tomato over couscous, sprinkle with cheese.
4 Bake about 30 minutes or until cheese is browned lightly.

prep + cook time 45 minutes **serves** 6
nutritional count per serving 5.9g total fat (3.6g saturated fat); 882kJ (211 cal); 29.6g carbohydrate; 8.5g protein; 1.9g fibre
tip To make this a vegetarian couscous, replace the chicken stock with vegetable stock.

Sweet breakfast couscous

4 x 5cm (2-inch) strips orange rind, shredded finely
1½ cups (375ml) orange juice
2 tablespoons honey
1 tablespoon olive oil
1 teaspoon orange blossom water
½ teaspoon ground cinnamon
1½ cups (300g) couscous
8 fresh dates (160g), seeded, quartered lengthways
⅓ cup (55g) coarsely chopped blanched almonds, roasted
⅓ cup (45g) coarsely chopped unsalted pistachios, roasted
¼ cup (40g) finely chopped dried apricots
1 cup (280g) greek-style yogurt

1 Combine rind and juice in medium saucepan; bring to the boil.
Remove from heat; stir in honey, oil, orange blossom water and cinnamon.
2 Combine couscous with orange mixture in large heatproof bowl,
cover; stand about 5 minutes or until liquid is absorbed, fluffing with
fork occasionally.
3 Stir dates, nuts and apricots into couscous; serve with yogurt.
Drizzle with a little extra honey.

prep + cook time 20 minutes **serves** 6
nutritional count per serving 15.6g total fat (3.4g saturated fat);
1927kJ (461 cal); 65.4g carbohydrate; 13.1g protein; 3.5g fibre

Saffron cinnamon couscous

3½ cups (875ml) chicken stock
1 teaspoon saffron threads
4 cinnamon sticks
3 cups (600g) couscous
2 tablespoons vegetable oil
2 medium red onions (340g), chopped finely
3 cloves garlic, crushed
2 small fresh red thai (serrano) chillies, chopped finely
2 teaspoons ground cumin
¾ cup (105g) slivered almonds, roasted
1 cup coarsely chopped fresh coriander (cilantro)

1 Bring stock, saffron and cinnamon to the boil in small saucepan.
Reduce heat; simmer, covered, 15 minutes. Remove cinnamon.
2 Combine couscous and hot stock in large heatproof bowl, cover; stand
about 5 minutes or until liquid is absorbed, fluffing with fork occasionally.
3 Meanwhile, heat oil in large frying pan; cook onion, garlic, chilli and
cumin, stirring, until onion softens.
4 Add couscous to pan; stir until heated through. Stir in nuts and
coriander; season to taste.

prep + cook time 20 minutes **serves** 8
nutritional count per serving 12.8g total fat (1.4g saturated fat);
1777kJ (425 cal); 61.3g carbohydrate; 14.3g protein; 3g fibre
tip This recipe is best made close to serving time.

Couscous with tomato and rocket

2 teaspoons olive oil
1 large red onion (300g), chopped finely
1 clove garlic, crushed
2 cups (400g) couscous
45g (1½ ounces) butter
2 cups (500ml) boiling water
4 medium tomatoes (600g), chopped coarsely
½ cup (80g) pine nuts, roasted
100g (3 ounces) baby rocket (arugula) leaves, chopped coarsely
2 tablespoons finely chopped fresh basil
1 tablespoon finely chopped fresh flat-parsley
1 tablespoon finely grated lemon rind
¼ cup (60ml) extra virgin olive oil
2 tablespoons lemon juice

1 Heat oil in small frying pan; cook onion and garlic, stirring, until onion softens.
2 Combine couscous, butter and the water in large heatproof bowl, cover; stand about 5 minutes or until liquid is absorbed, fluffing with fork occasionally. Cool.
3 Stir onion mixture and remaining ingredients into couscous; season to taste.

prep + cook time 20 minutes **serves** 4
nutritional count per serving 40.2g total fat (9.3g saturated fat); 3298kJ (789 cal); 85.5g carbohydrate; 18.8g protein; 5.4g fibre

Spiced lamb and spinach couscous

¾ cup (180ml) olive oil
1½ teaspoons caster (superfine) sugar
1 teaspoon each sweet paprika and ground cumin
1 fresh small red thai (serrano) chilli, chopped finely
2 cloves garlic, crushed
600g (1¼ pounds) lamb backstraps
⅓ cup (80ml) lemon juice
2 large carrots (360g), sliced thinly
1½ cups (300g) couscous
1½ cups (375ml) boiling water
400g (13 ounces) canned chickpeas (garbanzo beans), rinsed, drained
75g (2½ ounces) baby spinach leaves
¼ cup finely chopped fresh mint
⅓ cup firmly packed fresh coriander (cilantro) leaves

1 Reserve 1 tablespoon of the oil. Place remaining oil, sugar, spices, chilli and garlic in screw-top jar; shake well. Combine 2 tablespoons of the dressing in medium bowl with lamb; cover, refrigerate 3 hours. Add juice to remaining dressing.
2 Boil, steam or microwave carrots until tender; drain. Combine hot carrots and half the dressing in medium bowl.
3 Heat the reserved oil in large frying pan; cook lamb about 10 minutes or until browned all over and cooked as desired. Remove from heat, cover; stand 5 minutes, then slice thinly.
4 Meanwhile, combine couscous and the water in large heatproof bowl, cover; stand about 5 minutes or until liquid is absorbed, fluffing with fork occasionally.
5 Stir lamb, carrots, remaining dressing and remaining ingredients into couscous; season to taste.

prep + cook time 25 minutes (+ refrigeration) **serves** 6
nutritional count per serving 37.4g total fat (8g saturated fat); 2755kJ (659 cal); 48g carbohydrate; 30.8g protein; 4.6g fibre

Prawn and couscous salad with lemon coriander dressing

1 cup (200g) couscous
1 cup (250ml) boiling water
500g (1 pound) medium cooked king prawns (shrimp)
1 medium lebanese cucumber (130g), sliced thinly
1 medium red capsicum (bell pepper) (200g), chopped finely
1 cup loosely packed fresh coriander (cilantro) leaves
1 cup (115g) firmly packed trimmed watercress
lemon coriander dressing
1 teaspoon finely grated lemon rind
⅓ cup (80ml) lemon juice
2 cloves garlic, crushed
¼ cup (60ml) fish sauce
¼ cup coarsely chopped fresh coriander (cilantro)

1 Make lemon coriander dressing.
2 Combine couscous and the water in large heatproof bowl, cover; stand about 5 minutes or until liquid is absorbed, fluffing with fork occasionally.
3 Meanwhile, shell and devein prawns, leaving tails intact.
4 Stir prawns, dressing and remaining ingredients into couscous.
lemon coriander dressing Place ingredients in screw-top jar, season to taste; shake well.

prep time 25 minutes **serves** 4
nutritional count per serving 1.1g total fat (0.1g saturated fat); 1179kJ (282 cal); 42.5g carbohydrate; 22.7g protein; 3.9g fibre

Couscous, carrot and chickpea salad

2 cups (400g) couscous
2 cups (500ml) boiling water
½ cup (75g) dried currants
300g (10 ounces) canned chickpeas (garbanzo beans), rinsed, drained
2 medium carrots (240g), grated finely
1 cup loosely packed fresh coriander (cilantro) leaves
lemon paprika dressing
⅓ cup (80ml) olive oil
2 teaspoons finely grated lemon rind
2 tablespoons lemon juice
½ teaspoon each ground coriander, cumin and sweet paprika
1 clove garlic, crushed

1 Combine couscous and the water in large heatproof bowl, cover; stand about 5 minutes or until liquid is absorbed, fluffing with fork occasionally.
2 Meanwhile, make lemon paprika dressing.
3 Stir dressing and remaining ingredients into couscous.
lemon paprika dressing Place ingredients in screw-top jar, season to taste; shake well.

prep time 15 minutes **serves** 6
nutritional count per serving 13.4g total fat (1.9g saturated fat); 1839kJ (440 cal); 65.7g carbohydrate; 11.5g protein; 4.5g fibre

Spicy couscous salad

1 cup (250ml) chicken stock
2 cups (500ml) water
3 cups (600g) couscous
⅓ cup (50g) pine nuts, roasted
1 small red onion (100g), chopped finely
½ cup (75g) dried currants
⅓ cup each coarsely chopped fresh mint and flat-leaf parsley
harissa dressing
2 teaspoons harissa
⅓ cup (80ml) lemon juice
⅓ cup (80ml) olive oil

1 Bring stock and the water to the boil in medium saucepan.
2 Combine couscous and hot stock mixture in large heatproof bowl, cover; stand about 5 minutes or until liquid is absorbed, fluffing with fork occasionally.
3 Stir nuts, onion, currants and herbs into couscous.
4 Make harissa dressing.
5 Just before serving, pour dressing over couscous; toss gently.
harissa dressing Place ingredients in screw-top jar; shake well.

prep + cook time 15 minutes **serves** 8
nutritional count per serving 14.2g total fat (1.7g saturated fat);
1843kJ (441 cal); 65.3g carbohydrate; 11.4g protein; 2g fibre

Olive and herb couscous salad

2 cups (400g) couscous
2 cups (500ml) boiling water
6 green onions (scallions), chopped coarsely
4 large tomatoes (880g), seeded, sliced thinly
½ cup (80g) sliced black olives
1 cup each coarsely chopped fresh mint and flat-leaf parsley
lemon garlic dressing
½ cup (125ml) olive oil
1 tablespoon white wine vinegar
2 tablespoons lemon juice
1 clove garlic, crushed

1 Combine couscous and the water in large heatproof bowl, cover; stand about 5 minutes or until liquid is absorbed, fluffing with fork occasionally.
2 Meanwhile, make lemon garlic dressing.
3 Stir dressing and remaining ingredients into couscous.
lemon garlic dressing Place ingredients in screw-top jar, season to taste; shake well.

prep + cook time 15 minutes **serves** 6
nutritional count per serving 19.7g total fat (2.8g saturated fat); 1877kJ (449 cal); 56.3g carbohydrate; 9.9g protein; 2.9g fibre

Roasted pumpkin and spinach couscous

600g (1¼ pounds) pumpkin, chopped coarsely
1 tablespoon olive oil
1 cup (250ml) chicken stock
1 cup (250ml) water
2 cups (400g) couscous
150g (5 ounces) trimmed spinach, shredded coarsely
½ cup (50g) roasted walnuts, chopped coarsely
cumin dressing
¼ cup (60ml) lemon juice
¼ cup (60ml) olive oil
1 teaspoon honey
¾ teaspoon ground cumin
½ teaspoon cayenne pepper

1 Preheat oven to 220°C/425°F.
2 Place pumpkin, in single layer, on oven tray; drizzle with oil. Roast about 30 minutes or until tender, turning halfway through cooking time.
3 Meanwhile, bring stock and the water to the boil in medium saucepan. Combine couscous and hot stock mixture in large heatproof bowl, cover; stand 5 minutes, fluffing with fork occasionally. Stir in spinach, cover; stand 5 minutes.
4 Make cumin dressing.
5 Stir pumpkin, nuts and dressing into couscous mixture.
cumin dressing Place ingredients in screw-top jar, season to taste; shake well.

prep + cook time 45 minutes **serves** 4
nutritional count per serving 28.5g total fat (3.8g saturated fat); 2930kJ (701 cal); 89g carbohydrate; 19.5g protein; 4.5g fibre
tip You need about 300g (10 ounces) of spinach for this recipe, or you can use an equivalent weight of trimmed baby spinach leaves instead.

Olive and parsley couscous

1½ cups (375ml) vegetable stock
1½ cups (300g) couscous
30g (1 ounce) butter
1 cup (120g) seeded black olives
½ cup coarsely chopped fresh flat-leaf parsley

1 Bring stock to the boil in small saucepan.
2 Combine couscous, butter and hot stock in large heatproof bowl, cover; stand about 5 minutes or until liquid is absorbed, fluffing with fork occasionally.
3 Stir olives and parsley into couscous; season to taste.

prep + cook time 15 minutes **serves** 4
nutritional count per serving 7.3g total fat (4.4g saturated fat); 1572kJ (376 cal); 64.9g carbohydrate; 11.1g protein; 1.4g fibre

Fruity couscous

3 cups (750ml) chicken stock
3 cups (600g) couscous
1 medium red onion (170g), chopped finely
⅔ cup (110g) finely chopped dried apricots
200g (6½ ounces) red seedless grapes, halved
½ cup (75g) dried currants
½ cup (70g) flaked almonds, roasted
⅓ cup coarsely chopped fresh flat-leaf parsley
lemon dressing
⅓ cup (80ml) lemon juice
2 tablespoons olive oil
1 teaspoon dijon mustard

1 Bring stock to the boil in medium saucepan.
2 Combine couscous and hot stock in large heatproof bowl, cover; stand about 5 minutes or until liquid is absorbed, fluffing with fork occasionally.
3 Meanwhile, make lemon dressing.
4 Stir dressing and remaining ingredients into couscous.
lemon dressing Place ingredients in screw-top jar, season to taste; shake well.

prep + cook time 30 minutes **serves** 10
nutritional count per serving 8.5g total fat (1g saturated fat); 1522kJ (364 cal); 60.7g carbohydrate; 11.1g protein; 3.1g fibre
tip You can replace the chicken stock with vegetable stock or even water, if you prefer.

Pumpkin and pistachio couscous with grilled haloumi

1 cup (250ml) vegetable stock
⅔ cup (160ml) water
1 tablespoon finely grated
   lemon rind
⅓ cup (80ml) lemon juice
60g (2 ounces) butter
1½ cups (300g) couscous
1 tablespoon olive oil
1 medium red onion (170g),
   chopped finely
1 clove garlic, crushed
2 teaspoons sweet smoked
   paprika

1 teaspoon each ground turmeric
   and cumin
½ teaspoon cayenne pepper
½ cup (70g) roasted unsalted
   shelled pistachios
¼ cup (50g) finely chopped
   preserved lemon rind
¼ cup each finely chopped fresh
   flat-leaf parsley and mint
600g (1¼ pounds) pumpkin,
   sliced thinly
180g (6 ounces) haloumi cheese

1 Bring stock, the water, rind, juice and butter to the boil in medium saucepan.
2 Combine couscous and hot stock mixture in large heatproof bowl, cover; stand about 5 minutes or until liquid is absorbed, fluffing with fork occasionally.
3 Meanwhile, heat oil in medium frying pan; cook onion, garlic and spices, stirring, until onion softens.
4 Stir onion mixture, nuts, preserved lemon and herbs into couscous; cover to keep warm.
5 Cook pumpkin on heated oiled grill plate (or grill or barbecue) about 10 minutes or until tender.
6 Slice cheese lengthways into four pieces; cut each piece into triangles. Cook cheese on same grill plate (or grill or barbecue) until browned both sides.
7 Serve couscous topped with pumpkin and cheese, and sprinkled with more coarsely chopped parsley.

prep + cook time 1 hour 5 minutes **serves** 4
nutritional count per serving 34.8g total fat (15.3g saturated fat); 3018kJ (722 cal); 71.7g carbohydrate; 27.2g protein; 5.3g fibre
tip We used Jarrahdale pumpkin for this recipe.

Olive, chickpea and spinach couscous

1½ cups (300g) couscous
1½ cups (375ml) boiling water
20g (¾ ounce) butter
420g (13¾ ounces) canned chickpeas (garbanzo beans),
    rinsed, drained
⅓ cup (55g) sultanas
⅓ cup (50g) roasted pine nuts
100g (3 ounces) baby rocket (arugula) leaves, chopped coarsely
¾ cup finely chopped fresh flat-leaf parsley
1 cup (120g) seeded green olives
preserved lemon dressing
1 tablespoon finely grated lemon rind
¼ cup (60ml) lemon juice
¼ cup (60ml) olive oil
2 tablespoons finely chopped preserved lemon rind

1 Combine couscous and the water in large heatproof bowl, cover; stand about 5 minutes or until liquid is absorbed, fluffing with fork occasionally. Stir in butter. Stand 10 minutes.
2 Meanwhile, make preserved lemon dressing.
3 Stir dressing and remaining ingredients into couscous.
preserved lemon dressing Place ingredients in screw-top jar, season to taste; shake well.

prep + cook time 20 minutes **serves** 4
nutritional count per serving 29g total fat (5.5g saturated fat); 268kJ (686 cal); 85.6g carbohydrate; 17.2g protein; 6.5g fibre

Fennel and tomato couscous

250g (8 ounces) cherry tomatoes, halved
cooking-oil spray
1 cup (200g) couscous
1 cup (250ml) boiling water
2 baby fennel bulbs (260g), trimmed, sliced thinly
¼ cup (60ml) olive oil
1 tablespoon white wine vinegar
1 clove garlic, crushed
2 tablespoons finely chopped fresh oregano

1 Preheat oven to 200°C/400°F.
2 Place tomatoes on oven tray; spray with cooking oil. Roast about 10 minutes or until skins burst.
3 Meanwhile, combine couscous and the water in medium heatproof bowl, cover; stand about 5 minutes or until liquid is absorbed, fluffing with fork occasionally.
4 Stir tomato and remaining ingredients into couscous.

prep + cook time 20 minutes **serves** 4
nutritional count per serving 14.8g total fat (2g saturated fat); 1384kJ (331 cal); 40.8g carbohydrate; 7.1g protein; 2.7g fibre

Tagines

Chicken tagine with olives and lemon

2kg (4-pound) whole chicken
2 teaspoons each ground ginger,
    cumin and ground coriander
1 tablespoon olive oil
1 large brown onion (200g),
    sliced thickly
3 cloves garlic, crushed
¼ teaspoon ground turmeric
pinch saffron threads
1 cup (250ml) water
1 cup (250ml) chicken stock
625g (1¼ pounds) baby new
    potatoes, halved

375g (12 ounces) jap pumpkin,
    unpeeled, cut into wedges
1 cup (120g) seeded green olives
2 tablespoons thinly sliced
    preserved lemon rind
2 tablespoons lemon juice
½ cup coarsely chopped fresh
    flat-leaf parsley
¼ cup coarsely chopped fresh
    coriander (cilantro)

1 Rinse chicken under cold water; pat dry inside and out with absorbent paper. Using kitchen scissors, cut along both sides of backbone; discard backbone. Press down on breastbone to flatten out chicken. Combine half the combined ground ginger, cumin and coriander in small bowl; rub mixture over chicken.

2 Preheat oven to 220°C/425°F.

3 Heat oil in tagine or flameproof casserole dish on stove top; cook chicken until browned all over. Remove from tagine. Reserve 1 tablespoon pan drippings; discard remainder.

4 Heat reserved pan drippings in same tagine; cook onion and garlic, stirring, until soft. Add turmeric and saffron, and remaining ginger, cumin and coriander; cook, stirring, about 1 minute or until fragrant. Add the water, stock, potatoes and pumpkin; top with chicken. Bring to the boil.

5 Cover tagine, transfer to oven; cook about 1¼ hours or until chicken is cooked.

6 Stir olives, preserved lemon and juice into sauce; season to taste. Serve tagine sprinkled with herbs.

prep + cook time 2 hours **serves** 6
nutritional count per serving 34.5g total fat (9.6g saturated fat); 2316kJ (554 cal); 20.1g carbohydrate; 38.4g protein; 4.4g fibre

Chicken tagine with prunes

2kg (4 pound) whole chicken
2 tablespoons moroccan seasoning
¼ cup (35g) plain (all-purpose) flour
1 tablespoon olive oil
8 shallots (200g)
1 cup (170g) seeded prunes, halved
¾ cup (120g) blanched almonds, roasted
4 trimmed silver beet (swiss chard) leaves (320g), shredded finely
2 cups (500ml) chicken consommé
½ cup (125ml) prune juice
2 tablespoons finely chopped fresh flat-leaf parsley

1 Preheat oven to 200°C/400°F.
2 Rinse chicken under cold water; pat dry inside and out with absorbent paper. Using kitchen scissors, cut chicken into four pieces.
3 Combine seasoning and flour in large bowl; coat chicken with flour mixture, shake off excess.
4 Heat oil in tagine or flameproof casserole dish on stove top; cook chicken, in batches, until browned. Remove from tagine; drain on absorbent paper.
5 Meanwhile, peel shallots, leaving root ends intact. Cook shallots in same heated tagine, stirring, until browned. Add prunes, nuts, half the silver beet, consommé, juice and parsley; bring to the boil. Top with chicken.
6 Cover tagine, transfer to oven; cook about 50 minutes or until chicken is cooked. Remove from oven; stir in remaining silver beet. Season to taste. Stand tagine, covered, 10 minutes before serving.

prep + cook time 1 hour 5 minutes **serves** 4
nutritional count per serving 62.4g total fat (14.4g saturated fat);
3954kJ (946 cal); 33.5g carbohydrate; 61g protein; 7.9g fibre
tips Ask the butcher to cut the chicken into four pieces for you, or buy four chicken marylands.
Use either canned or packaged consommé for a good flavour, but you can use stock instead.

Chicken tagine with figs and walnuts

½ cup (55g) coarsely chopped walnuts
4 chicken drumsticks (600g)
4 chicken thigh cutlets (800g)
2 teaspoons cumin seeds
2 teaspoons each ground ginger and cinnamon
1 tablespoon olive oil
1 large red onion (300g), sliced thickly

pinch saffron threads
1½ cups (375ml) chicken stock
1 tablespoon honey
6 medium fresh figs (360g), halved
1 teaspoon white sugar
45g (1½ ounces) baby spinach leaves
¼ cup finely chopped fresh flat-leaf parsley

1 Dry-fry nuts in tagine until browned lightly. Remove from tagine.
2 Combine chicken and cumin seeds with half the ginger and half the cinnamon in large bowl.
3 Heat oil in same tagine; cook chicken, in batches, until browned. Remove from tagine. Reserve 1 tablespoon pan juices; discard remainder.
4 Heat reserved pan juices in same tagine; cook onion, stirring, until soft. Add saffron and remaining ginger and cinnamon; cook, stirring, about 2 minutes or until fragrant. Return chicken to tagine with stock; bring to the boil. Reduce heat; simmer, covered, about 30 minutes or until chicken is cooked.
5 Remove chicken from tagine; cover to keep warm. Add honey to tagine; simmer, uncovered, about 10 minutes or until sauce is browned and thickened slightly.
6 Meanwhile, preheat grill (broiler). Place figs, cut-side up, on a baking-paper-lined oven tray; sprinkle with sugar. Cook under grill about 5 minutes or until browned lightly.
7 Return chicken to tagine with spinach; simmer, covered, until heated through. Season to taste.
8 Serve tagine topped with figs; sprinkle with nuts and parsley.

prep + cook time 1 hour 10 minutes **serves** 6
nutritional count per serving 30.2g total fat (7.5g saturated fat); 1873kJ (448 cal); 12.9g carbohydrate; 30.5g protein; 3.1g fibre

Chicken tagine with prunes and honey

2 teaspoons sesame seeds
30g (1 ounce) butter
½ cup (80g) blanched almonds
1.5kg (3-pound) whole chicken
¼ cup (60ml) olive oil
1 medium brown onion (150g), sliced thinly
2 teaspoons ground ginger
1 teaspoon ground cinnamon
¼ teaspoon ground turmeric
pinch saffron threads
1½ cups (375ml) water
½ cup (175g) honey
¾ cup (125g) seeded prunes
1 tablespoon thinly sliced preserved lemon rind

1 Dry-fry sesame seeds in tagine until browned lightly. Remove from tagine.
2 Melt butter in same tagine; cook almonds, stirring, until browned lightly. Remove from tagine.
3 Rinse chicken under cold water; pat dry inside and out with absorbent paper. Using kitchen scissors, cut chicken into eight pieces.
4 Heat oil in same tagine; cook chicken, in batches, until browned. Remove from tagine. Reserve 1 tablespoon pan juices; discard remainder.
5 Heat reserved pan juices in same tagine; cook onion, stirring, until soft. Add spices; cook, stirring about 1 minute or until fragrant. Return chicken to tagine and toss to coat in onion mixture. Add the water; bring to the boil. Reduce heat; simmer, covered, about 30 minutes or until chicken is cooked.
6 Remove chicken from tagine; cover to keep warm. Add honey and prunes to tagine; simmer, uncovered, about 10 minutes or until sauce thickens slightly.
7 Return chicken to tagine; cook, covered, until heated through.
8 Serve tagine sprinkled with sesame seeds, almonds and preserved lemon.

prep + cook time 1 hour 15 minutes **serves** 8
nutritional count per serving 31.2g total fat (8.1g saturated fat); 1956kJ (468 cal); 24.6g carbohydrate; 21.6g protein; 2.5g fibre

Chicken and fig tagine

1 tablespoon olive oil
1kg (2 pounds) chicken thigh fillets, chopped coarsely
1 medium red onion (170g), chopped finely
1 stalk celery (150g), trimmed, chopped coarsely
2 cloves garlic, crushed
1 teaspoon each ground coriander, cumin, ginger, cinnamon and turmeric
2 cups (500ml) chicken stock
¾ cup (150g) dried figs, sliced thickly
1 medium red capsicum (bell pepper) (200g), chopped coarsely
1 teaspoon finely grated lemon rind
¼ cup coarsely chopped fresh coriander (cilantro)
¼ cup (35g) coarsely chopped roasted unsalted shelled pistachios

1 Heat oil in tagine, flameproof casserole dish or large saucepan;
cook chicken, in batches, until browned. Remove from tagine.
2 Add onion, celery, garlic and spices to same tagine; cook, stirring,
until onion softens.
3 Return chicken to tagine; stir to coat in spice mixture. Add stock;
bring to the boil. Reduce heat; simmer, covered, about 30 minutes or
until chicken is almost cooked.
4 Add figs, capsicum and rind to tagine; simmer, uncovered, about
15 minutes or until sauce thickens slightly.
5 Stir in fresh coriander; serve tagine sprinkled with nuts.

prep + cook time 1 hour 20 minutes **serves** 4
nutritional count per serving 27.9g total fat (7g saturated fat);
2441kJ (584 cal); 27.2g carbohydrate; 52.6g protein; 8g fibre

Quince and chicken tagine

2 medium quinces (700g), peeled, cored, cut into wedges
45g (1½ ounces) butter
⅓ cup (115g) honey
3 cups (750ml) water
2 teaspoons orange blossom water
2 teaspoons olive oil
4 chicken drumsticks (600g)
4 chicken thigh cutlets (800g), skin removed
1 large brown onion (200g), chopped coarsely
3 cloves garlic, crushed
1 teaspoon each ground cumin and ground ginger
pinch saffron threads
2 cups (500ml) chicken stock
2 large zucchini (300g), chopped coarsely
¼ cup coarsely chopped fresh coriander (cilantro)

coriander couscous
1½ cups (300g) couscous
1½ cups (375ml) boiling water
45g (1½ ounces) baby spinach leaves, chopped finely
2 tablespoons finely chopped fresh coriander (cilantro)
2 green onions (scallions), sliced thinly

1 Place quinces, butter, honey, the water and orange blossom water in medium saucepan; bring to the boil. Reduce heat; simmer, covered, 1 hour, stirring occasionally. Uncover, cook, stirring occasionally, about 45 minutes or until quinces are tender and red in colour.

2 Meanwhile, heat oil in tagine or flameproof casserole dish; cook chicken, in batches, until browned. Remove from tagine.

3 Cook onion, garlic and spices in same tagine, stirring, until onion softens. Return chicken to tagine with stock; bring to the boil. Reduce heat; simmer, covered, 20 minutes. Uncover; simmer, about 20 minutes or until chicken is cooked though. Add zucchini; cook, uncovered, about 10 minutes or until zucchini is tender. Stir in quinces and ½ cup of the quince syrup. Season to taste.

4 Meanwhile, make coriander couscous.

5 Divide tagine and couscous among serving plates; top with coriander.

coriander couscous Combine couscous and the water in large heatproof bowl, cover; stand about 5 minutes or until liquid is absorbed, fluffing with fork occasionally. Stir in spinach, coriander and onion.

prep + cook time 2 hours 15 minutes **serves** 4
nutritional count per serving 32.6g total fat (12.3g saturated fat); 3913kJ (936 cal); 99g carbohydrate; 56.7g protein; 12.5g fibre

Chicken and chickpea tagine with olives and preserved lemon

1 cup (200g) dried chickpeas
  (garbanzo beans)
2 tablespoons plain (all-purpose)
  flour
2 teaspoons hot paprika
8 chicken drumsticks (1.2kg)
8 chicken thigh cutlets (1.3kg)
45g (1 ½ ounces) butter
2 medium red onions (340g),
  sliced thickly
3 cloves garlic, crushed
1 teaspoon each cumin seeds,
  ground ginger and dried
  chilli flakes

½ teaspoon each ground
  coriander and turmeric
¼ teaspoon saffron threads
3 cups (750ml) chicken stock
2 tablespoons thinly sliced
  preserved lemon rind
⅓ cup (40g) seeded green olives
2 tablespoons finely chopped
  fresh coriander (cilantro)

1 Place chickpeas in medium bowl, cover with water; stand overnight, drain. Rinse under cold water; drain. Place chickpeas in medium saucepan of boiling water; return to the boil. Reduce heat; simmer, uncovered, about 40 minutes or until chickpeas are tender.
2 Preheat oven to 160°C/325°F.
3 Place flour and paprika in paper or plastic bag, add chicken, in batches; shake gently to coat chicken in flour mixture.
4 Melt butter in tagine or flameproof casserole dish; cook chicken, in batches, until browned. Remove from tagine.
5 Cook onion in same tagine, stirring, until soft. Add garlic and spices; cook, stirring, until fragrant. Return chicken to tagine with stock; bring to the boil.
6 Cover tagine, transfer to oven; cook 30 minutes. Add drained chickpeas; cook tagine, covered, in oven about 1 hour or until chicken is cooked. Stir in preserved lemon, olives and fresh coriander, season to taste; serve with rice, if you like.

prep + cook time 3 hours (+ standing) **serves** 8
nutritional count per serving 20.2g total fat (7.5g saturated fat); 1764kJ (422 cal); 14.3g carbohydrate; 46.1g protein; 4.3g fibre

Chilli fish tagine

4 x 200g (6½-ounce) white fish fillets, skin on
1 tablespoon finely grated lemon rind
2 teaspoons dried chilli flakes
2 cloves garlic, crushed
1 tablespoon mustard seed oil
30g (1 ounce) butter
2 baby fennel bulbs (260g), trimmed, cut into wedges
150g (5 ounces) green beans, halved lengthways
⅓ cup (50g) raisins
1 cup (250ml) dry white wine
pinch saffron threads
⅓ cup (45g) roasted unsalted shelled pistachios

1 Combine fish, rind, chilli, garlic and oil in large bowl. Cover; refrigerate 3 hours or overnight.
2 Melt butter in tagine or large frying pan; cook fennel, stirring, until browned lightly. Add beans, raisins, wine and saffron; top with fish. Bring to the boil. Reduce heat; simmer, covered, about 15 minutes or until fish is cooked as desired. Season to taste.
3 Serve tagine sprinkled with nuts.

prep + cook time 30 minutes (+ refrigeration) **serves** 4
nutritional count per serving 21.1g total fat (6.7g saturated fat); 1956kJ (468 cal); 13.1g carbohydrate; 44.8g protein; 4g fibre
tips We used blue-eye fillets in this recipe but you can use any firm white fish fillets. Fish or chicken stock can be used instead of wine. Mustard seed oil is available from health-food shops, delicatessens and some supermarkets. If you like, use olive oil instead.

Tuna tagine with lentils and beans

4 x 185g (6-ounce) tuna steaks
2 teaspoons each ground coriander and cumin
½ teaspoon dried chilli flakes
¼ cup (60ml) olive oil
⅓ cup finely chopped fresh flat-leaf parsley
2 large carrots (360g), cut into matchsticks
2 cups (500ml) chicken consommé
1 tablespoon honey
800g (1½ pounds) canned brown lentils, rinsed, drained
¾ cup frozen broad beans (90g), thawed, peeled
1 tablespoon coarsely chopped fresh flat-leaf parsley, extra

1 Combine tuna, spices, chilli, half the oil and half the parsley in large bowl. Cover, refrigerate 3 hours or overnight.
2 Heat remaining oil in tagine or large frying pan; cook carrots, stirring, until tender. Add consommé, honey, lentils and half the beans; top with tuna. Bring to the boil, reduce heat; simmer, covered, about 10 minutes or until tuna is cooked as desired. Season to taste.
3 Stir in remaining beans; stand tagine, covered, 5 minutes. Serve sprinkled with extra parsley.

prep + cook time 30 minutes (+ refrigeration) **serves** 4
nutritional count per serving 25.3g total fat (6.4g saturated fat); 2299kJ (550 cal); 21g carbohydrate; 56.2g protein; 7.2g fibre
tips Ask your fishmonger to cut thick tuna steaks; thin steaks can easily overcook and dry out.
Use either canned or packaged consommé for a good flavour, but if you prefer, use stock instead.

Chermoulla fish tagine

4 x 200g (6½-ounce) white fish fillets, skin on
¼ cup (60ml) olive oil
500g (1 pound) small red-skinned potatoes, unpeeled, sliced thickly
500g (1 pound) cherry truss tomatoes
½ cup (125ml) chicken stock
2 tablespoons tomato paste
1 teaspoon white sugar
¼ cup each loosely packed fresh flat-leaf parsley leaves and mint leaves
chermoulla
¼ cup each coarsely chopped fresh flat-leaf parsley and coriander (cilantro)
2 tablespoons lemon juice
1 tablespoon olive oil
2 cloves garlic, halved
2 teaspoons each ground cumin and sweet paprika
2 teaspoons harissa

1 Make chermoulla.
2 Combine fish and chermoulla in large bowl. Cover; refrigerate 30 minutes.
3 Heat half the oil in tagine or flameproof casserole dish; cook potato, stirring, about 10 minutes or until browned lightly. Cover; cook 5 minutes or until potatoes are almost tender.
4 Uncover potatoes; top with fish and tomatoes. Combine stock, tomato paste and sugar in medium jug; season to taste. Pour stock mixture over fish in tagine; bring to the boil. Reduce heat; simmer, covered, about 20 minutes or until fish is cooked.
5 Serve tagine drizzled with remaining oil; sprinkle with herbs.
chermoulla Blend or process ingredients until almost smooth.

prep + cook time 50 minutes (+ refrigeration) **serves** 4
nutritional count per serving 23.2g total fat (4.1g saturated fat); 2077kJ (497 cal); 22.8g carbohydrate; 45.6g protein; 5.9g fibre
tips We used snapper fillets for this recipe but you can use any white fish fillets.
We used desiree potatoes in this recipe.

Spicy prawn and tomato tagine

1 tablespoon olive oil
1 medium brown onion (150g), chopped finely
3 cloves garlic, crushed
1 teaspoon each ground ginger and cumin
¼ teaspoon chilli powder
pinch saffron threads
1kg (2 pounds) tomatoes, chopped coarsely
1.5kg (3¼ pounds) uncooked medium king prawns (shrimp)
¼ cup each finely chopped fresh flat-leaf parsley and coriander (cilantro)
¼ cup (30g) finely chopped roasted unsalted shelled pistachios
1 tablespoon finely chopped preserved lemon rind

1 Heat oil in tagine or flameproof casserole dish; cook onion and garlic, stirring, until onion softens. Add spices; cook, stirring, about 1 minute or until fragrant. Add tomato; cook, stirring, about 5 minutes or until tomato softens. Bring to the boil. Reduce heat; simmer, stirring occasionally, about 10 minutes or until sauce thickens slightly.
2 Meanwhile, shell and devein prawns leaving tails intact. Add prawns to tagine; cook, covered, stirring occasionally, about 5 minutes or until prawns are changed in colour. Season to taste.
3 Combine herbs, nuts and preserved lemon in small bowl.
4 Serve tagine sprinkled with herb mixture.

prep + cook time 40 minutes **serves** 6
nutritional count per serving 6.6g total fat (0.9g saturated fat); 857kJ (205 cal); 5.5g carbohydrate; 28.8g protein; 3.2g fibre

Fast fish tagine

4 x 200g (6½-ounce) firm white fish fillets, skin on, halved crossways
2 tablespoons moroccan seasoning
2 tablespoons olive oil
1 large brown onion (200g), sliced thinly
3 cloves garlic, crushed
1 medium lemon (140g), sliced thinly
12 seeded green olives (95g)
1 cup (250ml) salt-reduced chicken stock
1 teaspoon white sugar
2 tablespoons coarsely chopped fresh coriander (cilantro)
herb couscous
1 cup (200g) couscous
1 cup (250ml) boiling water
½ cup firmly packed fresh coriander (cilantro) leaves

1 Preheat oven to 200°C/400°F.
2 Combine fish and seasoning in large bowl.
3 Heat half the oil in large flameproof baking dish; cook onion and garlic, stirring, until soft. Remove from pan and set aside. Heat the remaining oil in same dish; cook fish, in batches, until browned. Return onion mixture to the pan with lemon, olives, stock and sugar; bring to the boil.
4 Transfer tagine to oven; cook, uncovered, about 10 minutes or until fish is cooked, season to taste.
5 Meanwhile, make herb couscous.
6 Sprinkle tagine with coriander; serve with herb couscous and steamed zucchini slices, if you like.
herb couscous Combine couscous and the water in medium heatproof bowl, cover; stand 5 minutes or until liquid is absorbed, fluffing with fork occasionally. Stir in coriander.

prep + cook time 30 minutes **serves** 4
nutritional count per serving 14.5g total fat (2.9g saturated fat); 2224kJ (532 cal); 48.7g carbohydrate; 49.3g protein; 3.1g fibre
tip If your baking dish isn't flameproof, cook the onion, garlic and fish in a large non-stick frying pan as per the recipe. Transfer to a baking dish with the lemon, olive olives, stock and sugar before placing in the oven.

Kingfish and tomato tagine

2 tablespoons olive oil
2 large brown onions (400g), chopped coarsely
6 cloves garlic, chopped finely
1 fresh small red thai (serrano) chilli, chopped finely
4 drained anchovy fillets, chopped finely
1 cup coarsely chopped fresh coriander (cilantro)
¾ cup each coarsely chopped fresh flat-leaf parsley and mint
200g (6½ ounces) button mushrooms, quartered
2 stalks celery (300g), trimmed, sliced thickly
2 teaspoons ground cumin
850g (1¾ pounds) canned diced tomatoes
4 x 250g (8-ounce) kingfish cutlets
1 medium lemon (140g), cut into wedges
2 tablespoons fresh flat-leaf parsley leaves

1 Preheat oven to 200°C/400°F.
2 Heat oil in tagine or large flameproof baking dish; cook onion, garlic and chilli, stirring, until onion softens. Add anchovy, chopped herbs, mushrooms, celery and cumin; cook, stirring, 5 minutes.
3 Add undrained tomatoes; bring to the boil. Add fish; return to the boil. Transfer tagine to oven; cook, uncovered, about 20 minutes or until liquid has almost evaporated and fish is cooked as desired.
4 Divide fish and lemon wedges among serving plates; sprinkle with parsley. Serve tagine with a tomato and herb salad (recipe page 85) and steamed long-grain white rice, if you like.

prep + cook time 1 hour **serves** 4
nutritional count per serving 14.9g total fat (3g saturated fat); 1672kJ (400 cal); 13.6g carbohydrate; 48.5g protein; 8.7g fibre

Meatball tagine with eggs

500g (1 pound) minced (ground) beef
1 clove garlic, crushed
¼ cup finely chopped fresh mint
2 tablespoons finely chopped fresh coriander (cilantro)
1 teaspoon each ground coriander and cinnamon
2 teaspoons ground cumin
½ teaspoon chilli powder
1 tablespoon olive oil
1 medium brown onion (150g), chopped finely
4 large tomatoes (880g), chopped coarsely
pinch saffron threads
4 eggs
½ cup loosely packed fresh coriander (cilantro) leaves

1 Combine mince, garlic, mint, chopped coriander, ground coriander,
cinnamon, half the cumin and half the chilli in large bowl; season.
Roll level tablespoons of mixture into balls.
2 Heat oil in tagine or large frying pan; cook meatballs, in batches,
until browned. Remove from tagine.
3 Cook onion in same tagine, stirring, until softened. Add tomato,
saffron and remaining cumin and chilli; bring to the boil. Reduce heat;
simmer, uncovered, about 15 minutes or until tomatoes soften.
4 Return meatballs to tagine; simmer, uncovered, about 10 minutes or
until meatballs are cooked and sauce thickens slightly. Season to taste.
Carefully crack eggs into tagine; simmer, covered, about 5 minutes or
until eggs are barely set. Sprinkle tagine with coriander leaves. Serve
with crusty bread.

prep + cook time 1 hour **serves** 4
nutritional count per serving 20.2g total fat (7.1g saturated fat);
1488kJ (356 cal); 6.6g carbohydrate; 35.3g protein; 3.5g fibre

Beef and eggplant tagine

2 tablespoons olive oil
625g (1¼ pounds) beef chuck steak, chopped coarsely
1 medium brown onion (150g), chopped coarsely
2 cloves garlic, crushed
2 teaspoons ground coriander
1 teaspoon each ground ginger, cumin and sweet paprika
½ cup (125ml) beef stock
3 medium tomatoes (450g), chopped coarsely
3 baby eggplants (180g), sliced thickly

1 Heat half the oil in tagine or large saucepan; cook beef, in batches, until browned. Remove from tagine.
2 Cook onion in same tagine, stirring, until softened. Add garlic and spices; cook, stirring, until fragrant. Return beef to tagine with stock and tomato; bring to the boil. Reduce heat; simmer, covered, 45 minutes. Uncover; simmer 30 minutes or until beef is tender and tagine thickens.
3 Meanwhile, heat remaining oil in medium frying pan; cook eggplant, stirring, about 10 minutes or until browned and tender.
4 Stir eggplant into tagine; season to taste.

prep + cook time 1 hour 30 minutes **serves** 4
nutritional count per serving 21.2g total fat (5.9g saturated fat); 1538kJ (368 cal); 5.7g carbohydrate; 37.3g protein; 3.1g fibre

Beef, raisin and almond tagine

1 tablespoon olive oil
625g (1¼ pounds) beef chuck steak, chopped coarsely
1 medium brown onion (150g), chopped coarsely
2 cloves garlic, crushed
2 teaspoons ras el hanout
½ teaspoon each ground ginger and ground cinnamon
1 dried bay leaf
1 cup (250ml) beef stock
¼ cup (35g) coarsely chopped raisins
¼ cup (40g) blanched almonds, roasted

1 Heat oil in tagine or large frying pan; cook beef, in batches, until browned. Remove from tagine.
2 Cook onion in same tagine, stirring, until softened. Add garlic, spices and bay leaf; cook, stirring, until fragrant. Return beef to pan with stock; bring to the boil. Reduce heat; simmer, covered, 1 hour. Add raisins; simmer, uncovered, about 15 minutes or until beef is tender and tagine thickens. Stir in nuts, season to taste; accompany with lemon wedges.

prep + cook time 1 hour 30 minutes **serves** 4
nutritional count per serving 22.1g total fat (5.6g saturated fat); 1630kJ (390 cal); 9.2g carbohydrate; 38.3g protein; 2.1g fibre

Beef and prune tagine with spinach couscous

2 large red onions (600g),
   chopped finely
2 tablespoons olive oil
pinch saffron threads
1 teaspoon ground cinnamon
¼ teaspoon ground ginger
1kg (2 pounds) beef blade steak,
   cut into 4cm (1½-inch) pieces
45g (1½ ounces) butter, chopped
410g (13 ounces) canned diced
   tomatoes
1 cup (250ml) water
2 tablespoons white sugar

¾ cup (100g) slivered almonds,
   roasted
1½ cups (250g) seeded prunes
1 teaspoon finely grated
   lemon rind
¼ teaspoon ground cinnamon,
   extra
spinach couscous
1½ cups (300g) couscous
1½ cups (375ml) boiling water
75g (2½ ounces) baby spinach
   leaves, shredded finely

1 Combine onion, oil, spices and beef in large bowl.
2 Place beef mixture in tagine or large saucepan with butter, undrained tomatoes, the water, half the sugar and ½ cup of the nuts; bring to the boil. Reduce heat; simmer, covered, 1½ hours. Remove 1 cup cooking liquid; reserve. Simmer tagine, uncovered, 30 minutes.
3 Meanwhile, place prunes in small bowl, cover with boiling water; stand 20 minutes, drain. Place prunes in small saucepan with rind, extra cinnamon, remaining sugar and reserved cooking liquid; bring to the boil. Reduce heat; simmer, uncovered, about 15 minutes or until prunes soften. Stir into tagine; season to taste.
4 Meanwhile, make spinach couscous.
5 Divide couscous and tagine among serving plates; sprinkle tagine with remaining nuts.
spinach couscous Combine couscous and the water in large heatproof bowl, cover; stand for about 5 minutes or until liquid is absorbed, fluffing with fork occasionally. Stir in spinach.

prep + cook time 2 hours 50 minutes **serves** 4
nutritional count per serving 50.3g total fat (16.5g saturated fat); 4799kJ (1148 cal); 102.3g carbohydrate; 72.1g protein; 11.6g fibre

Veal, quince and caramelised onion tagine

6 baby brown onions (150g)
6 thick pieces veal knuckle (1.6kg)
2 teaspoons each ground ginger and cinnamon
½ teaspoon chilli powder
1 tablespoon olive oil
1 tablespoon honey
2½ cups (625ml) beef stock
3 cloves garlic, crushed
3 medium quinces (1kg), peeled, cored, cut into thick wedges
⅓ cup coarsely chopped fresh coriander (cilantro)

1 Peel onions, leaving root ends intact; halve onions.
2 Combine veal and half the combined spices in large bowl.
3 Heat half the oil in tagine or flameproof casserole dish; cook veal, in batches, until browned. Remove from tagine.
4 Heat remaining oil in same tagine; cook onion, honey and ½ cup of the stock, stirring occasionally, about 5 minutes or until onion caramelises. Remove from tagine.
5 Add garlic and remaining spices to tagine; cook, stirring, about 1 minute or until fragrant. Return veal to tagine with remaining stock and quince; bring to the boil. Reduce heat; simmer, covered, about 1½ hours or until veal is tender.
6 Add onion to tagine; simmer, covered, about 5 minutes or until heated through. Season to taste.
7 Sprinkle tagine with coriander and serve with couscous, if you like.

prep + cook time 2 hours 15 minutes **serves** 6
nutritional count per serving 19.2g total fat (7.7g saturated fat); 1739kJ (416 cal); 18.7g carbohydrate; 38g protein; 9.2g fibre
tips Ask your butcher to cut the veal knuckle into 6 thick slices for you. You could use veal osso buco if you can't get veal knuckle.

Lamb tagine with ras el hanout

750g (1½ pounds) boned lamb shoulder, chopped coarsely
2 tablespoons ras el hanout
¼ cup (60ml) olive oil
8 baby new potatoes (320g), halved
2 small leeks (400g), sliced thinly
1 litre (4 cups) beef consommé
2 tablespoons finely chopped fresh flat-leaf parsley

1 Combine lamb, ras el hanout and 1 tablespoon of the oil in large bowl. Cover, refrigerate 3 hours or overnight.
2 Preheat oven to 200°C/400°F.
3 Heat 1 tablespoon of the remaining oil in tagine or flameproof casserole dish on stove top; cook lamb, in batches, until browned. Remove from tagine.
4 Heat remaining oil in same tagine; cook potato and leek, stirring, until potatoes are browned lightly and leek softens. Return lamb to tagine with consommé; bring to the boil.
5 Cover tagine, transfer to oven; cook about 45 minutes or until lamb is tender. Remove from oven; stir in parsley. Season to taste.

prep + cook time 1 hour (+ refrigeration) **serves** 4
nutritional count per serving 25.7g total fat (7.5g saturated fat); 2023kJ (484 cal); 16.9g carbohydrate; 44.2g protein; 4.7g fibre
tip Use either canned or packaged consommé for a good flavour, but if you prefer, use stock instead.

Lamb kefta tagine

625g (1¼ pounds) minced (ground) lamb
2 cloves garlic, crushed
1 medium red onion (170g), chopped finely
1 tablespoon each ground coriander, cumin and sweet paprika
1 cup firmly packed fresh coriander leaves (cilantro)
2 fresh small red thai (serrano) chillies, sliced thinly
2 eggs
1 cup (70g) stale breadcrumbs
½ cup (125ml) beef stock
800g (1½ pounds) canned diced tomatoes
1 cup (150g) drained semi-dried tomatoes, chopped coarsely
½ cup firmly packed fresh basil leaves, chopped coarsely

1 Preheat oven to 200°C/400°F.
2 Combine mince, garlic, onion, spices, coriander leaves, chilli, eggs and breadcrumbs in large bowl; season. Roll 2 heaped tablespoons of mixture into balls.
3 Cook meatballs, in batches, in heated oiled tagine or flameproof casserole dish, on stove top, until browned. Remove from tagine; drain meatballs on absorbent paper.
4 Return meatballs to tagine with stock, undrained tomatoes, semi-dried tomatoes and basil; bring to the boil.
5 Cover tagine, transfer to oven; cook about 35 minutes or until meatballs are cooked through. Season to taste.

prep + cook time 55 minutes **serves** 4
nutritional count per serving 17.5g total fat (6.6g saturated fat); 2086kJ (499 cal); 34.5g carbohydrate; 45.2g protein; 9.7g fibre

Lamb, artichoke and capsicum tagine

1kg (2 pounds) boned lamb shoulder, chopped coarsely
2 teaspoons each ground ginger and cinnamon
1 teaspoon hot paprika
2 tablespoons olive oil
1 large red onion (300g), sliced thickly
3 cloves garlic, crushed
1½ cups (375ml) beef stock
340g (11 ounces) bottled marinated artichoke hearts, drained, halved
½ cup (80g) drained, thinly sliced bottled roasted
    red capsicum (bell pepper)
¼ cup (40g) thinly sliced preserved lemon rind
¼ cup coarsely chopped fresh flat-leaf parsley

1 Combine lamb and half the combined spices in large bowl.
2 Heat half the oil in tagine or flameproof casserole dish; cook lamb, in batches, until browned. Remove from tagine.
3 Heat remaining oil in same tagine; cook onion and garlic, stirring, until soft. Add remaining spices; cook, stirring, about 1 minute or until fragrant. Return lamb to tagine with stock; bring to the boil. Reduce heat; simmer, covered, about 50 minutes or until lamb is tender.
4 Add artichokes, capsicum and rind; simmer, uncovered, until heated through. Season to taste.
5 Sprinkle tagine with parsley and serve with couscous, if you like.

prep + cook time 1 hour 30 minutes **serves** 6
nutritional count per serving 16.3g total fat (5.5g saturated fat); 1321kJ (316 cal); 4.6g carbohydrate; 36g protein; 2.7g fibre

Lamb tagine with chickpeas

2 tablespoons olive oil
1.6kg (3¼ pounds) diced lamb
2 medium red onions (340g), sliced thinly
3 cloves garlic, crushed
1 tablespoon ground cumin
2 teaspoons ground ginger
½ teaspoon ground turmeric
1 cinnamon stick
800g (1½ pounds) canned crushed tomatoes
3 cups (750ml) vegetable stock
600g (1¼ pounds) canned chickpeas (garbanzo beans),
    rinsed, drained
¼ cup finely chopped fresh flat-leaf parsley

1 Heat half the oil in tagine or large saucepan; cook lamb, in batches, until browned. Remove from tagine.
2 Heat remaining oil in same tagine; cook onion, garlic and spices, stirring, until onion softens.
3 Return lamb to tagine with undrained tomatoes and stock; bring to the boil. Reduce heat; simmer, covered, about 1 hour or until lamb is tender. Add chickpeas; simmer, uncovered, 5 minutes. Discard cinnamon; stir in parsley, season to taste.

prep + cook time 1 hour 30 minutes **serves** 6
nutritional count per serving 31.8g total fat (12g saturated fat); 2587kJ (619 cal); 17.3g carbohydrate; 63.3g protein; 5.8g fibre

Lamb tagine with couscous

6 lamb chump chops (800g)
1 tablespoon olive oil
2 large brown onions (400g), sliced thinly
2 cloves garlic, crushed
2 teaspoons ground cumin
1 teaspoon ground cinnamon
½ teaspoon ground ginger
pinch saffron threads
2 cups (500ml) water
2 small carrots (140g), chopped
2 medium zucchini (240g), chopped coarsely
300g (10 ounces) canned chickpeas (garbanzo beans), rinsed, drained
3 teaspoons lemon juice
1 tablespoon honey
2 cups (400g) couscous
45g (1½ ounces) butter
2 cups (500ml) boiling water
1 tablespoon finely chopped fresh coriander (cilantro)

1 Trim excess fat from lamb; cut in half.
2 Heat oil in tagine or large saucepan; cook lamb, in batches, until browned. Remove from tagine.
3 Cook onion and garlic in same tagine, stirring, until soft. Add spices; cook, stirring, until fragrant. Return lamb to tagine with the water; bring to the boil. Reduce heat; simmer, covered, 20 minutes. Add carrot; simmer, covered, 10 minutes. Add zucchini, chickpeas, juice and honey; simmer, uncovered, about 15 minutes or until lamb is tender and tagine thickens slightly. Season to taste.
4 Meanwhile, combine couscous, butter and the boiling water in large heatproof bowl. Cover; stand about 5 minutes or until liquid is absorbed, fluffing with fork occasionally. Stir in coriander.
5 Serve lamb with couscous.

prep + cook time 1 hour 25 minutes **serves** 4
nutritional count per serving 37.4g total fat (16.7g saturated fat); 3963kJ (948 cal); 97.6g carbohydrate; 51.3g protein; 6.7g fibre

Lamb tagine with baby carrots

2 tablespoons olive oil
1 teaspoon ground ginger
½ teaspoon saffron threads
2kg (4 pounds) boned lamb shoulder, chopped coarsely
2 medium brown onions (300g), sliced thinly
½ cup (125ml) water
3 stems fresh flat-leaf parsley
3 stems fresh coriander (cilantro)
500g (1 pound) baby carrots, trimmed
⅓ cup (40g) seeded black olives
2 tablespoons thinly sliced preserved lemon rind

1 Combine oil, ginger, saffron and lamb in large bowl.
2 Place onion and lamb mixture in tagine or flameproof casserole dish. Add herbs and the water; bring to the boil. Reduce heat; simmer, covered about 1½ hours or until lamb is tender.
3 Meanwhile, cut carrots in half lengthways and then in half crossways.
4 Remove parsley and coriander from tagine. Add carrot to tagine; simmer, uncovered, about 30 minutes or until carrots are tender.
5 Add olives and preserved lemon; simmer, uncovered, until heated through, season to taste.

prep + cook time 2 hours 25 minutes **serves** 8
nutritional count per serving 26.9g total fat (10.9g saturated fat); 1956kJ (468 cal); 6.2g carbohydrate; 49.2g protein; 2.5g fibre

Lamb, currant and quince tagine

45g (1½ ounces) butter
2 tablespoons olive oil
2 medium quinces (700g), peeled, cut into thick wedges
¼ cup (90g) honey
1kg (2 pounds) boned lamb shoulder, chopped coarsely
2 tablespoons finely chopped fresh coriander (cilantro) root and
   stem mixture
2 teaspoons each ground coriander and cumin
1 teaspoon ground ginger
1 cinnamon stick
1½ cups (375ml) beef stock
2 tablespoons tomato paste
¼ cup (40g) dried currants
½ cup loosely packed fresh coriander (cilantro) leaves

1 Heat butter and half the oil in tagine or flameproof casserole dish on
stove top; cook quince, stirring, about 10 minutes or until browned lightly.
Add half the honey; cook, stirring, about 5 minutes or until quince is
lightly caramelised. Remove quince from tagine.
2 Preheat oven to 180°C/350°F.
3 Heat remaining oil in same tagine; cook lamb, in batches, until browned.
4 Return lamb and quince to tagine with coriander root and stem mixture,
spices, stock, paste and remaining honey; bring to the boil.
5 Cover tagine, transfer to oven; cook about 1½ hours or until lamb
is tender.
6 Remove from oven; stir in currants and coriander leaves. Season to taste.

prep + cook time 2 hours **serves** 6
nutritional count per serving 22.1g total fat (9.5g saturated fat);
1902kJ (455 cal); 26.7g carbohydrate; 35g protein; 6.7g fibre
tip Some of the stems and roots of coriander are used in this recipe so
buy a bunch of fresh coriander with its roots intact. Wash the coriander
under cold water, removing any dirt clinging to the roots. Chop coriander
roots and stems together to obtain the amount specified.

Lamb tagine with sweet prunes

1kg (2 pounds) boned lamb shoulder, chopped coarsely
⅓ cup (80ml) olive oil
2 medium red onions (340g), grated coarsely
4 cloves garlic, crushed
1 teaspoon each ground ginger and sweet paprika
¼ teaspoon each dried chilli flakes and saffron threads
800g (1½ pounds) canned diced tomatoes
4 x 5cm (2-inch) strips orange rind
2 cinnamon sticks
½ cup coarsely chopped fresh coriander (cilantro)

sweet prunes
18 seeded prunes (145g)
¼ cup (90g) honey
2 tablespoons water

1 Combine lamb, oil, onion, garlic and spices in large bowl. Cover;
refrigerate 3 hours or overnight.
2 Preheat oven to 180°C/350°F.
3 Heat oiled tagine or flameproof casserole dish on stove top;
cook lamb, in batches, until browned.
4 Return lamb to tagine with undrained tomatoes, rind, cinnamon sticks
and half the coriander; bring to the boil.
5 Cover tagine, transfer to oven; cook about 1½ hours or until lamb is
tender, season to taste.
6 Meanwhile, make sweet prunes.
7 Serve tagine with sweet prunes; sprinkle with remaining coriander.
sweet prunes Bring ingredients to the boil in small saucepan.
Reduce heat; simmer, uncovered, 10 minutes.

prep + cook time 1 hour 50 minutes (+ refrigeration) **serves** 6
nutritional count per serving 22.1g total fat (6.2g saturated fat);
1969kJ (471 cal); 30.5g carbohydrate; 35.9g protein; 4.6g fibre

193

Lamb tfaya

1kg (2 pounds) boned lamb
   shoulder, chopped coarsely
1 tablespoon ground ginger
2 teaspoons ras el hanout
1 teaspoon ground cinnamon
2 tablespoons olive oil
1 litre (4 cups) water
2 cups (500ml) chicken stock
400g (13 ounces) canned
   chickpeas (garbanzo beans),
   rinsed, drained
2 cups (400g) couscous
2 cups (500ml) boiling water
15g (½ ounce) butter
¼ cup finely chopped fresh
   coriander (cilantro)

½ cup (80g) coarsely chopped
   blanched almonds, roasted
3 hard-boiled eggs, quartered
tfaya
2 large brown onions (400g),
   sliced thinly
¼ cup (90g) honey
½ cup (75g) raisins
45g (1½ ounces) butter, chopped
1 teaspoon each ground white
   pepper and ground cinnamon
½ teaspoon ground turmeric
pinch saffron threads
½ cup (125ml) water

1 Combine lamb and spices in large bowl. Heat oil in tagine or large saucepan; cook lamb, in batches, until browned. Remove from tagine.
2 Return lamb to tagine with the water, stock and chickpeas; bring to the boil. Reduce heat; simmer, covered, 30 minutes. Uncover; simmer, stirring occasionally, about 1 hour or until lamb is tender.
3 Meanwhile, make tfaya.
4 Combine couscous, the boiling water and butter in large heatproof bowl, cover; stand about 5 minutes or until liquid is absorbed, fluffing with fork occasionally. Stir in coriander and nuts; season to taste.
5 Serve lamb mixture with couscous; accompany with tfaya and eggs.
tfaya Bring ingredients to the boil in medium saucepan. Reduce heat; simmer, uncovered, stirring occasionally, about 30 minutes or until onion is caramelised.

prep + cook time 1 hour 50 minutes **serves** 6
nutritional count per serving 36.2g total fat (12.6g saturated fat); 3674kJ (879 cal); 83.2g carbohydrate; 53.5g protein; 5.3g fibre
tip Tfaya is an accompaniment of sweet and spicy caramelised onions and raisins.

Lamb, eggplant and prune tagine

2 medium eggplants (600g)
1 tablespoon coarse cooking salt (kosher salt)
2 teaspoons sesame seeds
2 tablespoons olive oil
1kg (2 pounds) diced lamb
1 large brown onion (200g), chopped finely
2 cloves garlic, crushed
2 teaspoons ground cumin
1 teaspoon ground turmeric
½ teaspoon ground ginger
2¾ cups (680ml) water
2 x 5cm (2-inch) strips lemon rind
1 cinnamon stick
¾ cup (125g) seeded prunes, halved
½ cup (80g) blanched almonds, roasted
1 tablespoon honey
2 tablespoons coarsely chopped fresh coriander (cilantro)

1 Cut eggplants into 1cm (½-inch) slices, place in colander, sprinkle with salt; stand 30 minutes. Rinse under cold water; drain, then cut into quarters.
2 Dry-fry sesame seeds in tagine or large saucepan until browned lightly. Remove from tagine.
3 Heat oil in tagine; cook lamb, in batches, until browned. Remove from tagine.
4 Cook onion, garlic and spices in same tagine, stirring, until onion softens. Return lamb to tagine with the water, rind and cinnamon stick; bring to the boil. Reduce heat; simmer, covered, about 1 hour or until lamb is tender.
5 Add prunes, nuts, honey, coriander and eggplants; simmer, covered, about 30 minutes or until eggplants are tender. Discard cinnamon stick and rind; season tagine to taste. Serve sprinkled with sesame seeds.

prep + cook time 2 hours **serves** 6
nutritional count per serving 29.5g total fat (8.1g saturated fat); 2082kJ (498 cal); 15.8g carbohydrate; 40g protein; 6g fibre

Lamb, apricot and almond tagine

2 tablespoons olive oil
1kg (2 pounds) diced lamb
12 shallots (300g), halved
1 medium red capsicum (bell pepper) (200g), chopped coarsely
2 cloves garlic, crushed
2.5cm (1-inch) piece fresh ginger (15g), grated
1 teaspoon ground cumin
1½ cups (375ml) water
1½ cups (375ml) chicken stock
½ teaspoon saffron threads
1 cup (150g) dried apricots, halved
1 tablespoon finely chopped preserved lemon rind
200g (6½ ounces) green beans, trimmed, chopped coarsely
½ cup (70g) slivered almonds, roasted

1 Heat half the oil in tagine or large saucepan; cook lamb, in batches, until browned. Remove from tagine.
2 Heat remaining oil in same tagine; cook shallots, capsicum, garlic, ginger and cumin, stirring, until fragrant.
3 Return lamb to tagine with the water, stock and saffron; bring to the boil. Reduce heat; simmer, covered, about 1 hour or until lamb is tender. Add apricots, preserved lemon and beans; simmer, uncovered, 15 minutes, season to taste.
4 Serve tagine sprinkled with nuts.

prep + cook time 1 hour 50 minutes **serves** 4
nutritional count per serving 41.7g total fat (12.1g saturated fat); 3018kJ (722 cal); 22.1g carbohydrate; 61.3g protein; 7.8g fibre

Lamb and quince tagine with pistachio couscous

45g (1½ ounces) butter
600g (1¼ ounces) diced lamb
1 medium red onion (170g),
  chopped coarsely
2 cloves garlic, crushed
1 cinnamon stick
2 teaspoons ground coriander
1 teaspoon each ground cumin,
  ginger and dried chilli flakes
1½ cups (375ml) water
425g (13½ ounces) canned
  crushed tomatoes
2 medium quinces (600g),
  peeled, quartered

1 large zucchini (150g),
  chopped coarsely
2 tablespoons coarsely chopped
  fresh coriander (cilantro)
pistachio couscous
1½ cups (300g) couscous
1 cup (250ml) boiling water
20g (¾ ounce) butter
½ cup finely chopped fresh
  coriander (cilantro)
¼ cup (35g) roasted unsalted
  shelled pistachios,
  chopped coarsely

1 Melt butter in tagine or large saucepan; cook lamb, in batches, until browned. Remove from tagine.

2 Cook onion in same tagine, stirring, until soft. Add garlic, spices and chilli; cook, stirring, about 1 minute or until fragrant.

3 Return lamb to tagine with the water, undrained tomatoes and quince; bring to the boil. Reduce heat; simmer, covered, 30 minutes. Uncover; simmer, stirring occasionally, about 1 hour or until quince is tender and sauce has thickened slightly.

4 Add zucchini; cook, stirring, about 10 minutes or until zucchini is tender, season to taste.

5 Meanwhile, make pistachio couscous.

6 Sprinkle tagine with coriander; serve with couscous.

pistachio couscous Combine couscous, the water and butter in large heatproof bowl, cover; stand about 5 minutes or until liquid is absorbed, fluffing with fork occasionally. Stir in coriander and nuts.

prep + cook time 1 hour 50 minutes **serves** 4
nutritional count per serving 31g total fat (14.7g saturated fat); 3214kJ (769 cal); 76.7g carbohydrate; 45.4g protein; 12.3g fibre

Sweet pumpkin tagine with harissa and almond couscous

20g (¾ ounce) butter
1 tablespoon olive oil
2 medium brown onions (300g),
   chopped coarsely
2 cloves garlic, crushed
4cm (1½-inch) piece fresh ginger
   (20g), grated
2 teaspoons each ground
   coriander and cumin
2 teaspoons finely grated
   lemon rind
1kg (2 pounds) pumpkin,
   chopped coarsely
400g (13 ounces) canned
   chopped tomatoes

2 cups (500ml) vegetable stock
400g (13 ounces) green
   beans, trimmed, cut into
   5cm (2-inch) lengths
⅓ cup (55g) sultanas
1 tablespoon honey
¼ cup each finely chopped fresh
   flat-leaf parsley and mint
harissa and almond couscous
2 cups (500ml) vegetable stock
1 cup (250ml) water
3 cups (600g) couscous
½ cup (70g) slivered almonds,
   roasted
1 tablespoon harissa

1 Heat butter and oil in tagine or large saucepan; cook onion and garlic, stirring, 5 minutes. Add ginger, spices and rind; cook, stirring, about 1 minute or until fragrant. Add pumpkin, undrained tomatoes and stock; bring to the boil. Reduce heat; simmer, covered, about 15 minutes or until pumpkin is tender.

2 Meanwhile, make harissa and almond couscous.

3 Add beans to tagine; cook, stirring, 5 minutes. Remove from heat; stir in sultanas, honey and herbs, season to taste.

4 Serve tagine with couscous.

harissa and almond couscous Bring stock and the water to the boil in medium saucepan. Combine couscous and hot stock mixture in large heatproof bowl, cover; stand about 5 minutes or until liquid is absorbed, fluffing with fork occasionally. Stir in almonds and harissa.

prep + cook time 1 hour **serves** 6
nutritional count per serving 14.5g total fat (3.5g saturated fat); 2780kJ (665 cal); 105.2g carbohydrate; 23.1g protein; 7.9g fibre

Harissa-braised vegetables with orange and mint couscous

2 medium carrots (240g)
2 medium zucchini (240g)
2 small leeks (400g)
1 teaspoon olive oil
1 medium brown onion (150g),
  chopped finely
1 clove garlic, crushed
1 stalk celery (150g), trimmed,
  chopped coarsely
3 teaspoons harissa
1 tablespoon tomato paste
425g (13½ ounces) canned
  crushed tomatoes
1¼ cups (310ml) water
1 tablespoon orange juice
¼ cup (20g) roasted flaked
  almonds

orange and mint couscous
1½ cups (300g) couscous
1 teaspoon olive oil
1½ cups (375ml) boiling water
2 teaspoons finely grated
  orange rind
1 tablespoon orange juice
2 tablespoons coarsely chopped
  fresh mint

1 Preheat oven to 180°C/350°F.
2 Quarter carrots and zucchini lengthways; cut into 4cm (1½-inch) lengths. Halve leeks lengthways; cut into 6cm (2¼-inch) lengths.
3 Heat oil in tagine or flameproof casserole dish; cook onion and garlic, stirring, until onion softens. Add carrot, zucchini, leek, celery, harissa, paste, undrained tomatoes and the water; bring to the boil. Cover tagine, transfer to oven; cook about 40 minutes or until vegetables are tender. Remove from oven; stir in juice, season to taste.
4 Meanwhile, make orange and mint couscous.
5 Divide couscous and tagine among serving bowls; sprinkle with nuts.
orange and mint couscous Combine couscous, oil and the water in medium heatproof bowl, cover; stand about 5 minutes or until liquid is absorbed, fluffing with fork occasionally. Stir in remaining ingredients.

prep + cook time 1 hour 10 minutes **serves** 4
nutritional count per serving 7.6g total fat (0.8g saturated fat); 1743kJ (417 cal); 71.1g carbohydrate; 15.1g protein; 8.6g fibre

Vegetable tagine

1 tablespoon each coriander seeds, cumin seeds and caraway seeds
1 tablespoon vegetable oil
3 cloves garlic, crushed
2 large brown onions (400g), chopped finely
2 teaspoons each sweet paprika and ground ginger
1 tablespoon tomato paste
2 cups (500ml) water
800g (1½ pounds) canned diced tomatoes
600g (1¼ pounds) pumpkin, chopped coarsely

8 yellow patty pan squash (240g), quartered
200g (6½ ounces) baby green beans, trimmed, halved
300g (10 ounces) canned chickpeas (garbanzo beans), rinsed, drained

lemon couscous
2 cups (400g) couscous
2 cups (500ml) boiling water
2 teaspoons coarsely grated lemon rind
2 teaspoons lemon juice
2 tablespoons coarsely chopped fresh flat-leaf parsley

1 Using mortar and pestle, crush seeds to a fine powder. Sift into small bowl; discard husks.
2 Heat oil in tagine or large saucepan; cook garlic and onion, stirring, until onion softens. Add crushed seeds and spices; cook, stirring, until fragrant.
3 Add paste, the water, undrained tomatoes and pumpkin; bring to the boil. Reduce heat; simmer, uncovered, 20 minutes. Stir in squash, beans and chickpeas; simmer, covered, about 10 minutes or until squash is tender, season to taste.
4 Meanwhile, make lemon couscous.
5 Serve tagine with couscous.
lemon couscous Combine couscous with the water in large heatproof bowl, cover; stand about 5 minutes or until liquid is absorbed, fluffing with fork occasionally. Stir in rind, juice and parsley.

prep + cook time 1 hour 5 minutes **serves** 6
nutritional count per serving 5g total fat (0.8g saturated fat); 1643kJ (393 cal); 69.9g carbohydrate; 16.2g protein; 7.8g fibre

Sweet and spicy vegetable tagine

2 tablespoons olive oil
1 medium brown onion (150g), sliced thinly
5cm (2-inch) piece fresh ginger (25g), grated
2 cloves garlic, crushed
2 teaspoons each ground coriander and cumin
1 teaspoon sweet paprika
500g (1 pound) pumpkin, chopped coarsely
1 medium kumara (orange sweet potato) (400g), chopped coarsely
2 small parsnips (240g), chopped coarsely
2 cups (500ml) vegetable stock
400g (13 ounces) canned diced tomatoes
2 tablespoons honey
8 small yellow patty pan squash (185g), halved
375g (12 ounces) baby carrots, trimmed
⅓ cup (50g) raisins
2 tablespoons finely chopped fresh flat-leaf parsley
¼ cup (20g) flaked almonds, roasted

1 Heat oil in tagine or flameproof casserole dish; cook onion, stirring, until softened. Add ginger, garlic and spices; cook, stirring, about 1 minute or until fragrant.
2 Add pumpkin, kumara, parsnip, stock, undrained tomatoes and honey; bring to the boil. Reduce heat; simmer, covered, 15 minutes. Add squash and carrots; simmer, uncovered, 20 minutes or until vegetables are tender, season to taste.
3 Stir in raisins and parsley; sprinkle with nuts.

prep + cook time 55 minutes **serves** 8
nutritional count per serving 6.8g total fat (1g saturated fat);
857kJ (205 cal); 28.4g carbohydrate; 5.4g protein; 5.3g fibre

White bean and lentil tagine

1 tablespoon olive oil
1 medium brown onion (150g), chopped coarsely
2 cloves garlic, crushed
2.5cm (1-inch) piece fresh ginger (15g), cut into matchsticks
1 teaspoon harissa
800g (1½ pounds) canned whole peeled tomatoes, chopped coarsely
1 medium red capsicum (bell pepper) (200g), chopped coarsely
½ cup (125ml) water
400g (13 ounces) canned white beans, rinsed, drained
400g (13 ounces) canned brown lentils, rinsed, drained
¼ cup finely chopped fresh mint
¼ cup finely chopped fresh flat-leaf parsley

1 Heat oil in tagine or large frying pan; cook onion, stirring, until
softened. Add garlic, ginger and harissa; cook, stirring, about 1 minute or
until fragrant.
2 Add undrained tomatoes, capsicum, the water, beans and lentils; bring
to the boil. Reduce heat; simmer, uncovered, about 15 minutes or until
tagine thickens. Remove from heat; stir in mint, season to taste.
3 Serve tagine sprinkled with parsley; accompany with grilled flatbread,
if you like.

prep + cook time 40 minutes **serves** 4
nutritional count per serving 5.8g total fat (0.8g saturated fat);
865kJ (207 cal); 23.8g carbohydrate; 10.6g protein; 10.2g fibre
tip We used cannellini beans in this recipe but you can use any canned
white beans you like.

Vegetable tagine with split peas

2 tablespoons olive oil
1 large red onion (300g), sliced thinly
¾ cup (150g) yellow split peas
2 cloves garlic, crushed
5cm (2-inch) piece fresh ginger (25g), grated
3 teaspoons ground coriander
2 teaspoons each ground cumin and sweet paprika
1 teaspoon caraway seeds
1 litre (4 cups) vegetable stock
400g (13 ounces) canned diced tomatoes
750g (1½ pounds) butternut pumpkin, cut into 2cm (¾-inch) pieces
350g (11 ounces) yellow patty pan squash, quartered
200g (6½ ounces) green beans, trimmed, halved widthways
½ cup (125ml) water
½ cup coarsely chopped fresh coriander (cilantro)

1 Heat oil in tagine or large saucepan; cook onion, stirring, until softened. Add peas, garlic, ginger, spices and seeds; cook, stirring, until fragrant.
2 Add stock and undrained tomatoes; bring to the boil. Reduce heat; simmer, uncovered, stirring occasionally, 15 minutes. Add pumpkin; simmer about 15 minutes or until peas are tender. Stir in squash, beans and the water, cover; cook about 5 minutes or until vegetables are tender, season to taste.
3 Serve tagine sprinkled with chopped coriander; accompany with thick yogurt, flavoured with grated lemon rind, if you like.

prep + cook time 1 hour **serves** 6
nutritional count per serving 8.3g total fat (1.6g saturated fat); 1070kJ (256 cal); 27.8g carbohydrate; 13.5g protein; 7.9g fibre

Pan-fries
& Barbecues

Chicken with olives and couscous

1 tablespoon olive oil
4 x 200g (6½-ounce) chicken breast fillets
1 medium brown onion (150g), sliced thinly
1 clove garlic, crushed
2 teaspoons ground cumin
¾ teaspoon ground turmeric
2 cinnamon sticks
3 x 6cm (2¼-inch) strips lemon rind
1 tablespoon lemon juice
2 cups (500ml) chicken stock
2 teaspoons cornflour (cornstarch)
1 tablespoon water
¾ cup (90g) seeded green olives
1 cup (200g) couscous
1 cup (250ml) boiling water
½ cup coarsely chopped fresh coriander (cilantro)

1 Heat oil in large frying pan; cook chicken until browned both sides. Remove from pan.
2 Cook onion, garlic and spices in same pan, stirring, until onion softens. Return chicken to pan with rind, juice and stock; bring to the boil. Reduce heat; simmer, covered, about 15 minutes or until chicken is tender. Add blended cornflour and the water; cook, stirring, until mixture boils and thickens. Discard rind and cinnamon sticks; stir in olives, season to taste.
3 Meanwhile, combine couscous and the boiling water in large heatproof bowl. Cover; stand about 5 minutes or until liquid is absorbed, fluffing with fork occasionally.
4 Serve chicken mixture with couscous, sprinkled with coriander.

prep + cook time 40 minutes **serves** 4
nutritional count per serving 16.7g total fat (4.4g saturated fat); 2312kJ (553 cal); 47.6g carbohydrate; 51.5g protein; 1.7g fibre

Spiced chicken with fruity couscous

4 x 200g (6½-ounce) chicken breast fillets
2 teaspoons each ground cumin and ground coriander
2 tablespoons plain (all-purpose) flour
2 tablespoons olive oil
½ cup (125ml) orange juice
1½ cups (375ml) chicken stock
1 teaspoon white sugar
1 cup (250ml) water
2 cups (400g) couscous
45g (1½ ounces) butter
½ cup (45g) coarsely chopped dried apricots
¼ cup (40g) sultanas

1 Combine chicken, spices and flour in large bowl. Heat oil in large frying pan; cook chicken, covered, until browned and cooked. Remove from pan; cover to keep warm.
2 Add juice, ½ cup of stock and sugar to same pan; simmer, uncovered, about 5 minutes or until sauce thickens slightly.
3 Meanwhile, bring remaining stock and the water to the boil in small saucepan. Combine couscous, hot stock mixture, butter, apricots and sultanas in large heatproof bowl, cover; stand about 5 minutes or until liquid is absorbed, fluffing with fork occasionally.
4 Serve chicken with sauce and couscous mixture; accompany with steamed green beans, if you like.

prep + cook time 25 minutes **serves** 4
nutritional count per serving 24.1g total fat (8.9g saturated fat); 3586kJ (858 cal); 97g carbohydrate; 60.7g protein; 2.6g fibre

Spicy chicken on couscous with spinach

1 tablespoon olive oil
1 clove garlic, crushed
1½ teaspoons ground cumin
1 teaspoon ground paprika
¼ teaspoon dried chilli flakes
4 x 200g (6½-ounce) chicken breast fillets
couscous with spinach
1 cup (250ml) chicken stock
1 cup (200g) couscous
45g (1½ ounces) butter
2 teaspoons finely grated lemon rind
155g (5 ounces) baby spinach leaves

1 Combine oil, garlic, spices and chilli in small bowl.
2 Split each chicken fillet in half horizontally to form 8 thin pieces.
Place chicken in large bowl with spice mixture; toss to coat chicken
in spice mixture.
3 Cook chicken on heated oiled grill plate or (or grill or barbecue) until
browned and cooked. Cover to keep warm.
4 Meanwhile, make couscous with spinach.
5 Serve chicken with couscous and lemon wedges.
couscous with spinach Bring stock to the boil in small saucepan.
Combine couscous and hot stock in large heatproof bowl, cover; stand
about 5 minutes until liquid is absorbed, fluffing with fork occasionally.
Heat butter in large frying pan; add couscous, cook, stirring, until the
couscous is separated and fluffy. Add the rind and spinach; toss gently,
season to taste.

prep + cook time 35 minutes **serves** 4
nutritional count per serving 19.1g total fat (8.1g saturated fat);
2286kJ (547 cal); 39.2g carbohydrate; 53.4g protein; 1.7g fibre
tip The chicken can be marinated a day ahead. Recipe best made
close to serving.

Chermoulla chicken with chickpea salad

1 cup (200g) dried chickpeas (garbanzo beans)
4 single chicken breast fillets (800g)
1 medium red capsicum (bell pepper) (150g), chopped finely
1 medium green capsicum (bell pepper) (150g), chopped finely
2 large egg (roma) tomatoes (180g), chopped finely
1 small white onion (80g), chopped finely
2 tablespoons lemon juice

chermoulla
½ cup each finely chopped fresh coriander (cilantro) and flat-leaf parsley
3 cloves garlic, crushed
2 tablespoons white wine vinegar
2 tablespoons lemon juice
1 teaspoon sweet paprika
½ teaspoon ground cumin
2 tablespoons olive oil

1 Cover chickpeas with cold water in large bowl; stand overnight, drain. Rinse under cold water; drain. Cook chickpeas in medium saucepan of boiling water, uncovered, until just tender; drain. Rinse, then drain.
2 Meanwhile, combine ingredients for chermoulla in large bowl; reserve half of the chermoulla for chickpea salad.
3 Place chicken in medium bowl with remaining chermoulla; turn chicken to coat in chermoulla. Cook chicken, in batches, on heated oiled grill plate (or grill or barbecue) until cooked through. Cover to keep warm.
4 Place chickpeas in large bowl with capsicums, tomato, onion and remaining chermoulla; toss gently to combine, season to taste.
5 Serve chickpea salad with sliced chicken, drizzled with juice.

prep + cook time 45 minutes (+ standing) **serves** 4
nutritional count per serving 21.6g total fat (4.6g saturated fat); 1994kJ (477 cal); 22.5g carbohydrate; 47.2g protein; 9g fibre

Harissa chickens with rocket and cucumber salad

4 x 500g (1-pound) small chickens (poussin)
1 tablespoon harissa
1 teaspoon finely grated lemon rind
¼ cup (60ml) olive oil
2 teaspoons cumin seeds
1 teaspoon ground coriander
200g (6½ ounces) yogurt
1 clove garlic, crushed
2 lebanese cucumbers (260g)
155g (5 ounces) baby rocket (arugula) leaves
2 tablespoons lemon juice

1 Rinse chickens under cold water; pat dry inside and out with absorbent paper. Using kitchen scissors, cut along each side of each chicken's backbone; discard backbone. Place chickens, skin-side up, on board; using heel of hand, press down on breastbone to flatten chickens.
2 Combine harissa, rind and 1 tablespoon of the oil in large bowl, add chickens; rub mixture all over chickens.
3 Cook chickens on heated oiled grill plate (or grill or barbecue), uncovered, 10 minutes. Cover, cook, over low heat, about 10 minutes or until chickens are cooked.
4 Meanwhile, dry-fry spices in small frying pan until fragrant. Cool. Combine spices with yogurt and garlic in small bowl.
5 Using vegetable peeler, slice cucumber lengthways into ribbons. Place cucumber in large bowl with rocket, juice and remaining oil; toss gently to combine, season to taste.
6 Serve chicken with yogurt and salad.

prep + cook time 45 minutes **serves** 4
nutritional count per serving 55.2g total fat (15.4g saturated fat); 3043kJ (728 cal); 4.9g carbohydrate; 52.8g protein; 1.5g fibre

Blood orange and chilli glazed quail

6 quails (960g)
1 teaspoon cumin seeds
½ cup (125ml) blood orange juice
1 fresh long red chilli, chopped finely
1 clove garlic, crushed
2 tablespoons light brown sugar
1 tablespoon finely chopped fresh coriander (cilantro)

1 Using kitchen scissors, cut along both sides of each quail's backbone; discard backbones. Halve each quail along breastbone; cut each in half again to give a total of 24 pieces.
2 Cook quail, covered, on heated oiled grill plate (or grill or barbecue) about 20 minutes or until cooked.
3 Meanwhile, dry-fry seeds in small saucepan until fragrant. Add juice, chilli, garlic and sugar; stir over heat, without boiling, until sugar dissolves. Bring to the boil; boil, uncovered, about 5 minutes or until mixture is thick and syrupy.
4 Combine hot quail, syrup and coriander in large bowl, season to taste.

prep + cook time 35 minutes **serves** 8
nutritional count per serving 6.6g total fat (1.7g saturated fat); 514kJ (123 cal); 4.4g carbohydrate; 11.3g protein; 0.1g fibre
tip Quails are available from specialist food stores and most poultry shops.

Chermoulla chicken with onion couscous

4 x 200g (6½-ounce) chicken
   breast fillets
2 tablespoons harissa
chermoulla
¾ cup (180ml) lemon juice
¼ teaspoon saffron threads
1 teaspoon each ground cumin
   and dried chilli flakes
½ teaspoon each smoked paprika
   and ground cinnamon
1 small brown onion (80g),
   chopped finely
¾ cup coarsely chopped fresh
   coriander (cilantro)
⅔ cup (160ml) olive oil

onion couscous
1½ cups (375ml) chicken stock
1½ cups (300g) couscous
1 tablespoon olive oil
1 large brown onion (200g),
   sliced thinly
4 wedges preserved lemon
300g (10 ounces) canned
   chickpeas, rinsed, drained
¼ teaspoon each ground allspice
   and cinnamon

1 Make chermoulla; reserve ⅓ cup chermoulla for serving.
2 Split each chicken breast in half horizontally to form 8 thin pieces.
Combine chicken and remaining chermoulla in medium bowl, cover;
refrigerate 3 hours or overnight.
3 Make onion couscous.
4 Drain chicken; cook on heated oiled grill plate (or grill or barbecue)
until browned and cooked.
5 Serve chicken and couscous with reserved chermoulla and harissa.
chermoulla Stand juice and saffron in bowl 10 minutes. Dry-fry spices
in small frying pan until fragrant. Combine spices, saffron mixture and
remaining ingredients in medium bowl, season to taste.
onion couscous Bring stock to the boil in small saucepan. Combine
couscous and hot stock in medium heatproof bowl, cover; stand 5 minutes
or until liquid is absorbed, fluffing with fork occasionally. Heat oil in
medium frying pan; cook onion, stirring, until soft. Remove flesh from
preserved lemon and discard; chop rind finely. Stir onion, preserved
lemon, chickpeas and spices into couscous; cover to keep warm.

prep + cook time 55 minutes (+ refrigeration) **serves** 4
nutritional count per serving 47.9g total fat (7.4g saturated fat);
4059kJ (971 cal); 72g carbohydrate; 60.6g protein; 5.2g fibre

Barbecued salmon with chermoulla sauce

6 x 180g (6-ounce) salmon fillets, skin on
2 tablespoons olive oil
2 medium red onions (340g)
3 medium zucchini (360g), sliced thinly lengthways
340g (11 ounces) asparagus, trimmed

chermoulla sauce
½ cup each firmly packed fresh flat-leaf parsley and
    coriander (cilantro) leaves
2 cloves garlic, chopped coarsely
1 teaspoon each chilli flakes, ground coriander and cumin
½ teaspoon ground turmeric
1 tablespoon lemon juice
1 tablespoon olive oil
½ cup (140g) greek-style yogurt

1 Make chermoulla sauce.
2 Rub fish skin with a little of the oil.
3 Cut each onion into 8 wedges, keeping root ends intact. Combine onion, zucchini and asparagus with remaining oil in medium bowl.
4 Cook fish on heated barbecue flat plate, skin-side down, until crisp; turn, cook as desired. Cook vegetables on heated oiled barbecue (or grill plate or grill) at the same time as the fish until tender.
5 Serve fish and vegetables with sauce; accompany with steamed couscous, if you like.

chermoulla sauce Blend or process herbs, garlic, chilli and ground spices until combined. Add juice and oil; process until smooth. Transfer to medium bowl; stir in yogurt, season to taste.

prep + cook time 30 minutes **serves** 6
nutritional count per serving 23.8g total fat (5.2g saturated fat); 1701kJ (407 cal); 7.2g carbohydrate; 39.6g protein; 3.1g fibre
tip Prepare the vegetables and the sauce up to a day ahead; keep the sauce, covered, in the refrigerator.

Crispy spiced fish

8 small white fish fillets (750g)
vegetable oil, for shallow-frying
2 eggs
1 teaspoon water
1 cup (150g) plain (all-purpose) flour
chermoulla
1 cup firmly packed fresh coriander (cilantro) leaves
1 clove garlic, crushed
1 tablespoon ground cumin
1½ teaspoons sweet paprika
pinch hot paprika
1 tablespoon olive oil
2 tablespoons water

1 Make chermoulla.
2 Cut fish fillets in half. Combine fish and chermoulla in large bowl.
Cover; refrigerate 2 hours or overnight.
3 Heat oil in large frying pan. Whisk eggs and the water in small shallow
bowl until combined. Drain fish, then toss in flour, shake off excess.
Dip fish in egg mixture, drain off excess. Shallow-fry fish, in batches,
until browned lightly; drain on absorbent paper.
chermoulla Blend or process ingredients until smooth; season to taste.

prep + cook time 35 minutes (+ refrigeration) **serves** 8
nutritional count per serving 13g total fat (2.2g saturated fat);
1104kJ (264 cal); 12.7g carbohydrate; 23.5g protein; 1.1g fibre
tip We used flathead fillets in this recipe.

Fish with chermoulla

1.2kg (2½ pounds) firm white fish fillets
chermoulla
3 cloves garlic, crushed
1 teaspoon ground cumin
½ teaspoon hot paprika
2 tablespoons each coarsely chopped fresh coriander (cilantro) and
   flat-leaf parsley
¼ cup (60ml) olive oil
2 teaspoons finely grated lemon rind
¼ cup (60ml) lemon juice

1 Make chermoulla
2 Cut fish into 8 even-sized pieces; place in large, shallow, non-metallic
dish. Pour half the chermoulla over fish; reserve remaining chermoulla
for serving. Cover fish and reserved chermoulla; refrigerate 3 hours.
3 Cook fish in heated oiled frying pan, in batches, about 2 minutes each
side or until browned lightly and just cooked.
4 Transfer fish to serving platter; drizzle with remaining chermoulla.
Sprinkle with extra coriander leaves, if you like.
chermoulla Combine ingredients in medium bowl; season to taste.

prep + cook time 20 minutes (+ refrigeration) **serves** 8
nutritional count per serving 10.2g total fat (2g saturated fat);
907kJ (217 cal); 0.4g carbohydrate; 31g protein; 0.3g fibre
tips We used a large snapper fillet cut into eight small portions in this
recipe. Other suitable fish fillets are perch, ling, barramundi or gemfish.
If hot paprika is unavailable, substitute ½ teaspoon of sweet paprika
and a good pinch of cayenne pepper.
This recipe is best prepared up to 3 hours ahead.

Spiced fried fish with lemon pistachio couscous

1 tablespoon plain (all-purpose) flour
1½ teaspoons each ground coriander and cumin
1 teaspoon sweet smoked paprika
¼ teaspoon cayenne pepper
8 white fish fillets (800g)
1 tablespoon olive oil
lemon pistachio couscous
1 cup (200g) couscous
¾ cup (180ml) boiling water
2 teaspoons finely grated lemon rind
¼ cup (60ml) lemon juice
2 teaspoons olive oil
1 small red onion (100g), chopped finely
1 clove garlic, crushed
½ cup (70g) roasted unsalted shelled pistachios
½ cup coarsely chopped fresh mint

1 Make lemon pistachio couscous.
2 Combine flour and spices in medium bowl; add fish, rub spice mixture all over fish.
3 Heat oil in large frying pan; cook fish, in batches, until browned and cooked as desired.
4 Serve fish with couscous and, if you like, wedges of lemon.
lemon pistachio couscous Combine couscous, the water, rind and juice in medium heatproof bowl, cover; stand about 5 minutes or until liquid is absorbed, fluffing with fork occasionally. Heat oil in small frying pan; cook onion and garlic, stirring, until onion softens. Stir onion mixture, nuts and mint through couscous, season to taste.

prep + cook time 35 minutes **serves** 4
nutritional count per serving 25.4g total fat (5.5g saturated fat); 2571kJ (615 cal); 44.8g carbohydrate; 49.7g protein; 2.9g fibre
tip We used bream fillets here, but you can use any firm white fish fillet, such as perch, blue-eye or ling, if you prefer.

Ras el hanout beef with couscous

2 tablespoons olive oil
4 x 220g (7-ounce) new-york cut steaks
1 tablespoon ras el hanout
1 tablespoon finely grated lemon rind
⅓ cup (80ml) lemon juice
⅔ cup (160ml) dry white wine
1 cup (250ml) water
1 small red onion (100g), chopped finely
2 cups (400g) couscous
¼ cup coarsely chopped fresh flat-leaf parsley
½ cup coarsely chopped fresh mint
¼ cup (50g) toasted pepitas
⅓ cup (95g) yogurt

1 Heat oil in large deep frying pan; rub beef with ras el hanout. Cook beef, uncovered, until cooked as desired, turning once only. Remove from pan, cover; stand 5 minutes, then slice thinly.
2 Meanwhile, add rind, juice, wine and the water to same cleaned pan; cover, bring to the boil then remove from heat. Add onion and couscous; cover, stand about 5 minutes or until liquid is absorbed, fluffing with fork occasionally. Stir in herbs and pepitas, season to taste.
3 Serve couscous topped with sliced steak and yogurt.

prep + cook time 20 minutes **serves** 4
nutritional count per serving 29.6g total fat (8.5g saturated fat); 3687kJ (882 cal); 82.3g carbohydrate; 64.3g protein; 2.5g fibre

Spicy beef and olives with citrus couscous

2 cloves garlic, crushed
1 tablespoon ground cumin
2 teaspoons ground coriander
1 teaspoon ground ginger
500g (1 pound) piece beef
  butt fillet or rump steak
1 tablespoon harissa
1 cup (250ml) beef stock
200g (6½ ounces) seeded green
  olives, crushed slightly
½ cup coarsely chopped fresh
  coriander (cilantro)

citrus couscous
2 medium oranges (480g)
1 cup (250ml) water
1 cup (250ml) orange juice
2 cups (400g) couscous
¼ cup (35g) roasted slivered
  almonds
1 tablespoon thinly sliced
  preserved lemon rind
1 small red onion (100g),
  sliced thinly
500g (1 pound) red radishes,
  trimmed, sliced thinly

1 Combine garlic and spices in medium bowl; reserve about a third of the spice mixture. Add beef to bowl with remaining two-thirds of the spice mixture; toss to coat beef. Cook beef on heated oiled grill plate (or grill or barbecue) until cooked as desired, cover; stand 10 minutes, then slice thinly.

2 Meanwhile, make citrus couscous.

3 Cook harissa and remaining spice mixture in heated small frying pan until fragrant. Add stock; bring to the boil. Reduce heat; simmer, uncovered, about 3 minutes or until harissa dressing reduces by half. Remove from heat; stir in olives and coriander.

4 Serve beef on citrus couscous, drizzle with warm harissa dressing.

citrus couscous Remove skin and white pith from oranges; cut in half, slice thinly. Place the water and juice in medium saucepan; bring to the boil. Remove from heat; stir in couscous, cover; stand about 5 minutes or until liquid is absorbed, fluffing with fork occasionally. Stir orange and remaining ingredients through couscous, season to taste.

prep + cook time 35 minutes **serves** 4
nutritional count per serving 15.1g total fat (4.4g saturated fat); 3164kJ (757 cal); 104.3g carbohydrate; 46.4g protein; 6.4g fibre

Spiced lamb leg with fruity couscous

2 tablespoons ras el hanout
2 tablespoons olive oil
1.5kg (3 pounds) butterflied lamb leg
fruity couscous
1 ½ cups (375ml) water
1 ½ cups (300g) couscous
2 medium oranges (480g)
1 cup (230g) fresh dates, seeded, quartered
1 cup (100g) roasted walnuts, chopped coarsely
⅓ cup coarsely chopped fresh flat-leaf parsley
½ cup (125ml) orange juice
2 tablespoons walnut oil
½ teaspoon ground cinnamon

1 Combine ras el hanout and oil in large bowl, add lamb; turn to coat in marinade. Cover; refrigerate 3 hours or overnight.
2 Meanwhile, make fruity couscous.
3 Cook lamb on heated oiled grill plate (or grill or barbecue), covered, about 35 minutes or until cooked, turning midway through cooking. Cover; stand 10 minutes, slice thickly.
4 Serve lamb with couscous.
fruity couscous Bring the water to the boil in medium saucepan, remove from heat; stir in couscous, cover; stand about 5 minutes or until liquid is absorbed, fluffing with fork occasionally. Segment oranges over pan. Add remaining ingredients, season to taste.

prep + cook time 1 hour (+ refrigeration & standing) **serves** 6
nutritional count per serving 37.6g total fat (8.1g saturated fat); 3490kJ (835 cal); 57.4g carbohydrate; 65.2g protein; 4.6g fibre

Crumbed lamb cutlets with orange, couscous and spinach salad

⅔ cup (50g) stale breadcrumbs
2 teaspoons each sweet paprika and ground cumin
½ teaspoon ground cardamom
12 french-trimmed lamb cutlets (600g)
¼ cup (35g) plain (all-purpose) flour
1 egg, beaten lightly
vegetable oil, for shallow-frying
½ cup (100g) couscous
½ cup (125ml) boiling water
2 medium oranges (480g)
1 cup (120g) seeded black olives
200g (6½ ounces) fetta cheese, cut into 1cm (½-inch) pieces
100g (3 ounces) baby spinach leaves
1 small red onion (100g), sliced thinly
⅓ cup (80ml) olive oil
2 tablespoons white wine vinegar

1 Combine breadcrumbs and spices in small shallow bowl.
2 Coat lamb in flour; shake off excess. Dip in egg, then in crumb mixture to coat.
3 Heat oil in large frying pan; shallow-fry lamb, in batches, until cooked as desired. Drain on absorbent paper.
4 Meanwhile, combine couscous with the water in large heatproof bowl, cover; stand about 5 minutes or until liquid is absorbed, fluffing with fork occasionally.
5 Segment oranges over small bowl; reserve ¼ cup juice.
6 Stir orange segments, reserved juice and remaining ingredients through couscous; season to taste.
7 Serve cutlets with salad.

prep + cook time 40 minutes **serves** 4
nutritional count per serving 60.1g total fat (18.6g saturated fat); 3658kJ (875 cal); 49.1g carbohydrate; 33.6g protein; 4.2g fibre
tip If blood oranges are in season, you can use them in place of regular oranges – they have a gorgeous salmon-coloured pulp and a slightly sweeter flavour than regular oranges.

Lemon and olive lamb with couscous

1kg (2 pounds) lamb backstraps
400g (13 ounces) green beans, trimmed
⅓ cup (80ml) dry white wine
½ cup (125ml) chicken stock
1 tablespoon lemon juice
20g (¾ ounce) butter
⅓ cup (50g) seeded black olives
COUSCOUS
1 cup (250ml) chicken stock
1 cup (200g) couscous
20g (¾ ounce) butter
2 tablespoons pine nuts
⅓ cup coarsely chopped fresh flat-leaf parsley

1 Cook lamb in large frying pan until cooked as desired. Remove from pan, cover to keep warm.
2 Meanwhile, make couscous.
3 Cook beans in medium saucepan of boiling water until tender; drain.
4 Drain the excess fat from the frying pan. Add wine to pan; bring to the boil. Add stock and juice; simmer, uncovered, about 1 minute or until sauce reduces slightly. Stir in butter and olives, season to taste.
5 Serve lamb and sauce with couscous and beans.
couscous Bring stock to the boil in small saucepan. Combine couscous and hot stock mixture in medium heatproof bowl, cover; stand about 5 minutes, or until liquid is absorbed, fluffing with fork occasionally. Heat butter in small frying pan; cook nuts, stirring, until browned lightly. Stir nut mixture and parsley through couscous, season to taste.

prep + cook time 30 minutes **serves** 4
nutritional count per serving 36.3g total fat (16g saturated fat); 3256kJ (779 cal); 44.8g carbohydrate; 63.2g protein; 3.9g fibre

Spicy lamb with garlic couscous

500g (1 pound) lamb backstraps
2 teaspoons bottled chopped chilli
2 teaspoons ground cumin
1 clove garlic, crushed
¼ cup coarsely chopped fresh coriander (cilantro)
2 cups (500ml) chicken stock
3 cloves garlic, sliced thinly
1 cup (120g) frozen peas
1½ cups (300g) couscous
2 teaspoons extra virgin olive oil
½ cup (125g) labaneh
2 teaspoons bottled chopped chilli, extra

1 Combine lamb, chilli, cumin, crushed garlic and coriander in medium bowl.
2 Cook lamb mixture on heated oiled grill plate (or grill or barbecue)
until cooked as desired. Remove from grill, cover; stand 5 minutes,
then slice thinly.
3 Meanwhile, combine stock, sliced garlic and peas in medium saucepan;
bring to the boil. Remove from heat, stir in the couscous and oil, cover;
stand about 5 minutes or until liquid is absorbed, fluffing with fork
occasionally, season to taste.
4 Divide couscous among serving dishes, top with lamb, labaneh and
extra chilli.

prep + cook time 30 minutes **serves** 4
nutritional count per serving 15.6g total fat (6.4g saturated fat);
2358kJ (564 cal); 62.8g carbohydrate; 40.6g protein; 3.3g fibre
tip Labaneh is a spreadable yogurt, and is available from some
supermarkets. You could use a low-fat yogurt instead.

Grilled spiced lamb with burghul salad

¾ cup (120g) burghul
1 tablespoon olive oil
1 tablespoon ras el hanout
800g (1½ pounds) lamb backstraps
½ cup (70g) roasted unsalted shelled pistachios, chopped coarsely
1 small red onion (100g), chopped finely
¾ cup each loosely packed fresh flat-leaf parsley and mint leaves
⅓ cup (55g) dried currants
1 tablespoon finely grated lemon rind
1 clove garlic, crushed
¼ cup (60ml) lemon juice
2 tablespoons olive oil, extra

1 Place burghul in medium bowl, cover with water. Stand 10 minutes; drain. Squeeze out as much excess water as possible.
2 Combine oil, spice and lamb in medium bowl, turn to coat lamb in mixture. Cook lamb, in batches, on heated oiled grill plate (or grill or barbecue) until cooked as desired. Cover lamb; stand 10 minutes then slice thickly.
3 Combine burghul in medium bowl with remaining ingredients, season to taste.
4 Serve salad topped with sliced lamb and, if you like, yogurt.

prep + cook time 40 minutes **serves** 4
nutritional count per serving 30.7g total fat (6.3g saturated fat); 2776kJ (664 cal); 38.5g carbohydrate; 53g protein; 10.8g fibre

Roasts & Kebabs

Roast chicken with fruity couscous stuffing

½ cup (100g) couscous
½ cup (125ml) boiling water
2 tablespoons honey
½ teaspoon each ground coriander and cumin
¼ teaspoon ground cinnamon
2 tablespoons each coarsely chopped raisins and dried apricots
1.6kg (3¼-pound) whole chicken
⅓ cup (80ml) orange juice
1 teaspoon dried oregano
½ teaspoon sweet paprika
1 cup (250ml) water
orange honey yogurt
¾ cup (200g) yogurt
2 teaspoons honey
1 teaspoon finely grated orange rind

1 Combine couscous with the boiling water and honey in small heatproof bowl, cover; stand about 5 minutes or until liquid is absorbed, fluffing with fork occasionally. Stir in spices and fruit, season to taste.
2 Preheat oven to 200°C/400°F.
3 Rinse chicken under cold water; pat dry inside and out with absorbent paper. Tuck wing tips under chicken. Trim skin around neck; secure neck flap to underside of chicken with skewers. Fill cavity with couscous mixture, fold skin to enclose stuffing; secure with skewers. Tie legs together with kitchen string.
4 Place chicken in oiled medium baking dish. Drizzle chicken with juice, sprinkle with oregano and paprika; pour the water into dish. Season. Roast chicken about 1½ hours, basting occasionally with juices, or until chicken is cooked.
5 Meanwhile, combine ingredients for orange honey yogurt in small bowl.
6 Serve chicken with stuffing and yogurt.

prep + cook time 1 hour 50 minutes **serves** 4
nutritional count per serving 33.5g total fat (10.8g saturated fat); 2776kJ (664 cal); 44.3g carbohydrate; 46g protein; 2.1g fibre

Roasted harissa chicken

1.8kg (3¾-pound) whole chicken
¾ cup (225g) harissa
1 large carrot (180g), halved lengthways
1 large red onion (300g), quartered
2 stalks celery (300g), trimmed
10 sprigs (20g) fresh lemon thyme
1 medium garlic bulb (70g), halved crossways
2 tablespoons olive oil

1 Rinse chicken under cold water; pat dry inside and out with absorbent paper. Tuck wing tips under chicken. Brush harissa all over chicken; tie legs together with kitchen string. Cover; refrigerate 3 hours or overnight.
2 Preheat oven to 200°C/400°F.
3 Combine remaining ingredients in large shallow baking dish; top with chicken, season.
4 Roast chicken about 1¼ hours or until chicken is cooked through. Cover; stand 10 minutes before serving.

prep + cook time 1 hour 35 minutes (+ refrigeration) **serves** 4
nutritional count per serving 47.4g total fat (13g saturated fat); 2968kJ (710 cal); 19.6g carbohydrate; 48.1g protein; 8.4g fibre

Honeyed orange quails

4 quails (640g)
1 tablespoon finely grated orange rind
½ cup (125ml) orange juice
4cm (1½-inch) piece fresh ginger (20g), grated
pinch ground turmeric
2 tablespoons olive oil
2 tablespoons honey
1 teaspoon sweet paprika
1 medium orange (240g), cut into 12 wedges
250g (8 ounces) rocket (arugula), trimmed

1 Rinse quails under cold water; pat dry inside and out with absorbent paper. Discard necks from quails. Using kitchen scissors, cut along each side of each quail's backbone; discard backbones. Skewer each quail lengthways with two skewers.
2 Combine rind, juice, ginger, turmeric, oil, honey and paprika in small bowl.
3 Cook quail on heated oiled grill plate (or grill or barbecue), basting with orange mixture, about 15 minutes or until cooked.
4 Cook orange wedges on heated oiled grill plate for last 10 minutes of quails' cooking time.
5 Serve quail with orange wedges and rocket.

prep + cook time 40 minutes **serves** 4
nutritional count per serving 18.4g total fat (3.6g saturated fat); 1300kJ (311 cal); 19.2g carbohydrate; 17.2g protein; 1.9g fibre

Lemony chicken kebabs

⅓ cup (80ml) olive oil
2 tablespoons coarsely chopped preserved lemon rind
2 tablespoons lemon juice
4 cloves garlic, halved
4cm (1½-inch) piece fresh ginger (20g), grated
1 teaspoon each ground coriander and cumin
½ teaspoon ground turmeric
¼ teaspoon ground cinnamon
1 tablespoon light brown sugar
2 tablespoons fresh marjoram leaves
1kg (2 pounds) chicken thigh fillets, chopped coarsely
1½ cups (420g) greek-style yogurt
⅓ cup finely chopped fresh coriander (cilantro)
1 medium lemon (140g), cut into wedges

1 Blend or process oil, preserved lemon, juice, garlic, ginger, spices, sugar and half the marjoram until almost smooth; reserve 1 tablespoon of the paste.
2 Combine chicken with remaining paste in large bowl. Cover; refrigerate 3 hours.
3 Thread chicken onto six metal skewers. Cook skewers on heated oiled grill plate (or grill or barbecue) until cooked.
4 Meanwhile, combine yogurt, coriander and reserved paste in medium bowl; season to taste.
5 Serve chicken kebabs sprinkled with remaining marjoram. Serve with yogurt and lemon wedges.

prep + cook time 35 minutes (+ refrigeration) **serves** 6
nutritional count per serving 29.1g total fat (8.6g saturated fat); 1843kJ (441 cal); 9.1g carbohydrate; 35.1g protein; 0.8g fibre

Chicken kebabs with blood orange

4 medium blood oranges (960g)
8 chicken tenderloins (600g)
1 tablespoon moroccan seasoning
¼ cup finely chopped fresh flat-leaf parsley
¼ cup (30g) finely chopped roasted unsalted shelled pistachios
1 tablespoon olive oil
1 tablespoon pomegranate molasses
pinch chilli powder

1 Finely grate 2 teaspoons rind from oranges.
2 Combine chicken, seasoning and rind in medium bowl; season.
Thread chicken onto 8 bamboo skewers.
3 Cook kebabs on heated oiled grill plate (or grill or barbecue) until
chicken is cooked.
4 Meanwhile, segment oranges over small bowl; reserve 1 tablespoon
juice, chop flesh finely. Combine juice and flesh with remaining
ingredients in small bowl, season to taste.
5 Serve kebabs with orange mixture and, if you like, toasted flatbread.

prep + cook time 45 minutes **serves** 8
nutritional count per serving 10.9g total fat (1.8g saturated fat);
1388kJ (332 cal); 19.4g carbohydrate; 36.7g protein; 4.3g fibre
tip Soak bamboo skewers in cold water for at least an hour before using
to prevent them burning during cooking.

Roast chicken with preserved lemon

¼ cup finely chopped preserved lemon rind
6 cloves garlic, crushed
1½ teaspoons ground ginger
1 teaspoon each ground cumin, sweet paprika and chilli flakes
½ teaspoon ground turmeric
2 tablespoons olive oil
2.5kg (5 pounds) chicken thigh cutlets
¼ teaspoon saffron threads
1 cup (250ml) boiling water
4 medium brown onions (600g), sliced thinly
4 wide strips preserved lemon rind
150g (5½ ounces) drained seeded green olives
1 cup loosely packed fresh coriander (cilantro) leaves

1 Combine chopped lemon rind, garlic, spices and half the oil in large bowl with chicken. Cover; refrigerate 3 hours or overnight.
2 Preheat oven to 180°C/350°F.
3 Combine saffron and the water in small heatproof bowl.
4 Heat remaining oil in large frying pan; cook chicken, in batches, until browned both sides. Remove from pan.
5 Add onion to same pan; cook about 5 minutes or until softened. Add saffron mixture to pan; bring to the boil. Spread onion mixture into large shallow baking dish; add chicken, in single layer. Roast, uncovered, in oven 20 minutes.
6 Sprinkle lemon rind strips and olives over chicken; roast, uncovered, about 25 minutes or until cooked through, season to taste.
7 Serve chicken sprinkled with coriander. Serve with steamed couscous combined with sliced red onion, parsley and roasted blanched almonds.

prep + cook time 1 hour 30 minutes (+ refrigeration) **serves** 6
nutritional count per serving 27.5g total fat (7.3g saturated fat); 2190kJ (524 cal); 11.9g carbohydrate; 56.3g protein; 2.8g fibre
tip We used brine-cured sicilian olives in this recipe for their lovely flavour and texture. Crack them open but leave the seeds in; use the flat blade of a knife to split the olives. Remember to warn your guests about the seeds before they start eating.

Citrus chicken with orange and pistachio couscous

3 cloves garlic, crushed
1 tablespoon finely chopped fresh oregano
¼ cup (60ml) lemon juice
½ cup (170g) orange marmalade
2 fresh small red thai (serrano) chillies, chopped finely
4 x 200g (6½-ounce) chicken breast fillets
2 cups (500ml) chicken stock
2 cups (400g) couscous
2 medium oranges (480g)
2 green onions (scallions), sliced thinly
⅓ cup (45g) roasted unsalted shelled pistachios, chopped coarsely

1 Preheat oven to 200°C/400°F. Oil oven tray; line with baking paper.
2 Combine garlic, oregano, juice, marmalade and chilli in medium bowl; add chicken, turn to coat in mixture.
3 Drain chicken, reserve marmalade mixture. Cook chicken on heated oiled grill plate (or grill or barbecue) until browned both sides. Place chicken on oven tray, drizzle with reserved marmalade mixture; roast in oven, uncovered, about 10 minutes or until chicken is cooked through.
4 Meanwhile, bring stock to the boil in medium saucepan. Combine couscous with hot stock in large heatproof bowl, cover; stand about 5 minutes or until liquid is absorbed, fluffing with fork occasionally. Segment oranges over couscous; stir in onion and nuts, season to taste.
5 Serve couscous topped with chicken.

prep + cook time 25 minutes **serves** 4
nutritional count per serving 18g total fat (4.4g saturated fat); 3620kJ (866 cal); 113g carbohydrate; 60.4g protein; 4.3g fibre

Chicken kebabs with harissa mayonnaise

2 tablespoons pistachio dukkah
1 ½ teaspoons mild paprika
2 tablespoons olive oil
6 chicken thigh fillets (600g), halved lengthways
1 medium lemon (140g), cut into wedges
harissa mayonnaise
½ cup (150g) whole egg mayonnaise
2 teaspoons harissa
2 teaspoons lemon juice

1 Combine dukkah, paprika and oil in medium bowl, season; add chicken, turn to coat in mixture. Thread chicken onto twelve bamboo skewers.
2 Cook kebabs on heated oiled grill plate (or grill or barbecue) until chicken is cooked.
3 Meanwhile, make harissa mayonnaise.
4 Serve kebabs with harissa mayonnaise and lemon wedges.
harissa mayonnaise Combine ingredients in small bowl.

prep + cook time 25 minutes **serves** 4
nutritional count per serving 21.4g total fat (4g saturated fat); 1208kJ (289 cal); 5.6g carbohydrate; 19g protein; 0.8g fibre
tips Dukkah is a Middle Eastern seed, nut and spice mix.
Soak bamboo skewers in cold water for at least an hour before using to prevent them burning during cooking.

Chicken with figs and couscous

1 tablespoon olive oil
1 large brown onion (200g), sliced thinly
2 cloves garlic, crushed
2 teaspoons coriander seeds
3 cups (750ml) chicken stock
pinch saffron threads
250g (8 ounces) dried figs
2 cinnamon sticks
2kg (4-pound) whole chicken
2 cups (500ml) chicken stock, extra
2 cups (400g) couscous
⅓ cup coarsely chopped fresh coriander (cilantro)

1 Preheat oven to 160°C/325°F.
2 Heat oil in large flameproof baking dish; cook onion, garlic and
seeds, stirring, until onion is soft. Add stock, saffron, figs and cinnamon;
bring to the boil.
3 Rinse chicken under cold water; pat dry inside and out with absorbent
paper. Tuck wing tips under chicken. Trim skin around neck; secure neck
flap to underside of chicken with skewers. Tie legs together with kitchen
string. Add chicken to dish, breast side up, season. Cover dish with foil;
roast 2 hours.
4 Uncover; roast about 1 hour or until chicken is browned and cooked.
Remove chicken and figs from dish, cover to keep warm; strain pan juices
into medium heatproof jug. Skim fat from top of pan juices.
5 Return pan juices to dish; boil, uncovered, until reduced to 1½ cups.
6 Meanwhile, bring extra stock to the boil in small saucepan. Combine
couscous and hot stock in medium heatproof bowl, cover; stand about
5 minutes or until liquid is absorbed, fluffing with fork occasionally. Stir in
coriander; season to taste.
7 Serve chicken and figs with sauce and couscous.

prep + cook time 3 hours 30 minutes **serves** 6
nutritional count per serving 31.4g total fat (9.3g saturated fat);
3311kJ (792 cal); 77.2g carbohydrate; 46.2g protein; 7.3g fibre

Chicken with couscous stuffing

1.6kg (3¼-pound) whole chicken
20g (¾ ounce) butter, melted
20 baby vine-ripened truss
  tomatoes (400g)
1 tablespoon olive oil
couscous stuffing
1 teaspoon olive oil
1 medium brown onion (150g),
  chopped finely
1½ cups (375ml) chicken stock
¼ cup (60ml) olive oil, extra

1 tablespoon finely grated
  lemon rind
¼ cup (60ml) lemon juice
1 cup (200g) couscous
½ cup (70g) roasted slivered
  almonds
1 cup (140g) seeded dried dates,
  chopped finely
1 teaspoon each ground cinnamon
  and smoked paprika
1 egg, beaten lightly

1 Make couscous stuffing.
2 Preheat oven to 200°C/400°F.
3 Rinse chicken under cold water; pat dry inside and out with absorbent paper. Tuck wing tips under chicken. Trim skin around neck; secure neck flap to underside of chicken with skewers. Fill large cavity loosely with couscous stuffing; tie legs together with kitchen string.
4 Half fill large baking dish with water; place chicken on oiled wire rack over dish. Brush chicken all over with butter, season; roast, uncovered, 15 minutes. Reduce oven to 180°C/350°F; roast, uncovered, about 1½ hours or until cooked through. Remove chicken from rack; cover, stand 20 minutes.
5 Meanwhile, place tomatoes on oven tray; drizzle with oil. Roast, uncovered, about 20 minutes or until softened and browned lightly.
6 Serve chicken with tomatoes.
couscous stuffing Heat oil in small frying pan; cook onion, stirring, until soft. Combine stock, extra oil, rind and juice in medium saucepan; bring to the boil. Remove from heat. Add couscous, cover; stand about 5 minutes or until liquid is absorbed, fluffing with fork occasionally. Stir in onion, nuts, dates, spices and egg; season to taste.

prep + cook time 2 hours 50 minutes (+ standing) **serves** 4
nutritional count per serving 67.4g total fat (16.7g saturated fat); 4565kJ (1092 cal); 67.8g carbohydrate; 54.9g protein; 7.2g fibre

Harissa and orange-roasted chicken and vegetables

1 small orange (180g),
cut into thin wedges
1.6kg (3¼ pound) whole chicken
1 tablespoon olive oil
300g (10 ounces) baby onions
500g (1 pound) baby new
potatoes
1 bulb garlic, separated into cloves
4 baby eggplants (240g),
halved lengthways
250g (8 ounces) cherry tomatoes

harissa
⅓ cup (15g) dried red chillies,
chopped coarsely
½ teaspoon each ground coriander,
cumin and caraway seeds
1 clove garlic, quartered
1 tablespoon tomato paste
2 teaspoons finely grated
orange rind
¼ cup (60ml) orange juice

1 Make harissa.

2 Preheat oven to 180°C/350°F.

3 Rinse chicken under cold water; pat dry inside and out with absorbent paper. Tuck wing tips under chicken. Fill large cavity with orange. Make a pocket between breast and skin with fingers; rub 2 tablespoons of the harissa under skin inside pocket. Tie legs together with kitchen string; brush chicken all over with 2 tablespoons of the harissa.

4 Half-fill large shallow baking dish with water; place chicken on oiled wire rack over dish, season. Roast, uncovered, about 1 hour.

5 Meanwhile, heat oil in large flameproof baking dish; cook onions, potatoes and unpeeled garlic, stirring, until vegetables are browned.

6 Cover chicken; roast about 50 minutes or until chicken is cooked through. Add eggplant and tomatoes to vegetable mixture in dish, season; place in oven for about the last 20 minutes of chicken cooking time or until vegetables are tender.

7 Serve chicken with roasted vegetables and remaining harissa.

harissa Place chilli in small heatproof bowl of boiling water; stand 1 hour. Drain; reserve ¼ cup soaking liquid. Dry-fry spices in small frying pan until fragrant. Blend or process spices, chilli, reserved soaking liquid, garlic and paste until mixture is smooth; transfer to small bowl, stir in rind and juice.

prep + cook time 2 hours 35 minutes (+ standing) **serves** 4
nutritional count per serving 37.5g total fat (10.7g saturated fat);
2717kJ (650 cal); 27.9g carbohydrate; 46.1g protein; 8.3g fibre

Chilli and coriander chicken skewers

1 fresh long green chilli, chopped finely
1 small white onion (80g), quartered
2 cloves garlic, quartered
1 tablespoon ground coriander
1 tablespoon lemon juice
2 tablespoons olive oil
8 chicken thigh fillets (1.6kg), cut into 2.5cm (1-inch) pieces
¼ cup firmly packed fresh coriander (cilantro) leaves

1 Preheat oven to 220°C/425°F. Line oven trays with baking paper.
2 Blend or process chilli, onion, garlic, ground coriander, juice and oil until mixture forms a smooth paste; season to taste.
3 Combine chicken and paste in medium bowl; thread onto 16 skewers. Place skewers on oven trays, in single layer; bake about 20 minutes or until cooked through. Serve with fresh coriander leaves.

prep + cook time 40 minutes   **serves** 8
nutritional count per serving 19g total fat (5g saturated fat); 1350kJ (323 cal); 0.8g carbohydrate; 37.5g protein; 0.4g fibre
tips Soak bamboo skewers in cold water for at least an hour before using to prevent them burning during cooking.
The paste can be made three days ahead (or even longer if frozen).

Sardines with preserved lemon salsa

2 tablespoons olive oil
1 medium brown onion (150g), chopped finely
6 drained anchovy fillets
2 cloves garlic, crushed
500g (1 pound) cherry tomatoes
800g (1½ pounds) canned diced tomatoes
¾ cup (90g) seeded black olives, chopped coarsely
¼ cup coarsely chopped fresh flat-leaf parsley
12 butterflied sardines (400g)
preserved lemon salsa
½ cup coarsely chopped fresh flat-leaf parsley
¼ cup (50g) finely chopped preserved lemon rind
1 clove garlic, crushed
2 tablespoons olive oil

1 Preheat oven to 220°C/425°F.
2 Heat oil in medium saucepan; cook onion, anchovy and garlic, stirring, until onion softens. Add cherry tomatoes, undrained canned tomatoes, olives and parsley; bring to the boil.
3 Pour tomato mixture into medium baking dish. Place sardines, skin-side up, over tomato mixture; season. Roast, uncovered, in oven about 15 minutes or until sardines are cooked.
4 Meanwhile, make preserved lemon salsa.
5 Serve sardine mixture topped with salsa.
preserved lemon salsa Combine ingredients in small bowl.

prep + cook time 40 minutes **serves** 4
nutritional count per serving 31.3g total fat (5.2g saturated fat); 1785kJ (427 cal); 12.5g carbohydrate; 20g protein; 7.2g fibre
tip Whiting or garfish fillets could be used instead of sardines.

Chermoulla-crusted fish

½ cup (35g) stale breadcrumbs
2 tablespoons each finely chopped fresh flat-leaf parsley and
    coriander (cilantro)
2 cloves garlic, crushed
1cm (½-inch) piece fresh ginger (5g), grated finely
½ teaspoon finely grated lemon rind
1 teaspoon each ground cumin and sweet paprika
1 tablespoon olive oil
4 x 200g (6½-ounce) white fish fillets
75g (2½ ounces) mesclun
1 medium lemon (140g), cut into wedges

1 Preheat oven to 220°C/425°F. Oil oven tray; line with baking paper.
2 Combine breadcrumbs, herbs, garlic, ginger, rind, spices and oil in
medium bowl; season.
3 Place fish on tray; press breadcrumb mixture onto fish.
4 Roast fish, uncovered, about 15 minutes, or until cooked through.
5 Serve fish with mesclun and lemon wedges.

prep + cook time 30 minutes **serves** 4
nutritional count per serving 9.4g total fat (2.1g saturated fat);
1200kJ (287 cal); 6.8g carbohydrate; 42.6g protein; 1.8g fibre
tip We used barramundi fillets in this recipe.

Roast trout with orange almond filling

45g (1½ ounces) butter
1 small red onion (100g), chopped finely
1 stalk celery (150g), trimmed, chopped finely
4cm (1½-inch) piece fresh ginger (20g), grated
1 cinnamon stick
½ cup (100g) white medium-grain rice
1 cup (250ml) chicken stock
¼ cup (40g) blanched almonds, roasted, chopped finely
2 teaspoons finely grated orange rind
3 medium red capsicums (bell peppers) (600g)
4 whole rainbow trout (1.2kg)
1 medium orange (240g), peeled, sliced crossways into thin rounds
90g (3 ounces) baby spinach
⅓ cup loosely packed fresh mint leaves

1 Melt butter in medium saucepan; cook onion, celery, ginger and cinnamon, stirring, about 5 minutes or until vegetables soften. Add rice; cook, stirring, 1 minute. Add stock; bring to the boil. Reduce heat; simmer, covered tightly, over low heat about 12 minutes or until water is absorbed. Remove from heat; stand rice, covered, 10 minutes, cool. Discard cinnamon stick; stir in nuts and rind; season to taste.
2 Meanwhile, preheat oven to 200°C/400°F.
3 Quarter capsicums through stems, leaving stem quarters attached to capsicums; discard seeds and membranes. Divide capsicum quarters between two oiled baking dishes.
4 Fill fish cavities with rice mixture; place fish on capsicums. Roast, covered, 20 minutes. Uncover; roast a further 10 minutes or until fish are cooked as desired.
5 Serve fish on capsicum; accompany with combined orange, spinach and mint.

prep + cook time 1 hour **serves** 4
nutritional count per serving 29g total fat (10.5g saturated fat); 2307kJ (552 cal); 31.5g carbohydrate; 39.3g protein; 5.1g fibre

Minted prawn kebabs

24 uncooked medium king prawns (shrimp) (1kg)
⅓ cup (80ml) lemon juice
¼ cup (60ml) olive oil
2 cloves garlic, crushed
¼ cup finely chopped fresh mint
1 medium lemon (140g), cut into wedges

1 Shell and devein prawns, leaving heads and tails intact. Combine prawns, juice, oil, garlic and mint in large bowl; season. Cover; refrigerate 30 minutes.
2 Thread prawns onto eight metal skewers. Cook skewers on heated oiled grill plate (or grill or barbecue) until prawns are changed in colour.
3 Serve skewers with lemon wedges; serve, if you like, with chopped fresh mint and extra virgin olive oil.

prep + cook time 40 minutes (+ refrigeration) **serves** 4
nutritional count per serving 14.6g total fat (2.1g saturated fat); 1028kJ (246 cal); 1.2g carbohydrate; 26.1g protein; 1g fibre

Roasted white fish with chermoulla

4 whole baby snapper (1.2kg)
1 teaspoon ground cumin
½ teaspoon hot paprika
2 teaspoons finely grated lemon rind
1 tablespoon olive oil
chermoulla
¼ cup (60ml) olive oil
⅓ cup each finely chopped fresh flat-leaf parsley and coriander (cilantro)
2 tablespoons lemon juice
1 clove garlic, crushed
1 fresh long red chilli, chopped finely

1 Preheat oven to 200°C/400°F. Oil oven tray.
2 Score fish through thickest part of flesh. Rub fish all over with combined spices, rind and oil; season. Place fish on tray; roast, uncovered, about 25 minutes or until cooked through.
3 Meanwhile, make chermoulla.
4 Serve fish drizzled with chermoulla; accompany with steamed couscous and a green salad, if you like.
chermoulla Combine ingredients in small bowl; season to taste.

prep + cook time 35 minutes **serves** 4
nutritional count per serving 20.8g total fat (3.5g saturated fat); 1346kJ (322 cal); 0.6g carbohydrate; 32.6g protein; 0.6g fibre
tip Baby bream would also work well in this recipe.

Chermoulla prawn skewers

16 uncooked medium king prawns (shrimp) (720g)
1 tablespoon olive oil
2 tablespoons each finely chopped fresh flat-leaf parsley,
   coriander (cilantro) and mint
2 cloves garlic, crushed
2 teaspoons finely grated lemon rind
1 tablespoon lemon juice
1 teaspon each ground allspice and caraway seeds

1 Shell and devein prawns, leaving tails intact. Combine prawns with oil, herbs, garlic, rind, juice, and spices in medium bowl; season.
2 Preheat grill (broiler).
3 Thread prawns, tail-end first, onto 16 bamboo skewers; cook prawns under grill about 5 minutes or until changed in colour.

prep + cook time 30 minutes **makes** 16
nutritional count per skewer 1.3g total fat (0.2g saturated fat); 130kJ (31 cal); 0.1g carbohydrate; 4.7g protein; 0.1g fibre
tip Soak bamboo skewers in cold water for at least an hour before using to prevent them burning during cooking.

Beef kebabs with roasted vegie salad

1kg (2-pound) piece beef eye fillet, chopped coarsely
1½ tablespoons ras el hanout
½ cup (125ml) olive oil
3 large red capsicums (bell peppers) (1kg)
2 medium red onions (340g), cut into wedges
4 cloves garlic, unpeeled
¼ cup (60ml) lemon juice
1 tablespoon finely chopped preserved lemon rind
½ teaspoon ground cumin
500g (1 pound) baby egg (plum) truss tomatoes, halved
¼ cup loosley packed fresh coriander (cilantro) leaves

1 Combine beef, ras el hanout and half the oil in large bowl. Cover; refrigerate 3 hours.
2 Quarter capsicums; discard seeds and membranes. Cook on heated oiled grill plate (or grill or barbecue), skin-side down, until skin blisters and blackens. Cover with plastic wrap or paper for 5 minutes; peel away skin then chop capsicum coarsely.
3 Cook onion and garlic on grill plate (or grill or barbecue) until tender; peel away garlic skin, slice garlic thinly.
4 Combine remaining oil, juice, preserved lemon, cumin, tomatoes, capsicum, onion and garlic in large bowl; season to taste.
5 Thread beef onto six metal skewers. Cook kebabs on heated oiled grill plate (or grill or barbecue) until cooked as desired.
6 Sprinkle kebabs with coriander; serve with roasted vegie salad and, if you like, warm flat bread.

prep + cook time 40 minutes (+ refrigeration) **serves** 6
nutritional count per serving 27.4g total fat (6.2g saturated fat); 1898kJ (454 cal); 11g carbohydrate; 38.5g protein; 4.1g fibre
tip You could substitute beef rump steak for the eye fillet, if you prefer.

Beef fillet with chermoulla

2 teaspoons grated lemon rind
1 tablespoon lemon juice
2 teaspoons sweet paprika
1 teaspoon each ground coriander and cumin
¼ cup coarsely chopped fresh flat-leaf parsley
2 tablespoons coarsely chopped fresh coriander (cilantro)
2 tablespoons olive oil
700g (1½ pound) piece beef eye fillet

1 Preheat oven to 200°C/400°F.
2 Combine rind, juice, spices, herbs and oil in large bowl.
3 Tie beef with kitchen string at 2cm (¾-inch) intervals; rub beef all over with herb mixture, season. Place beef on oiled wire rack over large baking shallow dish.
4 Roast, uncovered, about 30 minutes or until cooked as desired. Stand, covered, 10 minutes; remove string then slice thinly.
5 Serve beef with lemon wedges, if desired.

prep + cook time 45 minutes (+ standing) **serves** 4
nutritional count per serving 16.5g total fat (4.4g saturated fat); 1258kJ (301 cal); 0.2g carbohydrate; 37.8g protein; 0.4g fibre
tip The beef can be marinated for two hours, if you prefer. It is best cooked close to serving.

Beef kefta with green onion couscous

1kg (2 pounds) minced (ground) beef
1 medium brown onion (150g), chopped finely
2 cloves garlic, crushed
2 tablespoons lemon juice
1½ teaspoons each ground coriander and cumin
¼ cup (40g) roasted pine nuts
2 tablespoons finely chopped fresh mint
1 tablespoon finely chopped fresh coriander (cilantro)
1 egg
2 cups (500ml) beef stock
2 cups (400g) couscous
30g (1 ounce) butter
2 green onions (scallions), sliced thinly

1 Using hands, combine mince, onion, garlic, juice, spices, nuts, herbs
and egg in large bowl, season; roll heaped tablespoons of mixture into
balls, thread three balls on each of 12 bamboo skewers. Place kefta
skewers on tray, cover; refrigerate 30 minutes.
2 Bring stock to the boil in medium saucepan. Remove from heat,
add couscous and butter, cover; stand about 5 minutes or until
liquid is absorbed, fluffing with fork occasionally. Stir in green onion;
season to taste.
3 Meanwhile, cook kefta on heated oiled grill plate (or grill or barbecue)
until browned all over and cooked through.
4 Serve kefta with couscous, accompanied by a bowl of combined
yogurt and chopped cucumber, if desired.

prep + cook time 35 minutes (+ refrigeration) **serves** 4
nutritional count per serving 32.7g total fat (12.4g saturated fat);
380kJ (901 cal); 80.7g carbohydrate; 69g protein; 2.5g fibre
tip Soak bamboo skewers in cold water for at least an hour before using
to prevent them burning during cooking.

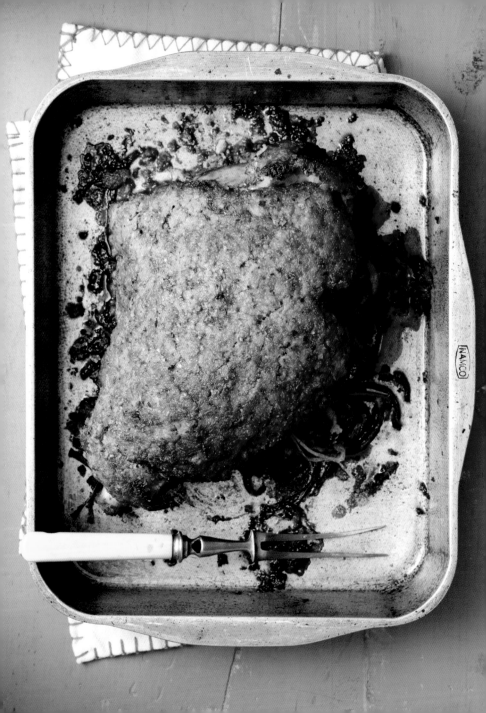

Almond harissa roast lamb

4 cloves garlic, halved
1 tablespoon harissa
2 tablespoons coarsely chopped fresh flat-leaf parsley
2 large brown onions (600g), sliced thinly
½ cup (125ml) olive oil
½ cup (60g) ground almonds
1.8kg (3¾-pound) leg of lamb

1 Preheat oven to 220°C/425°F.
2 Blend or process garlic, harissa, parsley, half the onion and ⅓ cup of the oil until smooth. Transfer mixture to medium bowl, stir in ground almonds.
3 Make deep cuts in lamb to the bone, at 2.5cm (1-inch) intervals. Rub almond mixture all over lamb.
4 Place remaining onion in oiled large baking dish; top with lamb. Drizzle with remaining oil; season. Roast lamb, uncovered, 25 minutes.
5 Reduce oven to 160°C/325°F.
6 Roast lamb a further 1 hour or until cooked as desired. Remove lamb from oven, cover loosely with foil; stand 20 minutes before slicing.

prep + cook time 1 hour 45 minutes (+ standing) **serves** 6
nutritional count per serving 38g total fat (9.5g saturated fat); 2424kJ (580 cal); 6.7g carbohydrate; 52.2g protein; 2.8g fibre

Spiced lamb roast with figs and honey

3 cloves garlic, chopped finely
4cm (1½-inch) piece fresh ginger (20g), grated
2 fresh long red chillies, chopped finely
⅓ cup each finely chopped fresh coriander (cilantro) and flat-leaf parsley
2 teaspoons each ground coriander and cumin
¼ cup (60ml) olive oil
2kg (4-pound) leg of lamb
9 medium fresh figs (540g), halved
2 tablespoons honey

1 Preheat oven to 180°C/350°F.
2 Combine garlic, ginger, chilli, herbs, spices and oil in small bowl.
3 Rub herb mixture all over lamb; season. Place lamb in oiled large baking dish; roast, uncovered, 1¼ hours.
4 Add figs to dish; drizzle honey over figs and lamb. Roast 15 minutes or until lamb is cooked as desired. Cover lamb; stand 10 minutes, before slicing.
5 Serve sliced lamb with figs; accompany with steamed couscous and a herb salad, if you like.

prep + cook time 1 hour 50 minutes **serves** 6
nutritional count per serving 24.3g total fat (8.4g saturated fat); 2115kJ (506 cal); 15.6g carbohydrate; 55.6g protein; 2.9g fibre
tip Make double the herb rub mixture and toss through steamed couscous to make a good accompaniment to the lamb.

Slow-roasted spiced lamb shoulder

2 teaspoons fennel seeds
1 teaspoon each ground cinnamon, ginger and cumin
¼ teaspoon chilli powder
2 tablespoons olive oil
1.2kg (2½-pound) lamb shoulder, shank intact
2 cloves garlic, sliced thinly
6 baby brown onions (150g)
375g (12 ounces) baby carrots, trimmed
1 cup (250ml) water

1 Preheat oven to 180°C/350°F.
2 Dry-fry spices in small frying pan until fragrant. Combine spices and half the oil in small bowl.
3 Using sharp knife, score lamb at 2.5cm (1-inch) intervals; push garlic into cuts. Rub lamb all over with spice mixture, season.
4 Heat remaining oil in large flameproof dish; cook lamb, turning, until browned all over. Remove lamb from dish.
5 Meanwhile, peel onions, leaving root ends intact. Add onions to dish; cook, stirring, until browned.
6 Add carrots and the water to dish, bring to the boil; top with lamb, cover loosely with foil. Transfer to oven; roast 1½ hours.
7 Reduce oven to 160°C/325°F.
8 Uncover lamb; roast a further 1½ hours or until lamb is tender. Cover lamb; stand 10 minutes, then slice thinly. Strain pan juices into small heatproof jug.
9 Serve lamb with onions, carrots and pan juices; accompany with steamed green beans, if you like.

prep + cook time 3 hours 30 minutes **serves** 4
nutritional count per serving 21.9g total fat (7.3g saturated fat); 1722kJ (412 cal); 6.5g carbohydrate; 45.7g protein; 3.1g fibre

Lamb kebabs

500g (1 pound) minced (ground) lamb
1 medium brown onion (150g), chopped finely
1 teaspoon each ground coriander and cumin
½ teaspoon each ground ginger, cinnamon and hot paprika
¼ cup finely chopped fresh mint
½ cup (140g) yogurt

1 Combine lamb, onion, spices and half the mint in medium bowl; season.
2 Shape lamb mixture into 8 sausages; thread onto 8 bamboo skewers.
3 Cook kebabs, in batches, in heated oiled large frying pan until browned and cooked through.
4 Sprinkle kebabs with remaining mint; serve with yogurt and lemon wedges, if you like.

prep + cook time 45 minutes **serves** 8
nutritional count per serving 10.1g total fat (4.7g saturated fat);
928kJ (222 cal); 4.2g carbohydrate; 27.9g protein; 0.7g fibre
tip Soak bamboo skewers in cold water for at least an hour before using to prevent them burning during cooking.

Lamb with minted couscous

1.3 kg (2½-pound) easy carve lamb leg
½ cup firmly packed fresh mint leaves
¼ cup (70g) yogurt
1 tablespoon ground cumin
½ teaspoon ground allspice
2 tablespoons lemon juice
1 cup (250ml) water
minted couscous
2½ cups (500g) couscous
2 cups (500ml) boiling water
60g (2 ounces) butter
½ cup (100g) coarsely chopped seeded prunes
½ cup (70g) slivered almonds, roasted
¼ cup (40g) sliced seeded black olives
2 tablespoons coarsely chopped fresh mint

1 Place lamb in large shallow dish. Blend or process mint, yogurt, spices and juice until smooth. Pour mint mixture over lamb, turn to coat well; season. Cover; refrigerate 30 minutes or overnight.
2 Preheat oven to 180°C/350°F.
3 Place lamb on oiled wire rack over large baking dish; pour the water into dish. Roast, uncovered, about 1½ hours or until lamb is tender. Cover loosley with foil; stand 15 minutes before slicing thinly.
4 Meanwhile, make minted couscous.
5 Serve lamb with couscous.

minted couscous Combine couscous, the water and butter in medium heatproof bowl, cover; stand about 5 minutes or until liquid is absorbed, fluffy with fork occasionally. Stir in remaining ingredients; season to taste.

prep + cook time 2 hours (+ refrigeration) **serves** 6
nutritional count per serving 26.6g total fat (11g saturated fat); 3231kJ (773 cal); 72.3g carbohydrate; 58.5g protein; 3.6g fibre

Honeyed lamb shanks

8 french-trimmed lamb shanks (1.6kg)
2 tablespoons plain (all-purpose) flour
¼ cup (60ml) olive oil
2 medium brown onions (300g), chopped coarsely
3 cloves garlic, crushed
1 teaspoon ground cinnamon
2 teaspoons each ground cumin and coriander
1 cup (250ml) dry red wine
1 litre (4 cups) chicken stock
2 tablespoons honey
2 small kumara (orange sweet potato) (500g), chopped coarsely

1 Preheat oven to 180°C/350°F.
2 Toss lamb in flour; shake away excess. Heat 2 tablespoons of the oil in large flameproof casserole dish on stovetop; cook lamb, in batches, until browned, drain on absorbent paper.
3 Heat remaining oil in same dish; cook onion, garlic and spices, stirring, until onion softens and mixture is fragrant. Add wine; bring to the boil. Reduce heat; simmer, uncovered, about 5 minutes or until liquid reduces by half.
4 Add stock and honey to dish; bring to the boil. Return lamb to dish dish; cook, covered, in oven about 1½ hours, turning shanks occasionally. Uncover dish, add kumara; cook, uncovered, about 50 minutes or until kumara is just tender and lamb is almost falling off the bone. Transfer lamb and kumara to platter; cover to keep warm.
5 Place dish with pan juices over high heat on stovetop; bring to the boil. Boil, uncovered, about 15 minutes or until sauce thickens slightly, season to taste.
6 Serve shanks with couscous, if you like.

prep + cook time 3 hours 15 minutes **serves** 4
nutritional count per serving 19.7g total fat (4.7g saturated fat); 2642kJ (631 cal); 36.8g carbohydrate; 66.5g protein; 3.5g fibre

Harissa-marinated lamb leg

30g (1 ounce) dried red chillies, chopped coarsely
1 teaspoon each ground coriander, cumin and caraway seeds
2 cloves garlic, crushed
1 teaspoon white sugar
⅓ cup (90g) tomato puree
⅓ cup (80ml) olive oil
2kg (4-pound) lamb leg

1 Place chilli in small heatproof bowl, cover with boiling water; stand 1 hour. Drain chilli; reserve ¼ cup of the soaking liquid.
2 Dry-fry coriander, cumin and caraway in small frying pan until fragrant. Blend or process spices with chilli, reserved liquid, garlic, sugar and tomato puree until mixture is almost smooth. With motor operating, add oil in thin, steady stream; process until harissa forms a smooth paste.
3 Reserve ⅓ cup harissa. Using sharp knife, pierce lamb all over; place in large bowl. Rub remaining harissa over lamb, pressing into cuts. Cover; refrigerate 3 hours or overnight.
4 Preheat oven to 200°C/400°F.
5 Pour enough water into large shallow baking dish to come about 5mm (¼-inch) up the sides; place lamb on oiled wire rack over dish, season. Roast, uncovered, about 1 hour or until cooked as desired. Cover lamb; stand 20 minutes before slicing thinly.
6 Serve lamb with a warm kumara and couscous salad, if you like.

prep + cook time 1 hour 45 minutes (+ standing & refrigeration)
serves 4
nutritional count per serving 38.3g total fat (11.5g saturated fat); 2847kJ (681 cal); 2.7g carbohydrate; 82.3g protein; 0.9g fibre

Roasted lamb racks with tomato and mint salad

4 x 4 french-trimmed lamb cutlet racks (720g)
2 teaspoons ground allspice
½ teaspoon cayenne pepper
1 tablespoon olive oil
250g (8 ounces) baby vine-ripened truss tomatoes
cooking-oil spray
1 cup firmly packed fresh mint leaves
1 small red onion (100g), sliced thinly
1 tablespoon lemon juice
⅔ cup (160g) baba ghanoush

1 Preheat oven to 220°C/425°F.
2 Combine lamb, spices and oil in large bowl, season. Place lamb in large shallow baking dish. Roast, uncovered, about 10 minutes.
3 Add tomatoes to dish; spray with oil. Roast about 10 minutes or until tomatoes soften and lamb is cooked as desired. Cover lamb; stand 5 minutes.
4 Place tomatoes in medium bowl with mint, onion and juice; toss gently to combine, season to taste.
5 Serve lamb with salad and baba ghanoush.

prep + cook time 25 minutes **serves** 4
nutritional count per serving 29.1g total fat (9.4g saturated fat); 1605kJ (384 cal); 5.3g carbohydrate; 23g protein; 8g fibre

Vegetable brochettes

12 shallots (300g), peeled
250g (8 ounces) cherry truss tomatoes
2 medium zucchini (240g), cut into six pieces each
12 baby beetroot (beets) (300g), trimmed
36 fresh bay leaves
dressing
2 cloves garlic, crushed
¼ cup (30g) dukkah
1 tablespoon finely grated lemon rind
½ cup (125ml) olive oil

1 Make dressing.
2 Combine shallots, tomatoes, zucchini and half the dressing in large bowl.
3 Place beetroot in medium saucepan, cover with cold water; bring to the boil. Boil 15 minutes; drain, cool. Using disposable gloves, squeeze skins from each beetroot.
4 Thread shallots, tomatoes, zucchini, beetroot and bay leaves onto 12 metal skewers.
5 Cook brochettes on heated oiled grill plate (or grill or barbecue) about 15 minutes or until vegetables are tender. Season to taste.
6 Serve brochettes drizzled with remaining dressing and yogurt, if you like.
dressing Place ingredients in screw-top jar; shake well.

prep + cook time 40 minutes **makes** 12
nutritional count per brochette 10.6g total fat (1.5g saturated fat); 493kJ (118 cal); 3.7g carbohydrate; 1.5g protein; 1.9g fibre
tips Cut vegetables the same size for even cooking.
If you have time, the shallot mixture will develop more flavour if it's covered and refrigerated overnight.

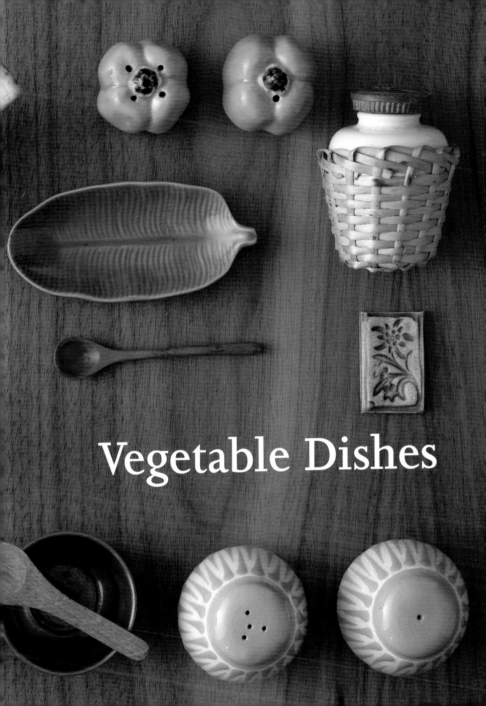

Vegetable Dishes

Minted carrots with goat's cheese

1.2kg (2½ pounds) baby carrots, trimmed
2 tablespoons olive oil
2 tablespoons cumin seeds
1 cup firmly packed fresh mint leaves
220g (7 ounces) soft goat's cheese, crumbled

1 Combine carrots and oil in large bowl; season.
2 Cook carrots on heated oiled grill plate (or grill or barbecue) about 5 minutes or until tender.
3 Meanwhile, dry-fry seeds in small frying pan until fragrant.
4 Combine carrots, seeds, mint and half the cheese in large bowl; sprinkle with remaining cheese.

prep + cook time 35 minutes **serves** 6
nutritional count per serving 12.1g total fat (4.7g saturated fat); 769kJ (184 cal); 10g carbohydrate; 6.5g protein; 5.6g fibre
tips You need 3 bunches of baby carrots, also known as dutch carrots; they're available from supermarkets and greengrocers.
We used an ash-coated goat's cheese in the recipe.

Vegetarian harira

15g (½ ounce) butter
1 large brown onion (200g), chopped finely
2 cloves garlic, crushed
4cm (1½-inch) piece fresh ginger (20g), grated
1 teaspoon ground cinnamon
pinch saffron threads
1 stalk celery (150g), trimmed, chopped finely
1 medium carrot (120g), chopped finely
8 cups (2 litres) water
410g (13 ounces) canned tomato puree
½ cup (100g) brown lentils
½ cup (100g) brown basmati rice
400g (13 ounces) canned chickpeas (garbanzo beans), rinsed, drained
2 medium zucchini (240g), chopped finely
3 medium tomatoes (450g), seeded, chopped finely
2 tablespoons lemon juice

1 Melt butter in large saucepan; cook onion, garlic and ginger, stirring, until onion softens. Add spices, celery, carrot, the water and puree; bring to the boil. Reduce heat; simmer, uncovered, about 10 minutes or until vegetables are tender.
2 Add lentils, rice and chickpeas; simmer, uncovered, about 20 minutes or until rice and lentils are almost tender. Add zucchini and tomato; simmer, uncovered, about 5 minutes or until zucchini is tender. Remove from heat; stir in juice, season to taste. Serve with crusty bread, if you like.

prep + cook time 1 hour **serves** 6
nutritional count per serving 4g total fat (1.6g saturated fat); 957kJ (229 cal); 33.4g carbohydrate; 10.7g protein; 8.6g fibre
tip Brown basmati rice is available from most major supermarkets. If it is not available, use white basmati rice instead.

Turnip soup

1 tablespoon olive oil
1 large brown onion (200g), chopped coarsely
2 cloves garlic, crushed
2 teaspoons each cumin seeds and ground coriander
½ teaspoon hot paprika
1.5kg (3 pounds) turnips, trimmed, chopped coarsely
1.5 litres (6 cups) chicken stock
½ cup (125ml) pouring cream
⅓ cup coarsely chopped fresh flat-leaf parsley

1 Heat oil in large saucepan; cook onion and garlic, stirring, until onion softens. Add spices; cook, stirring, until fragrant.
2 Add turnip and stock to pan; bring to the boil. Reduce heat; simmer, uncovered, until turnips are tender. Cool 15 minutes.
3 Blend or process soup, in batches, until smooth. Return to same pan with cream; stir until hot.
4 Serve bowls of soup sprinkled with parsley.

prep + cook time 50 minutes **serves** 4
nutritional count per serving 19.7g total fat (10.3g saturated fat);
1267kJ (303 cal); 17.5g carbohydrate; 9.9g protein; 10g fibre

Curried lentils with peas and potato

2 tablespoons olive oil
2 medium potatoes (400g), chopped coarsely
1 medium red onion (170g), chopped finely
2 cloves garlic, crushed
1 tablespoon curry powder
2 cups (500ml) chicken consommé
15g (½ ounce) butter
800g (1½ pounds) canned brown lentils, rinsed, drained
2 red banana chillies (250g), seeded, chopped finely
100g (3 ounces) baby spinach leaves, shredded finely
1 cup (120g) frozen peas

1 Heat oil in large frying pan; cook potato, stirring, until browned lightly. Add onion, garlic and curry powder; cook, stirring, until onion softens.
2 Add consommé, butter, lentils, chillies and half the spinach; bring to the boil. Reduce heat; simmer, uncovered, about 15 minutes or until potato is tender.
3 Stir in peas and remaining spinach; simmer, uncovered, until peas are hot. Season to taste.

prep + cook time 40 minutes **serves** 4
nutritional count per serving 13.6g total fat (3.6g saturated fat); 1271kJ (304 cal); 27.3g carbohydrate; 13.4g protein; 9.3g fibre
tip Use canned or packaged consommé for a good flavour, but if you prefer, use chicken stock instead.

Baked cabbage with tomatoes

400g (13 ounces) canned crushed tomatoes
1 small brown onion (80g), grated coarsely
1 clove garlic, crushed
1 teaspoon ground cumin
½ teaspoon white sugar
2 baby green cabbages (800g), quartered
2 tablespoons olive oil
2 tablespoons coarsely chopped fresh flat-leaf parsley

1 Preheat oven to 160°C/325°F.
2 Combine undrained tomatoes, onion, garlic, cumin and sugar in small bowl; season to taste.
3 Place cabbage in medium ovenproof dish; top with tomato mixture. Bake, covered, about 30 minutes or until cabbage is tender.
4 Serve cabbage mixture drizzled with oil; sprinkle with parsley.

prep + cook time 40 minutes **serves** 6
nutritional count per serving 6.4g total fat (0.9g saturated fat); 443kJ (106 cal); 6.7g carbohydrate; 2.8g protein; 5.9g fibre
tip If you can't find baby cabbage, use 1 small green cabbage and cut into eight wedges.

Saffron rice with zucchini flowers

12 zucchini flowers, stem attached (240g)
45g (1½ ounces) butter
1 large red onion (300g), cut into wedges
2 teaspoons caraway seeds
1 clove garlic, crushed
4 cups (850g) cooked white long-grain rice
1 teaspoon ground turmeric
pinch saffron threads
¼ cup (20g) flaked almonds, roasted

1 Remove flowers from zucchini; discard stamens from flowers.
Slice zucchini thinly.
2 Melt butter in large frying pan; cook onion, seeds and garlic,
stirring, until onion softens. Add sliced zucchini; cook, stirring,
until tender. Add rice, spices and zucchini flowers; cook, stirring,
until hot. Stir in half the nuts; season to taste.
3 Serve rice sprinkled with remaining nuts.

prep + cook time 30 minutes **serves** 4
nutritional count per serving 12.9g total fat (6.2g saturated fat);
1747kJ (418 cal); 65.3g carbohydrate; 8g protein; 3.6g fibre
tips The stem of zucchini is the baby zucchini attached to the flower.
You need to cook about 1½ cups (300g) white long-grain rice for this
recipe. Spread cooked rice on a flat tray and refrigerate, uncovered,
overnight before using.

Chickpea tomato stew

2 tablespoons olive oil
2 medium brown onions (300g), sliced thinly
1 tablespoon light brown sugar
2 teaspoons cumin seeds
1 teaspoon ground coriander
800g (1½ pounds) canned whole tomatoes
1 cup (250ml) vegetable stock
800g (1½ pounds) canned chickpeas (garbanzo beans), rinsed, drained
1 cup (150g) raisins
⅓ cup (70g) coarsely chopped preserved lemon rind
60g (2 ounces) baby spinach leaves

1 Heat oil in tagine or large saucepan; cook onion and sugar over low heat, stirring occasionally, about 15 minutes or until onions are lightly caramelised. Add spices; cook, stirring, about 1 minute or until mixture is fragrant.
2 Add undrained tomatoes, stock, chickpeas, raisins and lemon; bring to the boil. Reduce heat; simmer, covered, about 30 minutes or until thickened slightly. Stir in spinach; season to taste.

prep + cook time 1 hour **serves** 6
nutritional count per serving 8.7g total fat (1.3g saturated fat); 1195kJ (286 cal); 39.7g carbohydrate; 8.7g protein; 8.5g fibre

Spicy fried potatoes

1kg (2 pounds) baby new potatoes
2 tablespoons olive oil
1 tablespoon harissa
2 cloves garlic, crushed
2 teaspoons cumin seeds
2 teaspoons finely grated lemon rind
2 tablespoons finely chopped fresh flat-leaf parsley

1 Boil, steam or microwave potatoes until tender; drain, then cut in half.
2 Heat oil in large frying pan; cook potatoes, harissa, garlic and seeds, stirring occasionally, about 10 minutes or until potatoes are browned. Stir in rind and parsley; season to taste.

prep + cook time 35 minutes **serves** 6
nutritional count per serving 6.4g total fat (0.9g saturated fat); 732kJ (175 cal); 22.8g carbohydrate; 4.1g protein; 3.8g fibre

Minted beetroot

6 medium fresh beetroot (beets) (1kg)
1 cup (280g) yogurt
1 clove garlic, crushed
1 tablespoon tahini
1½ tablespoons lemon juice
½ cup loosely packed fresh mint leaves

1 Wash beetroot, trim leaves, leaving about 2.5cm (1-inch) of stem attached to beetroot. Cook unpeeled beetroot in large saucepan of boiling water about 45 minutes or until tender; drain.
2 Peel warm beetroot; cut into wedges.
3 Blend or process remaining ingredients until mint is finely chopped.
4 Serve beetroot topped with yogurt mixture.

prep + cook time 1 hour **serves** 6
nutritional count per serving 3.6g total fat (1.1g saturated fat); 518kJ (124 cal); 14.6g carbohydrate; 5.5g protein; 5.4g fibre
tip Wear disposable gloves when peeling the beetroot.

Grilled zucchini with pumpkin couscous

½ cup (100g) couscous
½ cup (125ml) boiling water
2 tablespoons lemon juice
2 teaspoons olive oil
¼ cup (40g) pine nuts
1 clove garlic, crushed
½ small red onion (50g), chopped finely
1 teaspoon sweet smoked paprika
½ teaspoon each ground cumin and cayenne pepper
½ small red capsicum (bell pepper) (75g), chopped finely
200g (6½-ounce) piece pumpkin, chopped finely
2 tablespoons finely chopped fresh flat-leaf parsley
6 medium zucchini (720g), halved lengthways
preserved lemon yogurt
½ cup (140g) greek-style yogurt
2 tablespoons finely chopped preserved lemon rind
2 tablespoons water

1 Make preserved lemon yogurt.
2 Combine couscous with the water and juice in large heatproof bowl, cover; stand about 5 minutes or until liquid is absorbed, fluffing with fork occasionally.
3 Heat oil in large saucepan; cook nuts, stirring, until browned lightly. Add garlic, onion and spices; cook, stirring, until onion softens. Add capsicum and pumpkin; cook, stirring, until pumpkin is just tender. Stir in couscous and parsley, season to taste.
4 Meanwhile, cook zucchini on heated oiled grill plate (or grill or barbecue) until tender.
5 Serve zucchini topped with couscous and drizzled with yogurt.
preserved lemon yogurt Combine ingredients in small bowl.

prep + cook time 40 minutes **serves** 4
nutritional count per serving 12.7g total fat (2.5g saturated fat); 1200kJ (287 cal); 30.1g carbohydrate; 10.1g protein; 4.9g fibre

Honey-spiced carrots and kumara

4 medium carrots (480g)
2 small kumara (orange sweet potato) (500g), sliced thickly
45g (1½ ounces) butter, melted
1 tablespoon olive oil
1½ teaspoons ground cumin
1 teaspoon cumin seeds
¼ cup (90g) honey
2 tablespoons coarsely chopped fresh flat-leaf parsley

1 Preheat oven to 220°C/425°F.
2 Cut carrots into 4cm (1½-inch) pieces. Cook carrot and kumara in large saucepan of boiling water 5 minutes; drain.
3 Combine butter, oil, cumin, seeds and honey in small bowl. Place vegetables on oiled wire rack over large baking dish. Brush vegetables with honey-spice mixture. Roast, uncovered, about 20 minutes, brushing with remaining honey-spice mixture, until vegetable are tender.
4 Serve vegetables sprinkled with parsley.

prep + cook time 45 minutes **serves** 4
nutritional count per serving 14g total fat (6.7g saturated fat); 1275kJ (305 cal); 39g carbohydrate; 3g protein; 5.4g fibre

Moroccan-style vegetables

2 tablespoons olive oil
2 large brown onions (400g), sliced thickly
2 cloves garlic, crushed
2 teaspoons ground coriander
1 teaspoon each ground cumin and sweet paprika
2 cinnamon sticks
pinch ground saffron
2 fresh small red thai (serrano) chillies, chopped finely
2 baby eggplant (120g), chopped coarsely
800g (1½ pounds) pumpkin, chopped coarsely
400g (13 ounces) canned chopped tomatoes
1 cup (250ml) vegetable stock
2 cups (500ml) water
300g (10 ounces) canned chickpeas (garbanzo beans),
    rinsed, drained
2 large zucchini (300g), chopped coarsely
½ cup loosley packed fresh coriander (cilantro) leaves
1 tablespoon lemon juice

1 Heat oil in large, deep frying pan; cook onion and garlic, stirring, until onion softens. Add spices, chilli and eggplant; cook, stirring, until fragrant.
2 Add pumpkin, undrained tomatoes, stock, water and chickpeas; bring to the boil. Reduce heat; simmer, covered, 10 minutes. Add zucchini; simmer, covered, about 5 minutes or until vegetables are tender.
3 Stir coriander and juice into vegetable mixture, season to taste; serve with steamed couscous.

prep + cook time 35 minutes **serves** 4
nutritional count per serving 11.6g total fat (2g saturated fat); 1091kJ (261 cal); 28.6g carbohydrate; 10.7g protein; 8.9g fibre

Zucchini with chermoulla dressing

2 tablespoons olive oil
30g (1 ounce) butter
8 medium green zucchini (960g), halved lengthways
chermoulla dressing
1 small red onion (100g), chopped finely
2 cloves garlic, crushed
½ teaspoon hot paprika
1 teaspoon each sweet paprika and ground cumin
½ cup (125ml) olive oil
2 tablespoons lemon juice
1 cup finely chopped fresh flat-leaf parsley

1 Heat oil and butter in large frying pan; cook zucchini until browned lightly and tender.
2 Meanwhile, make chermoulla dressing.
3 Serve zucchini drizzled with dressing.
chermoula dressing Place ingredients in screw-top jar; shake well.

prep + cook time 35 minutes **serves** 8
nutritional count per serving 22.3g total fat (4.7g saturated fat); 924kJ (221 cal); 2.8g carbohydrate; 1.9g protein; 2.6g fibre

Beans with tomato walnut sauce

1kg (2 pounds) green beans, trimmed
425g (13½ ounces) canned crushed tomatoes
1 tablespoon olive oil
2 cloves garlic, crushed
2 teaspoons each ground coriander and cumin
¼ teaspoon cayenne pepper
¾ cup (90g) coarsely chopped roasted walnuts
½ cup coarsely chopped fresh coriander (cilantro)
1 teaspoon white sugar
1 small red capsicum (bell pepper) (150g), sliced thinly
1 small yellow capsicum (bell pepper) (150g), sliced thinly

1 Boil, steam or microwave beans until tender; drain.
2 Blend or process undrained tomatoes until smooth.
3 Heat oil in large frying pan; cook garlic, spices and nuts, stirring, until fragrant. Add tomatoes, fresh coriander and sugar; cook, stirring, until heated through. Remove from heat, stir in capsicum and beans, season to taste.

prep + cook time 25 minutes **serves** 6
nutritional count per serving 14g total fat (1.1g saturated fat); 857kJ (205 cal); 9.3g carbohydrate; 7.3g protein; 7.3g fibre

Eggplant and capsicum with preserved lemon

3 medium eggplant (900g)
1 medium red capsicum (bell pepper) (200g)
vegetable oil, for shallow-frying
2 cloves garlic, unpeeled
1 tablespoon finely chopped preserved lemon rind
1 teaspoon each ground cumin and sweet paprika
1 tablespoon finely chopped fresh flat-leaf parsley

1 Using vegetable peeler, remove about half the skin from the eggplant in strips. Cut the eggplant into 1cm (½-inch) slices.
2 Preheat grill (broiler).
3 Quarter capsicum; discard seeds and membranes. Cook under grill, skin-side up, until skin blisters and blackens. Cover capsicum in plastic or paper for 5 minutes; peel away skin, chop finely.
4 Heat oil with garlic in large frying pan; shallow-fry eggplant, in batches, until browned lightly; drain on absorbent paper. Discard garlic.
5 Chop eggplant coarsely; combine eggplant with capsicum, preserved lemon, cumin and paprika, season to taste. Serve sprinkled with parsley.

prep + cook time 50 minutes **serves** 8
nutritional count per serving 10.3g total fat (1.2g saturated fat); 493kJ (118 cal); 3.8g carbohydrate; 1.6g protein; 2.9g fibre

Harissa and mint vegetable stew

45g (1½ ounces) butter
10 shallots (250g), halved
6 cloves garlic, crushed
2 tablespoons plain (all-purpose) flour
2 cups (500ml) vegetable stock
2 cups (500ml) water
1kg (2 pounds) baby new potatoes, halved
410g (13 ounces) canned crushed tomatoes
2 tablespoons harissa
1 cinnamon stick
½ cup firmly packed fresh mint leaves
500g (1 pound) yellow patty pan squash, halved
115g (3½ ounces) baby corn
½ cup (60g) frozen peas
250g (8 ounces) cherry tomatoes, halved

1 Heat butter in large saucepan; cook shallots and garlic, stirring, until shallots soften. Add flour; cook, stirring, 1 minute.
2 Add stock, the water, potato, undrained tomatoes, harissa, cinnamon and about two-thirds of the mint leaves; bring to the boil. Reduce heat; simmer, uncovered, 30 minutes.
3 Add squash; simmer, uncovered, 20 minutes. Add corn, peas and cherry tomato; simmer, uncovered, 10 minutes.
4 Serve stew sprinkled with remaining mint.

prep + cook time 1 hour 30 minutes **serves** 4
nutritional count per serving 10.3g total fat (5.7g saturated fat); 1705kJ (408 cal); 55.7g carbohydrate; 15.7g protein; 14.3g fibre

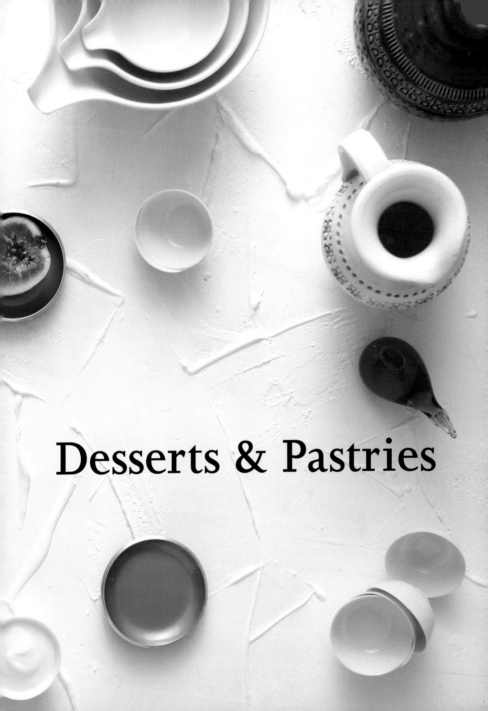

Desserts & Pastries

Honey-coated pistachio and rosewater palmiers

¾ cup (110g) roasted unsalted shelled pistachios
¼ cup (55g) caster (superfine) sugar
2 teaspoons rosewater
½ teaspoon ground cinnamon
20g (¾ ounce) butter
2 tablespoons demerara sugar
2 sheets puff pastry
1 egg, beaten lightly
½ cup (175g) honey
1 teaspoon rosewater, extra

1 Blend or process nuts with sugar, rosewater, cinnamon and butter until mixture forms a coarse paste.
2 Sprinkle board with half of the demerara sugar; place one sheet of pastry on the sugar. Using rolling pin, press pastry gently into demerara sugar. Spread half the nut mixture on pastry; fold two opposing sides of the pastry inwards to meet in the middle. Flatten folded pastry slightly; brush with a little of the egg. Fold each side in half to meet in the middle; flatten slightly. Fold the two sides in half again so they just touch in the middle, flattening slightly. Repeat process with remaining demerara sugar, pastry sheet, nut mixture and egg. Cover pastry pieces, separately, with plastic wrap; refrigerate 30 minutes.
3 Meanwhile, preheat oven to 200°C/400°F. Grease oven trays.
4 Cut rolled pastry pieces into 1cm (½-inch) slices; place slices, cut-side up, on trays about 2cm (¾ inch) apart.
5 Bake palmiers about 12 minutes or until browned lightly.
6 Meanwhile, bring honey and extra rosewater to the boil in small frying pan. Reduce heat; simmer, uncovered, 3 minutes. Remove from heat.
7 Add hot palmiers, one at a time, to honey mixture, turning to coat all over; drain on greased wire rack. Serve cold.

prep + cook time 45 minutes (+ refrigeration) **makes** 32
nutritional count per palmier 4.6g total fat; (0.7g saturated fat); 393kJ (94 cal); 11.5g carbohydrate; 1.4g protein; 0.4g fibre

Spiced crème caramel

¾ cup (165g) caster (superfine) sugar
½ cup (125ml) water
1¼ cups (310ml) pouring cream
1¾ cups (430ml) milk
4 cardamom pods, bruised
¼ teaspoon saffron threads
2 teaspoons rosewater
6 eggs
⅓ cup (75g) caster (superfine) sugar, extra

1 Stir sugar and the water in medium frying pan over medium heat until sugar dissolves; bring to the boil. Boil, uncovered, without stirring, until mixture is a dark caramel colour. Remove from heat; allow bubbles to subside. Pour toffee into deep 20cm (8-inch) round cake pan.
2 Bring cream, milk, spices and rosewater to the boil in medium saucepan. Remove from heat; stand 30 minutes, then return to the boil.
3 Whisk eggs and extra sugar in medium bowl; whisking constantly, pour hot milk mixture into egg mixture. Strain mixture into cake pan; discard solids.
4 Meanwhile, preheat oven to 160°C/325°F.
5 Place pan in medium baking dish; add enough boiling water to come half way up side of pan. Bake about 40 minutes or until set. Remove pan from baking dish. Cover crème caramel; refrigerate overnight.
6 Gently ease crème caramel from side of pan; invert onto deep-sided serving plate.

prep + cook time 1 hour (+ standing & refrigeration) **serves** 6
nutritional count per serving 30.4g total fat (18g saturated fat); 2027kJ (485 cal); 45.1g carbohydrate; 10.9g protein; 0g fibre
tip You can use a 300ml carton of cream for this recipe.

Almond rice pudding

1.5 litres (6 cups) milk
2 cups (320g) blanched almonds
¼ cup (55g) caster (superfine) sugar
5cm (2 inch) strip orange rind
⅔ cup (130g) arborio rice
½ teaspoon orange blossom water
1 large pomegranate (430g)
¼ cup (35g) roasted slivered almonds
pinch ground cinnamon

1 Blend milk and blanched nuts, in batches, until smooth. Strain milk mixture through fine sieve into large saucepan.
2 Stir sugar and rind into milk mixture over high heat; bring to the boil, stirring occasionally. Gradually stir in rice. Reduce heat; simmer, uncovered, over low heat, stirring occasionally, about 35 minutes or until rice is tender. Discard rind; stir in orange blossom water. Stand 10 minutes.
3 Remove seeds from pomegranate; serve warm rice sprinkled with seeds, slivered nuts and cinnamon.

prep + cook time 1 hour (+ standing) **serves** 6
nutritional count per serving 42.8g total fat (8.4g saturated fat); 2730kJ (653 cal); 43.5g carbohydrate; 22.4g protein; 6.8g fibre

Saffron panna cotta with honeyed figs

1 cup (250ml) pouring cream
½ cup (110g) caster (superfine) sugar
pinch saffron threads
8 cardamom pods, bruised
2 cinnamon sticks
4 teaspoons gelatine
2 tablespoons water
2 cups (500ml) buttermilk
honeyed figs
¼ cup (90g) honey
¼ cup (60ml) dry red wine
⅓ cup (65g) finely chopped dried figs

1 Stir cream, sugar and spices in medium saucepan over low heat until sugar dissolves. Bring to the boil. Strain mixture into large heatproof jug; cool 5 minutes.
2 Meanwhile, sprinkle gelatine over the water in small heatproof jug. Stand jug in small saucepan of simmering water; stir until gelatine dissolves, cool 5 minutes.
3 Stir gelatine mixture and buttermilk into cream mixture. Divide mixture into six ¾-cup (180ml) moulds. Cover; refrigerate 4 hours or until set.
4 Make honeyed figs.
5 Turn panna cottas onto serving plates; top with honeyed figs.
honeyed figs Bring ingredients to the boil in medium saucepan. Reduce heat; simmer, uncovered, about 5 minutes or until syrup thickens slightly. Cool.

prep + cook time 30 minutes (+ refrigeration) **serves** 6
nutritional count per serving 19.8g total fat (13g saturated fat); 1576kJ (377 cal); 42.4g carbohydrate; 6.7g protein; 1.5g fibre

M'hanncha

90g (3 ounces) butter, melted
1⅔ cups (200g) ground almonds
½ teaspoon almond extract
½ cup (80g) icing (confectioners') sugar
2 teaspoons rosewater
45g (1½ ounces) dark (semi-sweet) eating chocolate, grated coarsely
6 sheets fillo pastry
75g (2½ ounces) butter, melted, extra
1 egg, beaten lightly
½ teaspoon ground cinnamon

1 Preheat oven to 160°C/325°F. Grease 20cm (8-inch) springform tin.
2 Combine butter, ground almonds, extract, sifted icing sugar, rosewater and chocolate in medium bowl. Roll rounded teaspoons of mixture into balls. Roll balls into 2.5cm (1-inch) log shapes.
3 Brush 1 sheet of pastry with some of the extra butter; top with a second pastry sheet, brush with butter. Place one-third of the chocolate logs along one long end, 5cm (2 inches) from edge and leaving 2.5cm (1-inch) border on short ends. Roll pastry tightly to enclose logs. Repeat with remaining pastry, butter and logs. Brush pastry logs with butter.
4 Pinch one end of one pastry log to seal – this will become the centre of the spiral. Wind the pastry log into a tight spiral, brushing with egg to join. Continue adding pastry logs, end-to-end, in spiral pattern, brushing with egg to join and seal ends. Transfer spiral to tin. Brush with egg, sprinkle with cinnamon.
5 Bake m'hanncha about 25 minutes or until golden. Serve dusted with a little sifted icing sugar.

prep + cook time 55 minutes **serves** 8
nutritional count per serving 33.3g total fat (13.3g saturated fat); 1710kJ (409 cal); 20.5g carbohydrate; 7.4g protein; 2.5g fibre
tip M'hanncha, a Moroccan almond pastry, means 'the snake' and this coiled sweet pastry treat certainly represents that. However, instead of running away, our delicious chocolate almond recipe will have everyone running back for more.

Sweet orange blossom couscous

2½ cups (500g) couscous
1½ cups (375ml) boiling water
1 cup (250ml) milk
75g (2½ ounces) butter
2 tablespoons vegetable oil
1 cup (160g) blanched almonds
1 cup (160g) icing (confectioners') sugar
2 tablespoons orange blossom water
1 tablespoon ground cinnamon

1 Combine couscous, the water, milk and butter in large heatproof bowl, cover; stand about 5 minutes or until liquid is absorbed, fluffing with fork occasionally.
2 Meanwhile, heat oil in small frying pan; cook almonds, stirring, until browned lightly. Remove from pan; chop coarsely.
3 Stir half the icing sugar and the orange blossom water into couscous. Serve couscous dusted with remaining sifted icing sugar and sprinkled with cinnamon and nuts.

prep + cook time 35 minutes **serves** 8
nutritional count per serving 24.9g total fat (7.2g saturated fat); 2353kJ (563 cal); 70.3g carbohydrate; 13.1g protein; 2.3g fibre

Watermelon and fig salad

1.2kg (2½ pound) piece seedless watermelon
6 medium fresh figs (360g), sliced into rounds
¾ cup (200g) greek-style yogurt
1 teaspoon rosewater
¼ cup loosely packed fresh small mint leaves
⅓ cup (35g) roasted walnuts, chopped finely

1 Cut away skin and white pith from melon; cut melon into thin wedges. Arrange melon and figs on serving platter.
2 Combine yogurt and rosewater in small bowl; drizzle over fruit. Sprinkle with mint and nuts.

prep time 15 minutes **serves** 4
nutritional count per serving 10.2g total fat (2.7g saturated fat); 882kJ (211 cal); 21.8g carbohydrate; 5.9g protein; 4.2g fibre

Honey almond pastries

1½ cups (240g) blanched almonds, roasted
½ cup (110g) caster (superfine) sugar
1 tablespoon orange blossom water
1 teaspoon ground cinnamon
30g (1 ounce) soft butter
6 sheets fillo pastry
60g (2 ounces) butter, melted, extra
olive oil, for shallow-frying
1 cup (350g) honey
1 tablespoon sesame seeds, toasted

1 Blend or process almonds, sugar, 3 teaspoons of orange blossom water, cinnamon and butter until mixture forms a paste.
2 Lay pastry on board so the long sides are at the top and bottom; brush with a little butter. Cut into four rectangles. Form level tablespoons of almond mixture into a log shape at the short end of each rectangle. Roll pastry into tight cigar shape, folding in the sides as you roll to enclose filling. Brush with butter. Repeat with remaining pastry, butter and almond mixture to make 24 cigars.
3 Heat oil in large frying pan; shallow-fry pastries, in batches, until browned. Drain on absorbent paper.
4 Meanwhile, bring the honey and remaining orange blossom water to the boil in medium saucepan. Reduce heat; simmer, uncovered, 3 minutes.
5 Add hot pastries, in batches, to the honey mixture, turning to coat. Drain on greased wire rack. Sprinkle with seeds; cool.

prep + cook time 55 minutes **makes** 24
nutritional count per pastry 11.2g total fat (2.7g saturated fat); 790kJ (189 cal); 18.9g carbohydrate; 2.6g protein; 1g fibre
tip These pastries can be made a day ahead; store in an airtight container.

Figs in orange syrup with yogurt cream

2 medium oranges (480g)
1 cup (220g) caster (superfine) sugar
1 cup (250ml) water
½ cup (180g) honey
2 cinnamon sticks
1 vanilla bean
1 tablespoon orange blossom water
8 large fresh figs (640g), halved
yogurt cream
¾ cup (200g) greek-style yogurt
½ cup (125g) double thick (heavy) cream

1 Using vegetable peeler, remove 8 wide strips of rind from each orange. Remove any white pith from rind.

2 Place rind strips, sugar, the water, honey and cinnamon in small saucepan. Split vanilla bean; scrape seeds into pan with bean. Stir over low heat until sugar dissolves; bring to the boil. Reduce heat; simmer, uncovered, about 10 minutes or until syrup thickens slightly. Remove from heat; stir in orange blossom water.

3 Place figs, cut-side up, in large heatproof dish. Pour hot syrup over figs; cool.

4 Meanwhile, make yogurt cream.

5 Serve figs with yogurt cream.

yogurt cream Combine ingredients in small bowl. Cover; refrigerate until required.

prep + cook time 20 minutes (+ cooling) **serves** 8
nutritional count per serving 9.2g total fat (5.8g saturated fat); 1338kJ (320 cal); 55.1g carbohydrate; 2.7g protein; 2.3g fibre

Pastilla with sweet yogurt cream

90g (3 ounces) unsalted butter
1 tablespoon each honey and maple syrup
5 sheets fillo pastry
½ cup (65g) finely chopped roasted unsalted shelled pistachios
sweet yogurt cream
250g (8 ounces) mascarpone cheese
1 tablespoon caster (superfine) sugar
½ cup (125g) sheep's-milk yogurt
1 tablespoon finely grated lemon rind
50g (1½ ounces) chocolate-coated honeycomb bar, chopped finely

1 Preheat oven to 200°C/400°F. Grease oven trays; line with baking paper.
2 Stir butter, honey and maple syrup in small saucepan over low heat until smooth.
3 To make pastilla, brush 1 sheet of pastry with butter mixture, sprinkle with some of the nuts; top with another pastry sheet. Repeat layering with remaining pastry, butter mixture and nuts. Cut layered sheets into 24 squares; place on oven trays.
4 Bake pastilla about 10 minutes or until crisp; transfer to wire rack to cool.
5 Meanwhile, make sweet yogurt cream.
6 Serve pastilla with yogurt cream.
sweet yogurt cream Beat cheese and sugar in small bowl with electric mixer until smooth; fold in yogurt, rind and honeycomb bar.

prep + cook time 35 minutes **serves** 6
nutritional count per serving 43.9g total fat (26.1g saturated fat); 2144 kJ (513 cal); 25.6g carbohydrate; 5.2g protein; 1.4g fibre
tip Sweet pastilla is traditionally served with sweetened warmed milk to reduce the crunchiness of the layered pastille. We like to use the pastilla to dip into the sweet yogurt cream.

Ghoriba biscuits

90g (3 ounces) butter, melted
3 eggs
1¼ cups (200g) pure icing (confectioners') sugar
1¼ cups (200g) fine semolina flour
1½ cups (225g) self-raising flour
1 teaspoon vanilla extract
1 teaspoon orange blossom water
2 tablespoons pure icing (confectioners') sugar, extra

1 Preheat oven to 160°C/325°F. Grease oven trays; line with baking paper.
2 Combine butter, eggs and sifted icing sugar in large bowl. Stir in semolina, sifted flour, extract and orange blossom water.
3 Roll level tablespoons of mixture into balls, place about 7.5cm (3 inches) apart on trays; flatten slightly. Sift extra icing sugar over biscuits.
4 Bake biscuits about 15 minutes or until golden and sugar has 'cracked'. Transfer to wire rack to cool.

prep + cook time 35 minutes **makes** 30
nutritional count per biscuit 3.2g total fat (1.8g saturated fat); 443kJ (106 cal); 17.1g carbohydrate; 2.2g protein; 0.5g fibre

Orange shortbread cookies

½ cup (70g) roasted unsalted shelled pistachios
250g (8 ounces) butter, chopped
1 cup (160g) icing (confectioner's) sugar
1½ cups (225g) plain (all-purpose) flour
2 tablespoons cornflour (cornstarch)
¾ cup (90g) ground almonds
2 tablespoons orange blossom water
⅓ cup (55g) icing (confectioners') sugar, extra

1 Preheat oven to 150°C/300°F. Grease oven trays.
2 Finely chop ⅓ cup of the pistachios, leave remaining pistachios whole.
3 Beat butter and sifted icing sugar in small bowl with electric mixer until combined. Transfer mixture to large bowl; stir in sifted flours, ground almonds and chopped pistachios.
4 Shape level tablespoons of mixture into mounds about 2.5cm (1 inch) apart on trays, press a whole pistachio on each.
5 Bake cookies about 25 minutes or until firm. Transfer cookies to wire racks, brush with orange blossom water; stand 5 minutes. Dust cookies with extra sifted icing sugar; cool.

prep + cook time 50 minutes **makes** 40
nutritional count per cookie 7.4g total fat (3.6g saturated fat); 477kJ (114 cal); 10.3g carbohydrate; 1.5g protein; 0.6g fibre

Hazelnut and date tart

1 sheet shortcrust pastry
125g (4 ounces) butter, softened
⅓ cup (75g) caster (superfine) sugar
2 tablespoons finely grated lemon rind
2 eggs
1 cup (100g) ground hazelnuts
1 tablespoon plain (all-purpose) flour
1 teaspoon ground cinnamon
½ cup (60g) seeded dried dates, halved lengthways
½ cup (180g) honey, warmed
sesame cream
1¼ cups (310ml) thickened (heavy) cream
2 tablespoons caster (superfine) sugar
2 teaspoons black sesame seeds
1 teaspoon vanilla extract
1 teaspoon sesame oil

1 Preheat oven to 200°C/400°F.
2 Line greased 24cm (9½-inch) round loose-based flan tin with pastry; press into base and sides, trim edge. Refrigerate 30 minutes.
3 Meanwhile, beat butter, sugar and rind in small bowl with electric mixer until combined. Beat in eggs, one at a time. Stir in ground hazelnuts, flour and cinnamon. Spread hazelnut filling into pastry case; top with dates.
4 Bake tart about 35 minutes or until firm. Brush hot tart with half the honey. Cool in tin.
5 Meanwhile, make sesame cream.
6 Serve tart drizzled with remaining honey; top with sesame cream.
sesame cream Beat cream and sugar in small bowl with electric mixer until soft peaks form; fold in remaining ingredients.

prep + cook time 55 minutes (+ refrigeration & cooling) **serves** 8
nutritional count per serving 42.6g total fat (21.5g saturated fat); 2508kJ (600 cal); 49.4g carbohydrate; 6.5g protein; 2.6g fibre
tips You can use 300ml container of thickened cream for this recipe. You can use ground almonds instead of ground hazelnuts if you prefer. Black sesame seeds are available from specialty spice shops.

Spiced oranges with brown sugar toffee

1 cup (220g) firmly packed light brown sugar
1 cup (250ml) water
3 medium oranges (720g), peeled, sliced thickly
3 medium blood oranges (500g), peeled, sliced thickly
¼ teaspoon ground cinnamon
pinch ground cardamom
1 teaspoon orange blossom water

1 Stir sugar and the water in medium saucepan over medium heat until sugar dissolves; bring to the boil. Boil, uncovered, without stirring, about 10 minutes or until mixture is a dark caramel colour. Remove from heat; allow bubbles to subside.
2 Meanwhile, arrange orange slices, overlapping slightly, on large heatproof platter; sprinkle with spices and orange blossom water.
3 Pour half the toffee over oranges; pour remaining toffee onto greased oven tray. Stand oranges at room temperature about 2 hours or until toffee dissolves and forms a sauce over oranges. Allow toffee on tray to set at room temperature.
4 Break set toffee into pieces; sprinkle over oranges.

prep + cook time 25 minutes (+ standing) **serves** 6
nutritional count per serving 0.1g total fat (0g saturated fat); 815kJ (195 cal); 46.9g carbohydrate; 1.5g protein; 2.9g fibre
tip When you think the syrup has almost reached the colour we suggest, quickly remove the pan from the heat, remembering that the syrup will continue to cook and darken during this time. Let the bubbles subside, then drop a teaspoon of the syrup into a cup of cold water. The toffee should set the instant it hits the cold water; lift it out and break it with your fingers. If the toffee needs to be harder, then return the mixture to the heat and cook a little more. This test is easy, but a candy thermometer removes all the guess work for you. If you have a candy thermometer, boil the mixture until it reaches 138°C/280°F.

Fresh peaches and dates with orange blossom water

½ cup (110g) caster (superfine) sugar
pinch saffron threads
4 cardamom pods
½ cup (125ml) water
⅓ cup (80ml) lemon juice
1 teaspoon orange blossom water
6 large peaches (1.3kg), sliced thickly
12 fresh dates (240g), seeded, quartered
1 cup (280g) greek-style yogurt

1 Stir sugar, saffron, cardamom and the water in small saucepan over low heat, until sugar dissolves. Bring to the boil. Reduce heat; simmer, uncovered, about 5 minutes or until syrup thickens slightly. Cool 10 minutes. Stir in juice and orange blossom water.
2 Place peaches and dates in large bowl; strain syrup over fruit. Cover; refrigerate 2 hours.
3 Serve fruit with yogurt.

prep + cook time 15 minutes (+ refrigeration) **serves** 8
nutritional count per serving 1.4g total fat (0.8g saturated fat); 706kJ (169 cal); 33.8g carbohydrate; 3.3g protein; 3.3g fibre

Charosets

10 fresh dates (200g), seeded, chopped coarsely
½ cup (70g) raisins
½ cup (55g) coarsely chopped roasted walnuts
1½ tablespoons sweet red wine
200g (6½ ounces) dark eating (semi-sweet) chocolate
   (70% cocoa solids), melted
⅓ cup (40g) finely chopped roasted walnuts

1 Blend or process dates, raisins, coarsely chopped nuts and wine until mixture forms a smooth paste.
2 Using wet hands, roll level teaspoons of mixture into balls; place on baking-paper-lined tray. Cover; refrigerate overnight.
3 Dip half the balls in melted chocolate, place on foil-lined tray; leave to set at room temperature. Roll remaining balls in finely chopped nuts.

prep time 30 minutes (+ refrigeration) **makes** 50
nutritional count per charoset 2.5g total fat (0.8g saturated fat); 176kJ (42 cal); 4.4g carbohydrate; 0.5g protein; 0.4g fibre
tip You can use orange juice in place of the sweet red wine if you like.

Gazelles' horns

180g (6 ounces) butter, softened
⅔ cup (110g) icing (confectioners') sugar
2 eggs
2⅔ cups (400g) plain (all-purpose) flour
1 tablespoon orange blossom water
2 teaspoons iced water, approximately
1 tablespoon milk
½ cup (80g) icing (confectioners') sugar, extra
1 teaspoon ground cinnamon
almond filling
2 cups (240g) ground almonds
½ cup (80g) icing (confectioners') sugar
1 egg
45g (1½ ounces) butter, melted
1 tablespoon orange blossom water

1 Beat butter and sifted icing sugar in medium bowl with electric mixer until smooth. Beat in eggs, one at a time. Stir in sifted flour, orange blossom water and enough of the water to make a firm dough. Divide dough in half; cover, refrigerate 30 minutes.
2 Meanwhile, make almond filling.
3 Preheat oven to 160°C/325°F. Grease oven trays; line with baking paper.
4 Roll each dough half, separately, between sheets of baking paper until 2mm (⅛-inch) thick; cut 20 x 7.5cm (3-inch) rounds from each sheet of dough. Re-roll scraps of dough, if necessary, to make a total of 40 rounds.
5 Drop rounded teaspoons of almond filling into centre of rounds; brush edges with a little water. Fold rounds in half, press edges with a fork to seal. Pinch ends slightly to create horn shapes. Place horns on oven trays; brush with milk.
6 Bake horns about 20 minutes or until browned lightly. Roll warm horns in combined extra sifted icing sugar and cinnamon. Serve warm or cold.
almond filling Combine ingredients in medium bowl.

prep + cook time 1 hour (+ refrigeration) **makes** 40
nutritional count per horn 8.5g total fat (3.4g saturated fat); 606kJ (145 cal); 14.3g carbohydrate; 2.9g protein; 0.9g fibre

Rosewater and orange couscous

1 medium orange (240g)
1½ cups (375ml) water
⅓ cup (75g) caster (superfine) sugar
1½ cups (300g) couscous
30g (1 ounce) butter
1 teaspoon rosewater
½ teaspoon ground cinnamon
⅓ cup (65g) finely chopped dried figs
⅓ cup (45g) coarsely chopped roasted unsalted shelled pistachios
⅔ cup (190g) yogurt
¼ cup loosely packed fresh mint leaves

1 Finely grate 2 teaspoons rind from orange. Segment orange over small bowl.
2 Stir the water and sugar in small saucepan over medium heat until sugar dissolves; bring to the boil.
3 Combine couscous with the sugar syrup mixture, butter, rosewater, cinnamon and rind in medium heatproof bowl, cover; stand about 5 minutes or until liquid is absorbed, fluffing with fork occasionally. Stir figs and half the nuts into couscous.
4 Serve couscous topped with orange segments and yogurt; sprinkle with remaining nuts and mint.

prep + cook time 25 minutes (+ standing) **serves** 4
nutritional count per serving 13.5g total fat (5.5g saturated fat); 2362kJ (565 cal); 93.1g carbohydrate; 15.4g protein; 5.1g fibre
tip Use your favourite thick yogurt; sheep's-milk yogurt is delicious in this recipe.

glossary

almonds

blanched almonds with brown skins removed.

flaked paper-thin slices.

ground also known as almond meal; nuts are powdered to a coarse flour texture.

slivered small pieces cut lengthways.

anise also known as aniseed or sweet cumin, related to parsley. The seeds have a mildly sweet licorice flavour.

artichoke hearts tender centre of the globe artichoke; purchased in brine, canned or in glass jars.

baking paper also called parchment paper; a silicone-coated paper used to line baking pans and oven trays so cakes and biscuits won't stick, making removal easy.

baking powder a raising agent consisting mainly of two parts cream of tartar to one part bicarbonate of soda.

baharat see page 9.

basil an aromatic herb; there are many types, but the most commonly used is sweet basil.

beans

broad also called fava, windsor and horse beans; available dried, canned, fresh and frozen. Fresh and frozen should be peeled twice discarding the outer long green pod and the beige-green tough inner shell.

cannellini small white bean similar in flavour and appearance to haricot, navy and great northern, all of which can be substituted for each other.

beef

chuck steak from the neck and shoulder, and tends to be chewy but flavourful and inexpensive. A good cut for braising or stewing.

eye fillet a very tender cut from the area below the rib cage; also called beef tenderloin.

beetroot also called red beets or beets; firm, round root vegetable.

bicarbonate of soda also called baking soda.

blood orange a virtually seedless citrus fruit with a reddish rind and flesh; has a sweet, non-acidic pulp and the juice has slight strawberry or raspberry tones.

breadcrumbs, stale one- or two-day-old bread made into crumbs by blending or processing.

burghul also called bulghur wheat; hulled steamed wheat kernels that, once dried, are crushed into various sized grains. Is not the same as cracked wheat. See also page 9.

butter we use salted butter unless stated; 125g is equal to 1 stick (4 ounces).

buttermilk originally the term given to the slightly sour liquid left after butter was churned from cream, today it is commercially made like yogurt. Sold alongside fresh milk products in supermarkets. Despite the implication of its name, it is low in fat.

capsicum also called bell pepper. Discard seeds and membranes before use.

roasted available loose from delis or packed in jars in oil or brine.

caraway seeds a member of the parsley family; also available in ground form. Has a pungent aroma and a distinctly sweet but tangy flavour.

cardamom can be purchased in pod, seed or ground form. Has a distinctive aromatic, sweetly rich flavour and is one of the world's most expensive spices.

cayenne pepper long, thin-fleshed, extremely hot red chilli usually sold dried and ground.

cheese

fetta Greek in origin; a crumbly textured goat- or sheep-milk cheese with a sharp, salty taste. Ripened and stored in salted whey.

goat's made from goat's milk, has an earthy, strong taste; available in soft and firm textures, and in various sizes and shapes.

gruyère a hard-rind Swiss cheese with small holes and a nutty, slightly salty flavour.

mascarpone an Italian fresh cultured-cream product made in much the same way as yogurt. Whiteish to creamy yellow in colour, with a buttery-rich texture. Soft, creamy and spreadable.

chicken

drumsticks leg with skin and bone intact.

maryland leg and thigh still connected in a single piece; bones and skin intact.

small chicken also called spatchcock or poussin; no more than 6 weeks old, weighing a maximum of 500g. Spatchcock is also a term to describe splitting a small chicken open, flattening then grilling.

tenderloins thin tender strip of meat lying just under the breast.

thigh cutlets thigh with skin and centre bone intact; sometimes skinned.

thigh fillets thigh with skin and bone removed.

chickpeas see page 8.

chilli use rubber gloves when seeding and chopping fresh chillies as they can burn your skin. Removing seeds and membranes lessens the heat level.

banana chillies can be pale green, yellow and red in colour. Available from greengrocers and larger supermarkets.

long red available both fresh and dried; a generic term used for any moderately hot, long (6-8cm), thin chilli.

powder the Asian variety, made from dried ground thai chillies, is the hottest; can be used as a substitute for fresh chillies in proportion of ½ teaspoon ground chilli powder to 1 medium chopped fresh chilli.

red thai a small, hot, bright red chilli.

chocolate-coated honeycomb bar a honeycomb confectionery covered in milk chocolate.

chocolate, dark eating also called semi-sweet or luxury chocolate; made of a high percentage of cocoa liquor and cocoa butter, and little added sugar.

cinnamon dried inner bark of the shoots of the cinnamon tree; available in stick (quill) or ground form.

consommé a clear soup usually of beef, veal or chicken.

coriander also called cilantro or chinese parsley; bright-green leafy herb with a pungent flavour. The

stems and roots are also used in cooking; wash well before using. Also available ground or as seeds; these should not be substituted for the fresh herb as the tastes are completely different.

seeds have a mild, lemon-like taste. Ground coriander seeds are found in sweet mixed spice blends for cakes and biscuits as well as being used to thicken and flavour curries.

cornflour also called cornstarch. Available made from corn or wheat.

couscous see page 9.

cream

pouring cream also called pure cream; has no additives and contains a minimum fat content of 35%.

thickened a whipping cream that contains a thickener (minimum fat content of 35%).

cucumber, lebanese thin-skinned, short and slender. Probably the most popular variety because of its tender, edible skin, tiny, yielding seeds and sweet, fresh and flavoursome taste.

cumin also known as zeera or comino; has a spicy, nutty flavour.

currants, dried these tiny, almost black raisins are so-named after a grape variety originating in Corinth, Greece.

dates fruit of the date palm tree; green when unripe, they turn yellow, golden brown, black or mahogany red as they ripen. About 4-6cm in length, plump and oval, thin-skinned, with a honey-sweet flavour and sticky texture. Available fresh or dried, pitted or unpitted.

dukkah an Egyptian specialty spice mix made up of roasted nuts, seeds and aromatic spices.

eggplant also called aubergine.

baby also called finger or japanese eggplant; very small and slender so can be used without disgorging.

eggs we use large chicken eggs weighing an average of 60g unless stated otherwise. If a recipe calls for raw or barely cooked eggs, exercise caution if there is a salmonella problem in your area, particularly in food eaten by children and pregnant women.

fennel also called finocchio or anise; a white to very pale green-white, firm, crisp, roundish vegetable about 8-12cm in diameter. The bulb has a slightly sweet, anise flavour, but the leaves have a much stronger taste. Also the name given to dried seeds having a licorice flavour.

figs vary in skin and flesh colour according to type not ripeness. When ripe, figs should be unblemished and bursting with flesh; nectar beads at the base indicate when a fig is at its best.

fillo pastry also called phyllo; tissue-thin pastry sheets purchased chilled or frozen.

fish sauce called naam pla (Thai) and nuoc naam (Vietnamese); the two are almost identical. Made from pulverised salted fermented fish; has a pungent smell and strong taste. Available in varying degrees of intensity, so use according to your taste.

flour

plain also known as all-purpose.

self-raising all-purpose plain or wholemeal flour with baking powder and salt added; make at home in the proportion of 1 cup flour to 2 teaspoons baking powder.

gelatine a thickening agent; we use powdered gelatine. Also available in sheet form, known as leaf gelatine.

ginger

fresh also called green or root ginger; the thick root of a tropical plant.

ground also called powdered ginger; cannot be substituted for fresh.

harissa a sauce or paste made from dried chillies, cumin, garlic, oil and caraway seeds. The paste (in a tube) is very hot and should not be used in large amounts; bottled harissa sauce is more mild. Available from supermarkets and Middle Eastern grocery stores. See also page 13.

hazelnuts also called filberts; plump, grape-sized, rich, sweet nut with a brown skin that is removed by rubbing heated nuts together vigorously in a tea-towel.

ground is made by grounding the hazelnuts to a coarse flour texture.

honey the variety sold in a squeezable container is not suitable for the recipes in this book.

kumara Polynesian name of an orange-fleshed sweet potato often confused with yam.

leek a member of the onion family; resembles a green onion, but is much larger and more subtle and mild in flavour.

lemon thyme a herb with a lemony scent, which is due to the high level of citral in its leaves – an oil also found in lemon, orange, verbena and lemon grass. The citrus scent is enhanced by crushing the leaves in your hands before using the herb.

lentils (red, brown, yellow) dried pulses often identified by and named after their colour.

maple-flavoured syrup is made from sugar cane and is also called golden or pancake syrup. It is not a substitute for pure maple syrup.

maple syrup distilled from the sap of sugar maple trees found only in Canada and about ten states in the USA. Maple-flavoured syrup is not a good substitute for the real thing.

marjoram closely related to oregano; its flavour is distinctive but sweeter and milder than oregano and tastes slightly earthy.

mesclun pronounced mess-kluhn; also called mixed greens or spring salad mix. A commercial blend of assorted young lettuce and other green leaves, including baby spinach leaves, mizuna and curly endive.

milk we use full-cream homogenised milk unless stated otherwise.

mince also known as ground meat.

moroccan seasoning contains turmeric, cumin and cinnamon and adds an authentic Moroccan flavouring; available from most Middle Eastern food stores, spice shops and major supermarkets.

mushrooms, button small, cultivated white mushrooms with a mild flavour. When a recipe in this book calls for an unspecified type of mushroom, use button.

nutmeg the dried nut of an evergreen tree native to Indonesia; it is available in ground form, or you can grate your own with a fine grater.

oil

avocado is pressed from the flesh of the avocado fruit. Has a high smoking point. It is high in monounsaturated fats and vitamin E.

mustard seed is rich and full-bodied with a buttery, nutty flavour, but without the heat or strong mustard taste.

olive made from ripened olives. Extra virgin and virgin are the best, while extra light or light refers to taste not fat levels.

sesame made from roasted, crushed, white sesame seeds; a flavouring rather than a cooking medium.

vegetable sourced from plants.

olives

black have a richer and more mellow flavour than the green ones and are softer in texture.

green those harvested before fully ripened and are, as a rule, denser and more bitter than their black relatives.

rainbow cerignola olives, grown in Italy, are large oval-shaped olives that can be either black or bright green, depending on maturity. They may also come in a variety of colours, including yellow, red, green and brown; the colour depends on the curing medium – brine, lye or salt. Available from specialty food stores and delicatessens.

onions

baby brown are called cocktail onions and pickling onions; larger than shallots they are used raw, pickled in brine, or cooked in stews and casseroles.

green also called scallion or, incorrectly, shallot; an immature onion picked before the bulb has formed, it has a long, bright-green edible stalk.

red also called spanish, red spanish or bermuda onion; a sweet-flavoured, large, purple-red onion.

shallots also called french shallots, golden shallots or eschalots; small, brown-skinned, elongated members of the onion family. Grows in tight clusters like garlic.

spring have small white bulbs and long green leaves with narrow green-leafed tops.

orange blossom water a concentrated flavouring made from orange blossoms. Available from Middle Eastern food stores and some supermarkets and delis. Cannot be substituted with citrus flavourings, as the taste is completely different.

oregano also called wild marjoram; has a woody stalk with clumps of tiny, dark green leaves that have a pungent, peppery flavour. Used fresh or dried.

paprika a ground, dried, sweet red capsicum; varieties include sweet, hot, mild and smoked.

parsley, flat-leaf also called continental parsley or italian parsley.

patty pan squash also called crookneck or custard marrow pumpkins; a round, slightly flat summer squash being yellow to pale-green in colour and having a scalloped edge. Harvested young, it has a firm white flesh and distinct flavour.

pepitas are the pale green kernels of dried pumpkin seeds; available plain or salted.

pine nuts also called pignoli; not a nut but a small, cream-coloured kernel from pine cones. They are best roasted before use to bring out the flavour.

pistachios pale green, delicately flavoured nuts inside hard off-white shells. To peel, soak shelled nuts in boiling water about 5 minutes; drain, then pat dry with absorbent paper. Rub skins with cloth to peel. We use shelled nuts.

pomegranate molasses is thicker, browner and more concentrated in flavour than grenadine (the sweet, red pomegranate syrup used in cocktails). Possesses tart and fruity qualities similar to balsamic vinegar. It is available from Middle Eastern food stores, specialty food shops and better delis.

poppy seeds small, dried, bluish-grey seeds of the poppy plant, with a crunchy texture and a nutty flavour. Can be purchased whole or ground in delicatessens and most supermarkets.

potatoes

baby new also called chats; not a separate variety but an early harvest with thin skin.

desiree oval, smooth, pink-skinned, waxy yellow flesh; good in salads, roasted and boiled.

preserved lemon rind lemons preserved in salt and lemon juice or water. Sold in jars at delis and some supermarkets; once opened, keep refrigerated. To use, remove and discard pulp, squeeze juice from rind; slice rind thinly. Use the rind only and rise well under cold water before using. See also page 10.

prunes commercially or sun-dried plums.

quail related to the pheasant and partridge; a small, delicate-flavoured farmed game bird ranging in weight from 250g to 300g.

quince yellow-skinned fruit with hard texture and astringent, tart taste; eaten cooked or as a preserve. Long, slow cooking makes the flesh a deep rose pink.

radish a peppery root vegetable related to the mustard plant. The small round red variety is the mildest; it is crisp and juicy, and usually eaten raw in salads.

raisins dried sweet grapes.

ras el hanout see page 17.

rice

arborio small, round-grain rice well suited to absorb a large amount of liquid.

basmati a white, fragrant, long-grained rice. Wash several times before cooking.

roasting/toasting nuts and dried coconut can be roasted in the oven. Spread evenly on an oven tray then roast in oven at 180°C about 5 minutes. Desiccated coconut, pine nuts and sesame seeds roast more evenly if stirred over low heat in a heavy-based frying pan.

rocket also called arugula, rugula and rucola; a peppery-tasting green leaf. Baby rocket leaves are smaller and less peppery.

rosewater distilled from rose petals; do not confuse with rose essence, which is more concentrated.

saffron see page 8.

seafood

prawns also called shrimp. Can be bought uncooked (green) or cooked, with or without shells.

snapper a saltwater fish. The popular red snapper is so-named because of its reddish-pink skin and red eyes. Its flesh is firm and contains very little fat.

trout a delicately-flavoured fish belonging to the salmon family; classified as an oily fish. Most trout are freshwater, but some are saltwater. There are a number of different types including sea trout, rainbow trout and brown trout.

tuna reddish with a slightly dry, firm flesh. Varieties include bluefin, yellowfin, skipjack or albacore; substitute with swordfish.

white fish fillets, firm blue-eye, bream, ling, flathead, swordfish, jewfish, whiting or snapper are all suitable. Check for small pieces of bone and remove with tweezers.

semolina coarsely ground flour milled from durum wheat; the flour used in making gnocchi, pasta and couscous.

silver beet also known as swiss chard and, incorrectly, spinach; has fleshy stalks and large leaves, and both can be prepared as for spinach.

split peas see page 8.

star anise a dried star-shaped pod; its seeds have an astringent aniseed flavour.

sugar

brown a soft, finely granulated sugar retaining molasses for its characteristic colour and flavour.

caster also called superfine sugar.

demerara small-grained golden-coloured crystal sugar.

icing also known as confectioners' sugar or powdered sugar; pulverised granulated sugar crushed together with a small amount of cornflour.

pure icing also known as confectioners' sugar or powdered sugar.

sumac see page 9.

tomatoes

cherry also called tiny tim or tom thumb; small and round.

egg also called roma or plum; smallish, oval-shaped tomatoes.

paste triple-concentrated tomato puree.

truss small vine-ripened tomatoes with the vine still attached.

turmeric a member of the ginger family, its dried, ground root adds a yellow colour to dishes; is pungent but not hot.

vanilla

bean dried, long, thin pod from a tropical golden orchid; the tiny black seeds inside the bean are used to impart a luscious vanilla flavour.

extract obtained from vanilla beans infused in water; a non-alcoholic version of essence.

yeast (dried, fresh) a raising agent; dried (7g sachets) and fresh compressed (20g blocks) yeast can almost always be used one for the other.

yogurt we use plain full-cream yogurt unless stated otherwise.

za'atar see page 8.

zucchini also called courgette; small, pale- or dark-green, yellow or white vegetable from the squash family. Harvested when young, its edible flowers can be filled then cooked.

index

conversion chart

MEASURES

One Australian metric measuring cup holds approximately 250ml, one Australian metric tablespoon holds 20ml, one Australian metric teaspoon holds 5ml.

The difference between one country's measuring cups and another's is within a two- or three-teaspoon variance, and will not affect your cooking results. North America, New Zealand and the United Kingdom use a 15ml tablespoon.

All cup and spoon measurements are level. The most accurate way of measuring dry ingredients is to weigh them. When measuring liquids, use a clear glass or plastic jug with the metric markings.

We use large eggs with an average weight of 60g.

LIQUID MEASURES

METRIC	IMPERIAL
30ml	1 fluid oz
60ml	2 fluid oz
100ml	3 fluid oz
125ml	4 fluid oz
150ml	5 fluid oz (¼ pint/1 gill)
190ml	6 fluid oz
250ml	8 fluid oz
300ml	10 fluid oz (½ pint)
500ml	16 fluid oz
600ml	20 fluid oz (1 pint)
1000ml (1 litre)	1¾ pints

LENGTH MEASURES

METRIC	IMPERIAL
3mm	⅛in
6mm	¼in
1cm	½in
2cm	¾in
2.5cm	1in
5cm	2in
6cm	2½in
8cm	3in
10cm	4in
13cm	5in
15cm	6in
18cm	7in
20cm	8in
23cm	9in
25cm	10in
28cm	11in
30cm	12in (1ft)

DRY MEASURES

METRIC	IMPERIAL
15g	½oz
30g	1oz
60g	2oz
90g	3oz
125g	4oz (¼lb)
155g	5oz
185g	6oz
220g	7oz
250g	8oz (½lb)
280g	9oz
315g	10oz
345g	11oz
375g	12oz (¾lb)
410g	13oz
440g	14oz
470g	15oz
500g	16oz (1lb)
750g	24oz (1½lb)
1kg	32oz (2lb)

OVEN TEMPERATURES

The oven temperatures in this book are for conventional ovens; if you have a fan-forced oven, decrease the temperature by 10-20 degrees.

	°C (CELSIUS)	°F (FAHRENHEIT)
Very slow	120	250
Slow	150	300
Moderately slow	160	325
Moderate	180	350
Moderately hot	200	400
Hot	220	425
Very hot	240	475

First published in 2011 by ACP Magazines Ltd,
a division of PBL Media Pty Limited
54 Park St, Sydney
GPO Box 4088, Sydney, NSW 2001.
phone (02) 9282 8618; fax (02) 9267 9438
acpbooks@acpmagazines.com.au; www.acpbooks.com.au

ACP BOOKS
General Manager - Christine Whiston
Associate publisher - Seymour Cohen
Editor-in-Chief - Susan Tomnay
Creative Director & Designer - Hieu Chi Nguyen
Food Director - Pamela Clark

Published and Distributed in the United Kingdom by Octopus Publishing Group
Endeavour House
189 Shaftesbury Avenue
London WC2H 8JY
United Kingdom
phone (+44)(0)207 632 5400; fax (+44)(0)207 632 5405
info@octopus-publishing.co.uk;
www.octopusbooks.co.uk

Printed by Toppan Printing Co., China

International foreign language rights, Brian Cearnes, ACP Books bcearnes@acpmagazines.com.au

A catalogue record for this book is available from the British Library.
ISBN 978-1-74245-106-0

All by Grace

21 Years of Christian Headship

Jim Cockburn

Onwards and Upwards Publishers

3 Radfords Turf, Cranbrook, Exeter,
EX5 7DX, United Kingdom.
www.onwardsandupwards.org

This first edition published in the United Kingdom by Onwards and Upwards Publishers (2017).

ISBN: 978-1-911086-71-0
Typeface: Sabon LT
Editor: Sharon Fletcher
Graphic design: LM Graphic Design

Printed in the United Kingdom.

Endorsements

This is the book on school leadership I have been looking for. As a headteacher, I read a lot about leadership in an attempt to broaden my knowledge and understanding, however there is always something missing, something that doesn't quite connect. For me, the gap has been linking leadership reading to my faith as a Christian headteacher. Jim's words are poignant, insightful, heart-warming and encouraging – I know that I will come back to his words of wisdom regularly to refuel and refocus.

Kieran McGrane
Headteacher, Ponteland High School, Newcastle upon Tyne

It has been my privilege to know Jim and to be a frequent visitor to his school for thirty-seven years. My involvement in assemblies, lunch time meetings and classroom debates enabled me to present the Christian message from the standpoint of a believer and in ways that were sensitive, attractive and informative. It was also an opportunity to build relationships with staff and students and to be an encourager in the many challenges of school life. For these reasons I feel that it is so important that schools continue to remain open to the input of Christians like myself and to the message of faith and hope that we bring. I trust that this book will cause you to feel the same!

Dave Glover
Church Leader and Evangelist, Killingworth, Newcastle upon Tyne

I wholeheartedly recommend Jim's account of working in education as a committed Christian. The future generations of our society will gain opportunities to encounter God through leaders of influence in education who discover how to extend the kingdom of God in the schools of our nation. This book serves as an encouragement as well as offering practical wisdom for those who know the call to work with young people. God formed many young leaders in the Bible out of education and my prayer is that in reading this book you will be strengthened to partner with him to do the same.

Dr Tim Dunnett
Senior Pastor, Bethshan Church, Sunderland

About the Author

Jim Cockburn has spent thirty-seven years of his life in teaching, a career that he has loved. In December 2014 he retired from the school of which he had been headteacher for twenty-one years. During his time in teaching, he desired to live out the Christian life in a practical way and share the love of Jesus with others.

As a Christian headteacher he experienced God's grace and strength in dealing with many challenging situations as he sought to apply Christian principles in what he believes was a God-given role. He is keen to share his experience with other Christians involved in leadership in schools and other organisations.

Jim and his wife Ella have three grown-up sons, and are also experiencing the joy of their first grandchild. They are members of Jesmond Parish Church in Newcastle upon Tyne.

Contents

All by Grace

Preface

Looking out on to the Mediterranean from a Cypriot beach in April 2014 and thinking about my future retirement at Christmas of that year, the thought suddenly came to me that I should perhaps write a book about my experience of headship, particularly from the perspective of being a Christian. No matter how hard I tried, the thought would not go away, and was always there at the back of my mind.

Later on, I mentioned this to my vicar, David Holloway, who said to me very clearly, "You have to do it! When a person dies, they take a library with them." In saying this, he was adapting an African proverb, "When an old man dies, a library burns to the ground." In other words, we cannot simply take our collective wisdom to the grave with us, but we must write it down to pass it on to others.

I now felt that I had no alternative but to go ahead and write a book about my experience of headship over twenty-one years and how God's grace has been so evident over that time. It is not a book about how I took my school to the top of the local league table or how it was given an outstanding accolade by Ofsted; neither of these things happened. On the contrary, although the school received many blessings over that time, there were also many problems and difficulties that had to be faced, not all of which were overcome. Therefore, it is a book that I believe is grounded in reality, and so, hopefully, will be of great benefit and encouragement to Christian staff in schools, whatever leadership responsibilities (if any) they currently have.

Church members, particularly parents, will also find much of the book helpful in understanding some of the issues facing schools today. For example, chapter eight which covers sex and relationships education highlights an area of concern in our schools, but where, nonetheless, God can still shine his light. As Christians develop their understanding of today's schools, they will be able to pray more effectively for them and the Christian staff working within them.

The school of which I was head is a comprehensive school in the north-east of England, close to the city of Newcastle. During my time as headteacher it had a roll between 800 and 1150 students, occupying buildings mostly constructed in the 1950s. It served large former council housing estates with significant pockets of deprivation, as well as areas of private housing. It was a genuine comprehensive school that also served the local community through a large community education programme.

In many ways it was an ordinary school, but it was made very special through God having his hand upon it and showering his grace upon those who worked there. It was not a denominational school, but hopefully the book will show that God can use Christian staff to set his standards and share his love in any school. Where there are blessings, provision and protection, we can then say, "It is all by grace."

I am grateful to the people who have provided guidance, encouragement and support. I have already mentioned David Holloway who gave initial encouragement and advice. The following have read either all or part of the text, and have given very constructive comments for me to act upon: Tim Goodwin, Liz Jones, Lisa Lowery, Ken Matthews, Chris Richards and Eddie and Audrey Stringer. Luke Jeffery from Onwards and Upwards Publishers has provided me with excellent advice and guidance in what has been for me a new venture. Of course, I am particularly grateful to my wife Ella who has provided amazing love and support over forty years that has enabled me to do the things that I have described in this book.

This is a Christian book, and I have included extensive Bible references to illustrate my points. All references are taken from the New International Version.

May you capture a vision for God's grace in your own work as you read this book.

CHAPTER ONE

The End: The Last Fortnight

It was a strange feeling to lock the office door for the last time, leaving a room that had been my base for the past twenty-one years, and one which I might never enter again. It was December 2014 and I was about to begin my retirement from the headship I had held for the previous twenty-one years, as well as ending thirty-seven years in teaching, a profession I had loved.

There was one more event to take place, a staff celebration to mark my retirement that evening. The previous fortnight had been a whirlwind of events, with staff and students coming to make their farewells, passing on their best wishes and often leaving a card and a present.

The conversations I had with colleagues over that fortnight were very precious as it was an opportunity to reminisce over the good times that we had had together in the school. Many were very appreciative of the way that I had tried to support them both professionally and personally. What was particularly special was the fact that some former colleagues made the effort to come into school, along with those currently on maternity or on long-term sickness leave. Sometimes words could not be expressed as emotions ran high. Some of the conversations were more than simply reminiscing; some were deep spiritual conversations as we reflected on what God had done in individuals' lives and in the life of the school.

It was not only colleagues past and present from the school who expressed their best wishes. Those from beyond the school were also very kind in what they said and in the presents they gave. The head of a neighbouring school said very complimentary things about my role within the North Tyneside Secondary Heads' Group and made a presentation to me on behalf of the group. The heads of our primary feeder schools took me out for a meal, which again was a happy time of reminiscing on how we had worked together for all of the area's children and young people. The school's governors at the end of what was my last governors' meeting also thanked me for what I had done for the school over the past twenty-one special years.

Student Involvement

I appreciated all that was said by my colleagues, but what was just as important, if not more so, was my involvement with the students over that last fortnight.

We had special presentation events and it was a privilege to shake the hands of each Year 7 student in front of their proud parents as they received certificates to mark the end of their first term in the school. Likewise, at the other end of the student age spectrum, I very proudly welcomed back the sixth formers who had left the previous summer for university and elsewhere and presented them with their "A" level certificates. In a number of cases, I was able to embarrass them by reminding them of when they had been in my religious studies class in Year 7.

The Christmas concert in the school's theatre had been a traditional event in the school spanning many years, well before I arrived, although I was told that it was a pretty raucous event in these early years with very high-spirited youths sitting down the sides of the hall on the window ledges. Over time, however, audience behaviour improved phenomenally, as did the standard of the music. Performing arts was an area of school life of which I was exceptionally proud and the 2014 Christmas concert did not let me down, with the choir, orchestra, soloists and rock bands providing an exceptional evening of musical entertainment. I was not sure how I would be able to handle the emotions of my last concert 'thank you' address, but I kept them contained and I was able to thank the students for providing me with so much pleasure over many years.

It is part of the school's ethos to put the individual student at the heart of our work. To monitor progress, many students are given termly interviews to examine their grades and to see how they can be helped to improve their achievement. I had interviewed the members of one particular Year 11 tutor group since they were in their very first term in the school. This was to be their last interview with me and I was pleased to be able to congratulate many of them on the progress they were clearly making in their different subjects, as well as giving advice to those who were not making such good progress. I was particularly touched when each shook my hand, thanked me and wished me well before they left the room (probably as a result of firm instructions from their form tutor).

Occasionally, the contact with students went deeper than just academic grades. Sometimes there was a real spiritual dimension. One student had lost his father earlier that term and some particular class topics of discussion would get him upset. I picked him up one afternoon during that fortnight as he felt that he was too upset to stay in his class. He just needed to share his feelings with someone and I felt privileged that he trusted me enough to do that with me. For over an hour he did most of the talking, but I was able to give him some words of advice and I asked him if I could pray for him at the end. Praying with students does not appear in the manuals on school pastoral care, but I felt led to do it on this occasion and he appreciated it. I told him that even though I was leaving, I would always remember him and I still do pray for him.

Over my time at the school I had always maintained a teaching commitment as a way of keeping in touch with the young people and what was happening in the classroom. Therefore, I was especially pleased when Dot Lee and Lisa Lowery, the two Christian teachers who taught GCSE religious studies, asked me if I would be grilled by the students in their Year 11 classes in their last lesson of the term about my Christian faith. I have always loved that very demanding, interactive sort of session. Lessons are eighty minutes long, and we covered a lot of ground in that time. There were the expected questions on science and religion, the role of women in the church, suffering, sexual ethics and what heaven will be like, but also from their study of Mark's Gospel, issues related to whether Judas had been predestined to betray Jesus, what will happen at the Second Coming, why there will not be marriage in heaven and what our attitude to possessions should be.

As part of my answers to their questions, I was able to share with them how I became a Christian. I emphasised to them that the real issue which they needed to sort out for themselves was what they thought about the claims made in the Bible about Jesus, particularly that he was the Son of God who had died for them and had then risen from the dead. I also made it clear to them that although I had sometimes been accused of brainwashing young people into Christianity, I could not in fact force them to become Christians. They did, however, need to consider carefully what they had heard in their religious studies lessons and assemblies over the years (including what they would hear in the carol service the next day) and make up their minds for themselves.

Church Carol Service

The local parish church was absolutely packed out, and as I welcomed the congregation at the beginning of the carol service, I remarked that this was my twenty-first carol service, that I could remember my early ones when the numbers attending were relatively small, and that it was wonderful that so many people of all ages wanted to come to the service that extra seats had to be put out. I also repeated what I had said at the beginning of each of the previous twenty services, that it was only right that the school's Christmas celebrations should begin in the church so that we were fully aware of the real meaning of Christmas.

There was an atmosphere of expectancy and celebration during the service. As always, the choir sounded heavenly as they sang in the church, both singing their own pieces and leading the congregation in carol singing. Students read the traditional passages very clearly, as did Jonathan Sanders, one of our Christian governors, who read how the Word became flesh from John chapter 1.

God had laid it on my heart to preach about how the Christmas story shows how God wants to deal with our fears. I related to them that January 5th, 2015 might be a bit scary for me; whereas most other people would be going back to school or work after the Christmas break, I was not sure what I would be doing that day, as I was starting my retirement. (I also joked that my wife probably had plans for me that day and that was even more scary.) We all have fears, whether it be to do with exams, careers, our relationships, families, health, and, ultimately, what happens to us after we die.

Relating all this to the first Christmas, I reminded the congregation that the shepherds on the hillside were terrified when the angel appeared, but were reassured with the command and promise,

*Do not be afraid. I bring you good news of great joy that will
be for all the people. Today in the town of David, a Saviour
has been born to you; he is Christ the Lord.[1]*

The shepherds responded to that message and rushed off to
Bethlehem, saw the promised Saviour, and then told others who were
amazed at this good news.

That command and promise was given to others in the Christmas
story. Further back in the story, Mary, who was greatly troubled at the
words of an angel who appeared to her, was uplifted when she was
told,

*Do not be afraid, Mary, you have found favour with God.
You will be with child and give birth to a son, and you are to
give him the name Jesus.[2]*

The command was the same: "Do not be afraid" because God is
going to do amazing things.

Likewise, when Joseph heard that his fiancée was pregnant and he
felt that he should end the engagement, an angel appeared to him in a
dream and told him not to be afraid.[3] The promise was given in relation
to Mary,

*She will give birth to a son, and you are to give him the name
Jesus, because he will save his people from their sins.[4]*

The message in the Christmas story was always the same; there was
no need to be afraid because the most momentous series of events in the
whole of history was about to take place. The God of the universe was
about to enter the world through a virgin, and he would end up going
to the cross to do as his name means, to save his people from their sins.
Of course it would not end there as he would rise up from the dead,
dealing with the ultimate fear we have, that of dying. Jesus conquered
death and we too can conquer death by trusting in him!

He can deal with our fears, but only if we come and trust him, as
the shepherds, Mary and Joseph did. I related that to my own situation
by saying that although I did not know what I would be doing on

---

[1] Luke 2:10-11.
[2] Luke 1:30-31.
[3] See Matthew 1:20.
[4] Matthew 1:21.

January 5th, I was prepared to trust Jesus that he was going to see me through the next stage of my life, just as he had done in all the previous stages.

I went on to say that Jesus makes that same offer to all of us. He says, "Why not let me take over the running of your life? Why not let me save you from your sins? Why not let me take you to a place in heaven when you die? All you need to do is to ask me to come into your life and take control of it for you."

As I closed, I led the congregation in prayer and invited those who wished, to pray that God would forgive them for their sins and to ask Jesus to come into their lives. One of the parents who was in the congregation that evening approached me over a year later to thank me for what I had said, sharing that it had helped her in her new faith.

School Carol Services

The carol services held inside school were also special events when the gospel could be put across clearly and powerfully. For me, the 2014 services were particularly poignant, as they were the last assemblies that I would take with each year group, and my last opportunity to share God's message of love with them.

Again, the choir and soloists sang and readers read the appropriate lessons. There were, however, lighter moments within the services, with humorous dramatic sketches portraying the Christmas story, and a specially-made video starring members of staff, including myself, called "North-East Enders", to mark my leaving. This video was not particularly spiritual, but that did not matter, as it was highly enjoyable, particularly as it showed what bad actors the staff were.

It is always difficult to find a fresh slant in order to put the message across, but this year the John Lewis Partnership and St Thomas Church in Norwich came to the rescue. I showed the students pictures of "geeky gifts" that they may wish to buy as presents if they were short of ideas, such as a sonic screwdriver as used by Doctor Who, a periodic table shower curtain (perhaps for their favourite science teacher) or a Darth Vader mask.

I then went on to say that big stores such as John Lewis spend a lot of money trying to persuade us to buy gifts from them at Christmas. I showed them the 2014 John Lewis advert starring Monty the Penguin and playing the John Lennon composition "Real Love". The message of the advert was that real love could be found through gifts and finding that special person. I challenged the students to think that surely real love at Christmas must be more than that portrayed by big stores.

They were then shown an alternative video, but in the same format, produced by St Thomas Church, and presumably for much less than the million pounds that it cost John Lewis to make. At the end of this video, the child comes to the cross where real love can be found. I reminded the students of the real love that was shown at Christmas and displayed the verse,

> For God so loved the world that he gave his one and only Son, that whoever believes in him shall not perish, but have eternal life.[5]

Staff Meeting

Over the previous twenty-one years, I had led many staff meetings. Some were occasions for celebrating success, some reminders to staff of the standards expected of us, some training events, and more recently they were rather sombre events outlining budgetary problems and forthcoming redundancies. My last staff meeting on December 9th, 2014 had, however, to be a very special occasion, as it was my last major opportunity to encourage the whole staff, including Paul Quinn, my deputy who was taking over from me in January.

Usually in these meetings I used a slide presentation, which in effect was my script. This time, however, I felt that because it was more personal, a multimedia presentation was not appropriate, but in case my emotions got the better of me, I did type it all out and had it in front of me (although I did ad-lib on two or three occasions).

I shared with staff about how I had spent the previous half-term holiday going through twenty-one years of papers in the store cupboards, sending almost all of it to be shredded. These papers brought back memories of students and events from the past and what the school had been able to achieve over these years. I reminded colleagues of our successes over the years, including, in some years, excellent exam results that placed us high in local league tables, achieving technology college status, winning the bid to get a high-

---

[5] John 3:16.

technology learning centre on our site, our leadership in e-learning, and the magnificent music and drama performances put on over the years.

There were, however, difficult situations that needed to be mentioned. Our exam results, including our most recent ones, were on occasion disappointing. Failing our Ofsted inspection in 2008 over a safeguarding issue was a major blow, although I believe that God protected the school at that time, and indeed, despite Ofsted's judgement, numbers grew substantially in the forthcoming years.

The building, now sixty years old, had caused problems over the years with flooding, gas leaks, lack of heating and huge bills. Promises of new builds in the past had been thwarted by unsuccessful bids or a change in government. On the other hand, we were currently on track for a new build to be opened in 2016, which meant that although I personally would not work in it, Paul Quinn would be able to open it. I used the Old Testament illustration that King David had it in his heart to build the Temple, but God planned for David's son Solomon to build it instead.[6]

I paid tribute to the work of different groups of staff. The support staff were the backbone of the school and I said that we simply could not function as a school without them. I tried to encourage the young teachers on the staff to hold on to their values and enthusiasm; despite the buffetings they might receive from government or Ofsted, they would have a major influence on the lives of young people for many years to come. To reinforce this, I used the illustration of a young man whom I had taught over thirty years before and was now a parent at one of our feeder primary schools. He had got in touch with me having seen my photograph on our website; he expressed his appreciation of the influence I had had on him then. I assured the staff that they would also be appreciated by many students looking back in the years to come.

Curriculum leaders are key people in the leading of the school and I thanked them for the way in which they led their subject areas so effectively. I encouraged them to keep on raising academic standards, remembering particularly the vulnerable pupils in their classes and ensuring that they did not compromise their own personal standards by, for example, not adhering to examination board regulations. I also thanked the year leaders for doing a special job in leading our young

---

[6] See 1 Kings 8:18-19.

people to reach new heights, dealing with the many issues that they have on the way.

The senior leadership team had been reduced in size over time, but they were the members of staff with whom I worked most closely. I took the opportunity to thank each of them by name – Mark Elliott, Dot Lee, Val Short and Ian Williams – recognising the individual contribution that each of them had made.

Paul Quinn, the deputy headteacher, was given particular mention, as he would be taking over the helm in January. Paul has all the potential of being the "Level 5 Leader" that Jim Collins talks about in his book "Good to Great"[7], a leader who has a blend of personal humility coupled with professional will, ambitious for the organisation but not for themselves. I encouraged him to be that sort of leader and to do it under God. I then quoted the words of the Archbishop of Canterbury from the Queen's Coronation in 1953, "We present you with this Book, the most valuable thing that this world affords," referring of course to the Bible.[8] I presented Paul with a bible, asking him to be guided by it as he led the school. This was greeted by a spontaneous round of applause, showing that staff understood the significance of what was taking place.

I finished by referring to the first two assembly themes of the term, "School's Amazing!" and "You're Amazing!". The message that the students received from these assemblies was that they were part of an amazing school, that each individual was specially created, and that together with God's help we can do amazing things. I said to colleagues that whereas Ofsted might have certain views about us as a school, I strongly believed that God knows in which ways a school is really outstanding and that they played a major part in making this possible here, because they themselves were amazing.

The Full Reality of the Job

It would seem from discussion and emails afterwards that the staff meeting was well received. Indeed, so many events over that fortnight brought great pleasure to me and also seemed to be appreciated by staff and students that I might have been tempted to think that perhaps I was

---

[7] *Good to Great;* Jim Collins; Random House (2001); pages 17-40.
[8] *The Music with the Form and Order of Service to be performed at the Coronation of Her Most Excellent Majesty Queen Elizabeth II;* 1953.

making a mistake in leaving at all. Yet, I knew the reality of the job and that God had made it very clear to me that it was time to move on.

I did have certain remaining tasks to do over that fortnight that reminded me of that reality and how difficult the past year had been. It was not all about attending social functions and hearing nice things being said about me.

As will be explained in more detail in chapters ten and eleven, the school faced difficult financial circumstances with a large budget deficit and a number of staff having been made redundant, with more to follow. The local authority were reasonably supportive, but they were always breathing down our necks to make sure that we were not incurring unnecessary expenditure and that we were following our deficit reduction plan. It is only right that they should carry out this scrutiny in terms of accountability, but it did take away some of the pleasure of the post. Each month there were meetings with local authority representatives to discuss budget issues, and my last one took place during the final week of term. It was a tedious meeting and I was tempted to tell the local authority's finance officer to stop being so patronising, but I restrained myself (or perhaps, more accurately, the Holy Spirit restrained me), as it probably would not have really helped Paul and the governors in the future.

Linked to our financial position, I also wrote a bid during that last fortnight to obtain a special grant for schools that had suffered from falling rolls. Over the years, I had written a large number of bids to obtain resources for the school, and on occasion for groups of schools, and it is something that I quite enjoyed doing. This was to be my last and, if successful, would provide a one-off grant that would help to reduce the deficit. Having done my homework and then having received its approval from our chair of the finance subcommittee, I sent it off by the deadline. Subsequently, I did hear from Paul that the bid was successful and the funding received was able to help the school's financial position.

One last task was to rewrite the school's mission statement which appears on the school website. It might seem strange to write that sort of document in my last week in the post. The previous one, however, was out of date, and no longer really reflected where we were as a school. There was, however, a more sinister reason for doing it and that was in relation to British values which the British government insisted that schools actively promoted. I needed to write a statement that would incorporate these values without compromising where we stood over certain issues such as having mainly Christian assemblies.

This document was necessary should Ofsted decide to visit to inspect what we were doing in this area. Four Christian schools in the north-east of England had been inspected in November 2014 on the basis of looking particularly at the promotion of British values, with two of them suffering badly, and I obviously did not want my school to suffer at the hands of overzealous, misdirected inspectors. More detail on British values is covered in chapter three.

The issue of British values certainly made me realise that the freedom that I had enjoyed as a Christian head in proclaiming the gospel and maintaining biblical values may not be there in such fullness in the future. This may result in new challenges for future Christian leaders in schools.

Overview

The last event of the fortnight was a social occasion at a local Italian restaurant organised by some of the younger members of staff for me. Again, kind words were said, particularly in speeches made by Paul and by Sandra Belford, my longstanding deputy who had retired the previous Christmas. My response was to give special awards, often humorous, to various members of staff, including the lady who made Santa's grotto for me to sit in at the annual Christmas Fayre.

When I got home in the early hours of the morning, I spent a bit of time looking at my memory book with photographs compiled by Rowan Standish, my personal assistant for thirteen years, along with all the other cards I had received. People had been so kind.

Yes, they were very good years, but I was very conscious that they were not always easy, and certainly, I was leaving behind a school with lots of problems. Despite all the nice things that people said, I was well aware of my shortcomings and that whatever success had been achieved was very much by the grace of God. Throughout the twenty-one years, he has led me and provided for both me and the school. He has given his protection in times of difficulty and has answered prayer in many ways. He has allowed the gospel to be heard whether it be through assemblies, lessons, church services or other Christian activities. And it has all been through his grace.

"Oh, for more strong Christians in our schools," we might pray. Perhaps, however, we should also be praying for Christians who recognise their weakness and allow God's strength to work through them. That was the apostle Paul's experience, when he pleaded with the Lord to take away his thorn in the flesh. The Lord's response was to say,

> *My grace is sufficient for you, for my power is made perfect in weakness.*[9]

This gave Paul the ground for confidence so that he could say,

> *I will boast all the more gladly about my weaknesses so that Christ's power may rest on me.*[10]

Christian leaders in schools in an ever more difficult environment need to experience God's grace so that they can be led by his strength despite their weaknesses. My experience over twenty-one years of headship has been that he is willing to provide his strength by his grace as we seek him, and indeed even when we do not seek him, because it is *all* by grace.

That has also been my experience in the years before headship as the next chapter looking at my earlier Christian years will show.

[9] 2 Corinthians 12:9a.
[10] 2 Corinthians 12:9b.

CHAPTER TWO

The Beginning

I grew up in a very loving, stable, secure family in the Scottish town of Grangemouth, famous for its petrochemicals complex, and attended the local high school, where I was reasonably academically successful as well as ending up as school captain. My parents were members of the Old Parish Church of Scotland in the town and I attended children's and youth activities there. It would be true to say, however, that my knowledge of Christianity was academic rather than based on any sort of living faith. Certain events would fundamentally change that approach to Christianity.

The first and most significant of these events was the arrival in 1969 of a new principal teacher of chemistry in the school, Norman Reid, who would later in his career become rector of Bathgate Academy and professor of science education at the University of Glasgow. Norman, as well as revolutionising science teaching in the school, was a committed Christian who picked up the pieces of the school Scripture Union group that had fallen into disarray. He explained that his aim in running the group was to make Christianity fun, which seemed a novel concept to me. Of course, he had a more fundamental aim in that he hoped to see young people in the school come to a living faith in Jesus Christ.

New ideas and terminology were introduced to me such as "the nature of sin", "the atonement that Jesus made for us through his death on the cross", "the Bible as the Word of God", and "the need to invite Jesus to come into your life". I railed against these ideas, feeling that they were anti-intellectual or too emotionally charged. Certainly, they did not represent a form of Christianity that I was familiar with.

21

Norman, however, was very patient. He was of course an intellectual and, as I found out through working with him later, was very much against an over-emotional approach to Christianity that made coming to faith seem too easy without considering the cost of discipleship.

The next piece of the jigsaw was the study of Martin Luther and the European Reformation in history lessons in the autumn of 1970. What particularly struck me from looking at the ministry of Luther was the wonderful doctrine that he propounded, justification through faith alone, based on the text from Paul's letter to the Romans,

> *For in the gospel a righteousness from God is revealed, a righteousness from first to last, just as it is written: 'The righteous will live by faith.'* [11]

Paul was quoting from the prophet Habakkuk,[12] and in the Authorised Version, the word "just" is used for "righteous", thus the doctrine of justification through faith alone. It came to me that what Luther had rediscovered was the idea that we could not get to heaven by doing good works, but our salvation would come from simply putting our trust in Christ. I would later learn that "justified" for a Christian means "<u>just</u> as <u>if</u> I'd never sinned".

A particular event that was instrumental in bringing me to a faith in Christ was attending a conference run by Scripture Union for senior pupils in the last few days of December 1970. Norman persuaded five of us from the school to attend this conference. The speaker was an astonishing man, Jim Punton,[13] who had a passion for New Testament Greek, but who could also relate to all sorts of audiences, from disaffected young people with whom he worked through the Frontier Youth Trust wing of Scripture Union to intellectual theologians. Certainly, he related well to the young people at the conference.

He spoke about how Christianity was different from all other religions, in that in other faiths men and women are striving to find God, whereas in Christianity God came down to find us through the

---

[11] Romans 1:17.
[12] See Habakkuk 2:4.
[13] Jim Punton sadly died in 1986 at the young age of forty-eight. A website has been set up in his memory http://jimpunton.org.uk/

person of Jesus who died for us on the cross in our place and then rose again. This was a fundamental revelation to me.[14]

An analogy that stood out for me from Jim's teaching was about the difference between knowing about Jesus and actually knowing Jesus in a personal way. He used the illustration that many of Cliff Richard's fans (a rather dated illustration now!) would know lots of facts about him, such as all the key events in his life, the names of all of his hit songs, his likes and his dislikes, but they did not actually know Cliff in a personal way as a friend. It is the same with Jesus, as many people knew lots of facts about Jesus, but did they know him for themselves in a personal way? That difference between knowing facts about Jesus and knowing him personally absolutely hit me and I realised that God was speaking directly to me. I was at the same time reading the classic book "Basic Christianity" by John Stott,[15] which reinforced what Jim was saying and explained clearly how to take that step of faith.

As a result of all these Christian influences from the ongoing work of Norman Reid, the academic study of Martin Luther, and the powerful speaking of Jim Punton, to the writings of John Stott, I decided to commit my life to the Lord Jesus Christ. That decision would have a profound effect on what I did with the rest of my life.

The fact that it all happened through school influences rather than church influences also had a major impact on my thinking, as it was clear to me that there was such a great harvest of young people to be reaped in schools, obviously many more than churches were able to reach through their activities. By this stage, I intended to go into teaching as a career after university, and certainly saw through Norman the crucial importance of Christian teachers in our schools.

My coming to faith also made me realise the different ways in which God worked in a person's life. He used Norman Reid, Jim Punton, John Stott, and my history teacher Jim McHardy (who did not profess to be a Christian) to bring me to the point of committing my life to Jesus. The apostle Paul tried to make the church at Corinth understand that idea in order to prevent them from falling into factionalism. He wrote,

---

[14] I later thought more along these lines by reading Fritz Ridenour's commentary on Romans for young people: *How to be a Christian Without Being Religious;* Gospel Light Publications (1967).

[15] *Basic Christianity;* John R.W. Stott, Inter-Varsity Press (1958).

> *What, after all, is Apollos? And what is Paul? Only servants, through whom you came to believe – as the Lord has assigned to each his task. I planted the seed, Apollos watered it, but God made it grow.*[16]

I realised before I left school that in working with young people, God would graciously use me in particular ministries, and would use other people in other ministries. It was God, however, who would bring the growth.

The University Years, 1972-77

I obtained a place at Edinburgh University to study for a degree in economics and economic history, and started there in October 1972. These were good years, getting to grips with the demands of academic study, thinking through all sorts of issues, meeting lots of new people, growing in my faith and getting married.

Politically they were turbulent times, with an unpopular Conservative government forced out of office in 1974 through industrial relations issues, to be replaced by a minority Labour government led by Harold Wilson. The events of these years would later on provide the basis of many a good economics lesson. One of my earliest memories from October 1972 was sitting in a university debate on "The Troubles in Northern Ireland" that was chaired by a long-haired rather dour-looking young man. That young man was to rise to greater prominence a few months later when he was elected as University Rector, a post often held by "celebrities", but a post which this young man wanted to use more strategically in challenging the university authorities. This was Gordon Brown, later to become Chancellor of the Exchequer and British Prime Minister. (I thought back to these days again in 2004, when Stephen, our middle son, followed in Brown's footsteps and was elected as President of the Edinburgh University Students' Union; whether he will reach the same giddy heights of national public office remains to be seen!)

The university Christian Union played a key role in my spiritual growth. Looking back, the format of its meetings was very traditional, but the biblical teaching it provided through the foremost Scottish Christian preachers of the day and small group Bible study laid strong

---

[16] 1 Corinthians 3:5-7.

foundations for my ongoing development as a Christian. This included the annual residential weekend. I can still recall the impact that the ministry of David Searle had on the 1974 residential conference, when he stated, based on the sayings of Amos and other Old Testament prophets, that perhaps our prayers are not answered because we are deliberately holding on to sin in our lives.[17] There was much confession of sin that night!

Likewise, it was good to worship in the lively evangelical churches that Edinburgh had to offer and again receive strong biblical teaching. Most notable for me was Charlotte Baptist Chapel, with its large student population and its ministry led by Derek Prime. When, many years later, our eldest son, Andrew, went to live and work in Edinburgh, he asked my advice as to which church he should try; I suggested Charlotte Chapel. He followed that advice and became a Christian there as well as finding his future wife, Fiona. It was an emotional evening when, in 2009, Ella and I attended his baptism at the chapel and listened to his testimony.

Although the Christian Union and Edinburgh churches provided teaching and fellowship, I very much needed opportunities for service. God made it clear that these opportunities would take place amongst young people in Grangemouth, both in my home church and increasingly through helping to lead a fellowship of young people from across the town's churches. This included running a fortnightly Saturday evening evangelistic youth club and a weekly Sunday Bible Class. One Easter holiday, Christian friends and I also got permission to take over a vacant shop in the town centre to run a series of youth cafes with Christian speakers and groups, giving us the opportunity to share our faith with the young people of the town. Through these different activities, a number of young people became Christians, some of whom had a church background, whereas others had very little. One of those with a church background was Sheena Mathieson, (later Lightbody), who would be instrumental in carrying on with this work and who would many years later move to Newcastle and send her own children to my school.

---

[17] For example, in Amos 5:21-22 the Lord says that he despises the people's religious feasts and he will not accept their offerings, as a result of their complacency (6:1), their idleness and greed (:4-6) and their pride (:8).

Norman Reid was once more crucial in this work. He and I shared in the leadership of these activities and I learned so much from him in so doing. For him, it was crucial that the gospel was communicated clearly in a way that audiences, whether they be children, young people or adults, would clearly understand. Also, for Norman, it had to be the whole gospel that was proclaimed, including the call to discipleship, rather than easy conversion. He felt that this was particularly important in children's evangelism, as he had seen too much bad practice in whipping up children's emotions and getting children to say a prayer of commitment, just so that they would please their adult leader. For him, it was important to make it as hard as possible for a child to become a Christian so that any conversion would be a genuine work of the Holy Spirit.

Norman also believed strongly that any young people who became Christians should not just sit back as members of the fellowship, but rather that they should be involved in service. He was an arch delegator and he very quickly put new young people to work in the service of the Kingdom. Thus the Grangemouth Fellowship of young people grew and flourished in the 1970s.

One area of service in which I was involved with Norman was the summer missions programme run by Scripture Union Scotland. This involved working with a team of students normally led by Norman (although later on I led my own teams) for a week or a fortnight in reaching children, young people and adults, who were either on holiday, as in the case of the mission run at Whiting Bay in Arran, or who were residents of the place, as in the case of Holytown in Lanarkshire and Easterhouse in Glasgow. These missions were good fun, times of strong fellowship, but also times when many lives were touched by Christ.

The first mission I went on was at Whiting Bay in 1972 and one thing that I found odd was that four of the team of about sixteen came from a small mining village in Ayrshire that I had never heard of before called Muirkirk. I was soon to have stronger associations with that community. These four team members from Muirkirk invited me the following spring to speak at the coffee bar they ran every Saturday evening; that, however, ended up being a disastrous occasion, as the young people simply did not listen. They also invited me to join the Muirkirk summer mission team in July of that year, to be led by Charles Price, who would later become an internationally recognised

Christian speaker, broadcaster and writer, and ultimately pastor of The People's Church in Toronto. For me, however, even more important than meeting and working with Charles was to be meeting Ella, whom I would marry in 1976.

Muirkirk has a rich spiritual heritage, for this was covenanters' country in the seventeenth century, when staunch Christians in the area stood up in their support of the 1638 National Covenant against the desire of the English King to impose his brand of Christianity on the Presbyterian Scots. There was much brutality as a result, including the infamous murder near Muirkirk of John Brown in 1685 by Graham of Claverhouse. It was to the parish of Muirkirk that Reverend John Linkens came almost three hundred years later in 1964 and began a deep spiritual work, particularly with the children and young people of the village. Ella was one of a number of young people who were converted under John's ministry. As a group they continued to support each other even after John's departure in 1969.

I met Ella during my first Muirkirk mission in 1973, and in the following summer in 1974, I realised that she was the girl with whom I really wanted to spend the rest of my life. Our friendship and love grew from that point and as time went on we both realised that it was very much God's plan that we should share our lives together.

Our plan was to get married in August 1976 and for Ella to get a primary teaching job in Edinburgh, for us to buy a flat there, and for me to do my teacher training at Moray House. God had other plans, however, with the work in Grangemouth playing a significant part in our lives for one more year. Ella was not able to get a job in Edinburgh but she was given, on a plate, a job in Moray Middle School in Grangemouth without even an interview. We could not find a flat in Edinburgh that we could afford to buy that was not suffering from subsidence or had some other construction or planning issue, but Ella was given a council maisonette in Grangemouth as she was an incoming worker about to take up a teaching post. After our wedding, we honeymooned on the Isle of Skye, then set up home in Grangemouth with me teacher training in Edinburgh whilst doing my teaching, practices in more nearby Falkirk and Ella teaching eleven and twelve year olds. As well as that, we worked with Norman and his wife Gill in running the activities of the Grangemouth Fellowship for another year.

Sometimes we find that God has far better plans than the plans that we propose, no matter how good our plans seem to be.

"For my thoughts are not your thoughts, neither are your ways my ways," declares the Lord. "As the heavens are higher than the earth, so are my ways higher than your ways and my thoughts higher than your thoughts."[18]

Paul appreciated these truths as he undertook his missionary journeys. He was kept by the Holy Spirit from preaching in the province of Asia and prevented by the Spirit of Jesus from entering Bithynia. He did, however, have a vision of a man from Macedonia standing and begging that he would come and help them. That was a major decision as that call initiated the Christian mission into Europe.[19]

We very much experienced God's guiding hand as we set up our first married home, so much so that we included Paul's words from his letter to the Philippians in our wedding service booklet,

And my God will meet all your needs according to his glorious riches in Christ Jesus.[20]

We would rediscover that same experience a year later as I tried to obtain my first teaching post.

Cambridgeshire, 1977-85

If God had wanted us to stay working for him in Grangemouth we were sure that there would have been a suitable job teaching economics or modern studies in the school, where I was thoroughly enjoying my main teaching practice. That was not to be the case. Indeed there were no jobs at all in Scotland available for me. This was the era of the public spending cuts imposed by the International Monetary Fund on the Labour government in 1976 in a bid to force the government to deal with its high inflation and balance of payments difficulties. The result was that public spending was reduced with less money available to pay for new teachers. In those days, Scottish local authorities took responsibility for recruiting teachers and allocating them to schools. The way the system worked (or not, as the case may be) was that trainee teachers had priority in their home region; in my case this was the Central Region and there were simply no posts available for my

---

[18] Isaiah 55:8-9.
[19] See Acts 16:6-10.
[20] Philippians 4:19.

28

subjects. I then had the opportunity to apply in other regions in what was euphemistically called the "milk round". Any posts which had been available had by this time been snapped up by "home candidates", and there was nothing left. This once more repeated Paul's experience in Asia and Bithynia.

The next step was to apply for posts in England. Here the schools had greater autonomy and could advertise their own posts and do their own recruitment without local authority interference. One post which stood out for me was as a teacher of economics at a school in St Neots in Cambridgeshire. Although it seemed far from home, Ella and I felt that I should investigate it further. I wrote a letter asking for more details. This very sparse letter was taken to be my letter of application, and so I was invited down for interview on Friday, 3rd June, 1977. Unfortunately, however, I had a psychology exam that day, and if I did not sit it, I would fail the Diploma in Education course. God overruled, however, and the headteacher very graciously agreed to interview me on the Saturday morning instead.

I got the train down from Edinburgh about half an hour after I had finished the examination. It was a long, pretty gruelling journey with changes and long delays at Peterborough and Huntingdon. One reason for the delays was that there were lots of Scottish football fans travelling down to Wembley ready for battle the following day against the "auld enemy". I travelled down with a number of them on what started off as a very pleasant journey, but as the drink flowed I felt that I would be safer spending the journey in the corridor. As it happened, Scotland won 2-1, which was a famous victory, celebrated by the Scots fans that I travelled down with by invading the pitch and destroying one of the goals.

I also had a victory that Saturday as Brian Stevens, the headteacher, appointed me to be his sole economics teacher. It was an important appointment for him personally as his son was a member of the very small "A" level class that I would be inheriting. This was a very exciting job for me. I really believed that God could not have put me in a better place at that time. I was given freedom to teach the subject as I saw fit, and was mandated to improve results and ensure that numbers taking the subject at all levels rose. That was the sort of challenge that I relished and certainly, by the time I left the school in 1985, there were three of us who shared the teaching of the subject to much larger classes.

God prevented me from taking a post in Scotland and provided me with an ideal post in Cambridgeshire. He also gave us the resources to be able to make the move by allowing us to buy our first house and also our first car. Ella and I received rather large sums of money which were completely unexpected, including a large relocation grant. We also found in our bank account a large sum from British Petroleum. BP owned the oil refinery in Grangemouth where my father was an instrument engineer, and, because of government incomes policies, the company was not allowed to give any pay increases to their employees. Their solution was to give grants to the children of employees. We did not complain at the company's generosity!

In the first two weeks of the Scottish summer holidays of 1977 we were already committed to leading a fortnight's mission in Easterhouse in Glasgow, a large and, in the past, quite notorious housing estate. This was hard work, but it was a good time and we gave encouragement to the local church, St.George's and St Peter's Church of Scotland, who were hosting us. Immediately afterwards, Ella and I went down to St Neots to search for a house. We found one to our liking within our budget and started the ball rolling. We also went to a midweek meeting at the local evangelical church, and met Ted Fisher, a very lively, godly, caring pastor, who introduced us to some of the young couples in the church, including Janet and Graham Dolan, who immediately offered to allow us to stay with them if our house was not ready in time. We were so grateful for this offer, and took them up on it, as completion of our purchase did not in fact take place until October.

This was our beginning of involvement in St Neots Evangelical Church, where we were to have many close friendships, grow as Christians and serve the Lord in a variety of ways. As usual, we concentrated on children's and young people's work, but I was also called to become an elder, which added a new dimension to my experience of church leadership, including regular opportunities for preaching. It was also a safe haven for our new young family to grow up in, as our three sons were born during our St Neots years. Andrew was born in June 1979, Stephen in June 1981 and David in May 1984. They were of course very much a blessing to us, but they were also a blessing to young and old in the fellowship. Janet Arnott, a lovely Christian health visitor, was a great source of wisdom to us as young and, inevitably at times, struggling parents. Some of the young people

30

we worked with would come round after school and offer to help with the children.

There was a strong crossover between church and school. For example, two members of staff, John Norris and Pat Law, were both church members (indeed, John and Pat's husband John were both elders), and they were involved in helping to run Christian Union groups and prayer meetings. Most of the church young people attended the school and so I was involved with them throughout the week. One of the young people, Richard, was later to tell his wife Becky that he saw me every day, as I was his form tutor, economics teacher, young people's leader on a Saturday and church leader on a Sunday. We all, of course, had to be disciplined in this; it was, for example, formal titles ("Mr Cockburn") at school and Christian names ("Jim") in church. This seemed to work and, to my knowledge, none of the church young people ever abused the fact that they knew me outside school.

The paid work of course had to come first, and I believed that if I did that well, I would earn the respect of colleagues and the students as a Christian. Conversations about the Lord and what was happening at church often came up naturally. In a religious studies lesson, we had a discussion about the dangers of the occult and I was later told that the students were talking about it all day. On one occasion after we had moved on from St Neots, we returned to the church on a visit, when a young man called Craig approached me and said, "Do you remember that economics lesson when we discussed evangelism?" I did recollect talking about a gospel concert that the church was planning with the Christians in the school. He continued, "Well, I thought about that a lot and I decided later to become a Christian." I was so pleased that there had been fruit from within my normal class teaching.

The Northumberland Years, 1985-93

Although we were happy in St Neots, it was time to move on. I had had one promotion in the school, but I felt that it was right to seek further opportunities. Besides, the journey northwards to visit grandparents was becoming increasingly difficult as the family grew. In 1985, I decided to apply for the post of head of sixth form at a school in Northumberland. The headteacher was Angus Taylor, a name I recognised as he was chair of the Economics Association. As well as finding someone to lead the sixth form, he also wanted someone to look after the teaching of economics. Again, this seemed an ideal post, but the interview was much more demanding than the one I experienced eight years before. There were also very able, well qualified colleagues on interview with me. Nevertheless, Angus and the governors offered me the post, which I gladly accepted. Our family were now set for a move up north. We chose the small town of Bedlington for our new home.

I have often said that being head of sixth form was the hardest job that I ever did since it was like running a small school on one's own. When I joined the school, the sixth form was relatively small with very little sense of ethos or belonging about it. I felt that it was my responsibility to inject life and purpose into it and to ensure that it grew in size. Through curriculum change, better marketing, programmes of visits, speakers and residentials, and simply spending time with individuals, the atmosphere in the sixth form markedly improved and numbers grew. The sixth form became a real strength of the school.

In terms of church, it had not been as easy to find a church as it had been in St Neots since there was nothing that seemed obviously suitable within the town. I did attend one evening service at a small church in Bedlington called the Central Hall, although because of the shape of the building, the local people called it "The Coffin Chapel". There were twelve mostly elderly people in the service but they were all friendly and indeed quite surprised to see someone new come along. One couple, Neville and Mary Stuart, took us under their wing, came to visit us and recommended that we went to Jesmond Parish Church in Newcastle where as a family we would receive good age-appropriate teaching.

We had heard of Jesmond Parish Church before as it was the home church of one of our friends in St Neots, Helen Lewis. Also, we had heard the Vicar of Jesmond, David Holloway, on the radio as he was leading the outcry against the teachings of the about-to-be-enthroned Bishop of Durham, Professor David Jenkins. Professor Jenkins taught that there was no reliable, historical truth associated with the gospel and so, for example, the virgin birth and the bodily resurrection of Jesus could not be taken as historical facts. Through broadcasts, meetings and writings, David Holloway and others spoke out strongly against these heretical teachings. As David Holloway wrote, "People were being converted; lives were being changed; given time, this would have social and economic effects. There was no way that we could sit back and see someone come into the area from outside and undermine faith."[21] Although there were protests, the consecration went ahead in York Minster. Nevertheless, it was an exciting time to start going to Jesmond Parish Church!

We did, however, feel that we wanted to serve in Bedlington. Robin and Miriam Michie asked us if we would like to help run monthly family services in the church. This led to growth in the fellowship and, through time, we decided to reduce our links with Jesmond and concentrate on the work in Bedlington.

Within the school, I tried to have a Christian input. I ran sixth form assemblies every week, which aimed to assist students studying for "A" levels and applying for university, but where I also tried to include a spiritual input. We also had Tuesday afternoon talks with outside speakers on a range of subjects. I was able to include Christian speakers such as David Holloway on the Resurrection and local evangelist, David Glover, on the meaning of Christmas. There was a school Christian Union at which I occasionally helped. It was led by Dot Lee, a vivacious, highly imaginative teacher of physical education. Dot's clear Christian commitment and desire to help young people were outstanding and I know that she had a great influence on some of my sixth formers. Dot later became the north-east schools' worker for Scripture Union and I was a member of her support group. She would subsequently play a vital role in my own school as I searched for someone to lead the religious studies department.

I grew in my leadership and management strengths as head of sixth form under the guidance of Angus and his deputy, who would later become acting head, Mike Peck. Both of them were very approachable men and we were all on Christian name terms, which was not something I had been used to, as Brian Stevens, my first head, ran a well organised school but he tended to be rather distant from both staff and students. I did, however, learn from each of them and would mould my own style bearing in mind the strengths and weaknesses of the styles displayed around me. Angus, for example, was very forward-thinking, but he did tend to be out of school on many occasions attending conferences and sitting on national committees. I took the lesson for my own headship that I needed to have a presence around the site.

---

21 *The Church of England, Where is it Going?;* David Holloway; Kingsway Publications (1985); page 19.

After over three years as head of sixth form, I felt that I now wanted to try to obtain a deputy headship in preparation for taking on the headship of my own school. I applied for and obtained the post of deputy headteacher of another high school in Northumberland, this time in Alnwick, starting in January 1989. Again, it was a gruelling interview against some very capable, well-qualified, experienced practitioners. The headteacher was Roy Todd, a man who cared passionately about the welfare of his staff and students. Indeed, he probably knew most of his students by name! Being very hands-on with the students, he trusted his deputies to ensure that the school was well organised with everything running smoothly. This was a tremendous experience for me, especially with the introduction of the National Curriculum and the Local Management of Schools as a result of the 1988 Education Reform Act.

There were personnel challenges within the school as it was not a very united or forward-looking staff. The school had been the last school in Northumberland to go comprehensive and, indeed, had gone there shouting and screaming. The staff were made up of former boys' grammar school staff, former girls' grammar school staff and former secondary modern school staff. Colleagues were pleasant enough, but many held on to a lot of baggage from their previous school. In many cases, it was hard to get them to plan seriously for what was coming next. It took a lot of change management skills to get people to adapt their teaching styles and to try new approaches. Change did happen, however, partly through certain people moving on to be replaced by younger, more dynamic colleagues. Certainly, it was a happier, more united and more dynamic staff that I left in 1993 than I found in 1989.

There was a veneer of Christianity within the school, with lots of the staff being church members. Roy ensured that there was a Bible reading in each of the assemblies that he took. Kenneth, a youth worker from the New Life Church in Alnwick, helped to take Christian Union meetings each week and I encouraged him in this. If there were special youth speakers coming to the church, we would often get them to come into school religious studies classes or assemblies. Perhaps most notable was Steve Legg, the Christian escapologist who freed himself from chains at the top of a crane in the school playing field!

Interview for Headship, May 1993

I enjoyed my time in Alnwick. In 1989 we had moved to Morpeth to be a bit closer to the school while maintaining our ties with Bedlington. The journey to Alnwick was a lovely start to the day, and I had unique views from the classroom I taught in, seeing Alnwick Castle out of the front window and the Cheviot hills out of the back from the top floor of the nineteenth century Bailiffgate annexe. By 1993, however, it did seem time to seek the possibility of a headship.

An opportunity arose when the post of headship of an inner-city comprehensive in North Tyneside was advertised. Some people said that it could not have been more different from Alnwick, although I would retort that they had not seen Alnwick on a Saturday night.

I knew John Burn, the outgoing head and a fine Christian, and indeed I had invited him to preach at Bedlington on at least one occasion. Early in 1993, we had the chance to chat at a National Curriculum Council conference which he was hosting and I told him that Emmanuel College in Gateshead (one of the first City Technology Colleges to be established and which had a Christian foundation) was looking for a new principal, and that he would be ideal for it. He said that he was too busy, but, despite that, he did subsequently seek interview and was duly appointed to the post at Emmanuel.

I applied for John's post and was invited to a three-day interview at the school. This was the most difficult of the very few interviews that I had had. The field was very strong and I was probably the youngest of the eight candidates who were interviewed. Governors were very exacting in their interrogation of the candidates and were certainly not satisfied with vague answers.

John was not involved at all in the process, but we did have a brief chat on the second morning of the interview, when he reminded me of the conversation that we had had at the conference some weeks before. At that point, I got an absolute assurance from God that this was where he wanted me to be and that I would be appointed to the post. Although I still had two days of interviews left, I knew that the outcome was very much in God's hands. Sure enough, I was appointed to the post, and that evening I took the boys to St James' Park to celebrate, by watching Newcastle United defeat Oxford United, not that I took in much about the game that evening! I learned later that there was a school prayer group that had been praying for a Christian head to be appointed to replace John Burn; they were overjoyed that their prayers had been answered.

Throughout all of these career moves, I was sure of being in the right place at the right time, all according to God's purposes. I was conscious that if I had success in interviews (and indeed in my university examinations), it was all due to God's grace, and not because of particularly clever answers to questions I was asked. God had mapped out a career path for me to follow and step by step I had to follow his calling.

The apostle Paul wrote,

> *For it is by grace that you have been saved, through faith – and this not from yourselves, it is the gift of God – not by works, so that no man can boast. For we are God's workmanship, created in Christ Jesus to do good works, which God prepared in advance for us to do.*[22]

We cannot earn our own salvation by our good works and so we have nothing to boast about. We do not deserve God's mercy, but he pours it on us regardless. We do, however, have a lifetime of works ahead. God moulds us by his grace and enables us to do the works that he has called us to do. I would experience something of that grace in the twenty-one years that lay ahead in headship.

---

[22] Ephesians 2:9-10.

CHAPTER THREE

The Purpose of Education

Daniel is an amazing Old Testament character, a man of God with no recorded flaw, living out his life in exile in the high circles of the Babylonian court, far from his native Judah. He was without doubt a man of prayer who was prepared to co-operate with his new masters but not compromise his beliefs in the living God and the standards that God expected of him. He was prepared to point out the sin of kings Nebuchadnezzar and Belshazzar through his God-given ability to interpret dreams and visions, and he was brave enough to face the king's lions rather than give up his prayer regime that was fundamental to his walk with God. Undoubtedly he is a role model for our times.[23]

Likewise, his three friends, Shadrach, Meshach and Abednego (to use their better-known Babylonian names), refused to bow down and worship the image of gold that Nebuchadnezzar had set up, even though the threat for defiance was being thrown into a fiery furnace. They expressed their view by saying to the king,

> If we are thrown into the blazing furnace, the God we serve is able to save us from it, and he will rescue us from your hand, O king. But even if he does not, we want you to know, O king, that we will not serve your gods or worship the image of gold you have set up.[24]

---

[23] Daniel 1-6 provides a thrilling read.
[24] Daniel 3:17-18.

The three brave men were thrown into the furnace, but amazingly they were not harmed by the fire at all, and even more amazingly there seemed to be a fourth man walking in the furnace with them who was perhaps an angel or even the Son of God himself sustaining them. As a result, they were able to come out of the furnace without "a hair of their heads singed"[25].

The whole story, however, starts with the education that the four men received at the Babylonian court in their youth. They received an intensive curriculum of Babylonian language and literature over three years to prepare them for entry into the king's service. Of course they could have rebelled and refused to take part in learning about this alien culture, but they co-operated and ended up doing exceptionally well. As such, they were following the Lord's instruction as passed on by the prophet Jeremiah in a letter to the exiles,

> *Also, seek the peace and prosperity of the city to which I have carried you into exile. Pray to the Lord for it, because if it prospers, you too will prosper.*[26]

There was one area, however, over which Daniel resolved in his heart that he would not compromise, and that was over his diet. Rather than taking food and wine from the king's table, he wanted simply vegetables and water as a healthy diet that would comply with Jewish food regulations. This was a brave request to make, as it could be interpreted as an act of defiance against the king, and certainly, Ashpenaz, the chief court official, feared that he would lose his own head if the king found out. The guard over them, however, agreed to a ten-day test and, unsurprisingly, at the end of the ten days, the four young Jewish men looked far healthier than those who ate the royal food. They followed this diet over the next three years of their training, and their education was highly successful:

> *To these four young men God gave knowledge and understanding of all kinds of literature and learning. And Daniel could understand visions and dreams of all kinds.*[27]

---

[25] Daniel 3:27.

[26] Jeremiah 29:7.

[27] Daniel 1:17.

Furthermore,

> *In every matter of wisdom and understanding about which the king questioned them, he found them ten times better than all the magicians and enchanters in the whole kingdom.*[28]

I have always found the stories of Daniel and his friends inspiring, and have used them in a number of school assemblies. The story of their education is, however, fundamental to both their future wellbeing and that of their community. Perhaps the influence of these four men would have been much less and the miracles that took place in their lives might not have happened had they not shown resolve over eating the defiled food.

How does this relate to education today and my experience of twenty-one years of headship? First of all, education is vital, and plays a significant role in the "prosperity of the city" as Jeremiah wrote in his letter. This prosperity, I am sure, does not simply relate to economic growth and development, but rather to the whole spiritual and moral fibre of the community.

Secondly, what is taught, in other words the curriculum, has to be appropriate to meet the needs of those receiving it. Daniel and his friends were going to be used by God through high office in Babylonian society, and so the education they received, as heathen as we might think that it is, was what God wanted them to have as young men at the Babylonian court. Furthermore, they were chosen specially for it, indicating that although there has to be a basic curriculum for all, the curriculum should be tailored to meet the specific needs, talents and abilities of different young people.

Thirdly, how things are learned is also key to educational success. We have no idea from the chapter about Babylonian teaching and learning strategies, but I am greatly impressed that the guard in the story was willing to give the young men a degree of freedom and try a little bit of educational research. We who know so much more about how young people learn need to ensure that the right conditions for learning are in place and that the most appropriate learning strategies are adopted.

---

[28] Daniel 1:20.

Fourthly, the attitudes of the four Jewish young men were excellent, and were a key factor in their success. They were acting out of obedience to God and so wanted to learn to please and honour their Lord. Sadly, the attitudes of so many of our young people today are not so positive, with many of them unwilling to try new things, too prepared to give up at the first difficulty or simply not prepared to put effort in. On the other hand, I have seen young people inspired by amazing teachers to try things that they would have otherwise have thought to be too difficult or beyond their grasp. There is much work to be done in developing the attitudes and mindsets of our young people, including those who may seem to be initially successful but whose mindset cannot then cope with later setbacks. Of course, this includes teaching them the ways of the Lord, so that they know who it is they are ultimately serving.

Fifthly, we need to consider the outcomes of the education process. Daniel and his friends clearly obtained top marks and went on to achieve success in the land in which they were placed. Their characters would also be developed, preparing them for the trials that lay ahead. They were able people, but it was very much God who brought them through their education with academic success, and directly helped them as they made their stand for him in different situations. We have to pray that our young people will not only have examination success but will also turn into the men and women that God wants them to be for his glory and the good of their communities.

Your Vision and How You Put It into Practice

We need therefore to find the purpose of education for our day. As a head, when I interviewed candidates for appointment to promoted posts, I would almost always ask candidates the question, "What is your vision for the young people that you teach and how do you put that vision into practice?" There was a range of answers put forward by different candidates.

Some would talk about acquiring subject knowledge and skills with a view to doing well in examinations. Presumably for Daniel and his friends, this was the core of their curriculum, and for our students it is only right that they should develop appropriate subject knowledge and skills. There is of course always debate as to the balance between knowledge and skills. When I was at school as a pupil, history was very much content-based, where an excellent memory was required, and so it was a bit of a shock in my first year of teaching to teach a completely skills-based course following the Schools' Council History Project. There is now a more balanced approach by teaching skills through chronologically based content, although in history, perhaps more than most other subjects, there has been political interference over what that content should be.

Therefore, a key question for educators is what content should be covered. I do, however, prefer the Canadian educationalist John Novak's approach based on the work of Howard Gardner, where he talks about "uncovering" rather than "covering" material by "starting with students' present perceptions and connecting them to the logic and understanding of disciplinary experts". He also talks about "savouring" subject material which encourages students to appreciate the material in all its fullness.[29]

Other candidates in their answer to the question would talk about learning for employability and skills for life. The role and status of vocational education has been a contentious issue since the nineteenth century, it being viewed by many as very second class. This has not been helped by the poor quality of some vocational qualifications offered by schools, often with the aim of obtaining easy league table wins rather than preparing young people for future high quality careers. Professor Alison Wolf's 2011 report rightly lambasted much of what was provided for school students through statements such as "too many of our young people are being short-changed" and "large numbers of young people take vocational qualifications which the labour market does not reward in any way".[30]

There does, however, have to be a place for high quality vocational education. Although the American Christian educational philosopher Gordon Clark decried the role of vocational education as simply not appropriate for the curriculum,[31] from a biblical point of view it can be argued that there should be a strong place for a vocational curriculum. Timothy Keller argues in his book "Every Good Endeavour" that

---

[29] *Inviting Educational Leadership;* John M Novak; Pearson Education (2002): page 100.

[30] *Review of Vocational Education: the Wolf Report;* Department for Education (2011); page 44.

[31] *A Christian Philosophy of Education;* Gordon H Clark; The Trinity Foundation (1988): page 140.

because God has commanded us to "subdue the earth"[32], thus continuing God's creation process, we are expected to be involved in "rearranging the raw material of God's world in such a way that it helps the world in general, and people in particular, thrive and flourish."[33] The creation ordinance mandates high quality vocational education involving both our heads and our hands.

Coming back to the interview question, other candidates would talk about the qualities we would want to inculcate in our young people and the values we would want them to hold. Certainly, we would want to have our young people leave our schools with qualities such as persistence, resilience, loyalty, respect and a willingness to serve others. From a Christian point of view we would undoubtedly ideally want them to be God-honouring with a desire to serve him.

The British government currently[34] requires that schools in England actively promote fundamental British values as part of its "Prevent" strategy of countering terrorism, and has issued guidance to schools to assist them in doing so.[35] These values include promoting democracy, the rule of law, individual liberty and the mutual respect for those with different faiths and beliefs. At first sight, these values seem to be well worth promoting, and hard to argue against. They have, however, caused considerable controversy. Why are they uniquely British, and, for example, how would they be recognised if the Scottish referendum had yielded a different result in the autumn of 2014? The relatively moderate teachers' professional association, the Association of Teachers and Lecturers, passed a motion at their annual conference in March 2015 saying that the government's drive on British values was a "knee-jerk national policy 'solution' to localised governance issues" which risked "becoming the source of wider conflict rather than a means of resolving it".[36]

This presumably is referring to the fact that the then Education Secretary, Michael Gove, gave the British values instruction to schools as a result of the "Trojan Horse" investigations into certain

---

[32] Genesis 1:28.
[33] *Every Good Endeavour;* Timothy Keller; Hodder and Stoughton (2014); page 59.
[34] in 2017
[35] *Promoting Fundamental British Values as part of SMSC in schools;* Department for Education (November 2014).
[36] *Association of Teachers and Lecturers' Conference 2015,* motion 12.

Birmingham schools where there had been extremist Muslim infiltration on to some governing bodies. Professor David Starkey referred to the "utter banality" of them at the 100 Group conference in January 2015, arguing that values were intangible, would change over time and so could not be contained in a list.[37]

The debate over fundamental British values had more than mere academic implications, as accountability for promoting these values was, as always, to be verified by Ofsted. In late November 2014, four schools with a Christian ethos in the north-east of England were each given a no-notice safeguarding inspection looking at the promotion of fundamental British values, the implication being that their particular ethos would militate against the promotion of these values through Christian indoctrination.

On the second morning of these inspections, I remember sitting at the North Tyneside high school heads' meeting where there was discussion about how to prepare for Ofsted inspections, including having evidence that we were actively promoting these values. I reported to the group about the inspection of these schools from inside information that I had and said that the process seemed so unjust and that innocent people would be hurt. I also mentioned that the assembly that I had taken that morning would probably have been condemned as being too Christian, whereas a similar assembly I had done during our May 2012 Ofsted inspection was highly praised by the inspector who observed it. At the school prayer meeting the previous evening, I reported the same thing and we prayed that God's protection would be on these schools and also of course on our own school.

The outcome was rather frightening: two of the schools retained their previous Ofsted judgement, but found it to be a torrid experience, and the other two went into special measures with one of them being forced to close. There was a lot of intrusive questioning of the students reported, particularly with regard to matters of sexuality, along with their views of religions other than Christianity. Although there were other issues of concern at the two schools that failed their inspections, it was evident that both schools had been very harshly treated over British

---

[37] A helpful summary of that particular conference can be found in the headteacher's blog on Bede's school website.
http://www.bedes.org/senior-school/news-and-blogs/the-headmasters-blog/1/2015/02/values,-british-values,-and-educational-tensions.aspx

values. As mentioned in chapter one, one of my last tasks at my school before I retired was to rewrite the school mission statement so that reference was made to the promotion of British values. This would allow staff to follow a consistent line when Ofsted arrived and thus hopefully prevent the school from going the same way as the two unfortunate schools that failed their inspections.

A Christian Approach

All of the above answers given by candidates are of course correct, but our vision must have all of them working together, so that education develops subject knowledge and skills for learning, work and life in general, and the qualities and values that will allow young people to make a positive contribution to society.

For a Christian educator, this will mean endeavouring to ensure that young people have an understanding and appreciation of God's creation and his purposes, and how they may further his creative purposes in their stewardship of the earth and contributing to the wellbeing of others. It will mean seeking after truth with an understanding that the Lord Jesus Christ is the embodiment of that truth. Ultimately we would want our young people to be imbued with not simply knowledge and skills, but godly wisdom. The book of Proverbs encourages young people to desire this wisdom from the Lord: for example, in chapter 2, a father encourages his son to turn his ear to wisdom that comes from the Lord and which will enter his heart and keep him on the right path. We want our young people to find Christ,

> ...in whom are hidden all the treasures of wisdom and knowledge.[38]

Gordon Clark, the American Christian educational philosopher quoted earlier, sees it as imperative that we have a Christian theistic world view to guide our education system. He states,

> What is needed is an educational system based on the sovereignty of God, for in such a system, man as well as chemistry will be given his proper place, neither too high nor too low. ... In such a system, God, as well as man, will have his proper place. This alone will make education successful,

---

[38] Colossians 2:3.

*for the social, moral, political and economic disintegration of
a civilisation is nothing other than the symptom and result of
a religious breakdown.*[39]

We can clearly see that we are far away from having such an
educational system in the United Kingdom, and we can see so much
evidence for the disintegration of our society round about us. Some
might argue for a neutral approach, but Luc Bussiere at a conference in
Newcastle in June 2015 said,

*Education never takes place in a moral or philosophical
vacuum. If the larger questions about human beings and
their destiny are not being answered within a predominantly
Judaeo-Christian framework, they will be addressed from
within another philosophical or religious framework – but
not one that is neutral.*[40]

We may not have a system based on the Christian world view such
as Clark and Bussiere have been propounding, but we do have elements
of it within the United Kingdom through the establishment of faith
schools, the legal requirements to hold acts of collective worship and
teach religious education within a Christian framework (albeit they are
poorly observed), and the freedom of Christian teachers to share their
faith through Christian Unions or simply in classroom conversations.
We must hold on to what we have, however, as there are dangerous
elements at work trying to take these freedoms away. For example, in
June 2015, Charles Clarke, former Secretary of State for Education, and
Professor Linda Woodhead of Lancaster University published a report
recommending the abolition of the daily act of collective worship and
the adoption of a national syllabus for renamed religious and moral
education that would no longer be fundamentally Christian. The
recommendations in the report would also weaken the standing of faith
schools.[41] If Christians are not careful, the legislative backing of the

---

[39] Gordon H Clark; op. cit.; page 21.

[40] Luc Bussiere founder of a French Christian schools network was the speaker
at a conference on *Schools, the Battlefield for Worldviews* on June 13th,
2015 at Elswick Parish Church in Newcastle upon Tyne.

[41] *A New Settlement: Religion and Belief in Schools;* Charles Clarke and Linda
Woodhead; Westminster Faith Debates (2015).

place of Christianity in schools underpinned by the 1944 Education Act and the 1988 Education Reform Act may be reversed.

What of British values? Of course, we used to talk about promoting Christian values in our schools and there was at the time of the 1944 Education Act a general consensus that this was a right and proper thing to do. With increased secularism and pluralism in our society, this consensus based on a Judaeo-Christian framework is not nearly as strong. In the light of concern over the inspection of four Christian schools in the north-east of England, David Holloway, the vicar of Jesmond Parish Church, convened a conference in February 2015 to look at the British values in the light of Christian tradition in this country. I was fortunate to be invited to attend this conference along with others with an educational background. A statement was produced at the end of the conference adding the need for "the pursuit of truth" and "the Christian tradition" as fundamental values.[42]

Clearly without the pursuit of truth and the Christian tradition, there is a danger that the promotion of British values will not have the desired effect, and may even have a perverse effect. Democratic ideals, for example, may seem right to pursue, but just because a majority propound a particular view or elect a particular government, it does not mean that that majority is right.[43] After all, who is to say that the majority has the mind of God on a particular issue? Bad laws may be passed, and individual liberty without a sense of responsibility will lead to anarchy.

The School's Curriculum

How does all of this translate into a school's curriculum? Our curriculum changed over the years in response to different needs, including changes to the National Curriculum, league table pressures and a changed realisation as to the needs of our young people for their lives in the twenty-first century.

In many ways, our curriculum was quite traditional. In various statements produced, I would use words like "broad" to ensure that all

---

[42] The Jesmond Conference statement can be found on www.church.org.uk.
[43] Matthew Parris in *The Times* on March 12th, 2016 expressed concern about the state of democracy in Europe with the growth of far right parties standing on an anti-immigration platform or an extreme left party in Greece on an anti-austerity platform.

students would have a range of learning experiences across a range of different subjects, or "relevant" so that the curriculum met the current and perceived future needs of our students, including having a vocational experience, ideally out in the workplace. The curriculum was "differentiated" to allow each individual student to access the curriculum at their own particular level. Progression had to be incorporated so that students were able to build on previous experience to move on to higher order experiences, including taking the next steps to further education or work elsewhere. The curriculum needed to be "flexible" so that it was able to respond to meet the changing needs of individual students; for example, in 2008, mid-course we changed the science pathway that certain groups were taking from a traditional GCSE course to a vocational science course in which the students would have a greater chance of success. There also needed to be a degree of "student-centredness" within the curriculum to allow students to take more charge of their own learning so that, with guidance, they could "uncover" material, as Novak would recommend.

The curriculum should also be "coherent" so that it is not simply a plethora of unrelated subjects that are being studied, but rather coherent links are made to allow students to see their learning as a whole. This of course does not necessarily mean that subjects should be combined, and I resisted any attempt to combine, for example, religious studies with history and geography, but rather links should be created across subjects. Staff tried to create these links through joint projects involving problem solving, enquiry based learning or having projects with common themes. An example involving religious studies and history with Year 8 classes, including one which I taught, was to have the students investigate sources and answer the question, "Did Christianity hinder or help the slave trade?" Sometimes the timetable was suspended for a day or longer to allow students to be immersed in projects without the tyranny of the period bell getting in the way.

We also tried to develop students' attitudes, skills and knowledge using our ASK[44] programme across the curriculum with staff focusing on key words such as "resilience" and "perseverance" through subject content. Coherence also came about through promoting the students' spiritual, moral, social and cultural development by means of the assembly programme, cross-curricular themes and in extracurricular

---

[44] Attitudes, Skills, Knowledge.

activities which provided for students a wide-ranging set of experiences that helped to shape their attitudes and develop skills.

Finally, but perhaps most importantly, Christian values and the spiritual dimension need to have a key place in the curriculum. Ideally they should permeate the curriculum so that students understand the nature of God's creation and his purposes across all subjects. For example, the intricacies of God's creation can be seen in chemical bonding, and history is really "His story". When a school like ours does not have a Christian foundation, however, it is very difficult to have a consistent theological approach across the curriculum. In that situation, it is very much up to the individual teacher as to whether they can present specific Christian values in their lessons. Where, however, there is clear Christian leadership within the school, there is more chance that these values will come down from the top, for example, through assemblies, and into individual lessons. Therefore, as we shall explore in more detail in chapter seven, the role of assemblies and religious studies within the curriculum is crucial.

External Pressures

Whatever curriculum pathways a school offers its students, it has of course to be mindful of pressures from external sources, particularly the Department for Education. There are statutory requirements as to what should be taught through the imposition of the National Curriculum introduced in the 1988 Education Reform Act and modified thereafter. The original National Curriculum Programmes of Study for each subject were contained in large folders, outlining the content that should be taught from ages five to sixteen. Science, for example, had seventeen attainment targets for students to reach, although they were later reduced to four. I had always felt that there should be a national curriculum of some form or other, as in the 1960s and 70s there had been too much of a free for all, resulting in many students missing out on elements of the core curriculum. The large folders introduced, however, were an overreaction, as they were too detailed and unworkable. We have now, thirty years later, a more manageable curriculum, although, as usual, the speed expected for its implementation has put large pressures on schools. It is also ironic that the National Curriculum does not have to be taught in academies or free schools, which now account for well over half of all secondary schools in England, a figure which is likely to increase.

There is, however, another powerful influence on what is taught in secondary schools, particularly from age fourteen upwards, and that is where schools might end up in local league tables.

Part of the excitement of supporting a football team is seeing in which position it will end up in its league table. The second half of the 2014-15 season was excruciatingly painful for Newcastle United supporters as the team seemed to hurtle down the table at a rate of knots and was all set for relegation, only to be saved from that fate in the very last match of the season. The 2015-16 season ended up even more painful as the once proud club was relegated into the Championship, despite Rafael Benitez being brought in to try to save them. Much has been written and said about Newcastle's fall, but perhaps Newcastle United head coach, John Carver, summed it up best when he wrote in his last set of programme notes in May 2015,

...unfortunately the table doesn't lie and for the most part we haven't been good enough.[45]

A football team's league table position is very straightforward, with the table not lying, but a school's position in its league table is much more complex. There are so many performance indicators to consider, and there is an obvious bias in some of the indicators favouring schools that have more able cohorts and who can reach much higher standards of attainment. Although schools have to be accountable, and parents need to have information to make rational choices in order to decide to which school they should send their children, schools are much more than a collection of performance indicators; they are living communities, each with its own special ethos, and indeed that is how I always tried to view our school.

Nevertheless, schools do take their league table positions very seriously. Although I might try to take a more elevated view as to the purpose of education, it was always exciting seeing where the school would end up as the first tentative league tables were put together after results came out in August. In most years, we would be in the middle of the North Tyneside league table, which was a fair position, given the ability profile of our cohort. In some years, however, we would be

---

[45] Newcastle United match programme, 24th May, 2015.

ecstatic because we had reached the top three or four for either GCSE or "A" level. For example, in January 2006, I was over the moon when our son Stephen showed me an article in "The Independent" newspaper which placed us 44th out of all comprehensive schools in the country for "A" level results.[46] There were, however, other years when we were despondent because we had not done as well as our close neighbours or schools with a similar profile. League tables matter to schools because the position they end up in affects how they are perceived by some parents in the market for school places, which has financial implications, something that we shall consider in more detail in chapter ten. They can, however, also be a source of false pride, which I could be guilty of displaying in our good years, forgetting as I did that any success came through God's grace.

Many schools became very adept at manipulating their league table positions by choosing carefully the qualifications taken by their students. Sometimes this was done in the best interests of their students so that they would end up with more chance of success, but it was also likely to be the case that it was a mechanism to push their school up the local league table. Although I did not play this game as much as others did, I did on occasion go down this route. The earliest example which we adopted was GNVQ IT, originally a post-16 qualification, but one which ended up in the Key Stage 4 curriculum of many schools. For a few years we put almost the whole cohort in for this qualification, with most of the students achieving the equivalent of four GCSE grades C or above, but not requiring anything like the teaching time of four GCSEs. This propelled us up the league table and gave students a useful qualification, as well as giving the school great self-confidence that we could achieve excellent results. This qualification was later withdrawn by awarding bodies, and nothing quite replaced it that was so accessible and useful to large numbers of students.

Other qualifications came on stream that were adopted by schools and that gave them good league table points. This included various vocational qualifications each worth at least two GCSE qualifications, but some were of dubious validity. Schools were also making multiple entries for their students in GCSE mathematics with different examination boards and at different sittings until students finally struck lucky and achieved a grade C. This was tremendous for these students,

---

[46] *The Independent* (19th January, 2006).

as they got a grade C in maths, which was so necessary for their future careers, but I really doubted the depth of mathematical understanding as it just seemed to be an examination game that schools were playing. For that reason, we were slower than other schools in following this approach, and indeed we were criticised by Ofsted in 2012 for not bringing about curriculum change quickly enough.

In the summer of 2011, we did, however, feel that we had to adopt a more flexible curriculum, as our examination results were disappointing compared with other local and similar schools. In the marketplace and in the eyes of Ofsted, it seemed that we were being left behind. Therefore, we changed the curriculum diet of some of our students in their final GCSE year. Some were taken out of more academic courses where they were not performing well and moved to various online courses, in which they ended up having more success. GCSE photography provided phenomenal results for some of our less able students. Some did an intensive four-day practical course with an outside body, which gave them a Wider Key Skills qualification worth two GCSE B grades. We also applied the maths trick, thus ending up with our best set of GCSE maths results. The net effect was that in 2012 we achieved a massive 69% of students with 5 or more A* to C grades with English and maths, and were placed third highest in the local league table. This was a tremendous achievement, and very much an answer to prayer.

Needless to say, the government changed the rules so that some of these vocational qualifications would no longer count for as many GCSE equivalences, and some did not count at all. Likewise, the government moved away from modular exams to linear exams and stopped multiple entries, only allowing the first to count in league tables. Indeed, the rule of only counting first entry was announced by Michael Gove on the eve of the Conservative Party conference in September 2013. Schools up and down the country were apoplectic over the nature and timing of the announcement, coming at a time when they had decided to enter their students for GCSE English and maths in the November examination season, giving them the opportunity to resit in June. As a result, because lower results in November would penalise them in the league tables, many schools withdrew their students from these examinations. We decided, however, to maintain our original policy of entering all of our Year 11 students for English and most of our students for maths; this decision was taken on moral grounds as we were preparing our students for these exams, and it was in their best interests to give them the opportunity of two sittings, even although it was risky in terms of our league table position. As it turned out, the students did not do as well in November as we had hoped, with disastrous effects on our league table standing. Knowing that outcome, would we have done differently? That is a good question, but the students nonetheless did respect us for sticking to our original decision, having their best interests at heart.

Governments have also learned to manipulate the league tables to achieve their desired ends. For example, Mr Gove was keen that more (if not all) students should study a modern foreign language and either history or geography in Key Stage 4. Rather than making it statutory for these subjects to be studied, the power of the league table was used and a new composite qualification was introduced in 2012 called the English Baccalaureate including a modern foreign language and either history or geography. This was taken further with the introduction of a new accountability measure for 2016 onwards called Progress 8, which required as many students as possible to take these particular subjects to maximise progress point scores. As a result, many schools including ours encouraged students to take "Ebac" subjects. Thus the government's objective was reached without the need for statutory change.[47]

Teaching and Learning

As well as considering what subjects should be taught, I have always thought it vital that we adopt teaching and learning strategies that fully engage our young people and give them a zeal for learning. From my earliest days in the profession, I tried to make economics, dubbed "the dismal science", as interesting as possible by fully involving the students in their learning through games, simulations, research surveys and interactive worksheets that would enable them to build up their understanding of economic theory and its real-life applications. There was a place for didactic teaching, but I tried to minimise its use, along with copying notes from textbooks or from the board. Much later as a

---

[47] For a humorous account of how governments use key performance indicators to achieve their ends, and how schools try to manipulate league tables, see *Brave Heads;* Dave Harris; Independent Thinking Press (2012), especially the chapter on *Brave Politics.*

head, I still did a little bit of teaching, so that I could continue to relate to students in the classroom and keep up to date with best pedagogical practice. I was very conscious, however, that I had been left behind by the many highly effective teachers who surrounded me and who used very imaginative strategies to engage their students in their learning; I learned so much from them.

Particularly through the work of Professor John West-Burnham, I became increasingly aware of how learning may be categorised with a move from shallow to deep learning.[48] He considers shallow learning to be:

- an increase in knowledge;
- memorising; and
- acquisition of facts, to be retained and used when necessary.

I can relate to the above three in terms of much of my own learning at school when learning was rather superficial with the aim of getting through examinations. Sadly, I can also see many more recent examples of the above approach in my own and others' teaching. Increasingly deep learning would include:

- the abstraction of meaning, whereby students can derive genuine understanding of ideas, concepts and issues, often from a number of sources;
- an interpretative process aimed at understanding reality, whereby students can apply their understanding to new situations; and
- changing as a person as a result of learning.

It is this increasingly deep learning that I very much wanted students to experience, and I shared these ideas with leaders across the school at our Leadership Retreat Days in the mid 2000s.

At the same time as I was thinking about deep learning, I began to consider the possibility of ICT as a vehicle for developing this desired deep learning. ICT had been well developed at the school for standard work-related purposes, as the success of the GNVQ IT courses mentioned above demonstrated. Could we take things further so that e-

---

[48] See for example, *Effective Learning in Schools;* Christopher Bowring-Carr and John West-Burnham; *Financial Times;* Pitman Publishing (1997); page 76.

learning would be used to develop deep learning in our students? Was it possible to integrate technology into learning in a natural way so that our students could uncover new material, contact experts in their fields, solve real-life problems and be part of the global learning community with no barriers to learning?[49]

This was the learning journey that the school embarked on in the last ten or so years of my time in the school. Mark Elliott was appointed assistant headteacher with responsibility for E-learning and we invested large sums into our network and hardware, including our iPads for Learning scheme, which would hopefully ultimately enable all of our students to make use of mobile devices in lessons. There was of course a constant job to be done to ensure that students applied digital literacy skills so that they did not simply copy large chunks of material from the internet into their presentations, in the same way that previous generations copied from an encyclopaedia. This is an ongoing journey.

Conclusion

This has been a long chapter, and we have covered a lot of ground. We started with Daniel and how he excelled academically and how he was moulded into the man God wanted him to be through the education he received.

We must pray for our young people that God will do the same for them. As I look back, perhaps I have not prayed enough for examination success for our students. I have, however, seen God answer prayer over specific examinations. In November 2014, all of our Year 11 students sat their IGCSE English language examination. They had done a lot of work in preparation for that examination, and indeed I personally had helped to provide support for them. In the assembly immediately prior to the examination, I gave them some final advice and then prayed for them that they would be calm, that they would remember all the techniques they had learned and that they would do well. The results they achieved were excellent, and, I believe, were an answer to prayer.

---

[49] I am so grateful for the work of Alan November, for example, his course companion, *Empowering Students with Technology;* Skylight Professional Development (2001), for guiding me in my thinking about the power of e-learning.

I have also prayed for the students to be changed as people by the learning that they experienced in the school (in line with West-Burnham's final deep learning category). Seeing so many lovely young people come out at the other end of the process, I believe that God has answered and will continue to answer that prayer.

CHAPTER FOUR

Behaviour and Care

I always enjoyed taking prospective parents round the school, as it was an opportunity to show them what a calm, happy school it was, with learning and respect at the centre. Parents were always impressed, although some wondered where the naughty pupils had been hidden, as often their concept of a comprehensive school, particularly one taking young people from a council estate with a bit of a reputation, was one of unruly classes with teachers not able to control the pupils. Excellent behaviour, which means having engaged and not simply compliant students, is so important for effective learning, something which parents will expect to see. It is, however, also important in ensuring that the young people understand and apply God's standards of respect for other people and property.

Biblical Principles

Our starting point in looking at behaviour is that of inclusion, as seen in the concept given to us in the first book of the Bible, namely, that God has created us in his own image and as male and female.[50] This is tremendous when we reflect on it: we have amazing potential as human beings because we have all been created in the image of God. This includes creative potential, as we saw in the previous chapter when we considered God's command to subdue the earth.

This starting point has always had for me certain important implications in leading a school. Firstly, as educators, we need to maximise the creative potential of our young people so that they end up

---

[50] Genesis 1:27.

creating things that they never thought possible. Certainly, when I consider what our young people were able to create under the guidance of gifted teachers in areas such as music, drama, art, creative writing, design technology, gymnastics and dance, I am overwhelmed by the God-given talent that they were able to display. Likewise, the reasoning powers of our young people as shown in mathematics, science and analytical writing reflect, albeit in tiny ways, the reasoning powers of Almighty God. The importance of developing students' communication skills reflects the fact that we have a God who communicates with his creation.

Secondly, schools should be inclusive because *all* of us are created in God's image, and all need to have our potential maximised. For me, this has always been a strong argument in favour of comprehensive education, so that students of all abilities, both male and female, should be part of the same learning community, although within that community they may go down different learning pathways. This is not an argument that students of all abilities should be taught in the same classes or, that beyond an agreed core curriculum, they should all take the same courses; rather, there should be a differentiated curriculum with flexibility between pathways to allow crossover to take place.

Thirdly, taking the comprehensive ethos further, we need as far as possible to integrate students who have a variety of special educational needs and disabilities within the learning community. This may not be possible within the one school for the whole spectrum of learning and behavioural needs, but each school needs to make their particular contribution to meet the varying needs of our young people. Our learning support department, under the leadership over time of Dave Clarke, Moira Banks and Ian Little, had a well-deserved reputation and made a significant impact on the lives of students with a range of learning difficulties. In addition, I was pleased, although that pleasure was tinged with some trepidation, that we were commissioned by North Tyneside Council to host a centre for students with autistic spectrum disorder that we called the Melrose Centre. The students in the centre had a range of learning, communication and behavioural difficulties, which meant that they had to have a lot of specialist teaching and support within the centre, but we also tried wherever possible to integrate them into mainstream classes and activities. Indeed, it was a wonderful experience to see the first of the students achieve a GCSE maths qualification and to see them all perform at our Diamond Jubilee

Music Festival at the internationally renowned Sage Music Centre in Gateshead in the summer of 2014.

The Genesis creation story does not of course finish with idyllic life in the Garden of Eden, for as we well know, Adam and Eve disobeyed God, resulting in the Fall of mankind and Adam and Eve being cast out from the garden. That broken relationship with God is the root cause of poor behaviour in our schools and society as a whole, as sin had now entered the world.[51]

In the early 1980s, Philip May wrote a book "Which Way to Teach?", which I found helpful early on in my career. In thinking about behaviour in schools he draws out certain useful lessons from the Fall.[52] The first point that he brings out is that although Eden was a wonderful place in which to live, Adam and Eve still rebelled against God. On many occasions, I have emphasised to staff that if we teach boring lessons, we are bound to create behaviour issues, but the story of Eden suggests that there can still be some challenging behaviour in even the most exciting of lessons. That is because all of us have that tendency to put ourselves at the centre of attention, regardless of what behaviour is expected of us, due to our sinful natures.

Rules are still necessary in exciting lessons. The rules should not, however, be burdensome, and they should be clearly understood by all members of the community. In Eden, Adam knew that he had to look after the garden, implying that there was work before the Fall, but it would be most enjoyable work, and he also knew that there was one tree from which he should not take the fruit. Adam and Eve were also aware of the consequences of not obeying God, and that God would carry out his sanctions if they disobeyed him.

There are obvious lessons here for our behaviour management within schools. We need rules, but not so many that they become a burden to our young people and that they end up not being properly understood and, therefore, disregarded. When we first introduced Behaviour for Learning in the school, we had a system with a set of consequences that was far too complicated and so we had to simplify it to make it more workable. It is important that students understand the rules that are in force, the rationale behind these rules, and the

---

[51] The full account of the Fall is told in Genesis 3.
[52] *Which Way to Teach?*; Philip May; Inter-Varsity Press (1981); with chapter 5 being particularly helpful.

consequences of not following them. It is also important that the sanctions that are set out are enforced; too many teachers have created further problems for themselves by failing to follow through the threats that they have made.

God certainly followed through the sanctions that he had laid down with Adam and Eve. They were forced to leave the garden, and the work they would have to do to survive would be gruelling. Eve would have pain in childbearing. Finally, death would come upon them.

Even that, however, is not the end of the story, as despite all the sin and its consequences that are so evident in Genesis chapter 3, God demonstrated his grace to them; in an amazing way he promised undeserved mercy to humanity in that third chapter of the Old Testament. Eve was told that although childbearing would be painful, she would have a desire for her husband, indicating an intimate love between them.[53] Later she would give thanks to the Lord for helping her bring her firstborn son into the world.[54] Adam was told that although his toil would be painful, it would enable him to produce all the food necessary for his needs.[55] God provided for them further by making garments of skin, thus clothing them.[56] Although humanity had fallen, God was still very much involved in their lives.

Furthermore, when God rebuked the serpent, he hinted at a future spiritual battle between the offspring or seed of the serpent, who can be taken to be Satan, and the offspring or seed of the woman.[57] The apostle Paul saw this latter seed as the Lord Jesus Christ, who, by dying on the cross and rising from the dead, was able once and for all to defeat the power of Satan, sin and death.[58] God's grace was shown to a fallen world through the infinite cost of the sacrifice of his Son on the cross, which would ultimately reverse the actions of Adam and Eve in their rebellion in the garden.

Discipline and grace are seen together in Scripture. In Hebrews chapter 12, the writer asks us to...

---

[53] See Genesis 3:16.
[54] See Genesis 4:1.
[55] See Genesis 3:19.
[56] See Genesis 3:21.
[57] See Genesis 3:15.
[58] See Galatians 3:15-25.

...fix our eyes on Jesus, the author and perfecter of our faith, who for the joy set before him endured the cross, scorning its shame, and sat down at the right hand of the throne of God.[59]

This was God's grace at work, and of course, as a result, God "has seated us with him in the heavenly realms in Christ Jesus"[60]. The writer goes on to explain that discipline in the Christian life is necessary, quoting Proverbs chapter 3:

My son, do not make light of the Lord's discipline, and do not lose heart when he rebukes you, because the Lord disciplines those he loves, and he punishes those he accepts as a son.[61]

He also gives the reason for this discipline; it "produces a harvest of righteousness and peace for those who have been trained by it"[62]. If by God's grace we become his children, we can expect godly discipline to transform us so that we become more like Jesus.

What does all this mean for behaviour management in schools? There has to be a framework for acceptable behaviour that is clear and understood by all, with appropriate sanctions in place when rules are broken. At the same time, there also has to be in place a framework for the care of individuals allowing for forgiveness and restoration, reflecting the grace of God. Balancing the demands of these two frameworks is not easy and tensions can be created. This is inevitable, however, when we consider that we are dealing with young people who will make mistakes as they push at boundaries and as a result need to be corrected, but who also need to be shown deep care, love and forgiveness.

Pastoral Care

One of the consistently great strengths of the school is the quality of care that has been given to the students over the years. This was appreciated by both parents and students, as well as being recognised by Ofsted who said in their 2009 report, "Pastoral care for all students

---

[59] Hebrews 12:2.
[60] Ephesians 2:5.
[61] Hebrews 12:5-6; Proverbs 3:11-12.
[62] Hebrews 12:11.

and support for students with learning difficulties and / or disabilities is outstanding." There was a genuine caring concern for the overall welfare of all students, including the challenging ones, with a strong emphasis on treating them as individuals with their own particular needs. Staff from pastoral leaders to form tutors reflected God's grace and love towards the students in their care (although most would not have put it exactly in those terms).

When I arrived at the school in 1993, I recognised that strong pastoral ethos, but I did think that the actual pastoral structure was crazy. The school was divided into three sections: lower school, covering Years 7, 8 and 9; upper school, covering Years 10 and 11; and sixth form. The head of lower school had one assistant and was responsible for the overall welfare of about four hundred students, as well as all the transition arrangements with the primary schools. The head of upper school also had one assistant and was responsible for about three hundred students, but he was also examinations officer. One of the two deputy headteachers also had as one of his responsibilities the leadership of the sixth form.

New heads, when they come into post, usually look for areas where they can make significant changes, thus making their mark and hopefully improving the running of the school. This was to be one of my areas of change; after all, how could one senior member of staff take responsibility for so many students, albeit with an assistant? How could the immense and diverse needs of so many students be met by so few staff who also had a reasonably heavy teaching commitment? I was keen to introduce a house system, which had been the structure at the heart of all my previous schools, and which I felt might be more workable. There was, however, strong ill-feeling against having a house system, as the school had previously had such a pastoral structure, which had been tainted by rather poor quality heads of house. I took on board these strongly-held sentiments.

Indeed, it was twenty years before we changed the structure, as, despite its apparent clumsiness, it seemed to work. The strength of the system lay in the quality of the leadership of lower school and upper school. Key people inspired staff and students alike and ensured that systems operated. Two of the early holders of these positions were Helen Whitfield and Sandra Belford, both of whom were role models for future pastoral leaders. Helen lived in the community, was a member of the local parish church and was very well known to many families in the area. What amazed me was how well she knew the four hundred students in her care. Students were confident in approaching her with issues, knowing that she would be able to help them, while at the same time she was able to challenge them in terms of their behaviour and academic progress. Helen was very much one of the legends of the school. Sandra was another legend. With her PE background, she had learned how to get alongside young people and was perfect for a pastoral leadership role. She was one of those relatively rare teachers who were absolutely loved by students but who was also known as "Mrs Scary". It was said that students even owned up to things that they had not actually done as a result of her questioning, and even members of staff joked that they too were prepared to own up to crimes committed by students. If there was a problem, students and their parents knew that "Mrs Belford would sort it out".

Others came and took on pastoral leadership responsibility, each learning from Helen and Sandra, but each bringing their own areas of expertise. Paul Quinn, who would much later replace me as head, took on the role of head of upper school after Sandra became deputy headteacher having very successfully led the maths department. As a maths specialist, he brought a greater emphasis on the use of data in tracking students' academic progress. The pastoral leadership team was boosted by having others joining as assistant heads of school and also within the sixth form, which was necessary as it grew in size.

The pastoral structure is a necessary but artificial construct. It is important that there is support for students, but many students will often talk to a teacher whom they know and trust well. For that reason, Christian teachers need to be open to students coming to talk to them. Norman Reid, who had such a big influence on my Christian life, told me that as a Christian teacher he felt that he should always be available for students to come and talk to him on a whole range of issues, including spiritual ones. I have tried to follow that example. It was also good to see students coming to talk to the Christian staff over problems they had or in relation to what had been discussed in class or assemblies.

Support staff also had a role to play within the pastoral system. In 2000, the school became part of the Excellence in Cities programme, which was a government initiative to raise standards in inner city areas. Amongst other things, it introduced learning mentors to schools. These were members of support staff who would work alongside targeted students who were underachieving academically for all sorts of reasons. These members of staff had more time than teachers to talk through the issues that many students faced. Large numbers of students appreciated the help given by the learning mentors and made progress accordingly, giving very positive comments in any evaluation of the scheme.

Mentoring went on in other ways. For a number of years, we were able to mentor all students in Year 11 using certain teaching staff. This was to ensure that students were working towards their target grades in each of their subjects and, if they were not doing so, what action they were taking to get back on track. As part of this programme, each year I would have about a dozen students to mentor, some of whom I would have success with, although with others my intervention was less effective. In addition, we also trained some of our students as peer mentors to work alongside new Year 7 students in their first year within the school, within a special peer mentoring room that was officially opened by Peter Beardsley, former Newcastle United and England star, as well as being an old boy of the school.

Sandra Belford, as deputy headteacher with responsibility for student welfare, decided to retire in 2013. At that point it seemed opportune to review the workings of the pastoral system. The structure involving heads of school had served us well over twenty years, but there was now a feeling that it was time to have a more streamlined approach with year leaders responsible for particular year groups so that there was clearer accountability. Val Short, an experienced curriculum and pastoral leader and with strong Christian integrity, took overall responsibility for student welfare with other members of the team taking on the new posts of year leaders. There was strong pressure from the trade unions to appoint support staff into these posts, as many schools had done. I was convinced, however, that these posts should be taken by members of teaching staff, who would be more effective in leading year groups in assemblies and dealing with academic issues. I was not prepared to have excellent teachers made redundant to bring in cheaper support staff members, who would be much less effective in leading year groups. Although the unions did not agree, I was able to hold my ground over this issue.

Over all these years, care for the students was paramount with the welfare, including the academic welfare, of individual students at the centre of what we stood for. The pastoral system, however, also had a key role to play in behaviour management within the school.

Behaviour for Learning

In the first assembly of each academic year, I would remind the students of the expectations for excellent behaviour, and this would be constantly reinforced as the year went on. In the early years, however, it seemed very much like firefighting, dealing with behaviour issues as they arose, with a large number of fixed term exclusions and an average of five or six permanent exclusions each year. Some of the behaviour issues were related to poor conduct around the site, whereas others were related to low-level disruption in lessons, sometimes associated with the prevalence of mixed-ability teaching in the younger year groups.

New approaches were required, and over time introduced. For example, we introduced the 5 Cs for behaviour: consideration, consistency, co-operation, communication and commitment. Although we tried to reinforce them in assemblies and lessons, they were perhaps too abstract, and did not really deal with what happened if students did not abide by them. We needed a more comprehensive and consistent approach.

I read about the Behaviour for Learning system that seemed to be successfully operating at Ninestiles School in Birmingham and in March 2005 I took a small group of senior and middle leaders, consisting of Sandra Belford, Louise Skinner, Mike Clelland and Jon Haines, down to visit the school. (I have been reminded about that visit ever since, as we booked a rather second rate bed and breakfast for the night with a bed too short for the rather tall curriculum leader for science and my snoring during the night seemed to keep people awake.) The visit to the school was more positive, however, as we saw very clearly a behaviour system operating in a challenging school. It was understood by students, staff and parents, and it contributed to excellent examination results and an outstanding Ofsted judgement. The five of us who visited the school felt that this would help to give us the answer we were looking for.

By now, most schools have adopted a Behaviour for Learning structure similar to the Ninestiles model, but we were an early adopter, and we put a lot of resources into ensuring its success. We needed to customise the system so that it would work with our students and staff. A number of key members of staff spent a Saturday in May 2005 working together on policies and procedures that would be introduced to students, staff and parents. We consulted each group in the two months leading up to its launch in September 2005.

The system itself was very straightforward in that there was a stepped series of consequences leading up to isolation and exclusion if students did not keep to the school code of conduct both in the classroom and around the site. I explained it to staff and parents using my own experience of obtaining speeding penalties using a slide of a yellow speed camera. In the space of six months in 2005 I obtained six penalty points for speeding, and of course if I had gone on at that rate I would soon have been banned from driving. This had a marked effect on my driving behaviour. Behaviour for Learning consequences would work in a similar way. God's sense of humour was evident in giving me such a good illustration to introduce Behaviour for Learning.

Over time we had to modify the system a bit to make it work more effectively. For example, at the beginning of our second year we made it less draconian. Again I used the example of speed cameras, explaining to colleagues that drivers were often angry when excessive restrictions were put in place for no apparent reason. We needed to be sure that the consequences were appropriate for particular misdemeanours, otherwise we would alienate highly committed and conscientious students. There was also the danger that students who obtained lots of consequences leading to detention and isolation would simply not turn up for school. Consequently, work had to be done to help those students improve their conduct by having particular behaviour support sessions in place for them. It was also important to work with individual members of staff who were using the structure as a crutch and were giving out excessive consequences to students rather than using their own behaviour management skills to engage students. I would often encourage staff to give individual students a "glower"[63] before starting on the consequences route to make sure that these students understood that they were beginning to go down a slippery path.

The structure that was introduced in 2005 was still there when I left almost ten years later. It is not perfect, and students always point to a

---

[63] a significant stare (a word of Scottish origin).

degree of inconsistency among staff in their application of it. Part of this inconsistency is due to human error in failing to apply a system correctly. Part of it, however, is due to the need to deal with particular individuals in ways that are appropriate for them. For example, a student with a particular disorder is never going to manage an hour long detention in silence and to make them do so is to set them, and indeed the whole system, up to fail. God wants us to apply sanctions justly, but he also wants us to show grace to individuals who need that special approach to help them on their particular journeys.

Behaviour Improvement Programme

The Labour government that was in office from 1997 to 2010 was committed to using particular strategies to raise standards in targeted areas, with a lot of money being poured into each strategy. One of these strategies already mentioned was Excellence in Cities. Another was the Behaviour Improvement Programme, which aimed to improve standards of behaviour and attendance in particular secondary schools and some of their feeder primaries. In 2003, we were fortunate to be one of four secondary schools in North Tyneside to be given this funding. The choice of schools was based on a range of deprivation and behaviour indices. I did feel sorry for the schools not chosen because they were missing out on a large resource, but, on the other hand, diluting this resource would have made it less effective overall by failing to target where need was greatest.

One of our strategies through this programme was to have a base to which students who were excluded on a fixed term basis could go for a limited number of days both as a punishment and to receive some support for their behaviour. This was called first day response, as it meant that students who were excluded had education on their first day of exclusion. We looked at various properties for this, all of which were too expensive to rent, but we were then given a tremendous offer from Alan Giles, the head of one of our feeder primary schools, to rent some of his school's surplus area. The rooms available were brilliant for classroom work, small group and individual support and office bases. Thus the Farne Centre was established. It was staffed by a teacher and a support assistant who worked with the flow of students from the two high schools who needed to be taught away from the main site. Because these students were working within a school setting, albeit away from their home school, it did mean that fixed term exclusions fell to almost zero.

In addition, the Farne Centre was the outreach base from which staff were sent to work with students across the schools who needed behaviour support. This was particularly important for the primary schools in the programme, with the hope that sorting out children's problems at an early stage would prevent greater behavioural issues emerging later. Family support was a particularly successful part of the programme, with Susanne Wood forging very strong relationships with families where the children were causing concern across the schools.

There were many success stories of students and their families supported by the work of the Farne Centre staff and the outreach workers. Unfortunately, funding for the project came to an end in April 2013. We ended up incorporating it into the existing Behaviour for Learning structure on the school site. Staff were unfortunately made redundant, apart from Helen Kirk, the teacher in charge, who became a very valuable member of the new year leader structure, and Susanne Wood who continued her work supporting families as well as monitoring attendance. Indeed, it was a pleasure each Friday night in the months leading up to my retirement to read Susanne's weekly reports of home visits and the amazing effort she went to in order to get otherwise poor attending students into school. A number of students found her standing at the bottom of their beds cajoling them to get up and out for school.

Success Culture

One of the messages that we tried to put across to students was that of success, namely, "You have come to a successful school, and you too can be successful here." For example, the first assembly in the autumn term of 2014 was on the theme "School's Amazing!" and I shared with each year group the success that the school had achieved over the past year. Even though our overall summer results were not particularly good, I was able to put up on the screen the names of those who had done well in their GCSE, "AS" and "A" level examinations, along with some photographs. I also showed an interview that had been broadcast of one of our former students, Sarah Hunter, who had successfully captained the England Women's Rugby World Cup championship squad that summer. At the end we prayed thanking God for the success he had given us in the previous year and asking that he would give the school even more success in the coming year. The following week's assembly was on the theme "You're Amazing!" and I explained to the students how each of them was created in an absolutely unique way, and how each of them was special to God. Combining this with the previous week's theme, the message was that working together and with God's help, we can do even more amazing things.

Part of our success culture was the praise points element of Behaviour for Learning. The danger of concentrating on consequences and sanctions is that it might seem rather negative, and so in putting together the Behaviour for Learning programme it was felt to be essential that we have policies and plans for awarding praise points for good effort, achievement and contribution. I have, however, worried about the use of external motivators as I have always believed that motivation should come from within; in other words, motivation should be intrinsic. After all, in the world of work, employees do not get rewards for doing a good piece of work or speaking well in a meeting.

Daniel Pink in his book "Drive" (which as a senior leadership team we read week by week over a term) spells out the dangers of external motivators. In his summary[64] he says that...

- they can extinguish intrinsic motivation;
- they can diminish performance;
- they can crush creativity;
- they can crowd out good behaviour;
- they can encourage cheating, shortcuts, and unethical be-haviour;
- they can become addictive; and
- they can foster short-term thinking.

For example, he argues that rewarding a child to learn maths by paying her for each work book page completed will make her more diligent in the short term but make her lose interest in the long term.[65] Students may become less creative and innovative if they are simply rewarded for completing a piece of work.[66]

---

[64] *Drive;* Daniel H Pink; Canongate Books (2011): page 59.
[65] Pink; op. cit.; page 39.
[66] Pink; op. cit.; page 45.

In providing any merit system, we need to be aware of these dangers. Perhaps praise points work most effectively when they are seen as a means of appreciating what students have done. We all respond to appreciation, and that is more likely to produce the required effect than telling students that you will give them a praise point if they can tell you the capital of India. Certainly, Pink argues that extrinsic motivators work best if they are unexpected and awarded only after the task is completed, as holding out a prize at the beginning of a project will tend to focus attention on the prize rather than on the most innovative ways of attacking the problem.[67]

Sometimes Christians working in schools find themselves in a quandary; we want to build up students' self-esteem so that they obtain success, and yet do we not need to make them aware that they are, like all of us, wretched sinners who need to be saved by the grace of God? The answer is that we need to do both in line with the Creation story. We are all made in the image of God and as such we need to fulfil the amazing potential that he has given us. At the same time, we are part of fallen humanity and need to have our sins forgiven. Therefore, in some assemblies, I would share what sin was and how Jesus died upon the cross to save us from the consequences of our sin and to provide eternal life for us in heaven. I would also emphasise in other assemblies that God does not intend for us to try to get through life on our own, but rather that he wants to be with us to guide us and help us, if only we would let him, so that we end up achieving amazing things. The balance of the full Christian message has to be put across.

Overview

One of the highlights of the summer of 2012 for Ella and me was watching the London Olympics, the first week at home, and the second week as a whole family in London at a large number of events. We were, for example, fortunate to see Andy Murray live at Wimbledon winning the Olympic gold medal; indeed, we were seen on television by friends who videoed us, something which I have used in a number of assemblies since. Although we were not able to watch it live, we did watch the magnificent opening ceremony on television. One of the highlights was the Mr Bean sketch, in which he was supposed to be

---

[67] Pink; op. cit.; page 66.

playing the "Chariots of Fire" theme with the London Symphony Orchestra but he simply was not engaged with what was happening; he was not misbehaving particularly but rather he was daydreaming. I have used that video clip with staff and students to show that excellent classroom behaviour requires not simply compliance with rules but rather it requires deep engagement with the learning that is going on.

We need to use all of our behaviour management skills, our Behaviour for Learning structures and our use of praise points to enable that to happen. We do, however, also need to pray that our students will have the intrinsic motivation that will provide a love for learning so that they will want to give of their very best. We also need to ask God that we might have a loving care for our students so that when they do not reach the high standards we expect of them, we can patiently point them in the right direction, showing them God's grace as we do so.

Chapter Five

Staff

Appointing the right staff and developing them is one of the key roles of any headteacher. Using Jim Collins's analogy, heads need to ensure that they get "the right people on the bus" who will move the school forward under their leadership.[68] The "right people" will be self-motivated with a desire to do their best for the students and reach high standards of excellence. If the bus needs to change direction at any stage in time, the "right people" will be flexible enough to remain committed to the students and loyal to the organisation.

My experience as a head over twenty-one years was that on the whole we had the right people on the bus. I was surrounded by highly committed professional colleagues who gave their best for the students and were intensely loyal to the school. This was no accident as great care was taken in appointing new staff and promoting colleagues to more senior positions, including praying that God would make the right appointments. Staff were shown respect and were consistently trusted to do a good job, something which many staff over the years appreciated.

Relationships with Staff

In his letter to the Ephesians, Paul gives instructions to guide relationships between slaves and masters.[69] This of course can be transferred to the modern workplace in terms of relationships between employees and employers. Therefore, I, as a Christian teacher working

---

[68] Jim Collins; op. cit.; chapter 3.
[69] See Ephesians 6:5-9.

in a school, need to follow the instructions of my superiors "with respect, and fear, and with sincerity of heart", just as if I was obeying Christ.[70] Over my career, I worked under people that I greatly respected, and so did not find serving them to be a great burden, although I have to admit that I was perhaps a bit more rebellious in the early years of my career.

Paul goes on to give instructions to masters, whom we can consider to be employers, or anyone with authority in an organisation. The instruction is simply to treat slaves or employees in the same way, in other words, to serve them "with respect, and fear, and with sincerity of heart"[71], without threatening them. If we are going to lead staff effectively, we need to show them respect with godly fear and sincere hearts. As Christians, we need to let the love of Jesus overflow into our relationships with colleagues. Sometimes, with challenging members of staff, whom we would rather let off the bus, showing that love can be difficult to do, but nonetheless, we are called to demonstrate God's grace to our employees without threatening them, and hopefully win them round. Indeed, we should see ourselves as serving them, to help them get more satisfaction from their work and to enable them to do their jobs more effectively. This is a message I tried to get across to others. For example, in the leadership development courses which I ran over the years, I would include servanthood as being one of the qualities of excellent leadership, giving the example of Jesus washing the disciples' feet.

When I started at the school, I needed to put these biblical principles into practice. On the arrival of a new head, staff tend to be very unsure about what the future will hold for them. At the same time, it is also true that a new head is wary about how the staff will take to him or her, and I had lots of worrying thoughts about the staff going through my head. Will they accept my way of operating which may well be different from that of the previous head? When it comes to making changes, who will be allies and who will provide resistance? Who will see me as the new head that will help the school move forward in new directions and who will be concerned about being taken out of their comfort zones? Who will be gracious when I make mistakes and who will capitalise on errors of judgement that I shall inevitably make?

---

[70] Ephesians 6:5.
[71] Ephesians 6:9.

I knew two of the staff quite well before I started: Jon Foley, a geography teacher with whom I had worked at Alnwick, and Jo Bowden, a member of the religious studies department, who used to come with her husband Andy to take family services at our church in Bedlington. I needed to get to know other staff just as well. In my first month in the school, I made a point of meeting with each member of staff individually. I asked them to come and share with me about their own lives both professionally and personally, their hopes for the future and their thoughts about the school. I began to find out about them as people, including their family lives and interests, and about their aspirations. Heads of department were very keen to tell me about the exciting things that they were doing within their subject areas, as well as giving me wish lists in terms of needing more curriculum time and money for their departments. They all seemed exceptionally loyal to the school, but most also seemed open to the possibility of there being some change in aspects of the way in which the school was run.

Over the next twenty-one years, I endeavoured to make myself available to staff who wished to talk through issues. One of the ministries I believe that God has given me over the years is that of encouragement, and I believed that I should follow Paul's exhortation to those who have such a gift, "let him encourage"[72], whereas at times it can be so easy to dismiss or condemn people and their thoughts. Colleagues came and discussed ideas they had with regard to moving forward their areas of responsibility, or concerns they had with some aspect of their work. In extreme situations, it was a plea for help because they were not coping with their job very well at the time, and I would try to be as understanding as possible and help them formulate a plan of action to see them through. Very occasionally I would pray with the person, and certainly, during meetings over difficult situations, I would pray inwardly, seeking wisdom and handing the problem over to God.

I would often tell colleagues that they needed to guard their family lives, as the pressure of the job can so easily affect family relationships. Sometimes, they would come and talk through family concerns, perhaps relating to illness in the family, whether it be to do with their children or their parents. Occasionally it would be issues related to their marriages where things were not going well. Again, in these situations I

---

[72] Romans 12:8.

would listen, pray and where possible offer practical advice and help. If the person needed time to get things sorted out, I would try to arrange that for them. Although there were guidelines laid down for giving time off, I would sometimes be more generous than I needed to be to make sure that the colleague was able to have time to move things forward. Staff appreciated that, and to my knowledge never took advantage of it. This was all part of the trust and respect that I tried to show staff. I believe that I received it back in terms of extra commitment from colleagues, as well as kindness shown to me, for example, when I experienced bereavement on the deaths of both my own and Ella's mother.

Although I wanted staff to see me as being approachable, I chose, however, not to socialise privately with them, except at whole staff functions. I did not have a group of staff that I considered my "close friends", with whom I would meet out of school. I know that some headteachers feel free to do this, but I have always been concerned that this would lead to accusations of favouritism when it came to promotions, or worse, if I needed to discipline a member of staff who was also a friend, that would be difficult for both of us. Besides, it is better that colleagues are free to enjoy themselves without feeling that they are being watched. I believe that I am in good company there, as Sir Alex Ferguson adopted a similar philosophy in leading players and staff at Manchester United.[73]

As a result of what I believed to be trusting relationships, my involvement with trade unions up until my last year was minimal. I was not anti-union, but I was opposed to strike action, as I felt that in the public sector, if unions are in dispute with the government, it is innocent people such as parents or children who suffer, rather than government ministers. On the relatively rare occasions over twenty-one years when industrial action did take place, I did not do anything to undermine it, but I almost always managed to keep the school open so that the teaching of some year groups could take place.

Occasionally I made an error of judgement that led to discussions with trade union officials. For example, in 2011 we had decided to restructure the school day to allow longer lesson times and two hours of continuous professional development time for teaching staff on a

---

[73] *Leading;* Alex Ferguson with Michael Moritz; Hodder and Stoughton (2015): pages 119-120.

Tuesday afternoon, meaning an early finish for students that afternoon. These new arrangements were put in place to improve even further the already high quality of teaching. Governors were worried, however, that the early finish for students would be a matter of concern for parents. Therefore, it was agreed that there would be a programme of enrichment activities for all Year 7 students and for those older students whose parents insisted on them staying in school. These activities were to be run by an outside sports company and our own support staff. In an ideal world, support staff should have been involved in the training that was taking place, but it was a greater priority to ensure that the enrichment programme ran well, as long as other arrangements were made for the professional development of support staff.

We consulted with teaching staff, parents, students and partner schools, but I omitted to consult with support staff, as I took their co-operation for granted. This was a mistake, as a small minority objected and involved their union. I had to spend a fair bit of time negotiating with the union to get a compromise agreement, which we finally did, to allow us to go ahead with the scheme. It was a mistake, however, that I should not have made, as it was at odds with the principles of trust and respect that I tried to engender in my relationships with staff. God overruled in the end, but I felt bad that I had not dealt with this group of staff in the way they deserved to be treated.

Appointing Staff

One aspect of the role that I continued to find exciting over twenty-one years of headship was the appointment of new staff. No matter how good a school is, it can inevitability benefit from new blood coming in with fresh ideas, provided that the new blood can easily fit in with the culture of the school, in other words, getting "the right people on the bus".

During my first year, we appointed fourteen new staff to begin in September 1994. Some of the staff I had inherited in 1993 when I started were promoted to posts in other schools during the year, while others perhaps felt that it was time to move on as they found some of the changes being brought in by the new head rather uncomfortable. It was important that the induction of these new colleagues was of high quality, as two weeks after they started they were thrown in at the deep end as we faced our first Ofsted inspection.

In that first year, we also made a number of internal appointments. As mentioned in chapter four, we wished to bolster the pastoral leadership team, and so we appointed John Harrison as an additional assistant head of lower school and Steve Braysher as assistant head of sixth form. In addition, Bob Evans, the long-serving deputy head, obtained a headship in Sheffield, and I felt that rather than appointing a deputy from outside, I would pin my faith on existing middle leaders to be able to generate three assistant headteachers to strengthen the existing rather small and not particularly cohesive senior management team. (In those days, the emphasis was still on management rather than leadership). We interviewed a large number of middle leaders for these posts over a long day, and eventually appointed Sandra Belford, Dave Clarke and Ayleen Mills (later Weatherspoon) on to the team.

We always tried to make staff coming for interview feel welcome, and said to them that they should be looking at us to see if we were the sort of school that they wanted to join, always giving them the option of withdrawing from the process if they wished. This was important as we wanted staff who would fit in with our ethos and so be prepared to give of their best for the sake of the students. Occasionally candidates did withdraw, because they felt that either the post or the school was not quite right for them at that point in time. It was important to encourage them to do so in order to get the right match for the school.

Those coming for interview were always given at least one task to do; in the case of teachers an observation of them teaching a lesson and perhaps a student voice session, and in the case of support staff, possibly an ICT-related task. Making the candidates aware of the nature of the school and the post, along with particular tasks, were parts of the selection process that went well. In the early years, however, I was frustrated by the interview part of the process. Governors were always involved, which was important, as they were ultimately responsible for the employment of staff and did have lots of expertise to offer, but they tended to have pet questions that they wanted to ask, and I often wondered what the point was of asking some of these questions. There was the danger that the person appointed would be the person who could best answer a set of rather odd, and sometimes not particularly relevant, interview questions, rather than the person who would be most suitable for the post. It was rather similar to intelligence tests demonstrating who is best at doing intelligence tests rather than being able to measure intelligence. I am not saying that we ended up appointing the wrong people through this process, but the nature of the interview would not necessarily point to the person who would bring the most to the school.

I was very fortunate to be able to attend a course run by Marks and Spencer on how they recruited staff. This really opened my eyes, and it was as if God showed me through this course how the interview process could be made so much better for the candidates and also make us more confident that we had appointed the person who would make the most positive difference to the school. Governors allowed me to take charge of the new interview process. At the beginning of each interview session, I would emphasise to the selection panel that this should not be treated as an oral test to see how much candidates could remember as in an old-fashioned history exam, but rather we should aim to put candidates at their ease, and to get the best out of them. This might even mean helping them if they were struggling with answers by asking supplementary questions. I provided what I believed to be relevant questions grouped and weighted according to criteria that were essential for the post. Questions were less theoretical, in other words, not so much of "What would you do if...?" questions, but more of the candidates being allowed to talk from their own experience through answering "What have you done...?" type of questions. Not all of the candidates were asked exactly the same question, as it depended on their particular experience, but that did not matter as long as the specified criteria were met. This process was not perfect, and was indeed modified over time, but it did help us make excellent appointments.

Of course, I wanted to be sure that each appointment was covered in prayer, so that it was not just the product of a clever process, but rather that it was God's candidate who was appointed. Did that mean that all the appointments should be Christian? Certainly, we made some excellent appointments of teachers who were committed Christians. The maths department did at one point have a high proportion of Christian teachers, something which our youngest son David commented on when he spent some time in the department prior to the start of his own training as a maths teacher. These were, however, very good teachers who won their posts on merit, and they just happened to be Christians (although it did help in the case of Liz Burgess – later Tufton – that I had seen her relate well to young people at church). Over the years we did interview other Christians for different posts, and again some were appointed on merit, but unfortunately many did not show themselves to be by any means the best candidate for the job and so it would have been wrong to appoint them.

My first head, Brian Stevens, did not profess to be a Christian, but he liked appointing Christians because he believed that they would bring a strong commitment to the job, and perhaps cause fewer difficulties within the staff room of the strife-torn 1970s. His experience of Christians in schools was of people who followed Paul's instructions in Ephesians chapter 6, namely working with respect, fear and sincerity of heart. A Christian head would be even more keen to have Christian staff, to make it more likely that a Christian ethos would be embedded. If a school does not have a Christian foundation, however, it cannot discriminate in the appointments process in favour of Christian staff, but rather it has to take the people that God provides, whether they are Christian or not.

So then, does it matter if non-Christian staff are appointed? Provided that there are some strong Christians on the staff who will prayerfully support the Christian head and that those non-Christians who are appointed to the staff do not fight against the ethos of the school, it does not matter, and, besides, there is not really much that you can do about it. That has been my experience over twenty-one years. The fact that only two members of staff (and these were in the early years) refused to go into assemblies suggests that there was a compliance on the part of staff to the Christian message. Non-Christian staff do have so much to offer. The vast majority are very good people who are beneficiaries of God's common grace with so many gifts from God whether they overtly acknowledge him or not. As Timothy Keller says, "Deep in our hearts' operating systems, God has imprinted his story."[74] This means that staff who are not committed Christians can still work hard and do an excellent job for their students.

There was at least one post, however, where it was important to have a committed Christian, which was that of curriculum leader for religious studies and personal and social development. We shall go into more detail in chapter seven as to the importance of this post. A vacancy arose for this post in 2001 when David Priestley was appointed to a deputy headship in a school in County Durham (where he also later became head). The Christian governors involved in the selection wanted

[74] Timothy Keller; op. cit.; page 190.

to appoint a committed Christian to the post, but although we tried on two occasions, the normal processes of advertising and interviewing did not produce the desired candidate. One of Jim Collins' pieces of advice based on his research for "Good to Great" is very simple: "When in doubt, don't hire – keep looking."[75] In this case, I knew that this was a post that the Lord would want filled with absolutely the right person, and so I headhunted Dot Lee, with whom I had previously worked in Northumberland and who was currently working for Scripture Union. I knew that she had all the right skills and her Scripture Union experience was ideal for the post. I spent a long time talking to her about the post, and I persuaded her to put in an application. We interviewed Dot on her own having rejected all other candidates. She shone in interview and was appointed. This was a tremendous answer to prayer and a significant appointment for the development of the Christian life of the school.

The Development of Staff

In March 2010, I organised a residential conference for North Tyneside Secondary Leaders with the keynote speaker being John (now Sir John) Townsley, at that time headteacher of Morley High School in Leeds. One of his messages that really stuck with me was, "Do not waste a second of continuous professional development time." I had always realised that it was important that staff should continue in their professional development, but his remarks really hit home that this development was absolutely vital and urgent and should be of the highest quality. His comments were a spur to me to push ahead with restructuring the school day to raise the profile and improve the quality of training offered to colleagues.

Traditionally, the continuous professional development of staff meant sending staff on courses so that they could come back with fresh ideas with which they could stimulate their colleagues and thus bring about changes in the classroom. Over my whole career I have been on some excellent courses and attended some wonderful conferences that have influenced my thinking. The annual conference run by the Specialist Schools and Academies Trust in November in Birmingham was something that I greatly looked forward to as a source of

---

[75] Jim Collins; op. cit.; page 54.

inspirational ideas and thinking that I could bring back to school. That is where I first heard Alan November whom I mentioned in chapter three and Daniel Pink whom I mentioned in chapter four. Unfortunately, these particular conferences were expensive, and so latterly I felt that I could not attend them because of the state of the budget. Due to the expense of many courses on offer from different organisations, it became increasingly difficult to send staff out to attend them.

There were perhaps two further reasons why we were reluctant to send staff out on training courses. Courses were of variable quality and so often represented a wasted day and wasted finance. There was a second reason, in that even when courses were of high quality, it was very hard for one or two members of staff who were stimulated by an event to have a great impact on their colleagues who were unable to attend the event themselves. The bubble of initial enthusiasm was often met with apathy and even cynicism, and sadly the bubble was often burst and ideas were left stillborn.

As a result, schools have done more and more of their training in-house, either using the expertise of their own staff or buying in expertise from elsewhere. We needed to be increasingly aware of the skill set of our own staff so that knowledge could be shared and development needs met. Michael Fullan, one of the leading writers and thinkers in educational leadership, quoted Lew Platt, former chairman of Hewlett Packard, saying, "If only we knew what we knew at HP."[76] The implication was that there was a vast amount of knowledge available in any organisation just waiting to be found, tapped and shared with other members of the organisation. This is true within and across our schools, and I am also sure that it applies to our churches.

One way that is used in schools to see where staff expertise lies is in carrying out lesson observations. Over the years, I must have observed hundreds of lessons, and most were a delight to watch. Most teachers feel a bit uncomfortable and even quite nervous when they are being observed, but I always tried to make it a positive learning experience for colleagues, where we could discuss the many good points of the lesson, as well as areas for further development. Colleagues tended to appreciate the positive feedback given. Observations were necessary as

---

[76] *Leading in a Culture of Change;* Michael Fullan; Jossey-Bass (2001); page 79.

part of our monitoring processes to ensure that the quality of teaching remained high as well as preparing for future Ofsted inspections. It also enabled senior leaders to see where particular expertise lay so that it could be subsequently shared with others. The flip side of the coin is of course seeing where individual colleagues needed help, and starting a process to help these individuals improve their practice.

As well as using the expertise of our own staff, we occasionally brought in some from elsewhere. Whitley Bay High School had developed expertise in co-operative learning, and we arranged for them to lead a couple of whole staff training sessions, which were greatly appreciated and led to colleagues working through strategies for themselves. Over a number of years, we held in October what I called our annual learning conference, when we had a keynote speaker lead sessions on themes that we felt were important in moving us forward in teaching and learning. These speakers, such as Mike Hughes and Paul Ginnis, were well known nationally and provided inspirational and entertaining training sessions. Paul Ginnis has sadly since died, but I remember the evening before the 2012 conference when Dot Lee and I had a meal with him. During the meal he shared his love of Christian rock music from the 1970s and, in particular, the American Christian singer and songwriter Larry Norman; I really impressed him the following morning when I brought in a couple of Larry Norman vinyl albums that I had rooted out of the loft.

One of the strands of training that I concentrated on was leadership development. I felt very passionate about inspiring existing leaders to become better leaders as well as encouraging others to take on initial leadership roles or go for further promotion. This is one reason why so many promotions were internal, as staff had been well prepared to take on new leadership responsibilities, often against stiff external competition. As James Kerr writes in his leadership manual based on the experience of the development of the fearsome world championship All Blacks rugby team,

> *Leaders create leaders. They arm their subordinates with intent. And then step out of the way.*[77]

I felt that this was very much part of my calling as a headteacher.

---

[77] *Legacy;* James Kerr; Constable (2013); chapter IV.

I ran a series of leadership development courses over the years, initially for our own staff, but also subsequently for staff in other schools. I was later asked by the local authority to take responsibility for secondary leadership development in the borough, a role which I thoroughly enjoyed as I saw colleagues working and sharing together across schools, developing their understanding of leadership and applying it within their own contexts. To see colleagues becoming animated about penguins reacting to their melting iceberg and then applying the lessons of change management to their own school situations was absolutely invigorating.[78]

Getting the Wrong People off the Bus

Jim Collins would argue strongly that as well as getting the right people on the bus, it is only fair to all concerned that we get the wrong people off the bus. Again he has simple practical advice based on his research: "When you know you need to make a people change, act."[79]

Allowing the wrong person to stay on the bus saps everybody of energy as extra time is required to manage the person and to compensate for what that individual is failing to do. Besides, it is not really in that person's own best interests to remain on the bus as they may be able to find a more fulfilling post elsewhere. Of course, it may be that that individual is sitting in the wrong seat on the bus, and the answer may be to move them to a different seat. If that does not work, however, Collins would continue to argue strongly that that individual should be removed from the bus.

How does that apply in schools? It is much more difficult to get rid of teaching staff than it is in industry or commerce. Teaching has up until relatively recently been seen to be a job for life, and schools have often put up with bad practice, partly because there were so many hoops to go through in trying to get rid of staff. I know that I have been guilty of failing to make people changes quickly enough. It is, however, important that poor practice is challenged for the sake of the young

---

[78] This activity was based on a fable called *Our Iceberg is Melting;* John Kotter; Pan Macmillan (2006). The fable itself is based on John Kotter's book on change management, *The Heart of Change;* Harvard Business Review Press (2002).

[79] Jim Collins; op. cit.; page 56.

people who are being badly taught and badly prepared for examinations.

In my experience, most people action did not require removing people from the bus. If a department was consistently underachieving in examinations, it was important to be supportive to the curriculum leader and the staff in the department, and enable them to come up with strategies to improve results. Likewise, if it was recognised that a teacher was teaching poor lessons, then support would be given to help them improve the quality of their teaching. Sometimes staff can be in denial about the issues, and so the success of such approaches will depend on their willingness to be supported and learn from better practice elsewhere.

Ultimately, however, difficult decisions have to be made if improvement is not forthcoming. When a curriculum leader was simply not able to make progress, I have been able to persuade that colleague either to take on a different set of responsibilities that may be more appropriate for them, or stand down from leadership responsibility altogether. These are difficult conversations to have, and I have always found it such a wonderful answer to prayer when the colleague concerned has agreed to the proposal. If a teacher is not making progress in their classroom management, difficult conversations also need to be had as part of capability proceedings that may lead to dismissal. Again, it has been an answer to prayer when a colleague has come to the conclusion himself that he should leave his post; this allows the colleague to go with dignity rather than having to go through embarrassing capability hearings.

Fortunately, over the twenty-one years, there were very few occasions when staff had to be suspended pending an investigation into their conduct. When it was necessary, however, I was prepared to go ahead and do it. This took up a tremendous amount of time, particularly for the deputies who tended to be appointed as the investigating officers. The whole process was always by its very nature difficult, including for the governors who had to make the final decision in each case.

Overview

The prophet Isaiah proclaimed these inspiring words:

> *He gives strength to the weary*
> *and increases the power of the weak.*
> *Even youths grow tired and weary,*
> *and young men stumble and fall;*
> *but those who hope in the Lord*
> *will renew their strength.*
> *They will soar on wings like eagles;*
> *they will run and not grow weary,*
> *they will walk and not be faint.*[80]

I love that promise that the Lord gives strength to the weary, and I know that many times in my weariness over twenty-one years, he has given me strength though his grace. This has often been particularly true in dealing with staffing issues.

I also love the picture of soaring on wings like eagles to reach great heights. Obviously I wanted our students to soar to achieve great things. I also very much wanted my staff to soar on high, because if staff are soaring, then there is more chance that the students will start to take off as well. In some of the leadership development courses I ran, I would try to inspire leaders to soar and would show a slide of an eagle in flight and refer, among other more conventional leadership books, to one written by the American pastor and writer Charles R Swindoll, entitled "Living above the Level of Mediocrity: A Commitment to Excellence", which had an eagle in flight on its front cover.[81] My message was that as educators we had to soar and aim for excellence for the sake of our young people. It was a privilege to see over the years so many staff soaring and being committed to excellence, helping their students achieve great heights.

---

[80] Isaiah 40:29-31.
[81] *Living above the Level of Mediocrity;* Charles R Swindoll; Word Publishing (1987).

CHAPTER SIX

The Wider Community

Jeff Haden posted an article on "LinkedIn Pulse" entitled "What No One Ever Tells You about Being the Boss". His argument was that nobody can ever prepare you for becoming the chief executive officer of a company, and whereas before you had one boss, now you have lots of bosses. He quoted Jim Whitehurst, an American businessman, who said,

> *In my case I have a board, major investors, government officials (since we're a public company), Wall Street, employees – lots of bosses. Having greater latitude is one of the fun parts of being a CEO, but never assume you have free rein to do whatever you want.*[82]

The same is true for headship; as a deputy head, I had one boss, the headteacher, but now as a head I found that I had lots of people to whom I seemed to be answerable. Any school has to be at the centre of its community, and the headteacher has to be seen to be serving the community and working with the various stakeholding groups within the community. These groups include parents, governors, residents and businesses within the local community and other schools. As a Christian, I needed to be seen to be trustworthy in my dealings with members of the community, as well as being wise in balancing the demands of all my different bosses.

---

[82] *What No One Ever Tells You About Being the Boss;* Jeff Haden; LinkedIn Pulse (August 2015).

Partnership with Parents

From a biblical perspective, the family is seen as the core unit in the local community, with the ultimate responsibility for their child's education. The advice to young people in Proverbs 1 to listen to their fathers' instruction and not to forsake their mothers' teaching demonstrates the key role of the family in education.[83] Children are the responsibility first and foremost of their parents, and not the state, with the state only at liberty to step in if that responsibility is abused. This means that parents have the right and responsibility of deciding how and where their children should be educated, whether it be in the local state school, a state school some distance from the home, a faith-based school, an independent school, or even at home.

I have moved in my thinking over time, as I used to be opposed to children going to any school apart from the local comprehensive, and fee-paying education was an absolute anathema to me. This view, I increasingly realised, was at odds with how God saw things, as it put the state on a higher plane than the wishes of many parents as to how they wanted their children educated. As we have seen, Proverbs 1 indicates that parents have God-given responsibilities for the wellbeing of their children.

Having said that, many, and in some areas the vast majority of, parents are very happy to send their children to the local school and delegate the responsibility for their children's education to that school. It was very much a privilege for me to share in that responsibility and it was so important to meet the expectations of parents. It was also important that it should be a partnership, with parents delegating responsibility for their children's education without abdicating it; children were more likely to be successful when their parents supported them and encouraged them in their school work, including homework.

One of the messages that primary schools communicate very effectively with parents is the importance of reading at home. Most parents feel confident about being able to do that, although they may not necessarily feel that they can devote enough time to doing it properly. At secondary school, however, many parents feel out of their depth as subjects become more technical or are taught differently from what they remember from their own school days. The message that we

---

[83] See Proverbs 1:8.

tried to put across to our parents was that one of the main ways in which they could help was to encourage their children to do their very best in all of their subjects both in school and at home. This meant prioritising homework and ensuring that students had good study facilities available at home, including ICT facilities. We also encouraged parents to make sure that their children took advantage of all of the opportunities available to them through participating in the wide range of extracurricular activities that staff put on for them.

We talked positively about "Partnership with Parents", and parents seemed to appreciate the support and advice that they were given, whether it be through parental information evenings on issues such as changes to the examination system or discussions with individual parents on particular concerns that they had. It is not easy being parents of adolescents, and I felt that it was very much the duty of the school to be as supportive as possible, by encouraging parents to contact the school if they had any worries.

Parents did not usually feel the need to contact me personally, but I did occasionally meet with parents who felt that they wanted to draw a particular concern to my attention. When they brought genuine complaints, these discussions could sometimes be difficult. I had to pray that I would be both honest and discerning, and it was an answer to these prayers when we felt that progress had been made. Only rarely did I feel intimidated in these meetings, but when I did, prayer was always necessary, and the situation was calmed down.

It was absolutely vital that parents were brought in when there were behaviour issues with students. If a student was receiving an excessive number of consequences through the Behaviour for Learning system, parents needed to know so that they could be involved in working with their child to deal with the issues. Most parents appreciated being informed about their child's behaviour even when it was not particularly good news. Some parents, however, would become very defensive, and argue that their child should not have received a particular sanction, and that it was in some way the teacher's fault. In this situation, they had tended to rely too much on what the child had told them, which was often a distorted view of what had actually happened. When this was explained to them, most parents tended to back down, and we were able to explain how important it was that the child saw school and parents working closely together and that we must not allow the child to play one off against the other.

A growing area of concern over the years related to the misuse of ICT. We very much wanted students to use ICT at home in their learning, and we made use of various virtual learning environments and our iPads for Learning scheme to help them harness the power of ICT to carry out research, solve problems or be creative. Parents were very supportive, but increasingly faced difficulties in ensuring that their children were not spending endless hours playing games or going on inappropriate sites, rather than doing their homework. It was very easy for children and young people to become addicted to the content of particular sites, and too many students ended up tired the following morning, having spent too long on these sites. This can, of course, have seriously damaging academic effects. Recent research suggests that fourteen-year-olds who spent five hours of screen time each evening could possibly drop two grades at GCSE,[84] and those who spent more than six hours per evening are at risk of feeling lonely at school, arriving late for school or truanting.[85]

Likewise, social media easily got a hold over young people, and parents then found their children being upset over rumours spreading about them over these sites. This upset, through something said on "Facebook" or "Instagram", inevitably came into school the following morning and pastoral leaders spent an increasing amount of time on cyber issues.

The misuse of technology is very much part of our living in a fallen world. Technology is in itself a good thing, and helps us to carry out the creation mandate, enabling us to learn and to help people in ways that earlier generations never thought possible. Because of our sinful natures, however, we are prone to make the wrong use of technology, for example, becoming obsessed with social media or finding easy access to pornographic sites. Young people are particularly tempted to be caught up in what seems to be the exciting but inevitably dangerous side of the internet. As a school, we felt that it was important that students were made aware of the dangers inherent in misusing ICT.

---

[84] *Revising on the run or studying on the sofa: prospective associations between physical activity, sedentary behaviour, and exam results in British adolescents;* Kirsten Corder et al; International Journal of Behavioral Nutrition and Physical Activity 2015, volume 12.

[85] *Students, Computers and Learning: Making the Connection;* PISA, OECD Publishing (2015); chapter 1.

We also realised the importance of parents being made aware of these dangers and how to help their children. Through the Parent-Teachers' Association, for example, we had occasional E-safety evenings. Certainly, if we found individual students misusing ICT, we would always involve parents in following up the incidents. The Canadian pastor Tim Challies has suggested that parents have too often abdicated their responsibility for technology to their children, so that when a new technology comes along, parents profess ignorance about it and simply pass it on to their children. As a result, it is no wonder that so many young men are heavily into pornography. He suggests that parents should reject this ignorance of technology, but rather take the lead in their families in seeing how that technology should be appropriately used. For Christian parents, this would mean using technology to train their children in the discipline and instruction of the Lord.[86] As new technologies further develop, schools and parents need to work in closer partnership so that students can learn even more effectively, keeping themselves absolutely safe and not allowing technology to take over their lives.

Amidst all the behaviour issues and other worries that their children often bring them, parents also need to hear good news about their children. It must be very disheartening for many parents only to receive letters or phone calls from the school when their children have been behaving badly. It is no wonder that these parents end up with a very negative view of the school and are reluctant to attend events such as parents' evenings. As part of our success culture, we tried hard to work positively with these particular parents and to ensure that they received "good news" letters, postcards and phone calls as well.

Governors

Governors are key people within the English school system as they represent the wider community and have ultimate responsibility for the management of the school. Since the passing of the 1988 Education Reform Act, their responsibility has grown enormously, and even more so when schools have become foundation schools or academies, thus

---

[86] Tim Challies gives excellent advice to parents in a lecture entitled *Purity in a Digital Age.*
http://www.ligonier.org/learn/conferences/after-darkness-light-2015-national-conference/purity-in-a-digital-age/

leaving local authority control. Headteachers and governors need to have clear boundaries, so that, for example, governors do not involve themselves in the detailed day-to-day running of the school or carry out lesson observations without being accompanied by a senior member of staff. Likewise, headteachers need to ensure that governors have all the information that they need in order to make the decisions that are required of them.

Learning to have the right relationship with governors is a key task for any new headteacher. I am not sure that in the early days I always got that partnership correct, partly due to my inexperience, and partly due to certain governors pushing their own particular pet projects. As the school developed and, for example, examination results improved, I grew in confidence in working with the governors and saw them as less of a burden to bear and more as valuable partners to cultivate. There were still difficulties, however, and there was, for example, a period when political rivalries in the council chamber were being played out in our governing body meetings.

Overall, the expertise of governors was invaluable. Being able to see issues from a different perspective, while at the same time understanding that the world of education may be different in many respects from the world of industry or commerce, are tremendous assets that wise governors bring to the school. When it came to planning our new build, a number had experience of building projects in different sectors, and their advice was gladly taken. The new build subcommittee of governors worked exceptionally hard to ensure that the school ended up with the best building possible. Similarly, in dealing with budget deficits, a number of governors had financial experience that could be called upon in order to look at possible solutions. They also had contacts from their own networks that could be used in the classroom.

Part of the role of governors is to provide a degree of challenge to the headteacher. Nobody really likes what they believe to be their well thought-out plans to be challenged by others, particularly if they are lay people. Yet it is important that headteachers receive this challenge gracefully, as sometimes it can prevent serious mistakes from being made. Being asked why you are proposing to do things in a particular way makes you think more carefully about your plans in order to be absolutely sure that you have got the principles and details correct. For example, as mentioned in chapter five, in the spring term of 2011, we discussed the restructuring of the school day to allow longer teaching periods of eighty minutes, rather than the fifty-minute model we had had for years, along with an early finish on Tuesdays to accommodate quality training for staff. I was very keen to push forward with both aspects of the restructure. Most governors were happy with the principles, but there were particular concerns raised about childcare issues with an early finish. There was some forensic questioning, but finally a good solution was reached involving activities for all of the new intake students and those others whose parents did not want them alone at home.

Sometimes, however, the challenge was not so helpful, especially over pastoral-related issues when there may be some difference in values. One example was when Margery Tate, a lovely Christian lady who was a longstanding member of the religious studies department, decided to take early retirement from teaching in 1996. I was very keen to keep her on in some capacity because of the godly influence she had on the students. I came up with the idea of appointing a school counsellor, with Margery being the ideal candidate for the post. Some governors, however, quite rightly felt that we should interview for this post in order to have a wider field, although another reason for some was to avoid an overtly Christian appointment. The interview was very difficult, but a compromise was finally reached at a subsequent governors' meeting and we ended up appointing two counsellors, one of them being Margery.

I learned two very valuable lessons from this process. The first was that I had to do my homework and know exactly what I was really wanting. In this case, I had used the term "counsellor" too loosely, as there were technical specifications involved, which I discovered when I carried out research after the interview (something I should have done at the beginning of the process).[87] The other, and more important, lesson I learned was not to try to manipulate governors to get what I wanted. At the time I was preaching a series in Genesis at our church in Bedlington, and when I got to the story of Jacob and Esau,[88] I expounded how Jacob and his mother Rebekah were arch manipulators in obtaining the blessing and birthright from his father Isaac, privileges that should have gone to Esau, the firstborn son. Jacob manipulated the

---

[87] One Christian book on counselling that I found very helpful was
   Counselling in the Community; Roger Altman; Kingsway (1996).
[88] See Genesis 27.

outcome his way, rather than trusting in God. I realised that I had done the same over this appointment; the whole process would have been easier if I had prayerfully approached the governors and said that we should continue to employ Margery in some pastoral capacity. God, however, through his grace did bring me through this difficult period, and indeed we were able later on to shelve the counsellor posts and appoint Margery to the post of learning mentor as part of the government's Excellence in Cities initiative.

Although there were occasional difficulties, my overall experience with governors was very positive. This was very much helped by the fact that a number of governors over the years were Christians, although just as we saw in chapter five in relation to staff, non-Christian governors also had so much to offer. The chair for most of my twenty-one years was a very godly man, Tim Goodwin. In his own quiet way, he ensured that we did all that was possible to maintain a Christian ethos within the school. Tim was a man of prayer, and he constantly prayed for the school, occasionally praying with me and often for me; in this way he had a huge impact on the school, far beyond what is normally expected of a chair of governors.

The Local Community

Each of the schools that I worked in was designated a community school with a special vision to meet the educational needs of the community through the provision of adult education and facilities for leisure and recreation. I started off my career in Cambridgeshire which had a tradition of community education through the village college movement. This prepared me well for moving to Northumberland where each of the high schools had a deputy head (community) who took responsibility for adult education and outreach into the community.

When I came for my headship interview, I was amazed at the facilities which the school had for the local community. Under the leadership of my predecessor, John Burn, and his chair of governors, a prominent local councillor, Brian Flood, the school developed a vision to raise the educational aspirations of the whole community, and not just those of statutory school age. The school roll had declined over time, and so it made sense to use available space within the school for the learning and recreation of members of the community. Adults were encouraged to attend classes, not only in the evening, but during the day as well. There was a range of GCSE, vocational and leisure classes put on for adult students, and members of the community were also encouraged to join sixth formers in "A" level classes, although that latter provision had to be stopped for safeguarding reasons.

The facilities on site included a community library, the school's on-site public coffee shop with attached soft play facilities, and a crèche for children whose parents were attending classes in the school. One unique facility within a school setting was the Disability Resource Centre which was run by the council's social services department, and which hosted a number of wheelchair-bound ladies and gentlemen who had been brought in by minibus to receive various treatments within the centre, and then to attend community classes within the school accompanied by their carers. It was good for the school students to be in the same building as adults with disabilities, although there were inevitably logistical problems.

Age Concern, as it was then called, also had a base on site, which helped us do some intergenerational work. There was also what was called a People's Centre, although I have to confess that I was never very sure what its function was. Work was also beginning to start on building a sauna and sunbed suite, but after I arrived I quickly shelved these ideas as being expensive luxuries that did not really promote the health and wellbeing of the community.

In the early days of community education in the school, funding was very generous. When I arrived, there were lots of staff associated with community education working on the site including three leisure assistants to help with the leisure and sport programme, which was perhaps rather excessive. Funding had been reduced before I arrived, the deputy head (community) had been made redundant, and the governors were just going through the process of making the youth co-ordinator redundant. I could see that through time there would be further reductions in the funding of community education, but despite that, or even because of that, I was determined that there should be strong leadership in this aspect of our work. As part of the senior management restructure in 1994, we appointed one of our heads of department, Ayleen Mills (later Weatherspoon) as assistant headteacher with responsibility for community development. Ayleen had the vision, passion, temperament and Christian integrity to lead this work, which she did successfully until she retired in December 2010. Funding did decline, and we lost some of our facilities, but nonetheless community education still played an important part in the life of the school.

Working with the local community, however, did not simply mean providing classes and facilities; it also meant doing outreach work in the community. Over many years, groups of students undertook a large variety of projects where they were interacting with the local community. They included doing tidy-ups in the community and putting on art displays in community centres. Doing intergenerational work was very important, including visiting residential homes for the elderly, delivering gifts to elderly members of the community and doing a project on what the elderly people and students liked and disliked about the community with a jointly produced display at the end of it; all of these activities helped to reduce the barriers between the generations.

On these occasions our students were excellent ambassadors, but unfortunately there were other times when some of our students let the school down through poor behaviour such as dropping litter or running through people's gardens on the way to and from school. We did our best to make amends through cleaning up or showing our positive side by giving residents who had made complaints free tickets to concerts.

Businesses are also a key part of the local community, and it is important that schools interact positively with local employers. As an economics teacher, I believed strongly in the value of business-education links. In the summer term of 1977, I organised my first industrial visit: when on teaching practice, I took a class to the local lemonade factory which made the world famous Barr's Iron Bru. Since then, I have taken students on numerous visits so that they could see production processes and talk to key people in the business about running companies of different sizes. I have also endeavoured to get business leaders to come into school so that they can have a clearer picture of the world of education, and thus lay the foundation for joint projects. As part of our community programme, we were also able to provide courses for employees of local companies and public sector organisations. For example, the local Department of Work and Pensions office sent a number of employees to us to take our sign language courses.

One of the best ways that students related to the world of business was through work experience. Some of my fellow heads were a bit ambivalent about work experience, but I was passionate about it, and as a school we put a lot of resources into obtaining as many good placements as we could for our students. The less academically able students did have extended work placements as part of their curriculum, but I believed strongly that all students should have some experience in the workplace as part of the preparation for their future working lives. The vast majority of our students thoroughly enjoyed their work experience, and employers were also greatly impressed by how well motivated our students were.

Partnership with Schools

In their book, "Sustainable Leadership", Andy Hargeaves and Dean Fink argue the case very strongly that for educational change to have an effective impact and thus bring about a raising of standards and well-being, it has to be sustainable. The impact has to go well beyond the immediate, both in terms of time and place. One of the principles of sustainability that they describe in detail is justice. This is how they describe the impact of justice:

> *Sustainable leadership does no harm to and actively improves the surrounding environment. It does not raid the best resources of outstanding students and teachers from neighbouring institutions. It does not prosper at other schools' expense. It does no harm to and actively finds ways to share knowledge and resources with neighbouring schools and the local community. Sustainable leadership is not self-centred; it is socially just.*[89]

I desired the very best for the students, staff and community of my school, but I realised that this was not to be achieved at the expense of other schools. Rather, schools had to work in partnership for the sake of all the students in the area. I believed that we had so much to offer other schools, just as they had so much to offer us.

It was an absolute privilege to work with our feeder primary schools. Before I had arrived, Helen Whitfield, who was head of lower school, had established some excellent transition arrangements to make the move from primary to secondary as smooth as possible. One event which Helen organised was the Pyramid Music Festival when, over three nights, each school, along with our own choir and musicians,

---

[89] *Sustainable Leadership;* Andy Hargreaves and Dean Fink; Jossey-Bass (2006); page 19.

performed some highly acclaimed music. After Helen retired, Phil Abel and Adam Warkman continued the tradition. On three occasions we held the festival at the iconic Sage Music Centre in Gateshead to celebrate the twenty-fifth and thirtieth anniversaries of the festival and our own diamond jubilee. These were special celebrations that helped to cement our community of schools together.

When we became a specialist technology college in 1998, there was an expectation that we would use some of our additional funding to work with our feeder primary schools to raise standards in maths, science, design technology and ICT. This was an ideal opportunity to work even more closely with our partner primary schools. Designated teachers had weekly periods on their timetables labelled "Primary" which meant that they worked throughout the year in different primaries bringing their subject expertise and sometimes specialist equipment into the primary classroom. Sometimes it was more appropriate for the primary children to come up to our departmental suites to use facilities such as CAD-CAM[90] and Bunsen burners which they did not have in their own schools. Special "gifted and talented" days were also held when the most able children in maths and science from the primaries would come up to us and have an intensive day doing activities in these subjects. Later on, we expanded into other subject areas such as PE, music and modern languages. Although it seemed that we were giving a lot to the primaries, we gained by having more confident learners move up to the secondary school and who already had some contact with their future teachers. Our staff also learned a lot by improving their understanding of primary school pedagogy and applying it in their own teaching; this was real professional partnership at work.

There was another spinoff involved with working with primary schools, which was that their children and parents were our potential future customers, and so in terms of the market, this partnership would hopefully help parents in their decision to send their children to us. As we shall see in chapter ten, this had important financial implications in a world of autonomous schools with their own budgets to manage.

When it comes to undertaking collaborative work with secondary schools and local colleges, however, that meant working closely with potential (and actual) competitors, and this required trust on all sides. It

---

[90] computer-aided design and computer-aided manufacturing.

was very difficult to share educational resources if you felt that another school or college was taking your potential students.

Maturity was required on the part of all providers if partnership work was going to bring benefit to the students. One area where collaboration was essential was in post-16 education. North Tyneside had too many small sixth forms, which individually simply could not offer the range of courses to which students were entitled. We for many years had struggled to have a sixth form with over a hundred students, something commented on in successive Ofsted inspections. This was true of two other schools in our part of North Tyneside. In 1999, I was seconded to the local authority to work two days a week with Steve Rutland, then Vice Principal of Tynemouth College, to prepare for the introduction of Curriculum 2000 and the new "A" level structure of AS and A2. One of our key strategies was to divide the borough into four geographical clusters with the high schools in each cluster working closely together with each other and with the two colleges (who themselves eventually merged) and the work-based learning providers.

The degree of collaboration varied from cluster to cluster. After a hesitant start, our cluster did end up with a strong collaborative framework post-16, where we talked about having a collaborative solution for each course. The collaborative solution in some subjects such as English literature, which was popular enough to be taught in all three schools, was agreeing on common specifications and the sharing of materials. Where it was not possible to put on a particular course in all three schools, a decision had to be made as to which school would teach it, based on expertise and previous track records. We also tried videoconferencing lessons in the early days, but this was not found to be very effective for both technical and pedagogical reasons.

What this collaborative framework meant was that the students across all three schools could choose courses in any of the schools; they could still belong to the sixth form in their home school where they would be well known, but they would have access to a much wider range of courses and combination of courses. Collaboration is undoubtedly costly. Much time was spent in meetings negotiating solutions, timetables had to be realigned, a sixth form development officer had to be appointed and minibuses had to be hired to shuttle students across the three sites during the day. There also had to be trust that teachers in the other schools taught your students to very high standards. When issues of quality did arise, the headteachers and heads of sixth form knew that they had to sort it out. Despite the cost and occasional angst, collaboration was well worth it, as what was offered to the students across the cluster was of higher quality than any individual school could provide on its own.

Over the years since the introduction of Curriculum 2000, collaboration grew across North Tyneside. There were various projects, often initiated by the Blair-Brown governments that required schools to come together. I was humbled to think that both my fellow heads and the local authority trusted me enough to allow me to play a leading role in furthering collaborative work across the borough; this was important in terms of my Christian integrity. For most of my time as a head, I was either secretary or chair of the secondary headteachers' group, which gave me some influence to keep the system working together. I was also able to play a role by being on the steering committees for initiatives such as Excellence in Cities, the Behaviour Improvement Programme, the Education Improvement Partnership and the relatively short-lived Specialist Diploma Programme. There was some exciting work done that was aligned with Hargreaves and Fink's principle of justice. For example, through the Educational Improvement Partnership, all secondary schools on a pro-rata basis contributed to employing Lead Subject Professionals in key subject areas. These teachers would work where they were most needed. This meant that some schools put money into the pot, but did not themselves necessarily see much fruit for their contribution, if they did not have as much need as other schools at that time. That is an excellent example of collaboration for the benefit of the whole system rather than just individual schools.

The establishment of the North Tyneside Learning Trust was perhaps the most powerful collaborative project, involving most schools in the borough, a large number of local employers and further and higher education institutions. Most schools agreed to take on foundation status and join the learning trust to get the benefit of working in partnership with each other and with other organisations. The trust has been very powerful in getting resources into North Tyneside, particularly related to science, technology, engineering and maths (STEM) in a way that no individual school could possibly do.[91] This has so much potential for all the students in the borough. Sadly,

---

[91] The learning trust's website gives a strong flavour of the work of the trust: http://ntlearningtrust.org.uk/

prior to my retirement, the Trust was struggling a bit, as it came under attack from some schools that had decided not to join, but felt that they were entitled to some of the benefits that were clearly coming through the Trust; these schools were able to use legal arguments regarding delegated funding to press their point. In my leaving speech in front of all the North Tyneside heads, I reminded them how much the borough had changed over the years and encouraged them to continue in a true spirit of collaboration, even though there was a cost. Unfortunately, my plea fell on some deaf ears. Collaboration is not perfect, not even in North Tyneside.

Despite some of the problems that inevitably arise in trying to collaborate, North Tyneside had made huge strides in collaboration. One reason was that relationships with the local authority had greatly improved over time, largely because of the quality of new officers who came into the borough who strived to make sure that schools were given the freedom to work in a collaborative way. The period through both Labour and coalition governments was a time when schools could have gone in one of two ways, either to stay within the local authority or to be enticed by the so-called freedom offered by becoming an academy. At the time of writing, there are only three academies in North Tyneside, one that converted voluntarily, one that was previously an independent school but which merged with a local authority primary school and was given academy status, and one primary school that was forced to become an academy because of its position in special measures. That sends out a strong message about the strength of collaboration in North Tyneside and relationships between schools and the local authority. It is unlikely that this will continue for much longer, given the Conservative government's determination to see all schools become academies, as announced by the Chancellor, George Osborne, in his budget speech in March 2016,[92] although there was a significant U-turn when the Secretary of State announced on local election results day in May 2016 that academisation would no longer be mandatory for good and outstanding schools.

---

[92] https://www.gov.uk/government/speeches/budget-2016-george-osbornes-speech

The Global Community

Making students aware of the needs of the global community was an important part of our vision, and over the years a number of foreign links were established. In my first year in the school, I was amazed at the number of foreign exchanges with other schools that were in existence. There were two French exchanges, two German exchanges (one a science-based exchange), a Polish exchange and an Estonian exchange. Having students of different nationalities in the school was excellent for the whole school community, as these students were in different lessons and mixed very well with our students in their own homes. The host students also had the opportunity to go back to experience school, home and cultural life in France, Germany, Poland or Estonia. Unfortunately, these exchanges came to an end, partly for financial reasons, partly because the contacts in our partner schools moved on, and partly for safeguarding reasons, as we could not guarantee the wellbeing of our students in the homes of the families abroad, and we did have one bad experience which could have gone to the press.

More recently, we tried to broaden the students' horizons by creating links with schools in Kenya and China. The Kenyan school that we were linked with was Arina Primary in Kisumu in Western Kenya, and over the years we have provided the school with much needed equipment including stationery, toiletries, sports equipment and solar lamps. One of the nice touches was when as a school we changed our uniform from sweatshirts to blazers, we collected the unwanted sweatshirts and sent them out to Kenya; the Arina pupils absolutely loved wearing these sweatshirts. Most of the school's charity fundraising efforts went towards supporting the work in Arina. We placed a particular emphasis on sponsoring girls in their continuing education, as they were under threat of being married off at an early age in order to have children. Some of these girls wrote beautiful thank you letters in appreciation of the support they were given.

Initially, it was just members of staff who went out to forge the links with Arina prior to us taking students out. After their visit, members of the art department adapted their schemes of work to promote the work that was being done in Arina through a variety of Kenya-based projects, with some of the work being sold to raise funds for the school. In October 2015, Kat Lambert and Danielle Bernstone, having previously visited the school themselves, along with Dave and Sue Clarke, took a party of sixth formers out to work in Arina. This was life-changing for these students, and their eyes were opened, realising how materially fortunate they were compared with the children and young people in Arina. They also realised how much the Kenyan children valued their education making great sacrifices to learn. In 2014, we also welcomed to our school Wycliffe, a young Christian teacher from the school in Arina, and he very much won the hearts of our students.

The school also had strong links with a school in China called Tangshan Middle School Number 54, and this was a link that I personally was very involved in. In November 2009, I was approached by Eddy Tang, an education officer working for the education department of Hebei Province in China, but based in Newcastle and charged with creating foreign links with schools in Hebei. Eddy, who is also pastor of a church in Newcastle, asked if I would like the school to be part of a growing number of schools in the region which could be linked with schools in Hebei province. I agreed and, as a result, we were linked with a school in the city of Tangshan. Strangely, I remembered reading an article in "The Economist" in 1976 about the devastating earthquake that had taken place in the city killing half a million people. The point of the article was that in those days the Chinese authorities did not want to release information about disasters to the outside world as they preferred to have the power of the Chinese Communist Party solve problems without external help.[93] Little did I realise that Ella and I would have close ties with Tangshan over thirty years later.

Our first contact was in March 2010, when we welcomed Ms Shi, our Chinese link school headteacher, to the school and to our home in Morpeth. Fortunately, Eddy arranged a translator from the university to accompany her as she did not speak very much English, and our Mandarin was non-existent. (I did try to learn some by listening to a program on my iPod when I was at the gym, but that was a complete failure.) We had a lovely time with her, and a couple of months later Ella and I made a reciprocal visit to China with other heads from the region. We were treated like royalty when we visited the school and also when we made dumplings in Ms Shi's home.

---

[93] An excellent book that analyses the momentous events of 1976 in China is *The Death of Mao;* James Palmer; Faber and Faber (2012).

In July of that year, we welcomed our first contingent of Chinese students, when sixty young people from the school came on a UK tour, including three days at the school. Our students looked after them in their classes and on the special trips we arranged, as well as hosting them for an evening meal. This became an annual event. Finance was more of a problem for our students to make the return visit to China, but we managed to have two trips for sixth formers, one led by Sandra Belford and John Harrison in 2012, and a second led by Lisa Lowery, accompanied by Ella and me in 2014. We shall talk more about the 2014 visit in chapter eleven. A number of staff also went out to Hebei province during their summer holidays to take part in summer schools to help Chinese students learn English and to share teaching and learning strategies with the Chinese teachers.

Conclusion

At the beginning of the chapter, I quoted Jim Whitehurst talking about all the bosses he had and to whom he felt accountable as a CEO. Having expounded all the difficulties that that entails, at the end of the post, he says,

> But it will also be the best job you ever had. Running a business and being the CEO is incredibly rewarding. You can make a huge impact. You get to work with, and through, awesome people. You get to make a real difference. It's definitely a tough job … but it's also the best job.[94]

That was my experience as a head over twenty-one years. Despite the pressures of having so many bosses, God through his grace strengthened me and allowed me to experience so many blessings. Working with, and through, some awesome people both in school and the wider community was a privilege I am so grateful to have had.

---

[94] Jeff Haden; op. cit.

CHAPTER SEVEN

Assemblies and Religious Education

The first assembly that I led was a house assembly in my first school at St Neots, in November, 1977. The school was organised through a house system, with each house given a fair bit of freedom to develop its own ethos. The head of Darwin House, a rather terrifying man called Ivor Hunter (who actually was very nice when you got to know him) liked to get his form tutors to lead each of the weekly house assemblies. When it came to my week, I had to think and pray carefully about what I should do. As it was about the time of Remembrance Day, I used a Nigel Goodwin poem about the freedom God gives us, and how we often abuse it, thus leading to war, but how God loves us nonetheless. It was a bit nerve-wracking to do my first one, and it perhaps was not a great assembly, but it got me started and established as someone who could take assemblies. For my second assembly, I got my first year tutor group to do a Riding Lights Theatre Company play, "The Parable of the Good Punk Rocker", which everyone enjoyed, although some of the students suffered from a bit of stage fright. When I left the school, Ivor thanked me for the input that I had made to house assemblies, saying that he personally had appreciated what I had said.

For a Christian teacher, it is a privilege to be involved in taking assemblies and teaching religious studies lessons as a way of imparting the Christian faith to young people. In each of my first three schools, I had that privilege and took the opportunities that were offered to me to explain who Jesus is, what he has done for us and the response he expects from us. As I mentioned in chapter two, for example, as head of sixth form, I had weekly assemblies with the sixth form, and, as well as talking about studying for "A" level and applying to university, I felt able to share something of the love of God with my students. In Alnwick there was no religious education within the Key Stage 4 core curriculum, and so I introduced it, initially doing a high proportion of the teaching myself.

I have been asked the question as to whether putting across the Christian message in assemblies, classes and extracurricular activities was encouraged in the schools in which I spent the first half of my career. Encouragement is perhaps too strong a word; suffice to say that there was no formal discouragement of such activities. If a Christian teacher took the opportunities that were available and prayerfully and sensitively ran a Christian Union group, gave a Christian message in assembly, or explained what they believed in a religious studies class, that was seen to be quite acceptable. Where things went wrong were when Christian teachers showed a lack of common sense and proselytised in a way and at a time that was not appropriate. Christians also had to be respected for doing the main job for which they were paid, such as teaching economics or leading the sixth form; if that respect was missing, there would be less acceptance of Christian work within the school.

The law through the 1944 Education Act and the 1988 Education Reform Act was (and indeed still is) on the side of promoting the Christian message in schools. The 1988 Act makes it clear that collective worship and religious education should be wholly or mainly of a broadly Christian character, whilst taking account of the teaching and practices of the other principal religions represented in Great Britain. Nicky Morgan, when she was Secretary of State for Education, reinforced that in guidance sent out to schools in December 2015.[95] As we mentioned in chapter three in our discussion of British values, Christians need to hold on to the legal privilege we have in our schools, taking advantage of it without abusing our position, for the sake of our young people who desperately need to have an understanding of God's amazing love for them.

One of the many privileges of taking up my headship was the fact that I was going to lead a school that had played an important role in the formulation of the 1988 Act, as we shall shortly see.

---

[95] *Guidance for schools and awarding organisations about the Religious Studies GCSE,* Department for Education (December 2015).

Assemblies

When I arrived in the school, there was already in place a strong framework for collective worship. This was largely due to the influence of John Burn, my predecessor, who had actually provided advice to the government in framing the 1988 Education Reform Act and its requirement to have daily acts of collective worship that were mainly Christian in nature. The format that John established was very clear. Each morning, classes would spend up to ten minutes with their tutors and then proceed to one of two theatres for their assemblies. The school was fortunate in having two large theatres that could be used for assemblies, a throwback to the days when the site housed two separate schools, a boys' secondary modern school and a girls' secondary modern school. A Christian hymn or worship song was sung each morning with the music staff accompanying the singing, and a Christian message was given by either a member of staff or Christians from local churches or organisations such as Scripture Union or Youth for Christ. Some of these Christians have later told me that taking assemblies in the school played a key part in the development of their own ministries.

It was expected that I would continue with that format when I took over, and I gladly did so. I did two assemblies a week, one with lower school (Years 7 to 9) and one with upper school (Years 10 and 11). In my first term, I worked through many of the parables of Jesus, explaining how they showed God's grace to us and how we need to respond, as in the Parable of the Prodigal Son[96], or how they apply to our relationships with each other, as in the Parable of the Good Samaritan[97]. Other Christian speakers continued to come in and present the gospel. I am still very grateful to John for establishing that framework, both in the school and through national legislation, as it made this aspect of my new role so much easier.

That did not mean, however, that there was no scope to make improvements; there were aspects of the programme that perhaps did not work particularly well. One issue was the sheer number of students who had to be brought in and out of the theatre each morning in a short space of time. This was particularly true in lower school where there were about four hundred students assembled in the theatre, and

---

[96] See Luke 15:11-32.
[97] See Luke 10:25-37.

whose entry and exit did not always make for a calm, peaceful start to the day. The assembly programme was also disjointed, in that there were no common themes, and speakers brought in whatever message they felt that they had for the students. Singing was also an issue; students of secondary age feel very embarrassed about singing together, and, as a result, there was not a joyful noise heard in the theatre, with my lack of musical ability not really helping. Form tutors, although understanding the legal obligation for a daily act of collective worship, were also crying out for more time with their tutor groups so that they could get to know their students better and provide them the guidance and support that they needed.

During my second term in the school, I convened a small working group to look at how we could make the assembly programme more effective while maintaining our legal obligations. It was agreed that we would have year group assemblies on two or three mornings of the week and expect tutors to conduct tutor group assemblies on the other mornings. To help both tutors and the main assembly speakers, there was a set theme for each week and a termly booklet with ideas and materials which tutors could use with their classes. These were produced by the curriculum leaders for religious studies and personal and social development, David Priestley, Dot Lee and Lisa Lowery, respectively. A lot of work went into producing these booklets, and as a minimum, tutors could simply read to their classes the material that was included in the booklet, but from tutor assembly observations that we carried out, it was clear that the best tutors did much more than that.

The assembly programme now seemed more manageable, and over the following two decades, assemblies continued to play an important part in the life of the school and strongly reinforced the Christian ethos that was so important to many of us. The prominent position of assemblies was recognised even by those who were personally not quite so sympathetic to the Christian message. An anonymous comment was made by a member of staff, in a survey about the structure of the school day, that the school was "obsessed with assemblies". I am sure that that was not meant to be a complimentary comment, but it did show the importance of the assembly programme in the school. There was certainly agreement that having large groups come together to reinforce whole school values is extremely important, and when, for example, we had to reduce our programme significantly because of building work in the theatres, people realised that there was something missing and that there were more student conduct issues as a result. Of course, in addition, having a clear Christian message for the students to reflect upon may well have eternal repercussions.

The Christian Message in Assemblies

Not all of the pastoral and senior leaders who led assemblies over the years claimed to be Christians, and so they did not feel confident in giving a message from the Bible. None, however, were anti-Christian and so they never to my knowledge said anything that would be seen to be in conflict with the message of the gospel. Rather, they would give a very strong moral line which the students benefited very much from hearing, and it came from people that they greatly respected. Those members of staff who were Christians were also able to give a strong moral line, but they were able to go further by sharing God's love and grace with the students.

Outside Christian speakers were a great asset to have, and many of them were appreciated by even the most cynical of students, because of the particular rapport they had with young people. Dave Glover, a local church leader and evangelist, was able to use conjuring tricks and ventriloquism to put his message across. On one occasion, when the theme was "Love", Daniel McCarthy, a vibrant local curate, involved the students in playing a game, spoke about the special love of Jesus and then left copies of "Why Jesus?" for the students to take away. Each year over three years, the Tyneside Youth for Christ group "Dependance" spent a week in school and powerfully used humour and games in assemblies and lessons, encouraging students to come to an evening concert that was more overtly evangelistic, leading to a number of young people making a commitment to Christ.

Not all speakers were appreciated so much, however, and in a few cases we had to stop asking them to come in. Sometimes it was simply because they were boring and did not really relate to the young people. One or two felt that they had to give a long gospel message, just in case the students never got the chance to hear the gospel again, which given the nature of the overall programme was simply not true. Occasionally, they had a bee in their bonnet about something and used the gathering to get it off their chest in front of the young people.

It is not easy for people from outside to come in and take assemblies. A number of years ago, not long after I started at the school, a local Christian freelance writer, Richard Dyter, wrote a book, "School Assemblies Need You!" in which he encouraged Christians to embrace their local schools and seize the opportunity to take assemblies there. In the book he gives excellent advice with practical examples that could be used in assemblies. He also spoke about his first experience of taking an assembly and the hours of preparation that he put into it.[98]

It was of course important for me to take assemblies on a regular basis, both to put my own stamp on the leading of the young people in the school, setting the overall general standards that I expected, and to provide the Christian message that to me was absolutely fundamental. I have to confess now that, looking back, some of my assemblies were not particularly good, as I did not prepare them as carefully or as prayerfully as I should have done; I even prepared some of them in my head coming in the car in the morning, which of course was very last-minute, shoddy preparation. Whether these poorly prepared assemblies had any impact, I cannot tell. If they did, it would be solely by the grace of God.

What changed the level of preparation I had to do for assemblies was the "PowerPoint Revolution". This Microsoft product changed the way presentations were done in lecture halls, boardrooms, assembly theatres and eventually classrooms. I first of all used it in a big way when I was given a part-time secondment in 1999 to help prepare North Tyneside high schools for the introduction of Curriculum 2000, as mentioned in chapter six. This involved me in running courses and conferences, using PowerPoint as the medium for presentations whereas previously I would have used an overhead projector with acetate transparencies. I could clearly see the value of this medium in assembly presentations. Clear messages could be displayed including main headings, biblical texts, cartoons, photographs and eventually, once I learned how to create them, embedded video clips. There were now available powerful new visuals that would hopefully remain with the students. These presentations did take longer to be created, but of course they could be saved and adapted for future use. I did, however, have to remind myself that technology should not take the place of prayer. By God's grace, it was prayer that would change people's lives, with technology only being a means to put the message across.

---

[98] *School Assemblies Need You!;* Richard Dyter, Monarch Publications (1997).

Over the years I spoke on a number of themes. When it was "Harvest", I encouraged students to care about the less fortunate who had little to eat, using the example given to me by our son Stephen, who saw in Chad, in West Africa, a woman trying to get food from an ant hill; ants are supposed to live off human leftovers, not the reverse.[99] I also told them the Parable of the Rich Fool[100], reminding them not to worship their material possessions, but to be sure that they were ready to meet God.

In an assembly on "Faith and Science", I encouraged them to consider the need for both faith *and* science, as it was not a matter of considering one over the other. I quoted Einstein who said, "Science without religion is lame, religion without science is blind," as well as showing a video clip of how Professor David Wilkinson, an astrophysicist and theologian at the University of Durham, combined his faith with his pursuit of scientific understanding.

In a similar assembly to younger students on "Creation", I showed them a cartoon picture of the creation story, but rather than go down the line of arguments between creationists and evolutionists, I emphasised the need for us to be in awe of creation and to look after it. I pointed out that each one of us has been specially created by God, and that one day we can look forward to a new creation that will be perfect.

I loved doing assemblies on the theme of "Forgiveness", as it was here that I could really share God's love and grace. I used examples such as Corrie Ten Boom who related in her autobiography "The Hiding Place", how she was badly treated by guards at Ravensbruck Concentration Camp, but how God protected her and miraculously freed her from what would otherwise have been a horrible death.

After the war she was speaking at a meeting about her experiences when a former guard at the camp approached her at the end explaining who he was and how he had become a Christian. He stretched out his arm to shake Corrie's hand, but she felt that she was not able to do so, until something like an electric current went through her arm; this was the Holy Spirit enabling Corrie to forgive the man and shake his hand.[101]

---

[99] http://stevecockburn.blogspot.co.uk/2012/03/scavenging-from-ants-in-twenty-first.html
[100] See Luke 12:13-21.
[101] *The Hiding Place;* Corrie ten Boom: Hodder and Stoughton (1971).

I would finish with a picture of Jesus on the cross saying, "Father, forgive them because they do not know what they are doing."[102] Those who were concentration camp guards and those who put Jesus on the cross did not deserve to be forgiven, but God's grace provides us with forgiveness that we simply do not deserve; this of course applies to all of us.

In an assembly on the theme "I Believe", I spoke about the differences between believing facts and believing opinions, with examples of each. From there, I went on to speak about religious belief, which meant taking on a whole belief system. Which religion, however, should we choose, as there are so many? Should we pick and mix, or simply not bother at all? I suggested that what we needed to do was to look at the evidence and then take a step of faith. I told the story of the disciple Thomas who refused to believe that Jesus could possibly have risen from the dead, saying, "Unless I see the nail marks in his hands and put my fingers where the nails were, and put my hand into his side, I will not believe it."[103] When Jesus appeared again to the disciples, this time Thomas was with them, and he was given the opportunity to touch the Lord's hands and put his hand into his side. Thomas gave the response that each of us needs to give to Jesus: "My Lord and my God!"[104] I also gave the example of a pastor and evangelist who had spent some time working in RSD[105] classes; Rob Joy, a former drug addict, had responded to Jesus in the same way, thus experiencing his love and healing power.

There were three assemblies that I did almost every year: one was at Hallowe'en on the theme of "Good and Evil", one was our Christmas service and the other was our Easter service.

I felt strongly that we should make sure that students understood the satanic origins of evil in the world and that they should steer clear of dabbling with the occult. Hallowe'en seemed an appropriate time to do this, as it seems that so much effort goes into having fun celebrating the powers of evil. Probably most people, and particularly the children and young people who enjoy the celebrations so much, do not see any harm in Hallowe'en, and yet that is exactly what Satan wants us to

---

[102] Luke 23:34.
[103] John 20:25b.
[104] John 20:28.
[105] Religious studies and personal and social development.

believe. He does not want us to see him as a powerful force in the universe, as he is more able to manipulate us without us realising it. In "The Screwtape Letters", the senior devil Screwtape advises his nephew Wormwood that it is better that humans do not recognise the existence of demons and says to him,

> ...if any faint suspicion of your existence begins to arise in his mind, suggest to him a picture of something in red tights, and persuade him that since he cannot believe in that ... he therefore cannot believe in you.[106]

The truth is, however,

> ...our struggle is not against flesh and blood, but against the rulers, against the authorities, against the powers of this dark world and against the spiritual forces of evil in the heavenly realms.[107]

In other words, there are satanic forces at work and that is quite a battle! Therefore, my message to the students was that Satan is a real person, who wants to lead us astray and that we need to be aware of the dangers in dabbling with ouija boards, tarot cards and other tools of the occult, such as fortune tellers.

Each Christmas, we would hold a public carol service in the local parish church and special Christmas services for each of our year groups in school. In chapter one, I described my last Christmas service in the school, which for me was undoubtedly a very special event. Yet the Christmas services were always special events with music, readings and drama, leading up to my presentation of the message of Christmas. Each year I would finish off the service with a special message. For example, when the feature film "The Lion, the Witch and the Wardrobe" was released, I used a video clip and photographs from the film to show how the sacrifice of Aslan brought hope to Narnia, a land where it was always winter but never Christmas. In the same way, Jesus has brought hope and new life to us by dying upon the cross and rising again. On other occasions, I would ask them if they had completed their Christmas shopping and then show them the best-selling Christmas gifts for the year. I would tell them what God's special gift to us was:

---

[106] *The Screwtape Letters;* C. S. Lewis; Collins Fontana (1955); page 40.
[107] Ephesians 6:12.

> *For you know the grace of our Lord Jesus Christ, that though he was rich, yet for your sakes he became poor, so that you through his poverty might become rich.*[108]

There was one Christmas service where I changed the message at the last moment. On Sunday, 11th December, 2005, Ella and I sat in church next to Barnabas Okujagu, a Nigerian postgraduate student whom we had befriended. I asked him how he was, not expecting the disastrous story that he was about to tell me. That morning there had been an air crash in Nigeria, a country notorious for such accidents. This crash was particularly sad as, of the 103 people who died, 75 were children coming home on an internal flight for the Christmas holidays. One of Barnabas's brothers, a minister for education in one of the Nigerian states, was also a passenger on the flight and he too was killed. This moved me so much that I decided to change the message for the coming week's Christmas services. I told the students the story of the air disaster, but said that Jesus was even in that situation, and that he came into the world to identify with all of our problems and hurts. He knows what it is like to be poor, having been born in a stinking stable, and he knows what it is like to be rejected and suffer pain because he died on the cross bearing the burden of our sin. Jesus gives us fresh hope at Christmas, despite all of the suffering that we may be going through.

Many secondary schools have carol services, but far fewer have special Easter services. If, however, we believe that the death and resurrection of Jesus lie at the heart of the Christian gospel, it is important that we celebrate Easter and ensure that our young people understand its significance. Therefore, each year we had special Easter services that had a similar format to the Christmas services, with music, readings, drama and a message which I gave.

To many students, the idea of anybody rising from the dead was beyond belief. To try to overcome this misconception, I put forward what I believed to be incontrovertible evidence for the resurrection. For example, I used a series of "strange but true" stories such as the story of the court in Macedonia who put a bear on trial for stealing honey or the French mayor who banned people from dying in his village because of the lack of graveyard space. These were all true because there were

---

[108] 2 Corinthians 8:9.

witnesses who could testify to the fact that they happened. Likewise, there were witnesses who could testify that Jesus had risen from the grave because they had seen him.

In another assembly, I did a quiz on television detectives with Cadbury's Creme Eggs as prizes (ignoring for the occasion our Healthy Schools status), as a starter to think how detectives would look at the mystery of the missing body that first Easter Sunday. They might have a theory that Jesus did not actually die, but that went against all the evidence of what Jesus suffered through crucifixion; the Romans really knew how to kill people and do the job properly. Perhaps the body was stolen by the disciples, Jews or the Romans, but what could possibly be their motives? After all, the disciples were themselves persecuted because of their belief in the risen Lord Jesus; why would they suffer or even die for something they knew to be a lie? The Jews or the Romans could have stopped the spread of the Christian message at a stroke by producing the missing body if they had it. Then of course there were the witnesses who saw Jesus, and at that point I would display Paul's declaration,

> *He appeared to Peter and then to the Twelve. After that, he appeared to more than 500 of the brothers at the same time, most of whom are still living although some have fallen asleep. Then he appeared to James, then to all the apostles.*[109]

In another Easter message, I talked about how the fact of Jesus dying for our sins and rising from the dead changed so many lives. I got the choir to sing "Amazing Grace" and told the story of how the life of John Newton the eighteenth century slave trader was transformed by the risen Lord Jesus. I showed a clip from the classic film "The Cross and the Switchblade" to show how Nicky Cruz and other New York gang members had their lives turned upside down by the hope of the gospel. I finished by quoting from Paul's experience as to how Jesus appeared to him:

> *Last of all, he appeared to me also ... For I am least of all the apostles, and do not even deserve to be called an apostle because I persecuted the church of God.*[110]

---

[109] 1 Corinthians 15:5-7.
[110] 1 Corinthians 15:8-9.

113

If Jesus changed the lives of John Newton, Nicky Cruz and the apostle Paul, he could change the lives of any one of us.

In these different Easter assemblies, I tried to explain why Jesus had to die and the fact that he had risen from the dead. I also gave a challenge: if you accept the evidence, what are you going to do about it; ignore it or take a step of faith in following Jesus? At the end of the assembly, I prayed that people would respond to the Easter message of hope and new life.

In the preceding pages, I have provided examples of assemblies that I have given over many years. I know that staff inside the school such as Dot and Lisa and external speakers such as Dave Glover, Daniel McCarthy, John Stephenson, Geoff Brown and Ken Matthews were able to do more imaginative and exciting assemblies than I was able to do. I do, however, want to encourage Christian school leaders to see the importance of providing a strong Christian message within schools by taking assemblies.

We may have to face the challenge that most of the students sitting in our assemblies have no interest in the Christian faith or any desire to hear about it, and therefore some may say that it is wrong to impose the Christian message on them. It is a criticism that has sometimes been lodged against my assemblies. For those who refuse to accept the supremacy, let alone the existence, of the God of the Bible, that is a logical argument. For those of us, however, who live in obedience to the God of the Bible and see him as Lord, we shall want to share his truths with our young people, both because we love him and because we want the best for our students.

We cannot force young people to follow Jesus; that was certainly not his way in the New Testament. We do, however, have to hold on to God's promise that his word will not return empty but will accomplish what he desires and achieve the purpose for which he sent it.[111] By his grace, lives can be changed.

Prayer in Assemblies

Throughout this chapter, I have used the term "assembly" rather than "collective worship", and although of course there is a difference, as it is possible to assemble together without considering God, the term

---

[111] See Isaiah 55:11.

"assembly" is better understood and is more acceptable to staff and students. Perhaps I should have been more up front with everyone and used the correct term, but it did not seem a battle worth fighting as long as our practice was honouring to God and followed the spirit of the law.

Our first challenge in this area came not from humanists, secularists or atheists, but from Ofsted. Our first Ofsted inspection was in September 1994, and one of our key issues in their report was to ensure that we had a daily act of collective worship in line with statutory requirements. This was a shock to us, as we had our new programme in place with themes, main assemblies in the theatres and tutor group assemblies in classrooms. It was also a shock to other schools, because the feeling was, if we could not get this right, how could other schools which did not even try to comply with the law meet the demands of Ofsted? I can still hear the registered inspector saying to David Priestley and me, "I can see what you are trying to do with your theocentric programme, but there is not enough prayer or reflection in your assemblies to call it collective worship."

This just seemed to be a technicality, as we genuinely wanted to honour God and share his love with young people. It is also ironic, as I mentioned in chapter three, that twenty years later we were concerned that assemblies might be perceived to be too Christian as the promotion of British values were inspected. Anyway, from 1994 onwards we endeavoured to ensure that notices would be dealt with at the beginning of the assembly and that we would finish with either reflection on the message or a word of prayer.

I personally did not always specifically end with prayer, as sometimes it seemed more appropriate simply to allow the students to reflect on what had been said. Prayer, however, was very important. For example, in the first assemblies of the year which were always much longer, I would end by thanking God for all the success of the previous year and praying for the coming year. We would pray that each of us would respond to whatever the message was in that particular assembly. We would often pray for God's help in different situations, such as exams, and as I mentioned in chapter three, we prayed that Year 11 would do well in the English exam that they were just about to take. Occasionally when somebody was ill, we would pray specifically for them. When Phil Abel, the head of upper school, was quite seriously ill in 2011, we prayed for him in assembly, and one could sense that the young people were really joining in my prayer; they were later so glad to see him back in school and I reminded them how their prayers had been answered.

In the Ofsted inspection of 2012, I ended what was going to be the last assembly with this particular Year 11 cohort, with a prayer following a strong Christian message encouraging them to remember all that they had been taught over the previous five years, not just their academic lessons but the Christian values that had been shared in assemblies and RSD classes. One of the inspectors was observing and she approached two of our more challenging boys on their way out to ask them what they thought of the assembly. Although they were not the students I would have chosen to meet with an inspector, they said that it was fine, and when pressed specifically about the prayer, they responded by saying "that was just what we did". In her feedback to me she was very complimentary, saying that she had not heard such strong, practical Christian content in a secondary assembly before, along with the fact that the students accepted prayer in assemblies. Indeed, when I met her again in another school three years later, she immediately recalled that assembly and told her colleague and others about it.

I do still pray that these assembly prayers will be answered through the grace of God touching the lives of these young people.

The RSD Department

When I arrived in the school, the RSD department was well established and had a vibrant curriculum led by David Priestley, now a headteacher in County Durham. It took responsibility for Key Stage 3 religious studies (RS), Key Stage 3 personal and social development (PSD) and Key Stage 4 religious and social development (RSD), which was a course that combined RS and PSD. When Dot Lee took over, she added GCSE and "A" level courses to the curriculum offer.

The department covered a huge content as well as developing a large range of intellectual, emotional, social, spiritual and general life skills. One of the things that the department was very good at was engendering confidence in the students and developing excellent communication skills. I can remember in my first year taking a Year 7 PSD class, and one of the first exercises that the students had to do was to bring in some object from home which they cherished. One girl brought in her baby brother, Daniel, (along with her mother) and spoke about him, a fact that I was able to share with Daniel sixteen years later when he was in Year 11. The beauty of having PSD courses incorporated within a department that was responsible for religious studies was that topics could be covered from a Christian perspective. This was particularly important when teaching sex and relationships education and controversial topics such as abortion, euthanasia, poverty and suffering. I know that when I taught such topics in the Years 10 and 11 RSD courses, I believed that I was able to challenge the conventional mindsets of the students, and that the students enjoyed the discussions, even though they did not lead to an exam qualification.

It was my firmly held belief that the leadership of the department should be Christian. This was the case during my tenure, with David Priestley, Dot Lee, Lisa Lowery (the current curriculum leader) and, for a short time, John Hodgson, all being mature Christians. When we advertised for a curriculum leader for the department, we said that we were looking for someone who could teach courses from a Christian perspective and who could take responsibility for the leadership of Christian extracurricular activities. I have already indicated in chapter five how we appointed Dot Lee to the post in an unconventional way having exhausted the more conventional routes. I am so grateful that God did not allow us to go for a poor second best solution, as the spiritual development of the school would have been terribly damaged if we had made the wrong appointment. The same was true when we appointed Lisa as a newly qualified teacher; Dot and I prayed together that the right person would be appointed when we needed a main scale teacher for the department. Lisa was appointed, which was undoubtedly the right decision, and then four years later we appointed her with John Hodgson on an acting joint basis as curriculum leader when Dot joined the senior leadership team. Lisa was later given the post on a permanent basis.

The reason that it was so important to have a Christian curriculum leader of the RSD department was the central place that Christianity had within both the curriculum of the department and the wider life of the school such as the assembly programme and Christian extra-curricular activities such as Christian Union groups and Youth Alpha. It was imperative that someone committed to Christ should lead in these vital areas. As far as possible, the core staff of the department should also be Christian, although if they were not, at least they should not be against the Christian faith.

Placing Christianity in such a central position does not say that other faiths should not be taught. Indeed, the opposite is true. For students to have a whole picture of faith, it is essential that they have some understanding of other faiths and how adhering to these faiths affects people's lives. In my own teaching within the department in Key Stage 3 RS courses, I have taught aspects of Judaism, Islam, Sikhism and Hinduism. Some Christians worry that the teaching of other faiths will encourage young people to become adherents to these faiths. I tried to do justice to these faiths in my teaching, but there was no way in which my teaching could possibly encourage any student to become a member of another faith group.

I have been asked how students of different faiths deal with assembly and RSD programmes that have a Christian core. As it happened, there were very few students who were adherents to other faiths. In some cases, their parents withdrew them from the programmes. In most cases, however, they participated in the lessons and took part in assemblies. I taught the girls from one Muslim family, and they were excellent learners in the lessons. When the family returned to their homeland, Libya, the eldest girl, gave me a card thanking me for "leading the school in the right direction". A girl from another Muslim family took a role in the nativity scene in the Christmas service when she was in Year 7.

The work of the department was held in high regard in the school. When I conducted departmental reviews, I consistently saw very high quality lessons being taught. There was an absolute vibrancy and dedication on the part of members of the department in their approach to teaching their lessons, as well as a willingness to try out new teaching and learning strategies. When they had a chance to have their say during these reviews, students talked in a very positive way about their courses. Likewise, when the Ofsted inspector, whom I mentioned above, spoke to students in May 2012, she reported that she had never visited a school where the students spoke so positively about their RS courses, saying that lessons were fun and enjoyable and that they always learned so much.

One of the responsibilities of the department was the area of sex and relationships education. It is to this vexed topic that we shall turn in the next chapter.

CHAPTER EIGHT

Sex and Relationships Education

The current state of sex and relationships education is in crisis, with policymakers, encouraged by various lobbying groups, moving schools away from promoting a biblical Christian approach with an emphasis on heterosexual marriage. There is a desperate need to ensure that young people understand the beauty of sex within marriage and the physical, psychological and emotional dangers of early sexual activity outside marriage. The headline on the front page of "The Times" of February 11th, 2015, "Almost half of teenage girls coerced into sex acts", graphically demonstrated the need for a return to sex and relationships education based on Christian values.[112]

Dr Sharon James, Social Policy Analyst with the Christian Institute in a lecture at the Lovewise Conference in February 2015[113] spoke of the current prevailing worldview that sexual fulfilment is necessary for human flourishing, and anything, particularly traditional Christian teaching, which stands in the way must be damaging. This worldview, taking its lead from Freudian analysis, sees sex purely as a physical function, whereas the Bible sees sex as an intimate relationship between man and woman, reserved for marriage, reflecting in itself the relation-

---

[112] The article was based on the findings of an international study undertaken by the School for Policy Studies at the University of Bristol. The study also found that almost half of thirteen to seventeen-year-old girls in England sent and received sexual images and texts.

[113] Dr James spoke at the annual Lovewise Conference on February 28th, 2015. The place of Lovewise as an organisation will be explained in detail in subsequent pages.

ship between the Lord Jesus Christ, the bridegroom, taking the Church as his bride.[114]

Dr James traced the growing dominance of this worldview back to the so-called sexual revolution of the 1960s, with its emphasis on sexual liberation and gratification, encouraged by organisations such as the Family Planning Association, which in particular pushed for education on the use of contraception as a means of enabling sexual fulfilment to take place. Other groups believed that it was necessary for young people to have better sexual health information so that they could make their own decisions without being preached at. The Bible on the other hand tells us to "flee from sexual immorality"[115].

As Dr James pointed out, this approach has in itself led to further problems for young people, including increased depression, young men not seeing their responsibilities as fathers and young women feeling used and betrayed. This is not to say that sex in itself is wrong: far from it, as it is a gift of God to be enjoyed within the holy institution of marriage. Tim Chester gives an excellent summary of the beauty of sex as described in the Song of Songs. As he says,

To think negatively about sex is ingratitude towards God. It is to impugn God's goodness.[116]

Early Work

From an early stage, the school had taken a strong stand over the importance of marriage and the dangers of sexual activity outside marriage, including early sexual activity in adolescence. In the early 1990s the school had contact with Dr Lysabeth Duncan, a Scottish obstetrician and gynaecologist who had worked in Ethiopia and had observed and recorded the devastating medical, emotional and social effects of early sexual activity in that culture. She spoke to students and parents about the serious risks that such activity posed.

---

[114] Revelation 19:6-9 gives a wonderful picture of the wedding feast of the Lamb of God and his Church.
[115] 1 Corinthians 6:18. In this and the subsequent verses (19 and 20), Paul goes on to say that for Christians, our bodies are very special in that they are temples of the Holy Spirit, and that we have been bought with a price.
[116] *Captured by a Better Vision;* Tim Chester; Inter-Varsity Press (2010); pages 140-141.

Lysabeth also encouraged the school to produce a video promoting her message, to reach adolescents in the north-east of England. This seemed an exciting project in which to be involved. Members of the RSD department, Margery Tate, Jo Bowden, Phil Abel and David Priestley, were the creative driving forces behind it, and our drama teacher, Ian Williams, worked with the young people who would be taking leading roles. We also found a group of media students from Northumberland College who were willing to take responsibility for filming and editing the video. A storyline was written about young people who realised that they were in danger of making wrong choices in their relationships with members of the opposite sex. Local medical professionals, Christian youth workers and Phil Abel from the school were all interviewed and shared the dangers of early sexual activity, saying how much better it was to keep sexual relationships for marriage. A group of Year 11 students were asked to share their views, and they said, for example, that it was important not to bow to peer pressure. Margery and Jo also put together optional activity resources, including biblical material, to accompany the video. We were pleased with the final product, which we named "Just In Case You Didn't Know".

Once the video, graphically designed covers and resource packs were complete, we had to market the product to ensure that as much use as possible was going to be made of something that had such an important message and into which so much effort had been put. There was also the need to recoup our costs through sales of the product. We held a launch of the video in the school in the summer term of 1994, with those attending being very positive in their comments about the video. Sales, however, were very slow, and I was very concerned that we would not break even, a situation that I could not allow to happen, as limited school resources could not be used to subsidise the product. God, however, as always was very gracious to us, as he provided the funding for us through some generous donations from Christian people and from a bulk sale to one diocesan director of education who wanted to supply all of his schools with a copy of what he believed to be an excellent and essential resource.

We received some positive publicity in the local press about the video we produced. One bit of negative publicity, however, came in April 1997. A group of fathers on the local estate was established with the very laudable aim of promoting the role of fathers in families.

121

Unfortunately, one of the dads asked his daughter how many pregnant girls there were in the school. For some inexplicable reason, the girl said that there were forty! This was of course completely wrong, there being only two (which, of course was two too many). The group of fathers took it to the media where it got a few lines in "The Guardian" and a brief mention on the BBC Radio 4 "Today" programme. This was devastating publicity for us, and despite some retraction, I was concerned about the great amount of damage that might well have been done. To counter this publicity, I produced a letter for our parents, telling them what the true figure was, and the moral stand we took in teaching sex education. We mass-produced a similar letter for our feeder primary schools, three of which were church schools, and took them round by hand to be distributed to their parents.

My next dealings with the media came in the year 2000. The then Education Secretary, David Blunkett, issued guidance to schools that teachers were required to teach the importance of marriage, family life, love and more stable relationships, and not just about sex, which was a positive step forward. In September of that year, the Christian Institute was asked by BBC Radio Cleveland if they could find a secondary headteacher who would take part in a discussion by telephone about family values following the Secretary of State's guidance. I was approached and I agreed to take part in the discussion by telephone in my office with the presenter and another contributor who were in the studio.

I had learned from other interviewees that it was important to get across your points regardless of the specific question that was asked. As it happened, I was given great freedom to put my views across. I said that David Blunkett's proposals were very much in line with what we taught in assemblies and RSD lessons, and I mentioned the video that we had produced. I endeavoured to present marriage as being the ideal form of relationship between a man and a woman, as it was based on love and commitment and presented the most secure relationship for the couple and children, as well as being the most stable and cost-effective for society as a whole; it was the job of schools to challenge our young people with the very best.

I was glad when the interview was over, as I felt put on the spot, although I had prayed beforehand as I did my preparation. I did get a phone call later from one of the Christian Institute staff saying that they thought that it had gone well.

Lovewise

Despite the positive elements in David Blunkett's guidance, it was clear that the messages received by young people on sexual ethics from the media and many in education was that it did not matter how you behaved, as long as you kept yourself safe. Dr Chris Richards and Dr Liz Jones, two paediatricians working in Newcastle, became increasingly aware that many of the young people that they were working with in their clinics were being damaged by the breakdown in family relationships partially caused by the sexual revolution that was taking place. They both felt a strong calling from God to try to counter the prevailing sexual malaise by providing Christian teaching on marriage, sex and relationships to young people in schools and youth groups. As a result, they founded Lovewise in September 2002, with themselves as two of the trustees. They asked me if I would join them as a third trustee as they wanted someone with an education background. Lovewise obtained charitable status in February 2003.

The foundation of Lovewise was an exciting development, as this was an organisation formed with the specific objective of reaching young people with the purity and wholesomeness of God's message with regard to love, marriage, sex and relationships. A series of PowerPoint presentations was put together, written mainly by Chris and Liz, with assistance from a small team of one paid employee and a number of volunteers who did technical and administrative work. Because of the involvement of two highly experienced paediatricians, the materials produced were based on medical facts, and as such had greater credibility. They also of course had a Christian moral framework. Over time, the range of material produced has increased to include high quality DVDs and booklets.[117]

The aim was to take these materials into schools to present them to students to promote the dangers of early sexual relationships, together with the traditional Christian view of marriage, and thus challenge them about their own worldviews on sex and relationships. Although later on the resources were produced for sale to schools, churches and parents, it was initially felt that it was best to maintain the purity of the message by restricting presentations to a team of trained presenters who

---

[117] Full details of the work of Lovewise, including available resources, can be found on its website, lovewise.org.uk.

would deliver the school sessions themselves. These presenters included Chris and Liz along with Christian medical practitioners, students and parents. They were successful in getting into a number of schools to do a variety of types of presentations, and feedback suggested that the message was received positively by many young people. In addition, although Lovewise started in Newcastle, as its reputation spread amongst like-minded Christians, presenters were appointed in different parts of the country, including Cumbria, Hampshire, Northampton-shire, Warwickshire, Suffolk and Sussex, as well as Newcastle.

Not all schools were receptive, however, to having Lovewise presenters. There was often a fear of what was perceived to be an extremist view compared to the prevailing ideology, and so sometimes schools did not respond to invitations to have Lovewise in, or they did not allow presenters to come back. Sometimes it was a case of a key member of staff moving on elsewhere, and so the initial contact was lost. Certainly, it became more difficult to maintain contact with schools, although 120 presentations were still given nationwide over the year 2014-15. Because it was felt that it was becoming more difficult to get directly into schools, it was agreed that resources would be produced and sold to teachers who would use them in their own classrooms. Resources were also produced for church youth groups and for parents so that they could guide their own children, often to counter what was taught in schools.

The website shows the range of resources available for purchase. Flyers were occasionally sent out to contacts telling them of new and updated resources that were available. In 2007, for example, Chris and Liz wanted to send a mailshot out to church schools and they asked me if I would write a short piece to go with it on what they saw as a headteacher's perspective. This is what I wrote:

> *Being a headteacher at the beginning of the twenty-first century is a fascinating and rewarding job, but it brings with it all sorts of pressures. There are of course the same sort of pressures that football managers face, namely to achieve a high position in the league tables. A greater need, however, is for headteachers to help young people deal with the pressures they face, particularly sexual pressures.*

> *As a result of mixed messages from government and the presentation of promiscuous behaviour in the media as the*

norm, young people are in danger of growing up without being made fully aware of the values inherent in the traditional Christian approach to marriage and sex.

It is in this area that Christian headteachers need to take the lead and insist on their schools delivering a sex and relationships programme based on Christian moral standards. This is not easy as staff, governors and health agencies may not always be sympathetic, and certainly, the recent Ofsted report on PSHE has not helped in this matter. The role of Lovewise is of course crucial in this regard by providing a much needed support to schools who want to help their young people stand up to immoral sexual pressures and follow the biblical code on sex and relationships.

The School's Involvement with Lovewise

Inevitably, the school played a key role in the development of Lovewise, although this itself was later to bring problems. For example, the public launch of Lovewise took place in our West Theatre in March 2003, and was well attended.

Chris and Liz wanted to pilot the materials before they tried to get into Tyneside schools, and so they used a couple of our classes for trial presentations. This would be an important learning experience for Chris and Liz; the materials went down quite well with the students, but the approach was more like a lecture than what the students were used to. The team took this message on board as they further developed their presentations. They were later helped out by one of our former members of staff, Jenny Smithson. Jenny was a Christian geography teacher who felt that she would like to be involved more fully in Christian work, and so she left us in 2008 to take on appointments in paid Christian service, one of which was to work part-time for Lovewise. She was very gifted as a teacher in putting together presentations, and Chris and Liz made full use of her skills in improving the quality and attractiveness of the presentations used in schools.

When she became curriculum leader for RSD, Lisa Lowery also provided assistance in developing material for Lovewise. By this time, material was being produced for sale, including a high quality, professionally produced DVD on marriage, a topic that was at the heart of Lovewise's message. On behalf of the trustees, I asked Lisa to produce teaching material to accompany the video. She and I also trialled the DVD and material for our RSD classes before it went on general sale.

Chris and Liz were very concerned about the damaging effect that pornography was having on our young people. The complete sexualisation of our culture means that it is very hard for young people to escape it, and of course the insidious nature of pornography available to them through the internet presents a real danger to young people. Tim Chester, mentioned earlier in this chapter, quotes Pamela Paul in her description of the pornified culture:

> *Not only is pornography more ubiquitous, the entire culture has become pornified. By that, I mean that the aesthetics, values and standards of pornography have seeped into mainstream popular culture.*[118]

Lisa Lowery was also concerned about the issue and she had produced a lesson for our religious studies classes. With her permission, I shared this with Chris and Liz, and this became the basis for a Lovewise resource on pornography, available for sale.

Each year in the summer term, we had a special day for Year 9 students called "The Best of Health Day", co-ordinated by John Hodgson of the religious studies department. This involved students attending carousel sessions on health topics such as alcohol, drugs, healthy eating, exercise and, of course, sex and relationships. These sessions were led either by experts from outside or staff from within the school. The sex and relationships sessions were, up to 2008, led by Lovewise team members. These were good events, and many students indicated through their evaluations that they felt that they had benefitted from them.

The message put forward by the Lovewise team was so important that I felt that it would be valuable to have a presentation for parents so that they could understand the pressures faced by their young people. I invited Chris and Liz to come to a meeting for parents run by the Parent-Teachers' Association to do a presentation, with Dot Lee also taking part to provide information on what the overall school sex and relationships education programme looked like. The meeting was held

---

[118] Tim Chester; op. cit.; page 10.

126

in March 2008, just a few days after what had been a disastrous Ofsted inspection.

What to me seemed a very good idea and indeed a very valuable thing to do completely backfired. Some of the parents came to the meeting absolutely antagonistic towards Lovewise, possibly as a result of their children going home and sharing their perception of the message. There were parents who were more open-minded, and there were Christian parents who strongly believed the message. Chris and Liz gave a good presentation, but they were very strongly criticised by many of the parents who were convinced neither by the moral arguments or the statistical evidence used to back it up. For example, one of the slides likened sex to be a danger like fire, and this was misunderstood by parents thinking that the presenters were completely "anti-sex". The minority of Christian parents present felt too overwhelmed to provide their support to Chris and Liz. To this day, I cannot understand why good parents were so antagonistic towards what was undoubtedly a message that would help to keep their own children safe in terms of sexual relationships.

At the time, I was dealing with the aftermath of the March 2008 inspection (which I shall discuss in detail in chapter nine), and felt that this was another attack on the school. I was so glad when the Easter holidays came, as it gave me time to reflect, particularly as we had booked to fly out to the Algarve, where we also had some family time with Nan, one of Ella's sisters, and her husband, Brian.

Things, however, got worse on the Lovewise front in the summer term. One of the parents wrote to the Chief Education Officer complaining about the fact that this group had come into school with a pernicious message. Nothing could have been further from the truth, but we agreed that the letter of complaint be read out at a full governing body meeting.

At the meeting, I tried to counter the arguments put forward in the letter. One of the pieces of evidence that I used was from a paper written by David Paton, Professor of Industrial Economics at Nottingham University.[119] He used economic theory and econometric analysis to evaluate the effectiveness of the government's Teenage

---

[119] *Random Behaviour or Rational Choice? Family Planning, Teenage Pregnancies and STIs;* David Paton; presented at the Royal Economic Conference in Swansea (April 2004).

Pregnancy Strategy between 1998 and 2001. From 1999, as a result of the strategy, there was an expansion of community-based family planning services aimed specifically at adolescents, along with the provision of the "morning after pill". Effectively this meant that contraceptives, particularly non-barrier contraceptives, became cheaper (and indeed free) to young people. As economic analysis predicted, there was an increase in sexual activity. Empirical evidence indicated that sexual activity had increased over the period, resulting in no change in the very high teenage pregnancy rate but with a large increase in the prevalence of sexually transmitted infections. Basically, the Teenage Pregnancy Strategy resulted in worse sexual health amongst adolescents. My point was that there had to be an approach to sex education that showed students the dangers of sexual activity outside of a committed, stable relationship, preferably through marriage. The alternative contraceptive-based approach would result in disaster.

Governors were divided over the issue. Some wanted other groups to come in to provide balance, but I was very much against that, as the alternative groups would come with a different moral agenda and with a message that students would prefer because it was more liberal and thus seemed easier, and also, in their eyes, more fun. I would prefer no groups, including Lovewise, to come in rather than providing mixed and thus confusing messages for our young people. We would thus entrust the teaching of sex and relationships education to our own highly effective RSD staff.

This seemed a reasonable solution, although as a trustee of Lovewise, I was both disappointed and embarrassed that the group could not come into my school. The RSD staff, however, did use Lovewise resources in their teaching, and, as previously mentioned, Lisa did contribute to the production of resources on marriage and pornography.

The Present Scene: Opposition but Scope for Blessing

In her presentation, Sharon James, as we have seen, traced the development of a liberal worldview with regard to sex and relationships education back to the 1960s. That worldview is even more prevalent today, and so there is even greater opposition to traditional Christian teaching on sexual relationships.

One argument put forward against the traditional Christian approach is that the promotion of marriage as an ideal runs counter to the experience of so many young people whose family arrangements are totally different. Therefore they may feel stigmatised and alienated if they feel that their family is being criticised by teachers or Lovewise presenters. I have always struggled with that dilemma, but at the same time I have always believed that our young people do need to be presented with the very best, which in this case is marriage, for their own wellbeing, their children's wellbeing and the wellbeing of society as a whole. Teachers do, however, need to be sensitive in dealing with these issues. Because they had such good relationships with their students and are trusted by them, our religious studies staff were able to present the challenge of marriage to them in a positive way, and to quote Lisa in her leadership of the department, "We teach marriage as a noble, worthy, ascetic ideal and devote a lot of time to discussing it."

An example of the challenge to Lovewise took place in July 2012 when "The Journal", a regional newspaper for the north-east based in Newcastle, reported that the then shadow public health minister, Diane Abbott, had hit out at Lovewise because of claims that they had made about the consequences of abortion.[120] She was quoted as saying, "Sexual health education is supposed to be based on facts. These people are just peddling bigotry." Chris Richards was able to refute the arguments. He said, "We believe that young people, therefore, have a right to hear and discuss what might be positive about keeping sex for marriage and keeping their unborn child."

Chris was absolutely right. The message of Lovewise is of course one-sided, but so is that of so many other groups advocating greater sexual liberty or believing that contraception education is the answer. Young people, as we have seen, are constantly "pornified" through the media, and they need to be shown an alternative way that is pure and wholesome. If Lovewise and Christians in general cannot share that message, we are letting down generations of young people.

The situation becomes more complicated as a result of the legalising of same-sex marriage in England and Wales as from 2014. It is right for teachers to make their students aware of the change in the law and why people might want to choose that lifestyle. It is, however, also true that teachers do not have to promote that lifestyle against their own

---

[120] *The Journal*, Friday, July 20, 2012.

consciences, and they are also at liberty to explain why there are many people (including homosexual people) who opposed the introduction of that legislation.[121] It is here that Christians have to be wise in handling this and indeed other controversial issues, making sure that lessons in this area are backed up by much prayer.

Despite the opposition, I believe that God does want to bless organisations such as Lovewise. Satan knows the power of God's message in this area, which is why he is opposing it with so much vigour. God, however, will still bring victory. The resources produced by Lovewise are being used in schools and churches throughout the country and there are growing sales of Lovewise books in the United States. Lovewise is still able to make presentations to young people, and from comments made by students in their evaluations, some have been greatly touched by the message. God working in the hearts of young people in this most sensitive area of their lives is indeed a tremendous blessing.

---

[121] *Respecting beliefs about marriage;* Coalition for Marriage (2013) is a very helpful guide for teachers and school leaders.

CHAPTER NINE

Ofsted

If there is one factor that puts leaders in schools off becoming headteachers, it is the fear of Ofsted and, in particular, the consequences of a poor judgement. That phone call announcing their imminent arrival makes the mouth of the most confident head initially go dry and the stomach of the strongest churn. At least, that was my experience. I often said that it was a sad fact that I measured my career in terms of Ofsted inspections.

For the first nine years of my career, I had no contact with Her Majesty's Inspectorate, and that was not uncommon then. My first contact was in 1986 when I was head of sixth form and a large team spent a week scrutinising the work of the school, including the work of the sixth form.

The Ofsted inspectorate was going to play a crucial role in my time as a head, beginning in my very first year in headship.

The Early Inspections

The establishment of Ofsted was intended to raise standards in schools through a more consistent approach to inspection, so that teachers could not go through nine years of their careers without being inspected. The inspection in Alnwick in March 1993 was a pilot Ofsted inspection, prior to the new framework of inspections being rolled out in September of that year. This was very helpful to me, as it gave me a clearer idea as to what Ofsted expected when they came to inspect. It certainly gave me an advantage when I went for my interview for headship in May 1993, as some of the questions were around how we would prepare ourselves for Ofsted. Going through the Alnwick inspection was part of God's provision in preparing me for taking on my role as head.

It was in January 1994 that we received the initial letter saying that a team from Ofsted would visit the school to carry out an inspection in September of that year. This was in effect nine months' notice before the school was going to host its first Ofsted inspection, very different from the half-day's notice that schools now get. I used the forthcoming inspection to my advantage by making changes that I felt were necessary in my first year in the school on the basis that "this was what Ofsted expected". A couple of people used the counterargument that we could not possibly make changes such as introducing a fortnightly timetable with longer period lengths at this time, as this would destabilise the school and put extra pressure on the staff who would all be worried about the inspection. Most staff, however, understood the logic of changing the school organisation to make us as well prepared as possible for the forthcoming inspection.

It was a large team that came to the school in the third week of the autumn term of 1994, with subject specialist inspectors looking at the different departments. Although it lasted most of the week, the vast majority of staff coped very well with it, including the fourteen new staff who had started in the school only a fortnight before. There were some key issues that we were expected to deal with, including the problems associated with having a small sixth form, and also the fact that boys were achieving better than girls, in contrast to the overall national picture. There was also the absolutely baffling issue about not complying with the statutory requirements with regard to collective worship, which we looked at in chapter seven.

The next two inspections took place in 1999 and 2004. In both cases, huge amounts of paperwork were required beforehand, including folders of school policies, departmental schemes of work and data analysis. Each inspection lasted just under a week with about a dozen inspectors descending on the school in each case. These inspections were certainly thorough, and it was very difficult to try to hide anything, although it should be said that some inspectors were much more astute than others. The reports that they produced were, as a result, very detailed, stating the strengths of the school and individual departments, as well as providing lots of things for us to work on. As such, they were probably more helpful, particularly to departmental colleagues, than the much shorter, headline-making reports that are currently produced.

The 1999 inspection was carried out by our own local authority team who had won the contract to undertake our school's inspection. It seems strange now to think that local authorities were paid by Ofsted to inspect their own schools, with possible allegations of bias and whitewashing reports. In our case, the North Tyneside team was fair in its judgements, commenting positively on the quality of teaching and learning, but suggesting that achievement needed to be higher.

I received the phone call for the 2004 inspection on, of all days, my fiftieth birthday. This was my first contact with the registered inspector for the inspection, a retired senior inspector from another local authority, and who was a formidable man with a tremendous grasp of data analysis. He had a very clear understanding of the school's achievement data, and staff, governors and local authority officers were awestruck by his ability to reel off this data without using any notes whatsoever. In his use of data, he was a man slightly ahead of his time, but I could see that the effective use of data was the key to inspection success in the future. In his report, he was very complimentary about my leadership of the school, which was very gracious of him, as I was not so sure that I had a sufficiently robust grasp of our data, or that I was making the most effective use of it.

The reports from these inspections were overall positive, without being glowing. They certainly did not represent damning publicity for the school. This was probably true for most schools as they were so detailed that they did not provide headlines for the local press to use either to praise or condemn schools. We did know, however, that there was work to be done in the area of data analysis. I had thought that we were quite good in this area, but it was clear that the bar was being raised. We promoted Lorraine Smith, our excellent data clerk, to be data manager with a wider remit, and later Paul Quinn and Mike Clelland on the senior leadership team took increased responsibility for data analysis and tracking using a wider range of tools, including those provided by the Fischer Family Trust and Ofsted itself through its RAISE[122] reports.

---

[122] Reporting and Analysis for Improvement through school Self-Evaluation (more commonly referred to as "RAISE").

Building on the 2004 report, the school did move forward in terms of achievement with some excellent sets of examination results, putting us high up in local league tables at both GCSE and "A" level. We were now beginning to feel much more confident in facing future inspections. The inspection regime was, however, changing, as the government felt that they could no longer afford to spend lavish sums of money on sending large inspection teams into schools for a week. Teams would now be significantly smaller and only in school for two days, producing much more concise reports. Part of the inspection cost was also going to be passed on to schools as they were expected to carry out their own self-evaluation of their effectiveness, with the inspection team making judgements against the school's self-evaluation. With much improved examination results, the local authority encouraged me to go for "outstanding" by making that to be our judgement in the school's self-evaluation. It is one thing to go for "outstanding" in terms of making that your aim, but it is another to claim to be so. Looking back, there was undoubtedly arrogance on my part, but at the time I did feel that there was nothing to lose in putting down that judgement in our self-evaluation. I was soon to find out that Ofsted were not going to consider us as anything like "outstanding".

The 2008 Inspection

The next inspection took place in March 2008. Whereas in previous inspections, we had been given notice of a number of months (although this number markedly reduced over time from nine months including holidays in 1994 to three in 2004), this time we were only given two days' notice for colleagues to prepare excellent lessons and for us to finalise the necessary documentation and other arrangements. It was soon to be clear that we did not have all of the necessary documentation.

There is a warning verse that the apostle Paul wrote to which I had not paid close enough attention:

> *So if you think that you are standing firm, be careful that you don't fall!*[123]

---

[123] 1 Corinthians 10:2. I was to warn my secondary headteacher colleagues at my leaving presentation six years later of the dangers of ignoring this verse.

When I first met the HMI[124] leading the inspection I felt that I was standing firm. Almost immediately, however, she asked to have sight of our Single Central Record and other documents such as our Gender Equality Plan. I have to confess that I did not know what she was talking about. I was more keen to talk about our good examination results, the high quality of teaching and learning, our excellent pastoral care, our very good assemblies and the fact that this very week our students were mounting a high quality drama production written by local playwright Keith Williams. She was, however, insistent that she wanted to see this documentation.

I managed to write a Gender Equality Plan during the two days of the inspection with the help of Jean Griffiths, the Senior Secondary Inspector for North Tyneside, by adapting one from a London borough, as very few schools seemed to have one. It was the lack of a Single Central Record that caused us to fall.

The requirement for schools to have a Single Central Record goes back to the Soham murders of 2002 when a school caretaker, Ian Huntley, murdered two ten-year-old girls, Holly Marie Wells and Jessica Aimee Chapman. There had been separate complaints made previously about Huntley concerning sexual assaults and burglary, which had not been revealed by the police prior to his appointment as a caretaker. As a result of this tragic case, the vetting of staff who worked with children was tightened up, with all new staff on their appointment having to go through a Criminal Records Bureau (CRB) check. This is something that we did meticulously on all staff who joined us, which meant that we took our safeguarding responsibilities very seriously. We missed out, however, on the requirement introduced through new regulations in 2006 for the need to have a Single Central Record recording all of these CRB checks. Therefore, I had no idea to what the HMI was alluding. She did, however, very pointedly remark that we would not be getting an "outstanding" judgement. We were of course not the only school which did not have a record in place, and it may be that what happened to us was meant to be an example to other schools to make sure that they met this statutory requirement.

The failure to have this Single Central Record seemed to colour the whole inspection. For example, individual members of staff were given feedback indicating that a number had taught outstanding lessons, but

---

[124] Her Majesty's Inspector

the final report did not reflect that. It was almost as if our failure to have this record in place meant that we could not have outstanding teaching. The inspectors were also concerned about the large, open nature of the site. The overall outcome was that the college was judged to be "inadequate", particularly in relation to leadership and management, and care, guidance and support, and so we were given a "notice to improve".

This of course was devastating for the staff. Before the HMI gave her official feedback to a group consisting of the senior leadership team, Tim Goodwin, the chair of governors, and Jean Griffiths, the Senior Secondary Inspector for North Tyneside, I explained to them what had happened. They just could not believe it. Again, when I reported it to the whole staff, they too did not understand at all what had happened. Yet, once it had sunk in, there was a sense of resilient determination that we would show them next time. Jean actually said that was the reaction she expected from our staff, whom she had come to respect greatly.

After I had spoken to the staff, I sat in my office alone rather numb, thinking through what had happened. I could not actually go home at that point, as the final performance of the play was going to take place that evening, and I had to make a speech afterwards. I did, however, phone Ella and share with her what had happened. I also prayed that the Lord would bring the school through what seemed to be a devastating blow, and that he would sustain me by his grace. The last night of the play was superb, and I spoke at the end, congratulating the cast and the supporting staff and students for all of their efforts. I also encouraged them to hold on to what they had achieved as something that would have a major influence on their lives. Jean very kindly came to the play to provide support, and told me afterwards that I myself had to follow the advice that I had given the young people and hold on to what was really important.

The following morning when I came into school, Rowan, my personal assistant, told me that I needed to sit down before I looked at my in-tray. I thought that I was in for further devastating news, but in fact it was the opposite. Many colleagues had written me very kind letters of personal support, as well as leaving me gifts. This was very much the beginning of God answering my prayer the night before. Of course, it was not only I who prayed. Christians within the school and beyond were very much praying for me and for the school as a whole.

Indeed, one curriculum leader said to me that he had not prayed for a long time but he had very much prayed the previous night.

This sort of news spreads very quickly among schools, and in the days following the inspection I was inundated with phone calls and emails from heads in other schools, who simply could not believe that this could possibly have happened. A number confessed that it could so easily have happened to them.

I took full responsibility for what happened, and never thought about blaming anyone else. The costly error had to be my responsibility, and nobody else's. Did I think of resigning, doing what some might have considered to be the honourable thing? I have to confess that the thought never entered my head at all, and I am grateful to God for preventing me from thinking that way, and he used the support provided by colleagues to help me think positively about the future. Likewise, the governors could perhaps have sacked me. It has often been said that these days, headship is as risky as being a football manager (I am writing this the day after Jose Mourinho was sacked by Chelsea only months after the club won the Premiership!), but to my knowledge there was no discussion at all amongst governors of dismissing me. God protected me again. He also protected me from sinking into some depression that could even lead to something tragic. Sadly, a Scottish primary headteacher committed suicide at this time because her school had failed an inspection. God held me up and told me to go forward, despite what seemed to be a major setback for the school. In the days following the inspection, I very much saw God's grace at work in my life. God showed his mercy to me, even though I did not deserve it. That is grace!

I was warned, however, that there would be opposition. One of our parents who was a local Christian businessman came to see me shortly after the inspection. He told me how sorry he was about what had happened and that the school had a lot of support in the community. He asked me if I believed in visions, and I said yes. He then went on to say that he had had a vision from the Lord, which showed that I personally would be under attack. He also reassured me that people would be praying for me through this period. The attack started the following week with the Lovewise presentation to parents, which, like the inspection, had not gone the way I had expected. As discussed in chapter eight, the fallout from the presentation was something that I could have done without, but I saw it as part of an attack on the school and the standards we were trying to uphold. I knew that God would see us through it, and as mentioned in the previous chapter, he did give us a solution.

There was much work to be done to follow up the Ofsted inspection. One area was in carrying out damage limitation, in terms of our parents and prospective parents understanding what had happened so that they would have no fears about the care provided for their children. It was very fortunate that our School Improvement Partner had previously written a report outlining the ways in which we were an outstanding school. In writing a letter to parents, I used his judgement and quoted his examples to show that fundamentally Ofsted were wrong and that we could continue to be considered as at least a good school. I explained that Ofsted came to their conclusion because of an "administrative error" on our part, rather than there being genuine issues over safety, the quality of pastoral care, the quality of teaching or academic standards. This letter seemed to satisfy parents, and many passed on their personal views that Ofsted's judgement seemed to be complete nonsense.

This is where God's grace was very apparent. He lavished his protection on the school, and to my knowledge there was no adverse publicity in the local media; it was as if the inspection simply had not happened. There was no exodus of parents believing that because we had failed Ofsted we had somehow failed their children. Indeed, more than that, in the following two Septembers we experienced our highest ever intake numbers. God ensured that parents maintained and, amazingly, even increased their confidence in the school.

Tim Goodwin called an emergency governors' meeting two weeks after the inspection to discuss the way forward. My way of thinking through these situations is by mindmapping, and so I produced a mindmap of actions that we needed to take to meet the criticisms made by Ofsted to share with governors. The main criticism, that of failing to have a Single Central Record, was fairly easily rectified, and Rowan was already well underway in putting our record together. I was also very grateful to our finance and administrative officer, Ian Wallace, for producing a plan to increase student safety through the construction of a large, yet not obtrusive, fence around the site, to keep students inside the campus after they had entered it in the morning and unwanted visitors off the site. Jean Griffiths from the local authority was at the meeting, and she promised financial support for this project. Fence suppliers were going to have a field day as school after school followed our example in improving site security.

This meeting also accepted my recommendation that we did not appeal against the decision, but rather we should prepare ourselves for reinspection in a year's time, by which time the Single Central Record would be perfectly constructed as would be the fence around the site. The reason for this was that, at best on appeal, we would only get a judgement of "satisfactory", which would hang round our necks for perhaps three years, whereas it would be better to suffer the pain of being officially labelled "inadequate" for a year before we were re-inspected.

I did, however, feel that I needed to write to Ofsted to explain how I believed that we had been unjustly treated. This would not necessarily make any difference to our situation (although I do believe that the HMI who came to inspect us in 2009 did have sight of the letter), but it might prevent other schools from suffering the same fate. My two introductory paragraphs read as follows:

> *The judgement of the inspection team was that the overall effectiveness of the school was unsatisfactory, and, as a result, it was given a notice to improve. The issue that brought the school down was our failure to have our CRB checks recorded on a Single Central Record. We do accept that we should have had that in place, and under Ofsted's regulations, are deemed to be unsatisfactory. We have decided not to appeal against that decision.*

> *I need to point out, however, that this has resulted in the community not so much losing faith in the school, but rather in Ofsted as an organisation and the judgements that it makes. I have had nothing but support from both within the school and beyond, saying what an excellent school we have, and how ridiculous it is for Ofsted to fail us on an administrative technicality. You need to be aware that Ofsted has lost a significant amount of credibility over this particular inspection.*

Over the next few months the school worked hard in preparation for a monitoring visit in October and a full inspection in May 2009. The HMI who came to do the October monitoring visit had a reputation for taking no prisoners, but God allowed me to establish a good relationship with him. He was pleased with the Single Central Record, which he looked through forensically. On his way out, I did say to him that I expected the school to get record examination results in the following summer, perhaps getting as high as 60% 5 or more A*-C GCSE grades including English and maths. His response was that he could not see that happening. In August 2009, when we achieved 61%, I, perhaps arrogantly, emailed him to let him know how well we had done, and he very graciously replied, "I am delighted with your success – very well done. Lots of dedicated work by all."

The 2009 inspection was a different experience altogether. The HMI leading the inspection was very supportive, and her first comment to me was that I would have been angry about the previous outcome. I said that I was and that the punishment that the school had suffered was greatly disproportionate to the misdemeanour. The approach of the team was very much to look for the positives in the school, of which there were many. One of these positives was parental support, and the HMI and I together looked through the parental feedback that was sent in, which was very supportive, including from parents who appreciated the Christian emphasis (there were a couple of parents who felt that there was too much religion, but the inspector's response was, "What's wrong with that?"). The outcome was that our notice to improve was lifted and we were judged to be "good with outstanding features", to everyone's great relief.

The school had been through so much in the fourteen months following the March 2008 inspection, but it was undoubtedly a better school as a result of what we had been forced to do. Safeguarding was very high on our agenda, and we made sure that we had all procedures in place, no matter how unnecessarily bureaucratic they were. We were a much safer school as a result of the fence around our huge site, and our monitoring processes were now of a very high standard. I was reminded of one of my favourite verses in Paul's letters:

And we know that in all things God works for the good of those who love him, who have been called according to his purpose.[125]

---

[125] Romans 8:28.

The staff had to work very hard, and God protected the school; there were no casualties amongst the staff in the process, the school roll rose, and the school was a much better, safer place for staff and students.

How Did the 2008 Inspection Affect Me Personally?

It is fascinating to read in Scripture how different people coped with adversity. David spent much time in conflict and on the run from his enemies, particularly the armies of King Saul. In Psalm 22, he pours out his feelings to God. Initially, he feels that God has forsaken him.

> *My God, my God, why have you forsaken me?*
> *Why are you so far from saving me,*
> *so far from the words of my groaning?*
> *O my God, I cry out by day, but you do not answer,*
> *by night, and am not silent.[126]*

Towards the end of the Psalm, however, he is much more positive, and realises that God is there after all and is prepared to help him, and is indeed worthy of great praise.

> *For he has not despised or disdained*
> *the suffering of the afflicted one;*
> *he has not hidden his face from him*
> *but has listened to his cry for help.*
> *From you comes the theme of my praise in the great*
> *assembly;*
> *before those who fear you will I fulfil my vows.[127]*

My situation was nowhere near as desperate as David's; he was a fugitive on the run for his life, whereas my situation was only that my leadership was criticised by Ofsted for not ensuring that a particular record had been completed. There was simply no comparison.

Furthermore, Jesus used these same words as he hung upon the cross:

> *My God, my God, why have you forsaken me?[128]*

---

[126] Psalm 22:1-2.
[127] Psalm 22:24-25.
[128] Matthew 27:46.

Jesus suffered tremendous physical pain on the cross, but, more than that, to pay the punishment for our sins, he was separated from his Heavenly Father, and thus absolutely forsaken by God. Any dejection or disappointment that I had was of little significance compared with what Jesus had to go through in making the sacrifice that was necessary for my sins to be forgiven.

Yet, although it was of relatively little significance, God knew the pain I was going through and he poured out his grace on me and enabled me to lose very quickly any dejection that I felt. I was ultimately able to praise God as David did at the end of Psalm 22.

One event that God graciously used to put everything in perspective for me took place at the beginning of the week after the inspection. Ella and I had been earnestly praying for months over a family situation, but nothing seemed to be happening. It seemed as if God was going to allow a situation to develop that we were sure was not right and not in his will. God answered our prayer on the Monday after the inspection, which was also the same night as the fateful Lovewise meeting. This answer to prayer was very last minute and "just in time". It very much demonstrated God's love to our family, as well as making me realise that there were things more important than Ofsted. God showed to me once more that he was very much in control of all of our circumstances, and that he would protect the school despite the attacks upon it.

Another way in which God spoke to me was through a book which I read during the summer of 2008, R.T. Kendall's volume on the life of Joseph, "God Meant it for Good"[129]. I have always found Kendall's books stimulating in developing my understanding of biblical truth and very practical in terms of his application of that truth to my Christian life. This book was no different, and it was very apt for the situation I faced in that post-Ofsted year.

Kendall very vividly demonstrated how God worked his purposes out through the life of Joseph as he faced numerous difficulties including being sold by his brothers into slavery, false accusations of adultery and life in prison until he eventually became Pharaoh's prime minister. Joseph was in the pit (literally) but God had his hand on him throughout and through his different experiences God moulded him into the man he wanted him to be. God's refining comes so often through suffering. Joseph had been humbled from being a spoiled,

---

[129] *God Meant it for Good;* R.T.Kendall; Authentic Media (2006).

arrogant young man to becoming a slave and a prisoner. God's timing was perfect, however, and when his gift of interpreting dreams was most needed Joseph was brought before Pharaoh and shared God's plan for Egypt. As Kendall put it, he went from "humiliation today to exaltation tomorrow"[130]. He was finally able to meet his brothers and say to them, "You intended to harm me, but God intended it for good to accomplish what is now being done, the saving of many lives."[131]

God's grace was very evident in the life of Joseph, as he transformed this young man and brought him vindication at exactly the right time. I knew from reading this book and thinking again about the ever familiar story of Joseph that God's grace would be poured out on both me and the school, and that we would know God's vindication. I felt a degree of humiliation by the Ofsted experience, as I constantly had to explain to others what had happened. This was all part of God's refining in my life to make me more like the person he wanted me to be, and indeed to become more like Jesus. That should be the experience of all Christians as we are "transformed into his image with ever-increasing glory, which comes from the Lord, who is the Spirit."[132]

There was vindication in God's time. As mentioned before, the 2009 inspection was an excellent experience for us, removing the notice to improve and judging us to be a good school with outstanding features. I experienced some "exaltation", to use Kendall's word, in that my leadership was described as being "inspiring and visionary". If it was, it was very much by God's grace.

The 2012 Inspection

I experienced two more Ofsted inspections before I retired. The first was an inspection into economic and business education that took place in March 2011. This was judged to be "good", and indeed I would have been mortified if it had come out as any less than "good", given my own subject background.

My last inspection in the school took place in May 2012, and this turned out not to be a particularly easy one. Examination results rose significantly after the previous inspection in the summer of 2009, but then declined in 2010 and 2011. In comparison with other schools, the

---

[130] R.T. Kendall; op. cit.; chapter 15.
[131] Genesis 50:20.
[132] 2 Corinthians 3:18.

school's results did not seem particularly good, largely because we had not been playing the qualifications game that many others had, as described in chapter three. In the autumn of 2011, as a school we did change tack and became more flexible by taking students out of courses where they were not succeeding and putting them into more accessible courses such as GCSE photography and various vocational courses. We also gave students the opportunity to take GCSE mathematics a number of times using different examination boards. As a result, we were able to look forward to a much better set of results in August 2012, and so I felt that I could honestly say in our self-evaluation that we were a good school.

I was surprised, even shocked, when the phone call came in May 2012, as I had been praying that we would not be inspected until the autumn when our results would be so much better. This was clearly the wrong prayer, as God wanted to show me his gracious provision in a different way! During that initial phone call, the lead inspector made clear that our data based on previous examination results made the school look only satisfactory. She did, however, throw me a lifeline, challenging me to prove that our achievement data was good. This I felt was an amazing opportunity, and I said to staff when I briefed them on the Friday night prior to the inspection that those who prayed should pray that we would come through this inspection successfully. Indeed, there was much prayer over this locally and beyond. For example, on the day before the Ofsted inspection, I spoke at the Burnopfield Fellowship and shared with our friends Eddie and Audrey Stringer that Ofsted were due in the next day, and they promised to pray for the school.

There was hard work as well as prayer over that weekend. Paul Quinn, Mike Clelland and Lorraine Smith in particular worked on the data and Paul very convincingly presented our case to the inspectors. He was able to prove that the school was going to get excellent results in the summer, which we did, resulting in a "good" judgement for achievement, which allowed us to be judged "good" overall. In addition, spiritual, moral, social and cultural development was considered to be "outstanding", with the assembly programme, religious studies lessons, charity work and performing arts all contributing to that judgement. I was able to talk to the staff about the miracle that had taken place.

Overview

Schools and headteachers need to be held accountable, but Ofsted can often be cruel in its judgements. Too often, schools feel obliged to jump to the latest Ofsted pronouncement, whether it be to do with the height of fences or the promotion of British values. Mick Waters puts the Ofsted fear this way:

> *The secretary of state (Michael Gove), in a long line of those intent on school improvement, states publicly that headteachers have autonomy and freedom. Yet many heads smile wryly and see only their freedom to feel afraid. Fear for themselves, fear for their school and fear for its community being labelled a failure. With the wolf at the door, they focus more and more on trying to generate the data that might give temporary reprieve, knowing all the time that their school is becoming increasingly something that their pupils do not need and is far from their own belief about what education should be for. In some cases, integrity is replaced by increasingly desperate measures to meet and cheat the stats. It is a brave head who sticks to what is known to work in the long term when the pressure for a short-term fix is mounting.[133]*

If that is the outcome of Ofsted inspections, then that is a terrible indictment of our accountability system. I have always failed to understand how one number on a 1 to 4 scale can categorise as complex an institution as a school. Yet the judgement can be devastating for the school and its community if it receives a 3 or a 4. Indeed, as has happened to one of my previous schools, if a school falls off the precipice going from 1 ("outstanding") in a number of consecutive inspections to 4 ("requiring special measures"), there must be something inherently wrong with the system. Likewise, I have known a number of schools labelled "outstanding", which were no better than ours (although some were) but managed to play the Ofsted game well. These sorts of judgements distort the marketplace, and, as we shall see in the next chapter, this can be vital for any school's financial wellbeing.

---

[133] Paragraph taken from *Thinking Allowed: On Schooling* By Mick Waters © Mick Waters 2013; ISBN 9781781350560; page 125.

So much relies upon data, and many schools have been condemned by poor data. Certainly, I believe that we could have been judged to require improvement in 2012 on the basis of previous examination results, if it had not been for the lead inspector being prepared to accept more appropriate evidence. God once more very clearly answered our prayers. Data is very important, but it does not necessarily reflect the true spirit of an organisation.

In his excellent analysis of the devastating fall of RBS, Iain Martin is scathing about the tyranny of data when he says,

> *Data and modelling are useful in all manner of human activities, such as measuring performance in business, health, education or sport. The potential danger comes in elevating it to such an extent that insufficient room is left for the application of common sense. Data can point the way, but if we let it tell us what to think and feel we are in trouble.*[134]

Ofsted teams have been accused of being too data-driven to the detriment of many otherwise good schools.

In addition, too much has depended on the particular team sent to inspect a school. The team which failed us in 2008 was very different in its approach and attitude to that of 2009 which applauded the very good work of the school. Headteachers have often complained about inconsistencies between inspection teams, with some being much more hard-lined than others in the ways in which they interpret and apply the inspection framework. To quote Mick Waters again,

> *The only thing that has ever been consistent about Ofsted inspections is that they are inconsistent.*[135]

Besides, the frameworks have changed so much over time that a school that was judged "outstanding" under one framework would perhaps not be so judged under the framework introduced a few months later.

To make matters worse, Ofsted seems to be stretching its tentacles in all sorts of different directions. At the end of 2015, the government started consulting on giving Ofsted the power to inspect out-of-school settings that provided instruction for more than six hours in any week.

---

[134] *Making it Happen;* Iain Martin: Simon and Schuster (2013); page 316.
[135] Mick Waters; op. cit.; page 124.

This would undoubtedly include many church activities, such as summer missions, camps and holiday clubs. Ofsted would be looking to see whether the teaching complied with British values. A holiday club that taught children that only by trusting in Jesus can you receive salvation may well be accused of failing to tolerate other faiths and of encouraging extremism. This is frightening and potentially damaging. So many young people have come to faith or grown in their faith through these special activities. Even Sunday schools had seemed threatened, as indicated by Sir Michael Wilshaw, Her Majesty's Chief Inspector of Education, Children's Services and Skills, in a radio interview when he stated that he expected them to be registered to ensure the safety of the children attending, and where necessary to be inspected.[136] It almost seems like we are becoming more of a police state with the government attempting to use Ofsted to regulate what churches teach.

There is a need for schools to be made accountable, as we do not want weaknesses to be perpetuated and we want all of our schools to become better. We do, however, need to have a system that is based on support rather than fear. We also need to be sure that an organ of the state such as Ofsted does not obtain a remit to interfere in the teaching programme of churches. Christians need to be very much in prayer for their schools when the inspector calls, and praying that Christian values will direct the thinking and actions of government ministers and civil servants as they propose legislation relating to inspection, so that righteousness and common sense will prevail.

---

[136] Sir Michael Wilshaw in a radio interview on LBC on January 14th, 2016. He did, however, retract that statement when he appeared before Parliament's Education Select Committee on June 16th, 2016.

CHAPTER TEN

Finance and the Marketplace

A ny volume considering practical leadership in schools cannot escape the reality of finance and the need to ensure that available resources are used in the most effective ways for the benefit of children and young people. Over my experience of headship, budgetary constraints have at times prevented the school from doing everything it would like to do for the benefit of the students. It has also been true, however, that government grants have allowed the school to move forward in new directions particularly in the use of technology. Balancing the budget was often a headache, and was not always possible, and I often had to be reminded of the Lord's words, "...for every animal of the forest is mine, and the cattle on a thousand hills."[137]

Local Management of Schools

Prior to the passage of the Education Reform Act of 1988, schools were only given a limited amount of financial freedom, being allocated relatively small sums of money to buy books and pencils. Funding associated with a school's staffing and premises costs were held centrally, with the local authority, for example, deciding on the staffing complement of the school and paying the salary bill accordingly.

In the 1980s there was a growing international movement to give schools greater control of their own funding so that they could make their own spending decisions based upon local priorities. Two Australian educationalists, Brian Caldwell and Jim Spinks, wrote of their experience in Tasmania in what was to be a ground-breaking book

---

[137] Psalm 50:10.

on the subject, "The Self-Managing School"[138]. I was fortunate to attend a conference where they spoke and provided compelling arguments to support what in England was called the "Local Management of Schools". It all sounded eminently sensible and straightforward: the school would set its own priorities for the coming year, add up the costs, and if there was not enough money in the budget, subtract the costs of the least important priorities until the budget balanced. I was told that all you had to do was to add and subtract. Unfortunately, it was not going to be quite as straightforward as that.

I was deputy headteacher in Alnwick when Local Management of Schools was introduced. Finance was part of my area of responsibility and so I was thrown in at the deep end when delegated funding was introduced into schools, being responsible to the governors for the budgeting process. Each school was given funding based on a formula that was largely pupil-driven; AWPU (age weighted pupil unit) became another educational acronym to be added to the growing list. From that funding, all of the school's expenses had to be paid.

Inevitably, in going from one funding mechanism to another, there will be winners and losers. Prior to the introduction of the scheme, Northumberland County Council used some shadow figures, and worked out which schools would be winners and which schools would be losers. Unfortunately, when the scheme was actually introduced, it seemed that no schools were winners and that all schools would have to tighten their belts. It was not going to be so easy to apply the Caldwell and Spinks approach. One reason was that schools tended to have relatively fixed costs such as staffing and premises costs which were not particularly easy to cut.

Northumberland itself was poorly funded, not having areas of deprivation or ethnic mix that would tend to attract additional funding, and its wide geographical area with a sparse population brought further spending issues. There were also many small, relatively expensive schools which local politicians at the time were not very keen to close as they were at the centre of their communities. Spending cuts which local councils were forced to make in the early 1990s exacerbated the problem.

---

[138] *The Self-Managing School;* Brian J Caldwell and Jim M Spinks: Falmer Press (1988).

The school had its own problems within the Northumberland scheme. The funding formula was based on average salaries, which meant that if your salary bill was higher than average you would inevitably be a significant loser on the introduction of the system. We did have a relatively old and thus expensive staff, which greatly imbalanced the budget. Likewise, being a split site school, with one site dating back to the nineteenth century, considerably added to its costs.

There were some grants that helped fund the school, in particular funding through the Technical and Vocational Education Initiative (TVEI, yet another acronym), which provided a lot of extra computing power and other resources to pump prime curriculum change. This is where the Caldwell and Spinks approach came into its own. Priorities were ascertained and costed and if necessary spending plans were reduced until it was agreed that the grant funding available would be spent in the most beneficial way. The drawback with these grants, however, was that they were time-limited, thus giving the school further headaches when the funding came to an end.

When cuts have to be made, it is inevitable that the staffing budget has to take a hit, considering that it accounts for over eighty per cent of the total budget. Some of the reduction can come through natural wastage as staff move to other posts or retire. There may, however, have to be redundancies with staff leaving voluntarily or through compulsory notice, but without being replaced. It was as deputy head that I gained some experience of helping to administer redundancies. This was going to play an important part in my time as a headteacher, particularly in my latter years.

Finance and Headship

Moving to take up my headship meant moving from one local authority, Northumberland, to a neighbouring one, North Tyneside. For all sorts of demographic reasons, North Tyneside was much better funded than Northumberland. Heads' meetings, however, were still full of complaints about how poorly schools were funded. When headteachers get together, they tend to spend a lot of time talking about inequalities in the formula allocation between authorities and between schools and how much money the authority is holding back from schools.

Despite higher funding in North Tyneside, I had to grapple with budget deficits over a number of years, but they were never so bad as to require compulsory redundancies until my last two years (which will be covered in more detail in the following chapter). Voluntary redundancies, natural wastage and the judicious use of grants helped to deal with the financial problems the school faced. When we were in a deficit situation, I was usually able to convince the local authority that things were improving, and they usually were! Being allowed to carry a deficit forward was very much an answer to prayer, and at one governors' meeting I thanked those who prayed about the finances and encouraged others to do so as well.

The Lord did provide grants to us that helped our financial situation enormously and allowed us to give the new students new opportunities. For example, the school became a Technology College in 1998 after three unsuccessful bids and the fourth one finally being successful. At a staff end of term presentation evening, Mike Payling, who was my deputy at the time, gave me an award for perseverance with bagpipe music playing in the background and reminded everyone of the story of Robert the Bruce and the spider.

The first two bids were not particularly good and did not deserve to be successful, but the third one was judged to be excellent by consultants from the Technology Colleges Trust. Unfortunately, government ministers (or their civil servants) did not agree, but I did hear on the grapevine that we were held back for political reasons, with an unofficial promise that we would be successful next time. In 1997, Stephen Byers, our local Member of Parliament, became Minister of State for Education in the new Labour government and it was felt that it would not be appropriate to grant this award to a school in his constituency so soon after taking office. Whether that was true or not, what I do know is that we did not pray enough about our first three bids, probably as a result of complacency, and so when the fourth bid was submitted the school prayer group did cover it in much prayer.

Technology College Status brought in an abundance of riches in terms of new equipment particularly in the teaching of the technology subjects of maths, science, design technology and ICT. It also allowed us to employ more staff in these areas than the budget delegated by the local authority on its own would allow for. There was also an obligation to help our feeder primary schools deliver these subjects using the subject expertise of our staff and the increased equipment that we now had. As outlined in chapter six, this brought benefits to the primary schools involved as well as increasing our foothold in the schools, a development which was very important in our marketing strategy.

Excellence in Cities, an initiative introduced by the Labour government at the end of the 1990s, also brought additional funding into the school. Our most able students benefited from the gifted and talented programme, those who faced barriers to learning benefited from access to learning mentors and the whole community benefited from the building and equipping of the North Tyneside City Learning Centre.

The City Learning Centre (CLC) was a state-of-the-art high-tech centre that was to be at the forefront in the use of technology in education. North Tyneside was initially given in 2000 one such centre to be housed in one of its secondary schools, who were all asked to bid for it if they were interested in hosting the centre. I jumped at the opportunity of putting in a bid, in which I outlined the advantages which our school had, including space in a prominent position in the school, a brilliant network manager, Alastair Hetherington, who could lead ICT developments, a tradition of working with other schools and an adult education programme that would make excellent use of the new facilities. The bid, along with a presentation at Wallsend Town Hall, was successful, and the centre was open for business in the autumn of 2001. The centre did have its teething problems, but under the leadership of Jonathan Chicken it became an exciting place for young people and adults to learn, with many groundbreaking events taking place there. Although it was not a resource for our use alone, it did boost our budget, it provided excellent facilities for our students to use, and it was something that we could show off to parents who came to visit.

Marketing

The budget formula was very much pupil-driven, and so the more students who came on to the school roll, the greater the revenue the school would receive. This led schools to consider establishing marketing budgets. In the early years, I did not make direct marketing a major priority, apart from working closely with the designated primary schools in our pyramid of schools to ensure that a very high percentage came to us, and working with Year 11 students to ensure that as many of them as would benefit would continue into the sixth form.

The pyramid of schools worked very closely together and the heads were very supportive of the work that we did with their children who came to us. Mike Payling, one of whose responsibilities in the 1990s was pyramid liaison, spoke of his ideal of the pyramid as being one large split site school. Of course, there are now more formal groupings of schools in federations and multi-academy trusts, but in those early days it was a close partnership. It was not, however, inevitable that parents from our feeder schools would choose us as the secondary school for their children. Middle class parents in particular wanted to look round other schools, including high achieving schools in more affluent parts of North Tyneside and schools in the private sector. For some parents there was a stigma attached to the local estate, going back to the days of gangs in the 1970s.

Our strategy was very simple. Without using fancy brochures or giving out free gifts, we would encourage parents to visit the school for a guided tour. I would do the bulk of the tours myself, as it seemed to impress parents that the top person in the organisation would take time to show them round and answer their questions. They were almost always very impressed with the calm atmosphere and purposeful learning. If asked if we had bullying, I would be honest and say that there were instances of bullying, as in all organisations, but then would explain the various strategies we used to deal with it. We also had primary pupils come to the school to take part in various events which we put on for them.

In addition to encouraging parents to come into school, we would also ensure that we had a presence in the primary schools. Working with primary pupils in their own classrooms made our staff known to them, and if they had a good experience, they would hopefully want to come to us. I also tried to get into these schools as often as possible, even if it meant, as happened one year, taking Ella, her mother and her sister Betty to a local primary school summer fayre.

The strategy over time seemed to work and we heard of fewer parents from our feeder schools choosing to take their children elsewhere. We seemed an increasingly attractive option with improved examination results and the implementation of Behaviour for Learning. In addition, Christian parents liked the clear Christian ethos which came through assemblies, the strength of the RSD department and our stand on sex and relationships education.

Furthermore, some parents from outside the catchment area discovered the school, liked the ethos and sent their children to us. One Christian lady living in a neighbouring catchment area was very impressed, told her friends and that started the ball rolling. The parents of one particular primary school in another catchment area were so disenchanted with the secondary school that their children were meant to go to that en masse they decided to look for another school and many found us. This was helped by the fact that Paul Quinn sat close to the chair of governors of this school at St James' Park (the home of Newcastle United) and was able informally to share the strengths of the school at half time, or when the match got boring. Similarly, the parents of the music co-ordinator at the same school lived close to Dave Clarke, another member of the senior team, who explained how successful the Pyramid Music Festival was; the school's music co-ordinator was desperate to get her school involved in this major event.

In taking in pupils from outside our catchment area, there was no deliberate "poaching" of other schools' pupils by marketing the school in other catchment areas. This would have gone against the sustainable leadership principles propounded by Hargreaves and Fink, as explained in chapter six. Rather, I believe that God brought them our way, and even the conversations at St James' Park or between Dave Clarke and his neighbours were no accident, but were all part of God's provision for the school. The result was that by 2009, we were taking in year groups of over 200 students, compared with 140 when I first started at the school in 1993.

As well as ensuring that students came to us in Year 7, we also had to work hard to ensure that our Year 11 students stayed with us into the sixth form. I have never had a problem with students going elsewhere to do a course, particularly a vocational course for which we had neither the equipment nor expertise. I have, however, been extremely disappointed when students chose to go elsewhere to do courses that we offered so well in school. That was the situation I found when I arrived at the school, and indeed it was clear to me on interview that we had to make the sixth form more attractive. Year 11 students found the local sixth form college to be a very attractive option, and we were losing a sizeable number to them who would have benefited from staying with us. Our main strategy was to emphasise the advantages of staying with us, including the wide range of courses on offer, the high quality of teaching and the better care they would have from teachers who knew them. This seemed to be effective, and especially when examination results at "A" level improved, and gave us an even stronger selling point.

With our student roll rising through the work we were doing to get students into Year 7 and retaining students into the sixth form, our financial position greatly strengthened. I was grateful to God for his provision. Or was I? Perhaps I was relying on my own strength too much when it seemed that we were having success, and perhaps I was not giving God the glory for all that he had done for the school. Perhaps I was in essence a bit like the rich fool that Jesus spoke about in Luke chapter 12 and whom I talked about in harvest assemblies, who hoarded his wealth in ever bigger barns without seeing disaster round the corner. Perhaps I forgot about God's grace.

The Beginning of the Downturn

In his analysis of what the extraordinarily successful All Blacks rugby team can teach us about leadership, James Kerr makes use of a military acronym, "VUCA". This is what he says:

VUCA: Volatile, Uncertain, Complex and Ambiguous. VUCA describes a world prone to sudden change, unknown consequence and complex, shifting interrelationships; one that is impossible to decipher, impossible to predict. For the military-industrial complex, VUCA means asymmetric warfare, geopolitical instability and unreliable loyalties. For business, it means structural collapse, credit crises, reputation damage. For individuals, it represents career insecurity, rising prices, housing market illiquidity and an uncertain future. For leaders, it means dealing with decisions that involve incomplete knowledge, sketchy resources and the vicissitudes of human nature.[139]

We were at the top of our game by 2009 with good examination results, a growing roll, a very good Ofsted judgement and budget surpluses. The simple advice that Kerr gives is, "When you are at the

---

[139] James Kerr; op. cit.; page 26.

top of your game, change the game."[140] We were in a VUCA scenario with things about to change suddenly and I did not act quickly enough to change strategy. The basic mistake that I made was that I continued to expand the staff in response to a rising roll. This might seem to be the logical thing to do, but I failed to apply the OODA principle outlined by Kerr:[141]

O Observe, using all the senses like an animal sniffing in the wind.
O Orient, synthesising all the available data into one coherent map.
D Decide, determining the best course of action.
A Act, acting swiftly and decisively to take advantage of the moment.

There was a changing environment to which I did not react quickly enough. The local school that had been considered unpopular by many parents appointed a new headteacher who started to rebrand the school, market more persuasively and raise examination results, so that they were largely on a par with ours (better in some years and worse in others). Parents in that catchment area who in the past might have come to us stayed with that school as a result. I could hardly complain about that, although we did continue to compete over one particular primary school. Another school started to achieve much better examination results than we did, and also opened a beautiful new building. Their marketing was aggressive, and targeted a number of parents in our feeder primaries. The landscape had changed and I was caught on the backfoot.

Jim Collins and Morten T Hansen give good advice in their book "Great by Choice"[142], a book that I wish that I had read when we were starting on that upward trajectory. This book tries to explain why some companies thrive in times of uncertainty while others fail to do so. For example, they talk about "the 20 mile march" suggesting that organisations should aim at a constant target, not going below that when conditions are bad (which can be difficult), but also not going above it when conditions are good (which can also be difficult). The

---

[140] James Kerr; op. cit.; chapter II.
[141] James Kerr; op. cit.; pages 26-27.
[142] *Great by Choice;* Jim Collins and Morten T Hansen; Random House (2011).

aim is to be consistently good over a long period of time.[143] If I had read that earlier, I would have expanded the staff at a much slower rate in the good years. They also advise that you should "zoom out" to see the big picture and in particular any changes in conditions, and then "zoom in" to focus on the implementation of action plans.[144] This is similar to OODA, and again I wished that I had zoomed out earlier.

Reacting to the New Conditions

It was important that we kept our position in the marketplace, not simply for financial reasons, but also because we believed that we had something special to offer, not least of which was from a spiritual perspective. We could no longer simply rely on the parents of our feeder schools loyally sending their children to us or parents from other catchment areas finding us. Competition was now much more intense, and marketing had to be very high on our agenda.

As far as I was concerned, marketing meant celebrating the successes of the school and ensuring that our community knew what was special about us. It was not about making spurious claims or proclaiming that the school was better than it was. Neither did it involve saying that we were better than other schools, and thus diminishing their achievements.

Mark Elliott, one of our assistant heads, who had a sharp mind and a business studies background, was put in charge of the strategy, and he was ably assisted by Judith Spence, one of our longstanding members of the support staff who was very skilled at putting publicity materials together and organising events. Adam Warkman, our curriculum leader for history, was given extra responsibility for strengthening partnerships with our primary schools. We formed a marketing subcommittee of governors, and were very ably served by governors who had business expertise.

We felt that everything we did should become more professional, but without losing the personal touch. Our prospectus was a good example of that. Rather than having endless pages of dreary policies, we decided that we would set it out through themes such as teaching, caring and involvement, and have personal testimonies from students and their parents covering these different aspects, along with

---

[143] Collins and Hansen; op. cit.; chapter 3.
[144] Collins and Hansen; op. cit.; chapter 5.

professionally taken photographs. I interviewed a range of students and wrote the prospectus based on what they told me. This was a wonderful experience for me, as it was so affirming to hear how much the students loved their school and how much the staff of the school did for them. Parents likewise contributed excellent quotations; two Christian parents, Jonathan and Julia Sanders said,

> *The teachers seem to be genuinely enthusiastic about their subjects and we have often commented that we ourselves would like to have been taught by 'someone like that.' We are very grateful indeed for the provision and variety of musical experiences, and the Senior Choir in particular has been outstanding. How lucky the children are to have teachers who bother so much.*

Similarly, we produced a high quality video through a company recommended by one of our governors. The producers of the video asked members of staff and students questions based on the prospectus themes, allowing us to give answers that were unscripted and straight from the heart. It brought a lump to the throat every time we showed it at publicity events such as our Open Evening.

We made greater effort to get into primary schools to meet parents and work with their children. For example, I spent a few mornings standing in the playground of one of the schools talking to parents about the school, not something that necessarily comes easy to me.

I also did more assemblies in primary schools. These assemblies had a clear Christian message, which was of paramount importance, but I also tried to link their school to ours to ensure that they would think positively about choosing to come to us. In December 2013, our science department managed to obtain an exhibition from NASA of a collection of rocks from the moon, which was a focus for science and other lessons at the time. This was a tremendous coup for the school and we received a lot of positive publicity. We invited each of our feeder primaries to come and see the rocks and have a special lesson about them. In the following months I went to some of the schools to take an assembly, during which I showed the children photographs of them examining the rocks, before talking about the first moon landing. I shared with the children that the astronauts read from the Bible the following verses:

When I consider your heavens,
  the work of your fingers,
the moon and the stars,
  which you have set in place,
what is mankind that you are mindful of them,
  human beings that you care for them?[145]

From that, I left them with the message that God who made all the stars and planets cares for each one of us in a special way.

Our marketing had improved enormously and parents who came to the events we put on often said that they could not believe that anyone would want to send their child anywhere else because of the enthusiasm of our staff and the care we had for the students.

Marketing by schools does, however, pose ethical questions. Large sums of money intended to enhance the education of young people are used in advertising campaigns. It is, for example, very hard to justify the cost of advertising on the backs of buses travelling all around the city far from the school concerned. Yet it is also very hard in a competitive situation for individual schools to stop marketing as they may well lose that competitive edge. Schools do, however, need to ensure that what they say is truthful, as some ridiculous claims are made, such as, "_____ school is officially the best school in the borough." On more than one occasion, I reminded my headteacher colleagues both at meetings and privately that we should not be making spurious claims, including statements that may jeopardise the stability of another school.

Budgetary Outcomes

Despite our more intensive marketing, the school roll began to tumble at a fairly fast rate. For example, in September 2012 we took in a Year 7 cohort of only 151 to replace the Year 11 cohort of 196 that left the previous year. The following September was worse with a Year 7 intake of 118 that replaced a Year 11 of 193. Our total roll in September 2011 was 1,068, whereas our projection for September 2015 was only 825, representing a 23% decline in numbers over these four years. It was not only the fall in roll that caused us problems; the very fast rate of decline was the root cause of the financial headache we were about to face.

---

[145] Psalm 8:3-4.

There were other factors working against the school's finances as a result of changes in government policy. Sixth form funding was being reduced so that the allocation per sixth former was similar to that allocated for students in further education, in order to provide a level playing field in post-16 provision. Equity across the post-16 sectors is laudable but the value to society and the economy of post-16 education and training could have been better demonstrated by raising further education funding per student rather than lowering sixth form funding. In addition, the government decided to amalgamate all the separate grants, such as for technology college funding and the Behaviour Improvement Programme, into the total funding pot delegated to schools. This hit us more than most schools in North Tyneside.

Our finances were very badly hit. In November 2012, we predicted that we would end that financial year with a surplus of £10,000, but our predictions indicated that this would fall to a cumulative deficit of £294,000 in March 2014 and a massive deficit of £604,000 in March 2015. It was clear that we would have to take drastic action to reduce our costs, and particularly our staffing costs. We decided to take it step by step, and, following local authority guidance, governors agreed to aim to lose £250,000 worth of staffing by the summer of 2013.

Reducing staff is very difficult for everyone. For those who feel that their jobs and livelihoods are at risk, it is a very tense, painful time. For those administering the reductions, including the headteacher, it is a painstaking process knowing that the procedures have to be carried out carefully so that the correct decisions are made. Time also needs to be taken to counsel staff sensitively without compromising the process. As it happened, most of the job losses came through voluntary redundancies, but there were compulsory redundancies involved with the closure of the Farne Centre, our behaviour unit described in chapter four, which caused heartache for them.

Things, however, were going to get worse.

CHAPTER ELEVEN

2014: The Last Year

In many ways, 2014, my last year in the school, was an "annus horribilis", with many significant things going wrong. It did, however, start off very well. In the week before the Christmas holidays of 2013, we had a big celebration for the retirement of Sandra Belford, my long-serving deputy. I gave a major speech outlining some of her many achievements and how much she would be missed. It was an emotional occasion and so I tried to sprinkle the speech with doses of humour throughout. For example, I reminisced about how in March 2003, we drove round a good part of Newcastle when masses of our students decided to go on a protest march against the invasion of Iraq and we tried to get them back into school. In her reply, she commented on the speed that I drove at round the city. I ended my speech by recalling the telephone conversation we had when in 1994 I informed her that the governors had decided to appoint her as head of upper school; she said in reply, "I won't let you down, Jim." I told her and the whole gathering that in almost twenty years she never had. I knew that I would miss her terribly.

Sandra's retirement made me think more seriously about my own impending retirement. In June I was going to reach the age of sixty, the current normal retirement age for teachers, and I thought that following Sandra's example, Christmas would be a good time to go; it would give me a whole year to get used to the idea, as well as allowing me to take students to China in October as I had promised to do. Therefore, at the beginning of January 2014, I prayerfully made the decision that I would retire at Christmas that year. I did have great peace about it, contrary to how Ella and I thought I would feel, as the school had played such a massive part in my life.

In the week beginning Monday, 20th January, I started to tell colleagues, beginning with Paul Quinn, my very loyal deputy whom I saw as the ideal person to follow me, and Tim Goodwin, our very prayerful chair of governors. The following day, I individually informed the other members of the senior leadership team, who were all very shocked at what I was telling them, but at the same time very understanding. I made my formal announcement to the governors on the Wednesday of that week, and again there was an element of shock.

I told the staff the following day by email, and I got replies varying from "Congratulations!" to "How really sad!" and "You're too young, are you not?", this latter comment being not so much a compliment but a comment from a member of the support staff whose retirement age was unfortunately above that of teachers. As I told more people, including other heads and David and Jean Griffiths at the local authority, it was clear that there could be no going back. The Rubicon had been crossed. There was no need to go back, however, as I was convinced that God had led me to make that decision and my future was very much in his hands, as much as it was when I started teaching in 1977.

The year also got off to a very good start with our diamond jubilee service in the local parish church.

The Diamond Jubilee Service

As well as my reaching sixty that year, the school also reached that same milestone, and various diamond jubilee events were planned for the year. The first was the diamond jubilee service in the local parish church on Tuesday, 21st January, 2014. The aim of the service was to thank God for his goodness to us as a school over the past sixty years and to pray for his blessing in the years to come. The choir led the congregation in worship, and they themselves sang various pieces, including a wonderful rendition of "Amazing Grace". Nikki Holmes, our curriculum leader for performing arts, had trained the choir over the past few years, and they were well known in the area for their exceptionally high standards. Indeed, that evening I said that "Amazing Grace" had been sung by all sorts of famous artists at a huge range of special occasions, but that nobody sang it as well as our Senior Choir;

this was probably a massive exaggeration, but I was very proud of them. Unfortunately, Nikki was ill that evening, but the choir rose to the occasion under the baton of our other music teacher, Paul Kean.

Sixty years before, the schools that occupied the site were a boys' and a girls' secondary modern school, before the advent of comprehensive education. Alex Maughan, one of our drama teachers, arranged for some of her students to perform sketches based on the original opening of the schools and an interview with Miss Allan, a former headmistress of the girls' school. We also had four members of the teaching staff, Jon Foley, Adam Warkman, Katie Jackson and Nadia Motie, who were former students at the school. These very brave colleagues were interviewed by one of our sixth formers, causing much hilarity as they recounted their experiences as students of the school.

I interviewed my predecessor, John Burn, who was headteacher for fourteen years from 1979 to 1993. As I indicated in chapter seven, it was John who began to develop the Christian ethos of the school, and I asked him about his experience as headteacher in these years. He talked about having to deal with the local gangs in that era and about introducing religious education and assemblies with a Christian framework. Interestingly, he was told by the then Director of Education that he would face opposition from parents over this, but that did not materialise.

I preached at the end of the service on the theme of "Grace", following on from the singing of John Newton's wonderful hymn. I recounted the story of John Newton's conversion from being an immoral, depraved, foul-mouthed slave trader in the eighteenth century to a man who gave his life to the Lord Jesus Christ and who became a Christian minister. He knew, as he wrote in the hymn, that once he was lost, but now he had been found, and that he had once been blind, but now he could see. He had received God's mercy that he knew he did not deserve.

Earlier in the service, Tim Goodwin, our chair of governors, had read 1 Timothy chapter 1 verses 12 to 17, where Paul describes himself as "once a blasphemer and a persecutor and a violent man" and indeed "the worst of sinners". Paul was able to say that despite that, "the grace of our Lord was poured out on me abundantly, along with the faith and love that are in Christ Jesus". Paul knew why Jesus came into the world: "Christ Jesus came into the world to save sinners – of whom I am the worst."

I went on to say that as God saves us by grace, we need to go on and live by grace, and that as a school we have known God's grace over the past sixty years. The school at its foundation recognised that; at the official opening, all these sixty years ago the ceremony started with the hymn "Now Thank We All Our God". I emphasised that if we had been successful as a school, it was not so much because of what I, Mr Burn, Miss Allan or governors had done but rather because God had kept his hand on the school and people had prayed for it.

That is not to say that we did not have difficulties over the years; we had many, but God protected the school throughout. For example, I told the congregation that the government tried to change local authority boundaries between Newcastle and North Tyneside during Mr Burn's tenure, which would have resulted in splitting the catchment area and making the school unviable. God kept his hand on the school and the boundary change did not take place. I spoke about how God protected the school, despite the outcome of the disastrous 2008 Ofsted inspection. Even the calamity of the collapse of the East Theatre ceiling in June 2011 was part of God's protection on the school! I pointed out that it would have been unbelievably catastrophic if it had fallen on students eating their lunch, sitting in assembly or taking examinations, but by God's grace it had happened during the night and nobody was hurt. It had the bonus of giving us new ceilings in both theatres and more points to put us up the list to get a new school.

I emphasised that keeping God at the centre of what we do is important for our ethos, by ensuring that he has a central place in assembly programmes, that Christian values are paramount in the way we treat individuals seeing that each one is special because they are created in the image of God, and that in moral issues such as sex education a Christian view is promulgated. We need to maintain that in the future, as I pointed out that many are deliberately trying to marginalise Christianity in society, including in our schools. Sometimes this is done for seemingly good reasons such as equality, but it may have unintended consequences that affect Christianity and the beliefs and principles of Christians. I finished by saying that as we go into a new era for the next sixty years, which includes the building of a new school, we need to be sure that God stays at the centre and the school continues to know God's grace.

The service was a highly enjoyable occasion with, I believe, the Christian message going across strongly. At the end of the service, Paul

Quinn came up to me and said that having it all come together in this way, he understood how we were so different from most other schools. That of course is all by God's grace.

It was after that, however, that the attack on the school began.

Financial Meltdown

As outlined in the previous chapter, the school faced financial difficulties as a result of falling rolls, as well as national changes to the funding formula which took away separate grants that had been such a support to the school in the past. I worked with the local authority to set a target to cut £300,000 worth of staffing in the current academic year, which, although painful, seemed eminently possible.

Unfortunately, certain large budgetary errors came to light in January during the routine budget monitoring process. A number of key items of expenditure were either underestimated or omitted altogether. These errors had the effect of doubling the size of the in-year deficit, thus making projected cumulative deficits look huge, as each year's deficit was rolled over to the following year. The estimated deficit for 2016-17 was a massive £3.3 million. I spent hours going through the figures for myself just to be sure, but the logic of our plight was inescapable: the budget was out of control and of course such a situation was clearly unsustainable.

We were already in the process of making large staffing cuts, but they were clearly insufficient. One of the problems of making staffing cuts in schools is that there is a time lag between the fall in roll and thus budget income, and the time when staff can be released. As mentioned in the previous chapter, our roll was falling at a very fast rate, but we could not reduce our staffing costs quickly enough to balance the budget. The financial year finishes in March, whereas the academic year for which teachers have got timetables effectively finishes in August (as teachers have statutory summer holidays which have to be costed). This means that there is only a seven-twelfths saving of the salary of any teacher who leaves in August. Even to achieve these savings, strict timelines have to be adhered to so that appropriate notice periods are given.

Many people suggested that I could easily have walked away and let someone else deal with the crisis, but I believed that it was my responsibility to begin to find a solution. I met with local authority officers and discussed the situation. They were sympathetic that I was going to have to deal with this in my last year, and they offered their support. One of them, Mark Longstaff, kindly agreed to come to a joint governors and senior leadership team Saturday morning conference that was already calendared for March 1st, to ensure that everyone understood the magnitude of the problem. The message got through very clearly and everyone was in no doubt that we had to take action. I persuaded them to consider a full staff restructure led by myself and a governors' staffing restructure group.

It was important for this group to function in the best interests of the school, taking on the key values transmitted from the conference. Governors and SLT members divided themselves into groups to look at particular issues, some of which I suggested to them. For example, if we have to make cuts, what should we hold on to at all costs? Are we going to get rid of the oldest, most expensive staff to save money, but would this be at the cost of reduced academic standards? What sort of curriculum can we afford without driving students away to other schools because they cannot choose the subjects that they want?

Doing this exercise demonstrated that reducing our staffing budget was going to be difficult and would require a compromise between making economies and ensuring that standards were maintained. From the feedback there was clear agreement on certain key issues:

- the students remain at the centre of everything the school does;
- we keep all that is good about the school, such as the spirit of the staff, spiritual and moral values, extracurricular activities and performing arts;
- we offer a broad, balanced, attractive curriculum that meets the needs of the students and statutory requirements; and
- we have high quality teaching and thus keep our best teachers.

Staffing Restructure

The staffing restructure group met over a number of Saturday mornings, and I brought in some of Ella's home baking to make the work we had to do slightly more palatable. Although the decisions were ultimately made by governors, I led them in what I believed was the best direction for the school. Cuts had to be made, but it was imperative that academic standards, the quality of pastoral care and the overall ethos were maintained, otherwise the school would be destroyed. For example, there was discussion as to whether we should amalgamate departments and then make redundant the curriculum leaders who were no longer required, but it was clear that if we went down that route we would lose some very high quality teachers. Similarly, it was suggested that the RSD department could be part of a wider humanities department, but I emphasised the importance of the department in the wider life of the school and this was accepted. We looked at the option of replacing our teaching staff year leaders with support staff pastoral leaders, but it was realised that we could not make redundant excellent teachers to be replaced by support staff of unknown quality.

Although some compromises were made, I felt that the group was very supportive and made decisions that were most beneficial for the school. Nevertheless, there were going to be compulsory redundancies, including from the senior leadership team. I found all of this very difficult, as it meant job losses for first class people whom I had helped to build up.

Throughout the whole process, it was important to follow correct procedures, and I was grateful for the help given by Paul Stewart, our local authority link human resources officer, who ensured that I kept to the rules when I was tempted to cut corners. He also came to Saturday morning sessions to advise the governors. I was also very grateful to Rowan Standish, my PA, who produced reams and reams of paperwork that was essential for consultation to take place.

It was necessary to have consultation with the relevant trade unions, and this was another very difficult, even stressful, part of the process. I had experienced this in previous redundancy rounds, but it seemed so much worse this time. Long email correspondence was exchanged with union representatives, some of it being quite brutal towards me. There was particular concern on the part of the unions about the number of leadership posts, the rewards payable to those in leadership positions and who should be appointed as year leaders. Incredibly, there was much concern about the independence of the RSD department, which I believed was actually a satanic attack on the spiritual life of the school.

One of the North Tyneside union officers seemed to feel that he was on a crusade over these and other issues and whipped up a strong element of fear amongst his members, and even those who belonged to other unions. I did, however, have a lot of loyalty from the staff, many of whom reported to me what was happening in the meetings. This was of course against union rules, and so the union officials had to email their members and tell them not to report to me what was being said at meetings. More moderate members chose to stop attending the meetings.

Rather than continuing with long correspondence with this particular official, I decided that it would be far better to meet with him and have a frank face-to-face discussion. This I did, and it helped to improve the relationship between us, as he had a better understanding of where I was coming from. As in all negotiations, compromises were made, although not over what I believed to be fundamental issues such as having a strong, although much smaller, senior leadership team, teaching staff year leaders and an independent RSD department with its own curriculum leader.

Throughout the consultation process, staff wrote to me not only with their concerns, but also with positive suggestions for moving forward. At the end of the consultation period, on the afternoon of Friday, 13th June, Paul Stewart, a couple of members of the Staffing Restructure Committee and I met to go through the folder full of submissions. Although this was an important meeting, I did not want it to go on too long as Ella and I were set to go to Scotland that evening. Andrew our eldest son and his wife Fiona had organised a series of events to celebrate my sixtieth birthday which had taken place earlier in the week. Nevertheless, we did justice to all the submissions, and made decisions which I was scheduled to give to the staff at a full staff meeting the following Wednesday.

I was obliged at the staff meeting to give the outcome of the consultation and present the next steps in the process. I did, however, want to do more than that, as, for the first time that I could remember, there were serious divisions within the staff body and inevitably staff morale was low as jobs were being lost. I told them that I recognised that colleagues would be going through different emotions such as dismay at the extent of the problem, confusion about what it might mean for their livelihoods, and even anger that this should be happening at all. I asked them, however, not to direct their anger in the wrong direction, as I was concerned that serious divisions were now evident across the staff body: teaching staff against support staff; those who did not have a Teaching and Learning Responsibility (TLR) allowance against those who did; those who had a smaller TLR than others; and smaller departments against bigger departments. I said that this was never how we as a staff operated. I mentioned particularly the Physical Education and RSD departments as they seemed to be getting a lot of criticism, saying that although they did not enter a lot of students for examinations, nonetheless they played an immeasurable role in the development of our students, and had done so for many years.

I answered the criticism of those who felt that the process was unfair and worked against them by saying that there was no favouritism and the system was as fair as possible. Indeed, I said that the people who were being treated least favourably and were the most vulnerable were members of the senior leadership team who had to reapply for their jobs and if not successful would leave with nothing else to fall back on. These were the people I was closest to.

I admitted that the staffing cuts we had made had not solved the deficit problem; it would still remain, but taking one million pounds out of the staffing budget in the period 2014 to 2016 had put a big dent in the size of the deficit. I told the staff that to make any more cuts would absolutely destroy the school as we still needed to have an attractive curriculum, a strong system of care and robust leadership at all levels, otherwise we would be at the mercy of both Ofsted and the market.

I had prayed that this speech would raise morale and heal divisions, and although people spoke to me positively afterwards, I knew that it would take time before we experienced higher morale and the level of unity that we were used to in the school. Staff continued to work through to the summer holidays, the vast majority showing a high degree of professionalism, and morale certainly improved in the last week of term, with special events such as a spectacular performance of "Annie" at Whitley Bay Playhouse all helping to raise spirits. Colleagues also sent me encouraging emails which God used to raise my spirits.

There was one major piece of the staffing restructure to be sorted before the summer; this involved losing one more of our assistant headteachers. In our revised staffing structure, we would be moving from a situation where we had six assistant headteachers to one where we would have only three. This would be tight, but was more in line with the smaller size of school that we were moving towards. Two of the six asked for voluntary redundancy, which the governors granted. To eliminate one more post, it was agreed that those remaining had to put in an application for one of three generic assistant headteacher posts. Interviews were scheduled for Friday, 11th July.

I was dreading that morning; I valued each of them, and I could not face the prospect of there being a loser from the process. On the Monday morning of that week, as I was driving into work, I prayed, "Lord, please do something about Friday!" I did not have to say any more, because God knew exactly what was on my heart. About half an hour later, one of the team came in saying that they had decided on a change of lifestyle, and were going to ask for voluntary redundancy; there was no longer any need to go ahead with interviews on Friday. That was such an amazing answer to prayer.

How Did the Staffing Crises Affect Me Personally?

The uncertainty associated with the staffing restructure put a great strain on everyone. In my dealings with staff, I tried to be encouraging, but I could not give individuals the degree of certainty that they were looking for. I found it hard to see people hurting and not be able to come up with a solution. Every morning in the months leading up to the summer, I would wake up thinking about budget deficits, staff restructure and redundancies, which was not a healthy way to start the day. People said that I looked tired and worn out, as I worked long hours over these months trying to lead the school through the situation we found ourselves in. I knew that I was making errors of judgment, and indeed I joked with the staff, although apologetically, at my last staff meeting in December that I had probably made more errors of judgement in the past year than I had over the previous twenty.

I kept asking myself why all these things were happening to the school. I knew that there were technical reasons in terms of the falling roll, but why was God allowing these things to happen? Was it me? Had I committed sin that I had not confessed that was bringing the school down? David begins Psalm 7 by saying,

> LORD my God, I take refuge in you;
>   save and deliver me from all who pursue me,
>   or they will tear me apart like a lion
>   and rip me to pieces with no one to rescue me.[146]

I do not think that there were people looking to tear me apart or rip me to pieces (not even the trade union officers!). Events, however, were

---

[146] Psalm 7:1-2.

putting pressure on me and I needed constantly to take refuge in the Lord my God. David goes on to say,

> LORD my God, if I have done this
> and there is guilt on my hands –
> if I have repaid my ally with evil
> or without cause have robbed my foe –
> then let my enemy pursue and overtake me;
> let him trample my life to the ground
> and make me sleep in the dust.[147]

David was seeking God in case he had guilt on his hands, and I felt that I needed to do the same. Newcastle has a lovely park and set of nature walks called Jesmond Dene, given to the city by Lord Armstrong, a nineteenth century industrialist. One Sunday morning I stood on the bridge at the Old Mill in the Dene praying that God would forgive me for any ways in which I had offended him, in particular by glorifying myself as head rather than giving all the glory to him. I knew God's peace having sought God in that way.

I worked on towards the summer, looking forward to the end of term. As I mentioned above, the last week of term brought people's spirits up. There were lovely farewell speeches from colleagues, including some long-serving ones, who were leaving, all saying what a special place our school was. We continued our tradition of putting on musical productions at the Whitley Bay Playhouse with an amazing production of "Annie", staged by our new curriculum leader for performing arts, Mary Houlton, her assistant curriculum leader, Alex Maughan, and a very gifted learning support assistant, Robert Brent. After our annual rock festival in support of Team Kenya, I was ready for the holidays, but I felt that the summer term had ended better than it started.

Our main summer holiday that year was to attend a large number of events at the Commonwealth Games in Glasgow. The weather was glorious at the beginning of the games, although we were soaked watching the women's hockey final towards the end. It was very much a family occasion with David, Andrew and Fiona joining Ella and me for most of the events, and we stayed with my dad, which meant amongst

---

[147] Psalm 7:3-5.

other things that we did not have to pay highly overinflated Glasgow hotel prices.

I spent the second half of the summer holidays getting ready for going back to school. There was, however, one more shock to come in the shape of very disappointing examination results. As I outlined in chapter three, despite Mr Gove's announcement that only first entry results would count in the league tables, we kept to our original policy of entering GCSE students early for their English and maths exams. Unfortunately, their results were not nearly as good as we had hoped they would be. Using the early entry results, the score that would appear in the league tables would be only 43% of students achieving 5 or more A* to C grades with English and maths, and even counting the resits that they did in the summer the figure was only 54%, a very poor score for us. These results would put the school well down the local league tables and also might trigger an early Ofsted inspection. We seemed very vulnerable.

Was the coming term, my last one in the school, going to be as difficult as the two previous ones? From this latest blow it seemed that way, and I was not looking forward to going back to have to talk about poor results at our staff meeting on the first day of the new term. This meeting was normally a very buoyant one, which I would use to encourage the staff to reach new heights in the coming year. God, however, intervened in an amazing way. Ella and I were out walking on Alnmouth beach on the Sunday afternoon before term started when we could hear someone calling us from the bank above. God had sent Margery Tate, a godly lady who used to teach in the RSD department, to speak to me, and she reminded me of what God had done in the school over the previous twenty-one years, and that he was not going to let it go now. I left the beach with uplifted spirits, and indeed tears in my eyes.

The Final Term

The staff meeting on the first day of the new term was indeed positive, despite the disappointing exam results. Colleagues shared about their holidays, I showed slides of people's weddings and we had a Commonwealth Games quiz as a light relief starter activity. To boost morale, I put up on the screen a set of quotes from students and parents that I had used in the prospectus. I did, however, have to share the poor examination results at both GCSE and "A" level; our AS results were, however, fantastic, which showed staff that we could produce excellent results. Key messages were put across:

- We need to face the reality of the situation we are in; there is so much that is special about our school, but we do have a set of very disappointing results.
- We need to pick ourselves up.
- We need to work together without blaming anyone.
- We need to be determined that it will not happen again.
- We need to take appropriate action.
- We need to be prepared for Ofsted.

I then shared with the staff the ways in which we were going to take action.

The term had got off to a good start, and it continued that way. The first two assembly themes of the year, "School's Amazing" and "You're Amazing" set the tone for the students. Everything was harder with fewer staff but everybody was determined to do their best. I enjoyed working with Year 11 students as they prepared for their IGCSE English exam and with the Year 13 students with their UCAS applications, particularly those who were applying for Oxbridge courses. God was indeed gracious in allowing the term to go so well.

The highlight of the term, however, was the trip to China when Ella and I accompanied Lisa Lowery and twenty-three sixth formers as we together visited the sights of Beijing and the Great Wall, as well as spending a couple of days in Tangshan, working with the staff and students at our link Chinese school. Lisa had done the bulk of the paperwork and organisation, and although it was not quite a holiday for us, our role was to support her in leading the group and enjoy ourselves. As mentioned in chapter six, Ella and I had been out before in 2010, and Lisa had been out working as a team member on their summer school, and it was wonderful for the three of us to go back, but this time with a party of sixth formers. They had a tremendous time, even going to the Beijing Opera seen as being an "experience". They thoroughly enjoyed going to the homes of Chinese students where they were treated like royalty. The adults did not go to anyone's homes, but the Chinese teachers took us out for banquets and, to my consternation, a karaoke session.

Each year in November we held a Certificate Presentation Evening when examination certificates were presented to previous Year 11 students and progress certificates to current Year 11 students. Normally we would invite some eminent speaker to give an inspirational talk to the students, but this year as part of our diamond jubilee celebrations, I invited three former students whom I considered to be role models to talk about their experiences: Jack Cottrell, who had just graduated from Oxford with a degree in history, Jess Maughan, who was now practising as a dentist in Newcastle, and Sarah Hunter, who had become a real celebrity as she was vice-captain of the England ladies' rugby team who had won the women's rugby world cup in the summer of 2014. They each gave inspirational talks which would have made a significant impact on our young people.

Normally at this event I gave my report for the year, but this time, because it was my last, I wanted to talk about the past twenty-one years, and because it was our diamond jubilee, I wanted to create even further links with the past. I told our audience that by chance on the Friday evening before, an elderly gentleman visited the school with his wife and granddaughter who had just started that term studying at Northumbria University. This was Mr Missing, a former music teacher from the 1970s, and he wanted to show his granddaughter where he used to teach music. It was a bit difficult to find the exact room as inevitably we had moved rooms around over the previous forty years, but we finally found what he thought was his room. I also took him to meet Mary Houlton and Paul Kean who were rehearsing at the time with the Senior Choir. It was wonderful to have that musical link across the years. He talked about the concerts and productions his students put on, and we shared about our 2014 performances of "The Glastonbury Tales", "Annie" and the Diamond Jubilee Pyramid Music Festival. Interestingly, Mr Missing shared that he was a Christian and later left teaching to do full-time church work.

I gave the audience another illustration from the past. Vera Johnson, a friend of mine at whose church I occasionally speak, told me that she had met a lady who went to the former girls' school in its early days. This lady spoke fondly of her time there, including the assemblies at the beginning of the day with prayers. Vera told her that this still happens fifty or so years later. I was able to say that the Christian ethos of a respect for God and a respect for individuals as people specially created by God is still part of the culture of the school.

I shared with the audience that our examination results had improved markedly over time and showed photographs of some of our top performers. I shared how our sixth form had grown over time, and whereas it was a bit of an embarrassment when I first came to the school, it was now a source of pride, as our recent trips to China and Kenya demonstrated.

I finally talked about the future, which would of course be different with the brand new building due to be opened in September 2016. I said that my hope and prayer was that the same ethos which currently permeated the school would continue into the new building. I thanked God for the past twenty-one years that I had been at the school, and for the past sixty years of education on the site and wished everyone every success in the future.

The Importance of Prayer

The past year had been very difficult, although as I indicated above, the final term was much better, and as I described in chapter one, I very much enjoyed my last fortnight. Throughout all the difficulties, I had to cast myself on the Lord to seek his grace rather than relying on my own strength. When things got better, I had to keep going back and thanking God for his grace.

I had to apply again and again the words of Paul that he wrote to the Philippian church:

> *Rejoice in the Lord always. I will say it again: rejoice! Let your gentleness be evident to all. The Lord is near. Do not be anxious about anything, but in every situation, by prayer and petition, with thanksgiving, present your requests to God. And the peace of God, which transcends all understanding, will guard your hearts and your minds in Christ Jesus.*[148]

God does not want us to be anxious, but rather he wants us to come to him with thanksgiving and present our requests to him. I learned to plead for God's mercy on the school, and I learned to experience God's peace, even in difficult situations (because it transcended all understanding!).

---

[148] Philippians 4:4-7.

Instead of concentrating on budget deficits, staff restructure and redundancies, I had to learn to think in the way that Paul instructed in the verse which followed:

> *Finally, brothers and sisters, whatever is true, whatever is noble, whatever is right, whatever is pure, whatever is lovely, whatever is admirable – if anything is excellent or praiseworthy – think about such things.*[149]

Prayer was vital, and the support of others in prayer helped enormously. The school had a prayer group that met in my office over many years, going back to John Burn's day. For example, when John announced in 1993 that he was moving on, this group had prayed that another Christian would come to lead the school as head, which to their delight was answered through my appointment. Over the next twenty-one years the group met faithfully to pray for the school and for me as headteacher. Ian and Helen Longfield were key members of the group, bringing great spiritual wisdom and compassion to the meetings. Ian had been a general practitioner in the area over many years, and they both had a real passion for the area and the school. It was very humbling and such a privilege to know that such a wonderful group of Christians were praying for me and my school.

Throughout the difficulties of that last year, the group prayed that answers would be found, problems would be overcome and the school would know God's blessings. As part of the meeting, we would read a passage of Scripture for encouragement. For example, at the June 2014 prayer meeting, we read part of Psalm 107.

> *Let them give thanks to the LORD for his unfailing love*
> *and his wonderful deeds for mankind,*
> *for he breaks down gates of bronze*
> *and cuts through bars of iron.*[150]

These verses were tremendous encouragement, for we could indeed thank God for his love which never lets us down and for his wonderful deeds. I had this picture of God being able to cut through all the problems we had. This idea was very important to me as Tim Goodwin and I did have a difficult meeting coming up: our deficit clinic meeting

---

[149] Philippians 4:8.
[150] Psalm 107:15-16.

with local authority officers to discuss the progress that we had made with our budget deficit. I was quite worried about it, but Tim and I prayed in the car before we went into the meeting, holding on to the encouragement of Psalm 107. As it happened, the meeting was not nearly as bad as was feared, and the officers realised that we had made progress in dealing with our financial problems. Although the school was certainly not let off the hook, there was an understanding of our difficult situation.

Members of staff were also regular members of the group, particularly Dot Lee, Lisa Lowery, Caroline Foreman, Jo Dyer, Alastair Hetherington, as well as Margery Tate, a former member of staff. In between meetings, I would email them with regular updates of what was happening so that they could give thanks and pray through situations. They also asked their own families and church groups to pray for the school. Again, it was encouraging to know that there were Christians committed to praying for the school, and I was so grateful for their support.

God answered the prayers of his people for the school. I have mentioned above the way in which God answered prayer over the senior leadership team interviews and the budget deficit clinic. There were other instances. I was very concerned about a meeting between union representatives and the staffing restructure subcommittee. The union representatives had complained that in all the discussions they had never actually met governors, and so a meeting was set up for the fourth week in September. Knowing how difficult relationships with the unions had been in the past, I was not looking forward to this meeting. We brought this meeting to the Lord in prayer, and clearly saw his answer: the meeting ended up being simply a friendly, cosy chat with no confrontation at all, the absolute opposite of what I had expected. There is a time and place to be on your guard and be worldly wise, but more often we need simply to relax in God's grace and trust him to see us through whatever situation we are in.

The China visit was another example of how God answered prayer. I mentioned above that the group had a wonderful time under Lisa Lowery's leadership. Before we went, however, Lisa did have difficulty with some of the arrangements with the travel company, but she did not feel that she should bother me with them. One issue concerned the background colour of the visa photographs: should they be white or should they be blue, as there was conflicting information? It seemed so trivial, but the travel company were making a big issue about it, and of course we did not want to have any barriers affecting our entry into China. We felt, however, that we could not ask the students who had the "wrong" background colour to get these photographs taken again at such short notice. We held a parents' meeting just over three weeks before we were due to travel, but we decided not to say anything about the visa photographs. Instead, afterwards, Ella, Lisa and I prayed in the theatre where we had held the meeting and asked God to sort out the visa problem. The following day after both Lisa and I had spoken to the company, the company said that they would use software and change any offending colours. We received the visas back just in time for our departure. Lisa said later that she knew with certainty immediately after the meeting that God would directly answer our prayers; I have to confess that I did not quite have her faith.

The trip itself went exceptionally well. We had a wonderful set of students with us who were a credit to the school, themselves and their families. There were no major hitches; none of the students got lost (probably our worst fear in Beijing), the coach always arrived to pick us up on time, and nobody suffered any ill effects from smog (unlike the week before when the son of friends of ours was sick as a result of it). Perhaps the most important reason for everything going so smoothly was that we prayed intensively for it. Each evening after we sent the students off to bed, Ella, Lisa and I stayed in the hotel lounge and prayed for the students, the events of the following day, and each other's family circumstances. I am sure that not many prayer meetings had taken place before in these hotel lounges, but ours did make a great difference.

Prayer made such a difference throughout that last year; even being able to go into the cloakroom in my office and praying just prior to what may have otherwise been a difficult meeting was so helpful. God wants to buoy us up and give us victory in difficult situations. Prayer is a channel that allows his love to do just that.

CHAPTER TWELVE

An Overview: Advice to Christian Leaders in Schools

Over the previous eleven chapters, I have tried to give an insight into my experience of headship, and, in particular how I believe that God's grace was so evident as he provided for me and sustained me. In this final chapter, I want to give advice and encouragement to Christian leaders in schools, in the firm belief that God wants them to make a difference in their schools.

What Makes a Leader?

Textbooks and manuals will give many definitions of leadership, which may or may not be of help to those who wish to develop their leadership skills and capacity. One definition that I like is given by the American writer Dr Travis Bradberry, who says,

> *Leadership is a process of social influence which maximises the efforts of others toward the achievement of a greater good.*[151]

The source of leadership, as Bradberry points out, is social influence rather than a position of authority or power. There is no sense in which real leadership demands that you follow me because I am the boss. Leadership should be authoritative rather than authoritarian. Rather than simply telling people what to do, an effective leader is trusted

---

[151] *What makes a Leader?;* Travis Bradberry; LinkedIn Pulse (July 27th, 2015).

because they can explain why we should go in a certain direction. Leaders should be able to influence others positively.

In his book, "What Leaders Really Do", John P Kotter paints a picture of the day in the life of a successful president of an investment company.[152] It seems a chaotic, unplanned day with the executive going from one conversation to another, never writing business plans or making decisions. Amidst the seeming chaos, what the executive is doing is creating networks, setting agendas for these networks and persuading the networks to execute the agendas. Effectiveness comes from influence rather than power.

Bradberry in his definition and Kotter in his picture of the day in the life of a leader both emphasise the importance of others in the process. It is not a sole charismatic leader operating on their own, riding a white charger, moving the organisation forward, and solving problems as they do so. I often told staff and others I spoke to about leadership that I very rarely knew the solutions to complex problems on my own, but rather it was my role to harness the expertise of others to help move us forward. Leaders need to operate as part of a team, rather than believing that they can do things on their own, and they also need to be able to network with other teams.

The final part of Bradberry's definition talks about moving "toward the achievement of a greater good". Of course, who defines the "greater good" is a matter for debate, and Christians will have different aims relating to glorifying God and following his will, compared with those who do not believe. Leaders need to use their authoritative influence to persuade people that particular endpoints are worth going towards.

The use of the word "toward" in the definition indicates motion and thus highlights a fundamental difference between leadership and management. Leadership is about change, whereas management is about maintaining systems effectively and efficiently; both are required, as is administration, but for the school or any organisation to move forward, it is essential to have effective leadership. I have often suggested that administration is like tidying a path, whereas management is like following a path and leadership is creating a new path. At the same time, however, I have emphasised that leaders have to get their basic administration and management right. Leaders need to

---

[152] *What Leaders Really Do;* John P Kotter; Harvard Business Review (1999); chapter 7.

be sure, for example, that they have met the agreed deadlines for writing their student reports, otherwise they will let others down, and thus lose credibility as leaders.

Leadership, then, is fundamentally about change. Schools have gone through much turbulent change over the past three decades. As leaders, however, it is important that we take charge of change, rather than letting change take charge of us. If not, we shall become like the frog that did not realise that the water it was in was slowly being heated up to boiling point, and it ended up being boiled alive.[153]

Schools understand the importance of leadership far better now. At the beginning of my headship, we had a senior management team, which we began to call the senior leadership team at the turn of the century. Hopefully, the new term reflected reality. At the same time, heads of department became curriculum leaders, reflecting a change in emphasis from managing a department to leading a team.

Does that mean that leaders should not get involved in detail, but only work strategically? Far from it. The detail does matter, and there is a place for micromanaging. Jack Welch, the American business leader, encourages us to micromanage "when your help matters". He says,

> *Your help matters when you bring unique expertise to a situation, or you can expedite things by dint of your authority, or both. Your help matters when you have highly relevant experience that no one else on the team brings, and your presence sets an example of best practices – and prevents costly mistakes.*[154]

James Kerr in his analysis of the success of the New Zealand All Blacks puts it more bluntly:

> *Sweep the sheds. Never be too big to do the small things that need to be done.*[155]

---

[153] I first came across this illustration in *The Age of Unreason;* Charles Handy; Arrow Books (1995); pages 7-8, where he uses this as an example of discontinuous change, whereby a significant change takes place that is different from the past, and which requires radical action. Interestingly he quotes Jesus as a proponent of discontinuous change in his Sermon on the Mount, where the accepted norms were turned upside down (page 19).

[154] *Why I Love Micromanaging and You Should Too;* Jack Welch; LinkedIn Pulse; January 19th (2016).

[155] James Kerr; op. cit.; page 2.

As a head, for example, I very much enjoyed the detail of the timetable, and many a year I did spend a lot of hours working with our main timetabler in the massively complex exercise of constructing the school timetable. I believe that this help was appreciated and was not seen as gross interference. I do regret, however, not micromanaging the school budget a lot more in the years leading up to the financial crisis of 2012-13.

When I have led leadership development courses, I have often listed the qualities of excellent leaders. There are all sorts of variations of these lists, but the following list of qualities may be useful:

- being aware of the bigger picture;
- being aware of the higher order significance of what we do;
- having a vision of where the organisation should be going;
- having clear values articulately expressed;
- consistently modelling high performance behaviour;
- being able to trust team members;
- having excellent personal relationships;
- having the ability to articulate high performance standards;
- having the ability to keep the team moving in the same direction;
- being a creative thinker; and
- displaying servanthood.[156]

Christian leaders in schools should demonstrate all of the above. They should, however, also ensure that they follow the examples of Jesus and the apostles. In his book "To Corinth with Love", Michael Green explains how the apostle Paul authoritatively yet lovingly wrote to the young church in Corinth to help them with the issues they were facing.[157] He demonstrates a number of ways in which Paul suggests that effective Christian leaders should operate.

Some of the attributes of Christian leaders as described by Green from Paul's first letter to the Corinthians are what we would expect, such as being an example to those whom we are leading,[158] being a servant to those in our teams,[159] being a worker working hard for the

---

[156] I often used the example here of Jesus washing the disciples' feet; see John 13:1-17.

[157] *To Corinth with Love;* Michael Green; Hodder and Stoughton (1982).

[158] See 1 Corinthians 4:6.

[159] See 1 Corinthians 3:5.

Lord and the people we serve,[160] and being a master builder in creating new structures.[161] Some, however, are more surprising. Paul was prepared to be seen as a fool for Christ so that the gospel,[162] with the foolishness of the cross,[163] would spread and Jesus would receive all the glory. He was also prepared to be seen as "the scum of the earth, the garbage of the world"[164].

Christian leaders need to have all the attributes of other excellent leaders, but our "bigger picture" is eternal, serving the Lord as he commands, as well as the staff and students that he puts into our care. People may not accept all that we stand for, and some may think that our emphasis on eternity is foolishness, but hopefully we shall be respected for the love that shines through us as a manifestation of God's grace. Our leadership in schools should be seen as a calling from God.

Seeing Leadership as a Calling

Amazingly a young Jewish girl, living in captivity, became Queen of Persia. This was Esther who "won the favour of everyone who saw her"[165] including King Xerxes who "was attracted to Esther more than to any of the other women"[166]. God placed her in that influential position as part of his plan to save his people. The evil Agagite Haman had also been elevated by the king and he expected everyone including the Jews to bow down and honour him. Mordecai, Esther's guardian refused to do this, and so Haman looked for a way to destroy not only Mordecai, but all the Jews. He persuaded the king to issue an edict so that all Jews, men and women, young and old, would be killed on a particular day.

Mordecai persuaded Esther to go to the king to plead for her people with these words:

> Do not think that because you are in the king's house you alone of all the Jews will escape. For if you remain silent at this time, relief and deliverance for the Jews will arise from

---

[160] See 1 Corinthians 3:9.
[161] See 1 Corinthians 3:10.
[162] See 1 Corinthians 4:10.
[163] See 1 Corinthians 1:18.
[164] 1 Corinthians 4:13.
[165] Esther 2:15.
[166] Esther 2:17.

another place, but you and your father's family will perish.
And who knows but that you have come to your royal
position for such a time as this?[167]

It was a dangerous thing for anyone to approach the king without being summoned, but Mordecai believed that Esther had been placed in this position for this very purpose. (He also believed that God would send deliverance in another way if Esther refused to do this and remained silent, but she and her extended family would perish.) Esther did as she was asked and won the king's favour. Xerxes rescinded the previous decree, gave the Jews a new status in the land, destroyed Haman and elevated Mordecai to a new position as second in rank only to the king. All of this was possible because God placed Esther in a royal position "for such a time as this", and she was obedient to her calling.

To me, this story illustrates the importance of God's calling to his people that if they are open to him he will put them in the right place at the right time for his purposes. In chapter two I shared how I believe God called me to my first teaching post in Cambridgeshire in 1977, and how he led me to the further posts I held, leading to becoming a headteacher in 1993. This sense of calling should be true for all Christians working in schools. When Dot Lee was working for Scripture Union, she asked me if I would lead a session for Christian teachers. I encouraged them on that occasion to see their job as a special calling from God believing that he had put them in their schools with their classes for a particular reason. Perhaps, I suggested, they were the only person who could reach a particular individual with the love of God.

Again, James Kerr in his analysis of leadership lessons from the All Blacks and other successful sports teams has wise counsel to give. He quotes the architect Buckminster Fuller who asked himself questions which radically changed his life:

What is my job on the planet? What is it that needs doing,
that I know something about, that probably won't happen
unless I take responsibility for it?[168]

---

[167] Esther 4:13-14.
[168] James Kerr; op. cit.; page 8.

Christians should understand that that "job on the planet" is given by the Lord God himself! Timothy Keller refers to Paul's words,

> *Nevertheless, each person should live as a believer in whatever situation the Lord has assigned to them, just as God has called them. This is the rule I lay down in all the churches.*[169]

Keller goes on to say,

> *Remember that something can be a vocation or calling only if some other party calls you to do it, and you do it for their sake rather than for your own. Our daily work can be a calling only if it is reconceived as God's assignment to serve others. And that is exactly how the Bible teaches us to view work.*[170]

Leadership within schools should be seen as a calling from God, with God wanting us to take on specific roles within specific schools. Of course, not everyone is called to become a headteacher. My advice, however, is if you believe that God is calling you into that particular role, then follow his leading to serve others in a way that only you can. It will be hard, but you will have a unique chance to influence staff and students and to ensure that Christian values are instilled within your school. And of course, if it is God's calling, he will be with you every step of the way.

Vision

Christian leaders in schools need to have a vision for their schools and young people. It is important that they know the direction in which they are leading their schools. Without vision, even with a highly skilled staff and adequate resources, school leaders will find that there is confusion when they try to bring about change.

"Vision" is a very biblical word. In the Bible, God again and again gave his people visions. For example, Abraham was given a vision by God that he had to "look up at the sky and count the stars – if indeed

---

[169] 1 Corinthians 7:17.
[170] *Every Good Endeavour;* Timothy Keller; Hodder and Stoughton (2014); page 66.

you can count them," and he was told, "so shall your offspring be."[171] This was even more amazing as Abraham had no children; he was old and his wife Sarah was barren. When God met with Moses in the burning bush, he gave him a vision that his people would be led out of slavery with Moses being the leader who would be used by God to bring this miracle about.[172] The last book of the Bible, the book of Revelation, is a vision given by God to the apostle John concerning the end times culminating in the establishment of a new heaven and a new earth where...

> *He will wipe every tear from their eyes. There will be no more death or mourning or crying or pain, for the old order of things has passed away.*[173]

Christian leaders need to consider God's big picture as they plan out the vision for their schools.

The apostle Paul had a clear vision for his ministry. In his introduction to his letter to the Romans he expresses it like this:

> *Through him we received grace and apostleship to call all the Gentiles to the obedience that comes from faith for his name's sake.*[174]

He knew that he was the recipient of the mercy of God that he did not deserve, in other words, grace, and a position given by God, namely that of an apostle, despite the fact that he had persecuted the church. His vision was to see Gentiles become Christians by obediently believing in the name of Jesus.

Likewise, in writing to the Ephesian church, he says,

> *Although I am less than the least of all the Lord's people, this grace was given me: to preach to the Gentiles the boundless riches of Christ, and to make plain to everyone the administration of this mystery.*[175]

Again, he knows the extent of God's undeserved mercy shown to him and that his ministry was to share the infinite love of Christ with

---

[171] Genesis 15:5.
[172] Exodus 3.
[173] Revelation 21:4.
[174] Romans 1:5.
[175] Ephesians 3:8-9a.

the Gentiles and to explain how the mystery of God's plan has been revealed to all of us.

Later on in that same chapter he prays an absolutely amazing prayer for the Ephesian church:

> *I pray that out of his glorious riches he may strengthen you with power through his Spirit in your inner being, so that Christ may dwell in your hearts through faith. And I pray that you, being rooted and established in love, may have power, together with all the Lord's holy people, to grasp how wide and long and high and deep is the love of Christ, and to know this love that surpasses knowledge – that you may be filled to the measure of all the fullness of God.[176]*

When we pray for other people, we often limit our prayers to particular needs to do with their jobs, their families, their health, their house purchases, and so on. It is important that we should pray for these needs as, after all, Jesus taught us to pray for our daily bread.[177] It is, however, also vital that we pray for people's spiritual growth, that they will be strong in the Spirit, that Christ will be in their hearts, that they will be rooted in the love of Christ and that they will be able to begin to understand the extent of his wonderful love for them. Ultimately we should pray with Paul that they should be "filled to the measure of all the fullness of God". As we do so, we should by God's grace begin to see lives changed.

That prayer encapsulates Paul's vision for the people to whom he was ministering. Like Paul, Christian leaders in schools need to have a vision for their ministries, their schools and their young people. How we express that depends very much upon the context in which we are working. With the support of others, I produced a mission statement for the school as follows:

> *We will encourage all members of the school to have the power and aspiration to seek truth, knowledge and understanding by acquiring skills to think independently in order to take responsibility for their own learning. This will enable members of the school to become successful, adaptable learners, who will become responsible, caring,*

---

[176] Ephesians 3:16-19.
[177] See Matthew 6:11.

moral citizens able to make positive contributions to the local and global community.

This statement is not specifically Christian because there would not be sufficient agreement within the school to have explicit Christian values included. For those who are Christians, however, they can incorporate their own Christian values within the statement. For example, as mentioned in chapter three, I interpreted "seeking truth" through an understanding that the Lord Jesus Christ is the embodiment of that truth. In addition, later on in the document through explanations as to how the vision works in practice, I wrote the following:

In line with the 1988 Education Reform Act, school assemblies (or acts of worship) are in the main Christian, but tolerance is shown to those with different beliefs. Religious Studies also has a strong Christian basis, but the study of other faiths also takes place.

Hopefully, this made a clear statement about the primacy of Christianity while showing tolerance to those who followed other faiths or no faiths at all.

The vision that we have for our ministry and for our young people should be the driving force for us as we fulfil God's calling. Mark Batterson in his book on prayer and ministry, "The Circle Maker", says that one of the success criteria for his ministry is to "help people maximise their God-given potential". He says,

Potential is God's gift to us; what we do with it is our gift back to God. Helping people maximise their God-given potential is why God put me on this planet. That is what gets me up early and keeps me up late. Nothing is more exhilarating to me than seeing people growing into their God-given giftedness.[178]

However our vision is worded, it is important that it reflects our own personal values. For Christian leaders these values should have the sovereignty and love of God as reflected in Jesus at the centre of our lives. That will motivate us to "maximise the God-given potential" of our young people.

---

[178] *The Circle Maker;* Mark Batterson; Zondervan (2011); page 27.

Know the Grace of God

Roy Hession wrote a classic Christian book entitled "The Power of God's Grace"[179]. It was originally entitled "Good News for Bad People", which to me is an excellent description of the gospel. As Paul says,

> *For all have sinned and fall short of the glory of God, and all are justified freely by his grace through the redemption that came by Christ Jesus.*[180]

In other words, all of us are "bad people" through our sinful nature, but we have been set free from the bondage of our sin as a result of Jesus taking our punishment on himself on the cross. This is God's grace to us: mercy that we simply do not deserve. We first receive God's saving grace when we become Christians and accept the Lord Jesus Christ by repentance of our sins and faith.

God's grace, however, is not solely to be experienced when we first come to faith, but rather it should be an ongoing experience. Hession quotes the apostle John who writes in his Gospel,

> *Out of his fullness we have all received grace in place of grace already given.*[181]

Hession goes on to write,

> *It gives us the picture of ourselves standing on a river bank, looking down on the flowing waters. It is a beautiful sight; we can even see the fish and we would gladly retain that view. However, it soon flows past and that particular water is gone – but only to be replaced by another quantity of water carrying its own special beauty. It is water instead of water.*

> *So is the grace of God. From the point of view of the recipient it is not just an isolated experience, which at all costs he must retain and which, if it seems to disappear, he must do his best to recover. It is rather like a continuing*

---

[179] Taken from *The Power of God's Grace* by Roy Hession. Copyright © Roy Hession Book Trust. Used by permission.
[180] Romans 3:23-24.
[181] John 1:16.

flowing river, which means that he can afford to let the first experience go, for there is plenty more where that came from. There is grace instead of grace.[182]

God's grace is something we need to experience constantly as Christian leaders in schools. I know from my own experience that he does want to pour his grace out on us, by demonstrating his love to us despite the fact that we do not deserve it. When we do have success in our leadership, he, and not we, needs to receive all of the glory. When things are going badly we need to continue to trust him and believe that he is in absolute control of our particular situations.

The great danger for us when things are going well is that we start relying on our own strength and taking the glory ourselves. We end up in danger of arrogant triumphalism. I have seen too many heads display arrogance by proclaiming their successes without admitting areas where things are not so good, taking all the glory themselves without giving credit to others who have done much work, let alone giving glory to God.

Of course, this does not solely apply to education, as it can be manifest in all walks of life. Marshall Goldsmith, an American executive coach, warned against it in a post he published on LinkedIn Pulse as follows:

When your boss acts like he or she is perfect and tells everyone else they need to improve this is a sure sign that the leader isn't great. Worse yet, this behaviour can be copied at every level of management. Every level then points out how the level below it needs to change. The end result: No one gets much better.[183]

God starkly warned the people of Israel of the consequences of worshipping the gift rather than the Giver before they entered the Promised Land:

You may say to yourself, 'My power and the strength of my hands have produced this wealth for me.' But remember the LORD your God, for it is he who gives you the ability to

---

[182] Taken from *The Power of God's Grace* by Roy Hession. Copyright © Roy Hession Book Trust. Used by permission.
[183] *1 Sign Someone Isn't a Great Leader;* Marshall Goldsmith; LinkedIn Pulse (April 11th, 2016).

produce wealth, and so confirms his covenant, which he swore to your ancestors, as it is today. If you ever forget the LORD your God and follow other gods and worship and bow down to them, I testify against you today that you will surely be destroyed.[184]

It is so easy to be caught up in arrogant triumphalism, as it is human nature to promote ourselves or take undue credit when things go well; this basically means following other gods. As Goldsmith suggests, in the long run this ends up in much poorer performance for the organisation, and ultimately, as God says in Deuteronomy, it leads to destruction.

I have indicated in previous chapters that at times I have been guilty of that sin, probably more times than I care to remember. The warning verse which I quoted in chapter nine, "So if you think that you are standing firm, be careful that you don't fall!"[185], was one that I did not always pay enough attention to, and I needed to come back to the Lord and repent of my arrogant pride, seek his forgiveness and receive "grace in place of grace already given".

There are times, however, when we face trials in our leadership journeys. At these times, we need to throw ourselves on the Lord and let his light shine through. The apostle Paul very much knew that through the grace of God, God's light shone in his and other Christians' hearts "to give us the light of the knowledge of the glory of God in the face of Christ"[186]. To Paul this light was a treasure, but he knew human frailty, because he went on to say,

But we have this treasure in jars of clay to show that this all-surpassing power is from God and not from us.[187]

Sometimes God can only work through us when we are at a low point and we have to rely on his strength and not our own cleverness.

I wonder if Paul had in his mind the story of Gideon as he wrote about the treasure of God's light in jars of clay. In the book of Judges, the Midianites were terrorising the Israelites with their powerful armies. God called Gideon to lead the Israelites to drive out the Midianites

---

[184] Deuteronomy 8:17-19.
[185] 1 Corinthians 10:12.
[186] 2 Corinthians 4:6.
[187] 2 Corinthians 4:7.

from their land. He was a very reluctant leader, very unsure of his calling. What made it worse was that God insisted that he reduced the size of his army from 32,000 to only 300 men "in order that Israel may not boast against me that her own strength has saved her"[188].

Early in the morning when it was still dark, this tiny army approached the Midianite camp, each of the men holding trumpets and jars with torches inside. On hearing a signal from Gideon, the men blew their trumpets and smashed their jars, thus letting their light shine in the darkness of the camp. The sudden cacophony of trumpet sound and burst of light from the smashed jars resulted in tremendous confusion and panic within the Midianite camp, and so they made a hasty retreat.[189]

This was God's way of bringing victory, which would certainly not be our way. That, however, is the point; we need to trust him completely, and let him fulfil his purposes through our broken jars. As the writer of the book of Proverbs says,

Trust in the LORD with all your heart
and lean not on your own understanding;
in all your ways submit to him,
and he will make your paths straight.[190]

When we face difficulties in our leadership roles it is so easy to feel afraid, whether it be fear of opposition, or fear of the consequences of our actions. This is only natural, and indeed our heroes in the Bible also felt this fear at times. There were times when Paul was afraid for his own safety. He had, for example, to be reassured by the Lord when he was in Corinth through a vision when the Lord said,

Do not be afraid; keep on speaking, do not be silent. For I
am with you, and no one is going to attack and harm you,
because I have many people in this city.[191]

This reassurance was powerful enough to keep Paul in the city for another eighteen months teaching God's word.

After Moses died, it was Joshua's responsibility to lead the people of Israel across the Jordan and into the Promised Land. He must have felt

---

[188] Judges 7:2.
[189] The story of the Midianites' defeat can be found in Judges 7.
[190] Proverbs 3:5-6.
[191] Acts 18:9-10.

afraid going into new territory knowing that there would be many battles ahead and that he would have to make many difficult decisions. As we take on new leadership responsibilities in our schools, especially within an ever-changing educational landscape, we might feel exactly the same as Joshua. For Joshua there was also the challenge of stepping into Moses' shoes (or sandals!), and I can remember feeling the same before I started my headship, wondering how I could live up to the reputation of such an established, successful head as my predecessor, John Burn.

God, however, had words of reassurance for Joshua that also apply to us:

> *Have I not commanded you? Be strong and courageous. Do not be afraid; do not be discouraged, for the LORD your God will be with you wherever you go.*[192]

It is worth noting that this was a command, and not an option, that God gave Joshua. In our leadership battles, we should take the command and the accompanying promise with the utmost seriousness.

We need to rely on God's strength and not our own. Paul gives advice to Timothy, which also applies to Christian leaders:

> *You then, my son, be strong in the grace that is in Christ Jesus.*[193]

The strength we have is "in grace", meaning that it is undeserved, but it is also "in Christ Jesus", meaning that we can draw upon his unlimited power.

"Devote Yourselves to Prayer, Being Watchful and Thankful."[194]

If we are to receive strength from the Lord, then we have to maintain and develop our relationship with him through prayer. As Christian leaders in schools we need to take our needs and desires, along with those of our students, colleagues and communities, to the Lord in prayer, in the belief that he hears our requests and that he wants to answer our prayers.

---

[192] Joshua 1:9.
[193] 2 Timothy 2:1.
[194] Colossians 4:2.

Jesus gave a wonderful promise to his disciples that also applies to us:

> *You did not choose me, but I chose you and appointed you so that you might go and bear fruit – fruit that will last – and so that whatever you ask in my name the Father will give you.*[195]

The disciples were told by their master that he had selected them, rather than the other way round, and that they had been appointed to undertake his work by going out to bear fruit; in other words, as Jesus said in his great commission before he ascended into heaven, they had to "go and make disciples of all nations"[196]. That choice and appointment was all by grace, as these disciples were not from the educated elite, and had many personality issues that would have to be dealt with. It was a huge task that they had been given, but the promise was that they were not to try to do it in their own strength, but rather they could approach the Father in the name of Jesus and he would give them what they needed.

The disciples could only do their work if they remained in a close relationship with Jesus. He had previously taught them,

> *Remain in me, as I also remain in you. No branch can bear fruit by itself; it must remain in the vine. Neither can you bear fruit unless you remain in me. I am the vine; you are the branches. If you remain in me and I in you, you will bear much fruit; apart from me you can do nothing.*[197]

Prayer is the lifeblood of that relationship, listening to the Father, drawing strength from the Holy Spirit and praying to the Father in the name of Jesus.

These verses apply very much to Christian leaders in schools. We have been chosen and appointed by grace; we may be from the educated elite, but we should nonetheless be only too well aware of our shortcomings. God has called us to serve him in particular schools working with particular students and colleagues in order to bear much fruit. God has promised to answer our prayers and give us strength as

---

[195] John 15:16.
[196] Matthew 28:19.
[197] John 15:4-5.

we remain in close relationship with him. If we try to do our work in our own strength, we shall achieve nothing; certainly we shall not be able to bear fruit that will last. That has been my experience; I have seen God answer prayer in all aspects of my life, including my professional life, but when I have not been closely attached to the vine, there has been little, if any, fruit.

Prayer, however, can be hard. It is so easy to crowd it out through other things in our busy lives. We can fall into the trap of believing that we do not need God's help as we are doing well enough on our own. Sometimes it seems that we have been praying over a situation for a while and nothing seems to be happening, or things are even getting worse. We can feel tired and weak in our prayers.

If, however, we really believe that we are part of the vine, then God will help us through our difficulties in prayer. For example, he might prompt us to adopt a more disciplined approach to prayer, if we are tempted to neglect it through other pressures. If we are displaying the traits of arrogant triumphalism, he will bring us down to the right level. He will, perhaps through words of scripture, encourage us to continue to pray even although nothing seems to be happening. In many different ways, he will help us in our frailty. As Paul says,

> *In the same way, the Spirit helps us in our weakness. We do not know what we ought to pray for, but the Spirit himself intercedes for us through wordless groans. And he who searches our hearts knows the mind of the Spirit, because the Spirit intercedes for God's people in accordance with the will of God.*[198]

Even in our prayer life we are not left alone. Being attached to the vine means that God's Spirit will help us to pray.

Praying with others can also be a tremendous support to us as we seek the Lord. I have always found an illustration from the life of Moses to be very helpful in stressing the importance of corporate prayer. Towards the beginning of the Israelites' sojourn in the desert they were involved in a battle against the Amalekites. Moses stood on top of a hill overlooking the battle with the staff of God in his hands. Provided that Moses held his hands up high, the Israelites seemed to have the upper hand, but whenever he lowered his hands, the

---

[198] Romans 8:26-27.

Amalekites would seem to be winning. Moses inevitably found that his arms would tire, and so he needed the support of his two companions, Aaron and Hur, who held his arms up throughout the day until the Israelites won the battle at sunset.[199] This can be taken as a picture of prevailing prayer made possible through the support of others.

It is important that we find a group of prayerful Christians who will help us to keep our arms up in prayer. As I mentioned in chapter eleven, I was very fortunate as a head that there was a prayer group who had committed themselves for years to pray for the school, including praying for me.

So much is possible through prayer. Paul finished his prayer for the Ephesians with these words:

Now to him who is able to do immeasurably more than all we ask or imagine, according to his power that is at work within us, to him be glory in the church and in Christ Jesus throughout all generations, for ever and ever! Amen.[200]

God wants to answer our prayers mightily, doing more than we can even imagine, and so let us approach him with confidence and give him all the glory.

Maintain Your Integrity

In my last year in the school, when things were very difficult, I discussed the situation with my friend and home group leader, David Williams. He told me that he believed that people would be watching me and seeing how I reacted to all the difficult things that were thrown at me. Perhaps how I behaved would touch people's lives in ways that I might never see. These were wise words that I found reassuring.

It is vital for Christian leaders in schools to maintain their integrity despite the pressures that we face. Satan will want us to compromise over fundamental issues, but we need to stand firm. As Paul says,

Put on the full armour of God, so that you can take your stand against the devil's schemes.[201]

---

[199] See Exodus 17:8-13.
[200] Ephesians 3:20-21.
[201] Ephesians 6:11.

From its Latin root, "integrity" means "whole and undivided", as an integer in mathematics. We shall be pulled in different directions, but we need to remain wholly undivided for the Lord, seeking his will and maintaining his standards.

We shall of course make mistakes. Before I took up my deputy headship at Alnwick, Mike Peck, one of the deputies I worked closely with, advised me that staff would accept me as long as I did more good things than bad and that I said sorry for the mistakes I did make. The key, according to Mike, was to be honest, admit mistakes and say sorry. I tried to apply that simple advice both as a deputy and as a head. For example, during the staff restructure process throughout my last year as a head I did have to apologise to individuals when mistakes were made (even though the errors were not all necessarily of my making). Mike Peck was right; people appreciate honesty.

One of the ways in which we may be tempted as leaders is to consider ourselves better and more important than we really are, thus forgetting our true calling. After the mother of two disciples, James and John, asked Jesus for special places in his kingdom for her sons, the other disciples were indignant with them. Jesus, however, gave a timely warning and reminder to the whole group:

> You know that the rulers of the Gentiles lord it over them, and their high officials exercise authority over them. Not so with you. Instead, whoever wants to become great among you must be your servant, and whoever wants to be first must be your slave – just as the Son of Man did not come to be served, but to serve, and to give his life as a ransom for many.[202]

This is very much a warning and reminder to those of us in leadership positions in schools. We are not there to "lord it over" others, whether it be staff or students, but rather we have been placed there to serve. Christian leaders with integrity will be wholly undivided in their service for the Lord by meeting the needs of others, putting themselves last. When we are tempted to do otherwise, we need to come back to the example of Jesus: he bought us with the price of his own body, suffering and bleeding on the cross, separated from his Heavenly Father, so that our sins might be forgiven and that we might have

---

[202] Matthew 20:25-28.

fellowship with him now and for ever. That is the origin of the grace that we receive so abundantly.

As we fight our spiritual battles with integrity in the power of God's Spirit, we need to be wise. Jesus warned his disciples as he sent them out on mission to "be as shrewd as snakes and as innocent as doves"[203]. We need, for example, to decide which battles are worth fighting. The school had a very active Parent-Teacher Association, which raised money at events such as the Christmas Fayre, music concerts and drama productions. One source of funding was through selling raffle tickets for a variety of prizes that had been donated. I have to say that I loathe raffles and see them as a form of gambling. I did, however, feel that it was not worth fighting a battle over this issue, as I would have come across as being too negative amongst parent volunteers who wanted to do their best for the school, and besides, there were more important battles to fight. I did though draw the line at palm reading!

Another area where we need wisdom as leaders is in making promises. We are all aware of political leaders who make promises that they are not able to keep, and thus end up with a reputation for dishonesty. Sometimes it is not necessarily dishonesty, but rather a lack of wisdom on the part of politicians who find the reality of being in government a totally different experience from being in opposition, or who find that changing economic conditions prevent them from carrying out some promised programmes. Over my years of headship, I made a number of promises to parents about the school getting a new build, but for various political and financial reasons, these were promises that I was not able to keep until the very end of my headship when building work was just about to start. If I had considered the issues more carefully and not said anything publicly until the deal was signed and sealed, I would not have made what turned out to be broken promises. Rudolph Giuliani, the Mayor of New York at the time of the 9/11 tragedy, in his book "Leadership", refers to a principle that he tries to follow: underpromise and overdeliver.[204] This makes eminent sense, so that our promises are restrained, but our clients, whether they be students, staff or parents, will be pleased when we deliver more than they expected. If only more politicians followed that principle.

[203] Matthew 10:16.
[204] *Leadership;* Rudolph W Giuliani; Little, Brown Book Group (2002); chapter 7.

Conclusion

There is so much more that can be said about leadership and the strategies that should be used in different situations. For Christian leaders in schools, however, the key issue is that of attitude: how we see ourselves before God. It all comes back to grace, and grace is all that really matters.

Lee Strobel, an American Christian journalist, shared an experience at a low point in his life, when he was ill suffering from hyponatremia. His son prayed with him and he came to realise the extent of God's grace in his life. He wrote,

> *My eyes moistened as this truth crystallised: even if I were to actually lose everything – my house, my finances, my friends, my reputation, my position – it really wouldn't matter in the end, because I would still have God's grace. I would still be the Father's adopted and beloved son. And that would be enough.*[205]

For leaders, reputation and position are very often of paramount importance. God does want the best for us. He will want us to have a good reputation and he will place us in what for us is the best position. We are given these by grace, but, as Strobel says, if we lose them we shall still enjoy God's grace, having been adopted into his family.

In the passage that I preached on at our diamond jubilee service in January 2014, there is a key verse in which Paul explains what has happened to him:

> *The grace of our Lord was poured out on me abundantly, along with the faith and love that are in Christ Jesus.*[206]

Paul knew that he did not deserve God's mercy, but nevertheless he had received it in abundance, along with faith and love. In the knowledge that it is all possible by grace, Paul went on to do so much for his Saviour and Lord. Likewise, because of our sinful natures we do not deserve God's mercy, but he is prepared to shower it on us as we seek his forgiveness and ask Jesus to take control of our lives.

---

[205] *The Case for Grace;* Lee Strobel; Zondervan (2015); pages 168-169.
[206] 1 Timothy 1:14.

Paul instructed Titus that God's grace enables us to live godly lives:

> *For the grace of God has appeared that offers salvation to all people. It teaches us to say 'No' to ungodliness and worldly passions, and to live self-controlled, upright and godly lives in this present age, while we wait for the blessed hope – the appearing of the glory of our great God and Saviour, Jesus Christ, who gave himself for us to redeem us from all wickedness and to purify for himself a people that are his very own, eager to do what is good.*[207]

It is through grace that we shall be able to live the lives that will make a difference in our schools. By grace we can become role models to people around us, adopting the attitude of a servant, and pointing them to our Redeemer who is coming back again one day. That is the blessed hope we have.

---

[207] Titus 2:11-14.

C000175787

Beginning AutoCAD Release 14

for Windows NT and Windows 95

Robert McFarlane
MSc, BSc, ARCST, CEng, MIMech E, MIEE, MILog, MIED

Senior Lecturer, Department of Integrated Engineering,
Motherwell College

A member of the Hodder Headline Group
LONDON • SYDNEY • AUCKLAND
Copublished in North, Central and South America
by John Wiley & Sons Inc
New York • Toronto

Dedication
To Sam, a best pal who will never be forgotten

First published in Great Britain 1998 by Arnold,
a member of the Hodder Headline Group,
338 Euston Road, London NW1 3BH
http://www.arnoldpublishers.com

Copublished in North, Central and South America by John Wiley & Sons Inc.,
605 Third Avenue,
New York, NY 10158-0012

British Library Cataloguing in Publication Data
A catalogue record for this book is available from the British Library

Library of Congress Cataloging-in-Publication Data
A catalog record for this book is available from the Library of Congress

ISBN 0 340 72017 4
ISBN 0 470 32364 7 (Wiley)

2 3 4 5 6 7 8 9 10

Commissioning Editor: Sian Jones
Production Editor: James Rabson
Production Controller: Sarah Kett
Cover design: Stefan Brazzo

Produced by Gray Publishing, Tunbridge Wells, Kent
Printed and bound in Great Britain by The Bath Press, Bath
and The Edinburgh Press Ltd, Edinburgh

Contents

Preface

Wizard, Template, Scratch, Web, Folders – what have these to do with AutoCAD? They are some of the new phraseology associated with AutoCAD Release 14.

Release 14 is the latest AutoCAD from AutoDESK. It is a new package, incorporating several new features and concepts, and can only be used with either the Windows NT or Windows 95 operating systems.

This book is intended for:

a) new users to AutoCAD who have access to Release 14
b) experienced AutoCAD users wanting to upgrade their skills to Release 14.

The objective of the book is to introduce the reader to the essential basic 2D draughting skills required by every AutoCAD user, whether at the introductory, intermediate or advanced level. Once these basic skills have been 'mastered', the user can progress to the more 'demanding' topics such as 3D modelling, customization and AutoLISP programming.

The book will prove invaluable to any casual AutoCAD user, as well as the student studying any of the City and Guilds, BTEC or SQA (post-SCOTVEC) CAD courses. It will also be useful to undergraduates and post-graduates at higher institutions who require AutoCAD draughting skills. Industrial CAD users will be able to use the book, as both a textbook and a reference source.

As with all my AutoCAD books, the reader will learn by completing worked examples, and further draughting experience will be obtained by completing the additional activities which complement many of the chapters. All drawing material has been completed using Release 14, and all work has been checked to ensure that there are no errors.

I hope you enjoy learning with Release 14 as it is a very powerful draughting tool.

Your comments and suggestions for work to be included in any future publications would be greatly appreciated.

Bob McFarlane

Other titles from Bob McFarlane

Beginning AutoCAD   ISBN 0 340 58571 4

Progressing with AutoCAD   ISBN 0 340 60173 6

Introducing 3D AutoCAD   ISBN 0 340 61456 0

Solid Modelling with AutoCAD   ISBN 0 340 63204 6

Starting with AutoCAD LT   ISBN 0 340 62543 0

Advancing with AutoCAD LT   ISBN 0 340 64579 2

3D Draughting using AutoCAD   ISBN 0 340 67782 1

Beginning AutoCAD R13 for Windows   ISBN 0 340 64572 5

Modelling with AutoCAD R13 for Windows   ISBN 0 340 69251 0

Assignments in AutoCAD   ISBN 0 340 69181 6

Using AutoLISP with AutoCAD   ISBN 0 340 72016 6

Chapter 1

What's new in AutoCAD Release 14?

AutoCAD Release 14 is a new draughting package and requires either the Windows NT or Windows 95 operating system. The package has several new concepts when compared with Release 13, some of which are listed below:

- **Improved interactive display**
  - real-time pan and zoom
  - improves drawing performance.

- **Quick precision drawing**
  - three new automated tools for more precise drawing
  - autosnap, object snap button, tracking.

- **Object property access**
  - editing is quicker
  - object property toolbars
  - match properties command.

- **Window user interface integration**
  - toolbar dialogue box allows quicker access to toolbar command
  - command line editing allows standard editing support.

- **Layer and linetype management**
  - new easier to use layer control dialogue box
  - consolidation in management of named objects
  - new make layer current command.

- **Quality drawing presentation**
  - further enhanced text usability and display
  - solid fill option.

- **Learning tools**
  - start-up dialogue box assists when beginning a new drawing
  - accessibility of all documents from within AutoCAD.

- **Improved customization support**
  - creation of compound documents
  - object linking and embedding (OLE)
  - creation of scripts in languages such as Visual Basic.

- **Communicate and share designs**
  - improved XREF management
  - web site access for viewing drawings on the Internet.

- **Management tools**
  - improved preference dialogue box.

Chapter 2

System requirements and installation

The system requirements for Release 14 are:

1. RAM (random access memory) and hard disk space:
   - 32 MB of RAM (minimum)
   - 50 MB of hard disk space (minimum)
   - 64 MB of disk swap space (minimum)
   - 10 MB of additional RAM for each concurrent AutoCAD session
   - 2.5 MB of free disk space during installation (only temporary)
   - and for those using Windows NT 3.51: service pack 4 or 5 for networks.

2. Hardware:
   - Intel 486, Pentium or compatible (or better)
   - 640 × 480 VGA video (1024 × 768 recommended)
   - CD-ROM drive for installation
   - Windows supported display
   - mouse or other pointing device.

3. Hardware options:
   - printer or plotter
   - digitizer
   - serial or parallel port.

4. Installation. Release 14 can be installed:
   - for a single-user with single-user lock (dongle)
   - for a single-user with Sentinel driver
   - on a network.

Installation should follow the instructions given on the CD-ROM. It is recommended that the default names, e.g. ACADR4 are accepted.

Configuring AutoCAD Release 14

When Release 14 has been installed the 'system' can be customized to your own requirements using the **PREFERENCE** command. It is possible to configure the following:

- the display: colour and fonts
- the pointing device: digitizer or mouse
- the output device: printer or plotter.

In this book it is assumed that the system used has been configured to your own or your company's requirements.

Chapter 3

Using the book

This book is intended to assist you understanding AutoCAD Release 14 with a series of interactive exercises. These exercises will be backed up with tutorials, allowing you to practice your new skills. While no previous CAD knowledge is necessary, it would be useful if you knew how to use the following:

- the mouse to select items from the screen
- basic Windows commands, e.g. maximize/minimize windows.

Conventions used in the book

There are several simple conventions used in this book with which you should become familiar:

1 Menu selection will be in boldface type, e.g. **Draw**.

2 A menu sequence will be in boldface type and be either:
   a) **Draw**   or   *b*) **Draw–Circle–3 Points**
     Circle
     3 Points

3 User keyboard entry will also be highlighted in boldface type, e.g.
   a) coordinate entry: **125,36**; **@100,50**; **@200<45**
   b) command entry: **LINE**; **MOVE**; **ERASE**
   c) response to a prompt: **15**.

4 Icon selection will be displayed as a small drawing of the icon where appropriate – usually the first time the icon is used.

5 The AutoCAD R14 prompts will be in typewriter face, e.g.
   a) *prompt*   `from point`
   b) *prompt*   `second point of displacement`

6 The symbol **<R>** or **<RETURN>** will be used to signify pressing the return or enter key. Pressing the mouse right-button will also give the <RETURN> effect – called right-click.

7 The term **pick** is continually used with AutoCAD, and refers to the selection of a line, circle, text item, dimension, etc. The mouse left button is used to **pick an object** – called left-click.

8 Keyboard entry can be **LINE** or **line**. Both are acceptable.

Saving drawings

All drawing work should be saved for recall at some later time. Drawings can be saved:
- on a formatted floppy disk
- in a named folder on the hard drive.

It is up to you as to which method of saving drawings is used, but for convenience it will be assumed that a floppy disk is used. So, when a drawing is being saved or opened, the symbol **A:** will be used, e.g.

a) save drawing as A:WORKDRG
b) open drawing A:EXER_1.

Pre-Release 14 users should realize that the term 'directory' is no longer used. Folders replace directories, and are 'made' in the same way that a directory was created. Seek some help if you decide to save your work in a named folder.

Chapter 4

The Release 14 graphics screen and terminology

Starting AutoCAD Release 14

AutoCAD R14 is started as follows:
a) from the Windows 'start screen' with a double left-click on the AutoCAD R14 icon
b) by selecting the sequence: **Start–Programs–AutoCAD R14–AutoCAD R14**.

Both methods display the Release 14 logo screen and then the start-up (start from scratch) dialogue box. At this stage, pick (left-click) on cancel so that we may investigate the graphics screen.

The graphics screen

The Release 14 graphics screen (Figure 4.1) shows the following:

1 The title bar.

2 The 'windows buttons'.

3 The menu bar.

4 The Standard toolbar.

5 The Object Properties toolbar.

6 The Windows taskbar.

7 The Status bar.

8 The command prompt window area.

9 The coordinate system icon.

10 The drawing area.

11 The on-screen cursor.

12 The grips box at the cross-hair intersection.

13 Scroll bars.

14 The on-screen menu.

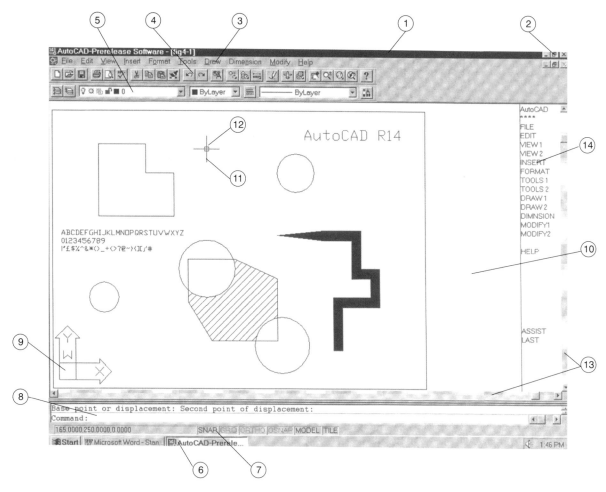

Figure 4.1 The Release 14 graphics menu.

Title bar

The title bar is positioned at the top of the screen and shows the Release 14 icon, the AutoCAD Release version and the current drawing name.

The Windows buttons

The Windows buttons are positioned to the right of the title bar, and are:
- left: minimize screen
- centre: maximize screen
- right: quit current application.

The menu bar

The menu bar displays the 'pull-down' menu headings. By moving the mouse into the menu bar area, the cursor cross-hairs change to a **pick arrow** and with a left-click on any heading the relevant pull-down menu will be displayed.

The full menu bar headings are:

File   Edit   View   Insert   Format   Draw   Dimension   Modify   Help

Figure 4.2 shows the full menu pull-down selections for five of the menu bar headings: File, View, Format, Draw and Modify.

Notes

1 Pull-down menu items which have '....' at the end of the name give a dialogue box when the item is selected.

2 Pull-down menu items which display ▶ result in a further menu (cascade) when selected.

3 Menu items in **bold** type are available for selection.

4 Menu items in grey type are not available for selection.

5 Menu items which display a ✓ are active, i.e. on

6 Menu bar and pull-down menu items can be selected (picked) with the mouse or by using the **Alt** key with the letter which is underlined, e.g.
   a) alt with M, activates the modify pull-down menu
   b) C press, activates the copy command.

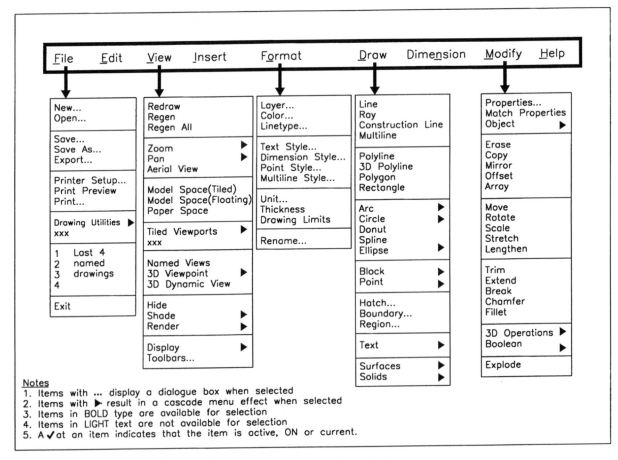

Figure 4.2 Complete pull-down menus from four menu bar selections.

The standard toolbar

The standard toolbar is normally positioned below the menu bar and allows you to access up to 24 icon selections including New, Open, Save, Print, etc. By moving the cursor pick arrow on to an icon and leaving it for about a second, the icon name will be displayed in yellow. The standard toolbar can be positioned anywhere on the screen or turned off if required.

The object properties toolbar

Normally positioned below the standard toolbar, this allows a further seven selections. The icons in this toolbar are Match Object's Layer Current (a new Release 14 command), Layer Control, Color Control, Linetype, Linetype Control and Properties.

The Windows taskbar

This is at the bottom of the screen and displays:
- the Windows NT or Windows 95 start button
- the name of any application which has been opened, e.g. AutoCAD
- the time and the sound control icon

By left-clicking on 'Start', the user has access to the other programs which can be run over the 'top' of AutoCAD, i.e. multi-tasking.

The status bar

The status bar, positioned above the Windows taskbar, gives the user information about drawing aids, e.g.
- on-screen cursor X, Y and Z coordinates at the left
- SNAP, GRID, ORTHO state, i.e. ON (in **bold**) or OFF (in grey)
- access to the OSNAP settings
- MODEL/PAPER space toggle.

Command prompt window area

The command prompt area is where the user 'communicates' with the program to enter:
a) a command, e.g. LINE, COPY, ARRAY
b) coordinate data, e.g. 120,150; @15<−30
c) a specific value, e.g. a radius of 25.

The command prompt area is also used by AutoCAD to supply the user with information, which could be:
a) a prompt, e.g. from point
b) a message, e.g. object does not intersect an edge.

The two-line command area can be enlarged by 'dragging' the bottom edge of the drawing area upwards. I generally leave the two-line command area as it is.

The coordinate system icon

This is the X–Y–W icon at the lower left corner of the drawing area. This icon gives information about the coordinate system in use. The default setting is the traditional Cartesian system with the origin (0,0) at the lower left corner of the drawing area. The icon (and origin) can be positioned anywhere in the drawing area, and can also be turned off by selecting the menu bar sequence **View–Display–UCS Icon–On** which removes the On tick. The same procedure is used to toggle the icon on. It is up to you as to whether the icon is on or off. I generally leave it on.

The drawing area

This is your drawing sheet and can be any size you want. Generally, we will use A3-sized paper, but will also investigate very large and very small drawings.

The cursor cross-hairs

The cursor cross-hairs are used to indicate the on-screen position, and movement of the pointing device will result in the coordinates in the status bar changing. The cursor is also used to 'pick' items for editing. Pre-Release 14 users will notice that the cursor is smaller than before, but it can be sized using PREFERENCES.

The grips box

The grips box is the small box which is normally 'attached' to the cursor cross-hairs. It has a limited use which will be discussed in a later chapter. As the grips box can cause confusion to new AutoCAD users I recommend that the box be turned off. This can be done with the following keyboard entries:

Enter	*Prompt*	*Enter*
GRIPS\<R>	New value for GRIPS\<1>	0\<R>
PICKFIRST\<R>	New value for PICKFIRST\<1>	0\<R>

Scroll bars

The scroll bars are positioned at the right and bottom of the drawing area and are used to scroll the drawing area. They are very useful for larger sized drawings and can be turned off if they are not needed.

The on-screen menu

The on-screen menu is positioned on the right of the drawing area and gives the same selection as the menu bar – although some items (e.g. Draw) have two selection names. It is for you as the user to decide if the screen menu is used; I never have it on.

Adapting the graphics screen

The graphics screen can be customized to the user's own requirements, i.e. screen colour, scroll bar, screen menu, etc. This is done with the menu bar sequence **Tools–Preferences** and the resulting preferences dialogue box has eight selections, two of which are as follows:

1 The display option gives:
   screen menu on or off
   scroll bars on or off
   screen colours to be changed
   number of lines for the command prompt area

2 The general option gives:
   time for automatic save
   whether back-up drawings have to be created or not

   My preferences are as follows:
   • white drawing area background
   • no screen menu
   • scroll bars
   • two lines in the command area.

Terminology

Release 14 terminology is basically the same as the previous releases, although there are a few new ideas. The following gives a brief description of the items commonly encountered by new users to AutoCAD.

Menu

A menu is a list of options from which the user selects (picks) the one required for a particular task. Picking a menu item is done by moving the mouse over the required item and left-clicking. There are different types of menus, e.g. pull-down, cascade and screen.

Command

A command is an AutoCAD function used to perform a task. This may be to draw a line, rotate a shape or modify an item of text. Commands can be activated by:
a) selection from a menu
b) selecting the appropriate icon from a toolbar
c) entering the command from the keyboard at the command line
d) entering the command abbreviation
e) using the Alt key as previously described.

Only the first three options will be used in this book.

Objects

Everything drawn in Release 14 is called either an **object** (**entity**), e.g. lines, circles, text, dimensions, hatching, etc. The user 'picks' the appropriate object with a mouse left-click when prompted.

Default setting

AutoCAD Release 14 has certain values and settings which have been 'preset' by the manufacturer (AutoDESK) and are essential for certain operations. These default settings are displayed within < > brackets, but can be altered by users as and when required. For example:

1 From the menu bar select **Draw–Polygon** and:
prompt   _polygon Number of sides<4>
respond   **press the ESC key** to cancel the command
Note that: *a*) <4> is the default value for the number of sides
          b) polygon is the active command.

2 At the command line enter **LTSCALE <R>** and:
prompt   New scale factor<1.0000>
enter   **0.5 <R>**
Note that: *a*) <1.0000> is the LTSCALE default value
          b) we have altered the LTSCALE value to 0.5.

The escape (Esc) key

The escape key is used to cancel any command at any time. It is very useful, especially when the user is 'lost in a command'. Pressing the Esc key will cancel any command and return the command prompt line.

Icon

An icon is a menu item in the form of a picture contained within a named toolbar. Icons will be used throughout the book, particularly when a command is being demonstrated for the first time.

Cascade menu

A cascade menu is obtained when an item in a pull-down menu with ▶ after its name is selected, e.g. by selecting the menu bar sequence **Draw–Circle–Tan,Tan,Radius** the cascade effect shown in Figure 4.3 will be displayed. Cascade menus can be cancelled by:

1 Moving the pick arrow to the right of Help in the menu bar area and left-clicking. The complete cascade effect is cancelled.

2 Pressing the Esc key – this cancels the last cascade menu.

Note that when the sequence **Draw–Circle–Tan,Tan,Radius** is selected, the status bar displays: Creates a circle tangent to two objects with a specified radius.

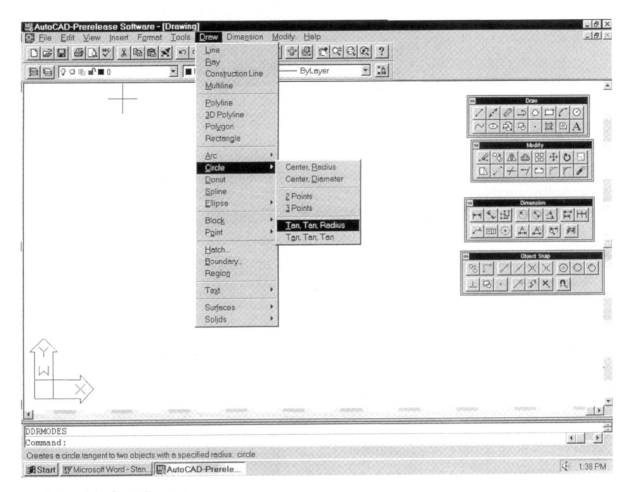

Figure 4.3   Cascade menu.

Dialogue boxes

A dialogue box is always shown when an item with '...' after its name is selected. When the menu bar sequence **Tools–Drawing Aids...** is selected, the drawing aids dialogue box (Figure 4.4) will be displayed. Dialogue boxes allow the user to alter parameter values or toggle an aid on/off. Aids are toggled using the small box adjacent to their name and:
a) a cross (×) in the box means that the aid is on
b) a blank box means that the aid is off.

Most dialogue boxes display the options On, Cancel and Help and are used as follows:
* OK   accept the values in the current dialogue box
* Cancel   cancel the dialogue box without any alterations
* Help   gives further information in Windows format. Windows can be cancelled with File–Exit or using the Windows close button.

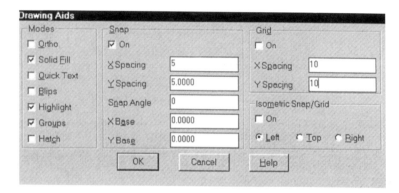

Figure 4.4 The Drawing Aids dialogue box.

Toolbars

Toolbars are aids for the user. They allow the Release 14 commands to be shown on the screen in icon form. The required command is activated by picking (left-click) the appropriate icon. The icon command is displayed in yellow by moving the pick arrow on to an icon and leaving it for a second or so. There are 17 toolbars available for selection, and two are already shown in the drawing area: the standard toolbar and the object properties toolbar.

Toolbars can be:
a) displayed and positioned anywhere in the drawing area
b) customized to the user's preference.

To activate a toolbar, select **View–Toolbars...** from the menu bar and the toolbars dialogue box will be shown. To display a toolbar, pick the box by the required name. Figure 4.5 shows the toolbar dialogue box with the object properties, standard, dimension and draw toolbars toggled on. When toolbars are positioned in the drawing area as shown in Figure 4.5 they are called **floating** toolbars.

Toolbars can be:

1 Moved to a suitable position on the screen by the user. This is achieved by moving the pick arrow into the blue title area of the toolbar and holding down the mouse left button. Move the toolbar to the required position on the screen and release the left button.

2 Altered in shape by 'dragging' the toolbar edges sideways or upwards and downwards.

3 Cancelled at any time by picking the cancel box at the left of the title bar.

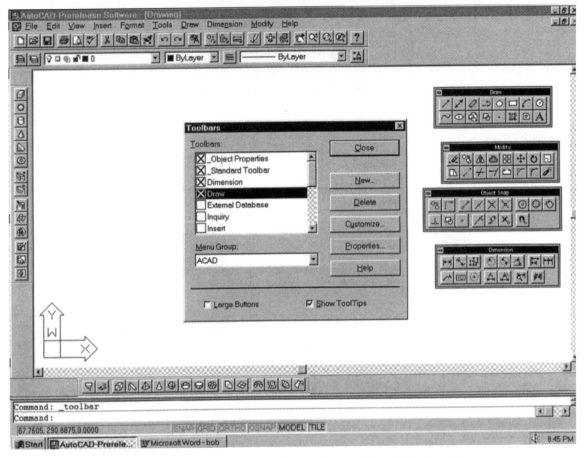

Figure 4.5 The Toolbars dialogue box and four floating toolbars and two docked toolbars.

It is your preference as to what toolbars are displayed at any one time. I always display the Draw, Modify, Dimension and Object Snap toolbars and others as and when required.

Toolbars can be **docked** at the edges of the drawing area by moving them to the edges. The toolbar will be automatically docked when the edge is reached. Figure 4.5 shows four floating and two docked toolbars.

Toolbars **do not have to be used** – they are an aid to the user. All commands are available from the menu bar, but it is recommended that toolbars are used, as they greatly increase draughting productivity.

When used, it is your preference if they are floating or docked.

Fly-out menu

When an icon is selected an AutoCAD command is activated. If the icon has a ◢ at the lower right corner of the icon box, and the left button of the mouse is held down, a fly-out menu is obtained. This gives access to other icons. Release 14 does not have as many fly-out menus as 13. The following fly-out menus are available from the standard toolbar:

Tracking	object snap icons
UCS	UCS options in icon form
Distance	properties icons
Named view	the viewpoint preset icons
Zoom	the various zoom options in icon form.

Wizard

Wizard is a new term and allows access to various parameters necessary to start a drawing session, e.g. units, paper size, etc. It has two options: quick and advanced. We will look at how to use the Wizard in later chapters.

Template

This is another new term and allows access to different drawing standards with different-sized paper. The following are supported in Release 14:

Standards	ansi, din, iso, jis
Sizes	A0, A1, A2, A3, A4 and A, B, C, D, E

The use of templates will be investigated later.

Toggle

Toggle is the term used when a drawing aid is turned on or off and usually refers to either:
a) pressing a key, or
b) activating a function in a dialogue box, i.e. × is on, no × is off.

Function keys

Several of the keyboard function keys can be used as aids while drawing:

F1	accesses the AutoCAD Help menu
F2	flips between the graphics screen and the Text window
F3	activates the OSNAP dialogue box
F4	toggles the tablet on/off (if attached)
F5	toggles the isoplane top/right/left
F6	coordinate on/off toggle
F7	grid on/off toggle
F8	ortho on/off toggle
F9	snap on/off toggle
F10	status line on/off toggle
F11	not used
F12	not used.

File types

When a drawing has been completed it should be saved for future recall and all drawings are called *files*. Release 14 has various file types with the extensions:

.dwg   drawing file
.dwt   drawing template file
.dwf   drawing web format.

Drawing names should be as simple as possible. It should be noted that both Windows NT and Windows 95 operating systems support drawing names that:
a) contain spaces
b) have full stops.

So, the following are acceptable drawing names:
MYDRG
MYDRAWING
MY DRAWING
MY.DRAWING
THIS IS MY FIRST DRAWING

This completes this long chapter. Now let's draw!

Chapter 5

Drawing, erasing and the selection set

In this chapter we will investigate how lines and circles can be drawn and then erased. Different methods will be used to draw the objects, and then we will look at the selection set – a powerful aid when modifying a drawing.

Starting a new drawing with Wizard

1   Start AutoCAD with a double left-click on the R14 icon and:
  prompt   Create New Drawing dialogue box
  respond   *a*) pick Use a Wizard
      b) pick Quick Setup – Figure 5.1
        pick OK
  prompt   Quick Setup screen with:
      a) Step 1 – Units
      b) Step 2 – Area
  respond   *a*) Units: pick Decimal units
      b) pick Next>>
      c) Area: Width 420 and Length 297
      d) pick Done
  prompt   Drawing screen returned set to decimal units and A3-sized paper.

With the menu bar sequence **View–Toolbars...** activate the Draw and Modify toolbars then close the toolbars dialogue box. Position the two toolbars to suit. The Standard and Object Properties toolbars should be docked at the top of the drawing area?

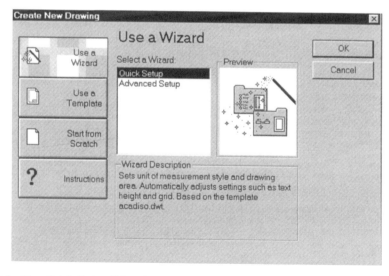

Figure 5.1   The Quick Setup Wizard.

Drawing line and circle objects

1   Activate (pick) the LINE icon from the Draw toolbar and observe the command prompt area. The prompt is _line From point. You now have to pick a **start** point for the line, so move the pointing device and pick (left-click) any point within the drawing area. Several things should happen:
    a) a small cross **may** appear at the selected start point – if it doesn't, don't panic
    b) as you move the pointing device away from the start point a line will be dragged from this point to the on-screen cursor position. This drag effect is termed **rubberband**
    c) the prompt becomes: To point

2   Move the pointing device to any other point on the screen and left-click. Another cross may appear at the selected point and a line will be drawn between the two 'picked points'. **This is your first R14 object.**

3   The line command is still active with the rubberband effect and the prompt line is still asking for the line endpoint.

4   Continue moving the mouse about the screen and pick points to give a series of 'joined lines'.

5   Finish the LINE command with a right-click on the mouse and the command line will be returned blank.

6   From the menu bar select **Draw–Line** and the From point prompt will again be displayed in the command area. Draw some more lines the end the command by pressing the RETURN/ENTER key.

7   At the command line enter **LINE <R>** and draw a few more lines. End the command with a right-click.

8   From the Draw toolbar activate the CIRCLE icon and:
    prompt   _circle 3P/2P/TTR/<Center point>
    respond   **pick any point on the screen as the circle centre**
    prompt   Diameter/<radius>
    respond   **drag out the circle and pick any point for radius**

9   From the menu bar select **Draw–Circle–Center,Radius** and pick a centre point and drag out a radius.

10 At the command prompt enter **CIRCLE <R>** and create another circle anywhere on the screen.

11 Using the icons, menu bar or keyboard entry, draw some more lines and circles until you are satisfied that you can activate and end the two commands.

12 Figure 5.2(a) shows some line and circle objects.

Blips

Several of you may have small crosses at the end of the lines drawn on the screen. These crosses are called **blips** and are used to identify the start and end points of lines, circle centres, etc. The are **not** objects or entities and will not be plotted out on the final drawing. I find them a nuisance and always turn them off. This can be done with the menu bar sequence:
Tools
Drawing Aids...
Blips box no cross, i.e. OFF
OK

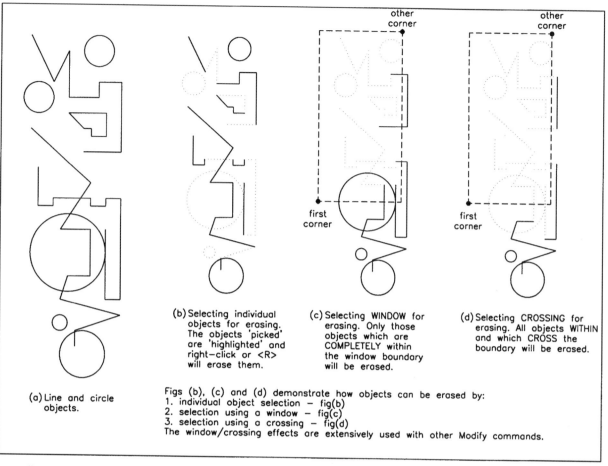

(b) Selecting individual objects for erasing. The objects 'picked' are 'highlighted' and right–click or <R> will erase them.

(c) Selecting WINDOW for erasing. Only those objects which are COMPLETELY within the window boundary will be erased.

(d) Selecting CROSSING for erasing. All objects WITHIN and which CROSS the boundary will be erased.

(a) Line and circle objects.

Figs (b), (c) and (d) demonstrate how objects can be erased by:
1. individual object selection – fig(b)
2. selection using a window – fig(c)
3. selection using a crossing – fig(d)
The window/crossing effects are extensively used with other Modify commands.

Figure 5.2 Drawing and erasing line and circle objects.

If you do not want to turn the blips off, then by selecting the REDRAW icon from the Standard toolbar, the drawing screen is regenerated and the blips are removed.

Erasing objects

Now that we have drawn some lines and circles, we will investigate how they can be erased – not as daft as it seems? The erase command will be used to demonstrate different options available to us when it is necessary to modify a drawing. The actual command can be activated by one of these three methods:

a) picking the ERASE icon from the Modify toolbar
b) with the menu bar sequence **Modify–Erase**
c) entering **ERASE <R>** at the command line.

Before continuing with the exercise, select from the menu bar the sequence **Tools–Selection...** to display the object selection setting dialogue box and ensure the following are set:

Noun/verb setting   OFF, i.e. blank box
Use shift to add   OFF
Press and drag   OFF
Implied windowing   ON, i.e. × in box
Object groups   ON
Pickbox size   set to suit
Pick OK when complete.

We will now continue with the erase exercise.

1   Ensure you still have several lines and circles on the screen similar to Figure 5.2(a).

2   Activate the ERASE command (icon, menu bar, keyboard?) and:

    prompt   `Select objects`
    and   cursor cross-hairs replaced by a 'pickbox' which moves as you move the mouse.
    respond **position the pickbox over any line and left-click**
    and   two things will happen:
                a) the selected line will 'change appearance', i.e. it will be highlighted
                b) the prompt displays Select objects: 1 found
    then   `Select objects`

3   Continue picking lines and circles to be erased (about six) and each object will be highlighted.

4   When you have selected enough objects, right-click the mouse.

5   The selected objects will be erased, and the command prompt will return.

6   Figure 5.2(b) demonstrates the individual object selection erase effect.

Oops

Suppose that you had erased the wrong objects. Before you do **anything** else, enter **OOPS<R>** at the command line.

The erased objects will be returned to the screen. Consider this in comparison to a traditional draughtsman who has rubbed out several lines/circles – it would be necessary to have to redraw each one.

OOPS must be used **immediately** after the last command and must be entered from the keyboard.

Erasing with a window/crossing effect

The individual selection of objects is satisfactory if only a few lines/circles have to be modified (we used erase). When a large number of objects need to be modified, the individual selection method is tedious. AutoCAD overcomes this by allowing you to position a 'window' over an area of the screen which will select several objects 'at one pick'.

To demonstrate the window effect, ensure you have several objects (about 20) on the screen and refer to Figure 5.2(c).

1 Select the ERASE icon from the Modify toolbar and:

prompt	Select objects
enter	**W <R>** (at the command line) – the window option
prompt	First corner
respond	**position the cursor at a suitable point and left-click**
prompt	Other corner
respond	**move the cursor to drag out a window (rectangle) and left-click**
prompt	??? found and certain objects highlighted
then	Select objects, i.e. any more to be erased?
respond	**right-click or <R>**

2 The highlighted objects will be erased.

3 At the command line enter **OOPS <R>** to restore the erased objects.

4 From the menu bar select **Modify–Erase** and:

prompt	Select objects
enter	**C <R>** (at command line) – the crossing option
prompt	First corner
respond	**pick any point on the screen**
prompt	Other corner
respond	**drag out a window and pick the other corner**
prompt	??? found and highlighted objects
respond	**right-click**

5 The objects highlighted will be erased – Figure 5.2(d).

Note on window/crossing

1 The window/crossing concept of selecting a large number of objects will be used extensively with the modify commands, e.g. erase, copy, move, rotate, etc. The objects which are selected when **W or C** is entered at the command line are as follows:

   window all objects *completely within* the window boundary are selected

   crossing all objects *completely within and also which cross* the window boundary are selected.

2 The window/crossing options **must** be entered from the keyboard, i.e. W or C.

3 Release 14 does not appear to support the Select Objects toolbar that was in Release 13. I think this a serious omission.

4 Figure 5.2 demonstrates the single object selection method as well as the window and crossing methods for erasing objects.

The selection set

Window and crossing are only two options contained within the selection set. The complete set contains the following options: All, Crossing, Crossing Polygon, Fence, Last, Previous, Window and Window Polygon.

During the various exercises in the book, we will use all of these options but will now consider three of them.

1 Erase all objects from the screen – individual or window?

2 Refer to Figure 5.3(a) and draw some new lines and circles – the layout is not important.

3 Refer to Figure 5.3(b), select the ERASE icon from the modify toolbar and:

prompt	Select objects
enter	**F <R>** – the fence option
prompt	First fence point
respond	**pick a point (pt 1)**
prompt	Undo/<Endpoint of line>
respond	**pick a suitable point (pt 2)**
prompt	Undo/<endpoint of line>
respond	**pick points 3, then 4, then 5, then right-click**
prompt	??? found and certain objects highlighted
respond	**right-click or <R>**.

4 The highlighted objects will be erased.

5 OOPS to restore these erased objects.

6 Menu bar with **Modify–Erase** and referring to Figure 5.3(c):

prompt	Select objects
enter	**WP <R>** – the window-polygon option
prompt	First polygon point
respond	**pick a point (pt 1)**
prompt	Undo/<endpoint of line>
respond	**pick points 2,3,4,5 then right-click**
prompt	??? found and objects highlighted
respond	**right-click** to erase the highlighted objects.

7 OOPS to restore the erased objects.

8 *a*) activate the ERASE command
b) enter **CP <R>** at command line – crossing polygon option
c) pick points in order as Figure 5.3(d) the right-click
d) right-click to erase objects.

9 The fence/window polygon/crossing polygon options of the selection set are very useful when the 'shape' to be modified does not permit the use of the normal rectangular window. With these three options, the user can 'make their own shape' for modifying.

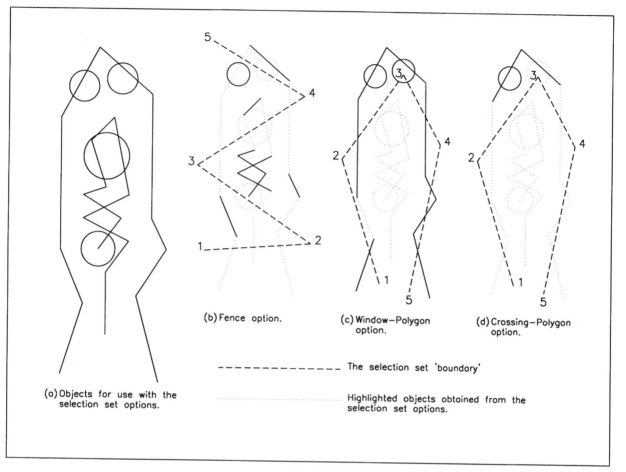

(b) Fence option.

(c) Window–Polygon option.

(d) Crossing–Polygon option.

– – – – – – – – – – – The selection set 'boundary'

(a) Objects for use with the selection set options.

··············· Highlighted objects obtained from the selection set options.

Figure 5.3 Further selection set options.

The pickbox

All the modify commands (e.g. ERASE) require you to position a pickbox over the objects which have to be modified. The 'size' of this pickbox may be 'too big' and can be altered at **any time** to your own specification. This is achieved by one of two methods:

a) from the command line by entering **PICKBOX <R>** and:

> *prompt* New value for PICKBOX<?>
> *enter* **3 <R>**

b) with the menu bar selection **Tools–Selection...** and:

> *prompt* Object selection settings dialogue box
> *respond* **alter pickbox size to suit then OK**

c) My preference is to set the pickbox size between 3 and 5.

Activity

Spend some time using the LINE, CIRCLE and ERASE commands and become proficient with the various selection set options for erasing – this will greatly help you in later chapters.

Read the summary and proceed to the next chapter. If possible, do not exit AutoCAD.

Summary

1   The LINE and CIRCLE draw commands can be activated:
    a) by selecting the icon from the draw toolbar
    b) with a menu bar sequence, e.g. **Draw–Line**
    c) by entering the command at the prompt line, e.g. **LINE<R>**.

2   The ERASE (modify) command can be activated:
    a) with the ERASE icon from the modify toolbar
    b) from the menu bar with **Modify–Erase**
    c) by entering **ERASE<R>** at the command line.

3   All modify commands (e.g. ERASE) allow access to the selection set.

4   The selection set has several options including Window, Crossing, Fence, Window-Polygon and Crossing-Polygon.

5   The appropriate selection set option can only activated from the command line by entering the letters W,C,F,WP,CP.

6   The term 'WINDOW' refers to all objects completely contained within the window boundary.

7   CROSSING includes all objects which cross the window boundary and are also completely within the window.

8   OOPS is a very useful command with 'restores' the previous command.

9   Blips are small crosses used to display the start and endpoints of lines. They are **not** objects and should be turned off.

10 REDRAW is a command which will 'refresh' the drawing screen and remove both blips and any 'ghost image' from the screen. The command is best used from the icon in the standard toolbar.

11 The pickbox size can be altered by the user at any time to suit the drawing requirements of the screen.

Note on the selection set

As stated previously, Release 14 does not seem to support the select objects toolbar that was available in the previous version. This toolbar allowed the selection set options to be activated in icon form. Users now have to enter the options from the command line.

AutoCAD recommends that objects which have to be modified be placed in a selection set **prior** to activating the modify command. While I can understand the logic behind this idea, I do not think it is practical and believe that the modify command should be activated first, and then the objects selected using one of the selection set options. This will be the method used with the modify command throughout the book.

Chapter 6

Using the drawing aids

Now that we know how to draw and erase lines and circles, we will investigate the drawing aids. Release 14 has three useful drawing aids, these being:

Grid   allows the user to place a series of imaginary dots over the drawing area. The grid spacing can be altered by the user at any time while the drawing is being constructed. As the grid is imaginary, it does **not** appear on the final plot.

Snap   allows the user to set the on-screen cursor to a predetermined point on the screen, this usually being one of the grid points. The snap spacing can also be altered at any time by the user.

Ortho   an aid which allows only horizontal and vertical movement.

Both the grid and snap spacing can be set using a dialogue box, or by keyboard entry. The ortho is a toggle on/off effect only.

Getting ready

1   Do you still have the objects from Chapter 5 on the screen?

2   Begin a new drawing with the menu bar sequence **File–New** and:

prompt   AutoCAD message dialogue box – Figure 6.1.

3   This dialogue box is displayed very regularly and can cause a great deal of confusion to new (and not so new) AutoCAD users.

4   The dialogue box is informing the user that since starting the drawing, changes have been made and that these alterations have not been saved. The user has to respond to one of the three options which are:

Yes   picking this option will save all changes to the named drawing. In my example this would be Figure 5.2.

No   selecting this option will mean that the original drawing (Figure 5.2 in my example) will be unaffected by the changes which have been made. It will also mean that these changes have not been saved.

Cancel   returns the user to the drawing screen.

5   In our case, pick no, i.e. we do not want to save the drawing used to investigate the erase command.

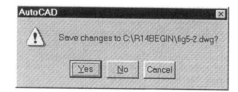

Figure 6.1 The AutoCAD message dialogue box.

6 When no has been selected, the create new drawing dialogue box – use a Wizard – will
be displayed, so:
a) pick Quick Setup then OK
b) pick Decimal units then Next>>
c) set width: 420 and length: 297 then pick Done.

7 We have again set an A3-sized sheet as before.

Grid and snap spacing – keyboard entry

1 At the command line enter **GRID <R>** and:
prompt   Grid spacing(X)...<?>
enter   **20<R>**

2 At the command line enter **SNAP<R>** and:
prompt   Snap spacing or...<?>
enter   **20<R>**

3 Refer to Figure 6.2 and use the LINE command to draw the letter H using the grid and
snap settings of 20.

4 Using the keyboard, change the grid and snap spacing to 15.

5 Use the LINE command and draw the letter E.

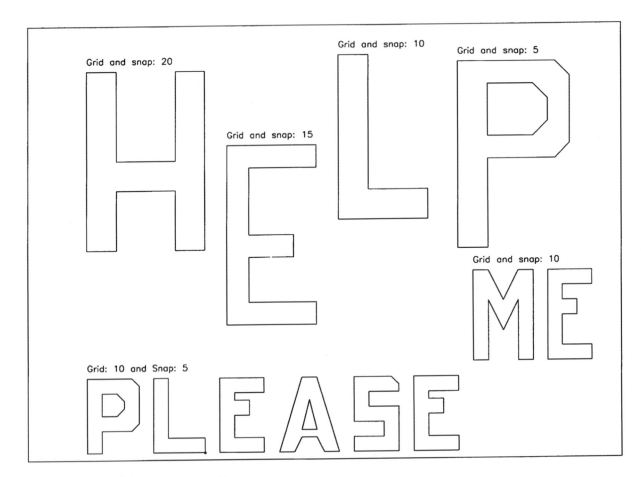

Figure 6.2   Using the drawing aids.

Grid and snap spacing – dialogue box method

1 From the menu bar select **Tools–Dialogue Box...** and:
   prompt   Drawing Aids dialogue box
   with   *a*) Snap on with spacing 15
            b) Grid on with spacing 15 – from previous setting
   respond 1) alter the Snap X spacing to 10 by:
             a) click to right of last digit
             b) back-space until all digits removed
             c) enter 10 then <R>
             d) Y snap spacing alters to 10?
         2) alter the Grid X spacing by:
             a) position pick arrow to left of first digit
             b) hold down left button and drag over all digits – they will be highlighted
                in blue
             c) enter 10 then <R>
             d) Y grid spacing alters to 10?
         3) pick OK

2 Use the LINE command to draw the letter L

3 Use the Drawing Aids dialogue box to set both the grid and snap spacings to 5 and draw the letter P.

Toggling the grid/snap/ortho

The drawing aids can be toggled on/off with:

1 the function keys, i.e. F7 – grid; F8 – ortho; F9 – snap

2 the Drawing Aids dialogue box where:
   a) tick in box – aid ON
   b) blank box – aid OFF.

3 The status bar with a double left-click on Snap and Grid.

4 My preference is to set the grid and snap spacing values from the dialogue box then use the function keys to toggle the aids on or off.

5 Take care if the ortho drawing aid is on. Ortho only allows horizontal and vertical movement and lines may not appear as expected. I tend to ensure that ortho is off.

Task

1 Refer to Figure 6.2 and:
   a) with the grid and snap set to 10, draw ME
   b) with the grid set to 10 and the snap set to 5, complete PLEASE but note that the S is harder than you think!

2 Proceed to the next chapter when you have completed the task, ensuring that you do not exit AutoCAD.

Chapter 7

Saving and opening drawings

It is essential that all users know how to save and open a drawing, and how to exit AutoCAD correctly. In my experience, in both industry and education, these operations cause new users to CAD a great deal of concern. This chapter will explain how these operations can be achieved quite easily, so make sure that:

a) you have a formatted floppy disk in the A: drive

b) the drawing from Chapter 6 is displayed on the screen.

Note that while all drawings will be saved to floppy disk, a named folder (the Windows NT/95 name for a directory) could also have been used. The name of this folder could be **mywork** or something similar. It is easier for me to use the A: floppy drive in exercises.

Saving a drawing

1 Select from the menu bar **File–Save As...** and:

prompt   Save Drawing As dialogue box

respond   1) observe the layout with:

   a) Save in box
   b) File name box
   c) Save as type box

2) pick the scroll arrow at the right of Save in box

3) pick 3.5 inch floppy (A)

4) alter File name to MYTEST

5) ensure save as type is AutoCAD R14 drawing (*.dwg)

6) dialogue box as Figure 7.1

7) pick Save.

2   The screen drawing will be saved to the floppy disk, but will still be displayed on the screen.

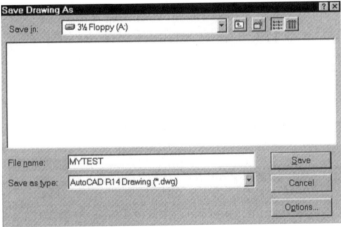

Figure 7.1   The Save Drawing As dialogue box.

Opening a drawing

1 Erase all objects from the screen by selecting the ERASE icon and:
   prompt Select objects
   enter **ALL <R>** – selection set option
   prompt ??? found
   respond **right-click** to leave a blank screen

2 From the menu bar select **File–Open** (No to message) and:
   prompt Select File dialogue box
   respond 1) ensure it looks in: 3.5 inch floppy (A) – should be the case?
   　　　　 2) pick **MYTEST** and:
   　　　　　　 a) it is highlighted in blue
   　　　　　　 b) MYTEST is displayed in File name box
   　　　　　　 c) File type: drawing (*.dwg)
   　　　　　　 d) preview of drawing displayed
   　　　　　　 e) dialogue box as Figure 7.2
   　　　　　　 f) pick Open.

3 The HELP ME PLEASE drawing will be displayed on the screen.

Replacing an existing drawing

1 Add some circles to your drawing – simple enough?

2 From the menu bar select **File–Save As...** and:
   prompt Save Drawing As dialogue box
   with MYTEST as File name
   respond **pick Save** and
   prompt AutoCAD message dialogue box – Figure 7.3.

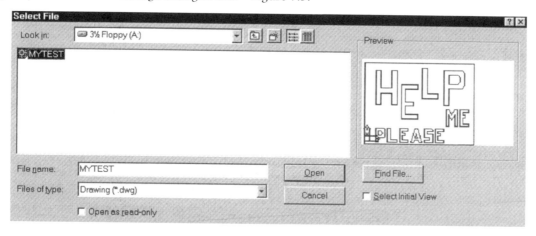

Figure 7.2 The Select File dialogue box.

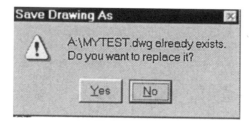

Figure 7.3 The Save Drawing As warning dialogue box.

3   This dialogue box is very common and can cause confusion to the new user and an explanation is required.

4   The drawing which was opened was MYTEST which contained the words HELP ME PLEASE. We have added some circles to this drawing and tried to save the modified drawing as MYTEST, i.e. the same file name as before. AutoCAD 'knows' that a drawing called MYTEST already exists and it is asking the user if it should be replaced and:

   Yes: will save MYTEST with the circles

   No: will return to the Save Drawing As dialogue box, waiting for your next instruction.

5   Respond by 1 picking no
                2 cancel the Save Drawing As dialogue box.

6   From the menu bar select **File–Save** and – nothing?

7   *a*) Now erase all objects from the screen – easy?
    b) Open the MYTEST drawing as before – 'no' to message?

8   The re-opened MYTEST drawing will display the circles.

Save and save as

The menu bar selection of **File** allows the user to pick either **Save** or **Save As**. The new AutoCAD user should be aware of the difference between these two options.

Save: will save the current drawing with the same name with which the drawing was opened. No dialogue box will be displayed.

Save as: allows you to enter a drawing name via a dialogue box. If a drawing already exists with the entered name, a warning is shown in a dialogue box.

Assignment

You are now in the position to try a drawing for yourself, so:

1   Erase all objects from the screen – save?

2   Refer to Activity drawing 1 (all of the activity drawing are grouped together at the end of the book).

3   Set a grid and snap spacing to suit, e.g. 10 and 5, respectively.

4   Only use the LINE and CIRCLE commands (and perhaps ERASE if you make a mistake) to draw some simple shapes. The size and position are not really important at this stage, the objective being to give you a chance to practice drawing using the drawing aids.

5   When you have completed the drawing, save it as **A:ACT_1**.

Summary

1 The **recommended** procedure for saving a drawing is:
   a) menu bar with **File–Save As**
   b) select A: (or named folder)
   c) enter the drawing name in the file name box
   d) pick save.

2 To open a drawing from **within** AutoCAD do as follows:
   a) menu bar with **File–Open**
   b) select A: (or named folder)
   c) pick the drawing name from the list
   d) a preview is obtained
   e) pick open.

3 To open a drawing from **start** do as follows:
   a) start AutoCAD
   b) pick **Open a drawing** from the start up dialogue box
   c) either pick the drawing name if it is displayed then OK
       or double left-click on **More-files...** and proceed as above.

4 The correct procedure to end an AutoCAD session is:
   a) complete the drawing
   b) save the drawing to floppy or your named folder
   c) menu bar with **File–Exit**.

5 The save and open command can be activated:
   a) by menu bar selection
   b) by keyboard entry
   c) from icon selection in the standard toolbar.

6 The standard toolbar SAVE icon, and the keyboard entry SAVE command, are the same
   as SAVE AS, i.e. both display the Save Drawing As dialogue box.

Chapter 8

Standard sheet 1

Traditionally, one of the first things that a draughtsperson does when starting a new drawing is to get the correct size sheet of drawing paper. This sheet will probably have borders, a company logo and other details already printed on it. The drawing is then completed to fit into the preprinted layout sheet. A CAD drawing is no different from this, with the exception that the user does not get a sheet of paper. Companies who use AutoCAD will want their drawings to conform to their standards in terms of the title box, text size, linetypes used, the style of the dimensions, and so on. Parameters which govern these factors can be set every time a drawing is started, but this is tedious and against CAD philosophy. It is preferable to have all standard requirements set automatically, and this is achieved by making a drawing called a **standard sheet** or **prototype drawing** – you may have other names for it. Standard sheets can be customized to suit all sizes of paper, e.g. A0, A1, etc., as well as any other size the customer wants. These standard sheets will contain the company's settings, and the individual draughtsman or draughtswoman can add their own personal settings as required.

It is the standard sheet which is the CAD operator's 'sheet of paper'.

We will create an A3 standard sheet, save it, and use it for all future drawing work. At this stage, the standard sheet will not have many 'settings', but we will continue to refine it and add to it as we progress through the book.

Note

While I realize that one of the new concepts in Release 14 is the **template** drawing, I would suggest that we leave this concept to a later chapter until you are reasonably proficient at using the draw and modify commands. The template drawing idea may not be as appealing to the CAD user as at first thought!

The A3 standard sheet will be created using the advanced wizard so:

1 Depending on AutoCAD being loaded, either:
    a) outside: start AutoCAD with a double left-click on the icon
    b) inside: menu bar with **File–New** (no changes).

2 Either method will give:
    prompt   Create New Drawing (Wizard) dialogue box
    respond   **pick Advanced Setup then OK**
    prompt   Advanced Setup dialogue box
    with   seven steps
    respond   to each step with the following selections:
        1) units: decimal with 0.00 precision then next>>
        2) angle: decimal degrees with 0.0 precision then next>>
        3) angle measurement: east for 0 degrees (default) then next>>
        4) angle direction: counterclockwise +ve (default) then next>>
        5) area: width 420 × length 297 (A3 drawing limits) then next>>
        6) title block: scroll and pick no title block then next>>
        7) layout: pick **no** to paper space layout capability.

3 When the seven advanced wizard steps have been complete, **pick Done** and the drawing screen will be returned with 'nothing', although we have set our paper size, units and so on.

Both the title block and the paper space concepts will be discussed in greater detail in later chapters.

4 From the menu bar select **Tools–Drawing Aids...** and set:
  a) blips: OFF
  b) grid: ON with 10 spacing – or to suit
  c) snap: ON with 5 spacing – or to suit
  d) ortho: OFF
  e) highlight: ON.

5 At the command line enter **PICKBOX<R>** and set to a value of 4.

6 Disable the grips and automatic selection from the command line by entering:
  a) **GRIPS<R>** and set to 0
  b) **PICKFIRST<R>** and set to 0.

7 Menu bar selection with **Tools–Preferences...** and set:
  a) general – automatic save active
          – minutes between save: set to suit, e.g. 30
  b) display – display scroll bars: active
          – command line window: 2 lines
          – colors: to suit.

8 Menu bar with **View–Toolbars...** and activate the Draw, Modify and Object Snap toolbars. Position to suit, i.e. floating or docked. Other toolbars (e.g. Dimension) will be activated as and when required.

9 Menu bar with **File–Save As...** and enter the file name as **A:STDA3**.

This completes our standard sheet (at this stage). We have created an A3-sized sheet of paper which has the units and screen layout set to our requirements. The status bar displays the coordinates to two decimal places and the snap and grid are on – both in bold type.

A final note

Although we have activated several toolbars in our standard sheet, you should be aware that these may not always be displayed when your A:STDA3 drawing is opened. AutoCAD displays the screen toolbars which were active when the system was last shut down. If other CAD operators have used your machine then the toolbar display may not be as you left it. If you are the only user on the machine then there shouldn't be a problem. Anyway it is easy now for you to display the required toolbars.

Chapter 9

Line creation and coordinate input

The line and circle objects created so far were drawn at random on the screen without any attempt being made to specify their position or size. To draw objects accurately, coordinate input is required and two 'types' are available as follows:

1 Absolute, i.e. from an origin point.

2 Relative or incremental, i.e. from the last point entered.

In this chapter we will use our standard A3 sheet to create several squares by different coordinate entry methods. The completed drawing will then be saved for future work.

Getting started

1 *From Windows*
Start AutoCAD and:
prompt Start Up dialogue box
respond 1) pick: Open a drawing
2) double left-click on **More files...**
3) scroll at left of look in box and:
   a) pick 3.5 inch floppy
   b) pick STDA3
   c) preview display
   d) pick open.

From AutoCAD
Menu bar with **File–Open** and:
prompt Select File dialogue box
respond as step 3 opposite.
respond 1) pick: Open a drawing
2) double left-click on **More files...**
3) scroll at left of look in box and:
   a) pick 3.5 inch floppy
   b) pick STDA3
   c) preview display
   d) pick open.

2 The previously saved standard sheet will be displayed.

3 Toolbars: Draw, Modify and Object Snap.

4 Refer to Figure 9.1.

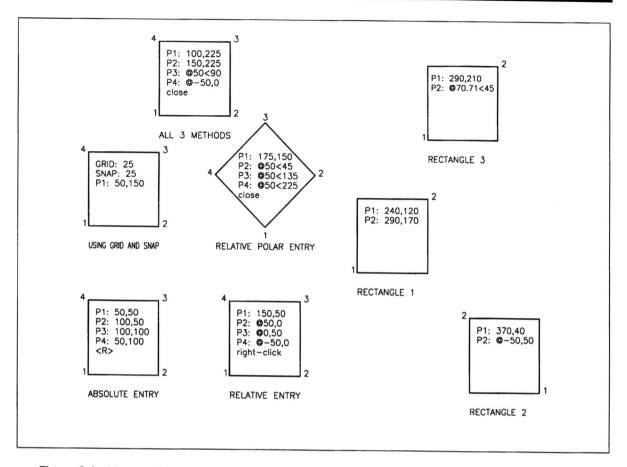

Figure 9.1 Line creation using different methods.

Absolute coordinate entry

This is the traditional *X–Y* Cartesian system, where the origin point is (0,0) at the lower left corner of the drawing area. This origin point can be 'moved' by the user, but this will be investigated in a later chapter.

Select the LINE icon from the Draw toolbar and:

prompt	From point	and enter: **50,50<R>**	start point P1
prompt	To point	and enter: **100,50<R>**	point P2
prompt	To point	and enter: **100,100<R>**	point P3
prompt	To point	and enter: **50,100<R>**	point P4
prompt	To point	and enter: **50,50<R>**	end point P1
prompt	To point	and enter: **<R>**	to end line command

Relative (absolute) coordinate entry

Relative coordinates are from the **last point** entered and uses the @ symbol for incremental entry.

From the menu bar select **Draw–Line** and enter the following *X–Y* coordinate pairs, remembering <R> after each entry.

From point	**150,50**	start point P1
To point	**@50,0**	
To point	**@0,50**	
To point	**@–50,0**	
To point	**@0,–50**	end point P1 again
To point	**right-click**	to end line command

The @ symbol has the following effects:
a) @50,0 is 50 units in the positive *X*-direction and 0 units in the *Y*-direction from the last point, which is 150,50
b) @0,–50 is 0 units in the *X*-direction and 50 units in the negative *Y*-direction from the last point on the screen.

Relative (polar) coordinate entry

This also allows coordinates to be specified relative to the last point entered and uses the @ symbol as before, but also introduces angular input using the < symbol.

Activate the LINE command (icon or menu bar) and enter the following coordinates:

From point	**175,150**	start point P1
To point	**@50<45**	
To point	**@50<135**	
To point	**@50<225**	
To point	enter **C<R>** to close square and end line command.	

Notes

1 The entries can be read as:
   a) @50<45 is 50 units at an angle of 45° from the last point which is 175,150
   b) @50<225 is 50 units at an angle of 225° from the last point.

2 The entry **C<R>** is the **CLOSE** option and:
   a) closes the square, i.e. a line is drawn from the current screen position (P4) to the start point (P1)
   b) ends the sequence, i.e. <R> not needed
   c) the close option works for any straight line shape.

3 There is **no** comma (,) with polar entries.

Using all three entry methods

Activate the LINE command then enter the following:

From point	**100,225**	start point
To point	**150,225**	absolute
To point	**@50<90**	relative polar
To point	**@–50,0**	relative absolute
To point	**c<R>**	close square and end sequence

Grid and snap method

The grid and snap drawing aids can be set to any value suitable for current drawing requirements, so:

a) set the grid and snap spacing to 25
b) draw a 50 unit square, the start point being **50,150**
c) set the grid and snap to original values, i.e. 10 and 5.

Rectangles

Rectangular shapes can be created by specifying two points on a diagonal of the rectangle, and the command can be used with absolute or relative input.

1 From the menu bar select **Draw–Rectangle** and:
prompt First corner
enter **240,120<R>**
prompt Other corner
enter **290,170<R>**

2 Select the rectangle icon from the Draw toolbar and:
prompt First corner and enter: **370,40<R>**
prompt Other corner and enter: **@–50,50<R>**

3 At the command line enter **RECTANG<R>** and:
prompt First corner and enter: **290,210<R>**
prompt Other corner and enter: **@70.71<45<R>**
question why 70.71?

Saving the squares

The drawing screen should now display eight squares positioned as shown in Figure 9.1, but without the text. This drawing must be saved as it will be used in other chapters, so from the menu bar select **File–Save As...** and:
prompt Save Drawing As dialogue box
respond 1 scroll at Save in
  2 pick 3.5 floppy
  3 enter file name as **DEMODRG**
  4 pick Save.

Conventions

Coordinate axes

The *X–Y* axes convention used by AutoCAD is shown in Figure 9.2 which also shows four points with their coordinate values. When using the normal *X–Y* coordinate system:
a) a positive *X*-direction is to the right, and a positive *Y*-direction is upwards
b) a negative *X*-direction is to the left, and a negative *Y*-direction is downwards.

Angles

When angles are being used:
a) positive angles are anti-clockwise
b) negative angles are clockwise.
Figure 9.3 shows the angle convention with four points with their polar coordinate values.

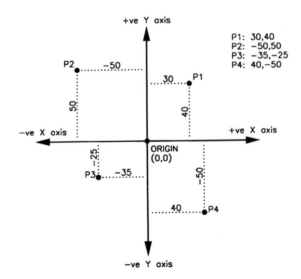

Figure 9.2 The *X–Y* Cartesian coordinate system.

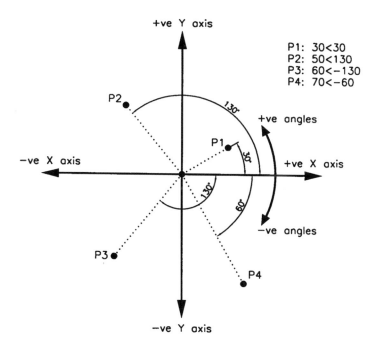

Figure 9.3 Angle convention with coordinates.

Task

Before leaving this exercise, try the following:

1 Make sure you have saved the squares!

2 Erase a rectangle. It is completely erased with a 'single pick'. Any idea why this is?

3 Now erase all the squares from the screen

4 Draw a line sequence using the following entries:
   From point: 30,40
   To point: −50,50
   To point: −35,−25
   To point: 40,−50
   To point: C <R>

5 Draw four lines, entering the following:
   From point: 0,0   To point: 30<30
   From point: 0,0   To point: 50<150
   From point: 0,0   To point: 60<−130
   From point: 0,0   To point: 70<−60

6 When these eight line segments have been drawn, only three are visible?

7 Menu bar with **View–Zoom–All** and:
   a) all eight lines are visible, i.e. we can draw 'off the screen'?
   b) move the cursor to the intersection of the four polar lines, and with the snap on, the status bar displays 0,0,0 as the coordinates
   c) now **View–Zoom–Previous** from the menu bar.

Notes

1 When using coordinate input with the LINE command, it is very easy to make a mistake with the entries. If the line 'does not appear to go in the direction it should', then: either
   a) enter **U <R>** from the keyboard to 'undo' the last line segment drawn or
   b) pick the **UNDO** icon from the Standard toolbar.

2 The symbol @ is useful if you want to 'get to the last point referenced on the screen'. Try the following:
   a) draw a line and cancel the command with a right-click
   b) re-activate the line command and enter @ **<R>**
   c) the cursor 'snaps to' the endpoint of the drawn line.

3 A right-click on the mouse, or pressing the <RETURN> key will always re-activate the last command – try it with line or circle.

Assignment

This activity only requires the LINE command (and ERASE?), but requires some coordinate entries for you to complete the drawing.

1 Open your A:SRDA3 standard sheet.

2 Refer to Activity 2 and draw the three template shapes using coordinate input. Any entry method can be used, but I would recommend that:
   a) position the start points with absolute entry
   b) use relative entry as much as possible.

3 When the drawing is complete, save it as A:ACT_2.

4 Read the summary then proceed to the next chapter.

Summary

1 Coordinate entry can be **ABSOLUTE** or **RELATIVE**.

2 ABSOLUTE entry is from an origin – the point (0,0). Positive directions are UP and to the RIGHT, negative directions are DOWN and to the LEFT. The entry format is **X,Y**, e.g. 30,40.

3 RELATIVE entry refers the coordinates to the last point entered and uses the @ symbol. The entry format is:
   a) relative absolute: **@X,Y**, e.g. @50,60
   b) relative polar: **@X<A**, e.g. @100<50 and note – no comma.

4 An angle of –45° is the same as an angle of +315°.

5 The following polar entries are the same:
   a) @–50<30
   b) @50<210
   c) @50<–150.
   Try them if you are not convinced.

6 All entry methods can be used in a line sequence.

7 A line sequence is terminated with:
   a) the <RETURN> key
   b) a right-click on the mouse
   c) 'closing' the shape.

8 The rectangle command is useful, but it is a 'single object' and not four 'distinct lines'.

9 The LINE command can be activated by:
   a) icon selection from the Draw toolbar
   b) menu bar selection with Draw–Line
   c) entering LINE <R> at the command line
   It is the user's preference what method is to be used.

Chapter 10

Circle creation

In this chapter we will investigate how circles can be created by adding several to the squares created in the previous chapter, so:

1 Open you A:DEMODRG to display the eight squares.

2 Refer to Figure 10.1 and activate the Draw and Modify toolbars.

AutoCAD R14 allows circles to be created by six different methods and the command can be activated by icon selection, menu bar selection or keyboard entry.

When drawing circles, absolute coordinates are usually used to specify the circle centre, although the next chapter will introduce the user to the object snap modes. These object snaps allow greater flexibility in selecting existing entities for reference.

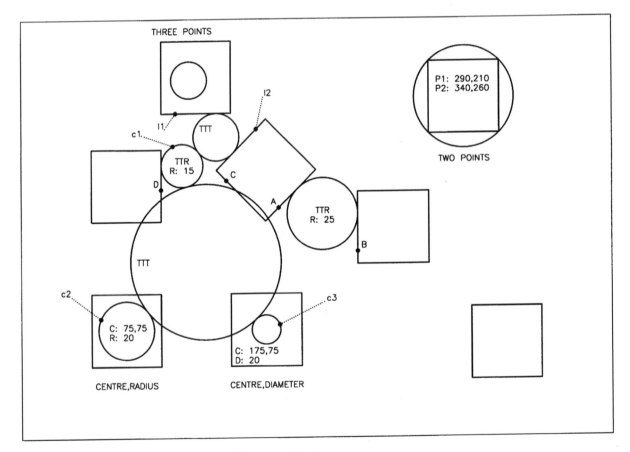

Figure 10.1 Circle creation using different methods.

Centre–radius

Select the CIRCLE icon from the Draw toolbar and:
prompt   3P/2P/TTR/<Center point>
enter   **75,75 <R>** – the circle centre point
prompt   Diameter/<Radius>
enter   **20 <R>** – the circle radius.

Centre–diameter

From the menu bar select **Draw–Circle–Center,Diameter** and:
prompt   .../<Center point> and enter: **175,75 <R>**
prompt   Diameter and enter: **20 <R>**.

Two points on circle diameter

At the command line enter **CIRCLE <R>** and:
prompt   .../<Center point>
enter   **2P <R>** – the two point option
prompt   First point on diameter and enter: **290,210 <R>**
prompt   Second point on diameter and enter: **340,260 <R>**.

Three points on circle circumference

Menu bar selection with **Draw–Circle–3 Points** and:
prompt   First point
respond   **pick any point within the top left square**
prompt   Second point
respond   **pick another point within the top left square**
prompt   Third point
respond   **drag out the circle and pick a point.**

TTR: tangent–tangent–radius

a) At the command line enter **CIRCLE <R>** and:
prompt   .../<Center point>
enter   **TTR <R>** – the tan–tan–radius option
prompt   Enter tangent spec
and   pickbox attached to the cursor
respond   **move cursor the line A and leave for a second**
and   1 small blue marker displayed
    2 deferred tangent highlighted in yellow
    3 more on this in next chapter
respond   **pick line A**, i.e. left click on it
prompt   Enter second tangent spec
respond   **pick line B**
prompt   Radius<???>
enter   **25 <R>**
and   circle drawn as tangent to the two selected lines.

b) Menu bar with **Draw–Circle–Tan,Tan,Radius** and:
prompt   Enter tangent spec and: **pick line C**
prompt   Enter second tangent spec and: **pick line D**
prompt   Radius<25> and enter: **15 <R>**
A circle is drawn tangential to the two selected lines, line C assumed to be projected.

TTT: tangent–tangent–tangent

a) Menu bar with **Draw–Circle–Tan,Tan,Tan** and:
prompt   First point: tan to and: **pick line l1**
prompt   Second point: tan to and: **pick line l2**
prompt   Third point: tan to and: **pick circle c1**.

A circle is drawn which is tangential to the three selected objects.

b) Activate the **Draw–Circle–Tan,Tan,Tan** sequence and:
prompt   First point... and: **pick circle c1**
prompt   Second point... and: **pick circle c2**
prompt   Third point... and: **pick circle c3**.

A circle is drawn tangential to the three selected circles – how long would this take by conventional methods?

Saving the drawing

Assuming that the CIRCLE commands have been entered correctly, your drawing should resemble Figure 10.1 (without the text) and is ready to be saved for future work.

From the menu bar select **File–Save As...** and:
prompt   Save Drawing As dialogue box
with   File name: DEMODRG
respond   **pick Save**
prompt   Drawing already exists message
respond   **pick yes** – obvious?

Task

The two tan–tan–tan circles have been created without anything known about their radii.

1 From the menu bar select **Tools–Inquiry–List** and:
   prompt   Select objects
   respond   **pick the smaller TTT circle**
   prompt   1 found and Select objects
   respond   **right-click**
   prompt   AutoCAD Text window with information about the circle.

2 Note the information then cancel the text window.

3 Repeat the **Inquiry–List** sequence for the larger TTT circle.

4 The information for my two TTT circles is as follows:

	smaller	*larger*
Centre point	139.52, 208,53	131.88, 122.06
Radius	16.47	53.83
Circumference	103.51	338.21
Area	852.67	9102.42

5 Could you calculate these figures as easily as demonstrated?

Assignment

1 Open your A:STDA3 standard sheet.

2 Refer to the Activity 3 drawing (at the end of the book) which can be completed with only the LINE and CIRCLE commands.

3 The method of completing the drawings is at your discretion.

4 Remember that absolute is recommended for circle centres and that the TTR method is very useful.

5 You may require some 'sums' for certain circle centres, but the figures are relatively simple.

6 When the drawing is complete, save it as A:ACT_3.

Summary

1 Circles can be constructed by six methods, the user specifying:
   a) the centre point and radius
   b) the centre point and diameter
   c) two points on the circle diameter
   d) three points on the circle circumference
   e) two tangent specification points and the circle radius three tangent specification points.

2 The TTR and TTT options can be used with lines, circles, arcs and other objects.

3 The centre point and radius can be specified by:
   a) coordinate entry
   b) picking a point on the screen
   e) referencing existing entities – next chapter.

Chapter 11

Object snap

The lines and circles drawn so far have been created by coordinate input. While this is the basic method of creating objects, it is often desirable to 'reference' existing objects already displayed on the screen, e.g. we may want to:
a) draw a circle, centre at the midpoint of an existing line
b) draw a line, from a circle centre perpendicular to another line.

These types of operations are achieved using **the object snap modes** – often referred to as **OSNAP** – and are one of the most useful (and powerful) draughting aids.

Object snap modes are used **transparently**, i.e. whilst in a command, and can be activated:
a) from the object snap toolbar
b) by direct keyboard entry.

While the toolbar method is the quicker, we will investigate the keyboard entry method.

Release 14 has several new additions to the object snap operation, which will become apparent to pre-R14 users as the exercise progresses. A full explanation of these new additions will be given later in the chapter.

Getting ready

1 Open your A:DEMODRG of the squares and circles.

2 Erase the two TTT circles.

3 Display the Draw, Modify and Object Snap toolbars and position then to suit.

4 Refer to Figure 11.1.

Using object snap from the keyboard

Activate the LINE command and:

prompt	From point
enter	**MID <R>**
prompt	of
and	aperture box on cross-hairs
respond	1 move cursor to line d1 and leave
	2 blue triangular marker at line midpoint
	3 Midpoint snap tip in yellow
now	**pick line d1**
and	line 'snaps to' the midpoint of d1
prompt	To point
enter	**PERP <R>**
prompt	of

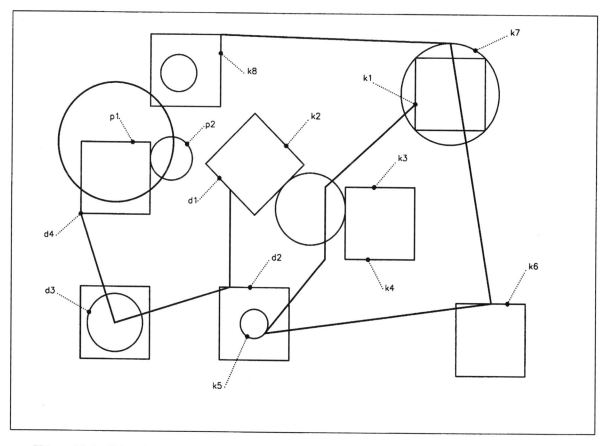

Figure 11.1 Using the object snaps with A:DEMODRG.

respond	**pick line d2** – note blue perpendicular marker
prompt	To point
enter	**CEN <R>**
prompt	of
respond	**pick circle d3** – note blue center marker
prompt	To point
enter	**INT <R>**
prompt	of
respond	**pick point d4** – note blue Intersection marker
prompt	To point and: **right-click** to end sequence.

Using object snap from the toolbar

Activate the LINE command and:

prompt	From point
respond	**pick the Snap to Nearest icon**
prompt	nea to
respond	**pick any point on line k1**
prompt	To point
respond	**pick the Snap to Apparent Intersection icon**
prompt	appint of
respond	**pick line k2**
prompt	and
respond	**pick line k3**
prompt	To point
respond	**pick the Snap to Perpendicular icon**
prompt	per to
respond	**pick line k4**
prompt	To point
respond	**pick the Snap to Tangent icon**
prompt	tan to
respond	**pick circle k5**
prompt	To point
respond	**pick the Snap to Midpoint icon**
prompt	mid of
respond	**pick line k6**
prompt	To point
respond	**pick the Snap to Quadrant icon**
prompt	qua of
respond	**pick circle k7**
prompt	To point
respond	**pick the Snap to Endpoint icon**
prompt	endpt of
respond	**pick line k8**
prompt	To point
respond	**right-click** to end sequence.

Object snap with circles

Select the CIRCLE icon from the Draw toolbar and:

prompt	Center point
respond	**pick the Snap to Midpoint icon**
prompt	mid of
respond	**pick line p1**
prompt	Radius
respond	**pick the Snap to Center icon**
prompt	cen of
respond	**pick circle p2**

Note

1 Save your drawing at this stage as A:DEMODRG.
2 The endpoint 'snapped to' depends on which part of the line is 'picked'. The blue marker indicates which line endpoint.
3 A circle has four quadrants, these being at the 3, 12, 9, 6 o'clock positions. The blue marker indicates which quadrant will be snapped to.

Running object snap

Using the object snap icons from the toolbar will increase the speed of the draughting process, but it can still be 'tedious' to have to pick the icon every time an ENDpoint (for example) is required. It is possible to 'preset' the object snap mode to ENDpoint, MIDpoint, Center, etc., and this is called a **running object snap**. Pre-setting the object snap does not preclude the user from selecting another mode, i.e. if you have set an ENDpoint running object snap, you can still pick the INTersection icon.

The running object snap can be set:

1 From the menu bar with **Tools–Object Snap Settings...**
2 Entering **OSNAP <R>** at the command line.
3 Selecting the Object Snap Settings icon
4 With a double left-click on OSNAP in the Status bar if it is in grey type.

Each of these methods displays the Osnap Settings dialogue box.

Task

1 Select **Tools–Object Snap Settings...** from the menu bar and:
   prompt   Object Settings dialogue box
   respond   **activate Endpoint, Midpoint and Center**
   by   picking the box – tick means active – Figure 11.2
   then   **pick OK**.

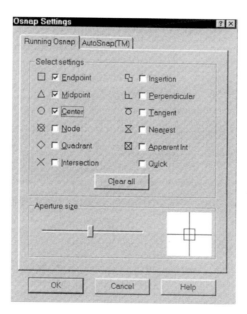

Figure 11.2 The Object Settings dialogue box.

2   Now activate the LINE command and move the aperture/cross-hairs onto any line and leave it.

3   A blue marker will be displayed at the Midpoint or Endpoint of the line, depending on where you position the aperture box.

4   Press the **TAB** key to cycle through the set running object snaps, i.e. the line should display the square and triangular blue markers for the Endpoint and Midpoint settings.

5   Cancel the command with **ESC**.

6   Note: OSNAP in the Status bar will be in **BOLD** type, indicating that a running object snap is set. When in bold, OSNAP cannot be used to display the dialogue box.

AutoSnap

The Object Settings dialogue box also allows the user to select the AutoSnap dialogue box – Figure 11.3. The user can control the object snap display from this dialogue box. The various terms should be easy to understand and:

Marker: is the geometric shape displayed at a snap point
Magnet: locks the aperture box on to the snap point
Snap Tip: is a flag describing the name of the snap location.

The rest of the options should be apparent. It is normal to have the three parameters, i.e. marker, magnet, and snap tip active (ticked).

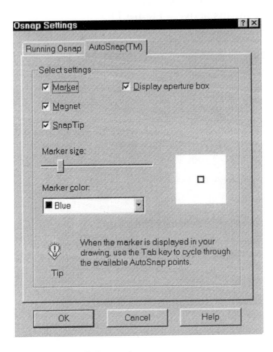

Figure 11.3   The Autosnap Settings dialogue box.

Cancelling a running object snap

A running object snap can be left 'active' once it has been set, but this can cause problems if the user 'forgets' about it. The running snap can be cancelled:

1   From the Object Settings dialogue box with **Clear All**.

2   Selecting the Snap to None icon from the toolbar.

Running object snap from keyboard

While the Object Settings dialogue box is the easiest way to set a running snap, it is possible to use keyboard entry.

1   At the command line enter **-OSNAP <R>** and:
   prompt   Object snap modes
   enter   **QUA <R>**

2   This entry sets the quadrant running object snap – check with the dialogue box.

3   The running snaps can be cancelled from the command line by entering **-OSNAP <R>** and:
   prompt   Object snap modes
   enter   **<R>**

Tracking

This is a new concept in Release 14 and is a sort of point filters (later) without the coordinate input. It is best demonstrated by example, which will be to draw a circle with its centre point at one of the square 'centres' without any coordinates being used.

1   Cancel any running object snap.

2   Select the CIRCLE icon and:
   prompt   Center point
   respond   pick the Tracking icon from:
              a) standard toolbar
              b) object snap toolbar
   prompt   First tracking point
   respond   *a*) pick the Midpoint icon
              b) pick a vertical line of top right square
   prompt   Next point (press ENTER to end tracking)
   respond   *a*) pick the Midpoint icon
              b) pick a horizontal line of rightmost square
   prompt   Next point (press ENTER to end tracking)
   respond   *a*) press ENTER, i.e. <R>
              b) enter radius value of 18.

3   A circle will be drawn with its centre at the square 'centre'.

4   Try and draw another circle at the 'centre' of another square using the tracking method in step 2.

5   Try and draw a line from one square 'centre' to another square 'centre' using tracking.

6   Do not save these additions to your drawing.

Assignment

1 Open your A:STDA3 standard sheet and refer to Activity 4.

2 Draw the three components using the lines and circles.

3 Object snap will require to be used and there are hints with each component.

4 When complete, save as A:ACT_4.

5 Read the summary then progress to the next chapter.

Summary

1 Object snap (OSNAP) is used to reference existing objects.

2 OSNAP is an invaluable aid to draughting and should be used where appropriate.

3 The user can 'preset' a running objects snap.

4 Geometric markers will indicate the snap points on objects.

5 The AutoSNAP dialogue box allows the user to 'control' the geometric markers.

6 Object snap is an example of a **transparent** command, as it is activated when another command is being used.

7 The object snap mode can be set and cancelled using the dialogue box, toolbar or by command line entry.

Chapter 12

Arc, donut and ellipse creation

These three drawings commands will be discussed in turn using our square and circle drawing. Each command can be activated from the toolbar, menu bar or by keyboard entry and both coordinate entry and referencing existing objects are permissible.

Getting started

1 Open your A:DEMODRG to display the squares, circles and object snap lines, etc.

2 Erase the objects created during the object snap exercise.

3 Refer to Figure 12.1 and activate the Draw, Modify and Object Snap toolbars.

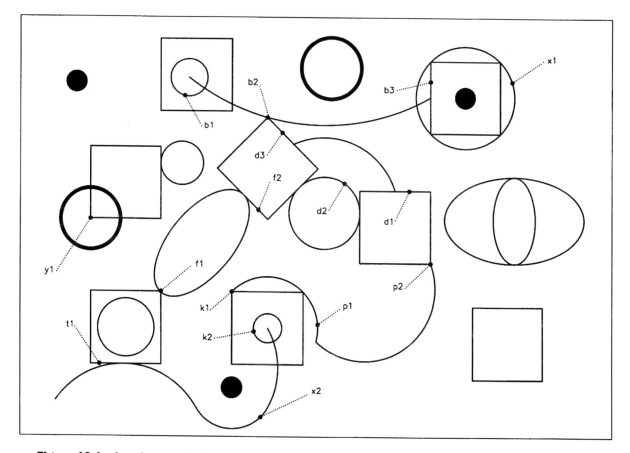

Figure 12.1 Arc, donut and ellipse creation with A:DEMODRG.

Arcs

There are ten different arc creation methods. Arcs are normally drawn in an anticlockwise direction with combinations of the arc start point, end point, centre point, radius, included angle, length of arc, etc. We will investigate five different arc creation methods, and you can try the others for yourself.

Start, Center, End

From the menu bar select **Draw–Arc–Start,Center,End** and:

prompt	Start point
respond	**Snap to Midpoint icon and pick line d1**
prompt	Center
respond	**Snap to Center icon and pick circle d2**
prompt	End point
respond	**Snap to Midpoint icon and pick line d3**

Start, Center, Angle

Menu bar with **Draw–Arc–Start,Center,Angle** and:

prompt	Start point
respond	**Snap to Intersection icon and pick point k1**
prompt	Center
respond	**Snap to Center icon and pick circle k2**
prompt	Included angle
enter	**–150 <R>**

Note that negative angle entries draw arcs in a clockwise direction.

Start, End, Radius

Menu bar again with **Draw–Arc–Start,End,Radius** and:

prompt	Start point and **snap to Endpoint of arc p1**
prompt	End point and **snap to Intersection of point p2**
prompt	Radius and enter **50 <R>**.

Three points (on arc circumference)

Activate the three points arc command and:

prompt	Start point and **snap to Center of circle b1**
prompt	Second point and **snap to Intersection of point b2**
prompt	End point and **snap to Midpoint of line b3**.

Continuous arcs

a) Activate the three points arc command again and:

prompt	Start point and enter **25,25 <R>**
prompt	Second point and **snap to Midpoint of line t1**
prompt	End point and enter **@50,–30 <R>**

b) Select from the menu bar **Draw–Arc–Continue** and:

prompt	End point – and snaps to end of last arc
enter	**@50,0 <R>**

c) Repeat the **Arc-Continue** selection and:

prompt	End point
respond	**snap to Center of circle k2**.

Donut

A donut (or doughnut) is a 'solid filled' circle or annulus (a washer shape), the user specifying the inside and outside diameters as well as the donut centre point.

1   Menu bar with **Draw-Donut** and:
   prompt   Inside diameter and enter **0 <R>**
   prompt   Outside diameter and enter **15 <R>**
   prompt   Center of doughnut and enter **40,245 <R>**
   prompt   Center of doughnut
   respond   **Snap to Center of circle x1**
   prompt   Center of doughnut
   respond   **Snap to Center of arc x2**
   prompt   Center of doughnut and **right-click.**

2   Repeat the donut command and:
   prompt   Inside diameter and enter **40 <R>**
   prompt   Outside diameter and enter **45 <R>**
   prompt   Center of doughnut and enter **220,255 <R>**
   prompt   Center of doughnut
   respond   **Snap to Intersection of point y1**
   prompt   Center of doughnut and **right-click.**

3   Note: the donut command allows repetitive entries, while the circle command only allows one – I don't know why!

Ellipse

The ellipses created with R14 are 'true' ellipses, i.e. they have a centre point which can be 'snapped to'. To draw an ellipse, the user specifies:
a) either the ellipse centre and axes endpoints
b) or three points on the axes endpoints.

1   Select from the menu bar **Draw–Ellipse–Center** and:
   prompt   Center of ellipse and enter **350,150 <R>**
   prompt   Axis endpoint and enter **400,150 <R>**
   prompt   <Other axis distance>/Rotation and enter **350,120 <R>**.

2   Select the ELLIPSE icon from the Draw toolbar and:
   prompt   Arc/Center/<Axis endpoint 1>
   enter   **C <R>** – the centre option
   prompt   Center of ellipse
   respond   **Snap to Center icon and pick the existing ellipse**
   prompt   Axis endpoint and enter **@0,30 <R>**
   prompt   Other axis endpoint and enter **@15,0 <R>**.

3   Menu bar with **Draw–Ellipse–Axis,End** and:
   prompt   Arc/Center/<Axis endpoint 1>
   respond   **Snap to Intersection of point f1**
   prompt   Axis endpoint 2
   respond   **Snap to Midpoint of line f2**
   prompt   <Other axis distance>/Rotation
   enter   **R <R>** – the rotation option
   prompt   Rotation about major axis and enter **60 <R>**.

Note

1 At this stage your drawing should resemble Figure 12.1.
2 Save it as A:DEMODRG for future recall – if needed.
3 Arcs, donuts and ellipses have centre points and quadrants which can be 'snapped to'. It is also possible to use the tangent snap icon and draw tangent lines, etc. between these objects. Try it!

Solid fill

Donuts are generally displayed on the screen 'solid', i.e. 'filled in'. This solid fill effect is controlled from the drawing aids dialogue box with a toggle effect and:
a) × at solid fill – on, i.e. donuts drawn 'filled'
b) blank at solid fill – off, i.e. donuts 'not filled'.

Use the drawings aids dialogue box to toggle the solid fill off, then enter **REGEN <R>** at the command line. The donuts should be displayed without the fill effect – note the lines. Toggle the Solid Fill back on, then REGEN the screen.

Summary

Arcs, donuts and ellipses are Draw commands and can be created by coordinate entry or by referencing existing objects.

General

1 The three objects have a centre point and quadrants.
2 They can be 'snapped to'.

Arcs

1 Several different creation options.
2 Normally drawn in an anticlockwise direction.
3 Very easy to draw in the wrong 'sense' due to the start and end points being selected wrongly.
4 Continuous arcs are possible.
5 A negative angle entry will draw the arc clockwise.

Donuts

1 Require the user to specify the inside and outside diameters.
2 Can be displayed filled or unfilled.
3 An inside radius of 0 will give a 'filled circle'.
4 Repetitive donuts can be created.

Ellipses

1 Two creation methods.
2 Partial ellipses (arcs) are possible.
3 The created ellipses are 'true', i.e. have a centre point.

Chapter 13

Layers and standard sheet 2

All the objects that have been drawn have had a continuous linetype and no attempt has been made to introduce centre or hidden lines, or even colour. All AutoCAD releases have a facility called **layers** that allow the user to assign different linetype and colours to named layers. For example, a layer may be for red continuous lines, another may be for green hidden lines, and yet another for blue centre lines. Layers can also be used for specific drawing purposes, e.g. there may be a layer for dimensions, one for hatching, one for text, etc. Individual layers can be 'switched' on/off by the user to mask out drawing objects which are not required.

The concept of layers can be imagined as a series of transparent overlays, each having its own linetype, colour and use. The overlay used for dimensioning could be switched off without affecting the remaining layers. Figure 13.1 demonstrates the layer concept with:

a) Five layers used to create a simple component. Each 'part' of the component has been created on 'its own' layer.

b) The layers 'laid on top of each other'. The effect is that all five layers 'are one'.

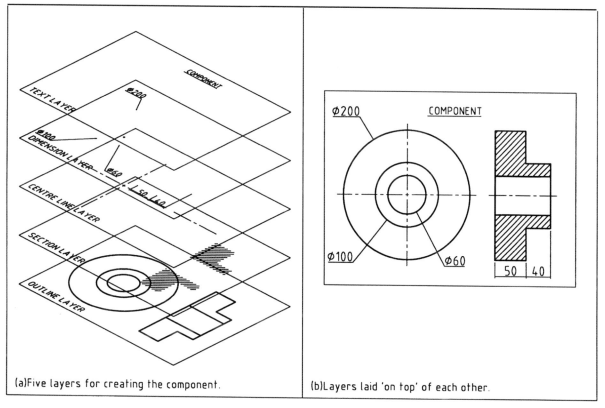

(a)Five layers for creating the component. (b)Layers laid 'on top' of each other.

Figure 13.1 The layer concept.

The following points are worth noting when considering layers:

1 All objects are drawn on layers.

2 Layers should be used for each 'part' of a drawing, i.e. dimensions should not be on the same layer as centre lines (for example).

3 New layers must be 'created' by the user, using the layer control dialogue box.

4 Layers are (in my opinion) the most important concept in AutoCAD.

5 Layers are essential for good and efficient draughting.

As layers are very important, and as the user must have a sound knowledge of how they are used, this chapter is therefore rather long (and perhaps a bit boring). I make no apology for this, as all CAD operators must be able to use layers correctly.

Getting started

Several different aspects of layers will be discussed in this chapter before we modify our existing standard sheet, so:

1 Open the A:STDA3 standard sheet.

2 Draw a horizontal and vertical line each of length 100, and a circle of radius 30 anywhere on the screen.

The layer control dialogue box

1 From the menu bar select **Format–Layer...** and:
   prompt   Layer & Linetype Properties dialogue box
   respond   study the information contained in the dialogue box.

2 The format of this dialogue box is:
   1 Display certain layers – generally all.
   2 The current layer – in our case 0.
   3 The layer information box with:
      a) layer name – only 0 at present
      b) five layer states – see later
      c) layer color – black
      d) layer linetype – continuous.
   4 Details about layers.
   5 New layer creation box – will use soon.
   6 Delete selected layers – use with care!

3 Layer 0 is the layer on which all objects have (so far) been drawn, and is 'supplied' with AutoCAD. It is the **current** layer and is displayed in the Objects Properties toolbar with the layer state icons.

4 Certain areas of the dialogue box are 'greyed out', i.e. inactive.

5 Move the pointing device arrow onto the 0 name and:
   a) pick with a left-click
   b) it turns blue
   c) the details section becomes active – Figure 13.2.

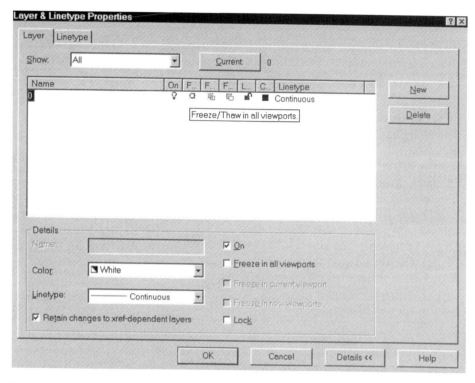

Figure 13.2 The Layer and Linetype Properties dialogue box.

6 Pick the On/Off icon – a yellow light bulb (ON) and:
  prompt AutoCAD warning message dialogue box – Figure 13.3
  respond **pick OK**
  and On/Off icon now a 'blue light bulb' – OFF
  respond **pick OK from the dialogue box**.

7 The drawing screen will be returned and no objects are displayed – they were drawn on layer 0 which has been turned off.

8 Re-activate the layer control dialogue box and:
  a) pick the 0 layer name – turns blue
  b) pick the 'blue light' and it changes to yellow (on)
  c) pick OK.

9 Line and circle objects displayed – layer 0 is on.

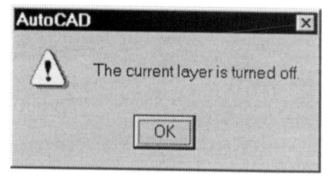

Figure 13.3 Warning!

Linetypes

AutoCAD allows you to display objects with different linetypes, e.g. continuous, centre, hidden, dotted, etc. Until now, all objects have been displayed with continuous linetype.

1 Activate the menu selection **Format–Layer...** and:
prompt	Layer & Linetype Properties dialogue box
respond	**pick Continuous from layer 0 'line'**
prompt	Select Linetype dialogue box
respond	**pick Load...**
prompt	Load or Reload Linetype dialogue box
with	Filename: **acadiso.lin**
respond	1 scroll and **pick Center** – Figure 13.4
	2 pick OK
prompt	Select Linetype dialogue box
with	Center linetype displayed, i.e. it has been 'loaded'
respond	1 **pick Center** – Figure 13.5
	2 pick OK
prompt	Layer & Linetype dialogue box
with	layer 0 – Center linetype
respond	pick OK.

2 The drawing screen will display the three objects with center linetype – remember it's an American program ('center' rather than 'centre').

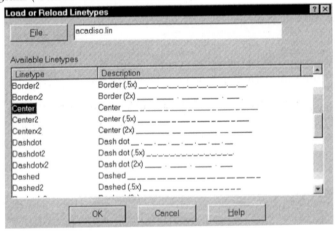

Figure 13.4 Load or Reload Linetypes dialogue box.

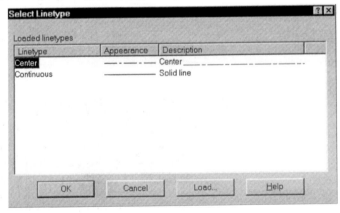

Figure 13.5 The Select Linetype dialogue box.

Colour

Individual objects can be shown on the screen in different colours, but I prefer to use layers for the colour effect. This is achieved by assigning a specific colour to a named layer.

1 Activate the layer control dialogue box.

2 *a*) pick line 0 to activate the layer 0 detailed information
   b) pick the scroll arrow at Color: White to display the seven standard colour names
   c) pick Red and:
      1 name Red appears the Color: box
      2 red square displayed in layer 0 line under C.
   d) pick OK

3 The screen displays the three objects with red centre lines.

4 Note the object properties toolbar:
   a) layer 0 has a red square
   b) red square in the color control icon
   c) center linetype in the linetype control icon.

Task

Using the layer control dialogue box:
a) set layer 0 linetype to continuous
b) set layer 0 colour to white/black
c) screen should display continuous white/black objects
d) note the object properties toolbar.

Note on colour

1 The default AutoCAD colour for objects is dependent on your screen configuration (preference):
   a) white background – black lines
   b) black background – white lines.

2 The white/black linetype can be confusing.

3 All colours in AutoCAD are numbered. There is a total of 255 colours, but the seven standard colours are:
   1 red   2 yellow   3 green   4 cyan
   5 blue   6 magenta   7 black/white.

4 The number or colour name can be used to select a colour. The numbers are associated with colour pen plotters.

5 The complete 255 'colour palette' can be activated from:
   a) layer control dialogue box by picking the coloured square under C
   b) from the details by scrolling and picking others... .

6 Generally only the seven standard colours will be used, but there may be the odd occasion when a colour from the palette will be selected.

Creating new layers

Layers should be made to suit company requirements, but for our purposes the layers which will be made for all future work are:

Usage	Layer name	Layer colour	Layer linetype
General	0	white/black	continuous
Outlines	OUT	red	continuous
Centre lines	CL	green	center
Hidden detail	HID	yellow	hidden
Dimensions	DIMEN	magenta	continuous
Text	TEXT	blue	continuous
Hatching	SECT	cyan	continuous

1 Activate the layer control dialogue box.

2 Pick **New** and:
   a) layer1 added to layer names – black and continuous
   b) detailed information active with layer1 as name.

3 Pick **New** five more times to display layer names Layer2–Layer6, all with black colour and continuous linetype.

4 *a*) Pick layer name Layer1 then pick it again
   b) enter OUT.

5 *a*) Pick layer name Layer2 then pick it again
   b) enter CL.

6 Repeat steps 4 and 5 and rename the layers using:
   Layer3: HID   Layer4: DIMEN   Layer5: TEXT   Layer6: SECT

7 Pick layer name OUT (probably Out) and:
   a) scroll at Color: White
   b) pick Red.

8 Pick layer name Cl, scroll and Color: White and pick Green.

9 Repeat the layer colour changes using the colours listed above.

10 Pick linetype name continuous on the 'Cl line' and:
   a) Select Linetype dialogue box
   b) pick center – should be displayed?
   c) pick OK.

11 Pick linetype name continuous on 'Hid line' and:
   a) Select Linetype dialogue box
   b) pick load to display Load/Reload Linetypes dialogue box
   c) scroll and pick hidden then OK
   d) from Select Linetype dialogue box, pick hidden then OK.

12 All layers have been:
   a) renamed to suit
   b) assigned colours
   c) assigned appropriate linetypes.

13 Now pick OK.

14 Reactivate the layer control dialogue box and:
   a) layers in numeric then alphabetic order
   b) pick **Details<<**
   c) dialogue box as Figure 13.6
   d) pick OK.

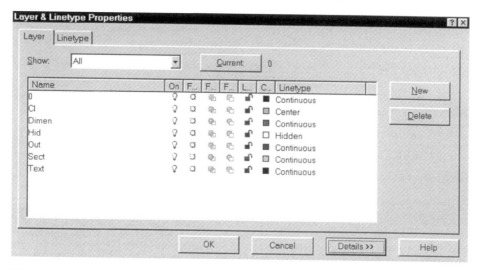

Figure 13.6 Layer and Linetype properties.

The current layer

The current layer is the one on which all objects are drawn. The current layer name appears in the layer control section of the object properties toolbar, which is generally docked below the standard toolbar at the top of the screen. The current layer is also named in the layer control dialogue box when it is activated.

The current layer is 'set' by the user:

1 From the layer control dialogue box by:
   a) menu bar with **Format–Layer**
   b) pick layer name to be current e.g. Out
   c) pick the current box to display – Current: Out
   d) pick OK.

2 Using layer control from the object properties toolbar by:
   a) pick scroll arrow at right of layer name box
   b) pick layer name, e.g. Out.
   The layer control dialogue box is used to create new layers with their colours and linetypes. Once created, the current layer is best set using layer control from the objects properties toolbar.

I generally start a drawing with layer OUT current, but this is a personal preference. Other users may want to start with layer CL or 0 as the current layer, but it does not matter.

Having created layers it is now possible to draw objects with different colours and linetypes, simply by altering the current layer. All future work should be completed with layers used correctly, i.e. if text is to be added to a drawing, then the TEXT layer should be current.

Saving the created layers

1 Erase all objects from the screen.

2 Make layer 0 current.

3 Using the LINE icon, draw:
   From: 0,0   To: @420,0   To: @0,290
   To: @–420,0   To: close.

4 This will give our drawings a 'border effect'.

5 Set the current layer to OUT.

6 Pick one of the following:
   a) Save icon from Standard toolbar
   b) Menu bar with **File–Save**.

7 This selection will automatically update the **A:STDA3** standard sheet drawing opened
   at the start of the chapter.

8 The standard sheet has now been saved with:
   a) units set to metric
   b) sheet size A3
   c) blips, grid, snap, etc. set to suit
   d) several new layers
   e) a border effect on layer 0.

9 With the layers having been saved to A:STDA3, the layer creation process does not need
   to be undertaken every time a drawing is started. Additional layers can be added to the
   standard sheet at any time – a fairly easy process?

Layer states

Layers can have six 'states' these being:
a) ON or OFF
b) THAWED or FROZEN
c) LOCKED or UNLOCKED.

The layer states are displayed both in the layer control box of the Objects Properties
dialogue box as well as in the Layer Control dialogue box itself. In both, the layer states
are displayed in icon form, and Figure 13.7 shows these icons from the Object Properties
dialogue box. The icon states:
a) yellow – ON, THAWED
b) bluey grey – OFF, FROZEN
c) lock and unlock; should be obvious?

Note

There is an additional icon displayed in the objects properties toolbar, and two additional
icons in the dialogue box. These icons are for multiple viewports and this topic will not
be discussed at present. These icons will therefore always be inactive, i.e. displayed in
bluey-grey.
   To investigate layers:

1 A:STDA3 on screen with black border and layer out current?

2 Using the seven layers (our created six and layer 0):
   a) make each layer current in turn

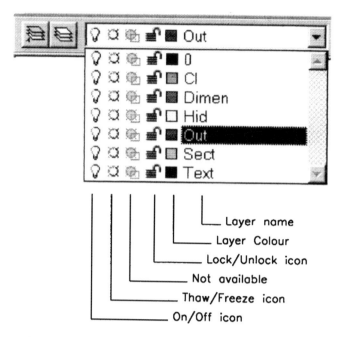

Figure 13.7 Layer control icons.

    b) draw a 50 radius circle on each layer
    c) make layer 0 current.

3 The green circle will be displayed with center linetype and the yellow circle with hidden linetype.

4 Activate the layer control dialogue box and:
    a) pick On/Off icon on Cl layer line – turns blue
    b) note the Details – no tick at On
    c) pick OK – no green circle.

5 Layer control dialogue box and:
    a) pick Freeze/Thaw icon on Dimen layer line – turns blue
    b) note the details – tick at freeze and on
    c) pick OK – no magenta circle.

6 Pick the scroll arrow at layer control in object properties dialogue box and:
    a) note Cl and Dimen display information!
    b) pick Lock/Unlock icon on Hid layer line – note appearance
    c) left-click to side of pull-down menu
    d) yellow circle still displayed.

7 With the pull-down layer control:
    a) pick freeze and lock icons for Sect
    b) no cyan circle.

8 Using layer control:
    a) turn off, freeze and lock the Text layer
    b) no blue circle.

9 Activate the Layer Control dialogue box and:
    a) note the icon display
    b) make layer Out current
    c) pick Freeze icon

d) Warning message – **Cannot freeze the current layer**
e) pick OK
f) turn layer 0 OFF
g) Warning message – **The current layer is turned off**
h) pick OK then OK – no red circle displayed.

10   The screen should now display:
   a) a black circle – drawn on layer 0
   b) a yellow hidden linetype circle – on locked layer Hid.

11   Thus objects will not be displayed if their layer is OFF or FROZEN.

12   Make layer 0 current.

13   Try to erase the yellow circle – you cannot. The prompt line displays:
   `1 was on a locked layer`

14   Draw a line from the centre of the yellow circle to the centre of the black circle. You can reference the yellow circle, although it is on a locked layer.

15   *a*) Make layer Out current
   b) warning message? – pick OK
   c) draw a line from 50,50 to 200,200 – no line obviously?

16   Using the layer control dialogue box, investigate the Show scroll arrow to display:
   a) all in use – seven layers
   b) all unused – none
   c) all – our seven as you would expect
   d) the other show options will not affect us.

17   From the layer control dialogue box:
   a) all layers to be – ON, THAWED and UNLOCKED
   b) all circles and lines displayed.

18   The layer states can be activated using:
   a) the icons in the pull-down layer control menu
   b) the icons in the Layer Control dialogue box
   c) the boxes in details in the Layer Control dialogue box.

Layer icons

There are three useful icons associated with layers and they are situated in the Objects Properties toolbar. They are:

1   Linetype: will activate the Linetype dialogue box of the Layer and Linetype Properties dialogue box.

2   Layers: when selected this icon will activate the Layer and Linetype dialogue box.

3   Make objects layer current. This is a new Release 14 command and when selected:
   prompt   `Select object whose layer will become current`
   respond   **pick the green circle**
   Cl will now be the current layer.

4   *Note*:
   a) The color control selection from the Object Properties toolbar will permit colours to be changed. This will allow objects to have different colours on the one layer.
   b) The linetype control selection from the Object Properties toolbar will allow objects to be displayed with different linetypes on the one layer.

c) These two operations **are not recommended**. Until you are **very** proficient with layers, I would always recommend one layer, one colour, one linetype.

d) The properties icon at the right of the object properties toolbar will be discussed in a later chapter.

Renaming and deleting layers

Unwanted or wrongly named layers can easily be renamed or deleted in Release 14.

1 Activate the layer control dialogue box and pick New twice. Two new layers will be added to the list: Layer1 and Layer2.

2 Rename Layer1 as NEW1 and Layer2 as New2.

3 Pick **Show–All unused** and the two renamed layers will be displayed. Pick Show-All again.

4 Pick OK from the dialogue box.

5 Making each new layer current in turn, draw a circle anywhere on the screen on each new layer.

6 Make layer Out current.

7 With the layer control dialogue box:
   respond **pick New1 then Delete** and
   prompt   AutoCAD message – `Selected layer was not deleted`

8 Cancel this dialogue box (Figure 13.8) and pick OK from Layer Control dialogue box.

9 *a*) Erase the two added circles
   b) activate layer control dialogue box
   c) pick New1–Delete
   d) pick New2–Delete
   e) Pre-Release 14 users, think about PURGE!

10 This completes this chapter, so exit AutoCAD (do **not** save changes). Hopefully your A:STDA3 standard sheet was saved with the layers and border earlier in the chapter.

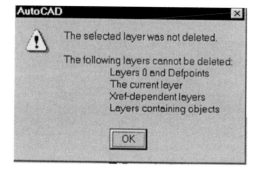

Figure 13.8

Assignment

There is no activity specific to layers, but all future drawings will be started using A:STDA3.

Summary

1 Layers are probably the most important concept in AutoCAD.

2 Layers allow objects to be created with different colours and linetypes.

3 Layers are created using the Layer and Linetype Properties dialogue box – I've called this layer control.

4 There are 255 colours available, but the seven standard colours should be sufficient for our use.

5 Linetypes are loaded as required for named layers.

6 Layers saved to a standard sheet need only be created once.

7 New layers can easily be added as and when required.

8 Layer states are:

    ON: all objects are displayed and can be modified
    OFF: objects are not displayed
    FREEZE: similar to OFF, but allows faster regeneration of screen
    THAW: undoes a frozen layer
    LOCK: objects are displayed but **cannot** be modified
    UNLOCK: undoes a locked layer.

9 Layer states are displayed and activated in icon form from the Layer Control dialogue box or using layer control from the Object Properties toolbar.

10 Care must be taken when modifying a drawing with layers which are turned off or frozen. More on this later.

11 Layers can be renamed at any time.

12 Unused layers can be deleted at any time.

Chapter 14

User exercise 1

By now you should have the confidence and ability to create line and circle objects by
various methods, e.g. coordinate entry, referencing existing objects, etc.

Before going on to other draw and modify commands, we will create a working drawing which will be used to introduce several new concepts, as well as reinforcing your
existing draughting skills. The exercise will also demonstrate how a 'new' drawing can
be created from the existing standard sheet.

1   Start AutoCAD R14 and:

     prompt   Startup dialogue box
     respond   **pick Open a Drawing**
     prompt   listed files in Select a file:
     and   A:\STDA3 **MAY** be displayed
     if yes   double left-click on A:\STDA3
     if no   *a*) double left-click on More files…
                   b) scroll at Look in: and pick 3.5 floppy
                   c) pick STDA3
                   d) pick open.

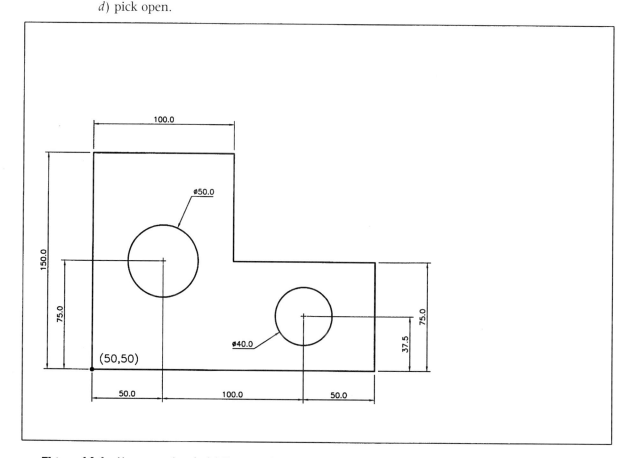

Figure 14.1   User exercise 1. (a) Draw to the sizes given. (b) Do **not** dimension. (c) Save as A:WORKDRG.

2 Either method will display the standard sheet with the black border and layer out current.

3 Refer to Figure 14.1 and:
   a) draw full size the component given
   b) a start point is given – **use it!**
   c) *do not attempt to add the dimensions*
   d) use absolute coordinates for the start point then relative coordinates for the outline
   e) use absolute coordinates for the circle centres – some 'sums' needed!

4 When the drawing is complete, select from the menu bar **File–Save As...** and:
   a) ensure the A floppy drive is current
   b) enter the file name as **WORKDRG**
   c) pick save.

5 We are now ready to investigate other commands.

Chapter 15

Fillet and chamfer

In this chapter we will investigate how the fillet and chamfer commands can be used to modify an existing drawing. Both commands can be activated by icon, menu bar selection or keyboard entry.

1 Open **A:WORKDRG** with layer Out current.

2 Activate the Draw and Modify toolbars.

3 Refer to Figure 15.1.

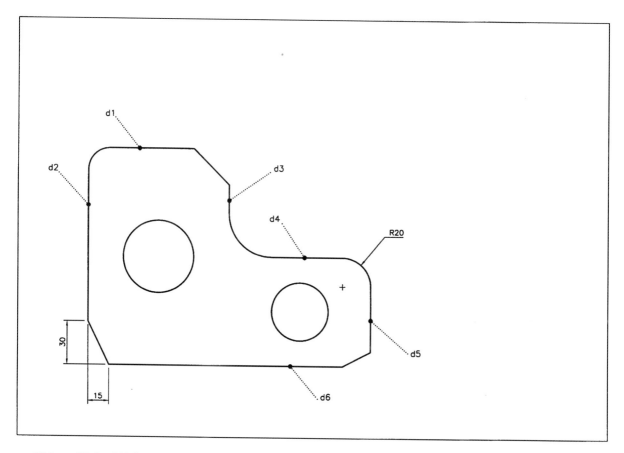

Figure 15.1 A:WORKDRG after using the fillet and chamfer commands.

Fillet

A fillet is a radius added to existing line/arc/circle objects. The fillet radius must be specified before the command can be used.

1   Select the FILLET icon from the Modify toolbar and:

    prompt   (TRIM mode) Current fillet radius = ??
                  Polyline/Radius/Trim/<Select first object>
    enter   **R <R>** – the radius option
    prompt   Enter fillet radius<??>
    enter   **15 <R>**.

2   Right-click the mouse to re-activate the fillet command and:

    prompt   ...<Select first object>
    respond **pick line d1**
    prompt   Select second line
    respond **pick line d2**.

3   The corner selected will be filleted with a radius of 15, and the two 'unwanted line portions' will be erased.

4   From the menu bar select **Modify–Fillet** and:

    prompt   Polyline/Radius...
    enter   **R <R>** – the radius option
    prompt   Enter fillet radius<15.00>
    enter   **30 <R>**.

5   Right-click to activate the fillet command and:

    prompt   ...<Select first object> and **pick line d3**
    prompt   Select second object and **pick line d4**.

6   At the command line enter **FILLET <R>** and:

    a) set the fillet radius to 20
    b) fillet the corner indicated.

Chamfer

A chamfer is a straight 'cut corner' added to existing line objects. The chamfer distances must be 'set' prior to using the command.

1 Select the CHAMFER icon from the Modify toolbar and:

prompt (TRIM mode) Current chamfer Dist1=? Dist2=?
Polyline/Distance/Angle/Trim/<Select first line>
enter **D <R>** – the distance option
prompt Enter first chamfer distance<?> and enter: **25 <R>**
prompt Enter second chamfer distance<25.00> and enter: **25 <R>**.

2 Right-click to reactivate the chamfer command and:
prompt ...<Select first line> and **pick line d1**
prompt Select second line and **pick line d3**.

3 The selected corner will be chamfered and the unwanted line portions removed.

4 Menu bar selection with **Modify–Chamfer** and:
prompt Polyline/Distance...
enter **D <R>**
prompt Enter first chamfer distance and enter: **10 <R>**
prompt Enter second chamfer distance and enter: **20 <R>**.

5 Right-click and:
prompt ...<Select first line> and **pick line d5**
prompt Select second line and **pick line d6**.

Note that the pick order is important when the chamfer distances are different. The first lines picked will have the first chamfer distance.

6 At the command line enter **CHAMFER <R>** and:
a) set first chamfer distance: 15
b) set second chamfer distance: 30
c) chamfer the corner indicated.

Saving

When the three fillets and three chamfers have been added to the component, save it as **A:WORKDRG**.

Error messages

The fillet and chamfer commands generally are used without any problems, but the following error messages may be displayed at the command prompt:

1 Radius is too large.

2 Distance is too large.

3 Chamfer requires two lines.

4 No valid fillet with radius of ??

These error messages should be self-evident.

Fillet and chamfer options

Although simple to use, the fillet and chamfer commands have several options. It is in your own interest to attempt the following exercises, so:

1 Erase all objects from the screen – saved?

2 Refer to Figure 15.2.

3 Fillet/chamfer with inclined lines. Our working drawing demonstrated the fillet and chamfer commands with lines which were at right angles to each other. This was not deliberate – just the way the component was drawn. Draw three to four inclined lines then use the fillet and chamfer commands. You only have to be careful with the fillet radius and chamfer distance values! The effect is displayed:
   a) fillet effect – Fig. (a)
   b) chamfer effect – Fig. (b).

4 Both commands have a polyline option. This will be covered after we have investigated the polyline command.

5 The commands have a TRIM option and the effect is displayed in Fig. (c). The option is obtained by entering **T <R>** when the commands are activated and:
   a) trim – corners removed. This is the default
   b) no trim – corners not removed.

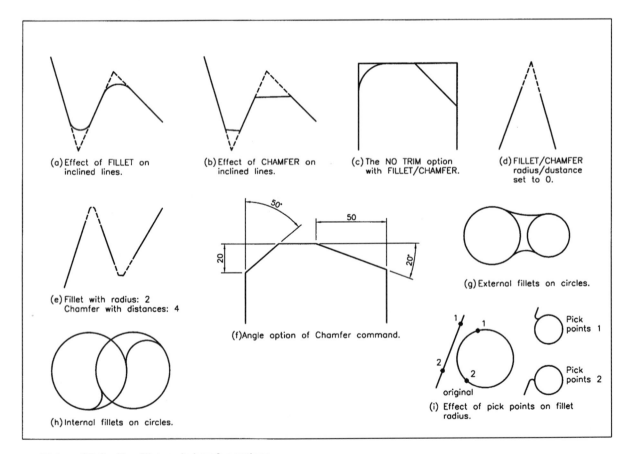

Figure 15.2 The fillet and chamfer options.

6   The two commands can be used to extend two inclined lines to a point – Fig. (d) – if:
    a) the fillet radius is set to 0
    b) both chamfer distances are set to 0.

7   Chamfer with one distance set to 0. Think about this!

8   Interesting effects with inclined lines if the fillet radius and the chamfer distances are 'small'. The lines are extended if required, and the fillet/chamfer effect 'added at the ends' as displayed in Fig. (e).

9   Chamfer has an angle option and when the command is selected:
    prompt   `Polyline/Distance/Angle...`
    enter   **A <R>** – the angle option
    prompt   `Enter chamfer length on the first line` and enter: **20<R>**
    prompt   `Enter chamfer angle from the first line` and enter: **50<R>**.

    The required lines can now be chamfered as Fig. (f) which displays:
    a) length of 20 and angle of 50
    b) length of 50 and angle of 20.

10 Circles can be filleted:
    a) externally as Fig. (g)
    b) internally as Fig. (h).

11 Circles cannot be chamfered. If any circle is selected:
    prompt   `Chamfer requires 2 lines (not arc segments)`

12 Lines–circles–arcs can be filleted, but the position of the pick points is important as displayed in Fig. (i).

13 Chamfer has a METHOD option, which when selected:
    prompt   `Distance/Angle` and:
    a) entering **D** sets the two distance method – the default
    b) entering **A** sets the length and angle method.

Summary

1   FILLET and CHAMFER are Modify commands, activated from the menu bar, by icon selection or by keyboard entry.

2   Both commands require the radius/distances to be set before they can be used.

3   When values are entered, they become the defaults until altered by the user.

4   Lines, arcs and circles can be filleted.

5   Only lines can be chamfered.

6   A fillet/chamfer value of 0 is useful for extending two inclined lines.

Offset, extend and trim

In this chapter we will investigate OFFSET, EXTEND and TRIM – three of the most commonly used draughting commands. We will also investigate the CHANGE and LTSCALE commands.
To demonstrate these new commands:

1 Open A:WORKDRG – should be easy by now.

2 Activate the Draw and Modify toolbars.

Offset

The offset command allows the user to draw parallel objects, and lines, circles and arcs can all be offset. The user specifies:
a) an offset distance
b) the side to offset the object.

1 Refer to Figure 16.1.

2 Select the OFFSET icon from the Modify toolbar and:

prompt	Offset distance or Through
enter	**50 <R>** – the offset distance
prompt	Select object to offset
respond	**pick line d1**
prompt	Side to offset
respond	**pick any point to right of line d1 as indicated**
and	line d1 will be offset by 50 units to right
prompt	Select object to offset, i.e. any more 50 offsets?
respond	**pick line d2**
prompt	Side to offset
respond	**pick any point to left of line d2 as indicated**
and	line d2 will be offset 50 units to left
prompt	Select object to offset, i.e. any more 50 offsets?
respond	**right-click** to end command.

3 Menu bar with **Modify–Offset** and:

prompt	Offset distance or Through<50.00>
enter	**75 <R>**
prompt	Select object to offset and **pick line d3**
prompt	Side to offset and **pick as indicated**.

4 At the command line enter **OFFSET <R>** and:
a) set an offset distance of 37.5
b) offset line d4 as indicated.

5 We have now created centre lines (of a sort) through the two circles. Later in the chapter we will investigate how these lines can be modified to be 'real centre lines'.

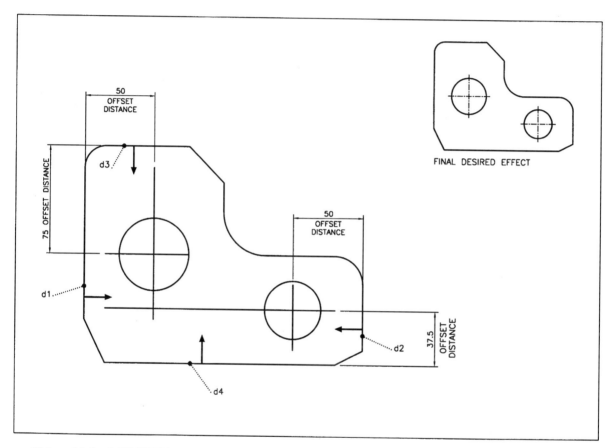

Figure 16.1 A:WORKDRG after the OFFSET command.

Extend

This command will extend an object 'to a boundary edge', the user specifying:
a) the actual boundary – an object
b) the object which has to be extended.

1 Refer to Figure 16.2(a) and select the EXTEND icon from the Modify toolbar and:

prompt	Select boundary edges (...)
	Select objects
respond	**pick line d1**
prompt	1 found
	Select objects, i.e. more boundary edges
respond	**pick line d2**
prompt	1 found then Select objects
respond	**right-click** to end boundary edge selection
prompt	<Select object to extend>...
respond	**pick lines d3, d4 and d5 then right-click.**

2 The three lines will be extended to the selected boundary edges.

3 From the menu bar select **Modify–Extend** and:

prompt	Select objects – boundary edges
respond	**pick lines p1 and p2 then right-click**
prompt	Select object to extend
respond	**pick lines p3 and p4 then right-click.**

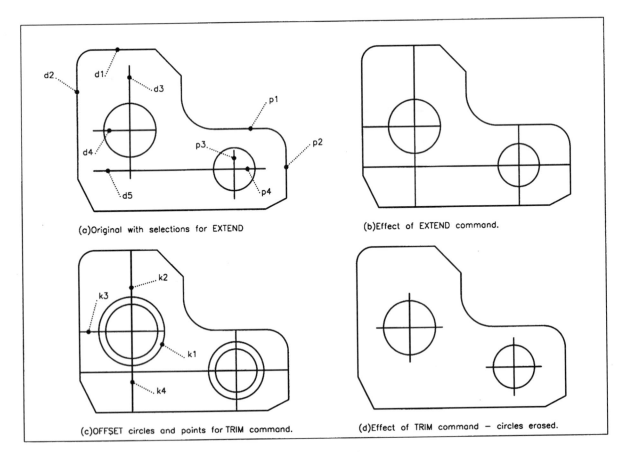

(a)Original with selections for EXTEND

(b)Effect of EXTEND command.

(c)OFFSET circles and points for TRIM command.

(d)Effect of TRIM command – circles erased.

Figure 16.2 A:WORKDRG with EXTEND and TRIM commands.

4 At the command line enter **EXTEND <R>** and extend the two vertical 'centre lines' to lower horizontal outline.

5 When complete, the drawing should resemble Figure 16.2(b).

Trim

Allows the user to trim an object 'at a cutting edge', the user specifying:
a) the cutting edge – an object
b) the object to be trimmed.

1 Refer to Figure 16.2(c) and OFFSET the two circles for a distance of 5 'outwards' – easy?

2 Extend the top horizontal 'circle centre line' to the offset circle – should be obvious.

3 Select the TRIM icon from the Modify toolbar and:

prompt	Select cutting edges...
	Select objects
respond	**pick circle k1 then right-click**
prompt	<Select object to trim>...
respond	**pick lines k2, k3 and k4 then right-click**

4 From menu bar select **Modify–Trim** and:

prompt	Select objects – the cutting edge
respond	**pick the other offset circle the right-click**
prompt	Select object to trim
respond	**pick four circle centre lines then right-click**

5 Erase the two offset circles and the drawing is displayed with 'neat centre lines' – Figure 16.2(d).

Saving

At this stage save your drawing as A:WORKDRG. We will recall it shortly.

Additional exercises

Offset, extend and trim are powerful commands and can be used very easily. To demonstrate the commands further:

1 Erase all objects from the screen – already saved?

2 Refer to Figure 16.3 and attempt the exercise which follows.

3 Offset for circle centre point. Using the OFFSET command to obtain a circle centre point is one of the most common uses for the command. Figure 16.3(a) demonstrates offset of 18.5 horizontally and 27.8 vertically to position the circle centre point. What about inclined line offsets?

4 Offset through. This is a very useful option of the command, as it allows an object to be offset through a specified point. When the command is activated:

prompt	Offset distance or Through
enter	**T <R>** – the through option
prompt	Select object to offset
respond	**pick the required object – a line**
prompt	Through point
respond	**Snap to Center icon and pick the circle**

The line will be offset through the circle centre – Fig. (b).

5 Extending lines and arcs. Lines and arcs can be extended to other objects, including circles – Fig. (c).

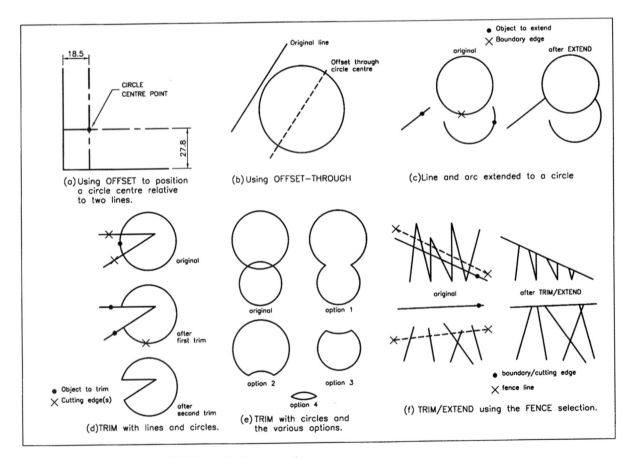

(a) Using OFFSET to position a circle centre relative to two lines.

(b) Using OFFSET–THROUGH

(c) Line and arc extended to a circle

(d) TRIM with lines and circles.

(e) TRIM with circles and the various options.

(f) TRIM/EXTEND using the FENCE selection.

Figure 16.3 OFFSET, EXTEND and TRIM examples.

6 Trim lines and circles. Lines, circles and arcs can be trimmed to 'each other' and Fig. (d) demonstrates trimming lines with a circle.

7 Trimming circles. Circles can be trimmed to each other, but the selected objects to be trimmed can give different effects. Can you obtain the options in Fig. (e)?

8 Trim/extend with a fence selection. When several objects have to be trimmed or extended, the fence selection option can be used – Fig. (f). The effect is achieved by:
   a) activating the command
   b) selecting the boundary (extend) or cutting edge (trim)
   c) entering **F <R>** – the fence option
   d) draw the fence line then right-click.

9 These exercises do not need to be saved.

Changing the offset centre lines

The WORKDRG drawing was saved with 'centre lines' obtained using the offset, extend and trim commands. These lines pass through the two circle centres, but they are continuous lines and not centre lines. We will modify these lines to be centre lines using the CHANGE command. This command will be fully investigated in a later chapter, but for now:

1 Re-open A:WORKDRG saved earlier in this chapter.

2 At the command line enter **CHANGE <R>** and:
   prompt   Select objects
   respond **pick the four offset centre lines**
   prompt   Properties/<Change point>
   enter   **P <R>** – the properties option
   prompt   Change what property...
   enter   **LA <R>** – the layer option
   prompt   New layer<OUT>
   enter   **CL <R>**
   prompt   Change what property... and **right-click.**

3 The four selected lines will be displayed as green centre lines, as they were changed to the CL layer. This layer was made with centre linetype and colour green. Confirm with Format-Layer if you are not convinced!

4 Although the changed lines are centre lines, their 'appearance' may not be ideal and an additional command is required to 'optimize' the centre line effect.

5 At the command line enter **LTSCALE <R>** and:
   prompt   New scale factor<1.0000>
   enter   **0.5 <R>**.

6 The centre lines should now be 'better defined'.

7 The value of LTSCALE depends on the type of lines in a drawing, and can be further refined – more on this later.

8 Now make sure you save your drawing as **A:WORKDRG**.

Question

In our offset exercise we obtained four circle centre lines using the offset command. These lines were then changed to the CL layer to display then as 'real centre lines'.

The question I am repeatedly asked by new AutoCAD users is: **'Why not use offset with the CL layer current?'** This question is reasonable so:

1 Is A:WORKDRG still on the screen?

2 Make layer CL current.

3 Set an offset distance of 30 and offset:
   a) any red perimeter line
   b) any green centre line.

4 The effect of the offset command is:
   a) the offset red outline is a red outline
   b) the offset green centre line is a green centre line.

5 The offset command will offset an object 'as it was drawn' and is independent of the current layer.

Assignment

It is now some time since you have attempted any activities on your own. Refer to the Activity 5 drawing (at the end of the book) and create the two template shapes as given. Use the commands already investigated and make particular use of FILLET, CHAMFER, OFFSET and TRIM as much as possible. **Do not attempt to add dimensions.**
   Start with A:STDA3 and save the completed drawing as A:ACT_5.

Summary

1 OFFSET, TRIM and EXTEND are modify commands and can be activated by icon selection, from the menu bar or by keyboard entry.

2 Lines, arcs and circles can be offset by:
   a) entering an offset distance and picking the side
   b) selecting an object and the point to be offset through.

3 Extend requires:
   a) a boundary edge
   b) objects to be extended.

4 Trim requires:
   a) a cutting edge
   b) objects to be trimmed.

5 Lines and arcs can be extended to other lines, arcs and circles.

6 Lines, circles and arcs can be trimmed.

Chapter 17

User exercise 2

In this chapter we will create another working drawing using previous commands, save it and then list all the drawings which have so far been completed.

1 Open your A:STDA3 standard sheet – layer Out current and required toolbars active.

2 Refer to Figure 17.1 and complete the drawing using:
   a) the basic shape and size – **use the 140,100 start point**
   b) three offset lines
   c) four extended lines
   d) trim to give the final shape.

3 When complete save as **A:USEREX**.

4 Do not exit AutoCAD.

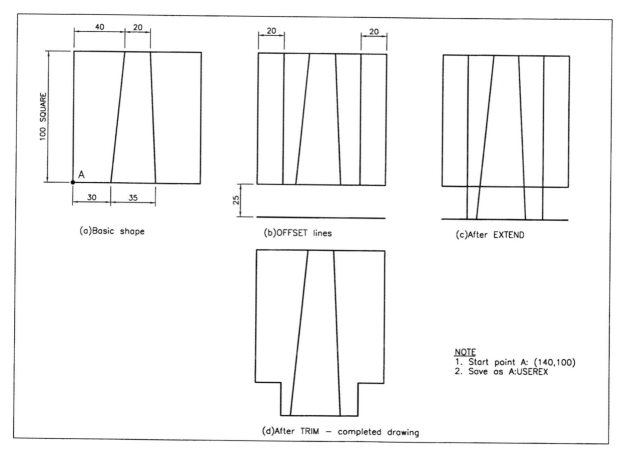

Figure 17.1 A:USEREX construction.

So far, so good

At this stage of our learning process, we have completed the following drawings:

1   A demonstration drawing A:DEMODRG, used in the creation of lines, circles, arcs and for object snap.

2   A standard sheet A:STDA3, which will be used for all new drawings.

3   A working drawing A:WORKDRG which was created after several new topics were discussed. This drawing will still be used to demonstrate new topics as they are discussed.

4   A new working drawing A:USEREX, which will also be used to demonstrate new topics.

5   Five activity exercises, ACT_1 to ACT_5, which you have been completing and saving as the book progresses. Or have you?

And now

Proceed to the next chapter in which we will discuss how text can be added to a drawing.

Chapter 18

Text

Text should be added to a drawing whenever possible. This text could simply be a title and date, but could also be a parts list, a company title block, notes on costing, etc. AutoCAD Release 14 has text suitable for:

a) short entries, i.e. a few lines

b) larger entries, i.e. several lines.

In this chapter we will consider the short entry type text, and leave the other type (multiple line entry) to a later chapter, so:

1 Is A:USEREX still on the screen? It should be.

2 Make layer Text (blue) current and refer to Figure 18.1.

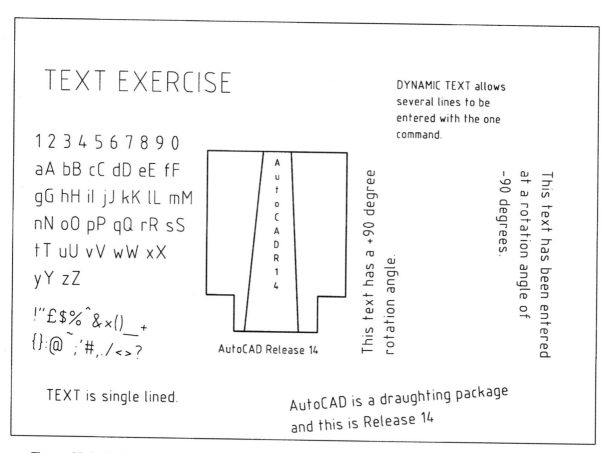

Figure 18.1 Text addition with A:USEREX.

One line of text

1 At the command line enter **TEXT <R>** and:
   prompt Justify/Style/<Start point>
   enter   **25,25 <R>**
   prompt Height<?> and enter: **8 <R>**
   prompt Rotation angle<0> and enter: **0 <R>**
   prompt Text
   enter   **TEXT is single lined. <R>**

2 The entered text item will be displayed at the entered start point.

3 Repeat the TEXT command with:
   a) start point: 20,240
   b) height: 15
   c) rotation: 0
   d) text: TEXT EXRECISE – this misspelling is deliberate!

Several lines of text

1 Select from the menu bar **Draw–Text–Single Line Text** and:
   prompt .../<Start point> and enter: **275,245 <R>** and:
   prompt Height and enter: **6 <R>**
   prompt Rotation angle and enter: **0 <R>**
   prompt Text and enter: **DYNAMIC TEXT allows <R>**
   prompt Text and enter: **several lines to be <R>**
   prompt Text and enter: **entered with the one <R>**
   prompt Text and enter: **command. <R>**
   prompt Text and enter: **<R>**, i.e. end of command.

2 At the command line enter **DTEXT <R>** and:
   prompt .../<Start point> and enter: **200,20 <R>**
   prompt Height and enter: **8 <R>**
   prompt Rotation and enter: **5 <R>**
   prompt Text and enter: **AutoCAD is a draughting package <R>**
   prompt Text and enter: **and this is Release 14 <R>**
   prompt Text and enter: **<R>** – to end command.

3 Using the DTEXT command, add the other items of text shown in Figure 18.1. The start point and height are at your discretion.

Note

1 The difference between the two text commands is:
   TEXT: *a*) must enter from keyboard
            b) only allows one single line of text
            c) not seen on screen as typed in
   DTEXT: *a*) this is dynamic text
            b) activated from menu bar or by keyboard entry
            c) allows several lines of text to be entered
            d) text is displayed on screen as it is typed at keyboard.

2 I generally prefer to use dynamic text (DTEXT).

Editing existing screen text

Text can be edited as it is being entered from the keyboard if the user spots a mistake. Screen text which needs to be edited requires a command.

1 From the menu bar select **Modify–Object–Text** and:

    prompt   `<Select an annotation object>...`
    respond   **pick the TEXT EXRECISE item**
    prompt   Edit Text dialogue box – Figure 18.2 with the text phrase highlighted in blue
    either   1 retype the phrase correctly then OK or:
               2 *a*) left-click at right of the text item
                    b) backspace to remove error
                    c) retype correctly
                    d) pick OK or:
               3 *a*) move cursor to TEXT EXR|ECISE and left-click
                    b) backspace to give TEXT EX|ECISE
                    c) move cursor to TEXT EXE|CISE and left-click
                    d) enter R to give TEXT EXER|CISE
                    e) pick OK.

2 The text item will be displayed correctly.

3 You could always erase the text item and enter it correctly.

4 Now save if required, but **not** as A:USEREX.

Figure 18.2 The Edit Text dialogue box.

Text justification

Text items added to a drawing can be 'justified' (i.e. positioned) in different ways, and Release 14 has several justification positions, these being:
a) six basic: left, aligned, fitted, centred, middled, right
b) nine additional: TL, TC, TR, ML, MC, MR, BL, BC, BR.

1 Open your A:STDA3 standard sheet and refer to Figure 18.3.

2 With layer Out current, draw the following objects:
   a) a 100 sided square, the lower left point at (50,50)
   b) a circle of radius 50, centred at (270,150)
   c) five lines:
      1) from: 220,20 to: 320,20
      2) from: 220,45 to: 320,45
      3) from: 120,190 to: 200,190
      4) from: 225,190 to: 275,250
      5) from: 305,250 to: 355,100.

3 Make layer Text (blue) current and activate the Draw, Modify and Object Snap toolbars.

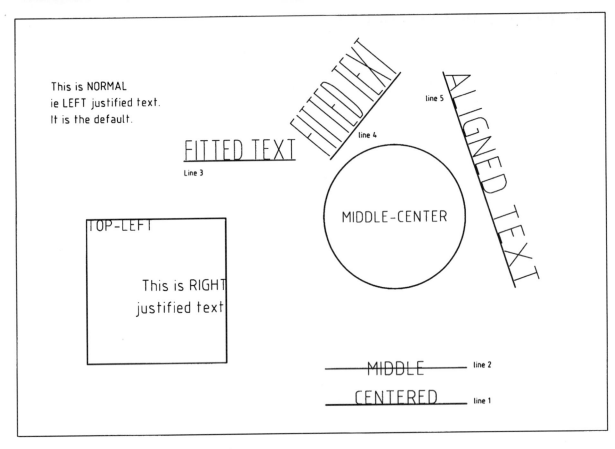

Figure 18.3 Text justification exercise.

4 At the command line enter **DTEXT <R>** and:
   prompt Justify/Style... and enter: **25,240 <R>**
   prompt Height and enter: **6 <R>**
   prompt Rotation angle and enter: **0 <R>**
   prompt Text and enter: **This is NORMAL <R>**
   prompt Text and enter: **i.e. LEFT justified text. <R>**
   prompt Text and enter: **It is the default <R>**
   prompt Text and enter: **<R>**

5 Menu bar with **Draw–Text–Single Line Text** and:
   prompt Justify/Style...
   enter **J <R>** – the justify option
   prompt Align/Fit/Center/Middle/Right...
   enter **R <R>** – the right justify option
   prompt End point
   respond **Snap to Midpoint icon and pick right vertical line of the square**
   prompt Height and enter: **8 <R>**
   prompt Rotation angle and enter: **0 <R>**
   prompt Text and enter: **This is RIGHT <R>**
   prompt Text and enter: **justified text <R><R>**

6 At the command line enter **TEXT <R>** and:
   prompt   Justify/Style... and enter: **J <R>**
   prompt   Align/Fit/Center... and enter: **C <R>** – center option
   prompt   Center point
   respond **Snap to Midpoint icon and pick line 1**
   prompt   Height and enter: **10 <R>**
   prompt   Rotation angle and enter: **0 <R>**
   prompt   Text and enter: **CENTERED <R>**.

7 Enter **DTEXT <R>** at the command line then:
   a) enter J <R> for justify
   b) enter M <R> for middle option
   c) Middle point: Snap to Midpoint icon and pick line 2
   d) Height: 10 and Rotation: 0
   e) Text: MIDDLE <R><R>.

8 Activate the TEXT command with the Fit justify option and:
   prompt   First text line point
   respond **Snap to Endpoint icon and pick left end of line 3**
   prompt   Second text line point
   respond **Snap to Endpoint icon and pick right end of line 3**
   prompt   Height and enter: **15 <R>**
   prompt   Text and enter: **FITTED TEXT <R>**
   Note: this option has no rotation prompt!

9 Using the DTEXT command with the fit justify option, add the text item FITTED TEXT with a height of 40 to line 4.

10 With DTEXT again:
   a) select the align justify option
   b) pick 'top' of line 5 as first text line point
   c) pick 'bottom' of line 5 as second text line point
   d) text item: ALIGNED TEXT
   Note: this option has no height or rotation prompt!

11 Activate the TEXT command and:
   a) justify with TL option
   b) top/left point: snap to intersection icon of top left of square
   c) height of 8 and rotation of 0
   d) text item: TOP-LEFT.

12 Finally the DTEXT command and:
   a) justify with MC option
   b) middle point: Snap to center of circle
   c) height of 8 and rotation of 0
   d) text item: MIDDLE-CENTER.

13 Your drawing should now resemble Figure 18.3. It can be saved, but we will not use it again.

14 The text justification options are easy to use. Simply enter the appropriate letter for the justification option. The letters used are:

A:	Align	F:	Fit
C:	Center	M:	Middle
R:	Right	TL:	Top left
MC:	Middle center	BR:	Bottom right.

Text style

When the TEXT or DTEXT command is activated, one of the options available is *Style*. This option allows the user to select any one of several previously created text styles. This will be discussed in a later chapter which will investigate text styles and fonts.

Assignment

Attempt Activity 6 which has four simple components for you to complete. Text should be added, but not dimensions.

The procedure is:

1 Open A:STDA3.

2 Complete the drawings using layers correctly.

3 Save as ACT_6.

4 Read the summary then progress to the next chapter.

Summary

1 Text is a draw command and can have:
   a) one line entry with TEXT, activated by keyboard entry
   b) several line entries with DTEXT, activated from the menu bar or by keyboard entry.

2 Dynamic text (DTEXT) allows the user to 'see' the text as it is entered from the keyboard.

3 Text can be entered with varying height and rotation angle.

4 Text can be justified to user specifications, and there are 15 justification options.

5 Screen text can be modified with:
   a) menu bar Modify–Object–Text
   b) keyboard entry: DDEDIT.

6 Fitted and aligned text are similar, the user selecting both the start and end points of the text item, but:
   a) fitted: allows the user to enter a text height
   b) aligned: text is automatically 'adjusted' to suit the selected points
   c) neither has a rotation option.

7 Centered and middled text are similar, the user selecting the center/middle point, but:
   a) centered: is about the text baseline
   b) middled: is about the text middle point.

8 *a*) Text style can be set by the user
   b) multiple line (or paragraph) text can be set by the user
   c) these two topics will be investigated in later chapters.

Chapter 19

Dimensioning

AutoCAD has both automatic and associative dimensioning, the terms meaning:

Automatic   when an object to be dimensioned is selected, the actual dimension text, arrows, extension lines, etc. are added.

Associative   the arrows, extension lines, dimension text, etc. which 'make up' a dimension are treated as a single object.

AutoCAD has different 'types' of dimensions which can be added to a drawing these being:

1 Linear: horizontal, vertical and aligned.
2 Baseline and continue.
3 Ordinate: both *X*-datum and *Y*-datum.
4 Angular.
5 Radial: diameter and radius.
6 Leader: taking the dimension text 'outside' the object.

Figure 19.1 displays the different dimension types.

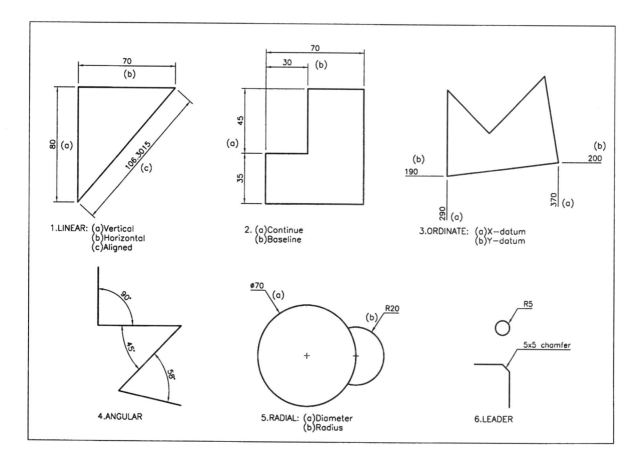

Figure 19.1   Dimension types.

Dimension exercise

To demonstrate how dimensions are added to a drawing, we will use one of our working drawings, so:

1 Open A:USEREX and with layer Out current add the following three circles:
   a) centre: 220,180, radius: 15
   b) centre: 220,115, radius: 3
   c) centre: 190,75, radius: 30
   d) trim the large circle to the line as Figure 19.2.

2 Make layer Dimen current and activate the Object Snap and Dimension toolbars.

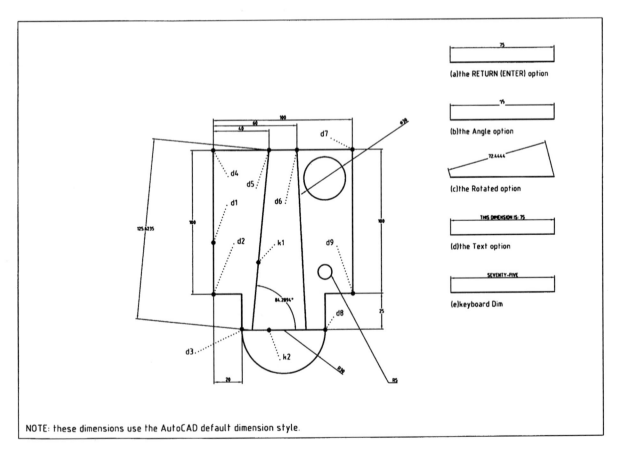

Figure 19.2 Adding dimensions to A:USEREX.

Linear dimensioning

1 Select the LINEAR DIMENSION icon from the Dimension toolbar and:
prompt   First extension line origin...
respond   **Endpoint icon and pick line d1**
prompt   Second extension line origin
respond   **Endpoint icon and pick the other end of line d1**
prompt   Dimension line location...
respond   **pick any point to the left of line d1**.

2 From the menu bar select **Dimension–Linear** and:
prompt   First extension line origin
respond   **Intersection icon and pick point d2**
prompt   Second extension line origin
respond   **Intersection icon and pick point d3**
prompt   Dimension line location
respond   **pick any point below object**.

Baseline dimensioning

1 Select the LINEAR DIMENSION icon and:
prompt   First extension line origin
respond   **Intersection icon and pick point d4**
prompt   Second extension line origin
respond   **Intersection icon and pick point d5**
prompt   Dimension line location
respond   **pick any point above the line**.

2 Select the BASELINE DIMENSION icon from the Dimension toolbar and:
prompt   Specify a second extension line origin
respond   **Intersection icon and pick point d6**
prompt   Specify a second extension line origin
respond   **Intersection icon and pick point d7**
prompt   Specify a second extension line origin
respond   **press the ESC key to end command**.

3 The menu bar selection Dimension–Baseline could have been selected.

Continue dimensioning

1 Select the LINEAR DIMENSION icon and:
prompt   First extension line origin
respond   **Intersection icon and pick point d8**
prompt   Second extension line origin
respond   **Intersection icon and pick point d9**
prompt   Dimension line location
respond   **pick any point to right of the line**

2 Menu bar with **Dimension–Continue** and:
prompt   Specify a second extension line origin
respond   **Intersection icon and pick point d7**
prompt   Specify a second extension line origin
respond   **press ESC**

3 The CONTINUE icon could have been selected.

Diameter dimensioning

Select the DIAMETER DIMENSION icon from the Dimension toolbar and:

prompt Select arc or circle
respond **pick the larger circle**
prompt Dimension line location
respond **pick a suitable point.**

Radius dimensioning

Select the RADIUS DIMENSION icon and:

prompt Select arc or circle
respond **pick the arc**
prompt Dimension line location
respond **pick a suitable point.**

Angular dimensioning

Select the ANGULAR DIMENSION icon and:

prompt Select arc, circle, line...
respond **pick line k1**
prompt Second line
respond **pick line k2**
prompt Dimension line location
respond **pick a point to suit.**

Aligned dimensioning

Select the ALIGNED DIMENSION icon and:

prompt First extension line origin
respond **Endpoint icon and pick line k1**
prompt Second extension line origin
respond **Endpoint icon and pick other end of line k1**
prompt Dimension line location
respond **pick any point to suit.**

Leader dimensioning

Select the LEADER DIMENSION icon and:

prompt From point
respond **Nearest icon and pick any point on smaller circle**
prompt To point
respond **drag to a suitable point and pick**
prompt To point...<Annotation>
respond **right-click**
prompt Annotation...
enter **R5 <R>**
prompt Mtext
respond **right-click** to end leader dimension command.

Dimension options

When using the dimension commands, the user may be aware of various options when the prompt is displayed. To investigate these options:

1 Make layer Out current and draw five horizontal lines at the right-side of the screen. Make layer Dimen current.

2 The RETURN option. Select the LINEAR DIMENSION icon and:
   prompt   First extension line origin or press ENTER to select
   respond **press the RETURN/ENTER key**
   prompt   Select object to dimension
   respond **pick the top line**
   prompt   Dimension line location
   respond **pick above the line** – Fig. (a).

3 The ANGLE option. Select the LINEAR DIMENSION icon, press RETURN, pick the second top line and:
   prompt   Dimension line location(Mtext,Text,Angle...)
   enter   **A <R>** – the angle option
   prompt   Enter text angle
   enter   **15 <R>**
   prompt   Dimension line location
   respond **pick above the line**.

4 The ROTATED option. LINEAR icon, right-click, pick third line and:
   prompt   Dimension line location(Mtext,Text,Angle...)
   enter   **R <R>** – the rotated option
   prompt   Dimension line angle
   enter   **15 <R>**
   prompt   Dimension line location
   respond **pick above the line**.

5 The TEXT option. LINEAR icon, right-click, pick the fourth line and:
   prompt   Dimension line location(Mtext,Text,Angle...)
   enter   **T <R>** – the text option
   prompt   Dimension text<75>
   enter   **THIS DIMENSION IS: 75 <R>**
   prompt   Dimension line location
   respond **pick above the line**.

6 Dimensioning with keyboard entry. At the command line enter **DIM <R>** and:
   prompt   Dim
   enter   **HOR <R>** – horizontal dimension
   prompt   First extension line origin...
   respond **right-click and pick the fifth line**
   prompt   Dimension line location
   respond **pick above the line**
   prompt   Dimension text<75>
   enter   **SEVENTY-FIVE <R>**
   prompt   Dim and **ESC** to end command.

Note

1 At this stage your drawing should resemble Figure 19.2.

2 The added dimensions (in my drawing) are not as I would accept. This is because I have used the AutoCAD default dimension style, and made no attempt to alter it. The object of the exercise was to investigate the dimensioning process.

3 Your dimensions may differ from mine if you are using a dimension style.

4 The <RETURN> selection is useful if a single object is to be dimensioned. It is generally not suited to baseline or continue dimensions.

5 Object snap is used extensively when dimensioning. This is one time when a running object snap (e.g. endpoint) will assist, but remember to cancel the running object snap!

6 From the menu bar select **Format–Layer** to display the layer control dialogue box. Note the layer **Defpoints**. We did not create this layer. It is *automatically* made by AutoCAD any time a dimension is added to a drawing. This layer can be turned off or frozen but cannot be deleted. **It is best left untouched**.

7 Dimension style will be discussed in the next chapter.

Dimension terminology

The dimensions used by AutoCAD have a terminology associated with them. It is important that the user has an understanding if this terminology especially when creating dimension styles. Figure 19.3 explains the basic dimension terminology.

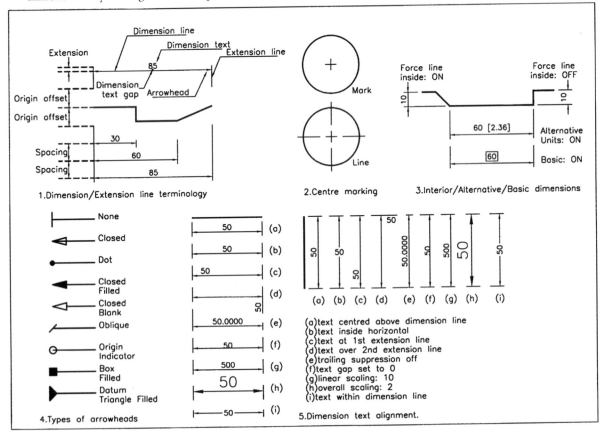

Figure 19.3 Dimension line terminology.

1 The dimension and extension lines

These are made up of:

a) dimension line
- the actual line
- the dimension text
- arrowheads
- extension lines

b) extension line
- an origin offset from the object
- an extension beyond the line
- spacing (for baseline).

2 Centre marking

This can be:

a) a mark
b) a line
c) nothing.

3 Dimension text

It is possible to:

a) force the interior dimension line on or off
b) display alternative units, i.e. [imperial]
c) display the dimension text in a box – referenced dimension.

4 Arrowheads

Release 14 has 18 arrowheads for selection and has the facility for user-defined arrowheads. A selection is displayed.

5 Dimension text alignment

It is possible to align the dimension relative to the dimension line by altering certain dimension variables. A selection of dimension text positions is displayed.

Summary

1 AutoCAD R14 has automatic, associative dimensions.

2 Dimensioning can be linear, radial, angular, ordinate or leader.

3 The diameter and degree symbol are automatically added when using radial or angular dimensions.

4 Object snap modes are useful when dimensioning.

5 A layer DEFPOINTS is created when dimensioning. The user has no control over this layer.

Chapter 20

Dimension styles 1

Dimension styles allow the user to set dimension variables to individual/company requirements. This permits various styles to be saved for different customers.

To demonstrate how a dimension style is 'set and saved', we will create a new dimension style called **STDA3**, use it with our A:WORKDRG drawing and then save it to our standard sheet.

Note

1 The exercise which follows will display several new dialogue boxes and certain settings will be altered within these boxes. It is important for the user to become familiar with the dimension style dialogue boxes, as a good working knowledge is essential if different dimension styles have to be used.

2 The settings used in the exercise are my own, designed for our A3 standard sheet.

3 You can always alter the settings to your own values at this stage.

Getting started

1 Open your A:WORKDRG drawing to display the component created from a previous chapter, i.e. red outline with green centre lines.

2 Activate the Draw, Modify, Dimension and Object Snap toolbars.

Setting dimension style STDA3

1 Either (*a*) menu bar with **Dimension–Style** or (*b*) Dimension Style icon from the Dimension toolbar

   prompt   Dimension Styles dialogue box
   with   ISO-25_WIZARDSCALED as the current style?
   respond 1 at Name, left click after ISO-25_WIZARDSCALED
          2 backspace to clear this name
          3 enter **STDA3**
          4 pick Save
   prompt   1 STDA3 becomes Current style name
          2 message **Created STDA3 from ISO-25_WIZARDSCALED**
          3 dialogue box as Figure 20.1.

2 Pick **Geometry** and:
   prompt   Geometry dialogue box and refer to Figure 20.2
   alter   1 spacing: 10
          2 extension: 2.5
          3 origin offset: 2.5
          4 overall scale: 1
          5 scaled to paper space: OFF
          6 arrowheads: both closed filled
          7 arrowhead size: 3
          8 center mark active, i.e. black dot
          9 center size: 2
          10 pick OK to return to Dimension Styles dialogue box.

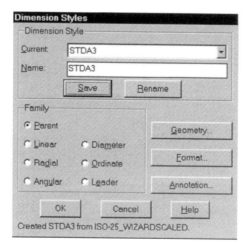

Figure 20.1 Dimension Styles dialogue box.

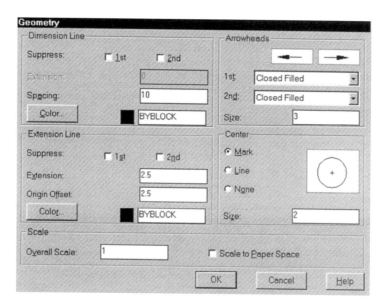

Figure 20.2 Geometry dialogue box.

3 Pick **Format** and:

prompt format dialogue box – refer to Figure 20.3

alter
1 user defined: OFF, i.e. blank box, no tick
2 forced line Inside: OFF
3 fit: best fit
4 horizontal justification: centered
5 text – inside horizontal: OFF; outside horizontal: ON, i.e. tick in box
6 vertical justification: above
7 pick OK to return to dimension styles dialogue box.

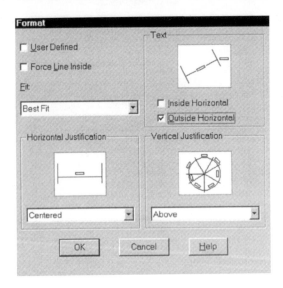

Figure 20.3   Format dialogue box.

4   Pick **Annotation** and:
    prompt   Annotation dialogue box – refer to Figure 20.4
    alter   1   tolerance method: none
                 2   enable units: OFF, i.e. blank box
                 3   Text:
                       • style: STANDARD (see note below)
                       • height: 3
                       • gap: 1.5
                 4   round Off: 0
                 5   pick **Units** for Primary Units dialogue box – Figure 20.5
    alter   1   units: decimal – they should be!
                 2   precision: 0.0
                 3   angles: decimal degrees
                 4   precision: 0.0
                 5   leading: OFF, i.e. blank box
                 6   trailing: ON, i.e. tick
                 7   linear scale: 1
                 8   pick OK – annotation dialogue box
                 9   from Annotation dialogue box, pick OK to return to the Dimension Styles
                     dialogue box.

5   As our 'settings' are now complete:
    a) pick **Save** from Dimension Styles dialogue box
    b) note message: **saved to STDA3** displayed at bottom of box
    c) pick OK from Dimension Styles dialogue box to return to the drawing screen.

6   Note: although I have stated that our Dimension Style 'settings' are now complete, this
    is not strictly true. We have still to set a text style in the Annotation dialogue box. This
    will be achieved when we have investigated this topic in a later chapter. For the present,
    we will accept and use the STANDARD default text style.

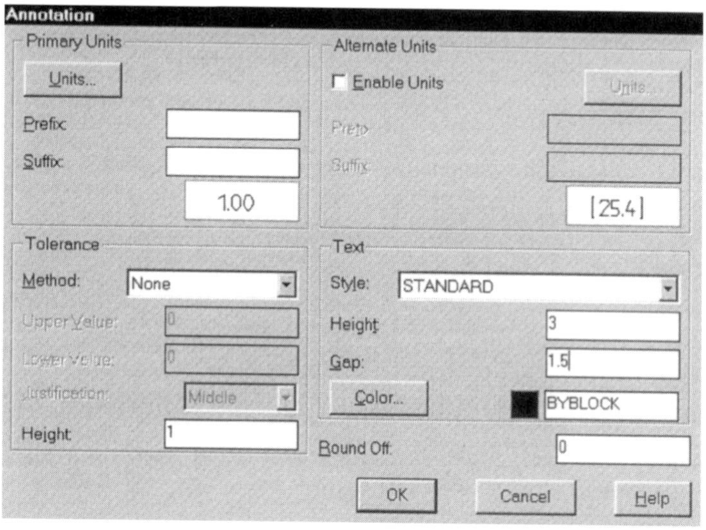

Figure 20.4 Annotation dialogue box.

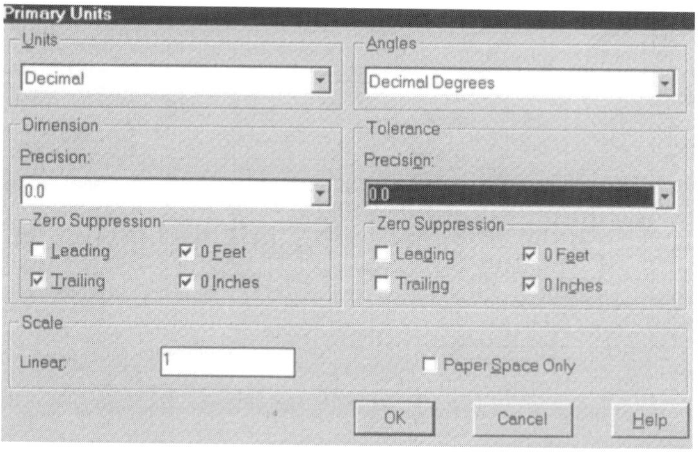

Figure 20.5 Primary Units dialogue box.

Using the STDA3 dimension style

1 A:WORKDRG drawing on the screen?

2 Make layer Dimen current.

3 Refer to Figure 20.6 and add the dimensions using the following:
   a) linear baseline
   b) linear continue
   c) diameter
   d) radius
   e) angular
   f) leader.

4 With layer Text current, add the text, the height being at your discretion.

5 When all dimensions have been added save the drawing, but **not** as A:WORKDRG

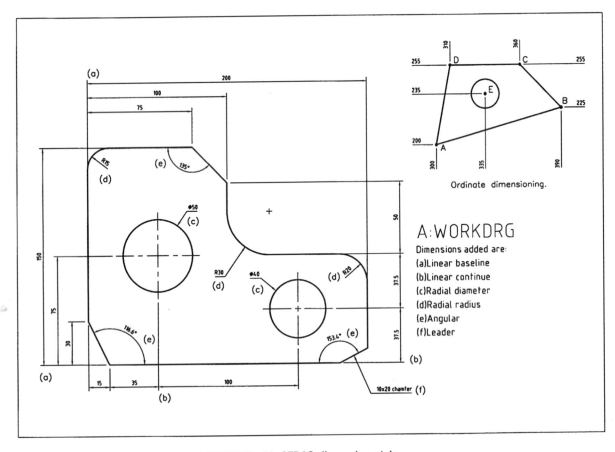

Figure 20.6 Dimensioning A:WORKDRG with STDA3 dimension style.

Saving the STDA3 dimension style to the standard sheet

The dimension style which we have created will be used for all future work when dimensioning is required. This means that we want to have this style incorporated in our A:STDA3 standard sheet. We could always open the standard sheet and redefine the STDA3 dimension style, but this seems a waste of time.

1 Make layer Out current.

2 Erase all objects from the screen **except** the black border.

3 Menu bar with **File–Save As** and:
   prompt   Save Drawing As dialogue box
   respond   **enter A:STDA3** as the File name
   prompt   A:STDA3.dwg already exists
   respond   **pick OK**

4 The A:STDA3 standard sheet now has STDA3 as the current dimension style, and can be used for all future dimensioning work.

Ordinate dimensioning

This type of dimensioning is very popular with many companies, and as it was not covered in the previous chapter, we will now investigate how it is used.

1 Refer to Figure 20.6.

2 Layer out current and toolbars to suit.

3 Draw the following objects:
   LINE   CIRCLE
   From: 300,200   centre: 335,235
   To: @90,25   radius: 10
   To: @–30,30
   To: @–50,0
   To: close.

4 Make the Dimen layer current.

5 Select the ORDINATE dimension icon from the Dimension toolbar and:
   prompt   Select feature
   respond   **pick point A** – osnap helps?
   prompt   Leader endpoint (Xdatum/Ydatum...
   enter   **X <R>** – the Xdatum option
   prompt   Leader endpoint
   enter   **@0,–10 <R>**

6 Menu bar with **Dimension–Ordinate** and:
   prompt   Select feature
   respond   **pick point A**
   prompt   Leader endpoint (Xdatum/Ydatum...
   enter   **Y <R>**
   prompt   Leader endpoint
   enter   **@–10,0 <R>**

7 Now add ordinate dimensions to the other named points, using the following *X* and *Y* datum leader endpoint values:

Point B:	Xdatum: @0,–35	Point C:	Xdatum: @0,10
	Ydatum: @10,0		Ydatum: @40,0
Point D:	Xdatum: @0,10	Point E:	Xdatum: @0,–45
	Ydatum: @–20,0		Ydatum: @–45,0

8 The result is hopefully as Figure 20.6 – save if required, but it will not be used again.

Assignments

As dimensioning is an important concept, I have included three activities which will give you practice with:
a) using the standard sheet with layers
b) using the draw commands with coordinates
c) adding text and dimensions.

In each activity the procedure is the same:

1 Open the A:STDA3 standard sheet.

2 Using layers correctly, complete the drawings.

3 Save the completed work as A:ACT_?
The three activities are:
a) Activity 7: two simple components to be drawn and dimensioned. The sizes are more awkward than usual.
b) Activity 8: two components created mainly from circles and arcs. Use offset as much as possible. The signal arm is interesting.
c) Activity 9: a component which is much easier to complete than it would appear. Offset and fillet will assist.

Summary

1 Dimension styles are created by the user to 'individual' standards.

2 Different dimension styles can be created and recalled at any time.

3 The standard A:STDA3 sheet has a 'customized' dimension style named STDA3 (obvious?) which will be used for all dimension work.

Chapter 21

The modify commands

The draw and modify commands are probably the most commonly used of all the AutoCAD commands and we have already used several of each. The modify commands discussed previously have been Erase, Offset, Trim, Extend, Fillet and Chamfer. In this chapter we will use A:WORKDRG to investigate several other modify commands.

Getting ready

1 Open A:WORKDRG to display the red component with green centre lines. There should be no dimensions displayed.
2 Layer Out current, with the Draw, Modify and Object Snap toolbars.
3 Freeze layer Cl – you will find out why shortly.

Copy

Allows objects to be copied to other parts of the screen. The command can be used for single or multiple copies.

1 Refer to Figure 21.1.

2 Select the COPY icon from the Modify toolbar and:

prompt	Select objects
enter	**C <R>** – the crossing selection set option
prompt	First corner and: **pick a point p1**
prompt	Other corner and: **pick a point p2**
prompt	11 found – note objects not highlighted
and	Select objects
enter	**A <R>** – the add selection set option
prompt	Select objects
respond	**pick objects d1, d2 and d3 then right-click**
prompt	<Base point or displacement>/Multiple
enter	**50,50 <R>** – note copy image as mouse moved!
prompt	Second point of displacement
enter	**300,250 <R>**.

3 The original component will be copied to another part of the screen and **may** not all be visible.

4 Don't panic! Select from the menu bar **View–Zoom-All** to 'see' the complete copied effect – Figure 21.2. You may have to reposition your toolbars.

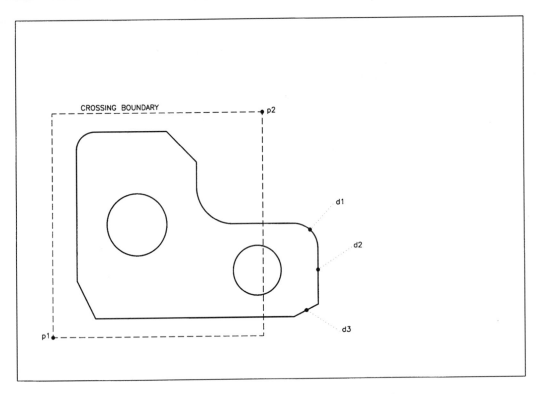

Figure 21.1 A:WORKDRG with selection points for the COPY command.

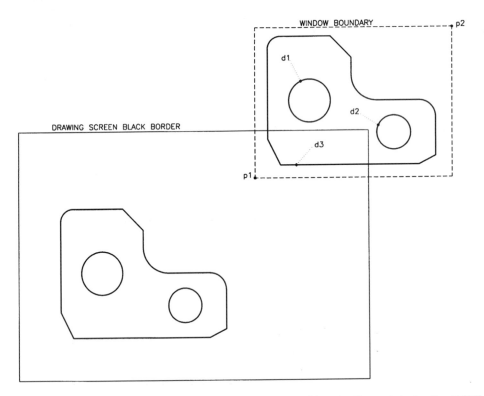

Figure 21.2 A:WORKDRG after the COPY command, with selection points for the MOVE command.

Move

Will move selected objects, the user defining the start and end points of the move by:

a) entering coordinates
b) pick points on the screen
c) referencing existing entities.

1 Refer to Figure 21.2 and select the MOVE icon from the Modify toolbar:

prompt	Select objects
enter	**W <R>** – the window selection set option
prompt	First corner and: **pick a point p1**
prompt	Other corner and: **pick a point p2**
prompt	14 found
and	Select objects
enter	**R <R>** – the remove selection set option
prompt	Remove objects
respond	**pick circles d1 and d2 then right-click**
prompt	Base point or displacement
respond	**Endpoint icon and pick line d3**
	(note image as cursor is moved)
prompt	Second point of displacement
enter	**@–100,–120 <R>**

2 The result looks like Figure 21.3, i.e. the red outline shape is moved, but the two circles do not – due to the Remove option.

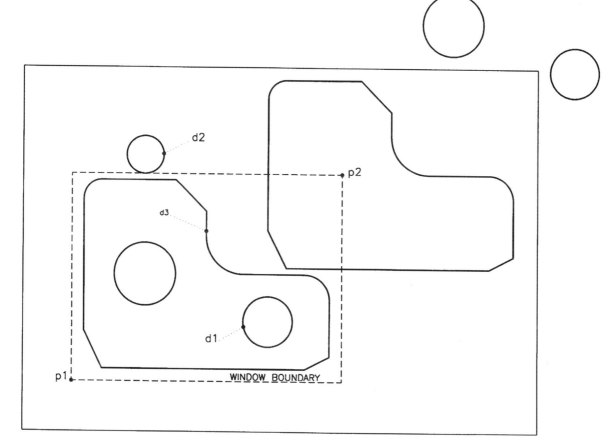

Figure 21.3 A:WORKDRG after the MOVE command, with selection points for the ROTATE command.

3 Task. Using the Layer Control dialogue box, THAW layer Cl and the centre lines are still in their original positions. They have not been copied or moved. This is a common problem with objects which are on frozen or off layers.

Now: *a*) freeze layer Cl

b) erase the copied–moved objects to leave the original

c) View–Zoom–Previous to 'restore' the original screen.

Rotate

Selected objects can be 'turned' about a designated point in either a clockwise (negative angle) or counterclockwise (positive angle) direction.

The base point can be selected as a point on the screen, entered as a coordinate or referenced to existing objects.

1 Refer to Figure 21.3 and draw a circle, centre: 100,220, radius: 15.

2 Select the ROTATE icon from the modify toolbar and:

prompt	`Select objects`
respond	**window from p1 to p2**
prompt	`Select objects`
enter	**R <R>**
prompt	`Remove objects` and: **pick circle d1**
prompt	`Remove objects` and enter: **A <R>**
prompt	`Select objects` and: **pick circle d2**
prompt	`Select objects` and **right-click** to end selection
prompt	`Base point`
respond	**Endpoint icon and pick line d3** – at 'lower end'
prompt	`<Rotation angle>/Reference`
enter	**–90 <R>**

3 The selected shape will be rotated as shown in Figure 21.4.

4 Note: two selection set options were used in the sequence:

a) R – removed a circle from the selection set

b) A – added a circle to the selection set.

Scale

The scale command allows selected objects or complete 'shapes' to be increased/decreased in size, the user entering the scale base point and the actual scale factor.

1 Refer to Figure 21.4 and erase the two circles 'outside the shape'.

2 Make layer Dimen current and using the icons from the Dimension toolbar:

a) linear dimension line AB

b) diameter dimension the circle.

3 At the command line enter **DIM <R>** and:

prompt	`Dim` and enter: **HOR <R>**
prompt	`First extension line origin` and: **Endpoint of X**
prompt	`Second extension line origin` and: **Endpoint of Y**
prompt	`Dimension line location` and: **pick above line**
prompt	`Dimension text<105>` and enter: **105 <R>**
prompt	`Dim` and enter: **RAD <R>**
prompt	`Select arc or circle` and: **pick the circle**
prompt	`Dimension text<25>` and enter: **R25 <R>**
prompt	`Dimension text location` and: **pick to suit**
prompt	`Dim` and **ESC** to end sequence.

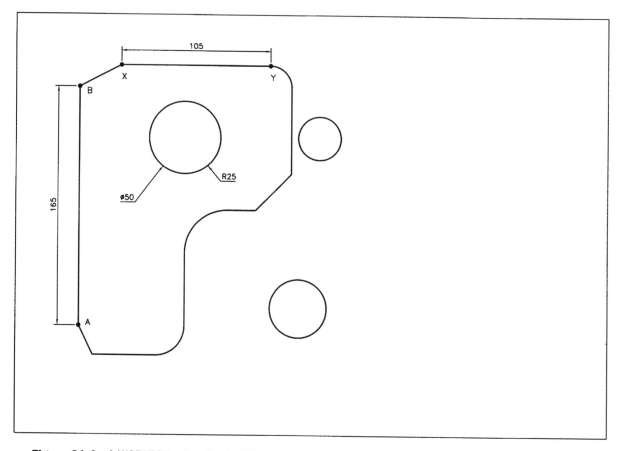

Figure 21.4 A:WORKDRG after the ROTATE command, with dimensions for the SELECT command.

4   Make layer Out current.

5   Select the SCALE icon from the Modify toolbar and:
    prompt   Select objects
    respond   **window the complete shape with dimensions then right-click**
    prompt   Base point
    respond   **Endpoint icon and pick point B**
    prompt   <Scale factor>/Reference
    enter   **0.5 <R>**.

6   The complete shape will be scaled by three-quarters as shown in Figure 21.5.

7   Note the dimensions:
    a) the vertical dimension of 165 is now 82.5
    b) the diameter value of 50 is now 25
    c) the horizontal dimension of 105 is still 105
    d) the radius of 25 is still 25.

8   Questions:
    a) Why have two dimensions been scaled by 0.5 and two have not?
    Answer: the scaled dimensions are those selected by icon and those not scaled had their dimension text values entered from the keyboard.
    b) Which of the scaled dimensions are correct? Is it the 82.5 and 25, or the 105 and 25?
    Answer: I will let you think this one for yourself!

Multiple copy

This is an option of the COPY command and does what it says – it produces as many copies of selected objects as you want.

1 Refer to Figure 21.5.

2 Using the Layer Control dialogue box, LOCK layer Dimen.

3 From menu bar select **Modify–Copy** and:

prompt	Select objects
respond	**window the shape including dimensions**
prompt	17 found and select objects
respond	**right-click**
prompt	<base point or displacement>/Multiple
enter	**M <R>** – the multiple option
prompt	Base point
respond	**Center icon and pick the circle**
prompt	Second point of displacement and enter: **145,150 <R>**
prompt	Second point... and enter: **@170,20 <R>**
prompt	Second point... and enter: **@170,–135 <R>**
prompt	Second point... and enter: **@275,0 <R>**
prompt	Second point...
respond	**Midpoint icon and pick right vertical line of the black 'border'**
prompt	Second point... and: **right-click** to end sequence

4 The result should look like Figure 21.5 with the dimensions copied, even although the layer Dimen was locked.

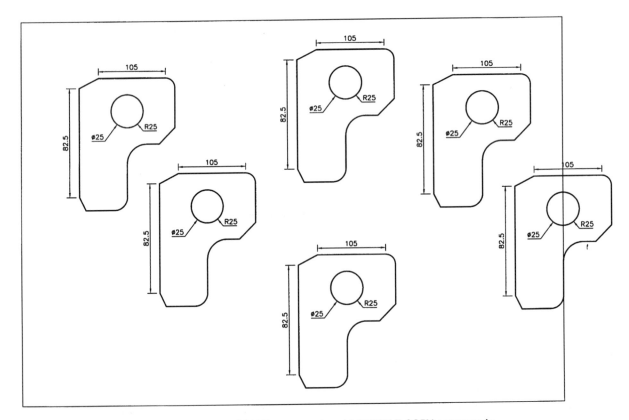

Figure 21.5 A:WORKDRG after the SCALE command and MULTIPLE COPY commands.

Mirror

A command which allows objects to be mirror imaged about a line designated by the user. The command has an option for deleting the original set of objects.

1 Erase the five multiple copied shapes to leave the original shape and dimensions. Layer Dimen must be unlocked before erasing the dimensions – did you forget this?

2 Move the shape and dimensions:
from   **Centre of circle**
to   **@120,20**

3 Draw the following lines:

AB	*MN*	*PQ*	*XY*
from: 140,270	*from*: 260,200	*from*: 240,150	*from*: 155,150
to: @0,–100	*to*: @0,70	*to*: @50<45	*to*: @60<0

4 Draw the following text items with 0 rotation:
 a) centred on 200,255; height: 6; item: AutoCAD
 b) centred on 185,180; height: 10, item: R14.

5 Select the MIRROR icon from the Modify toolbar and:
 prompt   Select objects
 respond   **window shape and dimensions then right-click**
 prompt   First point of mirror line
 respond   **pick point A**
 prompt   Second point of mirror line
 respond   **pick point B**
 prompt   Delete old objects<N>?
 enter   **N <R>**.

6 The selected objects are mirrored about the line AB. Note that the text has also been mirrored but the dimension text has not. The positions of the radial dimensions are interesting?

7 At the command line enter **MIRRTEXT <R>**
 prompt   New value for MIRRTEXTT<1>
 enter   **0 <R>**

8 Menu bar with **Modify–Mirror** and:
 prompt   Select objects
 enter   **P <R>** – previous election set option
 prompt   19 found and Select objects
 respond   **right-click** to end selection
 prompt   First point of mirror line and: **pick point M**
 prompt   Second point of mirror line and: **pick point N**
 prompt   Delete old objects and enter: **N <R>**.

9 The shape is mirrored – what about text?

10 At the command line enter **MIRROR <R>** and:
 a) select objects: enter P <R><R> – yes two returns – why?
 b) first point – pick point P
 c) second point – pick point Q
 d) delete – N.

11 Finally mirror the original selection about line *XY*.

12 The final result should be as shown in Figure 21.6.

13 As this exercise is now complete it can be saved if required, but not as A:WORKDRG. We will not use this modified drawing again.

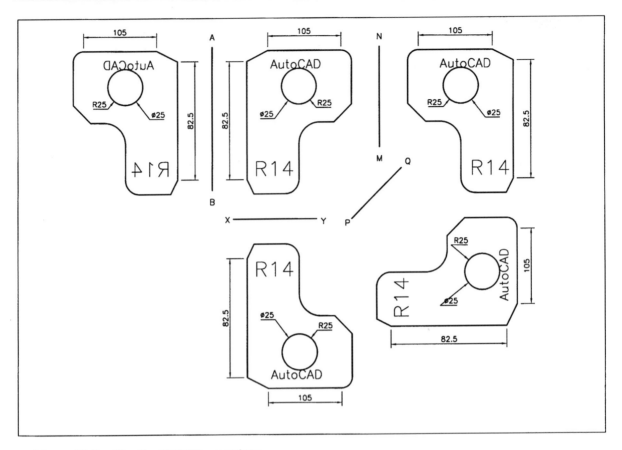

Figure 21.6 After the MIRROR operations.

Task

Before leaving the exercise, thaw layer Cl. The circle centre lines are still in their original positions.

Assignments

Three relatively easy activities have been included for the chapter. Each activity should be completed on the A:STDA3 standard sheet and layers should be used correctly. Remember to save your completed drawings as A:ACT_??, etc. The activities are:

1 Activity 10: An old-fashioned circuit.
Relatively easy to complete. Create the two 'gates' and then COPY or MULTIPLE COPY to other parts of the screen as required. As an addition, scale the complete layout by 0.5 then mirror.

2 Activity 11: A template.
This is easier to complete than you may think. Draw the quarter template using the sizes, then MIRROR twice. The text item is to be placed at your discretion. Copy and scale by 0.5 and 0.25. Additional: add the given dimensions to a quarter template.

3 Activity 12: A part memory cell.
Uses the SCALE, MIRROR and COPY commands. Creating the given reference drawing is not as easy as it may appear!

Summary

1 The commands COPY, MOVE, ROTATE, MIRROR and SCALE can all be activated:
   a) from the menu bar with **Modify–Copy**, etc.
   b) by selecting the icon from the Modify toolbar
   c) by entering the command at the command line e.g. **SCALE <R>**.

2 The selection set is useful for selecting objects, especially the add/remove options.

3 All of the commands require a base point, and this can be:
   a) entered as coordinates
   b) referenced to an existing object
   c) picked on the screen.

4 Objects on layers which are OFF or FROZEN are not affected by the modify commands. This could cause problems!

5 MIRRTEXT is a system variable with a 0 or 1 value and:
   a) value 1: text is mirrored – this is the default
   b) value 0: text is not mirrored.

6 Keyboard entered dimensions are not scaled.

Chapter 22

Grips

Grips are an aid to the draughting process, offering the user a limited number of modify commands. In an earlier chapter we turned grips off with the command line entry of GRIPS: 0. This was to allow the user to become reasonably proficient with using the draw and modify commands. Now that this has been achieved, we will investigate how grips are used.

Toggling grips on/off

Grips can be toggled on/off using (*a*) the grips dialogue box or (*b*) the command line entry.

1 Open your A:STDA3 standard sheet, layer Out current.

2 From the menu bar select **Tools–Grips** and:
   prompt   grips dialogue box
   respond   1   enable grips ON, i.e. tick in box
             2   grip colors:
                 a) unselected – blue
                 b) selected – red
             3   grip size: set to suit
             4   dialogue box as shown in Figure 22.1
             5   pick OK.

3 The drawing screen is returned, with the grip box 'attached' to cross-hairs.

4 At the command line enter **GRIPS <R>** and:
   prompt   New value for GRIPS<1>
   respond   **<RETURN>**, i.e. leave the 1 value.

5 The command entry is GRIPS: 1 are ON; GRIPS: 0 are OFF.
6 Note that:
   a) the grip box attached to the crosshairs should not be confused with the pick box used with modify commands. Although similar in appearance they are entirely different
   b) when any command is activated (e.g. LINE), the grips box will disappear from the crosshairs, and re-appear when the command is terminated.

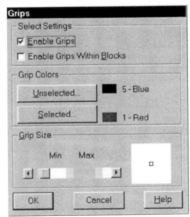

Figure 22.1   The Grips dialogue box.

What do grips do and how do they work?

1 Grips provide the user with five modify commands which can also be activated in icon form or from the menu bar. The five commands are Stretch, Move, Rotate, Scale and Mirror.

2 Grips work in the 'opposite sense' from normal command selection:
   a) the usual sequence is to activate the command then select the objects, e.g. COPY, then pick object to be copied
   b) with grips, the user selects the objects and then activates one of the five commands.

Types of grip

There are three types of grip, these being:
a) cold grip: appear on selected objects in blue, but the object itself is not highlighted. The grip options cannot be used in this state.
b) warm grip: appear as blue boxes and the selected objects are highlighted – dashed appearance. The grip options can be used in this state.
c) hot grip: appear as solid red boxes when a cold or warm box is 'picked'. The selected hot grip acts as the base point for the grip options.

1 Draw a line, circle, arc and text item anywhere on the screen.

2 Ensure grips are on.

3 Refer to Figure 22.2 and move the cursor to each object and 'pick them' with the grip box and:
   a) blue grip boxes appear at each object 'snap point' and the object is highlighted. These are warm grips – Fig. (b)
   b) move the grip box to any one of the blue boxes and 'pick it'. The box becomes red solid in appearance and the object is still highlighted. This is a hot grip – Fig. (c)
   c) press the ESC key – blue grips with highlighted object – warm
   d) press ESC – blue grips with objects not highlighted – cold grip as Fig. (a)
   e) ESC again to cancel the grips operation.

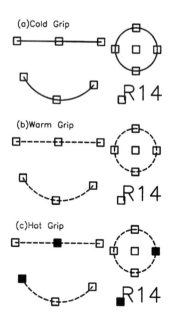

Figure 22.2 Types of grip.

Grip exercise 1

This demonstration is relatively simple but rather long. It is advisable to work through the exercise without missing out any of the steps.

1 Erase all objects from the screen, or re-open A:STDA3.

2 Refer to Figure 22.3 and draw the original shape using the sizes given – Fig. (a). Make the lower left corner at the point (100,100).

3 Grips on?

4 Move the cursor to the circle and pick it, then move to the right vertical line and pick it. Blue grip boxes appear and the two objects are highlighted. These are warm grips – Fig. (b).

5 Move the cursor grip box to the warm grip at the circle centre and left-click i.e. pick it. The selected box will be displayed in red as it is now a hot grip – Fig. (c). Observe the command line:

prompt　　** STRETCH **
　　　　　　　<Stretch to point>/Base point/Copy/Undo/eXit
respond　**<RETURN>**
prompt　　** MOVE **
　　　　　　　<Move to point>...
enter　　　**@25,25 <R>**.

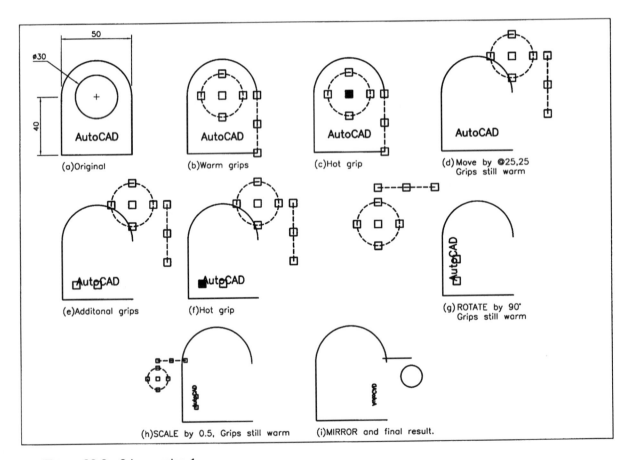

(a) Original

(b) Warm grips

(c) Hot grip

(d) Move by @25,25 Grips still warm

(e) Additonal grips

(f) Hot grip

(g) ROTATE by 90° Grips still warm

(h) SCALE by 0.5, Grips still warm

(i) MIRROR and final result.

Figure 22.3　Grip exercise 1.

6   Three things should have happened:
    a) the circle and line are moved
    b) the command prompt line is returned
    c) the grips are still warm – Fig. (d).

7   Move the cursor and pick the text item to add it to the warm grips – Fig. (e).

8   Make the left grip box of the text item hot, by moving the cursor pick box on to it and
    left-clicking – Fig. (f), and:
    prompt   ** STRETCH **
                 <Stretch to point>...
    enter   **<RETURN>**
    prompt   ** MOVE **
                 <Move to point>...
    enter   **<RETURN>**
    prompt   ** ROTATE **
                 <Rotation angle>...
    enter   **90 <R>**.

9   The circle, line and text item will be rotated and the grips are still warm – Fig. (g).

10 Make the same text item grip box hot (easy!) and:
    prompt   <STRETCH>...
    enter   **SC <R>** – the scale grip option
    prompt   ** SCALE **...
    enter   **0.5 <R>**.

11 The three objects are scaled, grips are still warm – Fig. (h).

12 Make the right box on the line hot and:
    prompt   <STRETCH>...
    enter   **MI <R>** – the mirror option
    prompt   ** <MIRROR>...
    enter   **B <R>** – the base point option
    prompt   *Base point*
    respond   **Midpoint icon and pick the original horizontal line**
    prompt   ** MIRROR **
                 <Second point>
    respond   **Midpoint icon and pick the arc**.

13 The three objects are mirrored about the selected 'line' and the grips are still
    warm – Fig. (i).

14 Press ESC – cold grips on the three objects.

15 Press ESC – removes the grips and ends the sequence.

16 The exercise is now complete. Do not exit yet.

Selection with grips

Selecting individual objects for use with grips can be tedious. It is possible to select a window/crossing option when grips are on.

1 Your screen should display the line, circle and text item after the grips exercise has been completed.

2 Refer to Figure 22.4(a) and move the cursor and pick a point 'roughly' where indicated. Move the cursor down and to the right, and pick a second point.

3 All complete objects within the window will display warm grip boxes.

4 Two ESC presses to cancel the grip effect.

5 Move the cursor to about the same point as step 2, and pick a point – Figure 22.4(b). Move the cursor upwards and to the left and pick a second point.

6 All objects within or which cross the boundary will display warm grips.

7 Two ESC presses.

8 The effect can be summarized as:
   a) window effect to the right of first pick
   b) crossing effect to the left of the first pick.

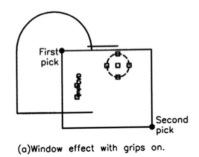

(o)Window effect with grips on.

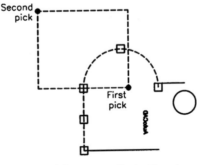

(b)Crossing effect with grips on.

Figure 22.4 Window/crossing selection with grips.

Grips exercise 2

1 Open A:USEREX to display the component used in the offset and text exercises and refer to Figure 22.5.

2 Erase all but the red objects – Fig. (a).

3 Grips on. Pick a point 1 and drag out a window and pick a point 2. Five lines will display warm grips – Fig. (b).

4 Make the rightmost grip hot and:
   prompt   `** STRETCH **`...
   respond **right-click** to display the grip options in a 'drop-down' menu
   then   **pick Rotate**
   prompt   `<Rotation angle>`...
   enter   **180 <R>**.

5 Now two ESC's to cancel the grips – Fig. (c).

6 Pick a point 3 and drag out a crossing window and pick a point 4 to display warm grips on another five lines – Fig. (d).

7 Make the lowest grip box on the right vertical line hot and:
   prompt   `** STRETCH **`...
   respond right-click to display the grip options
   then   **pick Move**
   prompt   `<Move to point>`...
   respond **Endpoint icon and pick line k**.

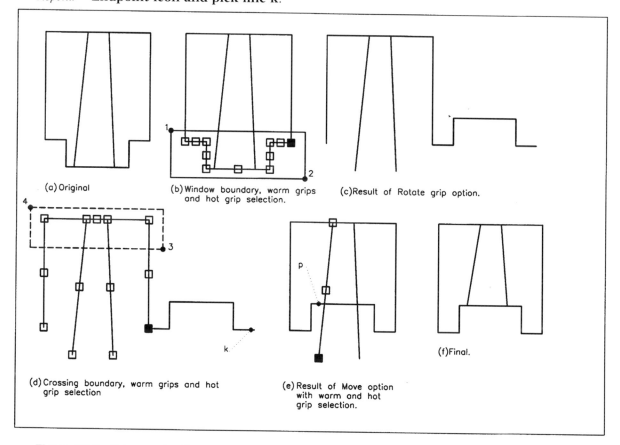

(a) Original

(b) Window boundary, warm grips and hot grip selection.

(c) Result of Rotate grip option.

(d) Crossing boundary, warm grips and hot grip selection

(e) Result of Move option with warm and hot grip selection.

(f) Final.

Figure 22.5 Grip exercise 2.

8   The lines are moved 'onto' the rotated lines – Fig. (e).

9   Two ESC's to cancel the grips.

10 Pick one of the inclined lines and:
    a) make the lowest grip box hot
    b) use the STRETCH option
    c) stretch the grip box perpendicular to line p
    d) repeat for the other inclined line
    e) final result – Fig. (f).

11 Note: this exercise could have been completed using the modify commands, e.g. rotate and trim. It demonstrates that there is no one way to complete a drawing.

Assignment

The grip activity 13 is the repositioning of a robotic arm, which was included in my *Beginning R13 book* with a reasonable amount of success, so:

1   Create the robotic arm in the original position using the reference sizes given – Fig. (a).

2   Upper arm rotate by 45°. Two circles and two lines need to be 'picked' – Fig. (b).

3   Both arms mirrored about line through large circle centre. Two more lines and a circle added to the grip selection – Fig. (c).

4   Both arms rotated to a horizontal position – Fig. (d).

5   Finally – Fig. (e) – three grip operations:
    a) lower arm stretch by 50
    b) upper arm move
    c) upper arm rotate.

Summary

1   Grips allow the user access to the modify commands STRETCH, MOVE, ROTATE, SCALE and MIRROR without icon or menu bar selection.

2   Grips work in the 'opposite sense' from the normal AutoCAD commands, i.e. select object first then the command.

3   Grips **do not have to be used**. They give the user another draughting tool.

4   Grips are toggled on/off using the grips dialogue box or by keyboard entry. The dialogue box allows the grip box colours and size to be altered.

5   Grips can be cold, warm or hot.

6   If grips are not being used, I would always recommend that they be toggled off, i.e. GRIPS: 0.

7   When a grip box is hot, the options can be activated by:
    a) return at the keyboard
    b) entering SC, MO, MI, etc.
    c) right-click the mouse.

Chapter 23

Drawing assistance

All objects have been created by picking points on the screen, entering coordinate values or by referencing existing objects e.g. midpoint, endpoint, etc.

There are other methods which enable objects to be positioned on the screen, and in this chapter we will investigate three new concepts, these being:

a) point filters
b) construction lines
c) ray lines.

Point filters

This allows objects to be positioned by referencing the *X* and *Y* coordinate values of existing objects.

Example 1

1 Open the A:STDA3 standard sheet and refer to Figure 23.1.

2 Draw a 50 side square, lower left corner at 20,220.

3 Multiple copy this square to three other positions.

4 A circle of diameter 30 has to be created at the 'centre' of each square and this will be achieved by four different methods:
   a) coordinates: activate the circle command with centre: 45,245; radius: 15
   b) Object snap:
     • draw in a diagonal of the square
     • pick the Circle icon
     • centre point: snap to midpoint of diagonal
     • radius: enter 15.
   c) Tracking:
     • pick the Circle icon
     • pick the Tracking icon
     • first tracking point: snap to midpoint icon and pick line AB
     • next point: snap to midpoint icon and pick line BC
     • radius: enter 15.
   d) Point filters: activate the circle command and:

prompt	Center point
enter	**.X <R>**
prompt	of
respond	**Midpoint icon and pick PQ**
prompt	(need YZ)
respond	**Midpoint icon and pick line PR**
prompt	Radius and enter: **15 <R>**.

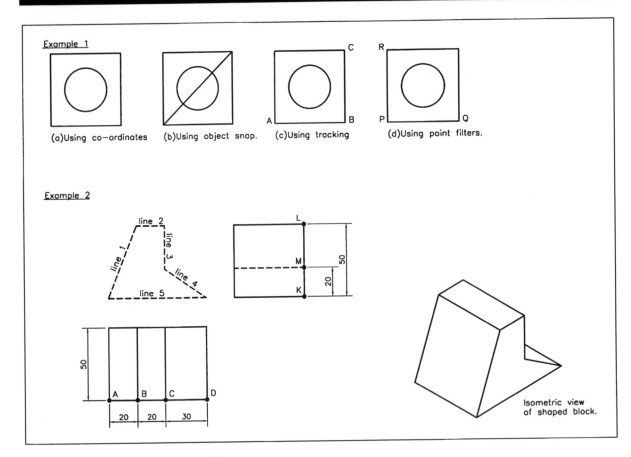

Figure 23.1 Point filter examples.

Example 2

Figure 23.1 shows the top, end and isometric views of a shaped block. The front view has to be created from the two given views, and we will use the point filter technique to achieve this.

1   Draw the top and end views using the sizes given. Use the lower part of the screen. Draw with the snap on.

2   Select the Line icon and:

prompt	From point
enter	**.X <R>**
prompt	of
respond	**pick point A** – snap on helps
prompt	(need YZ)
respond	**pick point K**
and	cursor 'snaps' to a point on the screen
prompt	To point
enter	**.X <R>**
prompt	of
respond	**pick point B**
prompt	(need YZ)
respond	**pick point L** – line 1 is drawn
prompt	To point
enter	**.X <R>** and: **pick point C**

prompt (need YZ) and: **pick point L** – line 2 is drawn
prompt To point
enter **.X <R>** and: **pick point C**
prompt (need YZ) and: **pick point M** – line 3 is drawn
prompt To point
enter **.X <R>** and: **pick point D**
prompt (need YZ) and: **pick point K** – line 4 is drawn
prompt To point and: **C <R>** to draw line 5.

3 The front view of the shaped block is now complete.

4 This exercise does not need to be saved.

5 Note: the point filter method of creating objects is rather 'cumbersome' to use. It has generally been superseded by tracking – a new Release 14 concept. Point filters is another aid to draughting, and it is user preference if it is used.

Construction lines

Construction lines are lines that extend to infinity in both directions from a selected point on the screen. They can be referenced to assist in the creation of other objects.

1 Open the A:STDA3 standard sheet, layer Out current and display toolbars Draw, Modify and Object Snap. Refer to Figure 23.2(a).

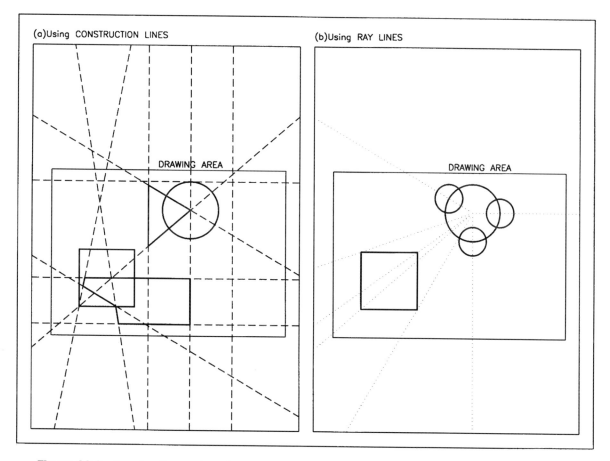

Figure 23.2 Construction and ray lines.

2 With layer Out current, draw:
   a) a 100 sided square, lower left corner at 50,50
   b) a circle, centred on 250,220 with radius 50.

3 Make a new layer (**Format–Layer**) named CONLINE, colour to suit and with a DASHED linetype. This layer is to be current.

4 Menu bar with **Draw–Construction Line** and:
   prompt   Hor/Ver/Ang/Bisect/Offset/<From point>
   enter   **50,50 <R>**
   and   line 'attached' to cursor through the entered point and 'swings' as the mouse is moved
   prompt   Through point
   enter   **80,200 <R>**
   prompt   Through point
   respond **Center icon and pick the circle**
   prompt   Through point and right-click.

5 At the command line enter **XLINE <R>** and:
   prompt   .../<From point>
   enter   **H <R>** – the horizontal option
   prompt   Through point
   enter   **100,20 <R>**
   prompt   Through point
   respond **Midpoint icon and pick a vertical line of square**
   prompt   Through point
   respond **Quadrant icon and pick top of circle**
   prompt   Through point and right-click.

6 Select the CONSTRUCTION LINE icon from the Draw toolbar and:
   prompt   options...
   enter   **V <R>** – the vertical option
   prompt   Through point
   respond **Center icon and pick the circle**
   prompt   Through point and right-click.

7 Activate the construction line command and:
   prompt   Through point
   enter   **O <R>** – the offset option
   prompt   Offset distance or Through and enter: **75 <R>**
   prompt   Select a line to offset
   respond **pick the vertical line through the circle centre**
   prompt   Side to offset?
   respond **offset to the right**
   prompt   Select a line to offset
   respond **offset the same line to the left**
   prompt   Through point and right-click.

8 Construction line command and at prompt:
   enter   **A <R>** – the angle option
   prompt   Reference/<Enter angle (0.0)>
   enter   **–30 <R>**
   prompt   Through point
   respond **Center icon and pick the circle**
   prompt   Through point
   enter   **135,40 <R>** then right-click.

9 Construction line command for last time and at prompt:
enter **B <R>** – the bisect option
prompt Angle vertex point
respond **Midpoint icon and pick top line of square**
prompt Angle start point
respond **pick lower left vertex of square**
prompt Angle end point
respond **Midpoint icon and pick square right vertical line**
prompt Angle end point and right-click.

10 Construction lines can be copied, moved, referenced to create other objects as displayed in Figure 23.2(a).

11 Think of how construction lines could have been used to create the front view of the point filters example completed earlier in this chapter.

12 I would recommend that construction lines are created on their own layer, and that this layer is frozen to avoid 'screen clutter'. I would also recommend that they are given a colour and linetype not normally used.

13 Task. Try the following:
a) at the command line enter **LIMITS <R>** and:
    prompt Lower left corner and enter: **0,0 <R>**
    prompt Upper right corner and enter: **10000,10000 <R>**.
b) From menu bar select **View–Zoom–All** and:
    i)   our drawing appears very small at bottom of screen
    ii)   the construction lines 'radiate outwards' to the screen edges
c) Enter LIMITS <R> and:
    i)   −10000,−10000 as the lower left corner
    ii)   0,0 as the upper right corner.
d) **View–Zoom–All** to 'see' the construction lines
e) Return limits to 0,0 and 420,297 then **View–Zoom–Previous** twice to restore the original drawing screen. A **REGEN <R>** from the keyboard may be required?

14 The construction line exercise is now complete. The drawing can be saved if required, but we will not use it again.

Rays

Rays are similar to construction lines, but they only extend to infinity in one direction from the selected start point.

1 Make a new layer called RAYLINE, colour to suit and with a dotted linetype. Make this layer current and refer to Figure 23.2(b).

2 Freeze layer CONLINE and erase any objects to leave the original square and circle.

3 Menu bar with **Draw–Ray** and:
prompt From point
respond **Center icon and pick the circle**
prompt Through point and enter: **@100<150 <R>**
prompt Through point and enter: **@100<0 <R>**
prompt Through point and enter: **@100<−90 <R>**
prompt Through point and right-click.

4 With layer Out current, draw three 25 radius circles at the intersection of the ray lines and circle.

5 Make layer RAYLINE current and at the command line enter **RAY <R>** and:

   prompt   From point
   respond **pick the circle centre point**
   prompt   Through point
   respond **Intersection icon and pick the four vertices of the square** then right-click.

6 Use the LIMITS command and enter:
   a) lower left: −10000,−10000
   b) upper right: 0,0.

7 Menu bar with **View–Zoom–All** and note position of 'our drawing'.

8 Return limits to 0,0 and 420,297 the **Zoom–Previous** to restore the original drawing screen – is REGEN needed?

9 As with construction lines, it is recommended that ray lines be drawn on 'their own layer' which can be frozen as required.

10 Using ray lines with Release 14 is slightly different to Release 13. R13 users will be pleased to note that the 'screen coverage' with ray lines has been eliminated.

Summary

1 Point filters allow the user a method of creating objects by referencing existing object coordinates.

2 Point filters are activated by keyboard entry.

3 The use of point filters in Release 14 has been slightly superseded by TRACKING.

4 Construction and ray lines are aids to draughting. The allow lines to be created from a selected point and:
   a) construction lines extend to infinity in both directions from the selected start point
   b) ray lines extend to infinity in one direction only from the selected start point.

5 Both construction and ray lines can be activated from the menu bar or by keyboard entry. XLINE is the construction line entry and RAY the ray line entry.

6 The default draw dialogue box only displays the construction line icon, although this can be altered to include the ray line icon.

7 Both construction and ray lines are very useful aids for the CAD operator, but it is personal preference if they are used.

Chapter 24

Viewing a drawing

Viewing a drawing is important. This may be to enlarge a certain part of the screen for more detailed work or perhaps to return the screen to a previous display. AutoCAD allows the user several methods of altering the screen display, and these include the scroll bars, the pan and zoom commands and the aerial view option. Release 14 has a new concept – realtime pan and zoom.

Getting ready

1 Open A:WORKDRG to display the red outline, two red circles, four green centre lines and a black border.

2 With layer Text current, use the DTEXT command with:
 a) start point: centred on 90,115
 b) height: 0.1 – yes 0.1
 c) rotation: 0
 d) text item: AutoCAD.

3 With layer Out current, draw a circle centred on 89.98,115.035 and radius 0.01.

4 These two objects cannot yet be 'seen' on the screen.

5 Ensure the zoom toolbar is displayed.

Pan

Allows the graphics screen to be 'moved' the movement being controlled by the user.

1 From the standard toolbar select the PAN REALTIME icon and:
 prompt   Press Esc or Enter to exit, or right-click to activate
         pop-up menu
 and   cursor changes to a hand
 respond 1 hold down the left button of mouse
         2 move mouse and complete drawing moves
         3 note that scroll bars also move
         4 move image roughly back to original position
         5 right-click and:
             a) pop-up menu displayed
             b) pan is active – tick
             c) pick exit.

2 Menu bar with **View–Pan–Point** and:
 prompt   Displacement and enter: **0,0 <R>**
 prompt   Second point and enter: **500,500 <R>**.

3 No drawing on the screen – don't panic!

4 Use PAN REALTIME to pan down and to the left, and 'restore' the drawing roughly in its original position, then right-click and exit.

Zoom

This is the one of the most important and widely used of all the AutoCAD commands. It allows parts of a drawing to be magnified/enlarged on the screen. The command has several options, and it is these options which will now be investigated. To assist us in investigating the zoom options:

a) use the COPY command and copy the red/green component from 50,50 to 200,500

b) refer to Figure 24.1.

Zoom All

Displays a complete drawing including any part which is 'off' the current screen.

1   From menu bar select **View–Zoom–All**.

2   The two components and the black border are displayed – Fig. (a).

Zoom Window

Perhaps the most useful of the zoom options. It allows areas of a drawing to be 'enlarged' for clarity or more accurate work.

1   Select the ZOOM WINDOW icon from the Zoom toolbar and:
    prompt   First corner
    respond   **window the original left circle** – Fig. (b).

2   At the command line enter **ZOOM <R>** and:
    prompt   All/Center/Dynamic...and enter: **W <R>**
    prompt   First corner and enter: **89.6,114.9 <R>**
    prompt   Other corner and enter: **90.4,115.2 <R>**.

3   The text item and circle will now be displayed – Fig. (c).

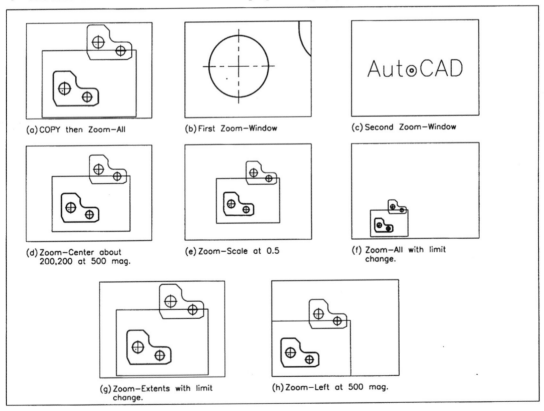

(a) COPY then Zoom–All

(b) First Zoom–Window

(c) Second Zoom–Window

(d) Zoom–Center about 200,200 at 500 mag.

(e) Zoom–Scale at 0.5

(f) Zoom–All with limit change.

(g) Zoom–Extents with limit change.

(h) Zoom–Left at 500 mag.

Figure 24.1   Various zoom operations.

Zoom Previous

Restores the drawing screen to the display before the last view command.

1 Menu bar with **View–Zoom–Previous** – restores Fig. (b).

2 At command line enter **ZOOM <R>** then **P <R>** – restores Fig. (a).

Zoom Center

Allows a drawing to be centred about a user-defined centre point.

1 Select the ZOOM CENTER icon and:
   prompt   Center point and enter: **200,200 <R>**
   prompt   Magnification or height<?> and enter **500 <R>**.

2 The complete drawing is centred on the drawing screen about the entered point – Fig. (d).

3 Note:
   a) the 'size' of the displayed drawing depends on the magnification/height value you
      enter and is relative to the displayed default value <?>:
      i) a value less than the default – magnifies drawing on screen
      ii) a value greater than the default – reduces the size of the drawing on the screen
   b) the grid effect with the centre option.

4 Menu bar with **View–Zoom–Center** and enter the following centre points, all with 1000
   magnification:
   a) 200,200
   b) 0,0
   c) 500,500.

5 Now Zoom–Previous four times to restore Fig. (a).

Zoom Scale

Centres a drawing on the screen at a scale factor and is similar (and easier?) than the
Zoom–Center option.

1 Select the ZOOM SCALE icon and:
   prompt   Enter scale factor and enter: **0.5 <R>**

2 Drawing is displayed centred and scaled – Fig. (e).

3 Menu bar with **View–Zoom–Scale** and enter a scale factor of 0.25.

4 Zoom to a scale factor of 1.5.

5 Zoom–Previous three times to restore Fig. (a).

Zoom Extents: zooms the drawing to extent of the current limits.

1 At command line enter **LIMITS <R>** and:
   prompt   Lower left corner and enter: **0,0 <R>**
   prompt   Upper right corner and enter: **1000,1000 <R>**.

2 Menu bar with **View–Zoom–All** – Fig. (f).

3 Select the ZOOM EXTENTS icon – Fig. (g)

4 Set limits back to 0,0 and 420,297 then Zoom–All to restore Fig. (a).

Zoom Dynamic

This option has not been discussed. The other zoom options and the realtime pan and zoom should be sufficient for all users needs?

Zoom Realtime

1 Menu bar with **View–Zoom–Realtime** and:

prompt Press Esc or Enter...
and cursor changes to a magnifying glass with a + and –
respond a) hold down left button on mouse and move upwards to give a magnification effect
  b) move downwards to give a decrease in size effect
  c) left-right movement – no effect
  d) right-click to display pop-up menu with Zoom active
  e) pick exit.

2 Zoom–All to display Fig. (a).

Zoom Left

An old zoom option not displayed but available.

1 At the command line enter **ZOOM <R>** then **L <R>** and:

prompt Lower left corner and enter: **0,0 <R>**
prompt Magnification and enter: **500 <R>**.

2 Complete drawing is moved to left of drawing screen and displayed at the entered magnification – Fig. (h).

3 Zoom–Previous to restore Fig. (a).

Aerial view

The aerial view is a navigation tool (AutoCAD expression) and allows the user to pan and zoom a drawing interactively.

1 The A:WORKDRG drawing should still be displayed from the zoom exercise?

2 From the Standard toolbar select the Aerial View icon and:

prompt aerial view dialogue box
respond **position on screen to suit** – Figure 24.2.

3 The black border displayed in the aerial view dialogue box is the 'drawing screen' and the user has control of a 'dotted cursor'. As the aerial view drawing is altered, the actual screen drawing will alter accordingly. The options available with the aerial view are:

Pan Zoom Zoom In Zoom Out Global

4 a) With the aerial view zoom active, window any area of the aerial view screen – drawing screen displays the same zoom effect
  b) with the aerial view pan active, pan the aerial view screen and the drawing screen will pan accordingly.

5 Experiment with the aerial view dialogue box, and decide if it would be useful for you?

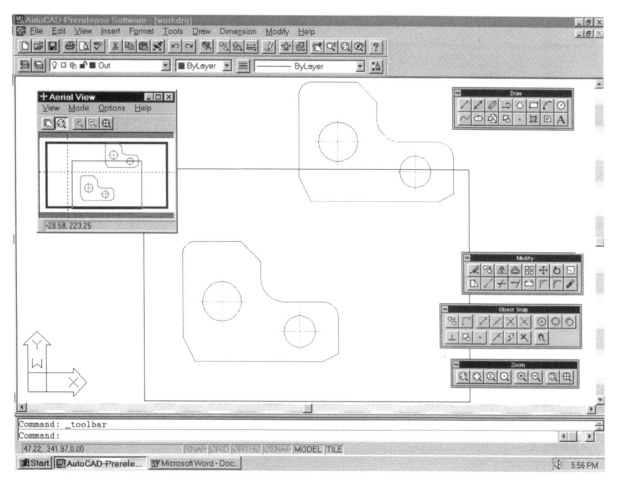

Figure 24.2 The aerial view.

Transparent zoom

A **transparent** command is one which can be activated while using another command and zoom has this facility.

1 Restore the original Fig. (a) – zoom all?

2 Select the LINE icon and:

prompt	From point
enter	**'ZOOM <R>** – the transparent zoom command
prompt	All/Center – the zoom options
enter	**W <R>**
and	window the leftmost circle
prompt	From point, i.e. back to the line command
enter	**89,115 <R>**
prompt	To point
enter	**'ZOOM <R>**
then	**P <R>** – the previous zoom option
prompt	To point, i.e. back to the line command
respond	**pick any point then right-click**.

3 The transparent command can be activated:
   a) by entering 'ZOOM as our example
   b) select View–Zoom–? from the menu bar.

4 Not all commands have transparency.

5 Do not save this drawing modification.

Summary

1 Pan and zoom are VIEW commands usually activated by icon.

2 Pan does 'not move a drawing' – it 'moves' the complete drawing screen.

3 The zoom command has several options, the most common being:

All:	shows the complete drawing
Window:	allows parts of a drawing to be displayed in greater detail
Center:	centres a drawing about a user-defined point at a user-specified magnification – very useful with multiple viewports
Previous:	displays the drawing screen prior to the last pan/zoom command
Extents:	zooms the drawing to the existing limits.

4 Both the pan and zoom commands have a REALTIME option.

5 The aerial view allows interactive pan and zoom.

6 The aerial view is more suited to large drawings.

Chapter 25

Hatching

AutoCAD Release 14 has associated boundary hatching. The hatching (sectioning) must be added by the user, and there are three types:
a) predefined, i.e. AutoCAD's stored hatch patterns
b) user defined
c) custom – not considered in this book.

When applying hatching, the user has two methods of defining the hatch pattern boundary:
a) by selecting objects which make the boundary
b) by picking a point within the boundary.

There are two hatch commands available:
a) HATCH: command line entry only
b) BHATCH: activated by icon, menu bar or command line entry. This command displays a dialogue box.

Getting ready

1 Open the A:STDA3 standard sheet and refer to Figure 25.1.

2 Draw a 50-unit square on layer Out and multiple copy it to ten other parts of the screen. Add the other lines within the required squares. Note that I have included additional squares to indicate appropriate object selection.

3 Make layer Sect (cyan) current.

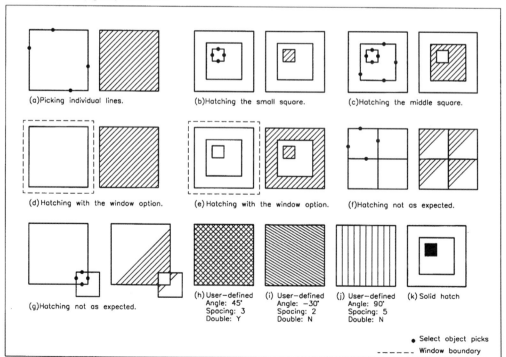

Figure 25.1 User-defined hatching using the select objects method.

User-defined hatch patterns – select objects method

User-defined hatching consists of straight line patterns, the user specifying:
a) the hatch angle relative to the horizontal
b) the distance between the hatch lines – spacing
c) whether single or double (cross) hatching.

1 At the command line enter **HATCH <R>** and:
prompt	Enter pattern name or [?/Solid/User defined]<Angle>
enter	**U <R>** – user-defined option
prompt	Angle for crosshatch lines<0>
enter	**45 <R>**
prompt	Spacing between lines<1.0000>
enter	**3 <R>**
prompt	Double hatch area<N>
enter	**N <R>**
prompt	Select objects
respond	**pick the four lines of first square the right-click**
and	hatching added to the square – Fig. (a).

2 Immediately after the hatching has been added, **right-click** and:
prompt	HATCH Select hatch boundaries or press ENTER for direct hatch options
then	Select objects
respond	**pick four lines indicated in second square then right-click**
and	hatching added to the small square – Fig. (b).

3 Select the HATCH icon from the draw toolbar and:
prompt	Boundary Hatch dialogue box
with	*a*) pattern: user-defined
	b) angle: 45
	c) spacing: 3, i.e. our previous entries!
respond	**pick Select Objects<**
and	dialogue box disappears
prompt	Select objects at command line
respond	**pick eight lines in third square then right-click**
prompt	Boundary Hatch dialogue box returned
respond	**pick Preview Hatch<**
and	1 drawing screen displayed with hatching added – check that it is correct
	2 continue dialogue box message
respond	**pick Continue**
prompt	Boundary Hatch dialogue box
respond	**pick Apply**
and	hatching added as Fig. (c).

4 Menu bar with **Draw–Hatch** and:
   prompt   Boundary Hatch dialogue box – settings as before?
   respond   **pick Select Objects<**
   prompt   Select objects
   enter   **W <R>** – the window selection option
   then   **window the fourth square then right-click**
   prompt   Boundary Hatch dialogue box
   respond   **Preview–Continue–Apply**
   and   square hatched – Fig. (d).

5 At the command line enter **HATCH <R>** then:
   a) pattern name: U
   b) angle: 45
   c) spacing: 3
   d) double: N
   e) select objects: window the fifth square then right-click
   f) hatching as Fig. (e).

6 Using HATCH from the keyboard, accept the four defaults of U,45,3,N and pick the four lines of the sixth square to give hatching as Fig. (f). Not as expected?

7 Repeat the hatch command and select the four lines indicated in the seventh square – Fig. (g).

8 Hatch the next three squares using the following entries:

	I	II	III
Pattern:	U	U	U
Angle:	45	−30	90
Spacing:	3	2	5
Double:	Y	N	N
	Fig. (h)	Fig. (i)	Fig. (j)

9 Finally enter **HATCH <R>** and:
   prompt   Enter pattern name...
   enter   **S <R>** – the solid option
   prompt   Select objects
   respond   **pick four lines of small square then right-click** and: a solid hatch pattern is added – Fig. (k).

10 The solid hatch pattern is new to Release 14.

11 This drawing does not need to be saved.

User-defined hatch patterns – pick points method

1   Refer to Figure 25.2 and:
   a) erase all hatching
   b) erase squares not required
   c) add squares and circles as shown – size not important.

2   With layer Sect current, pick the HATCH icon and:
   prompt   boundary hatch dialogue box
   respond   1   check/alter:
               a) pattern type: user-defined – should be
               b) angle: 45
               c) spacing: 3
            2   **pick Pick Points<**
   prompt   Select internal point
   respond   **pick any point within first square**
   prompt   various prompts at command line
   then   Select internal point
   respond   **right-click**
   prompt   Boundary Hatch dialogue box
   respond   **Preview–Continue–Apply**
   and   hatching added to square – Fig. (a).

3   Using the HATCH icon with the pick points option from the boundary hatch dialogue box, add hatching using the points indicated in Figure 25.2. The only 'problem' is hatching the outer square – Figs (d) and (e) – two pick points are required.

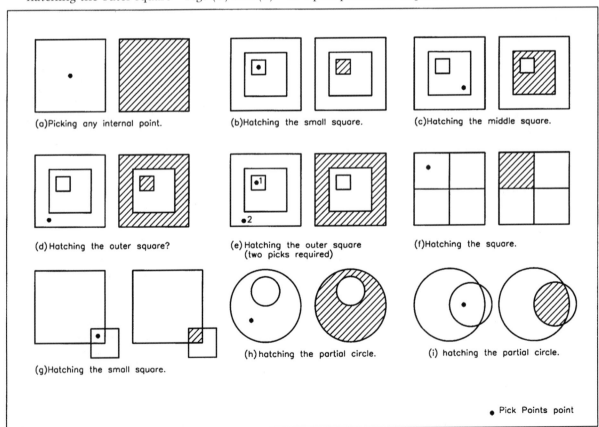

(a) Picking any internal point.

(b) Hatching the small square.

(c) Hatching the middle square.

(d) Hatching the outer square?

(e) Hatching the outer square (two picks required)

(f) Hatching the square.

(g) Hatching the small square.

(h) hatching the partial circle.

(i) hatching the partial circle.

• Pick Points point

Figure 25.2   User-defined hatching using the pick points method.

Select objects vs pick points

With two options available for hatching, new users to this type of boundary hatch command may be confused as to whether they should select objects or pick points. In general the pick points option is the simpler to use, and will allow complex shapes to be hatched with a single pick within the area to be hatched. To demonstrate the effect:

1 Erase all objects from the screen and refer to Figure 25.3.

2 Draw two sets of intersecting circles – any size. We want to hatch the intersecting area of the three circles.

3 Select the HATCH icon and from the boundary hatch dialogue box set: user-defined, angle of 45, spacing of 3, then:
 a) pick the select objects option
 b) pick the three circles
 c) preview–continue–apply – Fig. (a).

4 Select the HATCH icon again and:
 a) pick pick points option
 b) pick any point within the area to be hatched
 c) preview–continue–apply – Fig. (b).

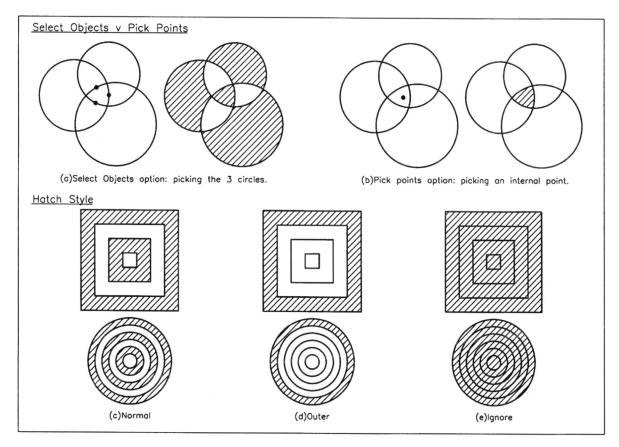

Select Objects v Pick Points

(a)Select Objects option: picking the 3 circles. (b)Pick points option: picking an internal point.

Hatch Style

(c)Normal   (d)Outer   (e)Ignore

Figure 25.3 Using the hatch command.

Hatch style

AutoCAD has a hatch style option which allows the user to control three 'variants' of the hatch command. To demonstrate the hatch style, refer to Figure 25.3 and draw:
a) a 70 sided square with three smaller squares 'inside it'
b) six concentric circles, smallest radius being 5
c) copy the squares and circles to two other areas of the screen.

1 Select the HATCH icon and:

prompt	Boundary Hatch dialogue box
check	user-defined, angle: 45, spacing: 3
then	**pick Advanced...**
prompt	advanced options dialogue box
note	*a*) boundary style 'picture'
	b) style: normal
respond	**pick OK**
prompt	Boundary Hatch dialogue box
respond	**pick Select Objects<**
prompt	Select objects at command line
respond	**window the first square and circle then right-click**
then	Preview–Continue–Apply – Fig. (c).

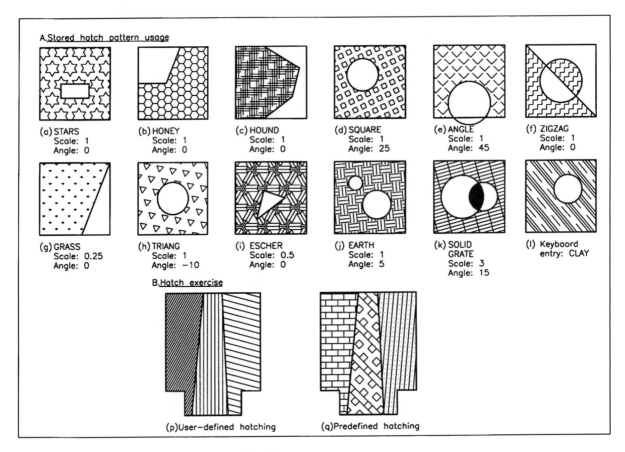

Figure 25.4 Using predefined (stored) hatch patterns.

2   Repeat the HATCH icon selection and:
    a) pick Advanced
    b) alter style to outer then pick OK
    c) select objects and window the second square and circle
    d) apply to give Fig. (d).

3   Using the Boundary Hatch dialogue box with the Advanced options, alter the style to ignore, then hatch the third square and circle – Fig. (e).

4   Note: it is usual to leave the style at 'normal' and the user controls the hatch area by picking the relevant points within the area to be hatched.

5   Save if required, but we will not use this drawing again.

R14's predefined hatch patterns

Release 14 has several stored hatch patterns which can be accessed using the command line HATCH entry or from the Boundary Hatch dialogue box, which is slightly easier. With predefined hatch patterns, the user specifies:
a) the scale of the pattern
b) the angle of the pattern.

1   Open your standard sheet, refer to Figure 25.4(A) and:
    a) draw a 50 unit square
    b) multiple copy the square to 11 other places on the screen
    c) add other lines and circles as required.

2   Select the HATCH icon and:
    prompt   Boundary Hatch dialogue box
    with   `pattern type: predefined`
    respond   **pick Pattern...**
    prompt   hatch pattern palette
    respond   *either*   scroll and pick STARS
                or   pick Next and then the STARS icon – Figure 25.5
    then   pick OK
    prompt   Boundary Hatch dialogue box
    with   Pattern: STARS

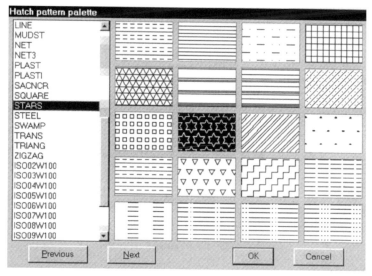

Figure 25.5

respond   1 scale: 1
           2 angle: 0 – Figure 25.6
           3 pick pick points
           4 select any internal point in first square
           5 right-click
           6 preview–continue–apply – Fig. (a).

3 Repeat the HATCH icon selection and using the following hatch pattern names, scales and angles, add hatching to the other squares using the pick points option:

Figure	Pattern	Scale	Angle
b	HONEY	1	0
c	HOUND	1	0
d	SQUARE	1	25
e	ANGLE	1	45
f	ZIGZAG	1	0
g	GRASS	0.25	0
h	TRIANG	1	−10
i	ESCHER	0.5	0
j	EARTH	1	5
k	SOLID		
	GRATE	3	15

4 Finally enter **HATCH <R>** and the command line and:
   prompt   `Enter pattern name[...]<GRATE>`
   enter   **CLAY <R>**
   prompt   `scale for pattern` and enter: **2 <R>**
   prompt   `angle for pattern` and enter: **−50 <R>**
   prompt   `select objects` and: **pick as required** – Fig. (1).

5 Save if required.

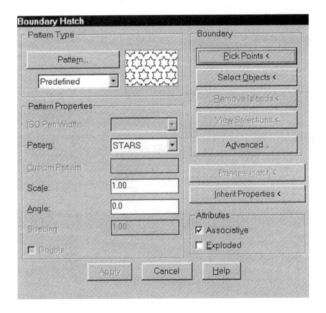

Figure 25.6

Hatch exercise

1 Open the A:USEREX and copy the component to another part of the screen. Refer to Figure 25.4(B). Layer Sect current.

2 Add the following hatching using the pick points option:

User-defined	*Predefined*
1 angle: 60, spacing: 2	1 BRICK, scale: 1, angle: 0
2 angle: 90, spacing: 4	2 SACNCR, scale: 2, angle: 40
3 angle: −15, spacing: 6	3 BOX, scale: 1, angle: 45

Save this exercise if required, but not as A:USEREX.

Associative hatching

Release 14 has associative hatching, i.e. of the hatch boundary is altered, the hatching within the boundary will be 'regenerated' to fill the new boundary limits. Associative hatching is applicable to both user-defined and predefined hatch patterns, irrespective of whether the select objects or pick points option was used. We will demonstrate the effect by example so:

1 Open A:STDA3 standard sheet, refer to Figure 25.7 and draw squares and circles as displayed. Note that I have drawn two sets of each squares to demonstrate the 'before and after' effect.

2 Make layer Sect current.

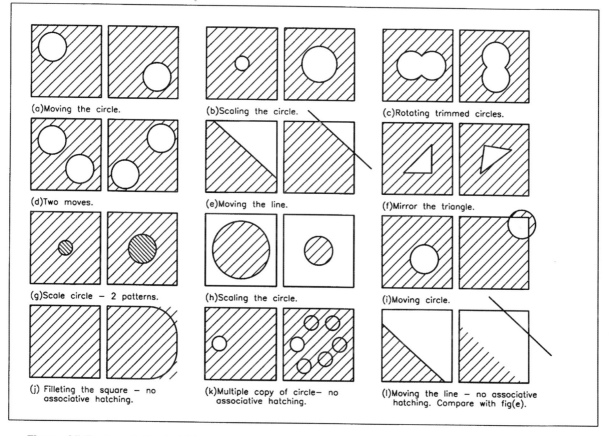

Figure 25.7 Associative hatching.

3   With the HATCH icon:
    a) pattern: user-defined; angle: 45; spacing: 5
    b) attributes: • associative ON, i.e. tick in box
                        • explode OFF, i.e. no tick in box
    c) add hatching to the first square.

4   Select the MOVE icon and:
    a) pick the circle in the first square
    b) move it to another position in the square
    c) hatching 'changes' – Fig. (a), i.e. it is associative.

5   Figure 25.7 displays some associative hatching effects, which you should try for yourself.
    The effects are:
    b) scaling the circle
    c) rotating two trimmed circles
    d) two circle moves
    e) moving the line
    f) mirror the triangle
    g) scaling the circle with two hatch areas
    h) scaling the circle
    i) moving the circle.

6   Associative hatch 'quirks'.
    Associative hatching does not occur with every modify operation as is displayed in
    Figure 25.7 with:
    j) filleting the square
    k) multiple copy of the circle
    l) moving the line – compare with Fig. (e) – why?

7   Task.
    Investigate the following:
    a) associative hatch OFF
    b) exploding hatching.

Modifying hatching

Hatching which has been added to an object can be modified, i.e. the angle, spacing or
scale can be altered, or the actual pattern changed.

1   Open A:STDA3 and refer to Figure 25.8(A). Display the MODIFY II toolbar.

2   Draw a square with two trimmed circles inside it.

3   Use the HATCH icon to add hatching to the square with user-defined pattern; angle: 45;
    spacing: 8 – Fig. (a); and check that associative hatching is on.

4   Menu bar with **Modify–Object–Hatch** and:
    prompt   Select hatch object
    respond   **pick the hatching**
    prompt   Hatchedit dialogue box
    respond   1   alter angle to –45
                2   alter spacing to 4
                3   pick apply – Fig. (b).

5 Select the EDIT HATCH icon from the Modify II toolbar and:
   prompt   `Select hatch object`
   respond   **pick the altered hatching**
   prompt   Hatchedit dialogue box
   respond   1 pattern type: predefined
               2 pick TRIANG
               3 scale: 1 and angle: 0
               4 apply – Fig. (c).

6 Rotate the trimmed circles by 45° – Fig. (d).

7 Using the Edit Hatch icon:
   a) pick pattern type: ESCHER
   b) scale: 0.6 and angle: 15 – Fig. (e).

8 Edit the hatching to user-defined, angle: 0, spacing: 2 – Fig. (f).

9 Scale the circles by 1.5 – Fig. (g). Zoom needed?

10 Move the circles – Fig. (h).

11 Finally: *a*) scale the circles by 0.667
                b) move the circles into the square
                c) change hatch pattern to SOLID
                d) Fig. (i).

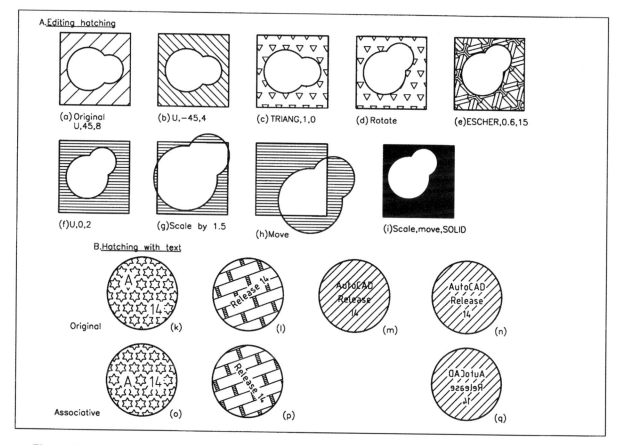

Figure 25.8 Modifying hatching and hatching with text.

Text and hatching

Text which is placed in an area to be hatched can be displayed with a 'clear border' around it.

1   Refer to Figure 25.8(B) and draw four 50 diameter circles.

2   Add any suitable text as shown. This text can have any height, rotation angle, position, etc.

3   With the HATCH icon:
    a) predefined: STARS, scale: 0.75, angle: 0
    b) pick points and pick any point in first circle
    c) apply – Fig. (k).

4   Use the HATCH icon with:
    a) predefined: BRSTONE, scale: 1, angle: 20
    b) pick points and pick any point inside second circle
    c) apply – Fig. (l).

5   HATCH icon using:
    a) user-defined at 45 with 4 spacing
    b) select objects and pick third circle only
    c) apply – Fig. (m).

6   Final HATCH with:
    a) user-defined, angle: 45, spacing: 4
    b) select objects and pick fourth circle **and** text items
    c) apply – Fig. (n).

7   Associative hatching works with text items:
    Fig. (o): moving the two items of text
    Fig. (p): rotating the text item
    Fig. (q): mirroring the text item.

8   Save if required – the exercise is complete.

Summary

1   Hatching is a draw command, activated:
    a) from the menu bar
    b) by icon selection
    c) with keyboard entry – HATCH or BHATCH.

2   AutoCAD has three types of hatch pattern:
    a) user-defined: this is line only hatching. The user specifies the angle for the hatch lines, the spacing between these lines and whether the hatching is to be single or double, i.e. cross-hatching
    b) predefined: these are stored hatch patterns. The user specifies the pattern scale and angle
    c) custom: are patterns designed by the user, but are outwith the scope of this book.

3   The hatch boundary can be determined by:
    a) selecting the objects which make the boundary
    b) picking an internal point within the hatch area.

4   Hatching is a single object and can be exploded.

5 Release 14 has associative hatching which allows the added hatching to change when the hatch boundary changes.

6 Added hatching can be edited.

Assignments

Some AutoCAD users may not use the hatch process in their draughting work, but they should still be familiar with it. The pick points option makes hatching fairly easy and for this reason I have included four interesting exercises for you to attempt. These should test all your existing CAD draughting skills.

1 Activity 14: Cover plate.
A relatively simple drawing to complete. The MIRROR command is useful and the hatching should give no problems. Add text and the dimensions.

2 Activity 15: Protected bearing housing.
Four views to complete, two with hatching. A fairly easy drawing.

3 Activity 16: Steam expansion box.
This activity has proved very popular in my previous books and is easier to complete than it would appear. Create the outline from lines and circles, trimming the circles as required. The complete component uses many commands, e.g. offset, fillet, mirror, etc. The hatching should not be mirrored – why?

4 Activity 17: Gasket cover.
An interesting exercise to complete. Draw the 'left view' which consists only of circles – layers correctly. The right view can be completed using offset, trim and mirror. Do not dimension.

Chapter 26

Point, polygon and solid

These are three useful draw commands which will be demonstrated by example, so:

1 Open A:STDA3 standard sheet with layer out current.

2 Activate the Draw, Modify and Object Snap toolbars.

3 Refer to Figure 26.1.

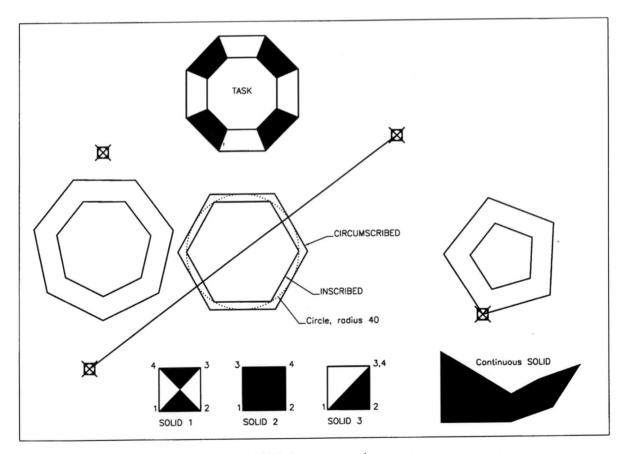

Figure 26.1 The POINT, POLYGON and SOLID draw commands.

Point

A point is an object whose size and appearance is controlled by the user.

1 From the Draw toolbar select the POINT icon and:
prompt   Point and enter: **50,50 <R>**
prompt   Point and enter: **60,200 <R>**
prompt   Point and **ESC** to end command.

2 Two point objects will be displayed in red on the screen. You may have to toggle the grid off to 'see' these points?

3 From the menu bar select **Format–Point Style** and:
prompt   Point Style dialogue box as shown in Figure 26.2
respond   1 pick point style indicated
    2 set point size to 5%
    3 check: set size relative to screen
    4 pick OK.

4 Menu bar with **Draw–Point–Multiple Point** and:
prompt   Point and enter: **330,85 <R>**
prompt   Point and enter: **270,210 <R>**
prompt   Point and **ESC**.
The screen will now display two additional points in the selected style.

6 *a*) At command line enter **REDRAW <R>** – no change
 b) At command line enter **REGEN <R>** – all four points are displayed with the new style.

7 Select the LINE icon and:
prompt   From point
respond **Snap to Node icon and pick lower left point**
prompt   To point
respond **Snap to Node icon and pick upper right point**
prompt   To point and right-click.

8 Task:
 a) set a new point style and size then REGEN the screen
 b) restore the previous point style and size the regenerated.

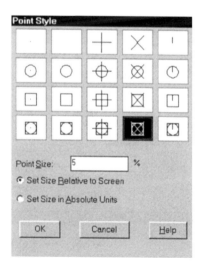

Figure 26.2 The Point Style dialogue box.

Polygon

A polygon is a multi-sided figure, each side having the same length and can be drawn by the user specifying:
a) a centre point and an inscribed/circumscribed radius
b) the endpoints of an edge of the polygon.

A polygon is a POLYLINE type object and has the 'properties' of polylines – see the next chapter.

1 Select the POLYGON icon from the draw toolbar and:

   prompt   Number of sides<4> and enter: **6 <R>**
   prompt   Edge/<Center of polygon>
   respond **Snap to Midpoint icon and pick the line**
   prompt   Inscribed in circle/Circumscribed about circle(I/C)
   enter   **I <R>** – the inscribed (default) option
   prompt   Radius of circle and enter: **40 <R>**.

2 Repeat the POLYGON icon selection and:
   prompt   Number of sides<6> and enter: **6 <R>**
   prompt   Edge/<Center...
   respond **Snap to Midpoint icon and pick the line**
   prompt   Inscribed/Circumscribed...
   enter   **C <R>** – the circumscribed option
   prompt   Radius of circle and enter: **40 <R>**.

3 The screen will display an inscribed and circumscribed circle drawn relative to a 40 radius circle as shown in Figure 26.1. These hexagonal polygons can be considered as equivalent to:
a) inscribed: ACROSS CORNERS (A/C)
b) circumscribed: ACROSS FLATS (A/F).

4 From the menu bar select **Draw–Polygon** and:
   prompt   Number of sides<6> and enter: **5 <R>**
   prompt   Edge/<Center... and enter: **E <R>** – the edge option
   prompt   First endpoint of edge
   respond **Snap to Node icon and pick right-most point**
   prompt   Second endpoint of edge
   enter   **@50<15 <R>**.

5 At the command line enter **POLYGON <R>** and:
a) number of sides: 7
b) edge/center: E
c) first point: 60,100
d) second point: @30<25.

6 Using the OFFSET icon, set an offset distance of 15 and:
a) offset the five-sided polygon 'inwards'
b) offset the seven-sided polygon 'outwards'.

Solid (or more correctly 2D solid)

A command which 'fills-in' lined shapes, the appearance of the final shape being determined by the pick point order.

1   With the snap on, draw three squares of side 30, towards the lower part of the screen – Figure 26.1.

2   Menu bar with **Draw–Surfaces–2D Solid** and:
   prompt   First point and pick point 1 of SOLID 1
   prompt   Second point and pick point 2
   prompt   Third point and pick point 3
   prompt   Fourth point and pick point 4
   prompt   Third point and right-click to end command.

3   At the command line enter **SOLID <R>** and:
   prompt   First point and pick point 1 of SOLID 2
   prompt   Second point and pick point 2
   prompt   . . . and pick points 3 and 4 in the order displayed.

4   Activate the SOLID command and with SOLID 3 pick points 1–4 in the order given, i.e. 3 and 4 are the same points.

5   The three squares demonstrate how 3 and 4 sided shapes can be solid filled.

6   Using the SOLID command enter the following:
   First point: 300,10
   Second point: @0,50
   Third point: 350,10
   Fourth point: 350,30
   Third point: 380,20
   Fourth point: 370,40
   Third point: 400,50
   Fourth point: 400,50
   Third point: right-click.

7   These last entries demonstrate how continuous filled 2D shapes can be created.

Task

1   *a*) Draw an eight-sided polygon, centre at 160,240, circumscribed in a 40 radius circle.
   b) Offset the polygon inwards by a distance of 15.
   c) Use the SOLID command to produce the effect in Figure 26.1.
   d) A running object snap to endpoint will help.

2   What are the minimum and maximum number of sides allowed with the POLYGON command?

3   From the menu bar select **Tools–Drawing Aids** and:
   a) set Solid Fill to OFF, i.e. no X in box
   b) REDRAW the screen – any change?
   c) REGEN the screen – any change?
   d) toggle Solid Fill ON, then regenerate the screen.

Summary

1 A point is an object whose appearance depends on the selection made from the point style dialogue box.

2 Only **one** point style can be displayed on the screen.

3 The snap to node icon is used with points.

4 A polygon is a multi-sided figure having equal sides.

5 A polygon is a polyline type object.

6 Line shapes can be 'solid filled', the appearance of the solid fill being dependent on the order of the pick points.

7 Only three- and four-sided shapes can be solid filled.

Chapter 27

Polylines and splines

A polyline is a single object which can consist of line and arc segments and can be drawn with varying widths. It has its own editing facility and can be activated by icon selection, from the menu bar or by keyboard entry.

A polyline is a very useful and powerful object yet it is probably one of the most under-used draw commands. The demonstration which follows is quite long and several keyboard options are required.

1 Open the A:STDA3 standard sheet with layer Out current. Refer to Figure 27.1 and activate the Draw, Modify, Object Snap and Modify II toolbars.

2 Select the POLYLINE icon from the Draw toolbar and:
  prompt   From point and enter: **15,220 <R>**
  prompt   Arc/Close/Half... and enter: **@50,0 <R>**
  prompt   Arc/Close/Half... and enter: **@0,50 <R>**
  prompt   Arc/Close/Half... and enter: **@−50,0 <R>**
  prompt   Arc/Close/Half... and enter: **@0,−50 <R>**
  prompt   Arc/Close/Half... and right-click.

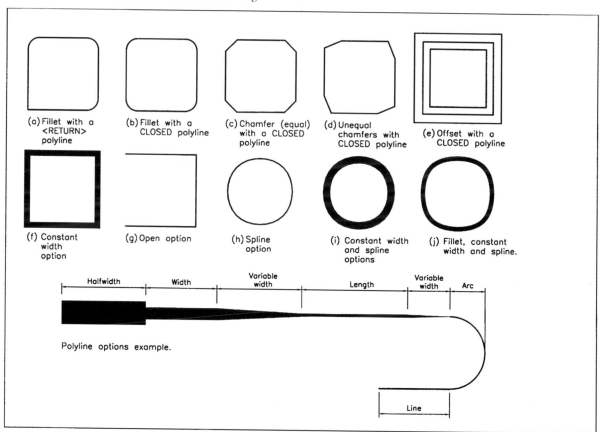

(a) Fillet with a <RETURN> polyline
(b) Fillet with a CLOSED polyline
(c) Chamfer (equal) with a CLOSED polyline
(d) Unequal chamfers with CLOSED polyline
(e) Offset with a CLOSED polyline
(f) Constant width option
(g) Open option
(h) Spline option
(i) Constant width and spline options
(j) Fillet, constant width and spline.

Halfwidth   Width   Variable width   Length   Variable width   Arc

Polyline options example.

Line

Figure 27.1 Polyline demonstration example.

3 From menu bar select **Draw–Polyline** and:
prompt Arc/Close/Half... and enter: **85,220 <R>**
prompt Arc/Close/Half... and enter: **@50<0 <R>** – polar
prompt Arc/Close/Half... and enter: **135,270 <R>** – absolute
prompt Arc/Close/Half... and enter: **@–50,0 <R>** – relative
prompt Arc/Close/Half... and enter: **C <R>** – close option.

4 Select the COPY icon and:
prompt Select objects
respond **pick any point on SECOND square**
and all four lines are highlighted with one pick
then right-click
prompt Base point
and multiple copy the square to eight other parts of the screen.

5 Selecting the appropriate icon:
a) set the fillet radius to 8
b) set chamfer distances to 8.

6 Select the FILLET icon and:
prompt Polyline/Radius...
enter **P <R>** – polyline option
prompt Select 2D polyline
respond **pick any point on first square**
prompt 3 lines were filleted – Fig. (a).

7 Repeat the fillet icon selection and:
a) enter **P <R>**
b) pick any point on second square
c) *prompt*: 4 lines were filleted – Fig. (b).

8 Note that the difference between the two fillet operations is:
Fig. (a) – not a 'closed' polyline, so only three corners filleted
Fig. (b) – a 'closed' polyline, so all four corners filleted.

9 Select the CHAMFER icon and:
a) enter **P <R>**
b) pick any point on third square
c) *prompt* 4 lines were chamfered – Fig. (c).

10 Task. Set chamfer distances to 12 and 5 then CHAMFER the fourth square remembering to enter **P <R>** to activate the polyline option. The result is Fig. (d). Note the orientation of the 12 and 5 chamfer distances.

11 *a*) Set the offset distance to 5 and offset the fifth square 'inwards'.
b) Set the offset distance to 6 and offset the fifth square 'outwards'.
c) The complete square is offset – Fig. (e).

12 Select the EDIT POLYLINE icon from the Modify II toolbar and:
   prompt   Select polyline
   respond **pick the sixth square**
   prompt   Open/Join/Width...
   enter   **W <R>** – the width option
   prompt   Enter new width for all segments
   enter   **4 <R>**
   prompt   Open/Join/Width...
   respond right-click – Fig. (f).

13 Menu bar with **Modify–Object–Polyline** and:
   prompt   Select polyline
   respond **pick the seventh square**
   prompt   Open/Join/Width...
   enter   **O <R>** – the open option
   prompt   Open/Join/Width...
   enter   **X <R>** – exit command option
   and   square displayed with 'last segment' removed – Fig. (g).

14 At the command line enter **PEDIT <R>** and:
   prompt   Select polyline and pick the eighth square
   prompt   options and enter: **S <R>** – the spline option
   prompt   options and enter: **X <R>**
   and   square displayed as a splined curve, in this case a circle – Fig. (h).

15 Activate the polyline edit command, pick the ninth square then:
   a) enter **W <R>** then **5 <R>**
   b) enter **S <R>**
   c) enter **X <R>** – Fig. (i).

16 *a*) set the fillet radius to 12
   b) fillet the tenth square – remember P
   c) use the polyline edit command with options:
     i)   width of 3
     ii) spline
     iii) exit – Fig. (j).

Polyline options

The polyline command has several options displayed at the prompt line when the start point has been selected. These options can be activated by entering the letter corresponding to the option. The options are:

Arc: draws an arc segment
Close: closes a polyline shape to the start point
Halfwidth: user enters start and end halfwidths
Length: length of line segment entered
Undo: undoes the last option entered
Width: user enters the start and end widths
Endpoint: the default option, the user entering, picking or referencing the polyline endpoint.

To demonstrate these options, at the command line enter **PLINE** <R> and:

prompt   From point and enter: **40,80 <R>** – or pick a suitable point
prompt   Options and enter: **H <R>** – the halfwidth option
prompt   Starting half-width<0.00> and enter: **8 <R>**
prompt   Ending half-width<8.00> and enter: **8 <R>**
prompt   Options and enter **@60,0 <R>** – segment endpoint
prompt   Options and enter: **W <R>** – the width option
prompt   Starting width<16.00> and enter **8 <R>**
prompt   Ending width<8.00> and enter **8 <R>**
prompt   Options and enter: **@50,0 <R>** – segment endpoint
prompt   Options and enter: **W <R>**
prompt   Starting width<8.00> and enter: **8 <R>**
prompt   Ending width<8.00> and enter: **2 <R>**
prompt   Options and enter: **@60,0 <R>** – segment endpoint
prompt   Options and enter: **L <R>** – the length option
prompt   Length of line and enter: **75 <R>**
prompt   Options and enter: **W <R>**
prompt   Starting width<2.00> and enter: **2 <R>**
prompt   Ending width<2.00> and enter: **0 <R>**
prompt   Options and enter: **@30,0 <R>** – segment endpoint
prompt   Options and enter: **A <R>** – the arc option
prompt   Arc options and enter: **@0,-50 <R>** – arc endpoint
prompt   Arc options and enter: **L <R>** – back to line option
prompt   Options and enter: **@–50,0 <R>** – segment endpoint
prompt   Options and right-click.

Task

Before leaving this exercise:

1 MOVE the complete polyline shape with a single pick from its start point by **@25,25**.

2 Menu bar with **Tools–Drawing Aids–Solid Fill OFF**, i.e. no tick.

3 REDRAW the screen – any difference?

4 REGEN the screen – any difference?

5 Toggle the solid fill ON, then redraw and regen the screen.

6 This exercise is now complete. Save if required, but it will not be used again.

Line and arc segments

A continuous polyline object can be created from a series of line and arc segments of varying width. In the demonstration which follows we will use several of the options and the final shape will be used in the next chapter. The exercise is given as a rather **LONG** list of options and entries, but persevere with it.

1 Open A:STDA3, layer out current, toolbars to suit.

2 Refer to Figure 27.2, select the Polyline icon and:

Prompt	*Enter*	*Ref*
From point	50,50	pt 1
options	L	
Length of line	45	pt 2
options	W	
Starting width	0	
Ending width	10	
options	@120,0	pt 3
options	A	
arc options	@50,50	pt 4
arc options	L	
options	W	
Starting width	10	
Ending width	0	
options	@0,100	pt 5
options	220,220	pt 6
options	W	
Starting width	0	
Ending width	5	
options	@30<−90	pt 7
options	A	
arc options	@−40,0	pt 8
arc options	@−50,30	pt 9
options	L	
options	W	
Starting width	5	
Ending width	0	
options	50,180	pt 10
options	C	pt 1 again.

3 If your entries are correct the polyshape will be the same as that shown in Figure 27.2. Mistakes with polylines can be rectified as each segment is being constructed with the **U** (undo) option. Both the line and arc segments have their own option entries.

4 Repeat the polyline icon selection and:

Prompt	*Enter*
from point	80,120
options	A
arc options	W
starting width	0
ending width	5
arc options	@60<0
arc options	W
starting width	5
ending width	15
arc options	@20,20
arc options	right-click.

5 Save the two polyshapes as **A:POLYEX** for the next chapter.

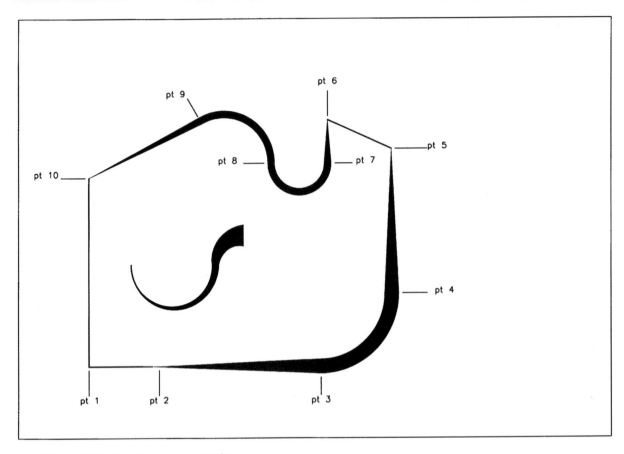

Figure 27.2 Polyline shape exercise.

Polyline tasks

Polyline shapes can be used with the modify commands. To demonstrate their use, open your A:STDA3 standard sheet and refer to Figure 27.3.

1 Draw a 100 closed polyline square and use the sizes given to complete the component in Fig. (a). It is easier than you may think. Commands are OFFSET, CHAMFER, FILLET.

2 Draw a 100 closed polyline square of width 7. Use the sizes from the first exercise to complete a solid filled component – Fig. (b).

3 Draw two 50 sided polyline squares each of width 5 but:
   a) first square to be drawn as four lines and closed with <RETURN>
   b) second square to be closed with close option.
   Note the difference at the polyline start point – Fig. (c).

4 Polylines can be trimmed and extended. Try these operations with an 'arrowhead' type polyline with starting width 10 and ending width 0 – Fig. (d).

5 *a*) Draw a polyline arc with following entries:

Prompt	Enter
from point	pick to suit
options	A
arc options	W
starting width	0
ending width	5
arc options	CE
center point	@0,–30
options	A
included angle	270
options	right-click

   b) Draw a donut with:
      inside diameter: 50
      outside diameter: 70
      centre: pick to suit
   c) draw two lines and trim the donut to these lines
   d) decide which method is easier – Fig. (e).

6 No need to save these tasks.

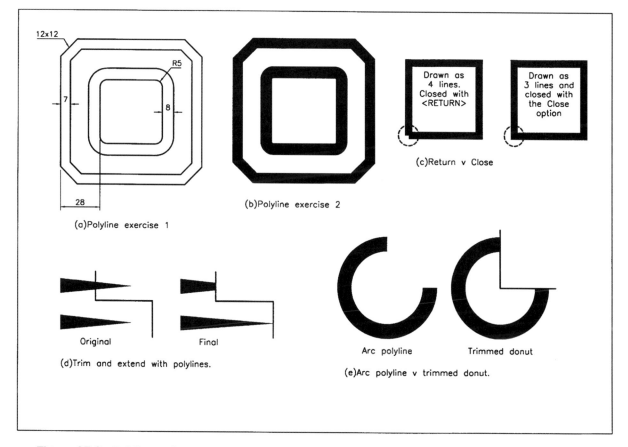

Figure 27.3 Polyline tasks.

Splines

A spline is a smooth curve which passes through a given set of points. These points can be picked, entered as coordinates or referenced to existing objects. The spline is drawn as a non-uniform rational B-spline or **NURBS**. Splines have uses in many CAD areas, e.g. car body design, contour mapping, etc. At our level we will only investigate the 2D spline curve.

1 Open your standard sheet or clear all objects from the screen.

2 Refer to Figure 27.4 and with layer Cl current, draw two circles:
   a) centre: 80,150 with radius: 50
   b) centre: 280,150 with radius: 25.

3 Layer Out current and select the SPLINE icon from the Draw toolbar and:
   prompt   `Object/<Enter first point>`
   respond **Snap to Center icon and pick larger circle**
   prompt   `Enter point` and enter: **90,220 <R>**
   prompt   `Close/Fit/Tolerance...` and enter: **110,80 <R>**
   prompt   `Close/Fit...` and enter: **130,220 <R>**
   prompt   `Close/Fit...` and enter: **150,80 <R>**
   prompt   `Close/Fit...` and enter: **170,220 <R>**
   prompt   `Close/Fit...` and enter: **190,80 <R>**
   prompt   `Close/Fit...` and enter: **210,220 <R>**
   prompt   `Close/Fit...` and enter: **230,80 <R>**
   prompt   `Close/Fit...` and enter: **250,220 <R>**

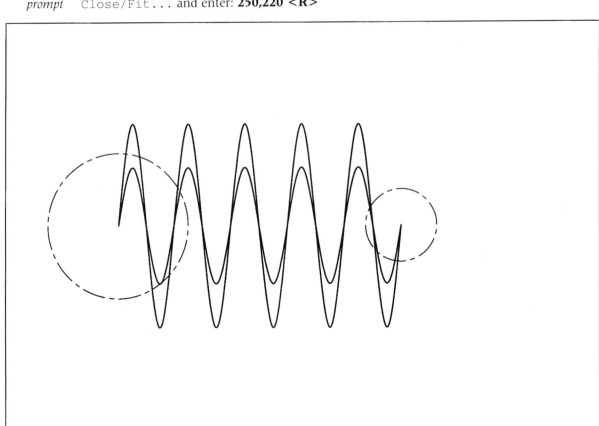

Figure 27.4 Spline curve exercise.

prompt	Close/Fit... and enter: **270,80 <R>**
prompt	Close/Fit... and right-click
prompt	Enter start tangent
respond	**pick larger circle centre point**
prompt	Enter end tangent
respond	**pick smaller circle centre point**.

4 Menu bar with **Draw–Spline** and:

prompt	Object/<Enter first point>
respond	**Snap to center of larger circle**
prompt	Enter point and enter: **90,190 <R>**
prompt	Close/Fit... and enter: **110,110 <R>**
prompt	Close/Fit...
respond	enter following coordinate pairs:

130,190	150,110	170,190	190,110	210,190
230,110	250,190	270,110		

then	right-click
prompt	Enter start tangent and pick large circle centre
prompt	Enter end tangent and pick small circle centre.

5 At this stage save drawing as **A:SPLINEX** for next chapter.

6 The spline options have not been considered at this introductory level, although they should be obvious.

Summary

1 A polyline is a single object which can consist of line and arc segment of varying width.

2 A polyshape which is to be closed should be completed with the close option.

3 Polyline shapes can be chamfered, filleted, trimmed, extended, etc.

4 Polylines have their own edit command – see the next chapter.

5 A spline is **not** a polyline but a NURBS curve with specific properties.

Assignments

Four activities of varying difficulty have been included for you to test your polyline ability.

1 Activity 18: Shapes.
Some basic polyline shapes created from line and arc segments. All relevant sizes are given for you. Snap on helps.

2 Activity 19: Backgammon board.
A slight digression but a nice simple drawing to complete. The filled triangles can be drawn as polylines or 2D solids. The copy and mirror commands are useful.

3 Activity 20: Printed circuit board.
An interesting application of the polyline command. It is harder to complete than you may think, especially with the dimensions being given in ordinate form. Can you add the dimensions given? All the relevant sizes are given on the drawing. Use your discretion when positioning the 'lines'.

4 Activity 21: Two 'components'.
  a) The flat uses polylines for the walls:
    outside: 3 wide; inside: 2 wide.
    The doors can be placed in the walls and the wall can then be trimmed.
  b) An integrated circuit – use your imagination for the hatching.
    The polylines are 5,3,2 and 1 wide.

Chapter 28

Modifying polylines and splines

Polylines have their own special editing facility which gives the user several extra options in addition to the existing modify commands.

1 Open the polyline exercise A:POLYEX and refer to Figure 28.1.

2 Select the EDIT POLYLINE icon from the Modify II toolbar and:
   prompt   Select polyline
   respond **pick any point on the polyline shape**
   prompt   Open/Join/Width...
   respond enter the following in respond to the prompt:

Prompt	Enter	Ref	Options
Open/Join...	W		constant width
new width	3	Fig. (b)	
options	D	Fig. (c)	decurve
options	S	Fig. (d)	spline
options	F	Fig. (e)	fit
options	D	Fig. (f)	
options	O	Fig. (g)	open
options	W		constant width
new width	0	Fig. (h)	
options	S	Fig. (I)	
options	D	Fig. (j)	
options	W		constant width
new width	5	Fig. (k)	
options	X		end command.

The join option

This is a very useful option as it allows several individual polylines to be 'joined' into a single polyline object. Refer to Figure 28.1 and:

1 Use the MIRROR command to mirror the polyarc shape about a vertical line through the right end of the object – ortho on may help, but remember to toggle it off.

2 At the command line enter **PEDIT <R>** and:
   prompt   Select polyline
   respond **pick any point on original polylarc**
   prompt   Close/Join/Width...
   enter   **J <R>**
   prompt   Select objects
   respond **pick the two polyarcs then right-click**
   prompt   2 segments added to polyline
   then   Close/Join/Width...
   enter   **X <R>**.

3 The two arc segments will now be one polyline object.

4 Select the Edit Polyline option and:
   a) pick the mirrored joined polyshape
   b) enter the same options as step 2 **except** enter C(lose) instead of O(pen).

5 Note: when the edit polyline command is activated and a polyline selected, the prompt is:
   a) Open/Join... if the selected polyshape is 'closed'
   b) Close/Join... if the selected polyshape is 'opened'.

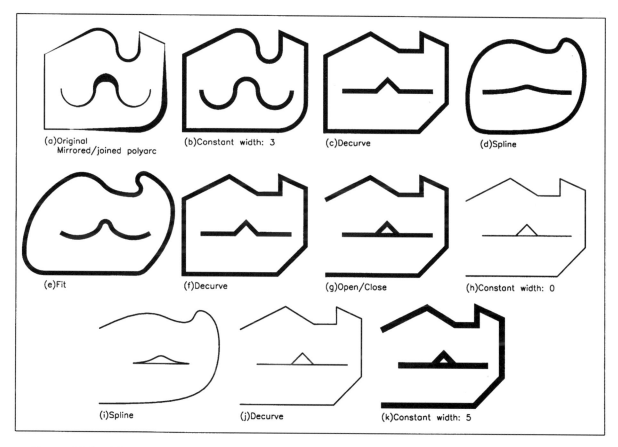

Figure 28.1 Editing polylines with A:POLYEX.

Edit vertex option

The options available with the edit polyline command usually 'redraws' the selected polyshape after each entry, e.g. if **S** is entered at the options prompt, the polyshape will be redrawn as a splined curve. Using the edit vertex option is slightly different from this. When **E** is entered as an option, the user has another set of options. Refer to Figure 28.2 and:

1 Erase all objects from the screen or open A:STDA3.

2 Draw an 80 sided **closed** square polyshape and multiple copy it to three other areas of the screen.

3 *Variable widths.*
    Menu bar with **Modify–Object–Polyline** and:

prompt	Select polyline
respond	**pick the first square**
prompt	Open/Join...
enter	**W <R>** and then: **5 <R>**
prompt	Open/Join/...
enter	**E <R>** – the edit vertex option
prompt	Next/Previous/Break...
and	an X is placed at the start vertex – lower left?
enter	**W <R>**
prompt	Enter staring width<5> and enter: **5 <R>**
prompt	Enter ending width<5> and enter: **0 <R>**
prompt	Next/Previous...
enter	**N <R>** and X moves to next vertex – lower right?
prompt	Next/Previous...
enter	**W <R>**

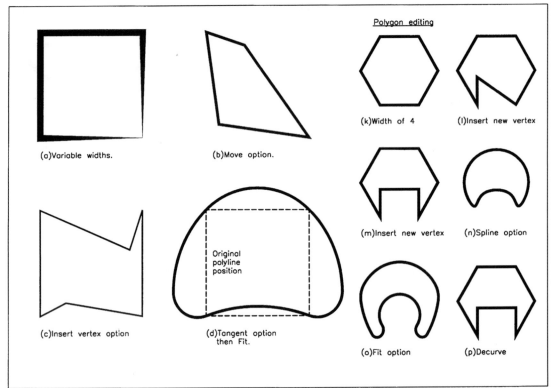

Polygon editing

(a)Variable widths. (b)Move option. (k)Width of 4 (l)Insert new vertex

(c)Insert vertex option (d)Tangent option then Fit. Original polyline position (m)Insert new vertex (n)Spline option

(o)Fit option (p)Decurve

Figure 28.2 Edit vertex option of the edit polyline command.

prompt	Enter starting width and enter: **0 <R>**
prompt	Enter ending width and enter: **5 <R>**
prompt	Next/Previous...
enter	**X <R>** – to exit the edit vertex option
then	**X <R>** – to exit the edit polyline command – Fig. (a).

4 *Moving a vertex.*
Select the edit polyline icon and:
a) pick the second square
b) enter a constant width of 2

c) *enter*	**E <R>** – the edit vertex option
prompt	Next/Previous...
enter	**N <R>** until X at lower left vertex – probably is?
then	**M <R>** – the move option
prompt	Enter new location
enter	**@10,10 <R>**
prompt	Next/Previous...
enter	**N <R>** until X at diagonally opposite vertex
then	**M <R>**
prompt	Enter new location and enter: **@–50,–10 <R>**
prompt	Next/Previous...
enter	**X <R>** then **X <R>** – Fig. (b).

5 *Inserting a new vertex.*
At the command line enter **PEDIT <R>** and:
a) pick the third square
b) enter a constant width of 1
c) pick the edit vertex option

d) *enter*	**N <R>** until **X** at lower left vertex then:
prompt	Next/Previous...
enter	**I <R>** – the insert new vertex option
prompt	Enter location of new vertex
enter	**@20,10 <R>**
prompt	Next/Previous...
enter	**N <R>** with X at the opposite diagonal the **I <R>**
prompt	Enter location of new vertex
enter	**@–10,–30 <R>**
then	**X <R>** and **X <R>** – Fig. (c).

6 *Tangent-fit options.*
Activate the Edit Polyline command with the fourth square, set a constant width of 2,
select the edit vertex option with the X at lower left vertex and:

prompt	Next/Previous...
enter	**T <R>** – the tangent option
prompt	Direction of tangent
enter	**20 <R>**
and	note arrowed line direction
prompt	Next/Previous...
enter	**N <R>** until X at lower right vertex
then	**T <R>**
prompt	Direction of tangent
enter	**–20 <R>** – note arrowed line direction
prompt	Next/Previous...
enter	**X <R>**
prompt	Open/Join...
enter	**F <R>**
then	**X <R>** – Fig. (d).

Note: the final fit shape 'passes through' the vertices of the original polyline square.

Editing a polygon

A polygon is a polyline and can therefore be edited with the edit polyline command. To demonstrate the effect:

1 Draw a six-sided polygon inscribed in a 40 radius circle towards the right of the screen.

2 Activate the edit polyline command, pick the polygon then enter the following option sequence:
   a) W then 4 – Fig. (k)
   b) E
   c) N until X at lower left vertex
   d) I
   e) @0,30 – Fig. (l)
   f) I
   g) @40,0 – Fig. (m)
   h) X
   i) S – Fig. (n)
   j) F – Fig. (o)
   k) D – Fig. (p)
   l) X.

Editing a spline curve

Spline curves can be edited in a similar manner to polylines, so open drawing A:SPLINEX and refer to Figure 28.3.

1 Select the EDIT SPLINE icon from the Modify II toolbar and:

prompt	Select spline
respond	**pick the larger spline curve**
and	blue grip type boxes appear
prompt	Fit Data/Close...
enter	**F <R>** – the fit data option
and	boxes at each entered vertex of curve
prompt	Add/Close/Delete...
enter	**M <R>** – the move option
prompt	Next/.../<Enter new location>
and	red box at left end of spline
enter	**N <R>** until red box at second from left lower vertex
then	**@0,-50 <R>**
prompt	Next/...
enter	**N <R>** until red box at third from left lower vertex
then	**@0,–50 <R>**
prompt	Next/...
enter	**X <R>**
prompt	Add/Close/Delete...
enter	**D <R>** the delete option
prompt	Select point
respond	**pick the sixth from left vertex then right-click**
prompt	Add/Close... and enter: **X <R>**
prompt	Fit Data... and enter: **X <R>**.

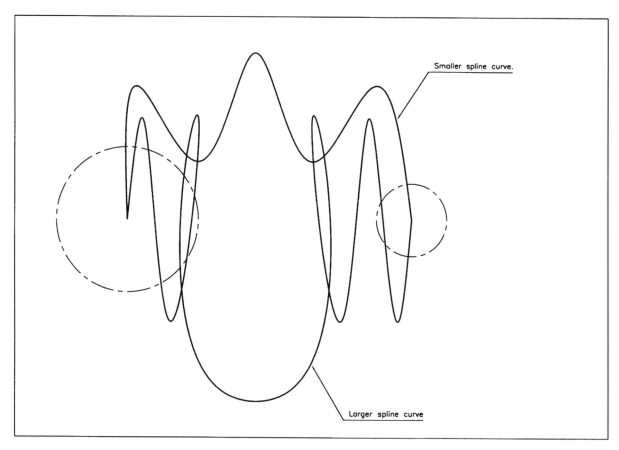

Smaller spline curve.

Larger spline curve

Figure 28.3 Editing the spline curves from A:SPLINEX.

2 Menu bar with **Modify–Object–Spline** and:

prompt	Select spline
respond	**pick the smaller spline**
prompt	Fit Data/Close... and enter: **F <R>**
and	blue boxes at entered vertices
prompt	Add/Close/Delete... and enter: **D <R>**
prompt	Select point and pick third vertex from left
prompt	Select point and pick fourth vertex from left
prompt	Select point and pick fifth vertex from left
prompt	Select point and pick seventh vertex from left
prompt	Select point and right-click
prompt	Add/Close/Delete
enter	**M <R>**
prompt	.../<Enter new location>
enter	**N <R>** until second left vertex is red
then	**@0,50 <R>**
then	**N <R>** until fourth left vertex is red
then	**@0,75 <R>**
then	**N <R>** until sixth left vertex is red
then	**@0,50 <R>**
then	**X <R>** and **X <R>** and **X <R>**.

3 Save modified drawing if required.

Summary

1   Polylines and splines can be modified using the appropriate icon selection.

2   Each edit command has several options.

3   This chapter has been an introduction only to the edit commands.

Chapter 29

Divide, measure and break

These are three useful commands which will be demonstrated by example, so:

1 Open your standard sheet with layer Out current.

2 Activate the Draw, Modify, Dimension and Object Snap toolbars.

3 Refer to Figure 29.1 and set the point style and size indicated (Format–Point Style).

4 Draw the following objects:
   a) LINE: from: 20,250 to: @65<15
   b) CIRCLE: centre: 125,250 with radius: 25
   c) POLYLINE: from: 170,270 to: @50,0 arc to: @0,−50 line to: @−30,0
   d) SPLINE: draw any spline to suit.

5 Copy the four objects below the originals.

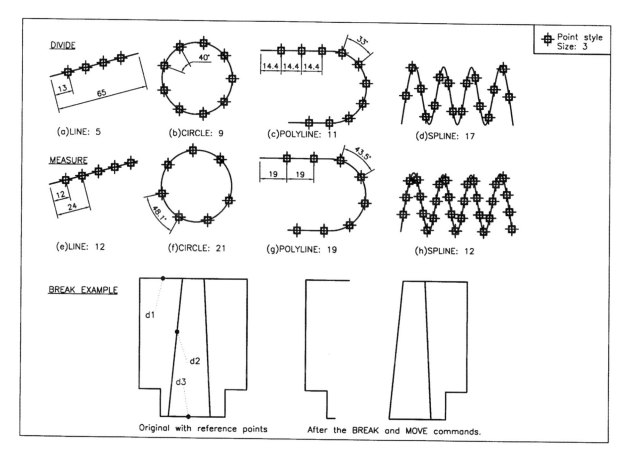

Figure 29.1 The DIVIDE, MEASURE and BREAK commands.

Divide

A selected object is 'divided' into an equal number of segments, the user specifying this number. The current point style is 'placed' at the division points.

1 Menu bar with **Draw–Point–Divide** and:

  prompt   Select object to divide
  respond **pick the line**
  prompt   <Number of segments>/Block
  enter   **5 <R>**.

The line will be divided into five equal parts, and a point is placed at the end of each segment length – Fig. (a).

2 At the command line enter **DIVIDE <R>** and:

  prompt   Select object to divide
  respond **pick the circle**
  prompt   <Number of segments>/Block
  enter   **9 <R>**.

The circle will be divided into nine equal arc lengths and nine points placed on the circle circumference – Fig. (b).

3 Use the DIVIDE command with:
  a) POLYLINE: 11 segments – Fig. (c)
  b) SPLINE: 17 segments – Fig. (d).

Measure

A selected object is 'divided' into a number of user-specified equal lengths and the current point style is placed at each measured length.

1 Menu bar with **Draw–Point–Measure** and:

  prompt   Select object to measure
  respond **pick the line** – the copied one of course!
  prompt   <Segment length>/Block
  enter   **12 <R>**.

The line is divided into measured lengths of 12 units from the line start point – Fig. (e).

2 At command line enter **MEASURE <R>** and:

  prompt   Select object to measure
  respond **pick the circle**
  prompt   <Segment length>/Block
  enter   **21 <R>**.

The circle circumference will display points every 21 units from the start point, which is where? – Fig. (f).

3 Use the MEASURE command with:
  a) POLYLINE: segment length of 19 – Fig. (g)
  b) SPLINE: segment length of 12 – Fig. (h).

4 Task. Dimension as shown – snap to node for points.

5 This completes the exercise – no need to save.

Break

This command allows a selected object to be broken at a specified point – similar to trim, but no erase effect.

1 Open A:USEREX and refer to Figure 29.1. We want to split the component into two parts and will use the break command to achieve the desired effect.

2 Select the BREAK icon from the modify toolbar and:
prompt   Select object
respond   **pick line d1**
prompt   Enter second point (or F for first point)
enter   **F <R>**
prompt   Enter first point
respond   **Snap to Endpoint of 'top' of line d2**
prompt   Enter second point
enter   **@ <R>.**

3 At command line enter **BREAK <R>** and:
prompt   Select object and: **pick line d3**
prompt   Enter first point (or...) and enter: **F <R>**
prompt   Enter first point
respond   **Snap to Endpoint of 'lower' end of line d2**
prompt   Enter second point and enter: **@ <R>.**

4 Now MOVE line d1 and the other lines to the 'right' of d1 (seven lines in all) from any point, by @50,0.

5 Note: the @ entry at the second point prompt, ensures that the first and second points are the same.

Summary

1 Objects can be divided:
a) into an equal number of parts – DIVIDE
b) into equal segment lengths – MEASURE.

2 The break command allows objects to be 'broken' at specified points.

3 The three commands can be used on line, circle, arc, polyline and spline objects.

Chapter 30

Lengthen, align and stretch

Three useful commands which will greatly increase drawing efficiency. To demonstrate the commands, open the A:STDA3 standard sheet and refer to Figure 30.1.

Lengthen

This command will alter the length of lines, arcs, polylines, rays and splines but cannot be used with CLOSED objects.

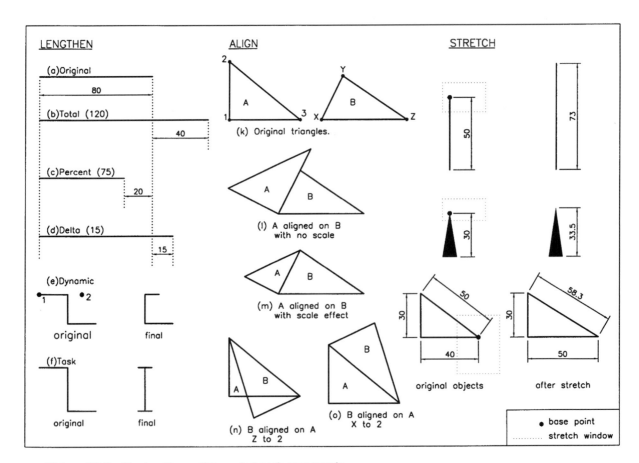

Figure 30.1   The lengthen, align and stretch commands.

1 Draw a horizontal line of length 80 – Fig. (a) – and multiple copy it to three other places.

2 Select the LENGTHEN icon from the Modify toolbar and:
   prompt   DElta/Percent/Total/DYnamic/<Select object>
   enter   **T <R>** – the total option
   prompt   Angle/<Enter total length>
   enter   **120 <R>**
   prompt   <Select object to change>/Undo
   respond **pick the second line** then right-click – Fig. (b).

3 Menu bar with **Modify–Lengthen** and:
   prompt   DElta/Percent...
   enter   **P <R>** – the percent option
   prompt   Enter percent length<100.00>
   enter   **75 <R>**
   prompt   <Select object to change>
   respond **pick the next line** then right-click – Fig. (c).

4 At the command line enter **LENGTHEN <R>** and:
   enter   DE <R> – the delta option
   enter   15 <R>
   respond pick the next line – Fig. (d).

5 *a*) Draw a Z-shape as Fig. (e)
   b) activate the lengthen command and:
     i)   enter DY <R> – the dynamic option
     ii)   pick point 1 on the line
     iii) move and pick a point 2
   c) the original shape is altered.

6 Task:
   a) dimension the lines (a), (b), (c) and (d)
   b) use the dynamic option of the lengthen command to produce the I-shape from the Z-shape – Fig. (f)
   c) use the lengthen command with a dimensioned line – will the added dimension be lengthened?

Align

A very powerful command which combines the move and rotate commands into one operation.

1 Draw any two triangles in the orientation shown – Fig. (k). Copy these two triangles to four other areas of the screen – the snap ON will help.

2 We want to align:
   a) side 13 of triangle A on to side XY of triangle B
   b) side XZ of triangle B on to side 23 of triangle A.

3 Menu bar with **Modify–3D Operation–Align** and:
   prompt   Select objects
   respond **pick the three lines of triangle A** then right-click
   prompt   Specify 1st source point and **pick point 1**
   prompt   Specify 1st destination point and **pick point X**
   prompt   Specify 2nd source point and **pick point 3**
   prompt   Specify 2nd destination point and **pick point Y**
   prompt   Specify 3rd source point and right-click
   prompt   Scale object to alignment points
   enter   **N <R>**.

4 Triangle A is moved and rotated onto triangle B with sides 13 and XY in alignment – Fig. (l).

5 Repeat the align selection and:
   a) pick the three lines of the next triangle A then right-click
   b) pick the same source and destination points as step 3
   c) enter **Y <R>** at the scale prompt
   d) triangle A will be aligned on to triangle B and side 13 scaled to side XY – Fig. (m).

6 At the command line enter **ALIGN <R>** and:
   prompt   Select objects
   respond **pick three lines of a triangle B** then right-click
   prompt   Specify 1st source point
   respond **Snap to Midpoint icon and pick line XZ**
   prompt   Specify 1st destination point
   respond **Snap to Midpoint icon and pick line 23**
   prompt   Specify 2nd source point and **pick point Z**
   prompt   Specify 2nd destination point and **pick point 2**
   prompt   Specify 3rd source point and right-click
   prompt   Scale object to alignment points
   enter   **Y <R>**.

7 The selected triangle B will be aligned on to triangle A as Fig. (n).

8 Repeat the align command and:
   a) pick three lines of a triangle B then right-click
   b) midpoint of side XZ as 1st source point
   c) midpoint of side 23 as 1st destination point
   d) point X as 2nd source point
   e) point 2 as 2nd destination point
   f) Y to scale option – Fig. (o).

9 The orientation of the aligned object is thus dependent on the order of selection of the source and destination points.

Stretch

This command does what it says – it 'stretches' objects. If hatching and dimensions have been added to the object to be stretched, they will both be affected by the command – remember that hatch and dimensions are associative.

1 Select a clear area of the drawing screen and draw:
   a) a vertical dimensioned line
   b) a dimensioned variable width polyline
   c) a dimensioned triangle.

2 Select the STRETCH icon from the Modify toolbar and:
prompt	Select object to stretch by crossing-window or crossing-polygon Select objects
enter	**C <R>** – the crossing option
prompt	First corner
respond	**window the top of vertical line and dimension**
prompt	2 found
then	Select objects
respond	**right-click**
prompt	Base point or displacement
respond	**pick top end of line** (endpoint)
prompt	Second point of displacement
enter	**@0,23 <R>**.

3 The line and dimension will be stretched by the entered value.

4 Menu bar with **Modify–Stretch** and:
prompt	Select objects
enter	**C <R>** – crossing option
prompt	First corner
respond	**window the top of polyline with dimension**
then	right-click
prompt	Base point and **pick top end of polyline**
prompt	Second point and enter: **@0,3.5 <R>**.

5 The polyline and dimension are stretched by the entered value.

6 At the command line enter **STRETCH <R>** and:
   a) enter C <R> for the crossing option
   b) window the vertex indicated then right-click
   c) pick indicated vertex as the base point
   d) enter @10,0 as the displacement.

7 The triangle is stretched as are the appropriate dimensions.

Stretch example

1   Open your A:WORKDRG and refer to Figure 30.2.

2   *a*) erase the centre lines
     b) add hatching – own selection
     c) dimension the two lines as shown.

3   Activate the STRETCH command and:
     a) enter C <R> – crossing option
     b) first corner: pick a point P1
     c) second corner: pick a point P2 then right-click
     d) base point: pick any suitable point
     e) second point: enter @15,0 <R>.

4   Repeat the STRETCH command and:
     a) activate the crossing option
     b) pick a point P3 for the first corner
     c) pick a point P4 for the other corner
     d) pick a suitable base point
     e) enter @0,–15 as the second point.

5   The component and dimensions will be stretched as required.

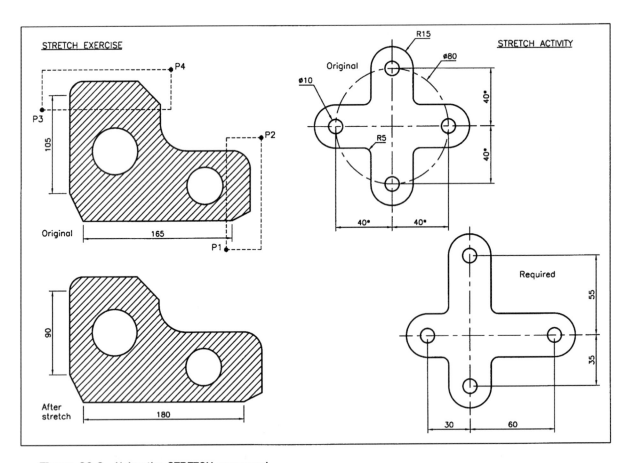

Figure 30.2   Using the STRETCH command.

Stretch activity

Refer to Figure 30.2 and:

1 Draw the original component as shown adding the four * dimensions.

2 Using the STRETCH command only, produce the modified component. The stretch command will need to be used ? times.

3 There is no need to save this activity, but do not exit AutoCAD just yet.

Pickfirst

Entering **W** or **C** to activate the window or crossing option with the modify commands is satisfactory but can be annoying to users. At the start of the book, we toggled a certain variable off which allows window and crossing selections to be obtained without the command line C or W entries.

1 Still with the completed stretch activity on the screen?

2 At the command line enter **PICKFIRST <R>** and:
prompt   New value for PICKFIRST<0> and enter **1 <R>**

3 A pick box will appear on the cursor cross-hairs.

4 *Using pickfirst.*
When pickfirst is activated (i.e. value of 1), the user can obtain window and crossing options without having to enter W or C. To demonstrate the effect:
a) activate the MOVE command
b) pick any point near your component
c) move up or down to the right of the pick point to drag out a window effect and pick a second point. This is a window selection – objects completely within window are highlighted
d) press ESC
e) move command again and pick any point near component
f) move up or down to left of first point and drag out a window.
This gives a crossing effect and all objects within or which cross the window boundary will be highlighted.

5 This window/crossing effect can be used at any time with all of the modify commands.

6 The W/C command line entries are still permissible with PICKFIRST on.

7 Decide for yourself if you want to use this method of selecting object with a window/crossing.

Summary

1 Lengthen will increase/decrease the length of lines, arcs and polylines. There are several options available.

2 Dimensions are not lengthened.

3 Align is a powerful command which combines move and rotate into one operation. The order of selecting points is important.

4 Stretch can be used with lines, polylines and arcs. It does not affect circles.

5 Dimensions and hatching are stretched due to association.

6 The variable PICKFIRST allows window and crossing selections without the keyboard W or C entry.

Chapter 31

Interrogating a drawing

Drawings contain information which may be useful to the user, e.g. coordinate data, distances between points, area of shapes, etc. We will investigate how this information can be obtained, so:

1 Open A:USEREX and refer to Figure 31.1.

2 Draw a circle, centre at: 190,140 and radius: 30.

3 Activate the Inquiry toolbar.

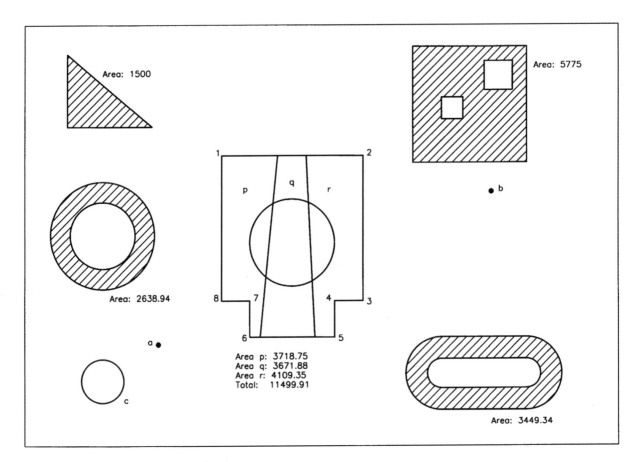

Figure 31.1 Interrogating a drawing.

Point identification

This command displays the coordinates of a selected point.

1 Select the LOCATE POINT icon from the inquiry toolbar and:
   prompt   Point
   respond   **Snap to Midpoint icon and pick line 23**

   The command line area displays:
   X = 240.00 Y = 150.00 Z = 0.00

2 Menu bar with **Tools–Inquiry–ID Point** and:
   prompt   Point
   respond   **Snap to Center icon and pick the circle**
   display   X = 190.00 Y = 140.00 Z = 0.00

3 The command can be activated with **ID <R>** at the command line.

Distance

Returns information about a line between two selected points including the distance and the angle to the horizontal.

1 Select the DISTANCE icon from the Inquiry toolbar and:
   prompt   First point and: **pick point 8** (snap on?)
   prompt   Second point and: **pick point 2**

   The command prompt area will display:
   Distance = 141.42, Angle in XY plane = 45.0,
   Angle from XY plane = 0.0
   Delta X = 100.00, Delta Y = 100.00, Delta Z = 0.00
   (Note: you may have to toggle the text screen – F2.)

2 Menu bar with **Tools–Inquiry–Distance** and:
   prompt   First point and: **pick centre of circle**
   prompt   Second point and: **pick midpoint of line 23**

   The information displayed will be:
   Distance = 50.99, Angle in XY plane = 11.3,
   Angle from XY plane = 0.0
   Delta X = 50.00, Delta Y = 10.00, Delta Z = 0.00

3 Using the DISTANCE command, select point 2 as the first point and point 8 as the second point. Is the displayed information any different from step 1?

4 Entering **DIST <R>** at the command line will activate the command.

List

A command which gives useful information about a selected object.

1 Select the LIST icon from the Inquiry toolbar and:

prompt	`Select objects`
respond	**pick the circle** then right-click
prompt	AutoCAD text window with information about the circle
respond	F2 to flip back to drawing screen.

2 Menu bar with **Tools–Inquiry–List** and:

prompt	`Select objects`
respond	**pick line 12** then right-click
prompt	AutoCAD text window
respond	*a*) F2 to flip back to drawing screen
	b) cancel icon from text window title bar.

3 Figure 31.2 is a screen dump of the AutoCAD Text window display for the two selected objects.

4 LIST at the command line will activate the command.

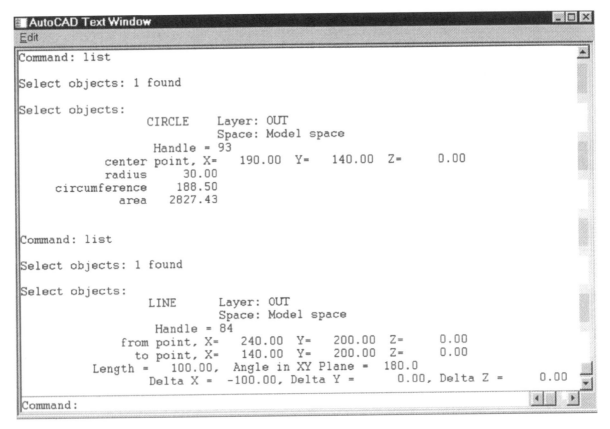

Figure 31.2 AutoCAD text window.

Area

This command will return the area and perimeter for selected shapes or polyline shapes. It has the facility to allow composite shapes to be selected.

1 Select the AREA icon from the Inquiry toolbar and:

prompt   <First point>/Object/Add/Subtract
enter   **O <R>** – the object option
prompt   Select objects
respond **pick the circle**

The command prompt area will display:
Area = 2827.43, Circumference = 188.50 – same as the list command?

2 Menu bar with **Tools–Inquiry–Area** and:

prompt   <From point>/Object...
respond **pick point 1**
prompt   Next point and: **pick point 2**
prompt   Next point and: **pick point 3**
prompt   Next point and:
respond **pick points 4,5,6,7,8** the right-click
prompt   Area = 11500.00, Perimeter = 450.00
Are these figures correct for the shape?

3 At the command line enter **AREA <R>** and:

prompt   <From point>/Object...
enter   **A <R>** – the add option
prompt   First point and: **pick point 1**
prompt   (ADD mode) Next point and **pick point 2**
prompt   (ADD mode) Next point and:
respond pick points 3,4,5,6,7,8 then right-click
prompt   Total area=11500.00
then   <First point>/Object/Subtract
enter   **S <R>** – the subtract option
prompt   <First point>/Object/Add
enter   **O <R>** – the object option
prompt   (SUBTRACT mode) Select objects
respond **pick the circle**
prompt   Total area = 8672.57
then   (SUBTRACT mode) Select objects
respond **ESC** to end command.

4 Is the area value of 8672.57 correct for the outline area minus the circle area?

Time

1 Gives information about the current drawing:
   a) when it was originally created
   b) when it was last updated
   c) the length of time worked on it.

2 The command can be activated from the menu bar with **Tools–Inquiry–Time** or by entering **TIME <R>** at the command line.

3 The command has options of ON, OFF or RESET.

4 A useful command for your boss?

Status

This command gives additional information about the current drawing as well as disk space information. Select the sequence **Tools–Inquiry–Status** to 'see' the status display.

Calculator

1 AutoCAD Release 14 has a built-in calculator which can be used:
   a) to evaluate mathematical expressions
   b) to assist on the calculation of coordinate point data.

2 The mathematical operations obey the usual order of preference with brackets, powers, etc.

3 At the command line enter **CAL <R>** and:
   prompt   Initializing..>> Expression:
   enter   **12.6*(8.2+5.1) <R>**
   prompt   167.58 – is it correct?

4 *enter*   **CAL <R>** and:
   prompt   >>Expression:
   enter   **(5*(7-4))^3.5 <R>**
   prompt   13071.3

5 What is answer to $((7 - 4) + (2 * (8 + 1)))/3$?

Transparent calculator

A transparent command is one which can be used 'while in another command' and is activated from the command line by entering the ' symbol. The calculator command has this transparent ability.

1 Activate the DONUT command and set diameters of 0 and 3, then:

prompt	Center of doughnut
enter	**'CAL <R>** – the transparent calculator command
prompt	>>Expression:
enter	**CEN/2 <R>**
prompt	>>Select entity for CEN snap
respond	**pick the circle**
and	donut at position (a)
prompt	Center of doughnut
enter	**'CAL <R>**
prompt	>>Expression:
enter	**(MID+INT) <R>**
prompt	>>Select entity for MID snap and: **pick line 65**
prompt	>>Select entity for INT snap and: **pick point 8**
and	donut at position (b)
prompt	Center of doughnut and right-click

2 Activate the circle command and:

prompt	Center point and enter: **55,45 <R>**
prompt	Radius
enter	**'CAL <R>**
prompt	>>Expression:
enter	**rad/2 <R>**
prompt	>>Select circle,arc or polyline segment for RAD function
respond	**pick the circle**
and	circle position at (c)

3 Check the donut centre points with the ID command. They should be: (*a*) 95,70; (*b*) 330,175. How are these coordinate values obtained?

Task

1 Refer to Figure 31.1 and create the following (anywhere on the screen, but use SNAP ON to help):

    a) triangle: vertical side: 50
       horizontal side: 60
    b) square: side 80, with two other squares, side 15 and 20 inside
    c) circles: radii 23 and 37 – concentric
    d) polyshape: outside horizontal length 60, outside radius 25, offset 15 'inwards'.

2 Find the shaded areas using the AREA command.

3 Obtain the areas of the three 'vertical strips' of the original USEREX, i.e. without the circle.

Summary

1 Drawings can be 'interrogated' to obtain information about:
   a) coordinate details
   b) distance between points
   c) area and perimeter of composite shapes
   d) the status of objects.

2 AutoCAD has a built-in calculator which can be used transparently.

Chapter 32

Text fonts and styles

Text has been added to previous drawings without any discussion about the 'appearance' of the text items. In this chapter we will investigate:
a) text fonts and text styles
b) text control codes.

The words 'font' and 'style' are extensively used with text and they can be explained as follows:

Font: defines the pattern which is used to draw characters, i.e. it is basically an alphabet 'appearance'. AutoCAD R14 has over 90 fonts available to the user, and Figure 32.1 displays the text item 'AutoCAD R14' using 30 of these fonts.

Style: defines the parameters used to draw the actual text characters, i.e. the width of the characters, the obliquing angle, whether the text is upside-down, backwards, etc.

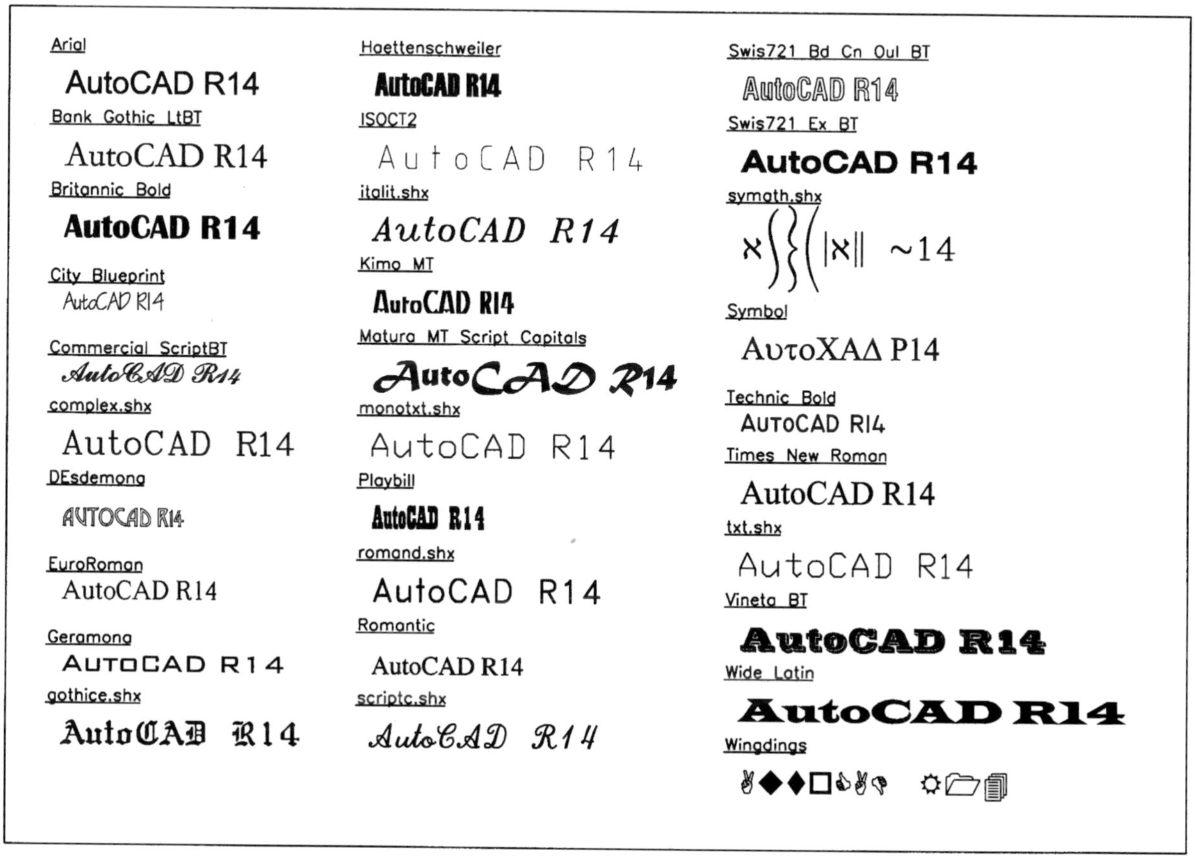

Figure 32.1 Some of AutoCAD Release 14's text fonts, all at height 8.

Notes

1 Text fonts are 'part of' the AutoCAD package.

2 Text styles are created by the user.

3 Any text font can be used for many different styles.

4 A text style uses only one font.

5 If text fonts are to be used in a drawing, a text style **must be created**.

6 New text fonts can be created by the user, but this is outside the scope of this book.

7 Text styles can be created: (*a*) by keyboard entry or (*b*) by a dialogue box.

Getting started

1 Open A:STDA3 with layer Text current.

2 At the command line enter **-STYLE <R>** and:
prompt	Text style name (or ?)<STANDARD>
enter	**? <R>** – the 'query' option
prompt	Text style(s) to list<*>
enter	**<R>**
prompt	AutoCAD Text Window with the display:

Style name:	STANDARD
Font files:	ISOCP
Height:	0.00
Width factor:	1.00
Obliquing angle:	0.0
Generation:	Normal.

3 This is R14's 'default' text style with the name STANDARD. The text font used is ISOCP – this may be different on your system?

4 Cancel the text window.

5 Using the DTEXT command with the default style (STANDARD), add the text item – AutoCAD R14 – at 145,270 with height 8 and rotation angle 0.

Creating a text style from the keyboard

1 At the command line enter **-STYLE <R>** and:
prompt	Text style name (or ?)<STANDARD>
enter	**ST1 <R>** – the style name
prompt	Specify full font name or font file name<ISOCP.shx>
enter	**romans.shx <R>**
prompt	Height and enter: **0 <R>**
prompt	Width factor and enter: **0 <R>**
prompt	Obliquing angle and enter: **0 <R>**
prompt	Backwards? and enter: **N <R>**
prompt	Upside-down? And enter: **N <R>**
prompt	Vertical? And enter: **N <R>**
prompt	ST1 is now the current style.

2 The above entries of height, width factor etc are the parameters which must be defined for every text style created.

Creating a text style from a dialogue box

1 From the menu bar select **Format–Text Style** and:

   prompt   Text Style dialogue box

   with   1 ST1 as the style name

              2 romans.shx as the font name

              3 height: 0.0

   respond **pick New** and:

   prompt   New Text Style dialogue box

   respond 1 alter style name to **ST2**

              2 pick OK

   prompt   Text Style dialogue box

   with   ST2 as the style name

   respond 1 pick the scroll arrow at right of romans.shx

              2 scroll and pick **italicc.shx**

              3 note the Preview box

              4 dialogue box as Figure 32.2

              5 pick **Apply** then **Close**.

2 With the menu bar selection Format–Text Style, use the Text Style dialogue box as step 1 to create the following text styles:

Style name	Font name	Ht	Width factor	Obl'g angle	Backwards	Upside down	Vert'l
				Effects			
ST3	gothice.shx	12	1	0	OFF	OFF	OFF
ST4	Arial Black	10	1	0	OFF	OFF	OFF
ST5	italict.shx	5	1	30	OFF	OFF	OFF
ST6	Romantic	10	1	0	OFF	ON	–
ST7	scriptc.shx	5	1	−30	OFF	OFF	OFF
ST8	monotxt.shx	6	1	0	OFF	OFF	ON
ST9	Lucinda Console	12	1	0	OFF	OFF	OFF
ST10	complex.shx	5	1	0	ON	OFF	OFF
ST11	isoct.shx	5	1	0	ON	ON	–
ST12	romand.shx	5	1	0	ON	ON	ON

3 Note: when using the Text Style dialogue box, a tick in a box means that the effect is on, a blank box means that the effect is off.

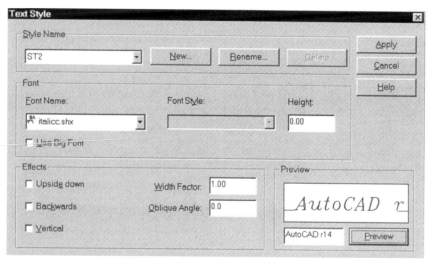

Figure 32.2 The Text Style dialogue box.

Using created text styles

1 Either: (*a*) enter **DTEXT <R>** at the command line or (*b*) menu bar with **Draw– Single Line Text**

prompt	Justify/Style/<Start point>
enter	**S <R>** – the style option
prompt	Style name (or ?)<ST12> – it should be
enter	**ST1 <R>**
prompt	Justify/Style/<Start point>
enter	**20,260 <R>**
prompt	Height and enter: **8 <R>**
prompt	Rotation angle and enter: **0 <R>**
prompt	Text and enter: **AutoCAD R14 <R>**.

2 Using the text command, add the text item AutoCAD R14 using the following information:

Style	Start pt	Ht	Rot
ST1	20,260	8	0 – already entered
ST2	225,265	8	0
ST3	15,145	NA	0
ST4	295,225	NA	0
ST5	25,175	NA	30
ST6	115,225	NA	0
ST7	145,195	NA	–30
ST8	215,235	NA	270 (default angle)
ST9	235,195	NA	0
ST10	365,165	NA	0
ST11	325,145	NA	0
ST12	385,135	NA	270 (default angle)

3 When completed, the screen should display 13 different text styles – the 12 created and the STANDARD default – Figure 32.3.

4 There is no need to save this drawing but:
   a) erase all the text styles from the screen
   b) save the 'blank' screen as **A:STYLEX** – you are really saving the created text styles for future use.

Notes

Text styles and fonts can be confusing to new AutoCAD users due to the terminology, and the following may be of assistance (refer to Figure 32.3):

1 *Effects*: three text style effects which can be 'set' are upside-down, vertical and backwards. These effects should be obvious to the user, and several styles had these effects toggled on.

2 *Width factor*: a parameter which 'stretches' the text characters and Fig. (a) shows an item of text with six width factors. The default value is 1.

3 *Obliquing angle*: this parameter 'slopes' the text characters as is apparent in Fig. (b). The default is 0.

4   *Height*: when the text command was used with the created text styles, only two styles prompted for a height – ST1 and ST2. The other text styles had a height value entered when the style was created – hence no height prompt. This also means that these text styles cannot be used at varying height values. The effect of differing height values is shown in Fig. (c).

5   *Recommendation*: I would strongly recommend that if text styles are being created, the height be left at 0. This will allow you to enter any text height at the prompt, when the text command is used.

6   The text items displayed using styles ST5 and ST7 are interesting, these items having:
   ST5   30 obliquing   30 rotation
   ST7   −30 obliquing   −30 rotation
   These styles give an 'isometric text' appearance.

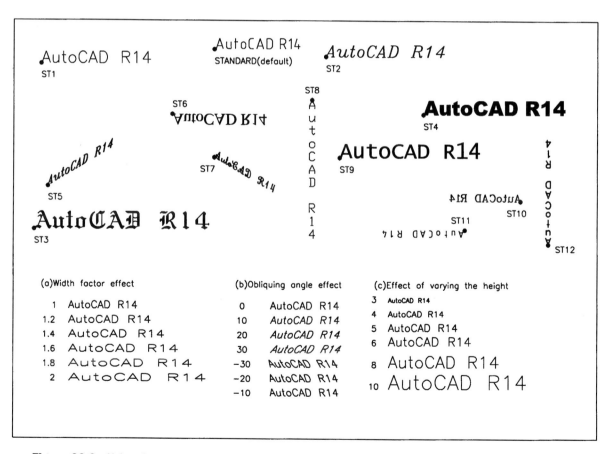

Figure 32.3   Using the created text styles.

Text control codes

When text is being added to a drawing, it may be necessary to underline the text item, or add a diameter/degree symbol. AutoCAD has several control codes which when used with text will allow underscoring, overscoring and symbol insertion.

The available control codes are:

%%O: toggles the OVERSCORE on/off
%%U: toggles the UNDERSCORE on/off
%%D: draws the DEGREE symbol for angle or temperature (°)
%%C: draws the DIAMETER symbol (∅)
%%P: draws the PLUS/MINUS symbol (±)
%%%:   draws the PERCENTAGE symbol (%).

1   Open A:STYLEX with the twelve created text styles.

2   Refer to Figure 32.4, select **Draw–Text–Single Line Text** and:

prompt   Justify/Style...
enter   **S <R>**
prompt   Style name (or ?)<??>
enter   **ST1 <R>**
prompt   Start point and enter: **25,250 <R>**
prompt   Height and enter: **10 <R>**
prompt   Rotation angle and enter: **–5 <R>**
prompt   Text and enter: **%%UAutoCAD R14%%U <R>**.

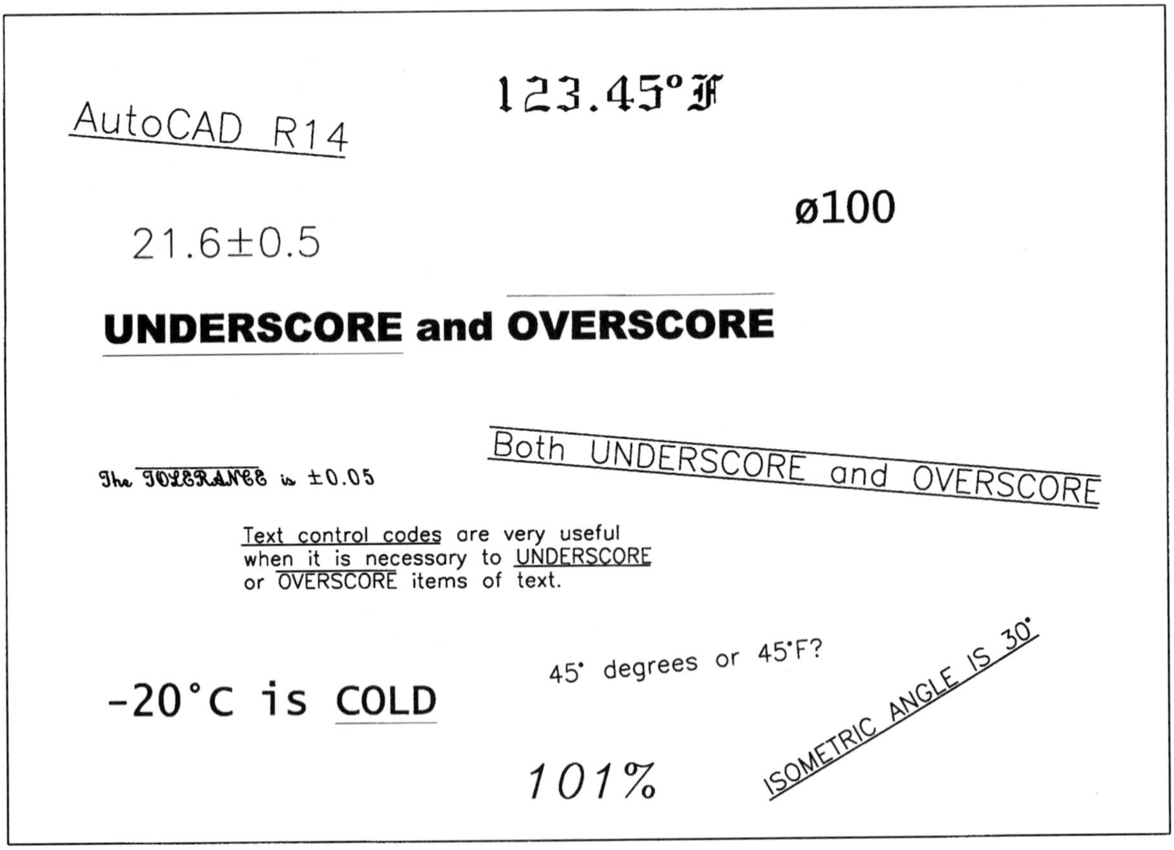

Figure 32.4 Text control codes.

3 At the command line enter **DTEXT <R>** and:
   a) style: ST3
   b) start point: 175,255
   c) angle: 0
   d) text: 123.45%%DF.

4 Activate the single line text command and:
   a) style: ST4
   b) start point: 35,175
   c) angle: 0
   d) text: %%UUNDERSCORE%%U and %%OOVERSCORE%%O.

5 With the DTEXT command:
   a) style: ST9
   b) start point: 285,215
   c) angle: 0
   d) text: %%C100.

6 Refer to Figure 32.4 and add the other text items – or text items of your choice. The text style used is at your discretion.

7 Save if required, but we will not use this drawing again.

Summary

1 Fonts define the pattern of characters.

2 Styles define the parameters for drawing characters.

3 Text styles must be created by the user.

4 A font can be used for several text styles.

5 Every text style must use a text font.

6 The AutoCAD R14 default text style is called STANDARD.

7 Text control codes allow under/overscoring and symbols to be added to text items.

Chapter 33

Multiline text

Multiline text is also called paragraph text and Mtext. It is a useful draughting tool as it allows large amounts of text to be added to a pre-determined area on the screen. The added text can also be edited.

1   Open the A:STYLEX with the created text styles.

2   Select the TEXT icon from the draw toolbar and:

prompt	Specify first corner
enter	**10,275 <R>**
prompt	Specify opposite corner or [Height...
enter	**S <R>** then **ST1 <R>** – the style option
prompt	*Specify opposite corner or [Height..*
enter	**H <R>** then **5 <R>** – the height option
prompt	Specify opposite corner or...
enter	**125,190 <R>**
prompt	Multiline Text Editor dialogue box
with	flashing cursor in the 'window area'
respond	1 enter the following text **including** the typing errors
	2 **do not press the return key**.
enter	CAD is a draughting <u>tol</u> with many benefits when compared to conventional draughting <u>techniches</u>. Some of these <u>benefitds</u> include <u>incresed</u> productivity, shorter lead <u>tines</u>, standardisation, <u>acuracy</u> <u>amd</u> rapid <u>resonse</u> to change.
and	dialogue box as Figure 33.1
respond	pick OK

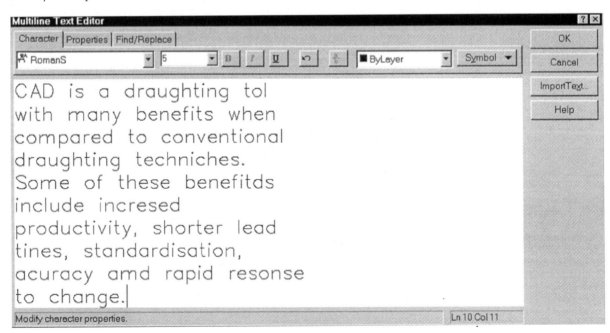

Figure 33.1   AutoCAD's Multiline Text Editor.

3 The entered text is displayed as Figure 33.2(a).
4 Notes:
   a) the text 'wraps around' the text editor window as it is entered from the keyboard
   b) the text is fitted into the **width** of the selected area of the screen – not the full
   rectangular area.

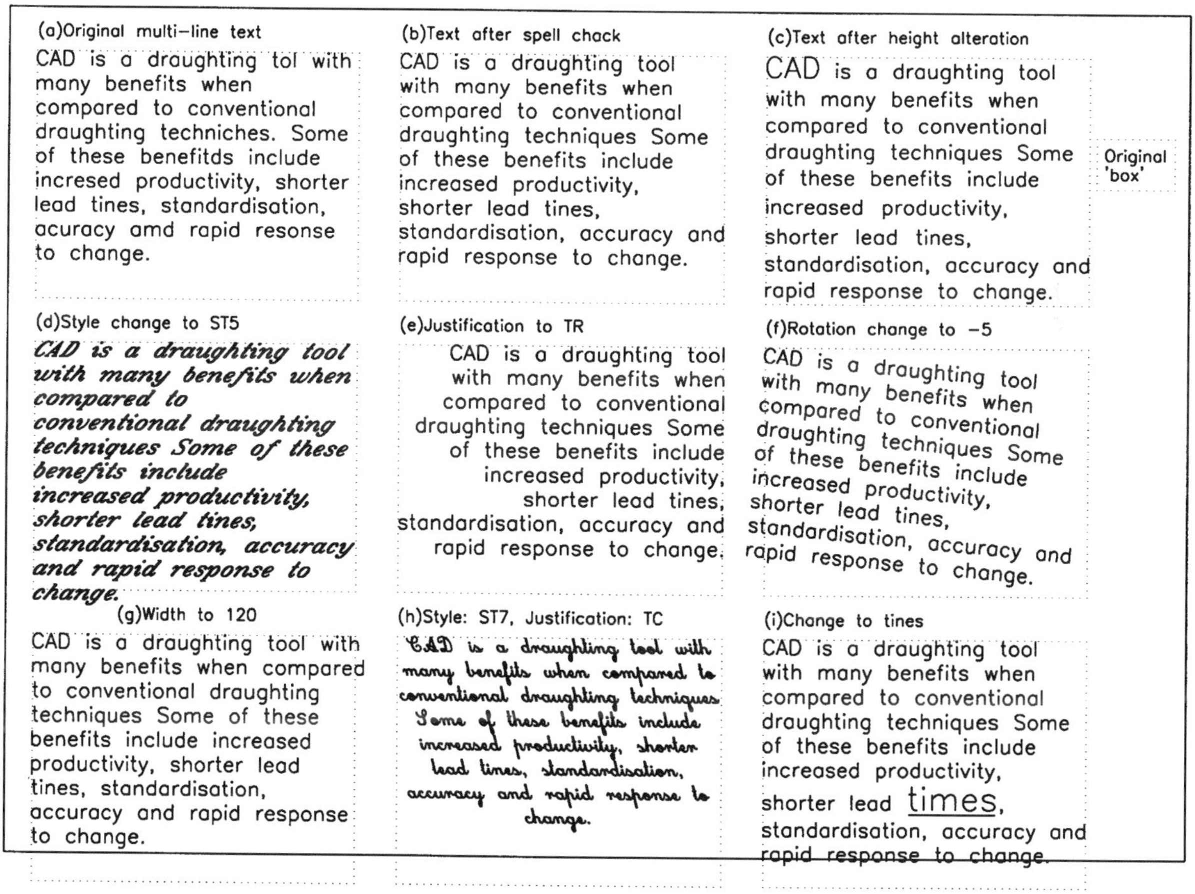

(a)Original multi–line text
CAD is a draughting tol with
many benefits when
compared to conventional
draughting techniches. Some
of these benefitds include
increased productivity, shorter
lead tines, standardisation,
acuracy amd rapid resonse
to change.

(b)Text after spell chack
CAD is a draughting tool
with many benefits when
compared to conventional
draughting techniques Some
of these benefits include
increased productivity,
shorter lead tines,
standardisation, accuracy and
rapid response to change.

(c)Text after height alteration
CAD is a draughting tool
with many benefits when
compared to conventional
draughting techniques Some
of these benefits include
increased productivity,
shorter lead tines,
standardisation, accuracy and
rapid response to change.
Original 'box'

(d)Style change to ST5
CAD is a draughting tool
with many benefits when
compared to
conventional draughting
techniques Some of these
benefits include
increased productivity,
shorter lead tines,
standardisation, accuracy
and rapid response to
change.

(e)Justification to TR
      CAD is a draughting tool
     with many benefits when
      compared to conventional
    draughting techniques Some
     of these benefits include
        increased productivity,
          shorter lead tines,
   standardisation, accuracy and
     rapid response to change.

(f)Rotation change to −5
CAD is a draughting tool
with many benefits when
compared to conventional
draughting techniques Some
of these benefits include
increased productivity,
shorter lead tines,
standardisation, accuracy and
rapid response to change.

(g)Width to 120
CAD is a draughting tool with
many benefits when compared
to conventional draughting
techniques Some of these
benefits include increased
productivity, shorter lead
tines, standardisation,
accuracy and rapid response
to change.

(h)Style: ST7, Justification: TC
CAD is a draughting tool with
many benefits when compared to
conventional draughting techniques
Some of these benefits include
increased productivity, shorter
lead tines, standardisation,
accuracy and rapid response to
change.

(i)Change to tines
CAD is a draughting tool
with many benefits when
compared to conventional
draughting techniques Some
of these benefits include
increased productivity,
shorter lead times,
standardisation, accuracy and
rapid response to change.

Figure 33.2 Paragraph text exercise.

Spellcheck

AutoCAD R14 has a built-in spellchecker which can be activated:
a) from the menu bar with **Tools–Spelling**
b) by icon selection from the Standard toolbar.

1 Activate the spell check command and:
  prompt   Select objects
  respond **pick any part of the entered text then right-click**
  prompt   check spelling dialogue box
  with   1 current word: probably *draughting*
            2 suggestions: probably *draughtiness*
            3 content: *CAD is a draughting tol …*
  respond 1 pick Change Dictionaries
            2 scroll at Main dictionary
            3 pick British English (ise)
            4 pick OK to return to Check Spelling dialogue box
            5 pick **Ignore All** – for draughting word
  prompt   Check Spelling dialogue box
  with   1 current word: *tol*
            2 suggestions: toll, tool, to...
  respond 1 pick **tool** – turns blue
            2 tool added to suggestion box
            3 dialogue box as Figure 33.3
            4 pick **Change**
  prompt   check spelling dialogue box
  with   1 current word: *techniches*
            2 suggestions: tech
  respond 1 alter *techniches* to **techniques**
            2 pick **Change**
  prompt   check spelling dialogue box
  respond change the following as the appear:
            benefitds →   benefits
            incresed   →   increased
            acuracy   →   accuracy
            amd   →   and (manual change required)
            resonse   →   response
  then   *AutoCAD message* Spelling check complete
  respond pick OK.

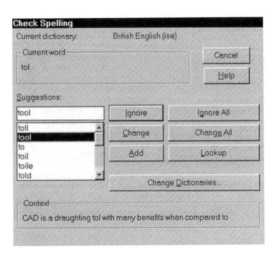

Figure 33.1 Check Spelling dialogue box.

2 The paragraph text will be displayed with the correct spelling as Figure 33.2(b).

3 One of the original spelling mistakes was '**tines**' (times) and this was not highlighted with the spellcheck. This means that the word 'tines' is a 'real word' as far as the Auto-CAD dictionary is concerned, although it is wrong to us. This is a major problem with spellchecks – they check the spelling, not the 'sense' of the word. This concept will probably be included in future spellchecks as technology progresses.

4 Multiple copy the corrected text to seven other places on the screen and refer to Figure 33.2.

Editing multiline text

1 Select the EDIT TEXT icon from the Modify II toolbar and:

   prompt   `<Select an annotation object>/...`
   respond **pick a paragraph text item**
   prompt   Multiline Text Editor dialogue box
   with   text displayed
   respond 1 alter text height to 7
               2 left-click and drag mouse over CAD
               3 pick height of 7 then OK
               4 pick OK – Fig. (c)
               5 right-click to end command.

2 Menu bar with **Modify–Object–Text** and:
   prompt   Select an annotation object
   respond **pick a text item**
   prompt   Multiline Text Editor dialogue box
   respond 1 pick properties label
               2 scroll at Style then pick ST5
               3 pick OK then right-click – Fig. (d).

3 Using the edit text command alter the other paragraph text items using the following information:
   a) properties: justification to Top Right – Fig. (e)
   b) properties: rotation to –5 – Fig. (f)
   c) properties: width to 120 – Fig. (g)
   d) properties: style to ST7 and justification to Top Centre – Fig. (h)
   e) replace *tines* with *times* and:
      i)   underline times
      ii) alter height of times to 8 – Fig. (i).

4 This exercise is now complete and can be saved if required.

Summary

1 Multiline text is also called paragraph text.

2 The text is entered using the Multiline Text Editor dialogue box.

3 The command can be activated by icon, from the menu bar or by entering **MTEXT** at the command line.

4 Multiline text has powerful editing facilities.

Chapter 34

The array command

Array is a command which allows multiple copying of objects in either a rectangular or circular (polar) pattern. It is one of the most powerful and useful of the commands available, yet is one of the easiest to use. To demonstrate the command:

1 Open the A:STDA3 standard sheet with layer Out current and the toolbars Draw, Modify and Object snap.

2 Refer to Figure 34.1 and draw the rectangular shape using the given sizes. Do **not** add the dimensions.

3 Multiple copy the rectangular shape from the mid-point indicated to the points A(25,175); B(290,235); C(205,110) and D(35,130). The donuts are for reference only.

4 Draw two circle, centre at 290,190 with radius 30 and centre at 205,65 with radius 15.

5 Move the original shape to a 'safe place' on the screen.

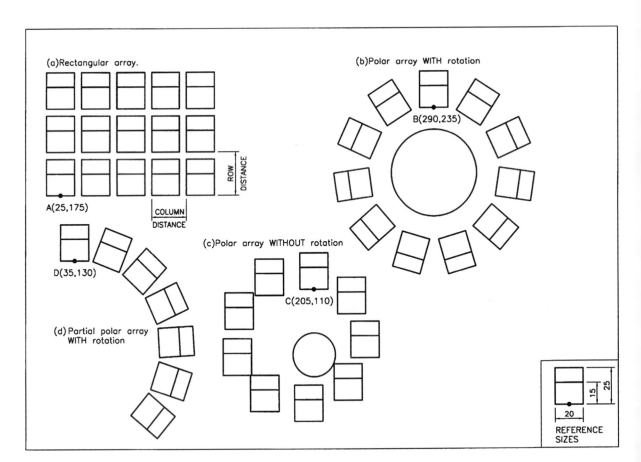

Figure 34.1 The ARRAY command.

Rectangular array

1 Select the ARRAY icon from the Draw toolbar and:

prompt `Select objects`
respond **window the shape at A then right-click**
prompt `Rectangular or Polar(<R>/P)`
enter **R <R>** – the rectangular option
prompt `Number of rows(−)<1>` and enter: **3 <R>**
prompt `Number of columns(||||)<1>` and enter: **5 <R>**
prompt `Unit cell or distance between rows(−)`
enter **30 <R>**
prompt `Distance between columns(||||)`
enter **25 <R>**.

2 The shape at A will be copied 14 times into a three row and five column matrix pattern as Fig. (a).

Polar array with rotation

1 Menu bar with **Modify–Array** and

prompt `Select objects`
respond **window the shape at B then right-click**
prompt `Rectangular or Polar` and enter: **P <R>**
prompt `Center point of array`
respond **Snap to Center icon and pick large circle**
prompt `Number of items` and enter: **11 <R>**
prompt `Angle to fill...` and enter: **360 <R>**
prompt `Rotate objects as they are copied?<Y>`
enter **Y <R>**.

2 The shape at B is copied in a circular pattern about the selected centre point. The objects are 'rotated' about this point as they are copied – Fig. (b).

Polar array without rotation

1 At the command line enter **ARRAY <R>** and:

prompt `Select objects`
respond **window the shape at C then right-click**
prompt `Rectangular or Polar` and enter: **P <R>**
prompt `Center point` and: **pick small circle centre**
prompt `Number of items` and enter: **9 <R>**
prompt `Angle to fill` and enter: **360 <R>**
prompt `Rotate option` and enter: **Y <R>**.

2 The original shape is copied about the selected centre point but is not 'rotated' as it is copied – Fig. (c).

Polar array with partial fill angle

1 Activate the array command and:
   a) objects: window the shape at D
   b) option: P
   c) centre: enter the point 35,70
   d) items: 7
   e) angle to fill: −130
   f) rotate: Y.

2 The result is as shown in Fig. (d).

   Your drawing should resemble Figure 34.1 and can be saved if required.

Array exercise
Polar array

The polar array command is very useful and will be further demonstrated so:

1 Erase the arrays from the screen (but not the original shape) and refer to Figure 34.2.

2 Draw three concentric circles:
   a) on layer Out with radii 40 and 10
   b) on layer Cl with radius 25.

3 Multiple copy these three circles to three other areas of the screen using Figure 34.2 for positioning.

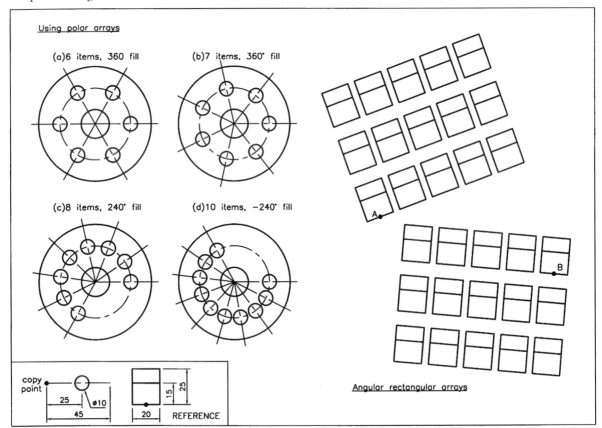

Figure 34.2 Array exercise.

iBS
www.bookshop.co.uk

The Internet Bookshop
www.bookshop.co.uk

iBS

www.bookshop.co.uk

- Over **1.2 million** titles

- Stock **range despatched** within 48 hours

- Secure **On-line** ordering

- **Guaranteed refund** or exchange for any reason

4 *a*) Draw a line (on layer Cl) and a circle (on layer Out) using the reference sizes given.
  b) Multiple copy the two objects to the centre of each circle.
  c) Use the Endpoint and Center icons.

5 With the polar option of the array command, array the centre line and circle using the following information:
  a) six items, fill angle 360
  b) seven items, fill angle 360
  c) eight items, fill angle 240
  d) ten items, fill angle −240.

Angular rectangular array

A rectangular array can be created at an angle using the **snap angle** variable, so:

1 Multiple copy the original rectangular shape from the point indicated to the points A(265,145) and B(390,105).

2 Rotate the shape at A by 20 and the shape at B by −5.

3 Menu bar with **Tools–Drawing Aids** and:
  prompt   Drawing Aids dialogue box
  respond   1 set snap angle to 20
          2 pick OK.

4 Note the grid points and cursor orientation – rotated by 20.

5 Use the array command and:
  a) window the shape at A
  b) select the rectangular option
  c) three rows and five columns
  d) row distance: 35 and column distance: 25.

6 At the command line enter **SNAPANG <R>** and:
  prompt   New value for SNAPANG<20.0>
  enter   **−5 <R>**.

7 Rectangular array the shape at B with:
  a) three rows and five columns
  b) row distance: −35 and column distance: −25.

8 Set the snap angle value to 0.

9 Exercise is now complete (Figure 34.2) and can be saved if required.

Summary

1 The ARRAY command allows multiple copying in a rectangular or circular pattern.

2 The command can be activated by keyboard entry, from the menu bar or in icon form.

3 Rectangular arrays must have at least one row and one column.

4 The rectangular row/column distance can be positive or negative.

5 Altering the snap angle will produce angular rectangular arrays.

6 Circular (polar) arrays require a centre point which:
  a) can be entered as coordinates
  b) picked on the screen
  c) reference to existing objects, e.g. snap to center icon.

7 Polar arrays can be full (360°) or partial.

8 The polar angle to fill can be positive or negative.

9 Polar array objects can be rotated/not rotated about the centre point.

Assignments

It has been some time since any activities have been attempted and four have been included at this stage. All involve using the array command as well as hatching, adding text, etc. I have tried to make these activities varied and interesting so I hope you enjoy attempting them. As with all activities:
a) start with your A:STDA3 standard sheet
b) use layers correctly for outlines, text, hatching, etc.
c) when complete, save as A:ACT_? or similar.

1 Activity 22: Ratchet and saw tip blade.
Two typical examples of how the array command is used. The ratchet tooth shape is fairly straightforward and the saw blade tooth is more difficult than you would think. Or is it? Draw each tooth in a clear area of the screen, then copy them to the appropriate circle points. The trim command is extensively used.

2 Activity 23: Nose adapter.
A typical engineering example requiring the array command. Fairly simple drawing to complete although the thread part is interesting – perhaps you could always forget the thread part and just draw lines. The countersunk hole arrangement is also interesting to complete. Why have I dimensioned one of the circles with '???'?. The mirror command is useful.

3 Activity 24: The light bulb.
This was one of my first array exercises and has proved very popular in previous AutoCAD books. It is harder than you would think, especially the R10 arc. The basic bulb is copied and scaled three times. The polar array centre is at your discretion. The position of the smaller polar bulb is relative to the larger polar array, but how is it positioned? – your problem! No hints are given on how to draw the basic bulb.

4 Activity 25: Bracket and gauge.
The bracket is fairly easy, the hexagonal rectangular array to be positioned to suit yourself. The gauge drawing requires some thought with the polar arrays. I drew a vertical line and arrayed 26 items twice, the fill angles being +150 and −150 – think about this! The other gauge fill angles are +140 and −140. What about the longer line? The pointer position is at your discretion. Another method is to array lines and trim to circles?

5 Activity 26: Pinion gear wheel.
Another typical engineering application of the array command. The design details are given for you and the basic tooth shape is not too difficult. Copy and rotate the second gear wheel – but what angle? Think about the number of teeth. I realize that the gears are not 'touching' – that's another problem for you to think about!

Chapter 35

Changing properties

All objects have properties, e.g. linetype, colour, layer, position, etc. Text has also properties such as height, style, width factor, obliquing angle, etc. This chapter will demonstrate how object properties can be changed, and this will be achieved by a series of simple exercises.

1 Open A:STDA3 with layer Out current, toolbars to suit and refer to Figure 35.1.

2 Draw a 40 unit square and copy it to four other places on the screen.

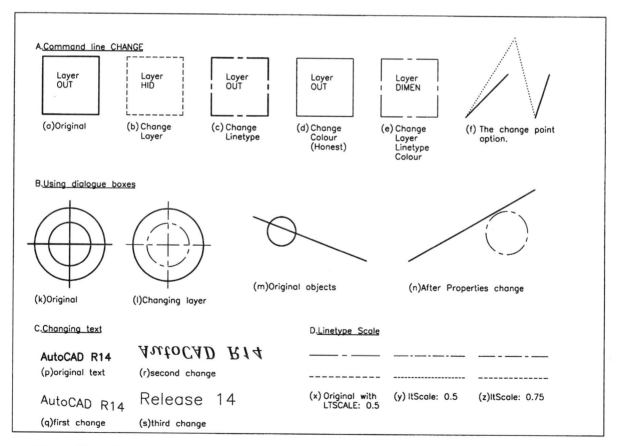

Figure 35.1 Change properties exercise.

Command line CHANGE

1 At the command line enter **CHANGE <R>** and:
   prompt   Select objects
   respond   **window the second square then right-click**
   prompt   Properties/<Change point>
   enter   **P <R>** – the properties option
   prompt   Change what property(Color/Elev/Layer...
   enter   **LA <R>** – the layer option
   prompt   New layer<OUT>
   enter   **HID <R>**
   prompt   Change what property... and right-click – Fig. (b).

2 The square will be displayed as yellow hidden lines.

3 Repeat the CHANGE command entry and:
   a) objects: window the third square then right-click
   b) options: enter P <R> for properties
   c) options: enter LT <R> for linetype
   d) new linetype: enter CENTER <R> for center linetypes
   e) options: right-click to end command – Fig. (c).

4 Use the command line CHANGE with:
   a) objects: window the fourth square then right-click
   b) options: enter P <R> then C <R> – the color option
   c) new color: enter BLUE <R>
   d) options: right-click – Fig. (d).

5 Finally CHANGE the fifth square with:
   a) options: enter P <R> then LA <R>
   b) new layer: DIMEN <R>
   c) options: enter LT <R>
   d) new linetype: CENTER <R>
   e) options: enter: C <R>
   f) new color: enter green <R>
   g) options: right-click – Fig. (e).

6 Menu bar with **Format–Layers** and:
   a) make layer 0 current
   b) freeze layer Out then OK
   c) only a yellow hidden line square and a green centre line square displayed?
   d) thaw layer Out and make it current.

7 Draw two lines:
   a) from: 320,220 to: 350,250
   b) from: 370,220 to: 380,250.

8 Activate the CHANGE command and:
   prompt   Select objects
   respond   **pick the two lines then right-click**
   prompt   Properties/<Change point>
   respond   **pick about the point 355,275 on the screen**.

9 The two lines are redrawn to this point – Fig. (f).

Changing properties using dialogue boxes

1 With layer Out current, draw:
   a) two concentric circles
   b) two 'centre' lines – Fig. (k).

2 Select the PROPERTIES icon from the standard toolbar and:
   prompt   Select objects
   respond **pick the two lines, small circle and right-click**
   prompt   Change Properties dialogue box
   respond **pick Layer**
   prompt   Select Layer dialogue box
   respond **pick CL then OK**
   prompt   Change Properties dialogue box – Figure 35.2
   respond **pick OK**.

3 The three objects are displayed as green centre lines – Fig. (l).

4 Draw the following objects:
   a) line, from: 170,150 to: 250,120
   b) circle, centre: 190,140 radius: 10 – Fig. (m).

5 With the properties icon, pick the line then right-click and:
   prompt   Modify Line dialogue box
   with   details on layer, linetype, startpoint and endpoint, etc.
   respond 1 alter From Point X: 160 Y: 100
            2 alter To Point X: 250 Y: 150
            3 dialogue box as shown in Figure 35.3
            4 pick OK.

6 Menu bar with **Modify–Properties**, pick the circle, right-click and:
   prompt   Modify Circle dialogue box
   with   details on Layer, Centre point, Radius, etc.
   respond 1 alter centre point X: 230 Y: 120
            2 alter radius: 15
            3 alter layer: CL
            4 pick OK.

7 The line and circle objects are displayed as Fig. (n).

Note on Change Properties dialogue boxes

When the properties command is activated by icon or from the menu bar, a dialogue box will be displayed. There are two types of dialogue box and the display is dependent on what objects are selected:

a) several objects: if more than one object is selected, the dialogue box is displayed as change properties as shown in Figure 35.2

b) single object: if a single object is selected, the dialogue box displayed is Modify Line, Modify Circle, etc. as shown in Figure 35.3. Each 'type' of object has a Modify Properties dialogue box.

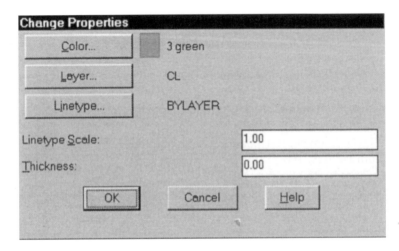

Figure 35.2   The Change Properties dialogue box.

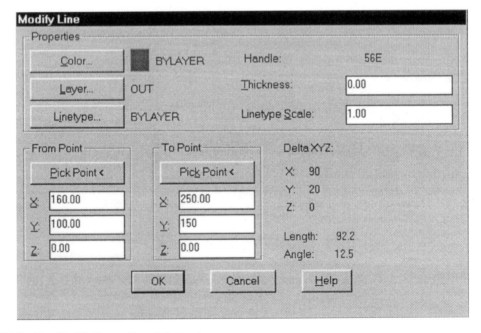

Figure 35.3   The Modify Properties dialogue box.

Changing text

Text has several properties which other objects do not, e.g. style, height, width factor, etc. as well as layer, linetype and colour. These properties can be altered with the properties command. To demonstrate how text can be modified:

1 Create the following text styles:

name	ST1	ST2
font	romant	italict
height	0	8
width	1	1
obliquing	0	0
backwards	N	N
upside-down	N	Y
vertical	N	N

2 With layer Out current and ST1 the current style, enter the text item AutoCAD R14 at height 5 and rotation 0 at a suitable part of the screen – Fig. (p).

3 Multiple copy this item of text to three other places.

4 With the Properties icon, pick the second text item and:
prompt Modify Text dialogue box
respond 1 alter layer to TEXT
       2 alter height to 6
       3 alter rotation to –5
       4 alter obliquing to –5
       5 pick OK – Fig. (q).

5 Repeat the properties icon selection, pick the next text item and alter:
a) layer to TEXT
b) Style to ST2 – Fig. (r).

6 Finally change the properties of the third text item:
a) layer: TEXT
b) text: Release 14
c) height: 8 – Fig. (s).

Changing linetype scale

The LTSCALE variable is 'global', i.e. if it is altered, all objects such as centre lines, hidden lines, etc. will alter in appearance and this may not be to the user's requirements. It is possible to alter the appearance of individual objects using the **ltScale** option of the CHANGE command. To demonstrate the effect:

1 Draw two horizontal lines, one on layer CL and one on layer HID as Fig. (x) and copy these lines to two other places.

2 At the command line enter **LTSCALE <R>** and:
 prompt New scale factor
 enter   **0.5 <R>**.

3 This is the global linetype value.

4 At the command line enter **CHANGE <R>** and:
 prompt   Select objects
 respond **pick the second 'set' of lines then right-click**
 prompt   Property/<Change point>
 enter   **P <R>**
 prompt   Change what property...
 enter   **S <R>** – the linetype scale option
 prompt   New linetype scale<1.00>
 enter   **0.5 <R>**
 prompt   Change what property...
 respond **right-click** – Fig. (y).

5 Select the properties icon and:
 prompt   Select objects
 respond **pick second set of lines then right-click**
 prompt   change properties dialogue box
 respond 1 alter linetype scale to 0.75
       2 pick OK – Fig. (z).

6 The linetype scale option of the change properties command is relative to the existing LTSCALE value. If LTSCALE is 0.5, then an ltScale value of 0.5 is effectively 0.25, and an ltScale value of 1 is effectively 0.5.

Combining ARRAY and CHANGE

Combining the array command with the properties command can give interesting results. To demonstrate the effect:

1 Open your standard A:STDA3 sheet and refer to Figure 35.4.

2 Draw the two arc segments as trimmed circles using the information given in Fig. (a).

3 Draw the polyline and 0 text item using the reference data.

4 With the ARRAY command, polar array (twice) the polyline and text item using an arc centre as the array centre point:
 a) for four items, angle to fill +30° with rotation
 b) for seven items, angle to fill −60° with rotation – Fig. (b).

5 Using the properties icon, pick each text item and alter:
 a) the text values to 10, 20, 30, ..., 90
 b) the text height to 8.

6 The result should be as shown in Fig. (c).

7 Save if required.

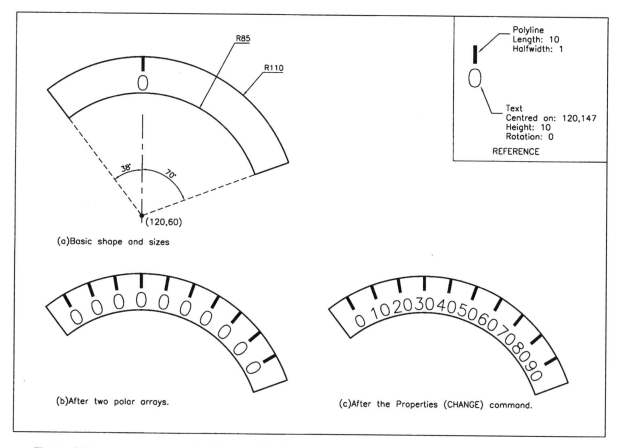

Figure 35.4 The combined ARRAY and CHANGE PROPERTIES exercise.

Note

The first exercise demonstrated that it was possible to change the properties of objects independent of the current layer. This means that if layer OUT (red, continuous) is current, objects can be created on this layer as green centre lines, blue hidden lines, etc. This is a practice I **would not recommend** until you are proficient at using the AutoCAD draughting package. If green centre lines have to be created, use the correct layer, or make a new layer if required. Try not to 'mix' different types of linetype and different colours on the one layer. Remember that this is only a recommendation – the choice is always left to you.

Summary

1 The properties command can be used to change the layer, colour, linetype, etc. of existing objects.

2 The command can be activated:
   a) using the properties icon – dialogue box
   b) from the command line with CHANGE – keyboard entry.

3 The dialogue box displayed depends on the object(s) selected.

4 Each individual selected object has its own modify dialogue box.

5 The properties command is very useful when text items are arrayed.

6 Individual objects can have specific linetype scale factors.

Format:	text inside horizontal: on
	text outside horizontal: on
	vertical justification: centred
Annotation:	units: scale linear: 2
	text style: ST1, height: 4

d) **DIMST5**

Geometry:	no change
Format:	no change
Annotation:	text style: ST3, height: 5
	text gap: 0

e) **DIMST6**

Geometry:	no change
Format:	no change
Annotation:	text style: ST4, height: 6
	text gap: 3.

4　At this stage save your drawing as **A:DIMST**, i.e. we are saving the six created dimension styles.

Using the created dimension styles

1　Using Figure 37.1 for reference, draw seven horizontal and vertical lines, seven circles and seven angled lines – the sizes are not of any significance but try and 'fit' all the objects into your drawing 'frame'.

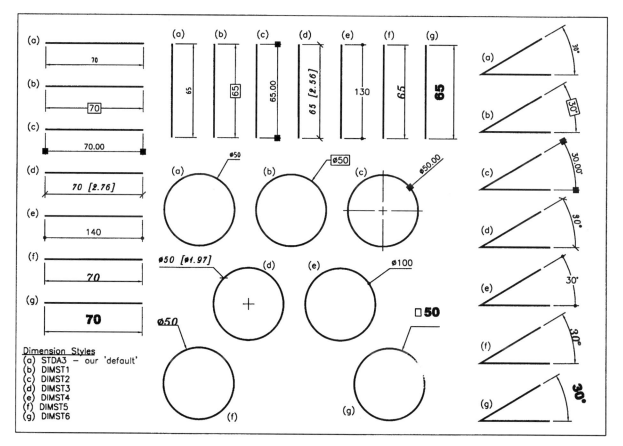

Figure 37.1　Dimension styles exercise.

2 Menu bar with **Dimension–Style** and:
   a) scroll until STDA3 is displayed
   b) pick STDA3 – it should be displayed as current?
   c) pick OK.

3 This sequence 'sets' STDA3 as the current dimension style.

4 Now dimension one set of objects, i.e. a horizontal line, a vertical line, a circle and an angled line – Fig. (a).

5 At the command line enter **DIMSTYLE <R>** and:
   prompt Dimension Style Edit...
   enter   **R <R>** – the restore option
   prompt ?/Enter dimension style name...
   enter   **DIMST1 <R>**

6 DIMST1 will now be the current text style. Dimension another 'set' of objects – Fig. (b).

7 Using either the dialogue box or command line entry:
   a) make each created dimension style current
   b) dimension a set of objects with each style.

8 Figure 37.1 displays the result of the exercise.

Comparing dimension styles

It is possible to compare dimension styles with each other and note any changes between them.

1 At the command line enter **DIMSTYLE <R>** and:
   prompt Dimension Style Edit and enter: **R <R>**
   prompt ?/Enter dimension style name and enter: **DIMST4 <R>**.

2 This sets DIMST4 as the current dimension style.

3 At the command line enter **DIMSTYLE <R>** and:
   prompt Dimension Style Edit...
   enter   **R <R>**
   prompt ?/Enter dimension style name
   enter   **~STDA3 <R>** – note the ~ symbol
   prompt AutoCAD text window with:

Differences between STDA3 and current settings

	STDA3	*Current settings*
DIMASZ	3.00	8.00
DIMBLK1		_DOTSMALL
DIMBLK2		_DOTSMALL
DIMLFAC	1.00	2.00
DIMSAH	Off	On
DIMTAD	1	0
DIMTIH	Off	On
DIMTXSTY	STANDARD	ST1
DIMTXT	3.50	4.00

4 Press **ESC** and cancel the text window.

Dimension variables

The above comparison between the two dimension styles displays some of the AutoCAD dimension variables. Some readers may remember using dimension variables before dimension styles were introduced. All dimension variables (**dimvars**) can still be altered by keyboard entry, although the Dimension Style dialogue box has tended to 'supersede' this method of altering dimension styles. There is however, one dimension variable which I would like to discuss, this being **dimtvp** – the dimension text vertical position.

1 Refer to your dimension style drawing, and note the dimensions which used DIMST1 – the second set of dimensioned objects.

2 This dimension style had the basic tolerance method set, and gave a box around the dimension text – the box is however above the dimension line and will now be modified.

3 Make DIMST1 the current dimension style.

4 At the command line enter **DIMTVP <R>** and:
   prompt   New value for DIMTVP<1.0000>
   enter   **0 <R>**.

5 Menu bar with **Dimension–Style** and:
   prompt   Dimension Styles dialogue box
   with   Current style: **+DIMST1**
   and   the + at the dimension style name means that there has been an alteration to some dimension variable which has not yet been saved
   respond **pick save then OK**.

6 All dimensions using DIMST1 will be altered to include the dimtvp value of 0, i.e. the basic box will be centred in the dimension line as Fig. (b).

7 This exercise is now complete and can be saved if you wish.

Task

1 Open your A:STDA3 standard sheet with the four saved text styles ST1–ST4.

2 Using menu bar **Dimension–Style**:
   a) check current style is STDA3
   b) with annotation, set text style to ST1 and height 3.5.

3 **File–Save** to update the A:STDA3 standard sheet with the modified STDA3 dimension style.

Summary

1 Dimension styles are created by the user and 'customized' according to user/customer requirements.

2 There would appear to be no limit to the number the dimension styles which can be created and saved.

3 Dimension styles use the Geometry, Format and Annotation dialogue boxes.

4 Dimension variables (dimvars) can still be entered and altered at the command line.

Chapter 38

Dimension families

Dimension styles are 'global', i.e. no matter whether a line, circle or angle is to be dimensioned, the current dimension style is applied to all objects. This is generally how dimensions are added to drawings.

It is possible to allocate a specific dimension style to a particular type of object, these objects being termed dimension families. There are six types of dimension families in AutoCAD, these being linear, diameter, radial, ordinate, angular and leader.

To demonstrate how dimension families are created:

1 Open A:DIMST which is a blank screen but has six saved dimension styles, DIMST1–DIMST6 from Chapter 37.

2 Refer to Figure 38.1 and draw a horizontal line, a circle and an angled line segment and copy them to two other places.

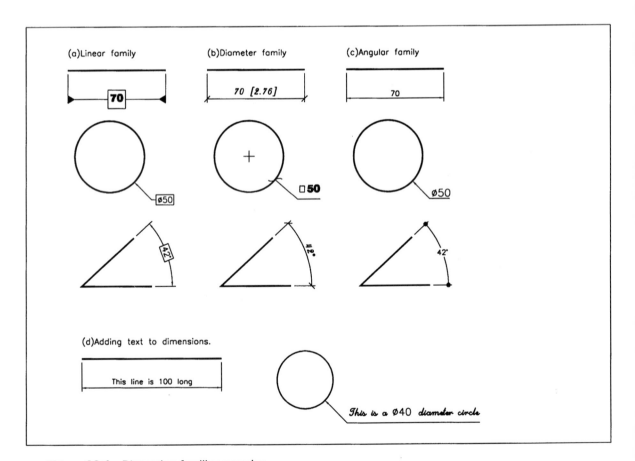

Figure 38.1 Dimension families exercise.

Linear family

1 Activate the Dimension Styles dialogue box and make DIMST1 the current dimension style.

2 Pick Linear family – black dot.

3 Pick Geometry and alter arrowheads to **datum triangle filled**, with size 5, then pick OK.

4 From Dimension Styles dialogue box, pick Save then OK.

5 Now dimension one 'set' of objects, i.e. a line, circle and angle.

6 The linear dimension will be displayed with the 'altered' style, the circle and angle with the 'normal' DIMST1 style – Fig. (a).

Diameter family

1 Using the Dimension Styles dialogue box, make DIMST3 the current style.

2 Pick Diameter family.

3 *a*) pick Geometry and alter arrowheads to **integral**, size 10 then OK.
   b) pick annotation and alter:
      i)   text style: ST4, height: 5
      ii) alternate units: off
      iii) pick OK.

4 Save then OK from Dimension Styles dialogue box.

5 Dimension the next set of objects.

6 The diameter dimension will be displayed with the modified style, i.e. with a different text style and without alternate units as Fig. (b). Angular dimensions have no alternate units.

Angular family

1 Dimension Styles dialogue box with STDA3 current style.

2 Pick Angular family.

3 Pick Geometry and alter arrowheads to **dot small**, size: 12.

4 Pick Format and alter text inside horizontal on.

5 Dimension Styles dialogue box with save then OK.

6 Dimension the last three objects and only the angular dimension will be displayed with the modified style – Fig. (c).

Adding text to dimensions

Dimensioning is automatic, i.e. the 'size' of the object is displayed when the dimension line location has been selected. It is possible to modify the actual dimension text before the dimension line position is selected.

1 Draw a horizontal line of length 100 and a 20 radius circle at a suitable area of the screen.

2 Using the Linear dimension icon, pick the endpoints of the line and

prompt	Dimension line location (Mtext/Text...)
enter	**M <R>** – the Mtext option
prompt	Multiline Text Editor
with	|<> – the | being a flashing cursor
enter	**This line is <> long**
then	pick OK
prompt	Dimension line location
respond	pick to suit

3 With the diameter dimension icon, pick the circle and:

prompt	Dimension line location (Mtext...)
enter	**M <R>**
prompt	Multiline Text Editor with |<>
respond	1 pick scroll arrow at RomanS then pick **ScriptC**
	2 enter: **This is a <> diameter circle** (some thought needed here)
	3 pick OK
prompt	Dimension line location
respond	pick to suit.

4 The dimensions are displayed as shown in Fig. (d).

Save if required, as the exercise is now complete.

Chapter 39

Tolerance dimensions

Dimensions can be displayed with tolerances and limits, the 'types' available being symmetrical, deviation, limits and basic. These are displayed in Figure 39.1(a) with the standard default dimension type, i.e. no tolerances displayed. To use tolerance dimensions correctly, different dimension styles should be created for each 'type' which is to be used in the drawing.

As usual we will investigate the topic with an exercise so:

1 Open your A:STDA3 standard sheet and refer to Figure 39.1.

2 Draw a line, circle and angled line and copy them to four other areas of the screen.

3 Dimension one set of objects with your standard (STDA3) dimension style setting – Fig. (p).

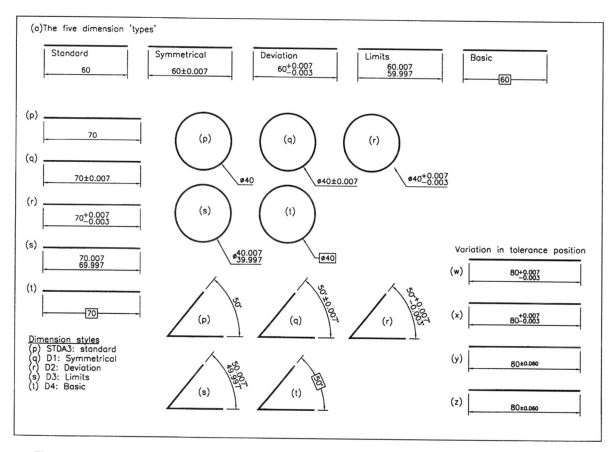

Figure 39.1 Dimension tolerances and limits.

Creating the tolerance dimension styles

1 At the command line enter **DIMTDEC <R>** and:
    prompt   New value for DIMTDEC<1>
    enter   **3 <R>** – more on this later.

2 Menu bar with **Dimension–Style** and:
    prompt   Dimension Styles dialogue box
    with   **+STDA3** as current style, i.e. it has been modified
    respond **pick Save**
    and   saved to STDA3 displayed.

3 Still with Dimension Styles dialogue box on the screen:
   a) alter name to **D1** and pick **Save**
   b) created D1 from STDA3 displayed.

4 Repeat step 3 and create dimension styles D2, D3 and D4 by:
   a) changing the name to D2 then D3 then D4
   b) picking save.

5 Pick OK from the Dimension Styles dialogue box – the four new styles have still to be modified.

Modifying the created styles

1 Activate the Dimension Styles dialogue box and:
   a) make D1 the current style – scroll and pick
   b) pick Annotation
   c) pick Tolerance method – symmetrical
   d) alter upper value to 0.007
   e) pick OK to return to the Dimension Styles dialogue box
   f) pick OK from Dimension Styles dialogue box.

2 Now dimension a set of objects with this style – Fig. (q).

3 Using step 1 as a guide alter the other three dimension style tolerance methods using the following information:
   a) style D2 – deviation, upper value: 0.007
                           lower value: 0.003
   b) style D3 – limits, upper value: 0.007
                       lower value: 0.003
   c) style D4 – basic with format, vertical justification: centered and DIMTVP = 0 entered from the command line.

4 Dimension a set of three object with each new style current as:
   Fig. (r): style D2
   Fig. (s): style D3
   Fig. (t): style D4.

5 Task: investigate the deviation and symmetrical justification options of top and bottom as well as the height option. The following are displayed:
   Fig. (w): deviation top, height 0.8
   Fig. (x): deviation bottom, height 0.8
   Fig. (y): symmetrical top, height 0.7
   Fig. (z): symmetrical bottom, height 0.7.

Geometric tolerancing

Release 14 has geometric tolerancing facilities, a concept first introduced to AutoCAD in Release 13. To demonstrate this feature:

1 Open your A:STDA3 standard sheet.

2 Menu bar with **Dimension–Tolerance** and:
   prompt   Symbol dialogue box as shown in Figure 39.2
   respond **pick the symbol highlighted then OK**
   prompt   geometric tolerance dialogue box
   respond **pick Cancel**.

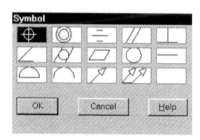

Figure 39.2   The Symbol dialogue box.

Feature control frames

Geometric tolerances define the variations which are permitted to the form or profile of a component, its orientation and location as well as the allowable runout from the exact geometry of a feature. Geometric tolerances are added by the user in **feature control frames**, these being displayed in the Geometric Tolerances dialogue box.

A feature control frame consists of two/three sections or compartments. These are shown in Figure 39.3(a) and are:

1 The geometric characteristic symbol – a symbol for the tolerance which is to be applied. AutoCAD Release 14 has 14 geometric symbols, representing location, orientation, form, profile and runout. The symbols include symmetry, flatness, straightness, angularity, concentricity, etc.

2 The tolerance value consisting of:
   a) an optional diameter symbol
   b) the actual tolerance value
   c) the material code which can be:
      i)   M: at maximum material condition
      ii)   L: at least material condition
      iii) S: regardless of feature size.

3 The primary, secondary and tertiary datum information which consists of the reference letter and the material code.

Typical types of geometric tolerance 'values' are shown in Figure 39.3(b).

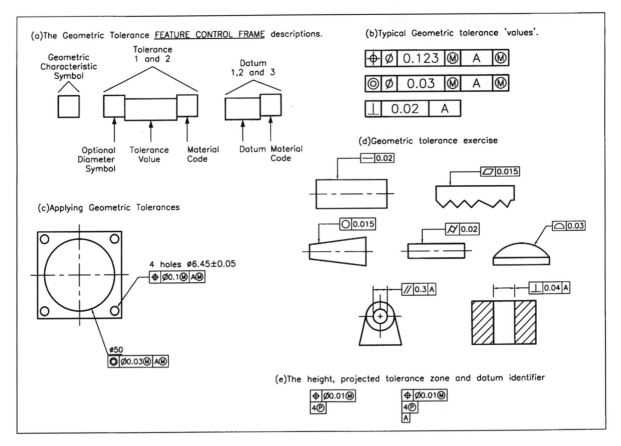

Figure 39.3 Geometric tolerance terminology and usage.

Note

1 Feature control frames are added to a dimension by the user.

2 A feature control frame contains all the tolerance information for a single dimension. The tolerance information must be entered by the user.

3 Feature control frames can be copied, moved, erased, stretched, scaled and rotated once 'inserted' into a drawing.

4 Feature control frames can be modified with DDEDIT.

Geometric tolerance example

1 Refer to Figure 39.3(c) and create a square with circles as shown. The size and layout is of no importance.

2 Diameter dimension the larger circle – use correct layer.

3 Select the TOLERANCE icon from the Dimension toolbar and:
   prompt Symbol dialogue box
   respond **pick Concentricity symbol then OK**
      (second left, top row)
   prompt Geometric Tolerance dialogue box
   with   Concentricity symbol displayed
   respond 1 at tolerance 1, pick Dia box
        2 at tolerance 1, enter 0.03
        3 at tolerance 1, pick MC box and:
   prompt Material Condition dialogue box
   respond **pick M then OK**
        4 at Datum 1, enter A
        5 at Datum 1, pick MC box, pick M then OK
        6 Geometric Tolerance dialogue box as shown in Figure 39.4
   then   **pick OK**
   prompt Enter tolerance location
   respond **pick 'under' the diameter dimension**.

4 Menu bar with **Dimension–Tolerance** and:
   prompt Symbol dialogue box
   respond **pick Position symbol then OK**
      (if in doubt **Help** helps!)
   prompt Geometric Tolerance dialogue box
   respond 1 at tolerance 1:
          a) pick Dia box
          b) enter value of 0.1
          c) pick MC box, pick M then OK
        2 at datum 1:
          a) enter datum A
          b) pick MC box, pick M then OK
        3 pick OK
   prompt Enter tolerance location
   respond **pick to suit**.

5 Now add the LEADER dimension information. I cheated here and used text with control codes.

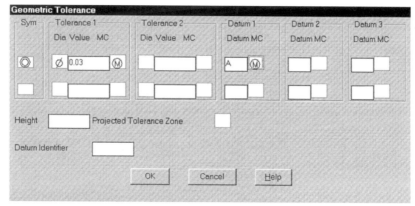

Figure 39.4 Geometric Tolerance dialogue box.

Geometric tolerance exercise

1 Refer to Figure 39.3(d) and create 'shapes' as shown – size is not important.

2 Add the geometric tolerance information.

3 Investigate the height, projected tolerance zone and datum identifier options from the Geometric Tolerance dialogue box as Fig. (e).

Summary

1 Geometric tolerances can be added to drawings using feature control frames.

2 There are 14 tolerance 'types' in Release 14.

3 All geometric tolerance information must be added by the user.

4 Feature control frames can be copied, moved, scaled, etc.

Assignments

Two assignments on tolerance dimensions and geometric tolerancing. Adding dimensions to a drawing is generally a tedious process and if dimension styles and geometric tolerancing are required, the process does not get any easier.

1 Activity 30: Tolerance dimensions.
The drawing is easy to complete. Adding the dimensions requires five created styles, all from the STDA3 default. The dimension styles use the symmetrical, limits and deviation tolerance methods, but you have the enter the upper and lower values. What about the diameter symbol in the five 'vertical' dimensions? Try dimension edit with the new option and enter %%C from the multiline text editor – unicodes revealed? If this does nor work, add the diameter symbol as text.

2 Activity 31: Geometric tolerances.
A slightly more complex drawing to complete. I created several dimension styles and used new arrowheads for two of the leader dimensions. The leader dimension allows access to the geometric tolerance dialogue box which you could investigate when adding the feature control frames?

Chapter 40

Drawing to different sizes

Two of the most common questions from new AutoCAD users are:

1 Can I draw in inches?
2 Can you set a scale at the start of a drawing?

The answer to the both these questions is yes:
a) you *can* draw in inches
b) you *can* set a scale at the start of a drawing, but remember that all drawing work should be completed full-size. This is a concept that some CAD users find difficult to accept.

In this chapter we will investigate both these topics with three exercises – a component drawn and dimensioned in inches, a large scale drawing and a small scale drawing. Each exercise will involve modifying the existing A:STDA3 standard sheet.

Drawing in inches

To draw in inches we require a new standard sheet which could be created:
a) from scratch
b) using the Wizard facility
c) altering the existing A:STDA3 standard sheet which is set to metric sizes.

We will alter our existing standard sheet, the only reason being that it has already been customized to our requirements, i.e. it has layers, a text style and a dimension style. This may save us some time. The conversion from a metric standard sheet to one which will allow us to draw in inches is relatively straightforward. We have to alter several parameters e.g. units, limits, drawing aids and the dimension style variables.

1 Open your A:STDA3 standard sheet and erase the black border – it is the wrong size.

2 *Units*: menu bar with **Format–Units** and from the Units Control dialogue box:
a) pick engineering
b) set precision to 0'–0.00"
c) angles: decimal to 0.00 precision
d) pick OK.

3 *Limits*   menu bar with **Format–Drawing Limits** and:
   prompt   Lower left corner and enter: **0,0 <R>** – default
   prompt   Upper right corner and enter: **16",12" <R>**

4 *Drawing area*:
a) with layer 0 current, draw a rectangular border from 0,0 to 15.5",11.75"
b) zoom-all.

5 *Drawing aids*:
a) set grid spacing to 0.5
b) set snap spacing to 0.25
c) set global LTSCALE value to 0.025.

6 *Dimension Style*: menu bar with **Dimension–Style** and using the Dimension Styles dialogue box:

a) current style: STDA3

b) rename to **STDIMP**

c) Geometry   spacing: 0.75
                     extension: 0.175
                     origin offset: 0.175
                     arrowheads: closed filled, size: 0.175
                     centre: none
                     overall scale: 1

d) Format   fit: best fit with no forced lines
                     text: inside horizontal ON, i.e. tick
                     outside horizontal ON, i.e. tick
                     vertical justification: centered
                     horizontal justification: centered

e) Annotation   text style: ST1
                     height: 0.18, gap: 0.09
                     units: engineering, precision: 0′–0.00″
                     zero suppression: 0 feet ON, i.e. tick
                     0 inches ON, i.e. tick
                     Trailing OFF, i.e. no tick

f) save to STDIMP

g) pick OK from Dimension Styles dialogue box to save the changes.

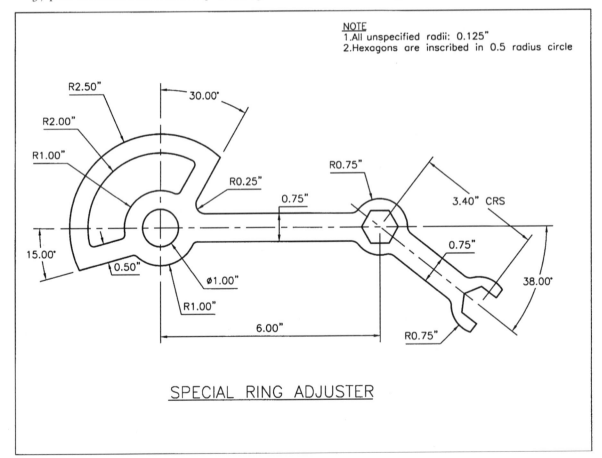

Figure 40.1   Working in inches.

7 Add all dimensions after altering the STDA3 dimension style with:
   geometry: overall scale 0.001
   annotation: units decimal with precision 0.0000.

8 Add text, but you have to decide on the height.

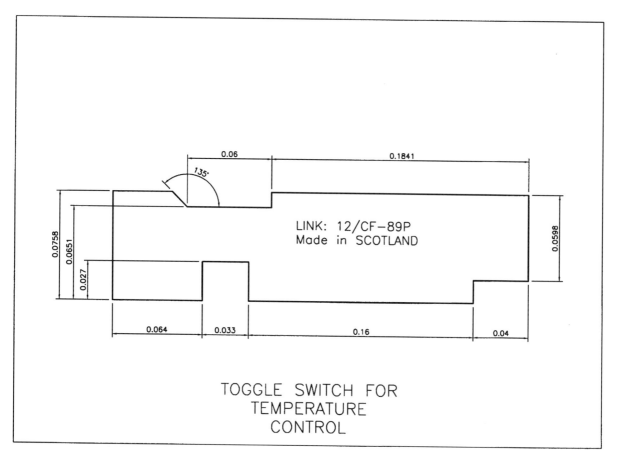

Figure 40.3 Small-scale drawing.

Summary

1 Scale drawings require the MVSETUP command to be used.

2 Large- and small-scale drawings can be 'fitted' on to any size of paper.

3 Dimensions with scaled drawings are controlled with the overall scale factor in the Dimension Styles dialogue box – geometry option. This is equivalent to altering the dimension variable **DIMSCALE**.

4 Text is scaled according to the overall scale factor.

Chapter 41

Multilines, complex lines and groups

Layers have allowed us to display continuous, centre and hidden linetypes, but AutoCAD has the facility to display multilines and complex lines, these being defined as:

Multiline: parallel lines which can consist of several line elements of differing linetype. They must be created by the user.

Complex: lines which can be displayed containing text items and shapes. They can be created by the user, although AutoCAD has several 'stored' complex linetypes.

In this chapter we will only investigate a two element multiline and only use the stored AutoCAD complex linetypes. Creating both multilines with several different elements and complex linetypes is outside the scope of this book.

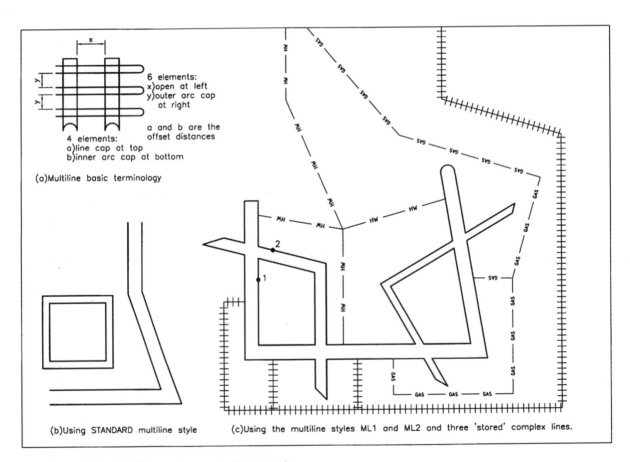

Figure 41.1   Multiline and complex line exercise.

Multilines

Multilines have their own terminology, the basic terms being displayed in Figure 41.1(a).
To investigate how to use multilines:

1 Open your A:STDA3 standard sheet with layer OUT current and refer to Figure 41.1.

2 Select the MULTILINE icon from the Draw toolbar and: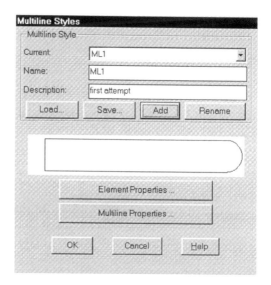
   prompt   `Justification=Top,Scale=1.00,Style=STANDARD`
   then   `Justification/Scale/Style...`
   enter   **S <R>** – the scale option
   prompt   `Set Mline scale<1.00>`
   enter   **10 <R>**
   prompt   `.../<From point>` and enter: **20,40 <R>**
   prompt   `To point` and enter: **@80,0 <R>**
   prompt   `To point` and enter: **@70<110 <R>**
   prompt   `To point` and enter: **@0,50 <R>**
   prompt   `To point` and right-click.

3 Menu bar with **Draw–Multiline** and:
   a) set scale to 5
   b) draw a square of side 40 from the point 20,60 using the close option – Fig. (b).

4 From the menu bar select **Format–Multiline Style** and:
   prompt   Multiline Styles dialogue box
   respond 1 alter Name to: **ML1**
             2 enter description as: **first attempt**
             3 pick Multiline Properties and:
   prompt   Multiline Properties dialogue box
   respond 1 pick **Line–Start**
             2 pick **Outer arc–End** – Figure 41.2
             3 pick OK
             4 Multiline Styles dialogue box returned
             5 pick Add – Figure 41.3
             6 pick OK.

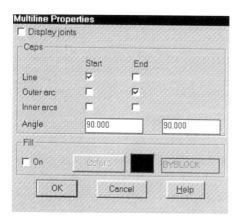

Figure 41.2 The Multiline Properties dialogue box.

Figure 41.3 The Multiline Styles dialogue box.

5 At the command line enter **MLINE <R>** and:

    prompt   Justification/Scale...
    enter   **ST <R>** – the style option
    prompt   Mstyle name and enter: **ML1 <R>**
    prompt   Justification... and enter: **S <R>** – the scale option
    prompt   Set mline scale and enter: **10 <R>**
    prompt   From point and enter: **170,170 <R>**
    prompt   To point and enter: **@0,–100 <R>**
    prompt   To point and enter: **@150,0 <R>**
    prompt   To point and enter: **@120<100 <R>**
    prompt   To point and right-click.

6 Menu bar with **Format–Multiline Style** and:

    prompt   Multiline Styles dialogue box
    respond   1 alter name to: ML2
               2 enter description as: second attempt
               3 pick Multiline Properties and:
                    prompt   Multiline Properties dialogue box
                    respond   1 cancel any existing end caps
                             2 pick line-start
                             3 pick line-end
                             4 alter angles to 45 and 30
                             5 pick OK
               4 Multiline Styles dialogue returned
               5 pick Add then OK.

7 Activate the MLINE command and:

    prompt   Justification/Scale/...
    enter   **ST <R>** – the style option
    prompt   Mstyle name (or ?)
    enter   **? <R>** – the query option
    prompt   AutoCAD text window with:
               Name   *Description*
               ML1   first attempt
               STANDARD
               ML2   second attempt
    respond **cancel the text window**
    prompt   Mstyle name and enter: **ML2 <R>**
    prompt   Justification/Scale...
    enter   **S <R>** then **8 <R>** – the scale option
    prompt   From point and enter: **210,40 <R>**
    prompt   To point and enter: **@0,80 <R>**
    prompt   To point and enter: **@–80,20 <R>**
    prompt   To point and right-click.

8 Repeat the MLINE command and:
    a) set the scale to 5
    b) draw from: 350,160 to: @100<–150 to: @80<–60 to: right-click.

9 Menu bar with **Modify–Object–Multiline** and:

    prompt   Multiline Edit Tools dialogue box – Figure 41.4
    respond **pick Open Cross then OK**
               (middle row left)
    prompt   Select first mline
    respond **pick multiline 1**

prompt Select second mline
respond **pick multiline 2**
prompt Select first mline
respond **pick as required** until all the 'crossed' multilines are opened – Fig. (c).

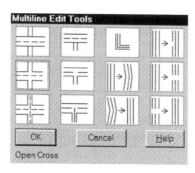

Figure 41.4 The Multiline Edit Tools dialogue box.

Complex linetypes

1 Continue with the exercise on the screen.

2 Menu bar with **Format–Layer** create a new layer:
   a) name: L1
   b) colour: to suit
   c) linetype: pick 'continuous' in L1 layer line and:

       prompt Select Linetype dialogue box
       respond 1 pick load
                    2 scroll and pick Gas_line then OK
       prompt Select Linetype dialogue box
       with Gas_line displayed
       respond pick Gas_line then OK
       and layer L1 displayed with gas_line linetype

   d) pick OK.

3 Using step 2 as a guide, create another two layers using the following information:

Name	Colour	Linetype
L1	to suit	Hot_water_supply
L2	to suit	Tracks

4 With each layer current, refer to Fig. (c) and draw gas, water and tracks lines.

5 *Task*: using the CHANGE PROPERTIES command, use the ltScale option to optimize the appearance of the new linetypes.

6 The exercise is now complete and can be saved if required.

Groups

A group is a named collection of objects. Groups are stored with a saved drawing and group definitions can be externally referenced. To demonstrate how groups are created:

1 Open your standard sheet, layer OUT current and refer to Figure 41.5.

2 Draw the reference shape using your discretion for any sizes not given. Ensure the lowest vertex is at the point 210,120.

3 Menu bar with **Tools–Object group** and:

prompt	Object Grouping dialogue box
respond	1 at group name enter: **GR1**
	2 at description enter: **first attempt**
	3 ensure selectable is ON, i.e. tick in box
	4 pick create group: **New<**
prompt	Select objects
respond	pick the two inclined lines and the large circle then right-click
prompt	Object Grouping dialogue box
with	group name Selectable
	GR1 yes
respond	pick OK.

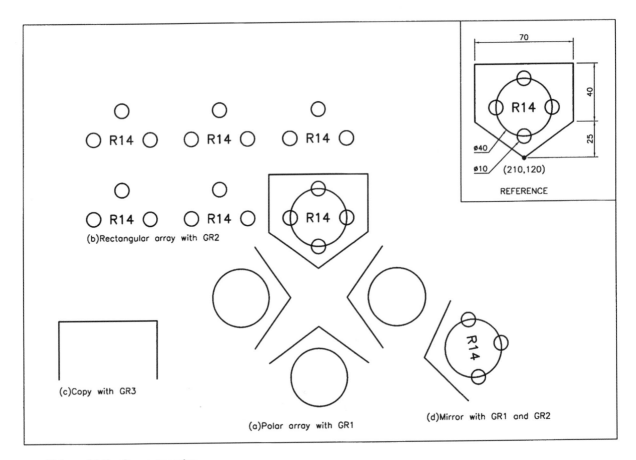

Figure 41.5 Group exercise.

4 At the command line enter **GROUP <R>** and:

   prompt   Object Grouping dialogue box

   respond   1 at group name enter: **GR2**

                 2 at description enter: **second attempt**

                 3 selectable ON? – it should be!

                 4 pick create group: **New<**

   prompt   Select objects

   respond   pick the text item and the top three small circles then right-click

   prompt   Object Grouping dialogue box with GR2 listed?

   respond   pick OK

5 Repeat the GROUP command and:

   a) name: GR3

   b) description: third group – or similar

   c) create group: New<

   d) objects: pick the two vertical and the horizontal lines

   e) dialogue box as Figure 41.6

   f) pick OK.

6 Activate the ARRAY command and:

   prompt   Select objects

   enter   **GROUP <R>**

   prompt   Enter group name and enter: **GR1 <R>**

   prompt   Select objects and right-click

   prompt   Rectangular or polar and enter: **P <R>**

   prompt   Center point and enter: **210,100 <R>**

   prompt   Number of items and enter: **4 <R>**

   prompt   Angle to fill and enter: **360 <R>**

   prompt   Rotate option and enter: **Y <R>**.

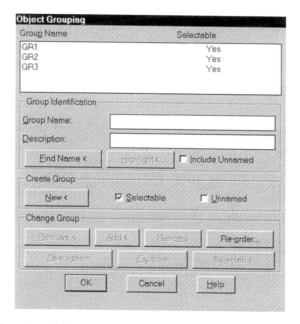

Figure 41.6   Object Grouping dialogue box.

7 The named group (GR1) will be displayed as shown in Fig. (a).

8 With the ARRAY command:
   prompt   Select objects
   enter   **GROUP <R>** then **GR2 <R><R>** – why two returns?
   prompt   Rectangular or polar and enter: **R <R>**
   prompt   Number of rows and enter: **2 <R>**
   prompt   Number of columns and enter: **3 <R>**
   prompt   Row distance and enter: **55 <R>**
   prompt   Column distance and enter: **–70 <R>** – Fig. (b).

9 With the COPY command:
   a) objects and enter: GROUP <R>
   b) group name and enter: GR3 <R><R>
   c) base point and enter: 210,120 <R>
   d) second point and enter: @–150,–100 <R> – Fig. (c).

10 Select the MIRROR icon and:
    a) select objects and enter: GROUP <R>
    b) group name and enter: GR1 <R>
    c) select objects and enter: GROUP <R>
    d) group name and enter: GR2 <R>
    e) select objects and right-click
    f) first point of mirror line and enter: 210,45 <R>
    g) second point and enter: @100<50 <R>
    h) delete old objects and enter: N <R> – Fig. (d).

11 The exercise is complete and can be saved if required.

12 Do not quit the drawing.

Task

1 Erase the original text item – complete group (GR2) erased?

2 Undo this effect with the UNDO icon.

3 Select the explode icon and select any group object and you will get:

   '? were not able to be exploded' displayed at prompt line.

4 At the command line enter GROUP <R> and from the dialogue box:
   a) pick GR2 line
   b) pick Explode
   c) pick OK.

5 Now erase the text item.

Summary

1 Multilines can be created by the user with different linetypes and can have several elements in their definition – not considered in this book.

2 Multilines have line or arc end caps.

3 Multilines have their own editing facility.

4 Complex linetypes can be have text or shape items in their definition.

5 Complex linetypes can be created by the user – not considered in this book.

6 Groups are collections of objects defined by the user.

7 Once created, a group can be exploded from the Object Grouping dialogue box.

Chapter 42

Blocks

A block is part of a drawing which is 'stored away' for future recall **within the drawing in which it was created**. The block may be a nut, a diode, a tree, a house or even a complete drawing. Blocks are used when repetitive copying of objects is required, but they have another important feature – text can be attached to them. This text addition to blocks is called **attributes** will be discussed in a later chapter.

Getting started

1 Open the A:STDA3 standard sheet and refer to Figure 42.1.

2 Draw the house shape using the reference sizes given with:
   a) the outline on layer OUT
   b) the circular windows on layer OUT but green (CHANGE)
   c) a text item on layer TEXT
   d) four dimensions on layer DIMEN

   Use your discretion for any sizes not given.

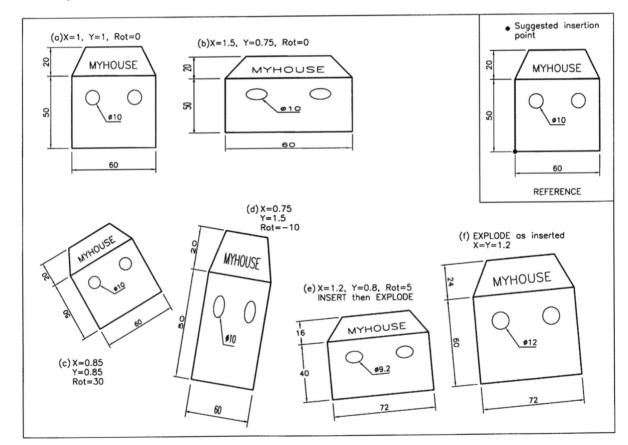

Figure 42.1 Block creation and insertion exercise.

Creating a block

1 At the command line enter **BLOCK <R>** and:

prompt	Block name (or ?)
enter	**HOUSE <R>**
prompt	Insertion base point
respond	**Intersection icon and pick lower left corner**
prompt	Select objects
respond	**window the house and dimensions**
prompt	14 found then Select objects
respond	**right-click**.

2 The house shape will disappear from the screen. It has been 'stored' as a block within the current drawing. This drawing has not yet been saved.

Inserting a block

Created blocks can be inserted into the current drawing by:
a) direct keyboard entry
b) with a dialogue box.

We will investigate both methods.

Keyboard insertion

1 At the command line enter **INSERT <R>** and:

prompt	Block name (or ?)
enter	**HOUSE <R>**
prompt	Insertion point and note the 'ghost' image
enter	**35,200 <R>**
prompt	X scale factor<1>/Corner/XYZ
enter	**1 <R>**
prompt	Y scale factor (default=X)
enter	**1 <R>**
prompt	Rotation angle<0>
enter	**0 <R>**.

2 The house block is inserted full-size as shown in Fig. (a).

3 Repeat the INSERT command and:

prompt	Block name and enter: **HOUSE <R>**
prompt	Insertion point and enter: **145,210 <R>**
prompt	X scale factor and enter: **1.5 <R>**
prompt	Y scale factor and enter: **0.75 <R>**
prompt	Rotation angle and enter: **0 <R>** – Fig. (b).

Dialogue box insertion

1 From the Draw toolbar select the Insert block icon and:

   prompt   Insert dialogue box

   respond   **pick Block...**

   prompt   Defined Block dialogue box

   with   *a*) pattern *

               b) HOUSE as only block name

   respond   **pick HOUSE then OK**

   prompt   Insert dialogue box with HOUSE as the block name

               (the above selection was probably not required as HOUSE was the block name from the previous exercise)

   respond   1 ensure Specify Parameters on Screen is active – tick

               2 pick OK

   prompt   Insertion point and enter: **55,75 <R>**

   prompt   X scale factor and enter: **0.85 <R>**

   prompt   Y scale factor and enter: **0.85 <R>**

   prompt   Rotation angle and enter: **30 <R>** – Fig. (c).

2 Menu bar with **Insert–Block** and:

   prompt   Insert dialogue box

   with   HOUSE as the block name

   respond   1 deactivate the Specify Parameters on Screen – no tick

               2 other parameters now available in black type

               3 alter Insertion Point to X: 120, Y: 40, Z: 0

               4 alter Scale to X: 0.75, Y: 1.5, Z: 1

               5 alter Rotation to angle: –10

               6 dialogue box as Figure 42.2

               7 pick OK – Fig. (d).

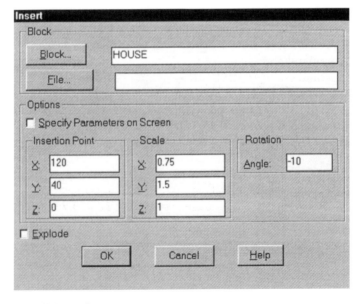

Figure 42.2 The Insert dialogue box.

Notes

1 An inserted block is a **single object**. Select the erase icon and pick any point on one of the inserted blocks then right-click. The complete block is erased. Undo the erase effect.

2 Blocks are inserted into a drawing with layers 'as used'. Freeze the DIMEN layer and the four inserted blocks will be displayed without dimensions. Now thaw the DIMEN layer.

3 Blocks can be inserted at varying X and Y scale factors and at any angle of rotation. The default scale is $X = Y = 1$, i.e. the block is inserted full size.

4 Dimensions which are attached to inserted blocks are not altered if the scale factors are changed.

5. A named block can be redefined and will be discussed later.

Exploding a block

The fact that a block is a single object may not always be suitable to the user, i.e. you may want to copy parts of a block. AutoCAD uses the EXPLODE command to 'convert' an inserted block back to its individual objects.

The explode option can be used:
a) after a block has been inserted
b) during the insertion process.

1 At the command line enter **INSERT <R>** and:
prompt   Block name and enter: HOUSE
prompt   Insertion point and enter: 220,25
prompt   X scale factor and enter: 1.2
prompt   Y scale factor and enter: 0.8
prompt   Rotation angle and enter: 5.

2 Select the EXPLODE icon from the modify toolbar and:
prompt   Select objects
respond   **pick the inserted block then right-click**.

3 The exploded block is restored to its individual objects and the dimensions are **scaled to the factors entered** – Fig. (e). The individual objects of this exploded block can now be edited if required. Note the dimensions 'style' of the exploded block!

4 Select the INSERT BLOCK icon and using the Insert dialogue box:
a) specify parameters on screen: ON, i.e. ticked
b) insertion point X: 325, Y: 35, Z: 0
c) scale X: 1.2, Y: 0.8, Z: 1
d) rotation angle: 5
e) explode: ON, i.e. ticked and *note the scale factor values*
f) pick OK.

5 The block is exploded as it is inserted at a scale of $X = Y = 1.2$ and the dimensions display this scale effect – Fig. (e). Note my 'style' for the inserted/exploded dimensions!

6 *Note*:
a) a block exploded after insertion will retain the original X and Y scale factors
b) a block exploded as it is inserted has $X = Y$ scale factors.

Block exercise

1 Open the A:STDA3 standard sheet and refer to Figure 42.3.

2 Draw the two components using the reference sizes given but do not add any dimensions.

3 Select the MAKE BLOCK icon from the draw toolbar and:
   prompt   Block Definition dialogue box
   respond   1   block name: enter **CAM**
                  2   pick Select Point<
   prompt   `Insertion base point`
   respond   pick point indicated
   prompt   Block Definition dialogue box – coordinates displayed
   respond   pick Select Objects<
   prompt   `Select objects`
   respond   window the CAM shape then right-click
   prompt   Block Definition dialogue box
   respond   pick OK.

4 The CAM shape is still displayed on the screen.

5 Menu bar with **Draw–Block–Make** and:
   prompt   Block Definition dialogue box
   respond   1   Block name: enter **FOL**
                  2   pick Select Objects<

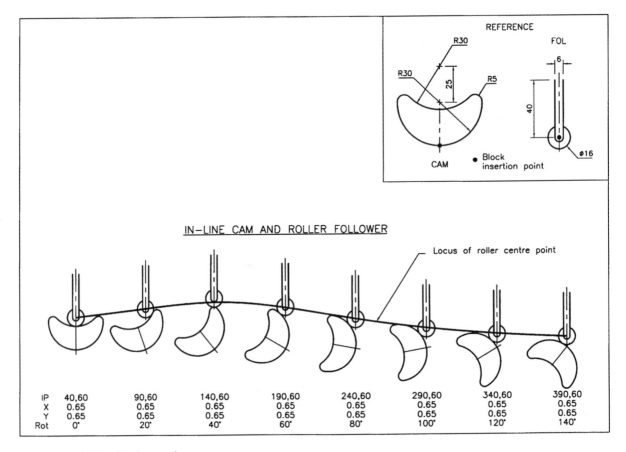

Figure 42.3   Block exercise.

prompt   Insertion base point
respond pick point as indicated – centre icon?
prompt   Block Definition dialogue box
respond pick select objects<
prompt   Select objects
respond window the FOL shape then right-click
prompt   Block Definition dialogue box – similar to Figure 42.4
respond pick OK.

6 The FOL shape will still be displayed on the screen.

7 Erase the CAM and FOL shapes.

8 With the command line INSERT command:
   a) block name: CAM
   b) insertion point: 40,60
   c) X scale: 0.65
   d) Y scale: 0.65
   e) rotation: 0.

9 Repeat the INSERT command with the CAM block using the insertion point and rotation values given in Figure 42.3. The *X* and *Y* scale factors are 0.65 for all insertions.

10 Insert the FOL block with:
   a) insertion point: 40,120
   b) X and Y scale factors: 0.75
   c) rotation: 0.

11 Rectangular array the inserted FOL block:
   a) for one row and eight columns
   b) column distance: 50.

12 The followers (FOL) have now to be moved vertically downwards until they 'touch' the cams. This sounds easier than it is, but I will leave this for you to complete.

13 When the followers are in their correct position:
   a) draw a 1 wide polyline through the roller centres
   b) edit this polyline to a spline fit
   c) this curve is the **locus of the roller centre points**.

14 Using the DISTANCE command, find the vertical distance between the leftmost and rightmost roller centre points. My value was 14.98.

15 Save the completed exercise if required.

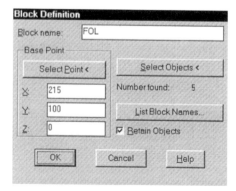

Figure 42.4 The Block Definition dialogue box.

Notes on blocks

Several points are worth discussing about blocks:

1 *The insertion point.* When a block is being inserted using the Insert dialogue box, the user has the option to decide whether the coordinates are entered via the dialogue box – the specify parameters on screen option. I prefer to have this option ON (tick in box) as I have 'more control' over the insertion point.

2 *Exploding a block.* I recommend that blocks are inserted before they are exploded. This maintains the original *X* and *Y* scale factors. Remember that blocks do not need to be exploded.

3 *The ? option.* Both the command line BLOCK and INSERT commands have a ? option which will list all current blocks in the current drawing. At the command line enter BLOCK <R> and:

    prompt   `Block name (or ?)` and enter: **? <R>**
    prompt   `Block(s) to list<*>` and enter: *** <R>**
    prompt   AutoCAD text window
    with   `Defined blocks`
              `CAM`
              `FOL`
              `User`
              `Blocks`
              `2`

4 *Making a block.* Blocks can be created by command line entry or by a dialogue box and the following interesting:
    a) command line: the original shape disappears from the screen
    b) dialogue box: the original shape 'stays' on the screen.

Using blocks

1 Open your A:STDA3 standard sheet, layer Out and refer to Figure 42.5.

2 Draw a 20 sided square with the diagonals and make a block:
    name: BL1
    insertion point: diagonal intersection
    objects: window the shape – no dimensions.

Draw an inclined line, a circle, an arc and a polyline shape of line and arc segments – discretion for sizes.

4 *Divide*   Menu bar with **Draw–Point–Divide** and:
           prompt `Select object to divide`
           respond **pick the line**
           prompt `<Number of segments>/Block` and enter: **B <R>**
           prompt `Block name to insert` and enter: **BL1 <R>**
           prompt `Align block with object` and enter: **N <R>**
           prompt `Number of segments` and enter: **4 <R>** – Fig. (a).

5 *Measure* Menu bar with **Draw–Point–Measure** and:
           prompt `Select object to measure` and: **pick the circle**
           prompt `<Segment length>/Block` and enter: **B <R>**
           prompt `Block name to insert` and enter: **BL1 <R>**
           prompt `Align block with object` and enter: **Y <R>**
           prompt `Segment length` and enter: **35 <R>** – Fig. (b).

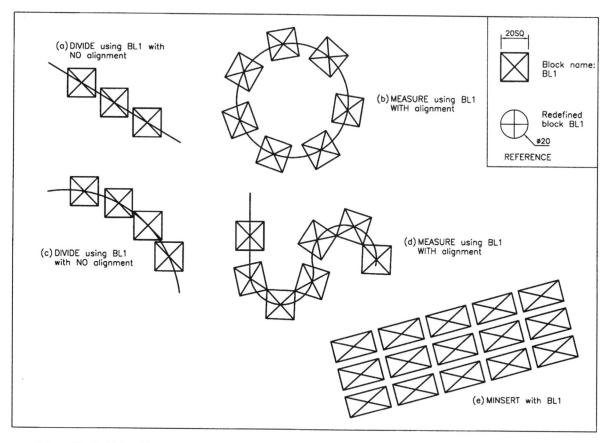

Figure 42.5 Using blocks exercise.

6 Using the DIVIDE and MEASURE commands:
   a) divide the arc: with block BL1, no alignment and with five segments – Fig. (c)
   b) measure the polyline: with block BL1, with alignment and a segment length of 30.

7 *MINSERT (multiple insert).* At the command line enter **MINSERT <R>** and:
   prompt Block name and enter: **BL1 <R>**
   prompt Insertion point and pick a suitable point on screen
   prompt X scale and enter: **1.5 <R>**
   prompt Y scale and enter: **0.75 <R>**
   prompt Rotation angle and enter: **15 <R>**
   prompt Number of rows and enter: **3 <R>**
   prompt Number of columns and enter: **5 <R>**
   prompt Unit cell or distance between rows and enter: **20 <R>**
   prompt Distance between columns and enter: **35 <R>**.

   The block BL1 is arrayed in a 3×5 rectangular matrix – Fig. (e).

8 Using the EXPLODE icon, pick any of the minsert blocks and:
   prompt 1 was minserted, i.e. you cannot explode minserted blocks.

9 *Redefining a block:*
   a) draw a circle of radius 10 and add the vertical and horizontal diagonals
   b) change the colour of the circle and lines to blue
   c) at the command line enter **BLOCK <R>** and:

prompt	Block name and enter: **BL1 <R>**
prompt	Block BL1 already exists Redefine it? <N>
enter	**Y <R>**
prompt	Insertion base point
respond	pick the centre of the circle
prompt	Select objects
respond	window the circle and lines then right-click

   d) interesting result? – all the red squares should be replaced by blue circles with the same alignment, scales, etc.

10 *Oops.* The OOPS command can be used to redisplay a block which has been defined with the command line BLOCK command. Entering **OOPS <R>** at the command line will 'restore' the block to the screen, but will not affect the 'saved block'.

Layer 0 and blocks

Blocks have been created with the objects drawn on their 'correct' layers. Layer 0 is the AutoCAD default layer and can be used for block creation with interesting results.

1 Erase all objects from the screen (save?) and draw:
   a) a 50 unit square on layer 0 – black
   b) a 20 radius circle inside the square on layer OUT – red
   c) two centre lines on layer CL – green.

2 Make a block of the complete shape with block name TRY, using the circle centre as the insertion point.

3 Make layer OUT current and insert block TRY at 55,210, full size with no rotation. The square is inserted with red continuous lines.

4 Make layer CL current and insert the block at 135,210, full size and with no rotation. The square has green centre lines.

5 With layer HID current, insert the block at 215,210 and the square will be displayed with yellow hidden lines.

6 Make layer 0 current and insert at 295,210 – square is black.

7 Freeze layer OUT and:
   a) no red circles
   b) no red square from first insertion when layer OUT was current.

8 Thaw layer OUT and insert block TRY using the Insert dialogue box with:
   a) explode option active, i.e. tick in box
   b) insertion point: 175,115
   c) square is black – it is on layer 0.

9 Explode the first three inserted blocks and the square should be black, i.e. it has been 'transferred' to layer 0 with the explode command.

10 Finally freeze layer 0 and:
   a) no black squares
   b) no objects from fourth insertion – why?

11 This completes the block exercises.

Summary

1 A block is a single object 'stored' for recall in the drawing in which it was created.

2 Blocks are used for the insertion of frequently used 'shapes'.

3 An inserted block is a single object.

4 Blocks can be inserted full size ($X = Y$) or with differing X and Y scale factors and varying rotation angles.

5 The explode command 'restores' an inserted block to its original objects.

6 The explode command can be used after insertion (command line) or during insertion (dialogue box).

7 Blocks are inserted with 'layers intact'.

8 Blocks can be used with the divide and measure commands.

9 Multiple block inserts are permissible with the MINSERT command in a rectangular array pattern.

10 Existing blocks can be redefined. The current drawing will be 'updated' to display the new block definition.

11 Unused blocks can be purged.

Assignment

One activity requiring blocks to be created has been included for you to attempt.

Activity 32:
Pneumatic circuit.

1 Draw the four pneumatic symbols below, using your discretion for any sizes not given. A snap of 2.5 may help.

2 Make blocks of each symbol selecting a suitable insertion point.

3 Complete the pneumatic circuit, inserting the blocks at 0.75 full size. The additional lines have to be added.

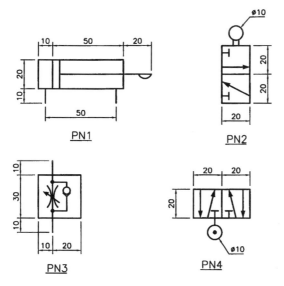

Chapter 43

WBLOCKS

Blocks are useful when shapes are required for repetitive insertion in a drawing, but they are **drawing specific**, i.e. they can only be used within the drawing in which they were created. There are however, blocks which can be created and accessed by all AutoCAD users, i.e. they are **global**. These are called WBLOCKS (world blocks) and they are created in a similar manner to 'ordinary' blocks. WBLOCKS are stored and recalled from a 'named folder/directory' which we will assume to be the A floppy drive – you may have an existing named folder/directory for your AutoCAD work.

Creating WBLOCKS

1 Open your A:STDA3 standard sheet with layer OUT current.

2 Refer to Figure 43.1 and draw a rectangular polyline shape – Fig. (a). The start point is to be 2.5,2.5 and the polyline has to have a constant width of 5. Close the shape with the close option. The rectangle sizes will become apparent during the insertion process.

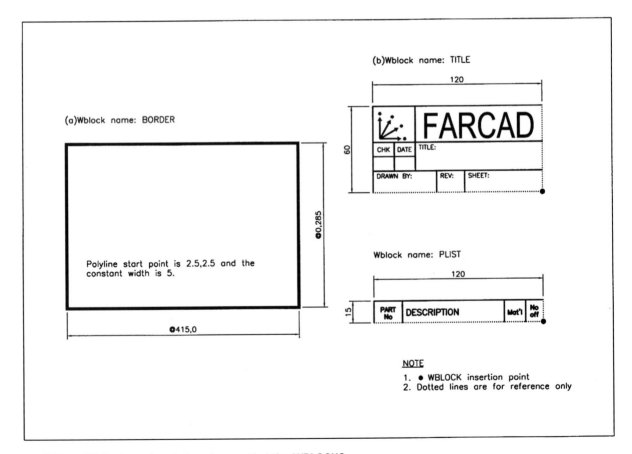

Figure 43.1 Layout and sizes for creating the WBLOCKS.

3 At the command line enter **WBLOCK <R>** and:
   prompt   Create Drawing File dialogue box
   respond   1 pick scroll arrow at Save in box
               2 pick your named folder or A drive
               3 enter **BORDER** as the file name
               4 ensure Drawing.dwg is the drawing type
               5 pick Save
   prompt   Block name and right-click
   prompt   Insertion base point and enter: **0,0 <R>**
   prompt   Select objects
   respond   **pick any point on the polyline then right-click**.

4 The polyline border will disappear – remember OOPS?

5 Construct the title box from the information in Fig. (b), the actual detail being to your
   own design, e.g. text style, company name and logo, etc. The only requirement is to use
   the given sizes – the donut and dotted lines are for 'guidance' only and should not be
   drawn.

6 Command line with **WBLOCK <R>** and:
   prompt   Create Drawing File dialogue box
   respond   1 scroll and pick your folder/directory/A drive
               2 BORDER displayed in drawing list?
               3 enter **TITLE** as the file name
               4 pick Save
   prompt   Block name and right-click
   prompt   Insertion base point
   respond   **pick point indicated by donut** (snap on helps?)
   prompt   Select objects
   respond   **window the title box then right-click**.

7 Create the parts list table headings using the basic layout in Fig. (c). Again use your own
   design for text, etc.

8 With the WBLOCK command:
   a) File name: **PLIST**
   b) pick Save
   c) block name: right-click
   d) insertion base point: pick as indicated by donut
   e) objects: window the shape then right-click.

9 Proceed to the next part of the exercise.

Inserting WBLOCKS

1 Open A:STDA3 – say no to any save changes prompt.

2 Refer to Figure 43.2 and draw the sectional pulley assembly. No sizes have been given, but you should be able to complete the drawing – use the snap to help. Add the hatching and the 'balloon' effect using donut-line-circle-middled text.

3 Select the INSERT icon from the draw toolbar and:
   prompt   Insert dialogue box
   respond **pick File...**
   prompt   Select Drawing file dialogue box
   respond 1 scroll and pick folder/directory/A drive
           2 pick BORDER and:
             a) File name: BORDER
             b) preview: displays the polyline
           3 pick **Open**
   prompt   Insert dialogue box with:
           a) Block: BORDER
           b) File: A:\BORDER.dwg
   respond **pick OK**
   prompt   Insertion point and enter: **0,0 <R>**
   prompt   X scale and enter: **1 <R>**
   prompt   Y scale and enter: **1 <R>**
   prompt   Rotation angle and enter: **0 <R>**.

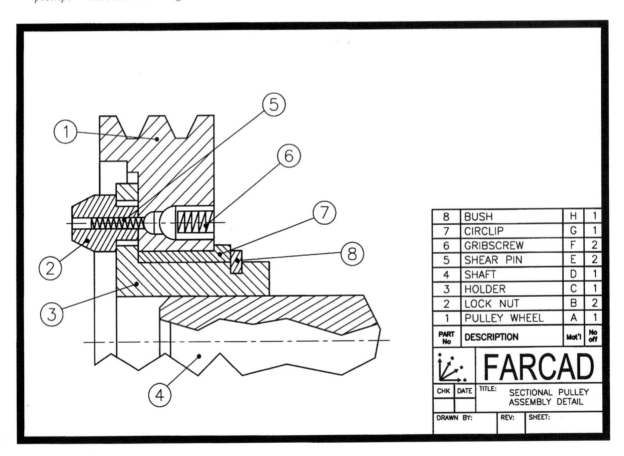

8	BUSH	H	1
7	CIRCLIP	G	1
6	GRIBSCREW	F	2
5	SHEAR PIN	E	2
4	SHAFT	D	1
3	HOLDER	C	1
2	LOCK NUT	B	2
1	PULLEY WHEEL	A	1
PART No	DESCRIPTION	Mat'l	No off

FARCAD

| CHK | DATE | TITLE: | SECTIONAL PULLEY ASSEMBLY DETAIL |
| DRAWN BY: | | REV: | SHEET: |

Figure 43.2 Inserting WBLOCKS exercise.

4 The polyline border should be inserted within the 'drawing frame' of the STDA3 standard sheet.

5 Menu bar with **Insert–Block** and:
prompt Insert dialogue box
respond pick File
prompt Select Drawing File dialogue box
respond 1 pick the A drive – or folder/directory
2 scroll and pick TITLE – preview displayed?
3 pick Open
prompt Insert dialogue box
with TITLE as the block name
respond pick OK
prompt Insertion point and enter: **415,5 <R>**
prompt scales: full size (1) and 0 rotation.

6 Using the WBLOCK command, insert file **PLIST**, full size with 0 rotation, the insertion point being 415,65 – or the ENDpoint of the top horizontal line of the TITLE box.

7 When inserted, add the additional lines and text items to the parts list table.

8 The drawing is complete – save?

9 *Notes*:
a) three saved WBLOCKS (BORDER, TITLE and PLIST) have been inserted into the drawing A:STDA3, these WBLOCKS having been 'stored' in our A floppy (or a named folder). If the computer is networked, then all CAD users could access the three WBLOCKS
b) the border and title box could be permanently added to the A:STDA3 standard sheet – you decide on this
c) the three wblocks could be used in every exercise and activity from this point.

About WBLOCKS

Every drawing is a WBLOCK and every WBLOCK is a drawing.

The above statement is true – think about it!

1 Open your A:STDA3 standard sheet and refer to Figure 43.3 which displays five saved activity drawings, inserted at varying scales and rotation angles. The drawings are:

Drawing file	IP	Xscale	Yscale	Rot
ACT_8	5,5	0.5	0.5	0
ACT_14	25,155	0.4	0.3	5
ACT_24	220,5	0.25	0.5	0
ACT_29	330,5	0.15	0.75	0
ACT_32	200,190	0.2	0.3	−5

2 Insert some of your previously saved drawings.

3 When creating a WBLOCK, if the file name entered has already been used, AutoCAD will display the message box with:
```
A drawing with this name already exists
Do you want to replace it? <N>
```

4 During the WBLOCK insertion process, there was a prompt to which we always entered <R>/right-click. This was:

prompt   Block name

This prompt allows the user to 'convert' an existing block into a wblock, and as we did not have any created blocks which were to be converted to WBLOCKS, we entered <R>.

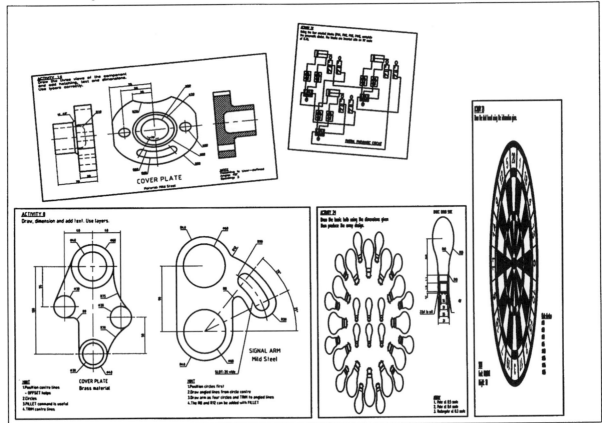

Figure 43.3   Inserting five activity drawings into A:STDA3.

Task

Can an inserted wblock be exploded? – investigate this!

Summary

1   WBLOCKS are global and could be accessed by all AutoCAD users.

2   WBLOCKS are usually saved to a named folder.

3   WBLOCKS are created with the command line entry WBLOCK <R>.

4   WBLOCKS are inserted into a drawing in a manner similar to ordinary blocks, the user selecting:
    a) the named folder
    b) the drawing file name.

5   WBLOCKS can be exploded after/during insertion.

6   All saved drawings are WBLOCKS.

Assignment

A single activity for you to attempt.

Activity 33:
Coupling.

1   Complete the drawing.

2   Insert BORDER at 0,0 – full size.

3   Insert TITLE – insertion point to suit.

4   Add all text and dimensions.

5   Save?

Chapter 44

Attributes

An attribute is an item of text attached to a block or a WBLOCK and allows the user to add repetitive type text to frequently used blocks when they are inserted into a drawing. The text could be:

a) weld symbols containing appropriate information
b) electrical components with values
c) parts lists containing coded, number off, material, etc.

Attributes used as text items are useful, but their main advantage is that attribute data can be **extracted** from a drawing and stored in an attribute extraction file. These data could then be used as input to other computer packages, e.g. databases, spreadsheets, word-processors, etc.

This chapter is only a 'taster' as the topic will not be investigated fully. The editing and extraction features of attributes are beyond the scope of this book. The purpose of this chapter is to introduce the user to:

a) attaching attributes to a block
b) inserting an attribute block into a drawing.

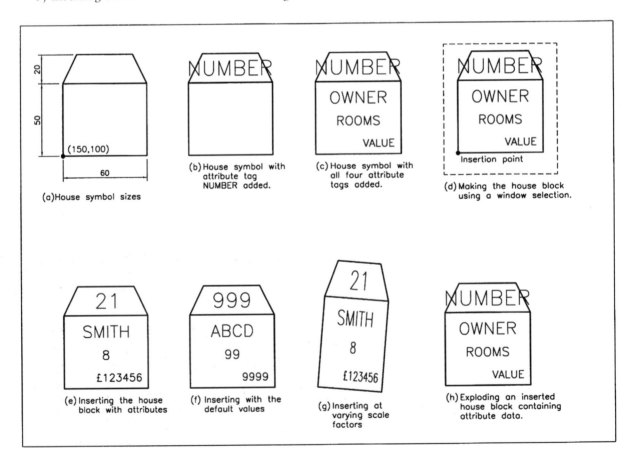

Figure 44.1 Making and using attributes with the block: HOUSE.

Getting started

The attribute example for discussion is a small select housing complex, each house being represented by a symbol – a block. On each symbol the street number, house owner, number of rooms and the current market value is to be displayed, and this will be achieved using attributes.

1 Open your A:STDA3 standard sheet with layer OUT current. Refer to Figure 44.1.

2 Create the house symbol using the sizes in Fig. (a) – discretion for sizes not given. Ensure that the lower left corner is positioned at the point 150,100 – this is important for the text which is to be added to the symbol.

Defining the attributes

1 Make layer TEXT current.

2 At the command line enter **ATTDEF <R>** and:

prompt	Attribute modes...
respond	**right-click**
prompt	Attribute tag and enter: **NUMBER <R>**
prompt	Attribute prompt and enter: **House number? <R>**
prompt	Default attribute value and enter: **999 <R>**
prompt	Justification/Style...
enter	**C <R>** – centre point option as text is involved!
prompt	Center point and enter: **180,155 <R>**
prompt	Height and enter: **10 <R>**
prompt	Rotation angle and enter: **0 <R>**.

3 The attribute tag NUMBER will be displayed in the roof area of the house symbol as Fig. (b).

4 Use the ATTDEF command three more times and enter the following attribute information using the same procedure as step 1

	First entry	Second entry	Third entry
Attribute modes	<R>	<R>	<R>
Attribute tag	OWNER	ROOMS	VALUE
Attribute prompt	House owner?	Number of rooms?	Current value?
Default value	ABCD	99	9999
Justification	Centred	Centred	Right
Text point	180,135	180,120	205,105
Height	8	6	5
Rotation	0	0	0

5 When all the attribute information has been entered, the house symbol will display the four tags – Fig. (c).

6 *Note*: when attributes are used for the first time, the words 'tag', 'prompt' and 'value' can cause confusion. The following description may help to overcome this:
   tag: is the actual attribute 'label' which is attached to the drawing at the specified text start point. This tag item can have any text style, height and rotation
   prompt: is an aid to the user when the attribute data is being entered with the inserted block
   value: is an artificial name/number for the attribute being entered. It can have any alpha-numeric value.

7 In our first attribute definition sequence, we were creating the house number and entered:
   1 Tag: NUMBER
   2 Prompt: House number?
   3 Default value: 999.

Creating the attribute block

1 At the command line enter **BLOCK <R>** and:
    prompt   Block name and enter: **HOUSE <R>**
    prompt   Insertion base point
    respond   **pick lower left corner of house symbol**
    prompt   Select objects
    respond   **window the house and tags then right-click** – Fig. (d).

2 The block will disappear as it has been made into a block with the command line BLOCK entry.

3 Remember OOPS, although it is not really necessary for us.

Testing the created block with attributes

Now that the block with attributes has been created, we want to 'test' the attribute information it contains. This requires the block to be inserted into the drawing, so:

1 Make layer OUT current.

2 At the command line enter **INSERT <R>** and:
    prompt   Block name and enter: **HOUSE <R>**
    prompt   Insertion point and pick a point to suit
    prompt   X scale and enter: **1 <R>**
    prompt   Y scale and enter: **1 <R>**
    prompt   Rotation angle and enter: **0 <R>**
    prompt   House number?<999> and enter: **21 <R>**
    prompt   House owner?<ABCD> and enter: **SMITH <R>**
    prompt   Number of rooms?<99> and enter: **8 <R>**
    prompt   Current value?<9999> and enter: **£123456 <R>**.

3 The house will be displayed with the attribute information as Fig. (e).

4 *Question*: do you recognize the prompts and defaults displayed at the command line?

5 *Note*: your order of the last four prompt lines (i.e. house number–current value) may not be in the same order as mine. This is not your fault.

6 Now insert the house block twice more:
    a) at any suitable point, full size with 0 rotation and accept the default values i.e. right-click at the prompt – Fig. (f)
    b) at another point on the screen with the *X* scale factor as 0.75, the *Y* scale factor as 1.25 and the rotation angle as –5. Use the same attribute entries as step 2, i.e. 21, SMITH, 8, £123456. The result should be as Fig. (g).

7 Explode any inserted block which contains attribute information and the tags will be displayed – Fig. (h).

8 We are now ready to insert the 'real' attribute data.

Attribute information

1 The housing estate is to consist of eight houses, each house being represented by the house symbol with the appropriate attribute information displayed. The attribute information is listed in Table 44.1.

Table 44.1 Attribute data

Tag	Number	Owner	Rooms	Value
Data	1	Brown	6	£85000
	2	Blue	6	£90000
	3	Cherry	8	£105000
	4	Donald	10	£150000
	5	East	7	£95000
	6	French	9	£120000
	7	Gray	5	£80000
	8	Horace	3	£50000

2 Attribute information can be added to an inserted block:
  a) from the keyboard – as previous example
  b) via a dialogue box which will now be discussed.

3 Erase all objects from the screen and make layer OUT current.

4 At the command line enter **ATTDIA <R>** and:
  prompt New value for ATTDIA<0>
  enter **1 <R>**.

5 At the command line enter **INSERT <R>** and:
  prompt Block name and enter: **HOUSE <R>**
  prompt Insertion point and enter: **30,180 <R>**
  prompt X scale factor and enter: **1 <R>**
  prompt Y scale factor and enter: **1 <R>**
  prompt Rotation angle and enter: **0 <R>**
  prompt Enter Attributes dialogue box
  with information displayed as shown in Figure 44.2(a); recognize the prompts and defaults?
  respond 1 alter House number 999 to: 1
       2 alter House owner ABCD to: BROWN
       3 alter Number of rooms 99 to: 6
       4 alter Current value 9999 to: £85000
       5 dialogue box as Figure 44.2(b)
       6 pick OK.

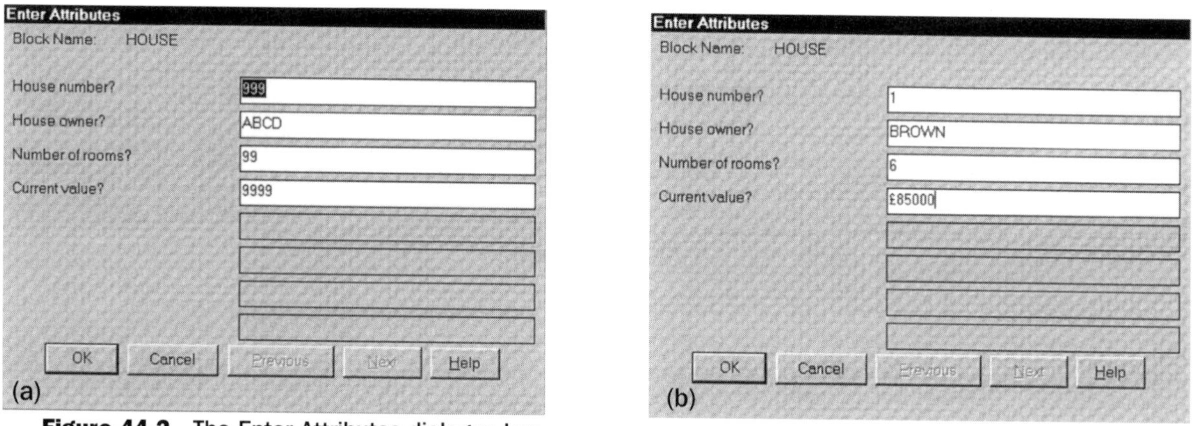

Figure 44.2 The Enter Attributes dialogue box.

6 The house block will be inserted with the attribute information displayed.

7 Using step 5 as a guide with the attribute data from Table 44.1, refer to Figure 44.3 and insert the HOUSE block to complete the housing estate – use your imagination with the scales and rotation angles.

8 Complete the estate layout and save?

9 This completes our brief 'taster' into attributes.

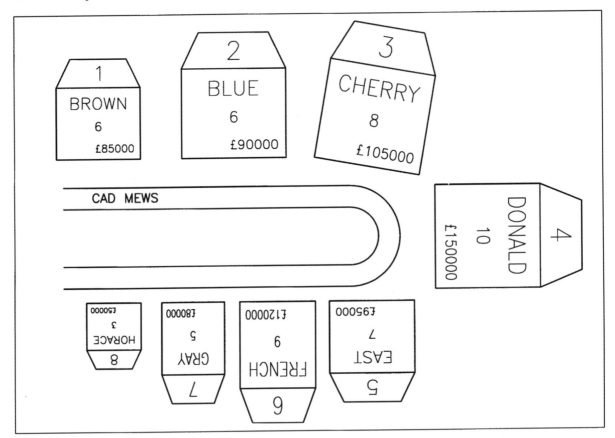

Figure 44.3 Estate layout with inserted HOUSE block and attribute data.

Point of interest?

In the previous chapter we created a title box as a WBLOCK. This title box had text items attached to it, e.g. drawing name, date, revision, etc. These text items could have been made as attributes. When the title box was inserted into a drawing, the various text items (attributes) could have been entered to the drawing requirements. Think about this application of attributes!

Summary

1 Attributes are text items added to BLOCKS or WBLOCKS.

2 Attribute must be defined by the user.

3 Attribute data are added to a block when it is inserted into a drawing.

4 Attributes can be edited and extracted from a drawing, but these topics are beyond the scope of this book.

Chapter 45

External references

WBLOCKS contain information about objects, colour, layers, linetypes, dimension styles, etc. and all this information is inserted into the drawing with the WBLOCK. All this inserted information may not be required, and it also takes time and uses memory space. Drawings which contain several WBLOCKS are not automatically updated if one of the original WBLOCKS is altered.

External references (**xrefs**) are similar to WBLOCKS in that they are created by the user and can be inserted into a drawing, but they have one major advantage over the WBLOCK. Drawings which contain external references are automatically updated if the original external reference 'WBLOCK' is modified.

A worked example will be used to demonstrate external references. The procedure may seem rather involved as it requires the user to save and open several drawings, but the final result is well worth the effort. For the demonstration we will:

a) create a WBLOCK
b) use the WBLOCK as an xref to create two drawing layouts
c) modify the original WBLOCK
d) view the two drawing layouts
e) use your named directory/folder or the A drive.

Getting started

1 Open your A:STDA3 standard sheet and refer to Figure 45.1.

2 Make a new current layer:
name: XREF
colour: red
linetype: continuous.

3 Draw
a) a circle of radius 18
b) the text item: AutoCAD, centred on the circle centre point with height 5 and rotation angle 0 – Fig. (a).

Creating the xref – a WBLOCK

1 At the command line enter **WBLOCK <R>**
prompt   Create Drawing File dialogue box
respond   1 file name: enter **XREFEX**
              2 pick save
prompt   Block name and right-click
prompt   Insertion base point
respond   **Snap to center icon and pick the circle**
prompt   Select objects
respond   **window the circle/text then right-click.**

2 The block disappears.

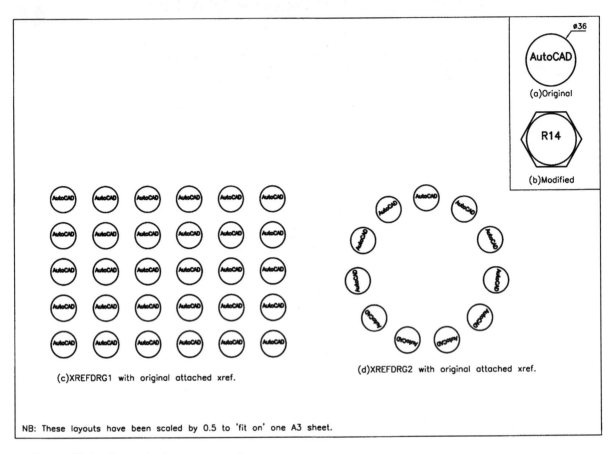

Figure 45.1 External reference example.

Inserting the xref – drawing layout 1

1 Open your A:STDA3 standard sheet – no to save changes.

2 Menu bar with **Insert–External Reference** and:
prompt External Reference dialogue box
respond **pick Attach**
prompt Select File to Attach dialogue box
respond 1 scroll and pick **xrefex**
   2 pick **Open**
prompt Attach Xref dialogue box as shown in Figure 45.2
respond pick OK
prompt Attach Xref XREFEX: A:\xrefex.dwg XREFEX loaded
then Insertion point
enter **50,50 <R>**.

3 Rectangular array the attached xref for:
a) five rows with row distance: 50
b) six columns with column distance: 60.

4 Save the layout as **A:XREFDRG1** – Fig. (c).

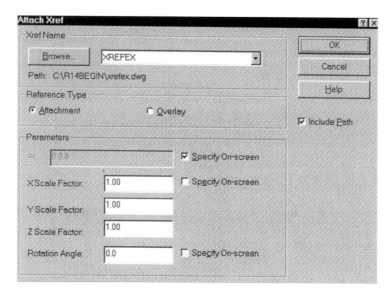

Figure 45.2 The Attach Cross-reference dialogue box.

Inserting the xref – drawing layout 2

1 Open A:STDA3 standard sheet.

2 At the command line enter **XREF <R>** and:
   prompt   External Reference dialogue box
   respond   1 scroll and pick **xrefex**
              2 pick open
   prompt   Attach Xref dialogue box
   respond   pick OK
   prompt   Insertion point and enter: **200,250 <R>**.

3 Polar array the attached xref with:
   a) centre point: 200,150
   b) number of items: 11
   c) full circle with rotation.

4 Save the layout as **A:XREFDRG2** – Fig. (d).

Modifying the original xref

1 Open the drawing A:XREFEX – the original WBLOCK.

2 Change the text item to R14.

3 Draw a hexagon, centred on the circle and circumscribed in a 19 radius circle – Fig. 45.1(b).

4 Change the three objects to blue colour.

5 Menu bar with **File–Save** to automatically update A:XREFEX.

Viewing the original layouts

1 Open A:XREFDRG1 – interesting?

2 Open A:XREFDRG2 – again interesting?

3 The layout drawings should display the modified XREFEX without any 'help' from us. This is the power of external references. Useful?

4 Menu bar with **Format–Layer** and note the layer: **xrefex|xref**.

   This indicates that an external reference (xrefex) has been attached to layer xref. The (|) is a pipe symbol indicating as attached external reference.

5 This completes our simple investigation into xrefs.

6 You could always modify the original XREFEX and view the two layout drawings – it could impress your colleagues or even your boss?

Chapter 46

Isometric drawings

An isometric is a 2D representation of a 3D drawing and is useful as it can convey additional information about a component which is not always apparent with the traditional orthogonal views. Although an isometric appears as a 3D drawing, the user should never forget that it is a 'flat 2D' drawing without any 'depth'.

Isometric drawings are created by the user with polar coordinates and AutoCAD has the facility to display an isometric grid as a drawing aid.

Setting the isometric grid

There are two methods for setting the isometric grid, both of which will be discussed.

Dialogue box

1 From the menu bar select **Tools–Drawing Aids** and:
   prompt   Drawing Aids dialogue box
   respond   1 pick isometric snap/grid ON, i.e. tick in box
            2 pick top – black dot
            3 set grid Y; spacing: 10
            4 set snap Y; spacing: 5
            5 dialogue box as shown in Figure 46.1
            6 pick OK.

2 The screen will display an isometric grid of 10 spacing, with the on-screen cursor 'aligned' to this grid with a snap of 5.

3 Use the Drawing Aids dialogue box to 'turn the isometric grid off', i.e. no tick in the box.

4 The screen will display the standard grid pattern.

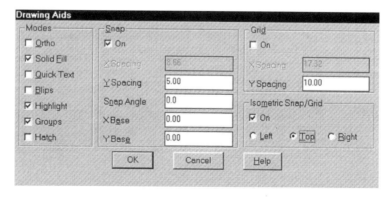

Figure 46.1 The Drawing Aids dialogue box.

Keyboard

1 At the command line enter **SNAP <R>** and:

prompt Snap spacing or ON/OFF/Rotate/Style<5.00>
enter   **S <R>** – the style option
prompt Standard/Isometric<S>
enter   **I <R>** – the isometric option
prompt Vertical spacing<5.00>
enter   **10 <R>**.

2 The screen will again display the isometric grid pattern with the cursor 'snapped to the grid points'.

3 Leave this isometric grid on the screen.

Isoplanes

AutoCAD uses three 'planes' called isoplanes when creating an isometric drawing – top, right and left. The three planes are designated by two of the X, Y and Z axes as shown in Figure 46.2 and are:
isoplane top: XZ axes
isoplane right: XY axes
isoplane left: YZ axes.

When an isoplane is 'set' or 'current', the on-screen cursor is aligned to the isoplane axes – Figure 46.3. The setting can be by one of three methods:

1 Drawing Aids dialogue box and:
a) isometric snap/grid ON
b) pick top
c) pick OK – Fig. (a).

2 At the command line enter **ISOPLANE <R>** and:
prompt Left/Top/Right
enter   **R <R>** – right plane – Fig. (b).

3 Using a 'toggle' effect by:
a) holding down the **Ctrl** key (control)
b) pressing the **E** key
c) toggles to isoplane left – Fig. (c).

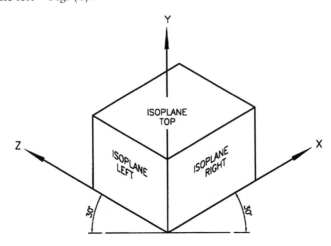

Figure 46.2 The isometric isoplanes.

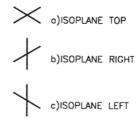

a) ISOPLANE TOP

b) ISOPLANE RIGHT

c) ISOPLANE LEFT

Figure 46.3 The cursor display with three isoplanes.

Note

It is the user's preference as to what method is used to set the isometric grid an isoplane, but my recommendation is:

1 set the isometric grid ON from the Drawing Aids dialogue box with a grid spacing of 10 and a snap spacing of 5

2 toggle to the required isoplane with Ctrl E

3 isoplanes are necessary when creating 'circles' in isometric.

Isocircles

Circles in isometric are called isocircles and are created using the ellipse command. The correct isoplane **must** be set. Try the following:

1 Set the isometric grid on with spacing of 10 and toggle the isoplane top.

2 Using the isometric grid as a guide and with the snap on, draw a cuboid shape as shown in Figure 46.4. The size of the sides is not important at this stage – only the basic shape.

3 Select the ELLIPSE icon from the draw toolbar and:
   prompt   Arc/Centre/Isocircle...
   enter   **I <R>** – the isocircle option
   prompt   Center of circle
   respond **pick any point on top 'surface'**
   prompt   <Circle radius>/Diameter
   respond **pick/drag as required**.

4 Toggle to isoplane right – Ctrl E.

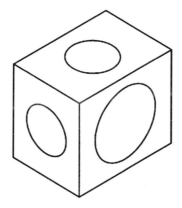

Figure 46.4 Drawing isocircles.

5 At the command line enter **ELLIPSE <R>** and:
   prompt `Arc/Centre/Isocircle...`
   enter   **I <R>**
   prompt `Centre of circle` and pick a point on 'right side'
   prompt `Circle radius` and pick/drag to suit.

6 Toggle to isoplane left, and draw an isocircle on the left side of the cuboid.

7 The cuboid now has an isocircle on the three 'sides'.

Isometric example

1 Open your A:STDA3 standard sheet and refer to Figure 46.5.

2 Set the isometric grid on, with a grid spacing of 10 and a snap spacing of 5.

3 With the LINE icon draw:
   From point: pick towards lower centre of the screen
   To point: @80<30 <R>
   To point: @100<150 <R>
   To point: @80<−150 <R>
   To point: @100<−30 <R>
   To point: @30<90 <R>
   To point: @80<30 <R>
   To point: @30<−90 <R><R> – Fig. (a).

4 With the COPY icon:
   a) objects: pick lines d1, d2 and d3 then right-click
   b) base point: intersection of pt 1
   c) displacement: intersection of pt 2.

5 Draw the two line (endpoint–endpoint) to complete the base, sides and top – Fig. (b).

6 Draw a top diagonal line as shown in Fig. (b).

7 Toggle to isoplane top.

8 With the ELLIPSE–Isocircle command:
   a) pick midpoint of diagonal as the centre
   b) enter a radius of 30.

9 Copy the isocircle:
   a) from the diagonal midpoint
   b) by: @50<90 – Fig. (c).

10 Erase the diagonal.

11 Draw in the two 'cylinder' sides using the quadrant snap and picking the isocircles.

12 Trim objects to these lines and erase unwanted objects to give the complete isometric – Fig. (d).

13 Save if required.

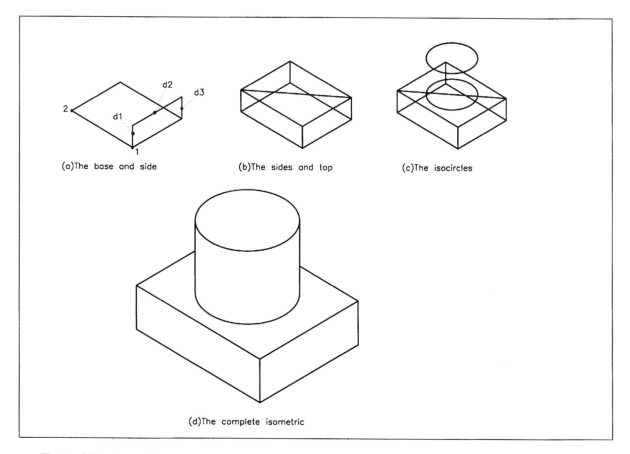

(a)The base and side   (b)The sides and top   (c)The isocircles

(d)The complete isometric

Figure 46.5 Isometric exercise.

Summary

1 An isometric is a 'flat' 2D drawing having 3D visualization.

2 An isometric grid is available as a drawing aid.

3 Isometrics are constructed with polar coordinates.

4 Circles are drawn with the ellipse–isocircle option and the correct isoplane must be set.

5 The objects snaps (endpoint, midpoint, etc.) are available with isometric drawings.

6 The modify commands (e.g. copy, trim, etc.) are available with isometrics.

7 The OFFSET command does not give the effect that the user would expect, and should not be used.

8 The isocircle option of the ellipse command is only available when the isometric grid is 'set on'.

Assignment

Activity 34:

Six into one.

This activity requires that isocircles are drawn with the three isoplanes. The recommended procedure is:

1 Draw an isometric cube of side 50.

2 Draw six isocircles, one at the centre of each face. The radius is 25.

3 Copy each isocircle by 50 at the appropriate angle, i.e. 30, 90, 150, −150, −90 and −30.

4 Draw in the 'cylinder sides' using the quadrant snap.

5 Trim as required with care.

6 Erase unwanted objects.

7 The sectional isometric is left for you to complete.

Chapter 47

Model space and paper space

AutoCAD has two drawing environments – model space and paper space:
model space: used to draw the component
paper space: used to layout the drawing paper.

The two environments are independent of each other and while the concept is particularly applicable to 3D modelling we will demonstrate its use with a previously saved 2D drawing.

Getting started

1 Open your A:STDA3 standard sheet and erase the black border and toggle the grid off.

2 Make a new layer named VP, colour to suit.

3 From the menu bar select **Tools–Paper Space** and:
   a) blank screen returned
   b) new icon displayed – the paper space icon as shown in Figure 47.1.

Figure 47.1   The paper space icon.

The sheet layout

Refer to Figure 47.2 and:

1   With layer 0 current, draw a rectangular border from 0,0 to 420,290.

2   Zoom all then pan to suit.

3   Make layer VP current.

4   Menu bar with **View–Floating Viewports–1 Viewport** and:
    prompt   ON/OFF...<First point>
    enter   **10,10 <R>**
    prompt   Other corner
    enter   **210,145 <R>**.

5   Repeat the View–Floating Viewports–1 Viewport selection and create two additional viewports using the following:
    a) first point: 230,75   other point: 380,170
    b) first point: 230,190   other point: 320,260.

6   The screen should display three viewport borders within a black drawing paper border. These viewports are three different 'drawing areas' on one A3 sized sheet of paper.

7   Menu bar with **View–Model Space (Floating)** and:
    a) icon changes to traditional *XY* display
    b) icon displayed in all three viewports
    c) one viewport (top?) is outlined in black with the on-screen cursor displayed – this is the **ACTIVE** viewport.

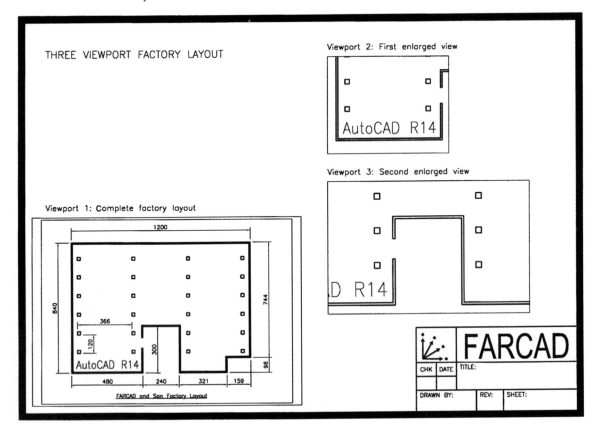

Figure 47.2   Model/paper space.

8 Move the pointing device arrow to another viewport and left-click – the selected viewport becomes active.

9 At the command line enter **PS <R>** – paper space environment.

10 At the command line enter **MS <R>** – model space environment.

The model

Rather than draw a new component we will insert an already completed and saved (I hope) drawing into our created viewports. This drawing is the large-scale factory layout (LARGESC) from Chapter 40.

1 Ensure the screen displays:
   a) model space environment – MS <R> if unsure
   b) lower left viewport active
   c) layer OUT current.

2 Menu bar with **Insert–Block** and:
   prompt　　Insert dialogue box
   respond　　1 pick File
   　　　　　　2 ensure your named folder (A drive) is current
   　　　　　　3 scroll and pick LARGESC
   　　　　　　4 pick Open
   prompt　　Insert dialogue box
   with　　　*a*) Block: LARGESC
   　　　　　　b) File: name\largesc.dwg
   respond　　1 ensure Explode ON, i.e. tick in box
   　　　　　　2 pick OK
   prompt　　Insertion point and enter: **0,0 <R>**
   prompt　　Scale factor and enter: **1 <R>**
   prompt　　Rotation angle and enter: **0 <R>**.

3 In each viewport Zoom-All and the screen will display the factory floor layout with dimensions?

Using the viewports

1 Make the top viewport active.

2 Menu bar with **Format–Layer** and using the Layer and Linetype dialogue box:
   a) pick Dimen layer line
   b) pick Freeze in Current Viewport box, i.e. tick
   c) pick OK.

3 Repeat step 2 with the lower right viewport active.

4 The model will be displayed without dimensions in these viewports.

5 With the top viewport active, use the Zoom-Window command with: first corner: 160,160 and other corner: 710,550.

6 With the lower right viewport active, Zoom-Window with: first corner: 575,170 and other corner: 1030,630.

7 Two viewports now display enlarged 'areas' of the factory layout.

Adding additional detail to the layout

1 Make layer TEXT current and left viewport active.

2 Menu bar with **Draw–Text–Single Line Text** and:
   prompt Start point and enter: **F <R>** – fit option
   prompt First text line point and enter: **230,230 <R>**
   prompt Second text line point and enter: **650,230 <R>**
   prompt Height and enter: **50 <R>**
   prompt Text and enter: **AutoCAD R14 <R><R>**.

3 The item of text is displayed in the three viewports.

4 Make layer OUT current and lower right viewport active.

5 Draw two lines:
   a) from: 650,430 to: 720,430
   b) from: 650,360 to: 720,360.

6 Use the TRIM command to trim these lines to give an opening into the factory – displayed in the three viewports.

Using the paper space environment

1 Enter paper space with **PS <R>**.

2 Try and erase any object from a viewport – you cannot as they were created in model space.

3 Make layer TEXT current and add the following to the layout:

Start	Height	Rot	Text item
a) 20,150	4	0	Viewport 1: Complete factory layout
b) 230,265	4	0	Viewport 2: First enlarged view
c) 230,175	4	0	Viewport 3: Second enlarged view
d) 20,260	5	0	THREE VIEWPORT FACTORY LAYOUT

4 Now enter model space with MS <R> and try to erase any of the added text items – you cannot as they were created in paper space.

Completing the layout

1 Enter paper space with PS <R> and layer OUT current.

2 Insert the following wblock drawings:

Name	Insertion Pt	Scale	Rot
BORDER	0,0	1	0
TITLE	415,5	1	0

3 The factory layout is now complete.

Task

1   If you have access to a printer/plotter:
    a) plot from model space with any viewport active
    b) plot from paper space.

2   In model space, investigate the coordinates of the top right corner of the left viewport – about 1725,1190?

3   In paper space investigate the coordinates of top right corner. They should be 420,290 i.e. our A3 paper size.

4   Question: how can a drawing area on 1725,1190 be displayed on an A3 sheet of paper? This is the 'power' of model/paper space.

5   Your inserted dimensions will probably be different from those displayed in Figure 47.2. Can you alter your dimensions to be readable? Think dimensions style!

Finally

This completes the introduction to the model/paper space environment available within AutoCAD. The concept is very powerful especially when working with 3D modelling techniques. This chapter has only been a very quick 'taster' for the user and I hope you have gained some insight into how the drawing environments can be used with 2D draughting.

Chapter 48

Toolbar customization

The toolbars supplied with AutoCAD Release 14 are more than adequate for the user's draughting requirements. It is possible to create a new toolbar and customize it with your own icons.

   We will demonstrate how a new toolbar can be customized to include six icons from four existing toolbars.

1   Open your A:STDA3 standard sheet.

2   Menu bar with **View–Toolbars** and:
   prompt   Toolbars dialogue box
   respond **pick New**
   prompt   New Toolbar dialogue box
   with   Menu Group: ACAD
   respond 1   Toolbar name: enter **MYOWN**
             2   dialogue box as Figure 48.1
             3   pick OK
   prompt   Toolbars dialogue box
   with   MYOWN added to the list
   respond 1   activate MYOWN, i.e. X in box
             2   pick close.

3   The new toolbar will be displayed on the screen – probably at the top. This toolbar is quite small – Figure 48.2(a), and does not yet contain any icons.

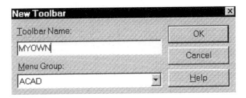

Figure 48.1 The New Toolbar dialogue box.

(a) New toolbar created

(b) LINE and CIRCLE
     icons added

(c) Other icons added

Figure 48.2 Toolbar customization example.

4 Move the new toolbar to the left-side of the drawing screen by
  a) left click in the blue title bar
  b) hold down the left button
  c) move to required position.

5 Menu bar with **View–Toolbars** and:
  prompt   Toolbar dialogue box
  respond   **pick Customize**
  prompt   Customize Toolbars dialogue box
  respond   1 pick scroll arrow at Categories
             2 scroll and pick Draw
  prompt   Draw icons
  respond   1 left-click on the LINE icon and hold down the button
             2 drag the LINE icon 'into' the new toolbar
             3 left-click on the CIRCLE Centre–Radius icon and hold down the button
             4 drag the CIRCLE icon onto the new toolbar
             5 the new toolbar extends
             6 pick close
  prompt   Toolbars dialogue box
  respond   pick Close.

6 The toolbar MYOWN is displayed with the LINE and CIRCLE icons as Fig. (b).

7 Select **View–Toolbars** again and:
  prompt   Toolbars dialogue box
  respond   pick Customize
  prompt   Customize toolbar dialogue box
  respond   scroll and pick Modify category
  prompt   Modify icons
  respond   1 pick ERASE icon
             2 hold down left button and drag icon into toolbar
             3 pick MOVE icon and drag into toolbar
             4 scroll and pick Dimensioning category to display the dimensioning icons
             5 pick LINEAR DIMENSION and drag into toolbar
             6 scroll and pick OBJECT SNAP category to display the object snap icons
             7 pick ENDPOINT icon and drag into toolbar
             8 pick Close
  prompt   Toolbars dialogue box
  respond   pick Close.

8 The new toolbar will display the six icons as Fig. (c).

9 It is as easy (or as hard) as that! You can now add other icons to your toolbar or create new toolbars as required.

Note

1 The new toolbar will always be displayed unless it has been cancelled with the close icon in the top-left corner.

2 The new toolbar MYOWN is permanently included in the list of named icons in the Toolbar dialogue box and can be activated from this dialogue box.

3 If required the new toolbar can be deleted from the list.

4 I have not investigated 'fly-out' icons in this brief introduction.

Chapter 49

Templates

This topic has been left to the end, when it should probably have been included nearer the beginning. There were two reasons for this, these being to allow you to:
a) become proficient at draughting with AutoCAD
b) understand the concepts of paper space and attributes.

What is a template?

A template is a prototype drawing, i.e. it is equivalent to our A:STDA3 standard sheet which has been used when every new exercise/activity has been started. The terms prototype/standard drawing are used whenever a drawing require to be used with various default settings, e.g. layers, text styles, dimension styles, etc.

With AutoCAD all drawings are saved with the file extension **.dwg** while template files have the extension **.dwt**. Any drawing can be saved as a template.

Template drawings (files) are used to 'safeguard' the prototype drawing being mistakenly overwritten – have you ever saved work on your A:STDA3 standard sheet by mistake? Templates overcome this problem.

AutoCAD has several templates which conform to the following drawing standards:
a) ansi: a0 to a4
b) din: a0 to a4
c) iso: a0 to a4
d) jis: a0 to a4.

There are also other templates available.

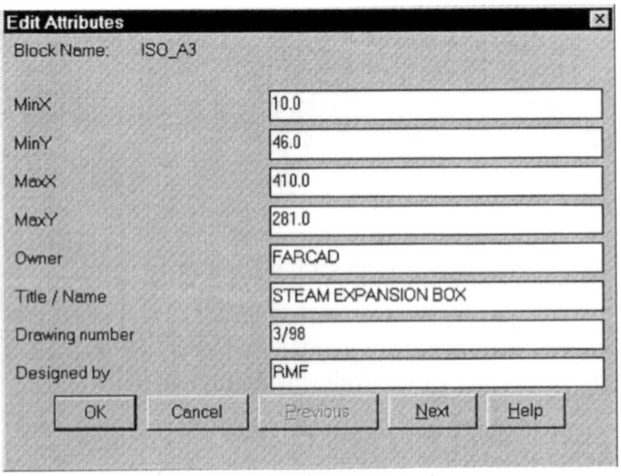

Edit Attributes		×
Block Name:	ISO_A3	

MinX	10.0
MinY	46.0
MaxX	410.0
MaxY	281.0
Owner	FARCAD
Title / Name	STEAM EXPANSION BOX
Drawing number	3/98
Designed by	RMF

| OK | Cancel | Previous | Next | Help |

Figure 49.1 Title block attribute editing – 1.

Summary

1 A template file is a prototype drawing with various defaults set to user requirements.

2 AutoCAD has several drawing standard prototypes.

3 Template files can be created by the user.

4 Template files 'safeguard' the prototype drawing being 'overwritten'.

Chapter 50

And finally ...

My objective in writing this book was to show you by means of exercises and activities how to produce drawings AutoCAD Release 14.

I hope you have overcome any fears you have had about using AutoCAD. You now have the ability to investigate topics I have not been able to cover for yourself. Your next stage is to consider 3D draughting, e.g. wire-frame models, surface models and solid modelling as well as topics such as customization of linetypes, hatch patterns, menus, etc.

Any comments you have about the exercises and activities would be greatly appreciated, and if there have been any mistakes I apologize for this – they were not intentional.

Good luck with your AutoCAD draughting.

ACTIVITY 1
Draw the simple shapes using the drawing aids
and the LINE and CIRCLE commands.

Function keys

F7	F8	F9
GRID	ORTHO	SNAP

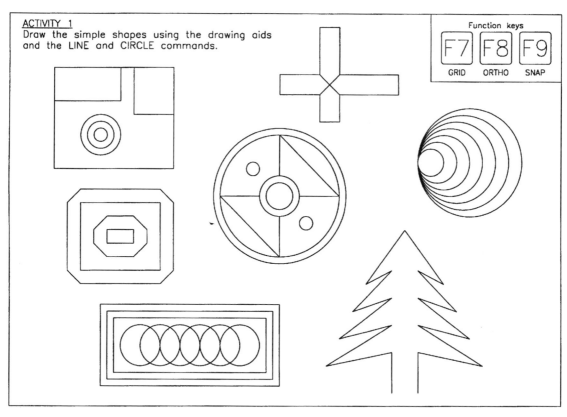

ACTIVITY 2
Draw the three templates using the sizes
given. The start points as A(40,70);
B(190,195) and C(375,155).

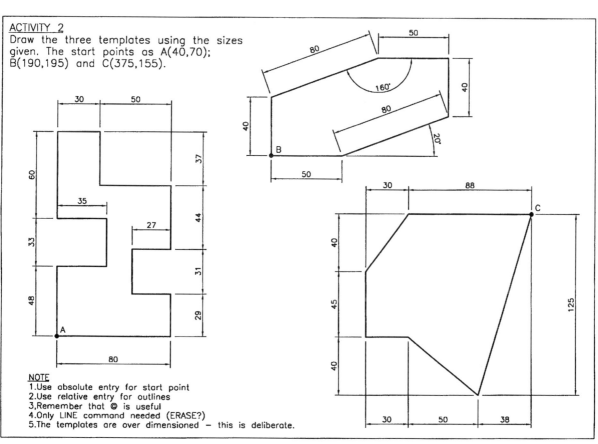

NOTE
1.Use absolute entry for start point
2.Use relative entry for outlines
3.Remember that @ is useful
4.Only LINE command needed (ERASE?)
5.The templates are over dimensioned – this is deliberate.

ACTIVITY 3
Draw the three shapes using the sizes given. The recommended start points are:
A: (90,100)
B: (220,180)
C: (380,30)

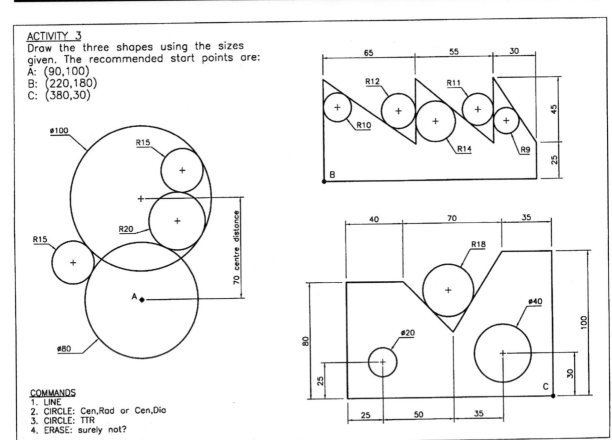

COMMANDS
1. LINE
2. CIRCLE: Cen,Rad or Cen,Dia
3. CIRCLE: TTR
4. ERASE: surely not?

ACTIVITY 4
Draw the three shapes using the hints provided.
The start points are:
A: (210,195)
B: (30,35)
C: (300,60)

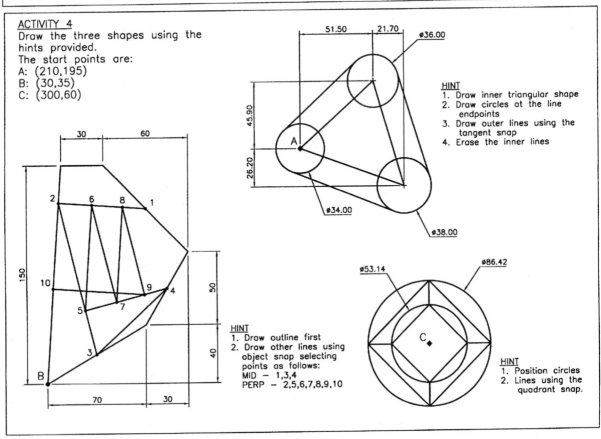

HINT
1. Draw inner triangular shape
2. Draw circles at the line endpoints
3. Draw outer lines using the tangent snap
4. Erase the inner lines

HINT
1. Draw outline first
2. Draw other lines using object snap selecting points as follows:
MID – 1,3,4
PERP – 2,5,6,7,8,9,10

HINT
1. Position circles
2. Lines using the quadrant snap.

ACTIVITY 5
Draw full size the two templates.
Suggested start points are:
A: (80,160)
B: (370,90)

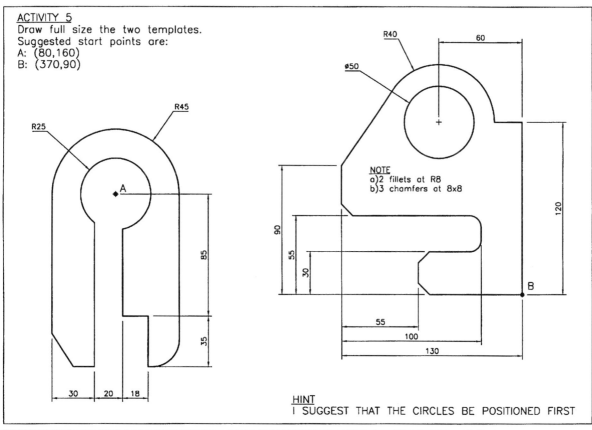

HINT
I SUGGEST THAT THE CIRCLES BE POSITIONED FIRST

NOTE
a)2 fillets at R8
b)3 chamfers at 8x8

ACTIVITY 6
Draw the four shapes to sizes given.
Make use of OFFSET and TRIM where possible.
Add all text.
Discretion for start points.

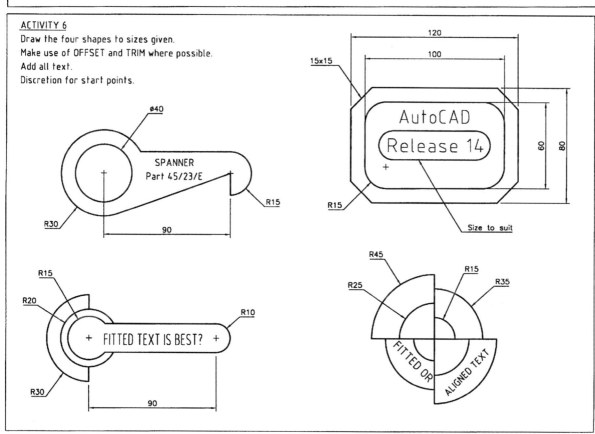

SPANNER
Part 45/23/E

AutoCAD
Release 14

Size to suit

FITTED TEXT IS BEST?

FITTED OR ALIGNED TEXT

ACTIVITY 7
1. Draw the two components full size
2. Add all text
3. Add all dimensions
4. Use layers correctly
5. Suggested start points are A: (50,70) and B: (380,220)

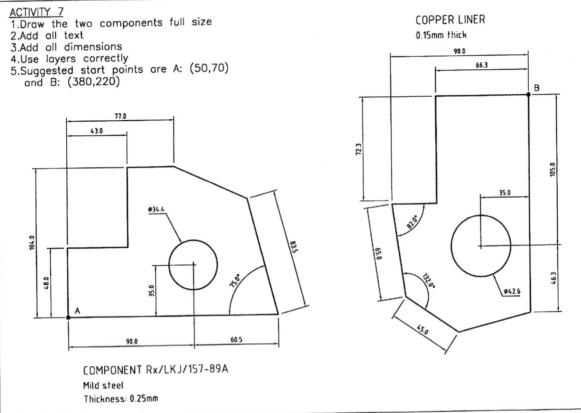

COMPONENT Rx/LKJ/157-89A
Mild steel
Thickness: 0.25mm

COPPER LINER
0.15mm thick

ACTIVITY 8
Draw, dimension and add text. Use layers.

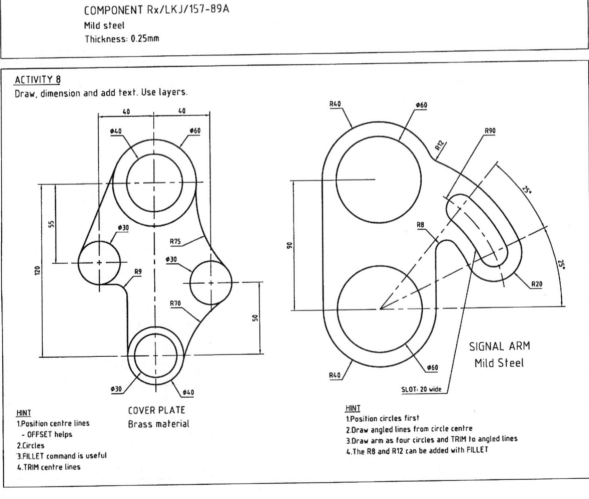

COVER PLATE
Brass material

SIGNAL ARM
Mild Steel

HINT
1. Position centre lines
   - OFFSET helps
2. Circles
3. FILLET command is useful
4. TRIM centre lines

HINT
1. Position circles first
2. Draw angled lines from circle centre
3. Draw arm as four circles and TRIM to angled lines
4. The R8 and R12 can be added with FILLET

ACTIVITY 9
Draw, fully dimension and add text
Easier than you think!!!

SPACER PLATE
Mild Steel

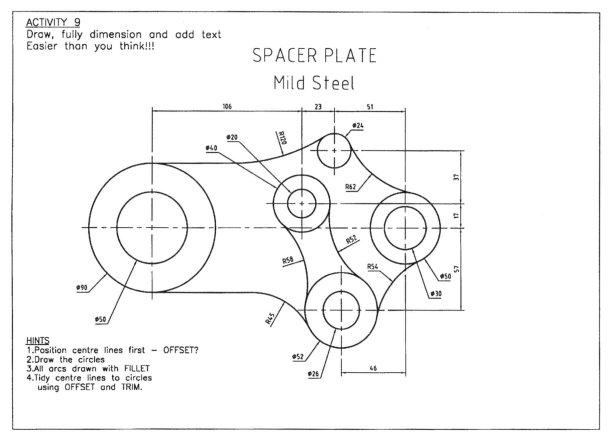

HINTS
1. Position centre lines first — OFFSET?
2. Draw the circles
3. All arcs drawn with FILLET
4. Tidy centre lines to circles
   using OFFSET and TRIM.

ACTIVITY 10
Draw the two components using the reference sizes given.
Complete the layout using your discretion.
COPY or MULTIPLE COPY
Connections are DONUT with ID: 0 and OD: 3

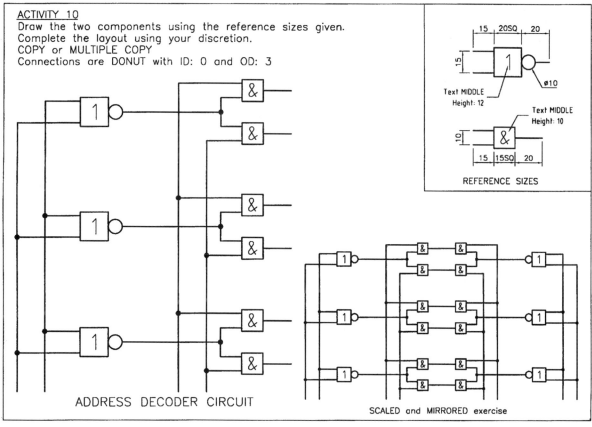

ADDRESS DECODER CIRCUIT

SCALED and MIRRORED exercise

REFERENCE SIZES

ACTIVITY 11
Draw the template full size
using the reference sizes
given.

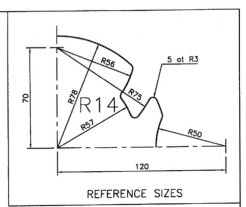

REFERENCE SIZES

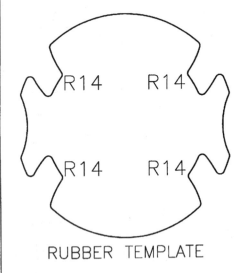

RUBBER TEMPLATE

HINTS
1.Position 4 centre lines – draw/offset
2.Draw 5 full circles using given radii
3.TRIM circles to each other and lines
4.Add the 5 R3 fillets
5.MIRROR twice?
6.MIRRTEXT value?

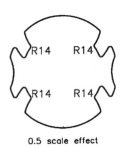

0.5 scale effect

0.25 scale effect

ACTIVITY 12
Draw the component using the sizes given.
Complete the circuit using the SCALE, MIRROR
and COPY commands.
The text item is at your discretion.

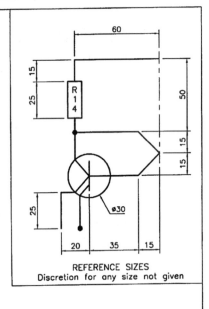

REFERENCE SIZES
Discretion for any size not given

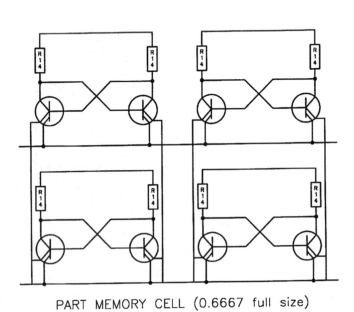

PART MEMORY CELL (0.6667 full size)

ACTIVITY 13
Robotic arm re-alignment using only grips.

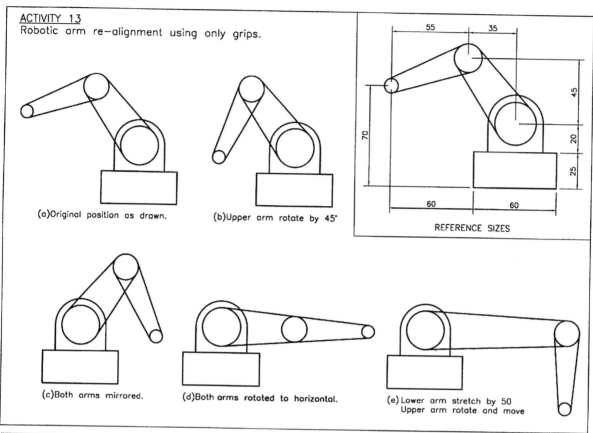

(a)Original position as drawn.

(b)Upper arm rotate by 45°

REFERENCE SIZES

(c)Both arms mirrored.

(d)Both arms rotated to horizontal.

(e)Lower arm stretch by 50
Upper arm rotate and move

ACTIVITY 14
Draw the three views of the component
and add hatching, text and dimensions.
Use layers correctly.

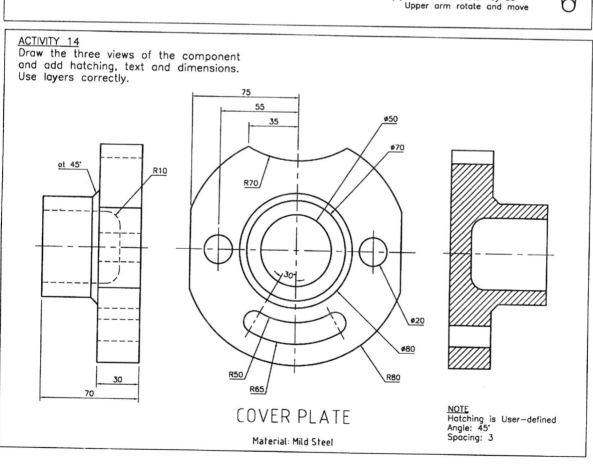

COVER PLATE

Material: Mild Steel

NOTE
Hatching is User-defined
Angle: 45°
Spacing: 3

ACTIVITY 15
Draw the four views and add the hatching, text and dimensions.

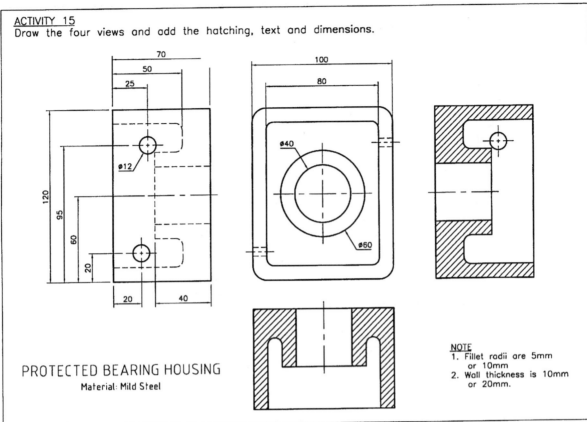

PROTECTED BEARING HOUSING

Material: Mild Steel

NOTE
1. Fillet radii are 5mm or 10mm
2. Wall thickness is 10mm or 20mm.

ACTIVITY 16
Draw the component and add text, hatching and dimensions.

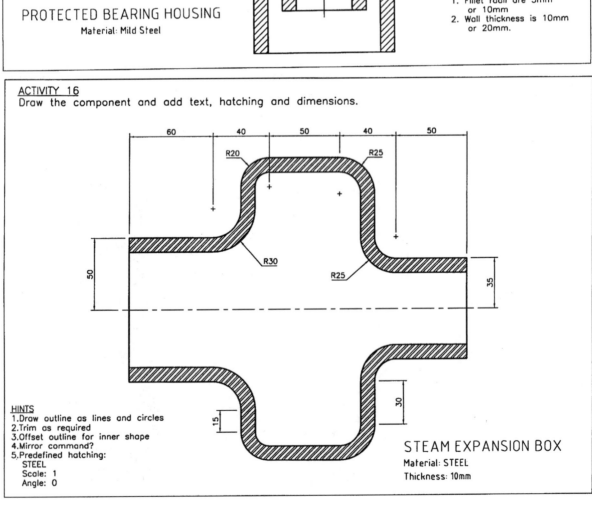

HINTS
1. Draw outline as lines and circles
2. Trim as required
3. Offset outline for inner shape
4. Mirror command?
5. Predefined hatching:
   STEEL
   Scale: 1
   Angle: 0

STEAM EXPANSION BOX

Material: STEEL

Thickness: 10mm

ACTIVITY 17
Draw full size, adding the hatching.

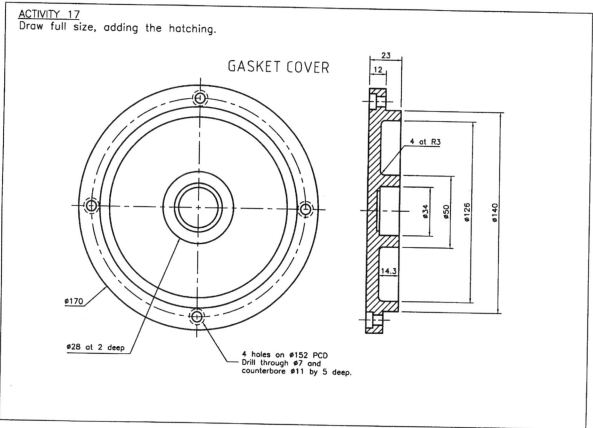

GASKET COVER

23
12
4 at R3
ø34
ø50
ø126
ø140
14.3

ø170
ø28 at 2 deep

4 holes on ø152 PCD
Drill through ø7 and
counterbore ø11 by 5 deep.

ACTIVITY 18
Draw the polyline shapes using the
sizes given.

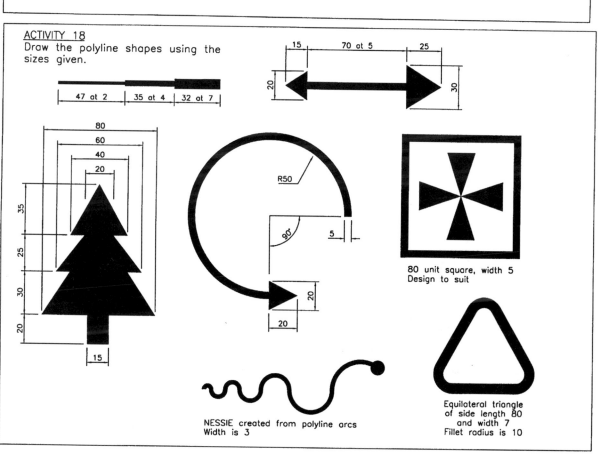

47 at 2 | 35 at 4 | 32 at 7

15 | 70 at 5 | 25
20
30

80
60
40
20
35
25
30
20
15

R50
90°
5
20
20

80 unit square, width 5
Design to suit

NESSIE created from polyline arcs
Width is 3

Equilateral triangle
of side length 80
and width 7
Fillet radius is 10

ACTIVITY 19
Draw the games board using the information given.

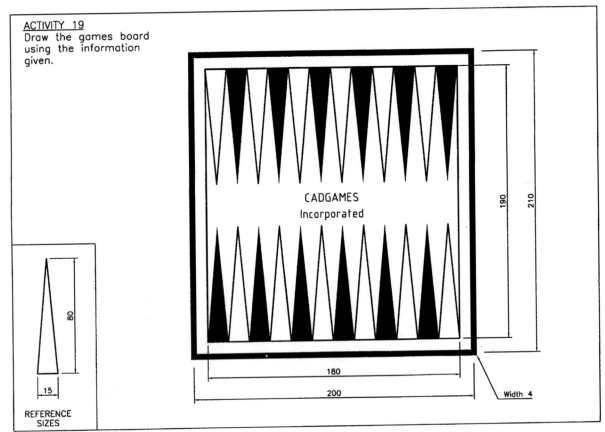

CADGAMES
Incorporated

REFERENCE
SIZES

ACTIVITY 20
Draw the printed circuit board using the information given.
Add the ordinate dimensions.

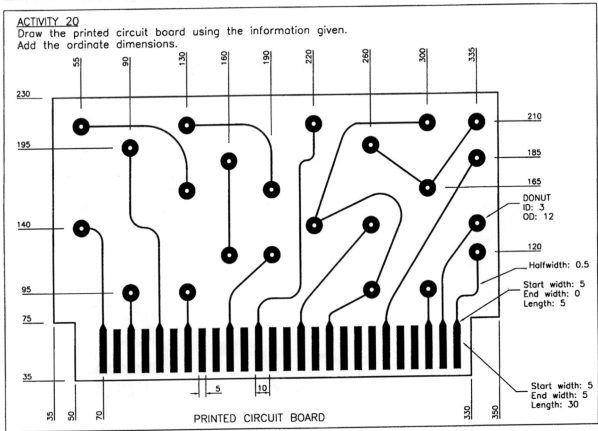

DONUT
ID: 3
OD: 12

Halfwidth: 0.5

Start width: 5
End width: 0
Length: 5

Start width: 5
End width: 5
Length: 30

PRINTED CIRCUIT BOARD

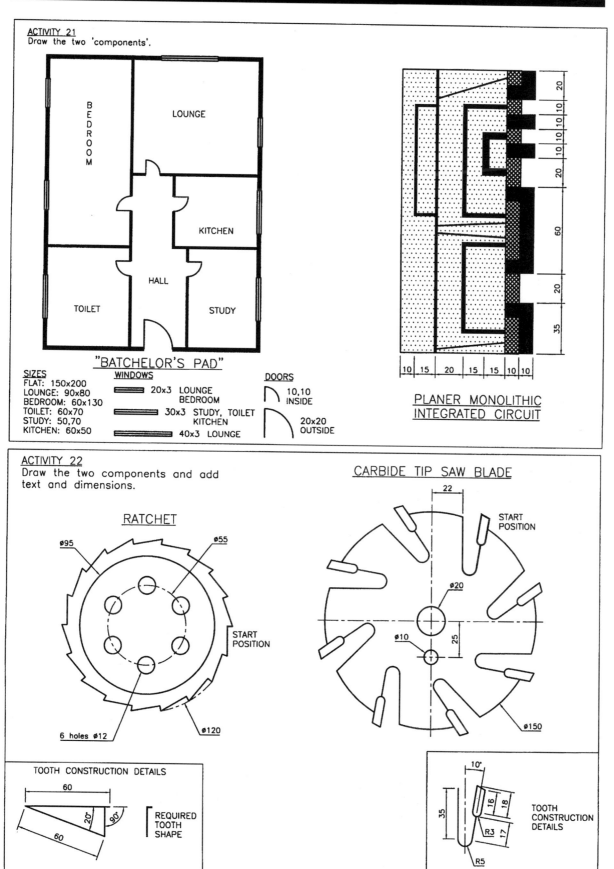

ACTIVITY 21
Draw the two 'components'.

"BATCHELOR'S PAD"

BEDROOM
LOUNGE
KITCHEN
HALL
TOILET
STUDY

SIZES
FLAT: 150x200
LOUNGE: 90x80
BEDROOM: 60x130
TOILET: 60x70
STUDY: 50,70
KITCHEN: 60x50

WINDOWS
20x3 LOUNGE BEDROOM
30x3 STUDY, TOILET KITCHEN
40x3 LOUNGE

DOORS
10,10 INSIDE
20x20 OUTSIDE

PLANER MONOLITHIC
INTEGRATED CIRCUIT

ACTIVITY 22
Draw the two components and add
text and dimensions.

RATCHET

Ø95
Ø55
6 holes Ø12
Ø120
START POSITION

CARBIDE TIP SAW BLADE

22
START POSITION
Ø20
Ø10
25
Ø150

TOOTH CONSTRUCTION DETAILS

60
20°
90°
60
REQUIRED TOOTH SHAPE

10°
16
18
35
R3
17
R5
TOOTH CONSTRUCTION DETAILS

ACTIVITY 23
Draw the two views full size.

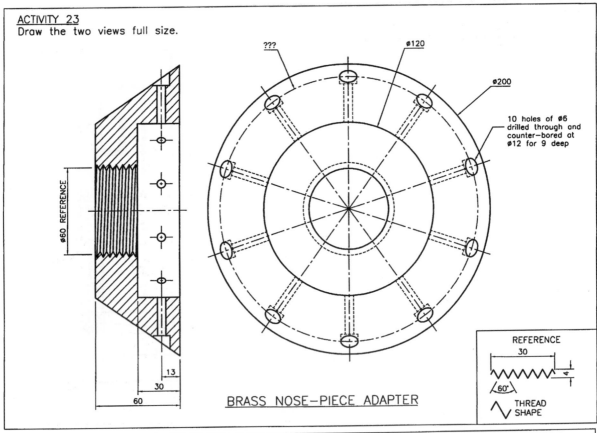

BRASS NOSE—PIECE ADAPTER

???
ø120
ø200

10 holes of ø6
drilled through and
counter—bored at
ø12 for 9 deep

ø60 REFERENCE

13
30
60

REFERENCE
30
60°
4
THREAD
SHAPE

ACTIVITY 24
Draw the basic bulb using the dimensions given
then produce the array design.

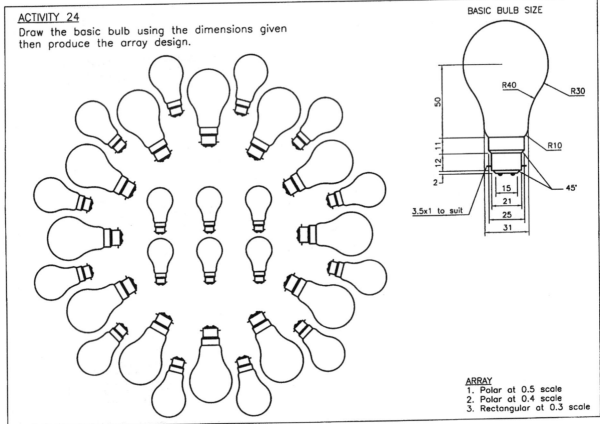

BASIC BULB SIZE

R40
R30
R10
45°

50
11
12
2

3.5x1 to suit

15
21
25
31

ARRAY
1. Polar at 0.5 scale
2. Polar at 0.4 scale
3. Rectangular at 0.3 scale

ACTIVITY 25

Draw the two components using the information given. Use your discretion for any sizes which are not given.

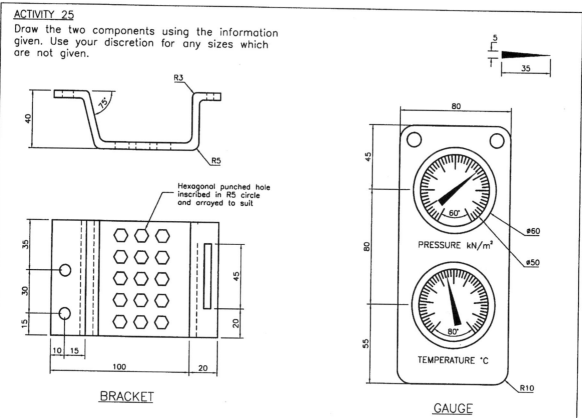

BRACKET

GAUGE

ACTIVITY 26

Draw the gear wheel arrangement using the information given.

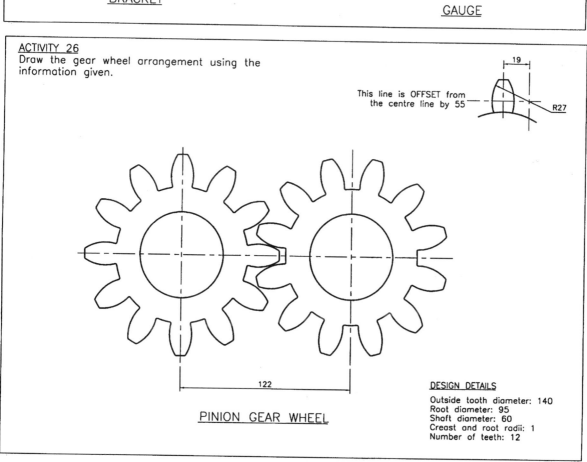

PINION GEAR WHEEL

DESIGN DETAILS

Outside tooth diameter: 140
Root diameter: 95
Shaft diameter: 60
Creast and root radii: 1
Number of teeth: 12

<u>ACTIVITY 27</u>
Draw the two types of telephone 'dials'
using the ARRAY command.

<u>OLD–FASHIONED?</u>

<u>MODERN?</u>

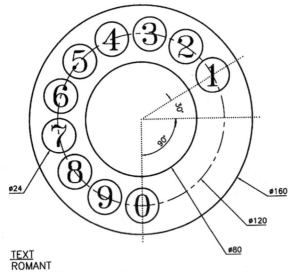

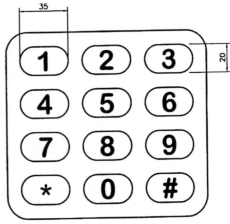

<u>TEXT</u>
ROMANT
Height: 15
Rotation: 0
Middle justify: at small circle centre

<u>TEXT</u>
ARIAL ROUNDED MT BOLD
Height: 14
Rotation: 0
Positioned to suit

<u>ACTIVITY 28</u>
Draw the flow gauge using the information given.

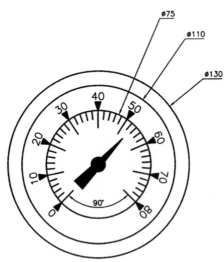

<u>FLOW GAUGE</u>

REFERENCE SIZES

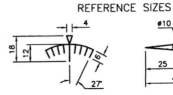

ACTIVITY 29
Draw the dart board using the information given.

Circle diameters
Ø10
Ø20
Ø80
Ø95
Ø160
Ø175
Ø215
Ø225

TEXT
Font: ROMANT
Height: 10

ACTIVITY 30
Draw the given component and add all
dimensions, creating appropriate dimension
styles for the tolerance dimensions.

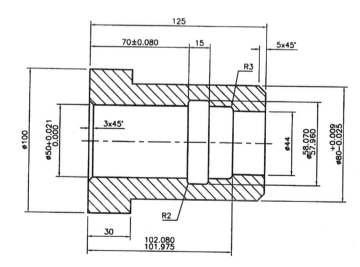

SPECIAL PLUG

ACTIVITY 31
Draw the component shown and add the
dimensions and geometric tolerance.

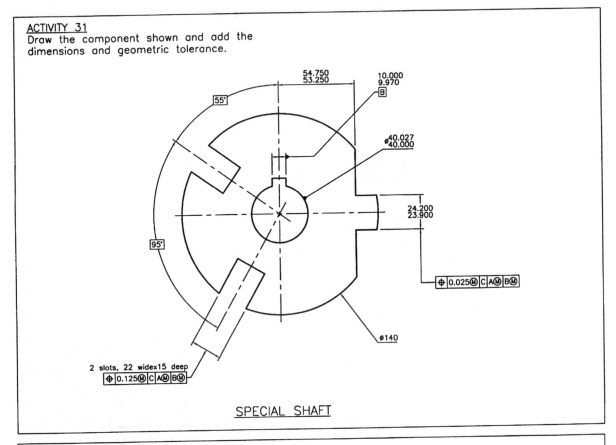

SPECIAL SHAFT

ACTIVITY 32
Using the four created blocks (PN1, PN2, PN3, PN4), complete
the pneumatic circiut. The blocks are inserted with an XY scale
of 0.75.

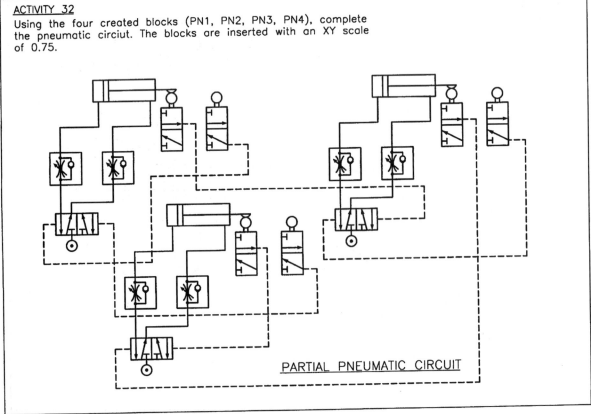

PARTIAL PNEUMATIC CIRCUIT

ACTIVITY 33
(a)Draw the two views
(b)Insert the WBLOCKS: BORDER, and TITLE
(c)Add all text and dimensions

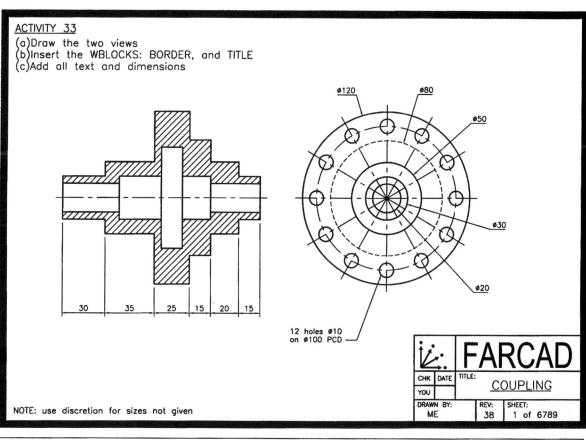

12 holes ⌀10
on ⌀100 PCD

FARCAD		
CHK	DATE	TITLE:
YOU		COUPLING
DRAWN BY: ME	REV: 38	SHEET: 1 of 6789

NOTE: use discretion for sizes not given

ACTIVITY 34
Create the isometric then produce
the section as given.

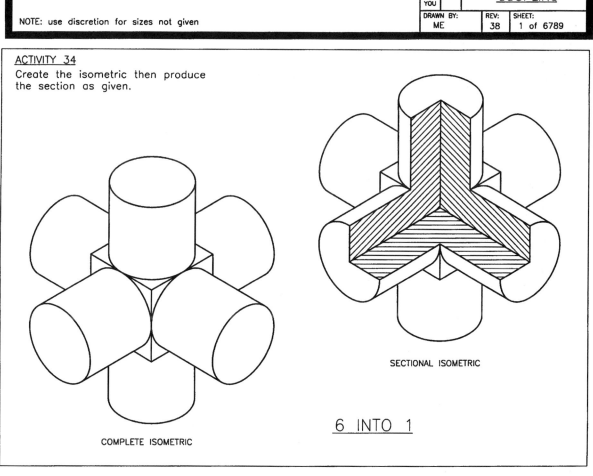

SECTIONAL ISOMETRIC

6 INTO 1

COMPLETE ISOMETRIC

Index